The Rate and Direction of Inventive Activity Revisited

A National Bureau of
Economic Research
Conference Report

The Rate and Direction of Inventive Activity Revisited

Edited by **Josh Lerner and Scott Stern**

The University of Chicago Press

Chicago and London

Josh Lerner is the Jacob H. Schiff Professor of Investment Banking at Harvard Business School, with a joint appointment in the Finance and the Entrepreneurial Management Units, and a research associate and codirector of the Productivity, Innovation, and Entrepreneurship Program at the National Bureau of Economic Research. Scott Stern is the School of Management Distinguished Professor of Technological Innovation, Entrepreneurship, and Strategic Management at the Massachusetts Institute of Technology Sloan School of Management and a research associate and director of the Innovation Policy Working Group at the National Bureau of Economic Research.

The University of Chicago Press, Chicago 60637
The University of Chicago Press, Ltd., London

Printed in the United States of America

21 20 19 18 17 16 15 14 13 12   1 2 3 4 5
ISBN-13: 978-0-226-47303-1 (cloth)
ISBN-10: 0-226-47303-1 (cloth)

Library of Congress Cataloging-in-Publication Data

The rate and direction of inventive activity revisited / edited by Josh Lerner and Scott Stern.
pages ; cm.—(National Bureau of Economic Research conference report)
Includes bibliographical references and index.
ISBN-13: 978-0-226-47303-1 (cloth : alkaline paper)
ISBN-10: 0-226-47303-1 (cloth : alkaline paper) 1. Inventions—Congresses. 2. Technological innovations—Economic aspects—Congresses. 3. Discoveries in science—Congresses. 4. Academic-industrial collaboration—Congresses. I. Lerner, Joshua. II. Stern, Scott, 1969– III.Series: National Bureau of Economic Research conference report.
HC79.T4R385 2012
338.'064—dc23

2011029618

♾ This paper meets the requirements of ANSI/NISO Z39.48-1992 (Permanence of Paper).

Relation of the Directors to the Work and Publications of the National Bureau of Economic Research

1. The object of the NBER is to ascertain and present to the economics profession, and to the public more generally, important economic facts and their interpretation in a scientific manner without policy recommendations. The Board of Directors is charged with the responsibility of ensuring that the work of the NBER is carried on in strict conformity with this object.

2. The President shall establish an internal review process to ensure that book manuscripts proposed for publication DO NOT contain policy recommendations. This shall apply both to the proceedings of conferences and to manuscripts by a single author or by one or more co-authors but shall not apply to authors of comments at NBER conferences who are not NBER affiliates.

3. No book manuscript reporting research shall be published by the NBER until the President has sent to each member of the Board a notice that a manuscript is recommended for publication and that in the President's opinion it is suitable for publication in accordance with the above principles of the NBER. Such notification will include a table of contents and an abstract or summary of the manuscript's content, a list of contributors if applicable, and a response form for use by Directors who desire a copy of the manuscript for review. Each manuscript shall contain a summary drawing attention to the nature and treatment of the problem studied and the main conclusions reached.

4. No volume shall be published until forty-five days have elapsed from the above notification of intention to publish it. During this period a copy shall be sent to any Director requesting it, and if any Director objects to publication on the grounds that the manuscript contains policy recommendations, the objection will be presented to the author(s) or editor(s). In case of dispute, all members of the Board shall be notified, and the President shall appoint an ad hoc committee of the Board to decide the matter; thirty days additional shall be granted for this purpose.

5. The President shall present annually to the Board a report describing the internal manuscript review process, any objections made by Directors before publication or by anyone after publication, any disputes about such matters, and how they were handled.

6. Publications of the NBER issued for informational purposes concerning the work of the Bureau, or issued to inform the public of the activities at the Bureau, including but not limited to the NBER Digest and Reporter, shall be consistent with the object stated in paragraph 1. They shall contain a specific disclaimer noting that they have not passed through the review procedures required in this resolution. The Executive Committee of the Board is charged with the review of all such publications from time to time.

7. NBER working papers and manuscripts distributed on the Bureau's web site are not deemed to be publications for the purpose of this resolution, but they shall be consistent with the object stated in paragraph 1. Working papers shall contain a specific disclaimer noting that they have not passed through the review procedures required in this resolution. The NBER's web site shall contain a similar disclaimer. The President shall establish an internal review process to ensure that the working papers and the web site do not contain policy recommendations, and shall report annually to the Board on this process and any concerns raised in connection with it.

8. Unless otherwise determined by the Board or exempted by the terms of paragraphs 6 and 7, a copy of this resolution shall be printed in each NBER publication as described in paragraph 2 above.

Contents

Introduction

Josh Lerner and Scott Stern

I.1 Introduction

Innovation—whether in the form of new products such as the iPad, new ways of incorporating process technologies such as bar coding, or new management practices—is critical to economic growth. This is particularly true in mature economies such as the United States and Europe, where pressing fiscal and demographic challenges preclude many other avenues to growth. But despite the critical nature of innovation, much remains unclear as to how nations, firms, and academic bodies can encourage this activity. While impressive strides have been made in understanding the economics of innovation over the past few decades, much about this activity remains uncertain or even mysterious.

This volume explores what we do and do not know about this critical area. It is based on the proceedings of the National Bureau of Economic Research (NBER) 50th Anniversary Conference in honor of the influential 1962 volume, *The Rate and Direction of Inventive Activity: Economic and Social Factors*, edited by Richard Nelson. We saw the anniversary of that volume—seen by many as having ushered in the modern era of study of the economics of technological change—as a timely opportunity to not only take stock of the economics of innovation and technological change,

Josh Lerner is the Jacob H. Schiff Professor of Investment Banking at Harvard Business School, with a joint appointment in the Finance and the Entrepreneurial Management Units, and a research associate and codirector of the Productivity, Innovation, and Entrepreneurship Program at the National Bureau of Economic Research. Scott Stern is the School of Management Distinguished Professor of Technological Innovation, Entrepreneurship, and Strategic Management at the Massachusetts Institute of Technology Sloan School of Management and a research associate and director of the Innovation Policy Working Group at the National Bureau of Economic Research.

but also to bring together leading scholars to identify the shape of the field going forward.

As the discussions by Arrow, Nelson, and Rosenberg and Stern later in this volume highlight, the backdrop for the 1960 conference was the growing recognition of the role of technological change in economic growth. This insight—which grew out of the insights of Abramovitz, Kendrick, and Schmookler, and the key work of Solow—highlighted that increased inputs (e.g., more capital expenditures and workers) could only explain a modest fraction of American economic growth over the past century. As Nelson noted in his introduction to the 1962 volume, "The lion's share had to be attributed to something else: to increased productivity or efficiency."

While this insight sparked a desire to understand the nature of technological innovation, there was also a more practical motivation. The Soviet Union's launch of the Sputnik satellite had raised alarms about the United States' competitive positioning, and led to a need to better understand the circumstances through which scientific insights could be translated into new defense and space technologies. Along with the creation of the National Science Foundation and the creation and availability of more data on research and development activities, the time was ripe for a more systematic research program in economics on both the causes and consequences of invention and technological change.

The 1960 conference brought together many leading thinkers of the era, and resulted in a volume whose influence extended well beyond the typical conference volume. A number of papers have resonated through the decades, but none more than the final essay, Arrow's "Economic Welfare and the Allocation of Resources for Invention." In it, Arrow lays out the implications of the conflict between the low social cost of using knowledge and the high cost of producing it, and the subtle ways in which information and knowledge are distinct economic goods. The implications for firms seeking to appropriate returns and for social welfare are substantial, as the author explicates. The five thousand-plus citations that this essay has on Google Scholar are a testimony to the power of these ideas.

But to focus on this one essay misses the richness and breadth of the 1962 volume. The conference brought together a rich array of methodologies, from theory to large-sample empirical analyses to economic history to case studies. The range of topics was broad, from the nature of appropriability to the role of organizational structure in shaping research and development productivity. Not surprisingly, (in light of both the times and the affiliation of a number of the authors with the RAND Corporation), there was a heavy emphasis on the nature of publicly funded innovation, particularly in the defense sector. The conference, as its subtitle suggested, also explicitly sought to draw in perspectives from other social sciences. Thus, the volume simultaneously provided general building blocks for understanding the innovation process and reflected the issues of its day.

The current volume builds on this legacy. Organized under the aegis of the NBER's Innovation Policy Working Group, the conference and this volume seek to honor and assess the original volume, and sponsor new theoretical and empirical contributions on fundamental questions in the economics of innovation and technological change. An explosion of empirical and theoretical research in the economics of technological change, as well as contemporary policy challenges, suggests an opportunity for reevaluation of the traditional innovation policy framework.

Among the questions that we sought to grapple with were:

- How do innovation and diffusion depend on the institutional environment in which new technology is developed and commercialized, and how are the drivers of innovation changing over time? Does the pervasive diffusion of information technology impact the economics of knowledge accumulation itself?
- What is the role of "open" research environments (from scientific communities to the open-source software movement) in innovation? What are the economic and institutional drivers of open-access versus proprietary innovation models, and how does institutional design impact innovation outcomes?
- What determines the allocation of research investment between the public and the private sector (and what should determine that allocation)? What role do universities (and other nonprofit research institutions) play in long-term technical change and economic progress?
- How do innovation and diffusion impact economic growth? Has technical change moderated or exacerbated macroeconomic fluctuations? What is the relationship between innovation and economic inequality, both within and across countries? What is the role of innovation—as a driver or a remedy—in the current economic crisis?

We sought to achieve these goals through two approaches. First, we circulated a call for papers, and encouraged submissions from leading scholars. These essays were refined through discussions in a July 2009 preconference at Laguna Niguel, California, and formal presentations and discussions in the September 2010 conference in Warrenton, Virginia. We recorded and edited the discussants' remarks from this conference to give a fresh perspective on the issues raised by the authors. In addition, we incorporated into the conference three panel discussions, which took a broader view of the issues under consideration. The key presentations from these discussions (though not the lively back and forth that ensued) are also captured in this volume.

At the same time, we should acknowledge that in some respects, we were less ambitious than the 1960 volume. Given the explosion of economics research into innovation, not to mention the great growth of work on the topic in the strategy, technology management, and social psychology literatures, we decided to keep a sharp disciplinary focus. (It should be noted, though, reflecting the broadening of the economics literature during this period, a number of papers cross over into topics that have typically been the purview of economic sociologists and other social scientists.) Nor did we try to explicitly duplicate the many case studies in the 1962 volume, though many papers use field research techniques.

The success of this conference was a function of many people and organizations. The Scientific Committee—Philippe Aghion, Ken Arrow, Richard Nelson, Manuel Trajtenberg, and Hal Varian—helped to shape the vision and agenda for the conference. They also helped considerably to boost this effort through their contributions. Both Marty Feldstein and Jim Poterba, the current and former NBER presidents, were uniformly supportive of this idea. Patrick Gaule, the 2010 to 2011 NBER Innovation Policy fellow, played a key role in organizing the conference and the production of the volume. Hal Varian gave a thoughtful and provocative after-dinner talk at the event. Carl Beck, Brett Maranjian, and Rob Shannon of the NBER conference department provided critical logistical support. The Kauffman Foundation was generous in their support of this initiative, playing a key role in supporting the Innovation Policy effort at the NBER more generally as well as funding this particular conference. We are particularly grateful to Bob Litan, Carl Schramm, and Bob Strom.

I.2 Broad Themes

In developing the agenda for the conference, we sought to focus on forward-looking research that offers direction for the field going forward. As one considers the essays as a whole, it is useful to highlight four thematic clusters: the university-industry interface, the interdependency between market structure and innovation, the sources of innovation, and the social impact of innovation.

I.2.1 The University-Industry Interface

One topic that received relatively little scrutiny in the 1962 volume, but much more attention here, was the university-industry interface. Certainly, many authors espoused a belief that basic research was important for innovation, and called for more work in the area. But to a large extent, much of the focus was on government and corporate research. This volume considers the consequences of academic research to a considerably greater extent.

Of course, this shift in emphasis largely reflects real-world developments over the past five decades. The passage of the Bayh-Dole Act in 1980 and the proliferation of multibillion-dollar companies founded on university research (from Genentech to Google) have vastly increased the economic profile of these activities. Moreover, the revolution in data availability—particularly, the detailed data on citations of papers and patents—has facilitated work in this area.

Gans and Murray take a broad, conceptual look at the issues associated with funding academic research. They begin with a paradox: when agencies funding scientific research emphasize basic research over translational projects, they are criticized for their impracticality, but when they emphasize near-term mission-oriented R&D projects, they are criticized for crowding out what industry would have done otherwise and backing redundant efforts. To help sharpen our thinking about these issues, the authors present a model in which the supply of and demand for public funds plays out in a world where private funding sources also exist.

In their model, public officials can decide not simply which projects to fund, but also what requirements regarding scientific openness to add. They show that the choices regarding funding sources—and the impact of publicly imposed requirements around disclosure—will vary not only with the scientific merit of the research proposal, but also with the immediacy of its applicability to commercial uses. In particular, they highlight that providing unrestricted public funds (i.e., without any disclosure requirements) may lead to many researchers who would otherwise be industry funded accepting public dollars: this can actually lead to fewer projects being funded overall without consequent gains in openness. Though some of the key issues raised here have long been recognized—indeed, both Nelson (1959) and Nelson's careful study of the transistor in the 1962 volume raised related issues—Gans and Murray provide fresh insight into the subtle ways that public and private funding interact, and the role that government policy (e.g., mandating openness) plays in shaping the production and use of knowledge.

Azoulay, Graff Zivin, and Sampat look at the consequences of academic mobility: to what extent does the movement of high-achieving faculty members affect both scientific and commercialization activities at their old and new schools? To examine this, they look at articles published by and patents granted to the mobile scientist before he departed for the new school, comparing these to similar outputs by scientists who did not move. In this way, they hope to limit the heterogeneity that can distort simpler comparisons.

The analysis suggests that the citations to a departing scientist's articles from the university where he or she departs are barely affected by the move. But citations to the departing scientist's patents (whether made in articles or patents) decline sharply at the originating school. This suggests that the physical proximity of the researcher is important to ensuring knowledge flows to industry. Not surprisingly, citations to the scientist's work at his or her new location increase dramatically once the move is complete. The authors offer the intriguing conclusion that barriers to scientific mobility may actually be socially detrimental, as they prevent the kind of knowledge gains from the mixing of ideas.

Kahn and MacGarvie also explore the impact of scientific mobility, focusing on the Fulbright Foreign Student Program, which since 1946 has brought students from many countries to undertake graduate studies in the United

States, with the expectation that they spend at least two years in their home nation before they can return. Like the prior paper (though with a substantially smaller sample and less exact controls), they compare the output of the Fulbright scientists with a set of otherwise similar scientists who studied in the United States without such a return requirement.

Tracing the subsequent career of these researchers, the authors find that the Fulbright scientists (relative to the controls) spent more than twice as many of their postgraduation years outside the United States when compared to controls. While the program does increase collaborations between US scientists and those based in the emerging world, Fulbright scientists from poorer nations or those with a weaker scientific tradition have fewer publications and less of an impact. This effect is not seen among those scholars from wealthier nations or those with a stronger scientific base.

These last two chapters suggest one profound difference between the two volumes: the vast increase in data availability. The richness of citation and personnel data has given us both the ability to test relationships that previously could only be discussed abstractly or else explored only in case studies. It also underlines the importance of phenomena that were previously not fully appreciated, such as the impact of geographic proximity on knowledge spillovers, a topic that received little mention in the 1962 volume.

I.2.2 Market Structure and Innovation

A second cluster of chapters focuses on a question that goes back at least to Schumpeter, but was brought back to prominence within economics with Arrow's 1962 paper: what is the relationship between market structure and innovation? Bresnahan, Greenstein, and Henderson focus squarely on a central puzzle in this line of research: why are incumbents who are able to succeed within a given technological trajectory often so ineffective at being able to take advantage of a new technological trajectory? This question is particularly salient once one considers the many advantages that incumbents are able to leverage in introducing new technology.

Bresnahan, Greenstein, and Henderson undertake detailed case studies of two historically important transitions—the introduction of the personal computer (PC) and the browser—to evaluate this question. Their analysis allows them to both assess the adequacy of existing theories (e.g., anticannibalization concerns, or the potential for organizational barriers within incumbents) and to identify key patterns that seem to characterize the process of creative destruction. Their analysis points to a novel driver of creative destruction—*diseconomies of scope* induced by the presence of necessarily shared assets within the firm. When the strategic commitments made by an incumbent are necessarily reflected in business activities for *both* the old and the new technological trajectory, the incumbent may not simply be able to create a "firm-within-a-firm" to preempt competitive entry. The fact that the incumbent must simultaneously sell both the new and the old technologies may put them at a disadvantage in both technologies relative to an entrant; these disadvantages can be observed through the significant organizational conflicts that accompany technological transitions.

The case study approach (though out of favor at traditional economics journals) allows Bresnahan, Greenstein, and Henderson to undertake a close reading of the evidence. This leads to a novel hypothesis about the underlying forces that may be at the heart of many cases of incumbent failure in the face of the gale of creative destruction.

Spulber offers a complementary perspective on this question by considering how the strategic interaction between incumbents and innovators in the market for ideas shapes (and is shaped by) the potential for product market competition. On the one hand, if the market for ideas is efficient (e.g., there can be perfect, low-cost transfer of both new designs and process innovations), then incumbents and entrants will have an incentive to cooperate (rather than compete) in the commercialization process. However, when technology transfer (of either product designs or processes) is imperfect, then innovators will have an incentive to enter the product market (and so start-up innovation will be associated with increased competition).

The question then arises: when is entry more likely? While Spulber considers a range of cases (and some of the results are subtle), an overarching lesson of the analysis is that the incentives for entry are higher when the underlying technologies are more (horizontally) differentiated from each other. Since the gains from cooperation are higher when the degree of differentiation is lower, the likelihood of entrepreneurial entry is higher under conditions of high product differentiation and imperfect technology transfer. Spulber highlights the idea that the impact of start-up innovation on market structure depends crucially on the nature of strategic interaction between start-ups and established firms, and that such strategic interaction is itself going to depend on the specific nature of the innovations impacting an industry at any point in time.

Daron Acemoglu also considers how strategic interaction impacts the relationship between innovation and incumbency, but places emphasis on a dynamic setting that incorporates not simply the rate but also the *direction* of innovative activity. Specifically, Acemoglu considers an environment where there are multiple potential "research lines," but only one research line is commercially active at any point in time. Acemoglu is particularly interested in cases where there is a chance that the commercially active research line will at some point be made obsolete (e.g., as the result of exhausting a natural resource), and focuses attention on the underlying incentives to invest in the alternative (but not yet commercially viable) technology line. Since the returns from innovation are only realized for those generations where the research line is commercially active, the private returns to innovation in the alternative line will be low unless there is a high likelihood that the currently active line is about to made obsolete.

This analysis highlights an important externality: while the social planner would prefer investments on the alternative research line (so that the level of this technology is at a high when the other technology is made obsolete), the private incentive to invest in the alternative research line is too low. In considering the impact of alternative policy approaches, Acemoglu surfaces a novel argument for public funding of a diverse set of research approaches: researchers with different incentives, capabilities, or perspectives may contribute to a more diverse research portfolio, and so contribute to economic growth.

Finally, Carl Shapiro turns our attention to how these types of analyses can inform innovation policy. In an essay that clearly captured the prize for the most clever chapter title, Shapiro offers a synthetic assessment of how the lessons of the economics of innovation inform merger analysis. Shapiro contrasts two dominant perspectives that inform merger analysis: Arrow versus Schumpeter. Where the Arrow approach suggests the positive impact of product market competition on innovation, the Schumpeter perspective focuses instead on the innovation inducements due to scale and the prospects of market power.

Shapiro emphasizes that these two perspectives—often taken to be contradictory—are not at all incompatible with one another, at least as they apply to policy analysis. While recognizing that the relationship between innovation and market structure is quite complex, Shapiro focuses on three key principles that build on the insights of both the Arrow and Schumpeter perspectives. By so doing, they can help us understand the impact of mergers on innovation incentives. Specifically, Shapiro highlights the idea that innovation is enhanced when (a) firms have the prospect of either gaining or protecting sales by providing additional value to consumers (the Contestability Principle), (b) the level of intellectual property protection is higher (the Appropriability Principle), and (c) complementary assets can be combined to enhance innovative capabilities (the Synergy Principle). Illustrating the role of these principles in clarifying the innovation impact of mergers in particular cases and circumstances, Shapiro's essay highlights the role of careful economic analysis in helping to clarify policy analysis, and how long-standing conceptual frameworks can be enriched by careful, formal reconsideration.

Taken together, this second group of essays provides a very useful delineation of our understanding of the relationship between innovation and market structure. Fundamentally, the economic analysis of market-based innovation incentives relies on a dynamic understanding of how innovation shapes (and is shaped) by industrial organization. These dynamics are themselves dependent on both the nature of competitive interaction between different technologies, and the organizational consequences of innovation. Interestingly, as a number of the authors and discussants remark, there are too few systematic studies of this process, and it has been difficult to bridge the gap between the types of qualitative and theoretical insights emerging from these chapters and the type of empirical research that tends to dominate scholarly discussion. That gap surely represents an important direction for future research.

I.2.3 The Sources and Motivations of Innovators

A third cluster of chapters focuses more directly on the incentives and motives of inventors and innovators, and highlights the role of institutions in shaping the behavior of individuals and firms in producing new technologies.

Moser and Rhode consider the impact of formal intellectual property rights—specifically, the Plant Patent Act of 1930—on innovation. While standard economic theory suggests that the introduction of formal intellectual property protection should enhance appropriability and the incentives to innovate, there are only a very small number of cases where economists are able to observe whether a *change* in intellectual property law results in a change in the degree or nature of innovation in a particular area. Moser and Rhode focus on the impact of the Plant Patent Act on patenting and innovation in roses, which were the plant variety most impacted by the Act (nearly half of all plant patents between 1930 and 1970 were for rose varieties). An important element of their analysis is that they are able to distinguish between the impact of the Act on patenting (which of course increased) versus the impact on innovation (which they measure in terms of new rose registrations).

Their empirical evidence poses an important challenge for the standard theory: after 1930, the number of registrations by American nurseries actually fell, and European nurseries accounted for an increasing share of new rose registrations. Instead of increasing the rate of innovation, it seems that the Plant Patent Act may have had the consequence of increasing the relative importance of commercial nurseries relative to hobbyists in the American industry, and spurred the use of patents as a defensive and strategic tool in the context of litigation. Importantly, the findings of Moser and Rhode are made more plausible by the fact that there are important nonpecuniary motivations on the part of (at least an important group of) innovators in this area; prior to the Plant Patent Act, both hobbyists and public sector breeders played an important role in establishing distinctive American rose varieties, but their role was diminished thereafter.

Mokyr and Meisenzahl offer a complementary perspective, offering an economic history approach of the peculiar nature of innovators and their motivations and interests during the British Industrial Revolution. Their analysis focuses in particular on the body of individuals who advanced technology and innovation during this period. Moving beyond the celebration of specific individuals responsible for macroinventions such as the steam engine, Mokyr and Miesenzahl focus in particular on “tweakers”—individuals involved in the process of incremental improvement and refinement central to cumulative technical progress. Their analysis builds on a novel database of such individuals, and offers a portrait of their careers.

Most notably, Mokyr and Miesenzahl provide suggestive evidence that formal intellectual property rights such as patents likely played (at best) a limited role in the incentives and compensation of tweakers. Instead, their primary incentives seem to be associated with the reputation-based and first-mover advantages associated with innovation, as well as the rewards to be gained through prize mechanisms or nonpecuniary rewards such as membership in societies and the like. Similar to Moser and Rhode, this analysis suggests that, in the presence of multiple innovation incentive instruments, the traditional arguments for patents may be weakened. Perhaps more importantly, the chapter opens up a critical window into both the motives and training underlying incremental innovation. As such, the chapter addresses an important concern: one of the enduring challenges among students of technology has been the difficulty of moving beyond the study of formalized, often patent-oriented innovation to the many more informal processes through which technologies are improved.

Finally, Boudreau and Lakhani directly confront the impact of innovator preferences on innovation and research productivity. Their chapter reports on an actual field experiment that tests for the influence of "sorting" on innovator effort. They focus in particular on the potential heterogeneity among innovators in whether they prefer a more cooperative versus competitive research environment. The focus of the field experiment is a real-world multiday software coding exercise in which participants are able to express a preference for being sorted into a cooperative or competitive environment (i.e., incentives in the cooperative environment are team-based, while incentives in the competitive environment are individualized and depend on relative performance). Half of the participants are indeed sorted on the basis of their preferences, while half of the participants are assigned to the two modes on a random basis.

Boudreau and Lakhani find strong evidence that sorting matters: those who prefer a competitive regime exert twice as much effort when they are assigned to that regime, and those who prefer a cooperative regime also increase their effort by 50 percent when they are assigned to their preferred regime. In addition to the sheer novelty of their experimental approach for the economics of innovation, their substantive results once again highlight the important role that motivation and preferences play in understanding innovative activity. Not simply a matter of providing appropriate incentives for effort, innovators exhibit strong preferences over the organization and incentives in their work environment, and the ability to match workers with their preferences has significant effects on overall research productivity.

Similar to the findings of the earlier volume, these detailed empirical studies of the motives of innovators pose a significant challenge to traditional economic models of incentives for innovators. For example, in all three studies there seems to be a significant role and interaction with the broader innovation "community." The historical evidence from the tweakers of Mokyr and Miesenzahl and the rose growers in Moser and Rhode suggests that the patent system, in particular, either played a limited role or (in the case of Moser and Rhode) may actually have undermined innovation incentives on the part of individual growers. As we discuss further later on, a great deal of the panel discussions and commentary at the conference focused on the drivers of volunteer contributors, which we may refer to as "wiki-motives." What is the impact of traditional innovation policy instruments such as patents or prizes in environments when innovators are motivated by recognition and community concerns rather than monetary payoffs? How important are such motives in understanding aggregate innovative effort, and how has this varied across time and context?

I.2.4 The Social Impact of Innovation

A final grouping of chapters grapples with what is undoubtedly the most challenging issue in the economics of technological change: assessing the social consequences of innovation. As Paul David points out in his discussion, an implicit assumption of policymakers today is that more innovation is undoubtedly a good thing. Economic theory takes a more cautious view, suggesting that the private sector can engage in too much as well as too little innovation.

Part of the reason for the presence of misconceptions, of course, is that the assessment of innovations' social impact is a daunting task. While industrial organization economists have made great strides in developing structural models that allow social welfare calculations over the past few decades, the types of dynamic changes that characterize important innovations defy ready characterization. The three chapters in this section take differing approaches to this challenging issue.

Lerner and Tufano explore the broader impacts of financial innovation. This class of breakthroughs—which attracted no real discussion in the 1962 volume—has broad impacts: not only do financial services represent a significant economic share (estimates in the United States run as high as over 30 percent[1]), but in an ideal world, they enable households to have new choices for investment and consumption, and firms to raise capital in larger amounts and at a lower cost than they could otherwise. At the same time, financial innovation has been criticized by Paul Krugman and others as a key driver of the recent global financial crisis.

In this chapter, the authors review the literature on financial innovation

1. Available at: http://www.ggdc.net/databases/10_sector.htm.

and highlight the similarities and differences between financial innovation and other forms of innovation. The chapter proposes a research agenda to systematically address the social welfare implications of financial innovation. To complement existing empirical and theoretical methods, the authors propose (and take some initial steps toward) the examination of case studies of systemic (widely adopted) innovations, explicitly considering counterfactual histories had the innovations never been invented or adopted.

Field takes a close look at the boom-bust pattern that characterizes many industries. During the boom period, there is a dramatic accumulation of physical capital—think of the huge efforts to lay broadband during the Internet boom of the late 1990s—followed by a contraction. In the short run, it is easy to see how such a contraction leads to a decline in productivity, as excess capacity lies unused.

But this chapter is interested in a more challenging question: what are the long-run consequences of these boom-bust cycles? To what extent are the resources accumulated during booms the appropriate ones, or do they represent wrong-headed investment decisions brought about by a frenzied market? To examine these questions, Field examines the experiences of railroads during the Great Depression. This was a difficult period for the industry: the economic downturn, along with increased competition from automobiles and trucks, led to a sharp contraction in demand for railroads. Moreover, access to capital was largely cut off after a period of heavy expenditures. He shows that the industry undertook a major restructuring to utilize labor and capital resources more effectively. Both capital and labor inputs declined substantially. Yet logistical innovation enabled railroads to record slightly more revenue ton miles of freight and book almost as many passenger miles in 1941 as they had in 1929. Adversity seems to have triggered a wave of innovation in this industry.

In the final chapter in this cluster, Bresnahan focuses on the recombination and reuse of key general purpose technologies (GPTs), which he defines as widely used discoveries capable of ongoing improvement that enable complementary innovations. He argues that a critical factor behind the creation of these key technologies is the extent to which the broad prospects for reuse can be anticipated.

Bresnahan distinguishes between two kinds of knowledge. He argues that technical knowledge—the understanding of how a firm can transform a technology into a product—is relatively commonplace. But an understanding of market demand and how an invention might be used in other sectors—which he refers to as entrepreneurial knowledge—is a rarer and more valuable asset. Because of the scarcity of entrepreneurial knowledge, the returns from developing a GPT may be much lower than they would be otherwise. But over time, through a process of innovations and product introductions, this scarce entrepreneurial knowledge may become much more widely known. He illustrates his theory with a number of cases from the information technology industry, where important GPTs were only developed after numerous false starts.

These three chapters take very different approaches to understanding the broader impact of innovation on social welfare. Despite the challenging nature of these questions, and the absence of well-accepted answers, the importance of this topic remains a major challenge to the economics of technological change.

I.3 Panel Discussions

In addition to the formal papers (and discussions), the conference included three panel discussions. By design, the panels were intended to be provocative, and to identify key research challenges going forward. Though each of the three panels were different in both style and substance, each significantly expanded the scope of discussion within the conference, and highlighted some of the central limitations of current models or empirical methodologies. The volume includes short contributions by nine of the panel chairs and participants, based on transcripts of their remarks.

The first panel—"The Impact of the 1962 *Rate and Direction* Volume: A Retrospective"—explicitly linked the 1960 and 2010 conferences, and included commentaries by two of the central participants in that earlier effort. Rosenberg and Stern began the discussion with a critical assessment of the 1962 volume, with a focus on identifying why that earlier volume turned out to be so influential on subsequent scholarship. The central contention of their remarks is that the Rate and Direction Conference can be interpreted as a reaction to the work by Solow and others highlighting the *aggregate* implications of technological change. More than simply a debate about the nature of the "residual," the 1960 conference focused attention on the central *economic* questions raised by inventive activity, innovation, and technological change. Specifically, the original conference highlighted (a) the nature of innovation as an economic good, (b) the economics of the organization of research and development, and (c) the industrial organization of innovation-intensive industries and sectors, with a particular focus on dynamics and evolution. As a marker in the history of economic thought in this area, a central contribution of the earlier conference was to crystallize the questions and issues that would come to dominate the *microeconomics* of innovation and technological change for the foreseeable future.

Nelson expanded on these themes. He focused on some broad lessons that have emerged since the earlier conference and also on important methodological issues that have been raised. Nelson noted that an important divide exists between the type of theory and empirical research emphasized within the United States (and within the NBER) and the interdisciplinary, evolutionary approach that has been emphasized by researchers such as those at the Science Policy Research Unit (SPRU) in the United Kingdom. Nelson argued that some of the underlying tensions between these two camps were foreshadowed in the earlier volume: the largely empirical tradition pioneered by Kuznets and Schmookler (and reflected in the NBER Productivity Program and its growth under Zvi Griliches) sat alongside (sometimes uncomfortably) the detailed case studies or innovation systems studies emphasized within the evolutionary tradition.

Arrow took a broad view of the issues that both conferences grappled with. His comments crystallized why economists have had such difficulty in clarifying the nature of innovation as an economic good: "How can you have a theory of the unexpected?" Arrow highlighted the idea that the economics of innovation must confront and incorporate some of the unusual properties of innovation, both in terms of its production (e.g., the significant level of uncompensated effort toward inventive effort, in areas ranging from medicine to Wikipedia) and use.

These panelist remarks (and subsequent discussion) highlighted how the peculiar nature of innovation poses an ongoing challenge to theory and measurement. They illustrated why the wide-ranging and exploratory nature of the 1962 volume has had such a significant and long-lived impact on subsequent work.

In many ways, the second panel—"Innovation Incentives, Institutions, and Economic Growth"—built on the first panel, reconsidering the implications of innovation and technological change. Paul David opened that panel with a deliberate mission—"mass provocation." He focused his remarks on the underlying (though often implicit) assumption among economists that a higher rate of innovation is almost always preferred. David pointed out that the social impact of technological change depends not only on innovation but on diffusion. The ultimate impact of research investments depends on how those research investments are organized, and the complex process by which technologies are improved and adapted over time and context. Without considering the dynamic process by which social systems adapt and incorporate technological change, it is difficult to consider the net impact of new technologies on human welfare.

Philippe Aghion looked at a related question, the implications of advances in endogenous growth for both macroeconomics and microeconomics. Aghion argued that a major contribution of theories of economic growth that explicitly endogenize the production and diffusion of technology is to identify the potential policy impacts of different types of intervention. Aghion stated that contemporary policy matters insofar as it facilitates a higher level of innovative investment and shifts the long-run growth rate. A range of recent evidence highlights the role of ensuring the ability to protect ideas (e.g., a stronger patent system) in economic growth, and the potential benefits of "industrial policy" measures.

Paul Romer also contributed remarks to the panel (not included in this volume), focusing on the dynamic interplay between different types of theory (e.g., verbal versus formal). Consistent with Aghion's discussion, Romer emphasized the specific contribution that models of endogenous growth have played; in one example, Romer highlighted the central role that appropriability conditions play in determining the rate of aggregate long-term technological change. The panel put a spotlight on the central role of policy and institutions in shaping the long-term rate and direction of technological change, and the value of bridging more narrow studies of the innovation process with more aggregate treatments in order to clarify the long-term drivers of economic growth.

These themes then were reinforced in the final panel discussion—"The Art and Science of Innovation Policy." After brief remarks by Bronwyn Hall, Glenn Hubbard focused on some of the challenges of developing and implementing well-designed innovation policy initiatives. Hubbard pointed out the disjunction between arguments for particular policies—for example, a particular tax rate or regulatory change—and the broader evidence that the rate and impact of innovation reflect broader measures of the overall innovation environment. Hubbard also emphasized the disjunction between academic and policy approaches. He also highlighted the role of certain types of institutions—for example, long-term interagency working groups—in facilitating a more sophisticated innovation policy-making process.

Dominique Foray reinforced these ideas, focusing in particular on the limited influence of economic science on policy making. Reflecting on his experiences within Europe, Foray argued that policy debates are often characterized by a low level of empirical sophistication, and that conditional statements or caveats often result in a diminished impact of rigorous economic analysis. Foray also highlighted that the bulk of innovation policy initiatives have been focused on enhancing the overall rate of innovation, but that an increasing share of innovation policy challenges are now about the direction of innovation (e.g., addressing climate change).

Finally, Trajtenberg considered the broader legacy of the Nelson-Arrow paradigm (with its focus on appropriability and the role of government support for early-stage research) on innovation policy. Trajtenberg highlighted that many of the central challenges facing innovation policymakers cannot be addressed directly through the Nelson-Arrow framework. For example, while the Nelson-Arrow framework assumes a single potential public funder, the question facing policymakers today is how much should an individual country fund, given the global nature of research and the potential to benefit from research conducted in other jurisdictions. Similar to the other panelists, Trajtenberg also remarked on the limited influence of rigorous economic analysis on actual policy, and suggests a focus on more policy-oriented research.

These panel discussions raised a rich array of issues. While there were more questions than answers, they suggested a variety of topics that should reward scrutiny by researchers in the years to come.

I.4 Crosscutting Insights and Themes

Taken as a whole, the chapters and discussions highlight some crucial and novel insights into the economics of innovation and technological change, and the role of policy and institutions in shaping innovation, diffusion, and ultimately, the social returns to technological change. While this volume cannot capture the full range of these more subtle implications, it is worthwhile to highlight a few central and novel ideas that were surfaced during the conference.

I.4.1 Innovation Externalities

The conference raised the hypothesis that the underinvestment problem is more pervasive, more subtle, and perhaps more pernicious that is usually understood. Building on the classic treatments of Nelson (1959) and Arrow (1962) emphasizing appropriability, a great deal of economics research has focused on how to provide sufficient market-based incentives for innovation (without inducing dissipative racing or rent-seeking).

A number of papers in the conference suggested, however, that our traditional understanding of the appropriability problem does not go far enough. Bresnahan, for example, emphasizes the idea that the history of general purpose technologies suggests that the conditions giving rise to their initial development usually arise in the context of a narrow application. This analysis suggests that innovation incentives are shaped by the prospective returns associated with that narrow application, rather than the returns associated with the diffusion of the general purpose technology. Externality problems can arise when the information about the potential impact of a new technology is widely diffused, so that commercialization of a general purpose technology depends on the coordination of multiple economic actors. In that case, no single actor can understand or appreciate the potential social impact of that innovation from an ex ante perspective. As Ben Jones emphasized in his discussion, "the fact that you can't identify the recombinant possibilities ex-ante means that you can't easily solve the bargaining problem in practice." Accordingly, the level of investment focused on general purpose innovations will be low.

Though different in its specifics, a similar theme runs through the analysis of Acemoglu. In that chapter, potential innovators will have little incentive to invest in an immature technology that cannot earn immediate commercial returns, even though the improvement of that technology over time will yield significant social benefits once an older technology becomes obsolete. Of course, it is possible that property rights could be specified in a way so that early innovators in alternative technologies retained some claim on the returns that ultimately arise from research lines that they are associated with; however, such rights would themselves pose a disincentive for later-stage innovators.

Gans and Murray broaden the scope further in their analysis of disclosure and knowledge accumulation. They highlight the idea that, even if the incentives for research investment are appropriate, the incentives for disclosing the knowledge resulting from that research are shaped by the strategic and institutional environment. Not only is there a significant gap between the private and social incentives for disclosure, but what seems to be a straightforward policy solution—such as mandating the disclosure of publicly funded research—can actually reduce the net level of disclosure (by pushing researchers to accept privately funded research contracts that mandate secrecy).

Together, these insights (and others dispersed throughout the volume) suggest that a central insight of the 1962 volume—the gap between the private and social returns to inventive investment—remains not only relevant today but is likely to stand as a central concern in the economics of innovation for the foreseeable future.

I.4.2 Agency Costs and Innovation

Another theme had to do with the impact of agency costs on the success of innovation projects. This theme—which was only dealt with implicitly in the 1962 volume—cut across a variety of the papers. Innovative projects are a natural place to see agency problems at work. Typically, there is substantial uncertainty as to whether a project will work or what the output will be, making the monitoring of effort or contracting on outputs difficult. The researcher is likely to have far more information about the intricacies of the project than his or her supervisors or financiers. In many cases, there are few tangible assets associated with the project making contracting particularly difficult. Market booms and bust may lead to dramatic shifts in the assessment of projects and availability of financing.

Against this backdrop, it is not surprising that economists have highlighted two important agency problems. The first has to do with the way in which innovators are rewarded. The second has to do with the way in which the firm itself is structured, and in particular the trade-offs associated with firm scope. While a number of the papers in the 1962 volume explored the role of individual researchers and the organization of firms, few (the Rubenstein paper is a notable exception) grappled with agency issues. Of course, this reflects the fact that agency theory was not formalized until the 1970s, and that the extent of agency problems in innovation was not thoroughly delineated until works such as Holmstrom (1989) and Aghion and Tirole (1994).

In this volume, the impacts of agency problems in innovation are far more widely recognized. Mokyr and Miesenzahl highlight the many incentives that were offered to British inventers during the Industrial Revolution, ranging from prizes to patents to consulting opportunities. The results from large-sample studies of the effects of incentives on individual researchers are more mixed. Boudreau and Lakhani show how incentives impact the output of software programmers, but that this relationship is mediated by the coders' preferences regarding incentive schemes. Moser and Rhode show that increased incentives—in the form of stronger intellectual property rights for plant varieties in the United States—seem to have not led to more innovation by American nurseries relative to their European counterparts.

At the firm level, Bresnahan, Greenstein, and Henderson explore why two very successful software firms became increasingly unable to respond to competitive threats from new rivals. They argue that neither fears of cannibalization nor the inability to recognize competitive threats were critical: rather, the need to share key assets across old and new businesses created severe organizational conflict.

This volume, then, reflects the increased appreciation of agency problems as a barrier to innovation, and the organizational response that can address them. In a theme we will return to in the final section of this essay, the proliferation of new organizational firms and incentive schemes in research-intensive industries suggests that opportunities for research into these issues are far from being exhausted.

I.4.3 The Analysis of Innovation Policy

A third commonality in the volume is the focus on policy analysis, and the role of innovation within economic policy more generally. While a whole collection of chapters in the current volume focus on the university-industry interface, these interactions were (essentially) in the background of the 1962 volume. Whereas universities were once seen as ivory towers, policymakers have increasingly come to regard innovation resulting from university research (or collaborative projects) as central drivers of regional economic growth.

Though the university-industry interface is seen as ever more important, there has been less attention to how the rules and policies governing these interactions matter. For one example, though the policy origins of the Fulbright program are remote, the program is a primary driver of how foreign graduate students in the United States are trained. The Fulbright program rules have an important impact on the ultimate research productivity of those involved in the program, particularly those from less developed environments. Similarly, Gans and Murray emphasize how the rules governing the disclosure of publicly funded research not only affect that research directly but also the governance of research that is funded by the private sector. As Scotchmer emphasized in her discussion of Gans and Murray, "disclosure rules and other details of public funding should be chosen with an eye to how they affect the funding choices of innovators." More generally, the conference highlights the central role of economic governance and policy for understanding the university-industry interface, and points toward the value of examining specific policies and institutions.

A second domain for policy analysis is the intersection between innovation and antitrust. As highlighted by Shapiro, the impact of antitrust policy on innovation is increasingly salient, and an emerging set of principles may allow economists to offer more concrete policy guidance for policymakers in this area. Indeed, Shapiro builds on a number of prior analyses published in the NBER's "Innovation Policy and the Economy" series in developing these principles. However, there is still a significant gap between the type of principles emphasized by Shapiro and the ability to apply those principles in real time to cases that pose potentially significant antitrust and innovation incentive concerns.

Finally, it is useful to note what might be seen as a nonfinding: in the one chapter in this volume that directly examines the impact of intellectual property policy, Moser and Rhode find little evidence that enhanced patent protection enhances the rate of innovation (and indeed one can interpret their findings as suggesting the opposite). Moreover, as emphasized in the panel discussion of Paul David, it is not clear that the primary goal of innovation policy should simply be to maximize the rate of innovation itself. Ultimately, the policy debate over intellectual property should be guided by the goal of maximizing social welfare, not simply innovations.

I.4.4 New Approaches for Studying Innovation

Over the past few decades, there has been a much greater emphasis placed in the economics literature—led by fields such as labor and development—on ensuring the careful identification of the causal effects behind the phenomena under study. A particular emphasis has been on the development of research methodologies that can address concerns about causality, such as experiments and regression discontinuity approaches.

This movement has posed real challenges for students of the economics of technological change. In the overwhelming majority of cases, given the substantial economic stakes at work and the magnitude of the investments, it is impossible to get a corporation or government to agree to run an experiment in lieu of its usual project management approach. It is a very different thing to randomize the teaching of a few third grade classes than the funding of a potentially multibillion-dollar drug! Moreover, the complexity of the innovation process does not lend itself well to the classic hour-long laboratory experiment.

As a result, the approach to addressing causality concerns has been twofold. First, there has been an emphasis on the development of careful matching approaches, which enables the undertaking of difference-in-difference analyses with a minimum of potential biases (as illustrated by the Azoulay, Graff Zivin, and Sampat chapter in this volume). The second has been to find circumstances where some exogenous shifts have allowed the use of an instrumental variable, such as the consequences of the rise of the Nazis and the consequent expulsion of Jewish scientists (Waldinger 2009) and the US pension reforms that greatly increased the flow of funds into venture capital in the early 1990s (Kortum and Lerner 2000).

This volume has two empirical chapters that represent substantial methodological departures in the economics of technological change, and thus deserve some special comment. First, Boudreau and Lakhani adopt a field experiment approach, exploiting the flexibility of web-based software development schemes to offer different incentive schemes to programmers. This approach seems to be an extremely promising one. While it can be argued that the incentive issues are different in software than other arenas—with the relatively finite project scale and the ability of skilled programmers to address a relatively broad array of challenges—this chapter should trigger many other innovation experiments in the years to come. Second, Lerner and Tufano adopt a counterfactual approach to explore the social consequences of a number of financial innovations. While this methodology remains controversial in economic history, it seems desirable to further explore its applicability to addressing some of the broad challenges in assessing the social impact of innovation.

Finally, the transformation of another methodology well represented in the 1962 volume deserves comment. As Nelson observes in his remarks, many of the participants in the original conference felt that some of the most valuable insights came from the case studies that represented a substantial share of the program.

The history of case studies—or to use the preferred modern parlance, clinical studies—in economics over the past century has been a bumpy one. The representation of such studies in major journals dropped precipitously after the 1950s, reflecting both the strides made by theoretical and empirical researchers and the uneven quality of many of the published cases. But some in the profession still feel that such studies can yield valuable insights into the richness of real-world phenomena, and suggest future directions for theoretical and empirical explorations. Such sentiments led to the initiation of the Sloan "Pin Factory" Project at the NBER and the launch of the clinical section of the *Journal of Financial Economics.*

Here, the field-based methodology is still present, though with a twist. There are a number of case-based chapters in the volume, including Bresnahan, Greenstein, and Henderson, Gans and Moser, Lerner and Tufano, and Moser and Rhode. These chapters can be seen as continuing the field-based tradition in the 1962 volume, but with a more developed theoretical and/or empirical structure than many of those earlier works.

I.5 The Agenda Going Forward

While the range of topics covered in this volume is substantial, there are also substantial lacunae. It is useful to highlight three critical issues that deserve more attention going forward.

The first of these has to do with the globalization of innovation. During the twentieth century, innovation was dominated by a handful of nations, such as the United States, Germany, and Japan. The twenty-first century—as witnessed, for instance, by the changing distribution of patent filings—has already seen a substantial disruption to this established order.

Lying behind this shift is a variety of factors. Governments such as those of China and Singapore have accepted the importance of academic science to economic development, and sought to lure faculty to their national universities, often with substantial investments. Corporations have increasingly sought to exploit the substantial cost savings associated with engineering talent in emerging economies, and what has often started with the overseas transfer of routine technical tasks has expanded in scope and magnitude. Venture capitalists, whether based in Silicon Valley or in emerging economies, have also been an important engine to the diffusion of research and innovative activities.

This rapid globalization of innovation poses many challenges to economists. How does the globalization of innovation affect our understanding of the economics of innovation? For example, the innovation system in many Western nations is characterized by a central role for university technology transfer offices in commercializing academic research, the prevalence of younger firms as strategic partners to and competitors with established players, and the challenges that many incumbents have faced in maintaining their initial innovative thrust. The extent to which these patterns will continue to hold in emerging economies is open to debate, and would reward close scrutiny.

A second area that deserves more scrutiny is the changing nature of incentives for innovators. Over much of the twentieth century, the structure of corporate research efforts, with their academic-type laboratories and weakly powered incentives for researchers, were largely static. However, the organization of research has seen a sharp transformation in recent years. Companies are increasingly relying on strategic alliances and other types of collaborations, and are increasingly proactive in aligning their internal research activities with the innovation system in which they reside. More strikingly, both private and public sector efforts have started to focus on relatively unfamiliar approaches, such as the widespread use of prizes, the proliferation of corporate venture schemes to facilitate spin-outs (and spin-ins), and attempts to harness the creativity and ideas of users and consumers. As was noted at various points in the volume, there seems to have been a significant increase (or at least an increasing awareness) of the roles that volunteers, freelancers, and users play in the innovation process. While a number of chapters in the volume touch on the changing nature of innovation incentives, only Boudreau and Lakhani directly address these issues (and probably not accidentally, do so using a quite novel methodological approach). The study of the subtle ways in which incentives matter for innovation will provide grist for research for the foreseeable future.

A third area is an old—but ongoing—one: the appropriate measurement of the consequences of innovation. As discussed earlier, the measurement of the social welfare consequences of innovation poses some daunting challenges, which defy easy solutions. But even more modest goals, such as accounting for the impact of innovative products in national accounts and price indexes, remain problematic.

It might be surprising that these issues remain problematic, given that economists have been thinking about them since the work of Kuznets, Schmookler, Abramowitz, Griliches, and Solow in the 1950s. Given the central role of innovation and technological change in long-term economic growth, it is perhaps surprising that so few of the chapters in this volume directly examine the welfare implications of innovation, and none of the empirical chapters undertake a detailed welfare analysis. At one level, this absence underscores the intellectual history of the conference and the participants, including the microeconomic and phenomenological orientation of the 1962 volume. At a deeper level, however, it highlights a challenge that was raised by Paul David, Ken Arrow, and Dick Nelson in their panel commentaries. The presumed benefits arising from innovation are indeed not only hard to measure, but are in many cases difficult to conceptualize. For example, while there has undoubtedly been progress in the ability to measure the rate of commercialization of particular types of technologies (e.g., university disclosed inventions), does an increase in this rate imply an increase in social welfare? As Acemoglu pointed out in the conference discussion, there are general equilibrium effects that can often be as important as the main effects when undertaking such welfare calculations, and therefore a great deal of caution should be applied.

Moreover, the nature of technological change—most dramatically, the growing importance of the Internet, particularly the set of applications often referred to as "Web 2.0"—has highlighted the limitations of earlier approaches. Perhaps the most dramatic limitation has been the inability of economic frameworks to account for activities that are free: people around the world are spending more time on blogs, Facebook, and YouTube, and consuming less of many traditional media. And while economists can account for the loss of revenue that newspapers have experienced or declining prime-time television advertising rates, the benefits of these alternative activities resist ready quantification. Building better tools for assessing innovations that are systemic in nature is an ongoing challenge.

The chapters collected in this volume are of necessity limited in scope, as is this survey of the broader territory. One conclusion, though, is inescapable: the study of the rate and direction of inventive activity remains highly vibrant, and is likely to reward scholars from multiple perspectives in the years to come.

References

Aghion, P., and J. Tirole. 1994. "On the Management of Innovation." *Quarterly Journal of Economics* 109: 1185–207.

Arrow, K. J. 1962. "Economic Welfare and the Allocation of Resources for Invention." In *The Rate and Direction of Inventive Activity,* edited by R. Nelson, 609–26. Princeton, NJ: Princeton University Press.

Holmstrom, Bengt. 1989. "Agency Costs and Innovation." *Journal of Economic Behavior and Organization* 12 (3): 305–27.

Kortum, S., and J. Lerner. 2000. "Assessing the Contribution of Venture Capital to Innovation." *RAND Journal of Economics* 31: 674–92.

Nelson, R. R. 1959. "The Simple Economics of Basic Scientific Research." *Journal of Political Economy* 49: 279–306.

Waldinger, Fabian. 2009. "Peer Effects in Science—Evidence From the Dismissal of Scientists in Nazi Germany." Centre for Economic Performance. Discussion Paper no. 910. London School of Economics.

I

Panel Discussion
The Impact of the 1962 *Rate and Direction* Volume, a Retrospective

Why Was *Rate and Direction* So Important?

Nathan Rosenberg and Scott Stern

One is tempted to start by saying: In the beginning was Simon Kuznets. We will not in fact start that way, because Kuznets would be more likely to point to larger social forces or institutions rather than specific individuals—he would have been more likely to point to the National Bureau of Economic Research (NBER)—where much of his early research was conducted, and where he trained and worked with his coauthors, colleagues, and former students, including Schmookler, Kendrick, Abramovitz, Fabricant, Denison, and others.

But our immediate task today is to understand how the 1962 conference volume has ended up playing such an important role in the development of the economics of innovation and technological change over the last half century. The volume includes an extremely diverse range of essays, from case studies of the organization of R&D to careful measurement studies to conceptual and theoretical papers, most notably Ken's paper on the nature of invention as an economic good. On their own, many of the papers would stand as important contributions to the field, and any assessment of their impact will necessarily be incomplete due to their diversity. However, our contention is to argue that the *Rate and Direction* volume had a separate and independent effect. Dick used the opportunity of the Rate and Direction Conference to bring together an extraordinary and diverse

Nathan Rosenberg is the Fairleigh S. Dickinson Jr. Professor of Public Policy Emeritus at Stanford University and an emeritus member of the Board of Directors of the National Bureau of Economic Research. Scott Stern is the School of Management Distinguished Professor of Technological Innovation, Entrepreneurship, and Strategic Management at the Massachusetts Institute of Technology Sloan School of Management and a research associate and director of the Innovation Policy Working Group at the National Bureau of Economic Research.

group of scholars, and focused those scholars on identifying a systematic research program to evaluate (a) the nature of innovation as an economic good, (b) the organization of research and development organizations, and (c) the interrelationship between innovation and the dynamics of industry structure. The volume initiated a systematic research program that offered a timely counterpoint to the macroeconomic approach that equated technological change to "the residual" and treated innovation as exogenous to the economic system. The 1962 volume served a decisive role in establishing the *microeconomics* of innovation and technological change.

To understand this contribution, it is worthwhile to take a brief but informative review of where the field stood in the late 1950s and how it had come to that place. Kuznets (working in large part through the NBER) began, first in the 1930s and then after the war, to systematically undertake a research program focusing on the measurement of economic inputs and outputs with the objective of relating them in some fashion. While measurement had always been a part of economic science, the efforts spearheaded by Kuznets and others involved a very significant increase in the sophistication and comprehensiveness of measurement. Indeed, it is no surprise that the first chapter of the 1962 volume is by Kuznets and is entitled "Inventive Activity: Problems of Definition and Measurement." It is also unsurprising that the commentary is by Jacob Schmookler.

Most importantly, this measurement work demonstrated that the relationship between measured economic inputs (capital and labor) and outputs (gross domestic product [GDP]) was changing dramatically over time and that there was no easy explanation for this. Simply put, the measurement program spearheaded by Kuznets at the NBER illuminated the central economic fact of US economic history.

Of course, the explanatory framework for understanding these empirical findings only emerged in the mid-1950s with the seminal studies of Moses Abramovitz ([1956], reprinted in 1990) and Bob Solow (1956, 1957). Both Abramovitz and Solow highlighted that, over time, the amount of inputs required to produce a given level of output had dramatically increased (an upward shift in productivity of 2 percent per year). Simply put, they had independently discovered—or more accurately, rediscovered—the residual (Copeland 1937; Griliches 1996).

Of course, the interpretation of this increase in total factor productivity (TFP) was more controversial. In 1956, Solow introduced a simple and tractable neoclassical equilibrium growth model. The Solow model simply stated that the relationship between inputs and outputs at a point in time can be described as the "level" of technology; as such, the *changing* relationship between inputs and outputs can be described as "technical change." While Solow was of course aware and recognized that technical change may itself be endogenous, the model took the growth rate in technology—A—to be exogenous. As Solow describes explicitly in his 1957 paper "Technical Change and the Aggregate Production Function," "It will be seen that I am using the term *technical change* as a short-hand expression for any kind of shift in the production function" (Solow 1957, 312).

Importantly, Abramovitz was less sanguine. Abramovitz memorably dubbed the residual "a measure of our ignorance." For example, in Abramovitz's review of Edward Denison's 1962 book *The Sources of Economic Growth and the Alternatives Before Us*. Abramovitz sharply comments that "as a residual, it is the grand legatee of all the errors of estimate embodied in the measures of national product, of inputs conventional and otherwise, and of the economies of scale . . . classified under productivity growth" (Abramovitz 1990, 162). Abramovitz notes that the original estimates of the residual—with more than 85 percent of the increase in income per capita unexplained—can be attributed to various sources, including changes in the intensity of work (i.e., reduction in work hours per worker), education, appropriately measured capital inputs, and changes in technology and organization. For Abramovitz, to understand the sources of growth is not simply a measurement exercise but requires an understanding of the economic forces inducing growth, including the determinants of investment toward invention, and the relationship between those forces and measured economic aggregates (Abramovitz 1990).

Ultimately, to understand the role of innovation in economic growth, it was necessary to move beyond a "black box" approach and build a meaningful microeconomics of technical change. Dick Nelson emphasizes this point exactly in his introduction to the volume, particularly in a section entitled "The Classical Economics Approach and the Black Box." While there had been earlier attempts to make progress—for example, a 1951 Social Science Research Council meeting at Princeton University, and the impactful publications arising from Zvi Griliches doctoral dissertation, it is fair to say that the microeconomics of innovation was at that time in an embryonic state. What was missing was an economics of technical change and innovation grounded in the microeconomic, historical, and institutional environment in which invention and innovation occur. The 1962 volume was in large part the first and a particularly important salvo in that cause.

Spurred by an initiative headed by Charles Hitch, then Chairman of the Economics Department at RAND, Dick Nelson brought together a group of junior and senior scholars to focus on the *rate and direction of inventive activity* as a key for understanding technological change as an economic problem. The volume takes an eclectic approach, with different papers offering different methodologies—from highly descriptive papers to systematic measurement to theory. How, then, does it "hang together" and what factors made the volume so influential?

Three distinctive areas are useful to highlight:

1. The nature of innovation as an economic good
2. The economics of the organization of research and development organizations
3. The industrial organization of innovation-intensive industries and sectors, with a particular focus on dynamics and evolution

Each of these areas is not only a central element of the microeconomics of innovation, but also one in which the 1962 volume serves as the essential starting point (or, more accurately, the starting point after Schumpeter) for the large literature that has been spawned since that time.

The Nature of Innovation As an Economic Good

The 1962 volume was a milestone in articulating how the nature of inventions and innovations as economics goods raise fundamental issues regarding appropriation, indivisibility, and uncertainty. Of course, Dick had raised these issues in his seminal 1959 paper, and issues regarding the nature of ideas as economic goods were an important area of contention among classical economists (see the penetrating summary and history of economic thought on the topic provided in Fritz Machlup's 1958 report for the US Congress, "An Economic View of the Patent System").

With that said, it is useful to consider Ken's distinctive contribution in his paper "Economic Welfare and the Allocation of Resources for Invention." Before diving into the substance, it is perhaps useful to note that, according to Google Scholar, this is Ken's third most highly referenced paper, with more than five thousand citations. Here is where Ken clearly articulates the disclosure problem: "there is a fundamental paradox in the determination of the demand for information; its value for the purchaser is not known until he has the information, but then he has in effect acquired it without cost." (Arrow 1962, 615). The traditional microeconomic notion of "willingness-to-pay" is undermined when one cannot formulate a willingness-to-pay. One cannot do so prior to having information about the idea. Most importantly, in the absence of enforceable intellectual property, once the potential buyer has the information that allows her to formulate a willingness-to-pay, the willingness-to-pay drops to zero.

Interestingly, though Machlup mentions in his 1958 essay that "Indeed, if one always cites only the 'fist and true inventor' of an argument concerning the patent system, one will rarely be able to cite an author from the 20th century" (Machlup 1958, 22), the distinctive role for intellectual property rights in enhancing the ability to negotiate and trade inventions is noted only obliquely (under the general rubric of appropriability issues).

A related contribution of the 1962 volume is the inclusion of early, persuasive empirical studies of appropriability. For example, Enos's careful study of invention and innovation in the petroleum refining industry offers sharp, early insights into the nature of innovation (see Rosenberg 1982, 8; Enos 2002). Enos carefully emphasizes the importance of incremental process innovations, and provides reasonable estimates of the private rates of returns (which he estimates to be quite high). The volume additionally provides evidence about the gap between the private and social rates of return. As Dick notes in the introduction, "A third major problem is that of external economies. Arrow, Kuznets, Machlup, Markham, Merrill, and Nelson all present argument or evidence that, given existing institutions, inventive activity generates values which cannot be captured by the inventor" (Nelson 1962, 14). Indeed, Arrow draws out these implications clearly in terms of the economywide incentives for research: "we expect a free enterprise economy to underinvest in innovation and research . . . because it is risky, because the product can be appropriated to only a limited extent, and because of increasing returns in use" (Arrow 1962, 619). This simple statement has certainly kept us busy.

By focusing on appropriability, the volume contrasts sharply with the treatment of innovation within the neoclassical growth literature. Not content to treat innovation as an exogenous feature of the economic environment, the papers in the volume suggest that the impact of innovation on the aggregate production function depends inherently on the microeconomic and institutional environment. For example, if a principal mechanism of appropriation is through embedding ideas into capital goods (which are protected by patent and sold at a premium), these innovations will be measured as increases in the value of the capital stock; in contrast, if the same idea is diffused for free in a perfectly competitive setting, the increase in labor productivity will be attributed to technical change. To understand the impact of innovation on economic growth, one must first understand the nature of innovation, and this requires a microeconomic orientation.

The Organization of Research and Development Organizations

Second, the 1962 volume is the first real collection of serious studies (in one place) that focuses on the economics of R&D organizations. Several studies in the volume highlight the distinctive ways that invention and innovation are managed, from the subtle structure of incentives to the development of infrastructure that communicates complex technical ideas across large organizations.

Consider Dick's wonderful study of the development of the transistor at Bell Laboratories. The case study is unusually careful, and gives a real sense of how the scientific insight—the transistor effect—resulted in the technological innovation that we have come to know as the transistor. Dick carefully discusses the motives of the scientists, of Bell, and explains how the research project was organized. He presciently highlights key aspects of the research process that have only recently come to be appreciated: the role of freedom on the part of scientists, the role of research teams in creativity, and the impact of private versus public funding on both the rate and direction of research.

Perhaps most notably, Dick clearly—and perhaps for the first time—articulates the *dual* nature of research. Dick emphasizes the fact that a single research program may simultaneously be of fundamental scientific interest (particularly from the perspective of the researchers) yet be associated with immediate and impactful commercial application (particularly from the perspective of the private research funder). He comments: "I have a feeling that duality of interests and results is far from unusual. I wonder how many scientists—university scientists—doing basic research do not think now and then about the possible practical applications of their work. . . . I have the feeling that many scientists in industrial research laboratories . . . are . . . internally torn about the dual nature of the research work" (Nelson 1962, 582). Of course, the dual nature of research has been at the heart of the economics of science and technology for the past half century.

Nelson's case study of the transistor is but one of seven or eight essays that begin to unpack the economics of research and development organizations. These include specific case studies of invention and innovation in the aluminum industry (Peck), the petroleum industry (Enos), DuPont (Mueller), and Bell Labs (Marschak and Nelson). These studies elucidate the impact of alternative incentive systems (e.g., whether to reward individual inventors for their discoveries), the flow of technology and knowledge within and across organizational boundaries (e.g., by examining the ultimate origin of the inventions that were ultimately impactful at companies such as DuPont), and distinctive mechanisms for appropriability, including speed, secrecy, and formal tools such as patents.

As well, the volume includes several essays emphasizing the importance of human capital and the motivation and supply of inventors, scientists, and engineers. Kuznets of course emphasized the role of education and the application of specialized researchers in his work (and also recognized the difficulties of inferring the *output* of innovation simply by measuring the *input* into innovation). Also, several papers highlight the distinctive nature of the human capital required for innovation: a preference for autonomy and freedom combined with the need to invest in specialized training at the early stages of the career.

From the perspective of the economics literature, few if any detailed case studies of the organization of research prior to this time continue to motivate theoretical and empirical research. The 1962 volume includes half a dozen, and ultimately motivated the type of systematic research seen in the work of David Mowery, Wes Cohen, and others. By bringing together a collection of careful case studies grounded in the phenomena yet attentive to economic theory, the volume offered a path for understanding the subtle interrelationship between the inventive process and the organization of R&D activities.

Innovation and the Dynamics of Industrial Organization

Finally, the 1962 volume is the beginning of serious industrial organization studies of strategy and innovation incentives. Notably, the section of Ken's paper entitled "Competition, Monopoly and the Incentive to Innovate" is perhaps the first important model of a nonobvious strategic effect regarding the incentives for innovative investment, and spawned the entire "patent racing" literature. Perhaps more saliently, the Arrow replacement effect serves as a powerful foundation for our modern understanding of Schumpeterian competition, and is present in the work of Aghion, Scotchmer, Segal and Whinston, and others.

More generally, the volume suggests that innovation incentives and the consequences of innovation are shaped by the microeconomic conditions of the product market. From the role of demand (as emphasized by Schmookler) to the potential for detailed strategic interaction (see Peck's detailed discussion of the market structure and innovation relationship in the aluminum industry), the 1962 volume highlighted the idea that the causes and consequences of innovation are grounded in the strategic environment in which firms and researchers operate.

Concluding Thoughts

Ultimately, the 1962 volume was among the first—and by far the most influential—volume that pointed economists toward the underlying phenomena of inventive activity and innovation as economic processes. The papers became the starting point for a microeconomic approach and lines of inquiry that have continued to this day—identifying the distinctive facets of information goods and knowledge, understanding how different research organizations are organized, and understanding the dynamic and evolutionary relationship between innovation and industrial organization.

A significant contributor to the volume's impact was its combination of detailed and concrete examples—the aluminum industry, the steel industry, Bell Labs, and so forth—with systematic measurement exercises and theoretical modeling. It is perhaps not too surprising that, by focusing a group of first-rate economists on the problems of invention and innovation, a great deal of progress was made.

Less obvious was the impact of placing the microeconomics of innovation at center stage. The volume ended up offering a constructive and ultimately quite powerful counterpoint to a more aggregate and linear view of innovation. By rendering invention as an endogenous process, one is forced to understand the historical context and institutional structures that motivate and facilitate the process of innovation. It is only then that the link between technological change and economic growth can be made. Looking back at the volume, it should come as no surprise that the key elements of endogenous growth theory as developed over the past two decades are the increasing returns to knowledge production, the impact of limited appropriability, and imperfect competition.

Perhaps more broadly, the volume and follow-on work have raised as many questions as they have settled. We are still involved in significant debates about the appropriate ways to fund research and development activities, the contribution of science and innovation to economic growth, and the endogenous nature of science and technological change. This anniversary conference aims to address some of questions in new ways. We look forward to that.

References

Abramovitz, M. (1989) 1990. *Thinking About Growth.* Cambridge: Cambridge University Press.

Arrow, K. J. 1962. "Economic Welfare and the Allocation of Resources for Invention." In *The Rate and Direction of Inventive Activity*, edited by R. R. Nelson, 609–26. Princeton, NJ: Princeton University Press.

Copeland, A. 1937. "Concepts of National Income." In *Studies in Income and Wealth.* Vol. 1, edited by the Conference on Research in Income and Wealth, 2–63. New York: National Bureau of Economic Research.

Enos, J. 2002. *Technical Progress and Profits: Process Improvements in Petroleum Refining.* Oxford: Oxford Institute for Energy Studies.

Griliches, Z. 1996. "The Discovery of the Residual: An Historical Note." *Journal of Economic Literature* 34 (3): 1324–30.

Machlup, F. 1958. "An Economic Review of the Patent System." Washington, DC: United States Government Printing Office.

Nelson, R. R. 1962. "Introduction." In *The Rate and Direction of Inventive Activity*, edited by R. R. Nelson, 1–16. Princeton, NJ: Princeton University Press.

Rosenberg, N. 1982. *Inside the Black Box: Technology and Economics.* Cambridge: Cambridge University Press.

Solow, R. 1956. "A Contribution to the Theory of Economic Growth." *Quarterly Journal of Economics* 70 (1): 65–94.

———. 1957. "Technical Change and the Aggregate Production Function." *Review of Economics and Statistics* 39 (3): 312–20.

Some Features of Research by Economists on Technological Change Foreshadowed by *The Rate and Direction of Inventive Activity*

Richard R. Nelson

The community of scholars studying technological change now draws from many disciplines. However, almost all of those participating at the 2010 National Bureau of Economic Research (NBER) conference whose proceedings are presented in this volume were economists by training. My observations here are mostly about economists who have been studying technological change. The basic points I want to make are first, that one can see foreshadowed in the papers presented and discussed at the old Conference on The Rate and Direction of Inventive Activity that this conference commemorates many of the directions and characteristics of the research on invention, and technological advance more generally, that has been done by economists since that time. And second, one can also see some of the difficulties and tensions that have marked this field in economics.

The essays by economists at the old conference are nearly unanimous in proposing the usefulness of the broad perspective provided by traditional economic analysis for research on inventive activity. They argued persuasively that inventors and organizations employing them are purposeful, and in a wide range of cases an important objective is profit. Their essays provided strong support for the proposition that the allocation of inventive effort is influenced by perceptions of where technically successful inventions will find a strong demand, and also by considerations of technical feasibility and the likely cost and time of achieving an advance. Much of the work on technological advance by economists since that time has been based on, and provided more evidence supporting, this perspective.

Richard R. Nelson is the George Blumenthal Professor of International and Public Affairs Emeritus at Columbia University and Director of the Program on Science, Technology, and Global Development at the Columbia Earth Institute.

However, the essays and discussion also display an uneasiness about treating invention as an activity in which the actors optimized in any nonsophistical sense of that term. The uncertainties involved in the process, the high failure rate, and the creativity often shown in both successes and failures, seemed to call for another way of characterizing their behavior. Also, while not discussed explicitly, recognition of the dynamics of competition in industries where innovation was important, and the continuing turnover of firms in such industries, clearly raised questions about the relevance of equilibrium concepts in analysis of technological advance. Several of the essays highlighted that a good share of the relevant activity needed to be understood as proceeding in contexts where profit was not the dominant objective. More generally, the participants at the conference recognized that inventing had properties that differed strongly from the standard productive activity depicted in the economics textbooks, and that an invention was not a standard commodity. A number of the participants clearly believed that there was a need for the development of theory tailored to the particularities of technological change.

As I suggested earlier, several of the essays and much of the discussion stressed the importance of uncertainty in the inventive process, and the fact that many efforts ended in failure. It was highlighted that, while individual inventors often had great confidence in their ideas, there generally were significant differences in how different inventors and firms laid their bets, and it was very difficult to predict in advance who would be the winners and losers. The idea that it was highly desirable to run parallel efforts was put forth in several of the papers, and several commentators observed that this is an important feature of market competition. I noted then that this certainly is not a feature of market competition highlighted in the standard economics text books.

There also was considerable discussion of the issue of how inventors were able to appropriate returns from their successful inventions. Several of the authors pointed out that inventions were new ways of doing things that not only were "nonrivalrous in use" but also often easily imitable, if they were not protected in some way. The threat of rapid imitation was flagged by Arrow and others as a deterrent to private inventing. However, it was also recognized that the total social gains from new technology were enhanced when the know-how went public, and that sooner or later most technology gets into the public domain. There clearly are some important issues here not treated or even recognized in standard microeconomic theory.

As I looked again at the essays, and tapped my memory of the conference discussion, it is interesting that explicit reference to Schumpeter is quite limited. Where there was such reference, it mostly was in discussion concerned with whether significant innovation in an industry required that the firms in it be large ones. However, as I noted previously, a Schumpeterian view that innovation is the principal means of competition in many industries is implicit in several of the papers. This perspective on the nature of competition diverges radically from the view in standard microeconomics.

In addition, there was widespread recognition that much more than the market system was involved in supporting and orienting inventive activity. It was proposed that in many sectors inventive activity drew heavily from science that was undertaken largely at universities. In addition to supporting much of the basic research done in the United States, government also played a major role in funding and directing applied research and development in several important fields. Thus it was apparent to many of the participants at the conference that effective analysis of technological advance would require a conceptual structure that encompassed a wider set of institutions and activities than were treated in the standard economic textbooks.

I also want to note here the apparent caution on the part of the scholars who were concerned with somehow measuring invention regarding the possibility of getting good quantitative measures. The various quantitative variables being discussed, and used in an exploratory way, generally were recognized as indicators of the phenomena being addressed, rather than being good measures of it. This was very much the case regarding the use of total factor productivity growth as a measure of the rate of technological advance, of patent numbers to indicate where and how much inventing was going on, and R and D numbers to "measure" inputs to inventing.

It is clear that many of the papers that attracted the most interest were detailed qualitative case studies, or analyses based on a collection of carefully detailed case studies. These were the studies that seemed to many of us to provide the most illumination regarding what inventive activity was all about.

While I did not recognize it at the time, with the advantage of hindsight one can see that this combination of features was going to make it difficult for empirically oriented study of technological advance to become fully conformable with the more general research orientation that the economics discipline increasingly was establishing as the norm. The theory of economic behavior that was coming to be treated as standard by the profession had apparent limitations as a way of orienting or interpreting research in this arena; thus, at least some of the research done by economists working in this field was going to proceed outside of this theoretical frame. The numbers that could be used in quantitative analysis had serious limitations as measures of the important variables and, therefore, much of our understanding of what is going on had to be qualitative, with numbers playing a useful role as indicators rather than accurate measures. However, since the time of the Rate and Direction Conference, the economics profession and the journals serving it have become less receptive to qualitative empirical studies. And the nature of the subject matter clearly called for an interdisciplinary approach to some of the key questions. Yet, economics as a general discipline was becoming increasingly separate from the other social and behavioral sciences.

In any case, the conference should be understood as part and parcel of a significant increase in interest by economists in technological advance that was occurring then in economics. Beginning around 1960, there was a burgeoning of research in this field.

That research has been quite varied in the questions explored, in the methodologies employed, and in the auspices of the research. Much of the research has been done by economists who have had their home in economics departments. A significant amount has been done by economists with appointments in business schools, some of that research on the topics economists in economics departments have been writing about, but some of it concerned with how firms develop the technological capabilities that they possess and the factors behind firm differences. Much of this research has been empirical and quantitative. Here I would like to specially recognize the work of the giants Jacob Schmookler, Edwin Mansfield, and Zvi Griliches. Nathan Rosenberg has done remarkable work on the history of technology. Some of the work has involved survey research. The NBER has been a sponsor and organizer of much of it. Much of it has been published in the regular economics journals.

However, a considerable amount of research in this broad field has been done by economists working in new research and teaching institutions, specifically oriented to the study of technological change, usually, but not always, oriented by a focus on issues of science and technology policy. The research done at the Science Policy Research Unit at the University of Sussex has made an especially important contribution to our understanding of how technological advance occurs. I note that these institutions, while providing a home for many economists studying technological advance, have had a definite interdisciplinary orientation. New journals like *Research Policy*, and *The Journal of Evolutionary Economics,* and *Industrial and Corporate Change,* have grown up around this intellectual community. Here I would like to specially recognize Keith Pavitt and Christopher Freeman as making enormous contributions to our understanding.

What are the major understandings that, as a result of this research, we now have that were not available to the scholars who participated in the Conference on the Rate and Direction? The discussion that follows obviously reflects my own judgments regarding what is important.

First of all, some of the arguments that might have been controversial at the time of the conference have been amply firmed up. There is no informed arguing now against the proposition that technological advance is the principal source of long-run productivity growth. We also now have much stronger evidence that, with few exceptions, industries where measured productivity growth and technological advance are great are characterized by high

R and D intensity, or high R and D intensity of some of their upstream supplying industries, or both. The important influence of perceptions of profit opportunities in motivating and orienting inventive effort also has been amply confirmed.

But second, we now are much more conscious that there are very great differences across industries in their rates of technological advance. While this cross industry variability clearly is related to differences in R and D intensity, scholars are still struggling with the reason for these differences. My belief is that one important factor is differences in the strength of the underlying sciences on which industrial R and D draws in different industries.

Third, it is now much better understood that much of scientific research is in fields, like electrical engineering, computer science, and oncology, where practical problems and objectives play a nontrivial role in orienting effort. That is, different fields of science are specifically oriented to helping the advance of different technologies. We have come a long way from earlier beliefs, implicit in a number of the old Rate and Direction Conference essays, that the technological payoffs from basic research are largely a matter of serendipity. On the other hand, the uncertainties about the particular applications of new scientific knowledge, which was a matter stressed by several authors at that conference, have been amply confirmed.

Fourth, our understanding has improved greatly regarding the means by which inventors and firms appropriate returns from the new products and processes they create. It now is recognized much more clearly than it was at the time of the conference that patents are only one of the means, and that they play a major role in only a few technologies. Many inventions are much more costly and time consuming to imitate than economists earlier believed, and in many technologies the advantage of a head start, particularly if complemented by rapid subsequent improvement of the initial invention, is the principal source of return to inventing and R and D. We also know now that the principal means of appropriation differ across technologies and industries.

Fifth, a lot has been learned about Schumpeterian competition in industries where innovation is important, and about the dynamics of industrial structure under these conditions. The old argument about whether large firms with considerable market power were necessary for there to be significant innovation in an industry has more or less been replaced by an understanding of the differences in the roles played by new firms and established firms at different times in the history of a technology. A significant body of empirical research and modeling of industrial dynamics has been structured by the conception of a technology life cycle. Differences in industry structure associated with this and other factors have been more clearly recognized.

I note that several of these understandings highlight major differences across technologies and industries. This suggests strongly that it is a mistake to argue in general about things like the role of university research, the importance of patents, or the importance of new firms in the innovation process, because these variables differ significantly across fields and economic sectors. I believe that many in the economics community have been slow in recognizing this.

I turn now to two matters that I and my working colleagues think we have learned, but are certainly controversial. First of all, a significant number of economists and other empirically oriented scholars of technological advance have come to propose that the process should be understood as evolutionary. The uncertainty involved in inventive activity leads to a diversity of efforts going on at any time to advance a technology, that are in competition with each other and with established technology. The winners and losers are determined to a considerable degree through actual comparison in use. And the results of today's competition and what has been learned today provide the context for the continuation of the competition tomorrow. This broad theoretical frame has provided the basis for a considerable amount of modeling, and also the orientation for a wide range of empirical research on technological change.

Second, a number of economists studying the subject empirically have come to the judgment that it is not helpful to view the institutional structure supporting innovation as essentially market organization, with nonmarket elements including public programs coming into the picture when markets fail, which is a point of view implicit in much of the main line economic writing. A considerable amount has been learned about the roles of nonmarket actors, particularly universities, since the days of the Conference on the Rate and Direction. For many scholars that have done that work it seems bizarre to propose that universities do what they do because of market failure. We also know much more now about the government programs, including programs of R and D support, that are important in many economic sectors, and many of these too, like those involved in defense contracting, seem not to be adequately rationalized in terms of responses to market failure. Several economists have developed the concept of an "innovation system" to characterize the range of different actors involved in the advancement of technology and the different roles they play.

These propositions about how technology advances and the range of actors involved in the process clearly are very different from the picture presented in today's standard economics textbooks (for example, in their treatment of growth theory). The divergence here testifies to the fact that the intellectual tensions I proposed were visible at the conference fifty years ago are very much evident today.

In any case, I suspect that while many of the readers of this essay are familiar with a number of the propositions I have just put forth, few are familiar with all. That is because different ones stem from the research of different groups of scholars, and unfortunately there is little cross-group communication. There are, first of all, economists relatively closely connected with the main line of the discipline. The NBER affiliates working on technological change are mostly in this camp. Economic historians in economics departments have also made significant contributions, but lately this group has been dwindling. There are, second, economists affiliated with research institutes dedicated to the study of issues of science and technology policy and of technological advance more broadly, and taking a transdisciplinary approach to the subject. Here, as I noted earlier, the research done by scholars at SPRU has been particularly important, but in recent years a number of other such institutions have become important loci of research.

In my view, while there is some overlap, for some time economists working in this area have been divided into two roughly separate camps each associated with different ways of dealing with the tensions that I suggested were visible at the Conference on the Rate and Direction. Economists in the first camp have stayed mainly within the confines of the discipline. They have accommodated to the tensions largely by being quantitative and empirical, and while urging caution about their numbers have tended to shun doing detailed qualitative case studies. They have been commonsensical in the theory they use and articulate in their work, while shying away from saying explicitly that the microeconomic theory of the textbooks does not work very well with the subject matter they are addressing.

Economists in the second camp have embraced the need to do detailed qualitative research and see quantitative data in the light of more qualitative understanding. They also have been more vocal in pointing out the inadequacies of standard microeconomics as a frame for understanding what is going on, and more active in entertaining and developing theory they think better suited to the subject matter. They have been active in developing a theory of the firm that is oriented to dynamic capabilities, and a neo-Schumpeterian theory of competition in industries where innovation is important that generates industrial dynamics. The development of evolutionary theory has largely been within this camp. They are comfortable with concepts like that of an innovation system that aims to encompass nonmarket as well as market actors in the process of technological advance.

Some economists have been able to bridge the divide, and act and think as members of both camps. But the divide clearly is there. Since the participants and presentations at the 2010 conference were largely those of the first camp, there was little opportunity for cross-group communication. However, we scholars of technological advance would benefit from more of it.

The Economics of Inventive Activity over Fifty Years

Kenneth J. Arrow

It is gratifying that a conference participated in fifty years ago is remembered as sufficiently influential and useful to be acknowledged as inspiring a new conference on the same subject. It is only natural that two of the survivors be trotted out to make the link and continuity more visible.

I will make a few remarks to emphasize the continuity and the change from today's viewpoint. Some seemingly promising leads have been followed up, some not. Some problems, empirical and conceptual, still persist. Other new ideas have appeared. Of course, the technical capacities of economists in all fields, including inventive activity, have changed, itself a reflection of inventive activity. The information and communication technology has changed econometric methodology from difficult to simple and made access to data far easier. Any economist will have to assume that lowering costs will lead to better and more abundant output.

Let me start with a universally valid remark. *Any* theory that purports to explain novelty, whether it deal with invention, innovation, or the emergence of new species of biota, is intrinsically difficult and paradoxical. How can you have a theory of the unexpected? If you can understand what novelties will emerge, they would not be novelties.

Biologists do not attempt to predict the specific characteristics of a species that will emerge in the future. Indeed, the theory of evolution through selection, especially in the form of the "modern synthesis," where mutations occur at random and favorable ones are selected for, virtually implies the impossibility of forecasting the novel elements in future new species. To be sure, there are known constraints. New species must have a lot in common with existing ones. If there is some successor to *Homo sapiens,* it will prob-

Kenneth J. Arrow is Professor of Economics Emeritus at Stanford University.

ably be bipedal. But it is precisely the way the new species (or the innovation) differs from the present that is of interest, and that is what is difficult to predict.

Biologists differ among themselves as to the extent to which the broad outlines of evolution could be predictable. The late Stephen Jay Gould argued that if evolution started all over again, the outcomes (the leaves on the evolutionary tree) could be totally different; others (e.g., Christian de Duve) argue that the movement toward greater complexity and greater intelligence would have emerged in any case, though the specific species embodying them might have been different in many ways. This issue has an exact parallel in varying views as to the importance of "path-dependence" in the history of adopted technologies.

A basic theme in both the previous conference (NBER 1962) and the current conference is the definition of the field; what are we studying under the heading of "inventive activity"? This concern is explicit in Simon Kuznets's lead essay in the 1962 volume (Kuznets 1962). He distinguishes between *invention,* a new combination of existing knowledge to create something useful (in some sense), and *discovery,* the development of new knowledge. He distinguishes both from, "the host of improvements in technique that are . . . the result of low-level and rather *obvious* attentiveness or know-how"; an invention, on the other hand, "must be the product of a mental effort above the average" (Kuznets [1962], 21; emphasis in original).

Before reverting to Kuznets's primary distinction, let us consider some implications of the distinction of both from routine improvements. Indeed, this leads to a basic question that the great pioneer in national income accounting might have pondered over: what is the relation between inventions, in Kuznets's (and most others') usage, and growth in total factor productivity (the Solow residual). This question was raised at the 1962 conference by Zvi Griliches (1962). I can do no better than to quote his remark (Griliches 1962, 347). "[I]nventions may be the wrong unit of measurement. What we are really interested in is the stock of useful knowledge or information and the factors that determine its rate of growth. Inventions may represent only one aspect of this process and be a misleading quantum at that. . . . [T]heir fluctuations may not be well correlated with changes in the over-all rate of growth."

Enos's (1962) paper cast some interesting light. He enumerated the basic significant steps in the improvement of petroleum refining to derive from crude oil its useful products (such as gasoline and kerosene), and the many types of "cracking." But he notes that the improvements in productivity between one major innovation and the next are at least as large as the improvements immediately due to each innovation (Enos [1962], table 5, 318, and discussion on 319). This illustrates the well-known phenomenon of progress curves found in airframes and other durable goods and a sequel to every major innovation, down to Moore's Law for integrated chips.

The hypothesis that inventions require a distinctive mental effort led to an emphasis in the 1962 volume on the psychological and social characteristics of inventors, reflected in the term "social" in the subtitle of the volume and in the presence of a whole part (part IV) dealing with, "nonmarket factors." No counterpart exists in the current volume. Part IV tried to discuss what kind of people become inventors and how decisions about invention are made in decentralized firms and in government departments. I am afraid that, both originally and on rereading, I felt that the ninety-six pages were a waste of space and effort. Some of the results are incredible; most are uninteresting even if correct. In the current volume, no parallel effort was even made.

Let me return to Kuznets's primary distinction between invention and discovery. Thomas Kuhn, in a comment later in the volume, prefers the terms "technology" and "science" (Kuhn 1962, 451–2), and these have been widely used since (e.g., Dasgupta and David 1994). The distinction, in any vocabulary, is associated with several rather different hypotheses:

1. Kuznets suggested that discoveries made in science provided the knowledge on which inventions or new technology, according to one's preferred terminology, were developed. Kuhn pointed out that this relation only begins to be true after 1860; before that, virtually none of the great inventions were based on scientific knowledge. Even today, many of the great improvements in information and communications technology do not depend on new scientific principles.

2. To the obviously considerable extent that scientific advance does provide the basis for technological improvement, a question arises as to the causes of scientific advance. To Kuznets (and, I think, implicit in the case studies in part III of the 1962 volume), scientific advance is essentially exogenous to technology and to the economy. It plays the role that Solow assigns to technological advance in general, causing but not caused. How sound and how fruitful this hypothesis is remains to be determined. I should note it is very distinct from that held by many, from Karl Marx to the present day, who ascribe the great growth in technology of the last quarter millenium to capitalist institutions and, in particular, the patent system. The latter point of view would imply that science is responsive to the needs of industry. I expand a little on this point later.

3. There are two further aspects of the relation between science and technology (invention and discovery) that have received mention in the 1962 volume and subsequent literature. One is the argument that the motivations of scientists and technologists differ. It is held that technologists are interested essentially in money, while scientists are primarily driven by curiosity or fame. (Actually, some of the 1962 authors suggested that curiosity might be a driving force in technology as well.) Certainly, many of the innovators in information and communications technology created concepts, such as the Internet, from which they benefited relatively little in a financial sense. They

were trying to solve some specific problem. Now, fame is certainly a reward for scientists. As John Milton put it, "Fame is the spur/that last impediment of a noble mind" (from *Lycidas,* lines 70–71). I noticed no concern with this question in the present conference.

I must add the somewhat atypical motivation of one major health discovery (one I learned about as chair of a study group on the introduction of a new antimalarial pharmaceutical) (Institute of Medicine 2004). Currently, the best treatments for falciparum malaria (the deadly form) are combinations of artmesinins, drugs derived from a plant popularly known as sweet wormwood. They were developed on the basis of ancient Chinese medical texts by a group of scientists who published their findings (tested by the best current scientific standards) *anonymously,* giving as author the Chinese Cooperative Research Group on Qinghaosu [sweet wormwood] and Its Derivatives as Antimalarials (1982). Of course, no patents or other intellectual property claims were filed. In short, neither fame nor wealth was implicated as a motive. The spread of open software and the anonymous writing of articles for *Wikipedia* may suggest that this example, if not common, is not entirely unique.

4. Finally, in this list of the problematic relations between science and technology, is the influence of technology on science. Once the point is made, it is entirely obvious that technological improvements have made science easier to perform, as they have improved performance in other human activities. I do not believe this proposition is at all discussed in the current conference, and I found only one brief remark in the 1962 paper of Irving Siegel (1962 448). When someone had the idea of using two lenses to create a telescope, Galileo was empowered to search the skies, to identify the complex surface structure of the Moon, and to determine that Jupiter had several moons. Later, someone put the lenses together in a different way, and Leeuwenhoek was enabled to see that a drop of water contained many very small animals. This audience may be young enough to need reminding that computers and the Internet have transformed economic analysis.

I have a few more, somewhat miscellaneous, remarks. I have already alluded to one, the role of patents and, more generally, institutions, legal and other, in encouraging and directing both science and technology. Despite a considerable number of individual remarks, neither conference has been much concerned with evaluating this role. As I have already indicated, many authors have ascribed an important role to capitalism in general and the institution of intellectual property in particular in stimulating technological progress. For vigorous defenses, of this point of view, see, for example, Rosenberg and Birdzell (1986) and Baumol (2003).

On the other hand, in informal conversations with presumably knowledgeable lawyers and businessmen, I derive the impression that patent protection is important only for a limited range of products, such as pharmaceuticals. There has also been an intellectual and theoretical case, arguing that the private information held by inventors enables them to reward themselves adequately without the need for patent protection (Hirshleifer 1971; Boldrin and Levine 2008). Is there no way of measuring the significance of the patent system as an incentive for invention, including bringing the new product or process into the market?

Patents indeed appear very frequently in the literature on invention but mostly as a measure of inventive activity rather than for their incentive implications. In turn, this measure has been repeatedly subject to criticism. We are sometimes told that counting the number of patents is meaningless. Most patents are, of course, of no importance; a few are of great importance. Does the total number have some significance for measuring technological progress in some sense? It is true that patent activity has one great advantage as a statistic: it is measurable with high accuracy.

To complete the items on my list of knowledge gaps, there is one more question related to incentives. It is generally accepted that the main source of profits to the innovator are those derived from temporary monopoly. Why is it that royalties are not an equivalent source of revenues? In simple theory, the two should be equivalent. Indeed, if there is heterogeneity in productive efficiency, in the use of the innovation in production, then it should generally be more profitable to the innovator to grant a license to a more efficient producer. This does happen, of course, but I have the impression that licensing is a minor source of revenues.

I conclude with a note about the genesis of the two volumes. A great deal of attention was paid to the role of government procurement of innovation in the first volume, primarily in relation to defense. A high percentage of the papers dealt with this topic. I do not believe there is a single chapter on this subject in the current volume.

References

Baumol, W. J. 2003. *The Free-Market Innovation Machine: Analyzing the Growth Miracle of Capitalism.* Princeton, NJ: Princeton University Press.

Boldrin, M., and D. K. Levine. 2008. *Against Intellectual Property.* New York: Cambridge University Press.

Chinese Cooperative Research Group on Qinghaosu and Its Derivatives as Antimalarials. 1982. "Clinical Studies on the Treatment of Malaria with Qinghaosu and Its Derivatives." *Journal of Traditional Chinese Medicine* 2:45–50.

Dasgupta, P., and P. David. 1994. "Toward a New Economics of Science." *Research Policy* 23:487–521.

Enos, J. L. 1962. "Invention and Innovation in the Petroleum Refining Industry." In *The Rate and Direction of Inventive Activity: Economic and Social Factors,* Universities-National Bureau Committee for Economic Research and the Committee on Economic Growth of the Social Science Research Councils, 299–321. Princeton, NJ: Princeton University Press.

Griliches, Z. 1962. “Comment on ‘The Origins of the Basic Inventions Underlying Du Pont’s Major Product and Process Innovations, 1920 to 1950,’ by Willard F. Mueller.” In *The Rate and Direction of Inventive Activity: Economic and Social Factors,* Universities-National Bureau Committee for Economic Research and the Committee on Economic Growth of the Social Science Research Councils, 346–53. Princeton, NJ: Princeton University Press.

Hirshleifer, J. 1971. “The Private and Social Value of Information and the Reward to Inventive Activity.” *American Economic Review* 61:561–74.

Institute of Medicine. 2004. *Saving Lives, Buying Time.* Washington, DC: The National Academies Press.

Kuhn, T. 1962. “Comment on ‘Scientific Discovery and the Rate of Invention,” by Irving Siegel.” In *The Rate and Direction of Inventive Activity: Economic and Social Factors,* Universities-National Bureau Committee for Economic Research and the Committee on Economic Growth of the Social Science Research Councils, 450–57. Princeton, NJ: Princeton University Press.

Kuznets, S. 1962. “Inventive Activity: Problems of Definition and Measurement.” In *The Rate and Direction of Inventive Activity: Economic and Social Factors,* Universities-National Bureau Committee for Economic Research and the Committee on Economic Growth of the Social Science Research Councils, 19–51. Princeton, NJ: Princeton University Press.

Milton, John. 1983. “Lycidas.” In *The Norton Anthology of Poetry*, 3rd ed., edited by A. A. Allison, H. Barrows, C. R. Blake, A. J. Carr, A. M. Eastman, and H. M. English Jr., 276. New York: W. W. Norton.

National Bureau of Economic Research. 1962. *The Rate and Direction of Inventive Activity: Economic and Social Factors.* Princeton, NJ: Princeton University Press.

Rosenberg, N., and L. E. Birdzell. 1986. *How the West Grew Rich.* Chicago: Basic Books.

Siegel, I. H. 1962. “Scientific Discovery and the Rate of Invention.” In *The Rate and Direction of Inventive Activity: Economic and Social Factors,* Universities-National Bureau Committee for Economic Research and the Committee on Economic Growth of the Social Science Research Councils, 441–50. Princeton, NJ: Princeton University Press.

II

The University-Industry Interface

1

Funding Scientific Knowledge
Selection, Disclosure, and the Public-Private Portfolio

Joshua S. Gans and Fiona Murray

1.1 Introduction

Funding agencies, philanthropists, and corporations agree that the funding of scientific progress provides essential knowledge for solving major global challenges. However, fifty years after the original *Rate and Direction* volume articulating the importance of public (and private) research funding (Arrow 1962), scholarly disagreement continues over the precise balance of funding, appropriate selection criteria for each funder, and the disclosure conditions to be enforced. In this chapter, we review the choices funders have made over the past fifty years and provide a model that yields an overarching framework in which to consider the diverse perspectives for research funders.

Over the past century, scholars and policymakers have provided at least two distinctive arguments for the public support of research—in particular, for basic research. The first contention, most famously articulated by Arrow, is grounded in the idea that there is a "funding gap" between the level of private support for research and the socially optimal level of its provision (1962). The second, more recent argument highlights differences in the institutional foundations of knowledge production, particularly as they pertain

Joshua S. Gans holds the Jeffrey C. Skoll Chair of Technical Innovation and Entrepreneurship at the Rotman School of Management, University of Toronto. Fiona Murray holds the David Sarnoff Chair of Management and Technology at the Massachusetts Institute of Technology (MIT) Sloan School of Management and is faculty director of the MIT Entrepreneurship Center.

Paper prepared for the NBER's Rate and Direction of Inventive Activity Conference, 2010. We are grateful to Suzanne Scotchmer and conference participants for helpful comments, an ARC Discovery Grant for financial assistance, and NSF Grant #0738394 for support from the Science of Science Innovation Policy Program. Responsibility for all errors lies with us. All correspondence to Joshua Gans, e-mail: joshua.gans@gmail.com.

to openness and disclosure (see Dasgupta and David 1994). Even if private funds are allocated to a critical research project under the "openness gap" argument, only public funding and the institutional arrangements that it supports enable optimal levels of disclosure and thus ensure effective accumulation of knowledge (Gans, Murray, and Stern 2010). These perspectives point to the importance of the *selection criteria* used by public (and private) funders in shaping both the overall level of funded research projects and their composition (across dimensions of contribution to understanding and to usefulness). They also suggest a second dimension to be considered: the *disclosure criteria* that funders (public or private) impose as they deploy their funding. The two schools of thought, however, fail to articulate how the evolution of private and public research funding have created a tangled relationship between openness and innovation, whereby corporate protection of intellectual property can lead to greater innovation and disclosure, while public funding can potentially restrict innovation and disclosure. A comprehensive review of the policies used by the major government and nonprofit funding institutions can highlight how the relationships between project selection and disclosure policies can affect outcomes for future research and innovation.

This chapter uses a theoretical model as a framework within which to examine and compare relationships between funders, including how differences shape the levels of research funding, the balance of public-private projects, and the disclosure of research results. Not only does this approach synthesize an otherwise complex area of enquiry, it also provides us with a much richer context within which to explore the role of public funders, the emerging role of philanthropic funding, and the potential for public funding to crowd out private sector research.

The historical arguments for the importance of public support of research provide the starting point for our chapter. Arrow first articulated the funding gap or *selection* perspective in 1962, arguing that since private incentives to fund research are well below social incentives, without public funding the rate of inventive activity will be suboptimal and its direction biased toward more applied, "close to market" outcomes. Even prior to this conceptualization, Nelson had argued that:

> if the marginal cost of research output is assumed to be no greater in non-profit laboratories than in profit-oriented laboratories, and if industry laboratories are assumed to operate where marginal revenue equals marginal cost, then the fact that industry laboratories do basic research at all is itself evidence that we should increase our expenditure on basic research. (1959, 304, emphasis in original)

In other words, the very fact that private activity continues is evidence that public grants to support invention do not displace private invention. Fifty years on, the theoretical rationale for public support of invention remains unchallenged; in the years following World War II, such public intervention has been recognized and institutionalized (Bush 1945). Nonetheless, public funders often find themselves at odds with policymakers and other constituencies as they balance the need to fund areas of basic research avoided by the private sector against the political need for real-world impact. Take, for example, the critique of cancer research spending by the National Cancer Institute (NCI): Forty years after Nixon's "War on Cancer," many have accused the NCI of overemphasizing basic research to the detriment of more translational projects that maximize patient impact (Groopman 2001). On the other hand, when agencies shift their funding toward near-term, mission-oriented R&D projects, they are criticized for crowding out what industry would have done otherwise or for funding (seemingly) redundant efforts.

An alternative openness gap or *disclosure* perspective rationalizes public funding on the basis that a stream of private sector research is not optimal for ensuring levels of disclosure that can spark longer-term innovation. Only publicly funded, public-sector researchers can ensure the broad disclosure of research findings that leads to long-term growth (Romer 1990). The institutional foundations that establish the setting, incentives, and mechanisms to ensure such freedom and openness have been elaborated by David (2008) and others. In addition, Mokyr (2004) emphasizes the importance of public funding for ensuring long-run knowledge accumulation and intertemporal spillovers. Together, these lines of scholarship build on and broaden Nelson's notion that basic research requires conditions of openness and emphasize that any type of research that is disclosed is far more socially valuable than research held secret. Disclosure is achieved through the contractual provisions of research funding and, more broadly, because of the norms and incentives for openness found in published research institutions. (Dasgupta and David 1994; David 2008). Moreover, different types of disclosure regimes can arise and even coexist, regardless of whether research is strictly basic or applied in nature.

Potential conflicts between the *selection* versus *disclosure* perspectives are most vividly illustrated by the calls to halt public funding of the Human Genome Project following the announcement that the for-profit company Celera would also undertake full genome sequencing and "race" the public effort to complete sequencing. Observers argued that the public funding was now redundant and wasteful. In response, public funders sought to emphasize and enhance the commitment of the public project to openness, rapid and full disclosure of sequencing data, and the provision of an entire information infrastructure for future generations of researchers—a claim that strongly countered Celera's tight control of their data (Williams 2010; Huang and Murray 2009).

To reconcile these two seemingly distinct perspectives on public research funding, we develop a theoretical model that considers demand and supply of research funds in relation to disclosure requirements. Our contention is that the conditions attached to public support of inventive activity will impact both on the mix of projects funded and the openness of those projects. This is achieved through a market that emphasizes the preferences of both the funders and the scientists in choosing the types of projects and disclosures they prefer. To elaborate this argument, we model the supply of funds, as determined both by the selection criteria of funding organizations and the disclosure conditions that organizations impose for funding. As we will detail later, we define the space in which funders select projects along two dimensions: usefulness to specific problems and contribution to basic knowledge (Stokes 1997; Murray 2002). The demand for funds comes from scientists who choose to accept or reject funding offers based on their other options and preferences for disclosure. This approach brings scientists back into a literature that has been centrally focused on funders and has only paid limited attention to the funding preferences of scientists themselves. Our analysis of disclosure relies on the assumption that knowledge can often be disclosed (or not) according to four different regimes: secrecy, publications, patents, or patent-paper pairs (Murray and Stern 2007; Gans, Murray, and Stern 2010). Our contention is that public funders (governmental and nongovernmental) do not contribute to invention solely by adding resources to knowledge production projects. Their impact arises in the way they select projects for support *and* in the conditions they attach to the disclosure and commercialization of those projects. Both selection and disclosure, we argue, have an impact on the direction of inventive activity. In our model some projects—depending on their characteristics—are able to attract private funding. The supply of those funds is determined by the selection criteria of funding organizations and by those organizations' choice of (disclosure) conditions on funding. The demand for private funds is shaped by the relative desirability of accepting private funds.

Our context for understanding the role of public and private research funding is a period in which total US R&D expenditures have risen from \$72.5 billion in 1962 (the year of the *Rate and Direction* volume) to US\$350 billion in constant 2000 dollars by 2008 (S&E Indicators, Figure 4-1). This represents not simply a rise in federal (public) funding, which grew around \$47 billion to over \$85 billion (over the same period), but also in R&D funding from industry which experienced its highest growth, from being about 50 percent of the federal contribution level (\$23 billion) to dwarfing the federal contribution at over \$200 billion. Given the high levels of private sector funding of R&D, the possibility that at least some public funding is purely duplicative of enlarged private efforts only strengthens the case that opportunities exist to target public funding to promote more socially valuable inventive activity. When combined with the question of what conditions should be attached to research contracts (for example, disclosure and commercialization), this approach provides a framework within which to examine and inform research selection and research contract design by public (government and philanthropic) funding agencies.

We pursue our analysis by gathering (the somewhat sparse) empirical evidence and developing a theoretical model. Our findings motivate a broader agenda for the study of the contract design problem facing research funders. To this end, our chapter does three things: First, in sections 1.2 and 1.3, we provide an overview of preferences of funding organizations across different types of research projects and disclosure regimes: Section 1.2 reviews the selection criteria in government and nongovernment funding organizations—specifically focusing on their choice of projects along the two dimensions of scientific merit and immediate applicability. Then in section 1.3, we examine conditions for disclosure and commercialization of research project outcomes. In section 1.4, we provide a model of the demand and supply of public research funds. Finally, in section 1.5, based on our analysis, we outline an agenda for future research. This agenda is motivated by the fact that we have limited knowledge of the actual outcomes—selection and openness—of publicly funded projects as well as the baseline trade-offs that our theoretical model has identified.

1.2 How Public Institutions Select Academic Projects for Funding

In prescribing the role of public research support (in universities and elsewhere), Nelson, Rosenberg, and others have classified research projects along a continuum from basic to applied.[1] Under this schema, a key concern for public funders and academic observers is that private funders pursued too little basic research relative to their emphasis on applied "mission-oriented" research. The funding landscape turns out to be more complex: First, industry itself provides funding to universities to undertake research. Second, industry also does some basic research. Third, public funding is spent in academia on both basic research and more near-term, mission-oriented objectives. For example, some projects given government funding, such as the development of theories of plate tectonics or the big bang theory (funded by the National Science Foundation [NSF]), are explicitly generated to advance basic scientific understanding. Others have been focused specifically on meeting particular short-run practical objectives, such as the Department of Defense's (DoD) funding of gallium arsenide RF technology to enable cellular commercial infrastructure. Projects such as the Human Genome Project (noted earlier) were funded by the Department of Energy (DOE) and the National Institutes of Health (NIH) to generate knowledge considered useful *and* scientifically interesting. Not confined to the life sciences, research on chip design in the 1960s and 1970s (funded by

1. See also the definition formalized in 1963 in the Frascati Manual of the Organization for Economic Cooperation and Development (OECD).

the Defense Advanced Research Projects Agency [DARPA]) was also considered to be critically useful *and* scientifically important.

Given the complexity of the funding choices previously described, the simple basic-to-applied continuum as a model of selection is too simple to capture the current research landscape *and* fails to capture important findings in scientific history. As an alternative, we have chosen to consider a two-dimensional space for projects characterized by the degree of scientific merit on one dimension and the extent of immediate valuable application on the other. In other words, research projects cannot simply be characterized as basic (contributing to the advance of scientific knowledge) or applied (leading to immediate applications) but may also involve both: Galileo not only developed significant scientific insights that contributed to astronomy while observing the moons of Jupiter, Venus, and other plants; he also made useful advances in optics with implications for the nautical community (Biagioli 2000). Another eponymous example of this blurring between basic and applied research is Pasteur's simultaneous discovery of the small pox vaccine and advances in microbiology. His work, like Galileo's, has been described as lying in Pasteur's Quadrant (Stokes 1997). (See figure 1.1.)

By mapping research projects along two dimensions, their contribution to fundamental advances in knowledge and their application to useful problems, we can define (at least) three distinct classes of research (see Stokes 1997):

- Pure basic research (exemplified by the work of Niels Bohr, early twentieth century atomic physicist)
- Pure applied research (exemplified by the work of Thomas Edison, inventor)
- Use-inspired basic research (described as Pasteur's Quadrant)

		Immediate Application	
		NO	YES
Contribution to Fundamental Knowledge	YES	Bohr's Quadrant	Pasteur's Quadrant
	NO	Other research!	Edison's Quadrant

Fig. 1.1 Selection matrix of knowledge production projects

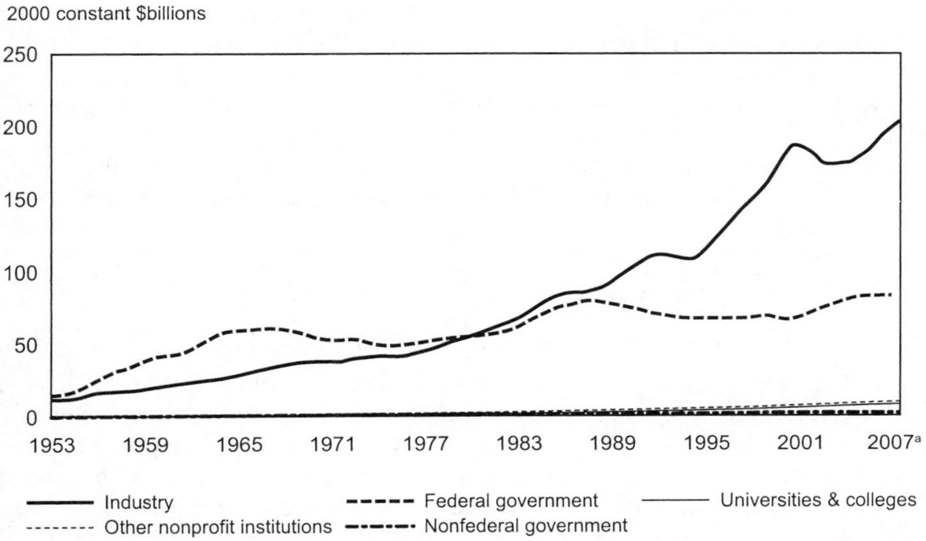

Fig. 1.2 R&D in 2000 constant $billions by source of funding

[a]Figures for 2007 are estimates.

Source: National Science Foundation, Division of Science Resources Statistics, National Patterns of R&D Resources (annual series).

The criteria used by funding organizations in the selection of their research portfolio have been the subject of surprisingly little empirical analysis; however, it is clear that there is no simple mapping of public (and private) funding to specific quadrants as defined earlier. In what follows, we therefore provide the broad context for public R&D funding (to universities) and data to elaborate trends in the fifty-year period since the *Rate and Direction* volume (1962).

As figure 1.2 illustrates, United States federal funding (the major source of public funding in the United States) has grown fourfold in this period. Not all of this funding flows to universities; they perform about 10 to 15 percent of the total (public and private) research with around 50 to 60 percent of this funding coming from public federal sources and 5 percent from private sources.[2]

1.2.1 Public Funding—Federal Agencies

University-based academics perform more than 60 percent of the research funded by the federal government (with much of the remainder by government laboratories)—what amounts today to approximately $40 bil-

2. One note, however: because private funders generally do not use public "calls for proposals," information on their selection criteria are limited.

lion annually. The following graph (fig. 1.3) illustrates both funding agency sources and research performer. It highlights that the majority of funds are disbursed via four major funding agencies (who receive their budget via congressional appropriations). In recent years, the NIH has dominated federal R&D, followed by the NSF (Clemins 2010). The DoD is the third-largest sponsor of academic research (when only "science and technology" funding is included), with the DOE distributing a small (but growing) budget to academia.[3]

1.2.2 Selection Criteria of the Four Major Funding Agencies

The National Science Foundation—Funding Bohr's Quadrant

At its current funding level, the NSF accounts for about 20 percent of all research funding in academic institutions—one third of all public federal funds. The NSF and the funds it provides are most closely associated with a single funding Quadrant—"Bohr's Quadrant"—and uses as its selection criteria measures long-term scientific merit. At the broadest level, this reflects its founding mission, as articulated in 1945 in the letter written by Vannevar Bush—later to become the first director—to President Truman. In it, he articulated the "Endless Frontier"—the power of public (government) support for basic research to advance our understanding. While formulated as ultimately leading to innovation, economic growth and wealth creation, at its core Bush and his supporters established the NSF on the understanding that advances in knowledge must be funded in their purest form. Thus, the funding for basic research in US academia was established in its modern form.

The NSF awarded its first grants to academics in 1952 and since then the agency's mission has remained "to promote the progress of science; to advance the national health, prosperity, and welfare; to secure the national defense."[4] The funding criteria focus on their mission "chiefly by issuing limited-term grants—currently about 10,000 new awards per year, with an average duration of three years—to fund specific research proposals that have been judged the most promising by a rigorous and objective merit-review system."[5] To be specific, the NSF defines its goals as:

> discovery, learning, research infrastructure and stewardship—provide an integrated strategy to advance the frontiers of knowledge, cultivate a world-class, broadly inclusive science and engineering workforce and expand the scientific literacy of all citizens, build the nation's research capability through investments in advanced instrumentation and facilities, and support excellence in science and engineering research and education

3. The DoD Science & Technology (S&T) spending includes basic and applied research, medical research, and technology development categorized as 6-1 "basic," 6-2 "applied," and 6-3 "technology development."

4. http://www.nsf.gov/about/glance.jsp.

5. Ibid.

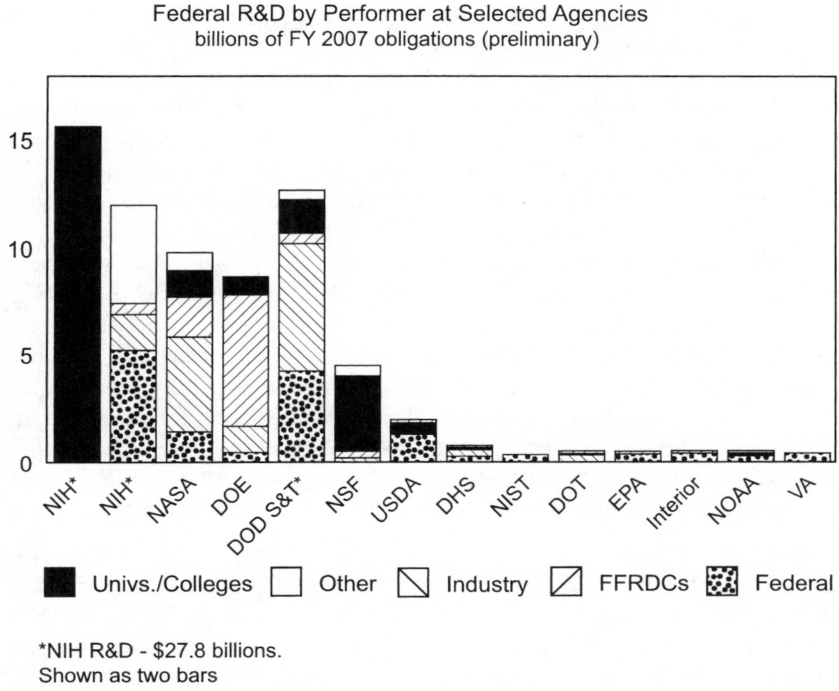

Fig. 1.3 Federal R&D by performer at selected agencies
Source: AAAS, based on NSF, Federal Funds for Research and Development, Fiscal Years 2005, 2006, and 2007, 2008. The R&D includes research, development, and R&D facilities. *DOD R&D in "6.1" through "6.3" categories. Feb. '08 © 2008 AAAS.

> through a capable and responsive organization. We like to say that the NSF is "where discoveries begin."

These goals led the NSF in the 1950s to fund a series of national observatories (1955), the South Pole Station (1957), and in the 1980s, the Internet backbone. In addition to major research infrastructure projects, most NSF funding is disbursed in the form of competitive grants to individual investigators. Its selection criteria highlight the intellectual merit of the proposed activity as well as the broader impacts resulting from the proposed activity in their proposals. However, these impacts are also defined not in terms of usefulness (in an Edisonian sense) but rather their contribution to education and training; in other words, the NSF funds Bohr's Quadrant. More specifically, the NSF review panels guide applicants to address two questions, both emphasizing knowledge advancement over applicability or usefulness:[6]

6. http://www.nsf.gov/pubs/policydocs/pappguide/nsf10_1/gpg_3.jsp.

- *What is the intellectual merit of the proposed activity?* How important is the proposed activity to advancing knowledge and understanding within its own field or across different fields? How well qualified is the proposer (individual or team) to conduct the project? (If appropriate, the reviewer will comment on the quality of prior work.) To what extent does the proposed activity suggest and explore creative, original, or potentially transformative concepts? How well conceived and organized is the proposed activity? Is there sufficient access to resources?
- *What are the broader impacts of the proposed activity?* How well does the activity advance discovery and understanding while promoting teaching, training, and learning? How well does the proposed activity broaden the participation of underrepresented groups (e.g., gender, ethnicity, disability, geographic, etc.)? To what extent will it enhance the infrastructure for research and education, such as facilities, instrumentation, networks, and partnerships? Will the results be disseminated broadly to enhance scientific and technological understanding? What may be the benefits of the proposed activity to society?

More recently, the NSF has initiated a new mechanism—EAGER—focused on early stage research. However, this is not a move toward application. Instead, it is intended to move researchers into more high risk-high return areas of Bohr's Quadrant by supporting "exploratory work in its early stages on untested, but potentially transformative, research ideas or approaches."[7]

The NIH, DoD and DOE—Funding Multiple Quadrants

The more mission-oriented funding for academic research provided by the NIH, DoD and DOE stands in contrast to the NSF. All three agencies' focus on their explicit mission-based approach (at least in theory) pushes them to evaluate and select projects along criteria of basic intellectual merit and immediate mission-oriented impact. However, in the mix of funding decisions, projects have been funded in Bohr's and Edison's Quadrants as well as Pasteur's Quadrant.

National Institutes of Health

As of 2010, the NIH budget reached over US$25 billion (excluding American Recovery and Reinvestment Act [ARRA] funding) with more than 80 percent funding research undertaken at over 3,000 US universities and research institutions.[8] The need to spend its appropriations through

7. http://www.nsf.gov/pubs/policydocs/pappguide/nsf10_1/gpg_2.jsp#IID2.

8. Research grants are defined as extramural awards made for Research Centers, Research Projects, Small Business Innovation Research/Small Business Technology Transfer (SBIR/STTR) Grants, and Other Research Grants. Research grants are defined by the following activity codes: R, P, M, S, K, U (excluding UC6), DP1, DP2, D42, and G12.

project selections that blend scientific knowledge advancement with immediate application is evident in the current NIH mission "to improve human health by increasing scientific knowledge related to disease and health."[9] In its past history, the NIH was more mission-oriented and at the outset more closely focused on immediate applications of research to critical social problems; that is, it was strongly associated with Edison's Quadrant. In 1798 the Marine Hospital Service, which served as the founding organization of today's NIH, was established by President John Adams for the treatment of seamen and (later) officers of the US Navy. Its role in application-focused research was initiated almost 100 years later when Congress appropriated funds to study the causes of epidemic diseases, "especially yellow fever and cholera."[10] This was rapidly followed in 1879 by the establishment of the first comprehensive medical research effort on a national scale and the creation of the National Board of Health. Among its first research investments were a bacteriology laboratory on Staten Island focused on useful research. By 1918, the research program expanded beyond communicable diseases and extended its grants to outside institutions (thus establishing the precedent that the federal government might turn to scientists other than their own employees in institutions around the country for research assistance through a grant-making mechanism).[11]

The shift in orientation away from research of immediate practical application toward Pasteur's Quadrant and more basic contributions to the advancing of knowledge in Bohr's Quadrant can be traced to the 1950s and the rise of molecular biology. This field offered a deep knowledge base for the study of health and disease and for the development of specific treatments and cures (Judson 1979). Not surprisingly, it led to the NIH's hybrid goal of research to "advance the understanding of biological systems, improve the control of disease, and enhance health." Nonetheless, the current orientation is toward more "Bohr-like," less problem-oriented research. This orientation is evident in the criteria outlined to external peer reviewers: In selecting external awardees, the NIH uses a peer review system as legally required through sections 406 and 492 of the PHS Act with an underlying system to "provide a fair and objective review process in the overall interest of science" (NIH Grants Policy Statement [12/03], 7). Surprisingly, given the orientation toward practical applications as well as basic knowledge advance, the NIH review criteria are strikingly similar the NSF. Five selection criteria are defined in the Congressional guidelines:[12]

9. NIH Grants Policy Statement General Information 12/03.

10. NIH Almanac.

11. Today the NIH allocates awards (for research rather than infrastructure) through PAs or RFAs. A PA describes new, continuing, or expanded program interests. An RFA is a more targeted solicitation focused on well-defined scientific areas or for a one-time competition.

12. http://grants.nih.gov/grants/policy/nihgps_2003/NIHGPS_Part3.htm#_Toc54600045.

- *Significance:* Does this study address an important problem? If the aims of the application are achieved, how will scientific knowledge be advanced? What will be the effect of these studies on the concepts or methods that drive this field?
- *Approach:* Are the conceptual framework, design, methods, and analyses adequately developed, well integrated, and appropriate to the aims of the project? Does the applicant acknowledge potential problem areas and consider alternative tactics?
- *Innovation:* Does the project employ novel concepts, approaches, or methods? Are the aims original and innovative? Does the project challenge existing models or develop new methodologies or technologies?
- *Investigator:* Is the investigator appropriately trained and well suited to carry out this work? Is the work proposed appropriate to the experience level of the PI and other researchers (if any)?
- *Environment:* Does the scientific environment in which the work will be done contribute to the probability of success? Do the proposed experiments take advantage of unique features of the scientific environment or employ useful collaborative arrangements? Is there evidence of organizational support?

The lack of mention of immediate application is striking. Specific funding choices at the level of particular grant mechanisms emphasize this shift toward a basic knowledge orientation. For example, in selecting projects in the R21 category (Exploratory Research Grant Program) that, like the NSF EAGER grants, are designed to support "novel scientific ideas or new model systems, or technologies that have the potential for significant impact on biomedical . . . research," reviewers are directed to focus their evaluation on the "conceptual framework, the level of innovation and the potential to significantly advance our knowledge."

Department of Defense

The United States DoD spent $82 billion on research, development, testing, and evaluation (RDT&E) in 2008—nearly 50 percent more than the rest of the federal government combined.[13] Little of this funding reaches academic institutions—only $2 billion to academia for research purposes—2.1 percent of the DoD's RDT&E budget to so-called basic research, and 5.3 percent to applied research (DoD Budget: Fiscal Year 2009, 2008).

The limited emphasis on research in academia is further reflected in its organizational structure; university research is one of several mandates supported by one of four organizations within the Research Directorate, which

13. The DoD classifies RDT&E into seven activities: basic research, applied research, advanced technology development, advanced component development and prototypes, system development and demonstration, RDT&E management support, and operational system development (DoD Financial Management Regulation 2008).

itself is one of four directorates under the Office of Defense Research & Engineering. Nearly all of the basic research and much of the applied research supported by the DoD is funded through DARPA, administratively independent from the Office of Defense Research & Engineering. Founded in 1958 as the Advanced Research Projects Agency in response to the launch of Sputnik and renamed DARPA in 1972, its mission is "to maintain the technological superiority of the U.S. military and prevent technological surprise from harming our national security by sponsoring revolutionary, high-payoff research bridging the gap between fundamental discoveries and their military use."[14] The DARPA can thus be squarely identified as searching for and selecting research opportunities in Pasteur's Quadrant or, when appropriate, in Edison's Quadrant—solutions to specific problems.

This problem orientation is evident in DARPA's organization around seven independent offices: Adaptive Execution, Defense Sciences, Information Processing Techniques, Microsystems Technology, and so forth. These offices are similar to the NIH's Institutional Centers in that they have independent missions and identify their own research agendas, but their selection criteria are more closely tied to their missions. Each office posts solicitations for research proposals in the form of Broad Agency Announcements (BAAs) (similar to NIH RFAs and DOE FOAs) in the specificity of research requested (DARPA Solicitations 2010). While the independence given to each office leads to variability within the evaluation criteria used across BAAs, the following criteria are present in each BAA, illustrating a tighter focus on useful applications in Edison's Quadrant:[15]

- *Overall scientific and technical merit:* The technical merit of the research and the soundness of the plan to perform it will be evaluated. The proposed research must be highly innovative and show promise of sufficient technical payoff to warrant the technical risk. The research must have the potential to make a radical impact on future technology. The proposed technical approach is feasible, achievable, complete, and supported by a proposed technical team that has the expertise and experience to accomplish the proposed tasks. Task descriptions and associated technical elements provided are complete and in a logical sequence with all proposed deliverables clearly defined such that a final outcome that achieves the goal can be expected as a result of award. The proposal identifies major technical risks and planned mitigation efforts are clearly defined and feasible.
- *Potential contribution and relevance to the DARPA mission:* The potential contributions of the proposed effort with relevance to the national technology base will be evaluated and its relevance to DARPA's par-

14. DARPA Mission 2010.
15. Taken from DARPA-BAA-10-35 2010, DARPA-RA-10-76 2010.

ticular mission and methods assessed. Specifically, DARPA's mission seeks to maintain the technological superiority of the US military and prevent technological surprise from harming US national security. The DARPA aims to accomplish this by sponsoring revolutionary, high-payoff research that bridges the gap between fundamental discoveries and their ultimate military use.

- *Cost realism:* The objective of this criterion is to establish that the proposed costs are realistic for the technical and management approach offered, as well as to determine the proposer's practical understanding of the effort. The proposal will be reviewed to determine if the costs proposed are based on realistic assumptions, reflect a sufficient understanding of the technical goals and objectives of the BAA, and are consistent with the proposer's technical approach (to include the proposed Statement of Work). At a minimum, this will involve review, at the prime and subcontract level, of the type and number of labor hours proposed per task as well as the types and kinds of materials, equipment, and fabrication costs proposed. It is expected that the effort will leverage all available relevant prior research in order to obtain the maximum benefit from the available funding. For efforts with a likelihood of commercial application, appropriate direct cost sharing may be a positive factor in the evaluation.

Department of Energy

The smallest of the federal funding agencies in terms of funding of research in academia, the Department of Energy—unlike the NSF and NIH—has not historically been an organization devoted to funding research. Created in 1977 in response to the energy crisis of the 1970s from organizations that regulated the nuclear power industry and managed nuclear weapons development (Origins & Evolution of the Department of Energy 2010), the DOE has been "principally a national security agency" (DOE Program Offices 2010). It originally emphasized "energy development and regulation," "nuclear weapons research, development, and production" in the 1980s, and "environmental cleanup of the nuclear weapons complex, nonproliferation stewardship of the nuclear stockpile, energy efficiency and conservation, and technology transfer and industrial competitiveness" in the 1990s and early 2000s (Origins & Evolution of the Department of Energy 2010).

As of 2008, the DOE's mission is more focused on research and development, specifically "discovering the solutions to power and secure America's future" (DOE Summary of Performance and Financial Information 2009). In fact, the DOE now funds 40 percent of the basic research in the physical sciences in the United States, making it the single largest supporter of such research. (The majority of DOE supported research is performed internally in 17 national laboratories rather than in academic university labs.) Nonetheless, the DOE's strategic theme of science, discovery, and innovation accounted for only 16 percent ($4.1 billion) of its total program expenditures in 2009 (DOE Summary of Performance and Financial Information 2009). While this was supplemented by appropriations from ARRA, the DOE is not primarily focused on research funding despite its current mission.

The DOE selection criteria can be observed in its external grant solicitations through its Office of Science. Like the other mission-oriented agencies, the Office of Science is subdivided into six program offices, each reflecting a key mission area: Advanced Scientific Computing Research, Basic Energy Sciences, Biological and Environmental Research, Fusion Energy Sciences, High Energy Physics, and Nuclear Physics. Each office provides funding opportunity announcements (FOAs) focused on well-defined research goals. The DOE criteria for peer review (as legally required through the Office of Science Financial Program Rule [10 CFR Part 605 2006]) listed in descending order of importance, reflect funding in Edison's quadrant and, to a lesser extent than the NIH, Pasteur's Quadrant:[16]

- *Scientific and/or technical merit of the project:* For example, the influence that the results might have on the direction, progress, and thinking in relevant scientific fields of research; the likelihood of achieving valuable results; and the scientific innovation and originality indicated in the proposed research.
- *Appropriateness of the proposed method or approach:* For example, the logic and feasibility of the research approaches and the soundness of the conduct of the research.
- *Competency of the personnel and adequacy of proposed resources:* For example, the background, past performance, and potential of the investigator(s), and the research environment and facilities for performing the research.
- *Reasonableness and appropriateness of the proposed budget.*
- *Other appropriate factors, established and set forth in a notice of availability or in a specific solicitation.*

In response to the 2007 "Rising Above the Gathering Storm" report (National Academy of Sciences 2007), the America COMPETES Act established the Advanced Research Projects Agency-Energy (ARPA-E) within the DOE to "explore creative 'outside-the-box' technologies that promise genuine transformation in the ways we generate, store and utilize energy" (ARPA-E 2010c).

The ARPA-E is modeled after DARPA and received $400 million in initial funding through ARRA. Its mission is to "fund projects that will develop transformational technologies that reduce America's dependence on foreign

16. Basic Energy Sciences: Review and Selection of Research Projects 2010; 10 CFR 605.10.

energy imports; reduce U.S. energy related emissions (including greenhouse gasses); improve energy efficiency across all sectors of the U.S. economy and ensure that the U.S. maintains its leadership in developing and deploying advanced energy technologies" (ARPA-E 2010b). Furthermore, ARPA-E is not intended to support the traditional energy research agenda of the DOE, but to focus "exclusively on high risk, high payoff concepts—technologies promising genuine transformation in the ways we generate, store and utilize energy" (ARPA-E 2010b). The ARPA-E has released seven FOAs to date, six of which have a narrow research focus similar to traditional DOE FOAs (ARPA-E 2010c). However, "ARPA-E's inaugural program . . . was open to all energy ideas and technologies, but focused on applicants who already had well-formed research and development plans for potentially high-impact concepts or new technologies" (ARPA-E 2010a) suggesting a shift toward Pasteur's Quadrant with a specific focus on energy applications.

The ARPA-E uses a peer review process to select awardees with the following evaluation criteria:[17]

- *Impact of the proposed technology relative to state of the art:* The proposed technology must directly address one or more ARPA-E Mission Areas. Quantitative material and/or technology metrics must be proposed that demonstrate the potential for a transformational (not incremental) advancement in one or more energy-related fields. The applicant must demonstrate an awareness of competing commercial and emerging technologies and identify how its proposed concept/technology provides significant improvement over these other solutions. The applicant must have a strong and convincing transition strategy, including a feasible pathway to transition the program results to the next logical stage of R&D or directly into industrial development and deployment. The applicant must address the program-specific requirements identified for the Full Application phase as described in Section II of this FOA.
- *Overall scientific and technical merit:* The work must be unique and innovative. The proposed work should be high risk, but must be feasible. The applicant must demonstrate a sound technical approach to accomplish the proposed R&D objectives. The outcome and deliverables of the program, if successful, should be clearly defined. The applicant must address the program-specific requirements identified for the Full Application phase as described in Section II of this FOA.
- *Qualifications, experience, and capabilities:* The proposed Principal Investigator or technical team should have the expertise and experience needed to accomplish the proposed project. In addition, the applicant should have access to all facilities required to accomplish the R&D

17. DE-FOA-0000289; DE-FOA-0000290.

effort or has proposed the necessary missing equipment as part of the effort. The applicant's prior experience must demonstrate an ability to perform R&D of similar risk and complexity.

- *Sound management plan:* The proposed effort must have a workable plan to manage people and resources. Appropriate levels or people and resources should be allocated to tasks. The application should identify major technical R&D risks and have adequately planned mitigation efforts that are clearly defined and feasible. The proposed schedule should be reasonable. The applicant's prior experience in similar efforts must clearly demonstrate an ability to manage an R&D project of the same proposed complexity that meets the proposed technical performance within the proposed budget schedule.

Overall, it is clear that today's federal agencies select academic research projects across a mix of quadrants.

1.2.3 Public Funding—Philanthropic Foundations

Philanthropic foundations serve as an alternative source of public (i.e., not for profit) funding for research in academia. They have played a critical role in supporting US university research since the contributions of James Smithson to the establishment of the Smithsonian Foundation, which served not only to fund the now renowned museum but also one of the first extramural grant-making programs. According to his will (drafted in 1826) this Englishman's money would go "to the United States of America, to found at Washington, under the name of the Smithsonian Institution, an establishment for the increase and diffusion of knowledge."[18] After that time, wealthy individuals in the United States continued the practice of supporting academic research, selecting mainly on their interest in specific individual beneficiaries and missions. Many of the earliest gifts to university-based researchers focused on astronomy, botany, and zoology. In later years, more highly organized philanthropy shifted attention toward biomedical research.

The current landscape of philanthropic support for research includes a broad variety of criteria, with almost as much variation for funding university researchers as the federal agencies themselves. Traditionally, most foundations—for instance, the Sloan Foundation and the Howard Hughes Medical Institute, have followed selection criteria emphasizing scientific rather than applied outputs; Howard Hughes Awards are well-known for their provision of long-term support for high-risk research based on scientific merit and contributions to fundamental knowledge; that is, Bohr's Quadrant (see Azoulay, Graff Zivin, and Manso 2010).

The more recently founded Bill & Melinda Gates Foundation is a strik-

18. Available from http://siarchives.si.edu/history/exhibits/documents/smithsonwill.htm.

ing example of a foundation with significant resources that places a much greater emphasis on solving problems of immediate social and economic value. The overall foundation statement highlights a strong mission orientation by outlining its commitment to projects by asking the following questions:[19]

- What affects the most people?
- What has been neglected?
- Where can we make the greatest change?
- How can we harness innovative solutions and technologies?
- How can we work in partnership with experts, governments, and businesses?

In the arena of Global Health (which constitutes more than 60 percent of the $22 billion in funding that the foundation has committed from 1994 through 2010), the Foundation's priority areas are defined by disease. Its work in areas such as diarrhea, malaria, polio, and tuberculosis closely mirrors the priorities and emphasis of the NIH in the late half of the nineteenth century and early twentieth century. In selecting funding recipients, the Foundation uses criteria that are significantly at odds with the NIH (even in the same programmatic arenas) and emphasize problem-focus in Edison's Quadrant.

Like most of the federal funding agencies, the Gates Foundation also has a program to fund high-risk, high-reward research: the Grand Challenge Explorations program. At only $100k per project, the foundation emphasizes "unorthodox thinking . . . essential to overcoming the most persistent challenges in global health . . . to expand the pipeline of ideas to fight our greatest health challenges."[20] Not only is the mission of this program more tightly coupled to the production of useful knowledge to address key problems, but the funding criteria are also dramatically different from the approach used in federal funding. At the start of an Explorations program, a topic area is outlined. For example, a 2010 Grand Challenge Explorations theme was focused on new technology for contraception. The topic was defined with the articulation of a key "roadblock." Specifically, they state that:[21]

> there have been tremendous improvements in the reproductive health of men and women in the developing world. Nonetheless, many do not have access to health supplies and services that enable planning the number and timing of pregnancies, safe delivery of children, and management and treatment of sexually transmitted infections.

19. http://www.gatesfoundation.org/grantseeker/Pages/foundation-grant-making-priorities.aspx.
20. www.grandchallenges.org/explorations/.
21. http://www.grandchallenges.org/Explorations/Topics/ContraceptiveTechnologies/Pages/round4.aspx.

The Foundation argues that barriers to uptake arise because:

> current methods do not meet their needs. For those whose income is less than $2 per day, cost is an specially important issue . . . and side effect[s] that can occur [are] not acceptable in certain cultural contexts. Skilled health care workers are often unavailable in resource poor settings so self-administration or options that allow for non-medical staff—such as community health volunteers—can increase access to new methods.

They conclude with their statement for proposals:

> that are "off the beaten track," daring in premise, and clearly different from the approaches currently being developed or employed. Technologies or approaches should enhance uptake, acceptability and provide for sustained use; enable or provide for low-cost solutions; promote effective delivery and administration of new solutions; and ensure or enhance safety.

Proposals are not explicitly subject to traditional peer review. Instead, the review panel has "broad expertise and a track record in identifying innovations." Members may not be deep domain experts in the field. Review is executed in four stages: In stage 1, foundation staff review proposals to determine a match between the proposal and key needs described in the topic, or proposals considered to be more incremental advances. In the second step, external reviewers make evaluations, but rather than seek consensus, they can make funding recommendations based on the best proposals they see. Three criteria are deemed critical.[22]

- *Topic responsiveness:* How well does the proposal address a key need illustrated in the topic description?
- *Innovative approach:* Does the idea offer an unconventional, creative approach to the problem outlined in the topic?
- *Execution plan:* Is the work described feasible within the budget and time allocated for a Phase I GCE award and if successful, would it be sufficient to show a clear path to further support?

The Gates criteria, in contrast to all the federal funding criteria, illustrate a much tighter coupling for selection to specific areas of need and immediate application. More akin to the French wine industry funding much of Pasteur's work on fermentation, the criteria couple the hybrid generation of fundamental knowledge to the solution of specific problems, thus reemphasizing the degree to which—at least in selection—funders have a rich array of choices available to them as they establish selection criteria.

In figure 1.4 we map each of the agencies and several of their larger programs, as well as a number of the major foundations, into the two-by-two selection matrix outlined earlier. What is clear is that there is significant

22. Rules and Guidelines: Grand Challenges Explorations Round 4.

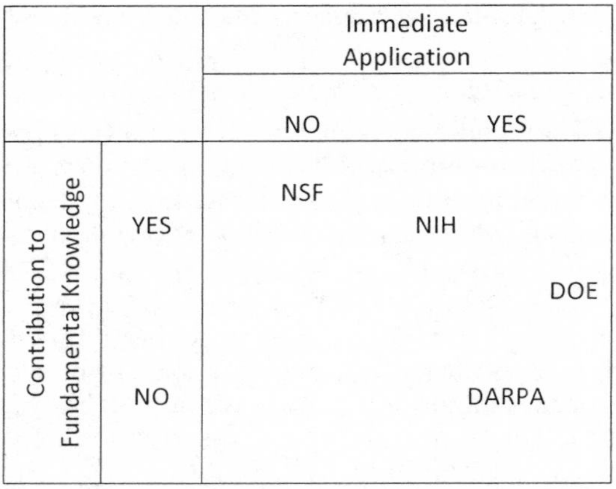

Fig. 1.4 Mapping federal funding to the selection matrix

diversity across the agencies, even among those three with a well-articulated mission orientation. And, among foundations there is even greater variation and a willingness to experiment with a broader space of selection criteria (although the effectiveness of these criteria, either in terms of selecting distinctively different research projects or achieving different outcomes, remains to be fully analyzed).

1.3 Disclosure and Commercialization

Disclosure is a key element in shaping the economic impact of investments in research by both the public and the private sector; however, the disclosure conditions imposed by funders received only limited scrutiny from policymakers and scholars until the 1980s. Contemporary scholarship brought the recognition that the mere production of knowledge was inadequate to ensure its role in knowledge accumulation: intertemporal knowledge spillovers require that knowledge be disclosed and accessible to others, a feature of knowledge production that is far from axiomatic (Mokyr 2004). What remains to be understood and analyzed in the context of the research funding is the range of possible disclosure choices, the preferences of researchers and funders for these conditions, and whether and how disclosure conditions influence the level and type of projects funded by the public and private sector respectively.

Building on the two-by-two framework elaborated in section 1.2, we argue that there exist at least four distinctive disclosure strategies; secrecy (nondisclosure), publication, patenting, and patent-paper pairs (Murray 2002). Each of these options map into several of the four research quadrants previously described. Specifically for research that lies in Pasteur's

Quadrant, all four disclosure strategies are viable alternatives—research that is useful and makes a contribution to fundamental knowledge can be patented or published (or both), but can also be subject to secrecy. For Bohr's quadrant, secrecy and publication are viable strategies. Edison's quadrant research can remain secret or be patented, as illustrated by the high levels of patenting achieved by Edison and his laboratory.

In what follows, we provide some insight into each of the four disclosure choices (for more detail see Gans, Murray, and Stern 2010). Nondisclosure or secrecy may be preferred by some funders (particularly those in the private sector or government agencies funding particular types of research with national security implications) but is generally not compatible with researchers in academia. Far from being a modern practice, secrecy was widely used by funders of research, particularly patrons who had utilitarian motives for maintaining at least some of the discoveries that they funded a secret (David 2008). Even in the case of Galileo, the telescopes he prepared for his patron were presented only at the Grand Duke's orders to the other European rulers (David 2008, 13). In later periods, researchers funded on botanical expeditions also maintained their plant specimens, drawings, and maps as secrets for their wealthy commercial sponsors (Stroup 1990; Schiebinger and Swan 2005). More contemporary examples of secrecy in government-funded research include the Manhattan Project—among the best known "secret" research projects undertaken by academic scientists. Most recently, the so-called "climategate" argument over research performed in the UK identified researchers at the University of East Anglia who had "an unacceptable culture of secrecy."[23] Indeed, as a leading analyst of medical science has argued, "secrecy in science reduces the efficiency of the scientific enterprise by making it harder for colleagues to build on each other's work" (Blumenthal et al. 2006).

The three disclosure strategies that provide an alternative to secrecy rely upon complex institutions to provide incentives for scientists and those who fund them to engage in disclosure: the patent system or *commercial science,* and the system of publications often termed *open science* (Dasgupta and David 1994).

Disclosure in patents is supported by commercial science, which, among other functions, provides incentives to ensure that knowledge locked within labs might instead be disclosed (Machlup and Penrose 1950; Kitch 1977; Scotchmer and Green 1990). As a quid pro quo for exclusionary rights of a limited term, patent holders (whether they be the funder or the researcher) must disclose knowledge at the level that enables a person "skilled in the art" to replicate that knowledge and potentially build upon it. This strategy is most likely to be appropriate for knowledge that is of immediate applica-

23. Chairman of the Science and Technology Committee blamed the University for encouraging a "reprehensible culture of withholding information."

tion (in Edison's or Pasteur's Quadrant), given the requirement for patent grant that an idea be not only novel and nonobvious but also useful. And, with the passage of the 1980 Bayh-Dole Act title to patents was clearly given to universities for researchers funded by the federal government, a norm that has extended to many other funders (with some institution specific variations).

For researchers working within academia, publication disclosure associated with open science is the dominant institutional logic: when knowledge is disclosed through scientific publication in the academic literature, researchers are rewarded with kudos and other private benefits (Dasgupta and David 1994; David 2008). In other words, to receive credit for the intellectual priority of their scientific discoveries, scientists publicize their findings as quickly as possible but retain no other rights over their ideas (Merton 1957). Of course, journals require that an idea make a contribution to fundamental knowledge, and therefore knowledge in Bohr's and Pasteur's quadrant are most likely to be potentially disclosed via publication. Interestingly (as we outline in more detail later), public funders rarely place publication *requirements* on those whom they fund, assuming instead that broader institutional norms promote publication.

The fourth disclosure strategy—patent-paper pairs—is widespread among academic scientists (using a variety of funding sources). When research projects are in Pasteur's Quadrant and lead to research of immediate usefulness and make a contribution to long-run knowledge, then we see many observe disclosure in the form of patent-paper pairs regardless of funding source (Murray 2002; Murray and Stern 2007). For example, with funding from Geron Corporation, Professor James Thomson from the University of Wisconsin developed both monkey and then human embryonic stem cells and disclosed the research in the form of an academic publication. However, only a few weeks prior to publication, he filed patents. The more formal disclosure requirements provided by funders do not, to our knowledge, explicitly make provisions for patent-paper pairs. Instead, by making provisions that allow for publication hold-up to enable patent filing, they implicitly acknowledge the possibility of patent-paper pairs and enable researchers, their universities, and the flow of funding to follow the complex timing requirements that enable disclosure through patent-paper pairs.

Disclosure outcomes are typically negotiated between researchers or their organizations (for example, universities) and funders as they match on particular research projects. A control rights approach to the selection of disclosure strategy has recently been developed by Gans, Murray, and Stern (2010). They argue that scientists and those who fund them have clear (and potentially diverging) preferences for disclosure. In particular, while researchers have strong preferences for disclosure in the form of academic publications (Stern 2004), some funders—particularly those in the private sector—may have expectations that research is disclosed through patents or may prefer secrecy. This disjuncture highlights the important role of public (versus private) support in shaping the conditions influencing the level of research dissemination (or patenting) as well as the level of inventive activity (Furman, Murray, and Stern 2010).

In what follows, we examine the ways in which funders (as well as researchers and the universities in which they are employed) shape the selection among the four disclosure strategies for knowledge generated by the projects they fund. The precise nature of these requirements can be defined either through formal contracts (as is typically now the case for private funding) or via informal normative expectations (as is broadly true for public funding, although specific regulations do exist).

1.3.1 Disclosure Criteria for Public Funding—Government Agencies and Foundations

If public funding agencies, particularly the federal government, have been vague with regard to their expectations around the selection of research projects, their stipulations regarding disclosure of the results of these projects is even less precisely articulated.

In broad strokes, our analysis suggests that government funders make few active provisions to limit *nondisclosure*; the National Science Foundation asks researchers to make best efforts in disclosure but has no formal requirement limiting secrecy. The specific contractual provisions hold few obligations of publication disclosure. The NSF outlines:

> 38. Sharing of Findings, Data, and Other Research Products
> a. NSF expects significant findings from research and education activities it supports to be promptly submitted for publication, with authorship that accurately reflects the contributions of those involved.
> b. Adjustments and, where essential, exceptions may be allowed to safeguard the rights of individuals and subjects, the validity of results, or the integrity of collections or to accommodate legitimate interests of investigators.

Overall, there is a strong adherence to the notion of autonomy and self-regulation for the scientific community. This is based both on a view that incentives for academic publication will eventually ensure that knowledge production will indeed be disclosed via publications, and through the use of publications as a selection mechanism for future awards.[24]

With regard to patenting, the regulations are more precise. Provided for by the Bayh-Dole Act, the National Science Foundation and other US govern-

24. Scotchmer and Maurer (2004) demonstrate that a reputation-based funding mechanism can substitute for a public funder's difficulty in evaluating research outcomes ex ante.

ment agencies have provisions for the patenting of inventions outlined in the Federal Register ([35 U.S.C. § 200 et seq.]).

Specifically:

> Unless otherwise provided in the award, if this award is for experimental, developmental or research work the following clause will apply:
> b. Allocation of Principal Rights
> The grantee may retain the entire right, title, and interest throughout the world to each subject invention subject to the provisions of this Patent Rights clause and 35 U.S.C. §203. With respect to any subject invention in which the grantee retains title, the Federal Government shall have a non-exclusive, nontransferable, irrevocable, paid-up license to practice or have practiced for or on behalf of the U.S. the subject invention throughout the world.

Of particular note is the requirement to disclose inventions to the NSF within two months (and include in that notification information about other publications and manuscripts).

> c. Invention Disclosure, Election of Title and Filing of Patent Applications by Grantee
> 1. The grantee will disclose each subject invention to NSF within two months after the inventor discloses it in writing to grantee personnel responsible for the administration of patent matters. . . . It shall be sufficiently complete in technical detail to convey a clear understanding of the nature, purpose, operation, and, to the extent known, the physical, chemical, biological or electrical characteristics of the invention. The disclosure shall also identify any publication, on sale or public use of the invention, whether a manuscript describing the invention has been submitted for publication and, if so, whether it has been accepted for publication, at the time of disclosure.

This is the most salient element of the contractual regulation of federal funding that *requires* rather than expects disclosure, although it is not clear whether in practice this is always fulfilled and there is considerable discretion on the part of investigators.

While the NSF rules are closely followed by other US federal funding agencies, more stringent disclosure requirements have been imposed by government agencies elsewhere such as the UK's Medical Research Council. They place a greater emphasis on publication as a strong expectation (BBSRC 2011):

> GC 23 Publication and Acknowledgement of Support
> The Grant Holder should, subject to the procedures laid down by the Research Organisation, publish the results of the research in accordance with normal academic practice.

This is augmented by specific provisions making publications themselves more available:

AC30 Self archiving of publications
For proposals (for grants or fellowships) submitted after 1 October 2006, electronic copies of any original research papers accepted for publication in a peer-reviewed journal, which are supported in whole or in part by MRC funding, must be deposited at the earliest opportunity, and certainly within six months of publication, in UK PubMedCentral. This applies whether the manuscript was submitted during or after the period of the grant. The condition is subject to compliance with publishers' copyright and licensing policies. Whatever possible, the article deposited should be the published version.

Some foundations follow a similar line and, in fact, use disclosures as critical inputs into funding decisions. For instance, the Sloan Foundation specifically requests tangible outputs "(such as number of students whose training or careers are affected, data collected, scientific papers produced) and outcomes (such as new knowledge, institutional strengthening, etc.)" or other measures of success including "big sales of a book, a prize awarded for research, a government grant to continue the project, web traffic, high enrollments, better salaries, etc." in evaluating grant effectiveness (Sloan Foundation 2008). Similarly, the criteria of the Gates Foundation (as it pursues a selection model that emphasizes immediate value) emphasize what they term "actionable measurement" in follow-on grant selection process but places no specific requirements on disclosure.[25]

1.3.2 Disclosure Criteria for Public Funding—Special Provisions of Defense Funding

In comparison to most public funding from government agencies and philanthropic foundations, research funding for defense-oriented research, including research funded by DARPA, places greater limitations on disclosure, particularly when associated with research of immediate application. Of course, as Senator Moynihan quoted in an address on Secrecy in Science to the American Association for the Advancement of Science in 1999:[26] "What is different with secrecy is that the public cannot know the extent or the content of regulation."[27] Thus it is difficult to precisely calibrate the extent of secrecy for defense research.

The secrecy (nondisclosure) of publically funded research can be required through the 1951 Invention Secrecy Act,[28] which empowers federal defense agencies to prevent the disclosure of new inventions that pose a potential national security threat by sharing with the United States Patent and Trade-

25. http://www.gatesfoundation.org/learning/Documents/guide-to-actionable-measurement.pdf.
26. http://www.aaas.org/spp/secrecy/Presents/Moynihan.htm.
27. Commission on Protecting and Reducing Government Secrecy, Secrecy: Report of the Commission on Protecting and Reducing Government Secrecy (Washington, D.C.: Government Printing Office, 1997), p. xxi.
28. 35 U.S.C. § 181–188.

mark Office (USPTO) a classified list of sensitive technologies in the form of the "Patent Security Category Review List" (PSCRL).[29] Prior to this time, during World War I and throughout World War II, Congress authorized the USPTO to classify certain defense-relevant patent applications, and patent secrecy was used to maintain secrecy over information considered critical to national security particularly the Manhattan Project. The formal language of the 1951 statute is informative:

> Whenever publication or disclosure by the grant of a patent on an invention in which the *Government has a property interest* might, in the opinion of the head of the interested Government agency, be detrimental to the national security, the Commissioner upon being so notified shall order that the invention be kept secret and shall withhold the grant of a patent therefore under the conditions set forth hereinafter.
>
> Whenever the publication or disclosure of an invention by the granting of a patent, in which the *Government does not have a property interest,* might, in the opinion of the Commissioner, be detrimental to the national security, he shall make the application for patent in which such invention is disclosed available for inspection to the Atomic Energy Commission, the Secretary of Defense, and the chief officer of any other department or agency of the Government designated by the President as a defense agency of the United States. Each individual to whom the application is disclosed shall sign a dated acknowledgment thereof, which acknowledgment shall be entered in the file of the application.

A secrecy order not only prevents patent award and orders that the invention be kept secret, it restricts the filing of foreign patents, and specifies procedures to prevent disclosure of ideas contained in the application.[30] The number of patents subject to this treatment as of 2009 is just over 5,000 with 103 new secrecy orders imposed on patents in 2009.[31]

It is generally within the more narrow constraints of specific research funding contracts used by Defense funding agencies, particularly DARPA, that other disclosure limitations are imposed on researchers (in academia

29. It should be noted that this provision is not limited to ideas generated with federal funding. It can be imposed even when the application is generated and entirely owned by a private individual or company without government sponsorship or support.

30. The inventor does have some recourse for compensation: According to Section 183, An applicant, his successors, assigns, or legal representatives, whose patent is withheld as herein provided, shall have the right, beginning at the date the applicant is notified that, except for such order, his application is otherwise in condition for allowance, or February 1, 1952, whichever is later, and ending six years after a patent is issued thereon, to apply to the head of any department or agency who caused the order to be issued for compensation for the damage caused by the order of secrecy and/or for the use of the invention by the Government, resulting from his disclosure. See the Project on Government Secrecy at http://www.fas.org/sgp/othergov/invention/index.html.

31. See Invention Secrecy Statistics as reported annually by the USPTO available at: http://www.fas.org/sgp/othergov/invention/stats.html. Also, see Foerstel, Herbert N., *Secret Science: Federal Control of American Science and Technology.* Westport: Praeger, 1993, 165–172.

and elsewhere). All DARPA BAAs are composed of the same basic requirements (although details differ from office to office and announcement to announcement) regarding disclosure with the obligations and requirements on intellectual property, publications, and export control restrictions dependent upon whether the research is funded as basic research (6.1), applied research (6.2), or advanced technology development (6.3).

In general, all research performed on a university campus will have no publishing restrictions and is distinguished from proprietary research and from industrial development, "the results of which ordinarily are restricted for proprietary or national security reasons" (DARPA-BAA-10-35 2010). For research that meets the basic or applied classification, BAAs have a publication approval subsection under award administration information that states that it is "the policy of the Department of Defense that the publication of products of fundamental research will remain unrestricted to the maximum extent possible" (DARPA-BAA-10-35 2010, DARPA-RA-10-76 2010). However, DARPA may change the research designation (and hence the disclosure provisions) after research has been completed at the discretion of the DARPA contracting officer according to this language:

> in those rare and exceptional circumstances where the applied research effort presents a high likelihood of disclosing performance characteristics of military systems or manufacturing technologies that are unique and critical to defense, and where agreement on restrictions have been recorded in the contract or grant. Such research is referred to by DARPA as "Restricted Research." (DARPA-BAA-10-35 2010, DARPA-RA-10-76 2010)

Depending on the designation imposed by the Contracting Officer, a variety of publication disclosure limits may be imposed (see table 1.1).

With regards to noncommercial and commercial technical data and computer software, as well as patents and other forms of intellectual property, disclosure and control is governed by the Defense Federal Acquisition Regulation Supplement (DFARS). However, rather than disclosure per se, the main concern of the funding agency lies in maintaining control rights over ideas. For procurement contracts, the proposer must identify all commercial and "noncommercial technical data and . . . computer software that it plans to generate, develop, and/or deliver under any proposed award instrument in which the Government will acquire less than unlimited rights, and to assert specific restrictions on those deliverables" (DARPA-BAA-10-35 2010). It is important to note that the government assumes unlimited rights to any technical data and software not delineated. Researchers who undertake nonprocurement contracts must disclose similar information, primarily restrictions on government use of technical data and software. Just as the NSF and NIH require that patent filings be documented, DARPA requires documentation proving "ownership of or possession of appropriate licens-

Table 1.1 **US Department of Defense publication restrictions**[a]

DoD distribution statement	Description
The statement below requires review through DISTAR	
A	Approved for public release; distribution is unlimited
The statements below are assigned by the sponsoring DARPA Program manager	
C	Distribution authorizes US government agencies and their contractors (fill in reason) (date of determination). Other requests for this document shall be referred to (insert DoD controlling office).
D	Distribution authorized to the Department of Defense and US DoD contractors only (fill in reason) (fill in date). Other requests for this document shall be referred to (insert DoD controlling office).
B	Distribution authorized to US government agencies only (fill in reason) (date of determination). Other requests for this document shall be referred to (insert DoD controlling office).
E	Distribution authorized to DoD components only (fill in reason) (date of determination). Other requests for this documents shall be referred to (insert DoD controlling office).
X	Distribution authorized to US government agencies and private individuals or enterprises eligible to obtain export-controlled technical data in accordance with DoD Directive 5230.25, Withholding Unclassified Technical Data from Public Disclosure (date of determination). DoD controlling office is (insert).
F	Further dissemination only as directed by (insert DoD controlling office) (date of determination) or higher DoD authority.

[a]DARPA Distribution Statements 2010

ing rights to all patented inventions (or inventions for which a patent application has been filed)" (DARPA-BAA-10-35 2010). In addition, DFARS 227.303 gives patent rights to the contractor for all inventions discovered while under contract. Thus, overall, DARPA's standard contractual obligations on disclosure are relatively unrestrictive with respect to intellectual property ownership and the dissemination of information.

1.3.3 Disclosure Practices of Private-Sector Funders

The disclosure practices of private-sector-funded research taking place within private-sector firms is beyond the scope of this chapter. However, of the $200 billion in private-sector funds spent on R&D, over $2 billion are spent on research taking place within US universities, which constitutes 5 percent of the university research budget. Private-sector funding is particularly widespread among life science researchers: A survey of more than two thousand life scientists at the fifty US universities receiving the most National Institutes of Health funding found that more than 25 percent of the most productive researchers received industry funding—over 36 percent in clinical departments compared to 21 percent in nonclinical departments (Blumenthal et al. 1996).

Table 1.2 **Commercial outcomes of research by life-science faculty members according to type of outcome**

Industrial support	Outcome of research (Percent of respondents)						
	Applied for patent	Patent issued	Patent licensed	Trade secret	Product under review	Product on market	New company
Yes	42.0	25.0	18.5	14.5	26.7	26.1	14.3
No	24.0	12.6	8.7	4.7	5.5	10.8	6.0

Note: $P < 0.001$ for all comparisons between the subgroup with industrial support and the subgroup without such support.
Source: Reproduced from Blumenthal et al. 1996, 1,737.

With regards to disclosure, industrial funders are more closely associated with attempts to enforce *secrecy* on the scientists they fund. The challenge of limiting secrecy falls to sponsored research administrators within universities as well as on academic scientists themselves. In current industry-funded medical science, for example, secrecy appears to be widespread. The precise disclosure requirements placed on recipients of industry funding are not systematically documented. However, several recent surveys of life science researchers found that faculty members with industrial support were significantly more likely than those without industrial support to report that their research had resulted in trade secrets (14.5 percent vs. 4.7 percent), thus suggesting more limited disclosure linked to industrial funding (this figure rises to over 17 percent for the subset of over 500 researchers whose area of focus is in biotechnology—including recombinant DNA, monoclonal antibodies, and gene sequencing; however, these researchers are also more likely to apply for patents and are more productive in publication terms as illustrated in table 1.2).

Concerns over delays in publication disclosure, while less concerning than secrecy, are still salient in research. As leading commentators have noted: "The enormous legal and financial power of the pharmaceutical industry puts clinical investigators in a very difficult position if there is a major controversy about the outcome of a particular study." (Nathan and Weatherall 2002). In several cases, scientists have accused their funders of attempting to limit disclosure, particularly of negative clinical results (Haack 2006), exemplifying the complex relationship between researchers, their funders, and the universities (and medical schools) who serve as the intermediaries in constructing and executing these contracts and in setting appropriate levels of disclosure.[32] As noted in a leading medical journal "[t]he intense pressure on individuals at academic institutions to publish and on the sponsoring

32. Kern, D., Crausman, R. S. Durand, K. T. Nayer, A. and Kuhn, C., III. Flock worker's lung: chronic interstitial lung disease in the nylon flocking industry. *Ann Intern Med* 1998;129:261–272. [Erratum, *Ann Intern Med* 1999;130:246.] Rennie D. Thyroid storm. *JAMA* 1997;277:1238–1243. [Erratum, *JAMA* 1997;277:1762.]

companies to get their drugs on the market sometimes produce[s] tensions between the two parties, and if results are not favorable, disagreements can develop[,] leading to disputes, innuendos, and even legal action."[33] More pragmatic is the voice from leading journal *Nature Biotechnology* that asks, "When is it reasonable for academics to expect total freedom over the data they have gathered on a company's behalf, especially if they have signed a confidentiality agreement?"[34]

The debate over privately funded medical research and, more broadly, regarding all industrial funding of academic research is grounded in the contracts that are signed between academic scientists and the private corporations who fund them. Certainly, scandals, such as those experienced in academic medical centers, have exacerbated the need for clearer rules. Early examples of industry-university contracts gave many of the rights to the knowledge produced (and its disclosure) to the funder (usually referred to as the sponsor). In the past decade, universities have become more sensitive to charges of "research-for-hire" and the possibility that knowledge is being withheld to serve corporate interests. However, while the Technology Transfer Office (TTO) function has received considerable attention among scholars of innovation and the academic-industry boundary (Owen-Smith 2005; Mowery et al. 2004), the ways in which universities contract over the incoming funding (rather than the outgoing licensing of completed projects) is poorly understood. We have little systematic knowledge of the disclosure provisions put into place for privately (commercially) sponsored research. To fill this gap, we have gathered some preliminary data in this regard to catalogue the contractual practices of twenty major US research universities.[35]

The contractual provisions shaping disclosure (and ownership) of industry-funded research in academia are rarely established via a bilateral agreement between researcher and funder. More typically, the negotiation is carried out and the contract signed by an "Office of Sponsored Projects," which seeks to represent the broader interests of the university in maintaining the disclosure of research findings. Our analysis focuses on the standard contractual terms offered to industrial sponsors in single-sponsor research agreements with regard to publications, rights to tangible research property, university project inventions, university copyrightable software and databases and university copyrightable works other than software. There

33. Donald M. Poretz, Letter to the Editor, Outcomes of a Trial of HIV-1 Immunogen in Patients with HIV Infection, 285 *JAMA* 2192, 2192–93 (2001).

34. Editorial, Knee-Jerk Response, 18 *Nature Biotechnology* 1223 (2000)

35. The twenty universities in alphabetical order are Dartmouth College, Carnegie Mellon University, Case Western Reserve University, Cornell University, Emory University, Georgia Tech, Harvard, Johns Hopkins University, Massachusetts Institute of Technology, Rochester Institute of Technology, Stanford, University of Arizona, University of California at Berkeley, University of Florida, University of Pennsylvania, University of Pittsburgh, University of Texas at Austin, University of Washington, University of Wisconsin, and Washington University.

appears to be significant heterogeneity among the terms surrounding publications and rights in tangible research property across universities, whereas the terms for university project inventions, university copyrightable works other than software, and university copyrightable software and databases are similar across the sample.

Publication

With regards to disclosure via publication, sixteen of the twenty universities in our sample explicitly address publication restrictions in single-sponsor research agreements with industrial entities including terms governing the public disclosure of information gained in research, the existence of prepublication sponsor review, the time for review (if permitted), exceptions in permitted reviews for theses or dissertations and sponsor acknowledgment.[36] We present Article VI of the research contract used by the University of California at Berkeley's Sponsored Projects Office (2011) as an example of common terms presented to corporate sponsors with regard to publications:

> ARTICLE VI. PUBLICATION California will have the right to copyright, publish, disclose, disseminate and use, in whole and in part, any data or information received or developed under this agreement. Copies of any proposed publication will be provided to Sponsor thirty (30) days prior to submission for Sponsor's review, comment, and identification of any of Sponsor's proprietary data which has inadvertently been included and which Sponsor wishes to have deleted. During this review period, Sponsor may also identify patentable inventions for which it wishes California to file for patent protection. In such case, California will delay publication up to an additional sixty (60) days in order to file such patent application.

The University of California at Berkeley and nine other universities in our sample permit the disclosure of all information that is not marked as confidential by the sponsor, five universities allow full disclosure, and the University of Texas at Austin has a more complex policy: it allows full disclosure if it has exclusive rights to the intellectual property produced in the project, but it gives the sponsor the right to mark information as confidential and nonpublishable if the sponsor has some claim to the intellectual property produced. Nonetheless, every university permits presponsor publication review, even though the sponsor may not necessarily have rights to restrict the information divulged in the publication. A majority of universities give the sponsor thirty days for review and allow between a thirty-day and sixty-day extension. However, some universities gave more favorable terms, such as a 180-day extension and even a three-month standard review with a three-

36. The four universities that did not address publication restrictions are the University of Arizona, University of Washington, University of Wisconsin, and Washington University.

month extension. This heterogeneity across universities is surprising and merits further investigation into its causes and effects.

Patenting

While the terms surrounding publications are heterogeneous across universities, the terms governing rights in tangible research property are dichotomous.[37] When addressed, the university is always given the right to use all tangible research property. Ownership rights generally require further negotiation and/or separate agreement. Harvard is the only university we examined that claims ownership rights over the research property and only gives the sponsor rights for internal research use. While firm conclusions cannot be drawn from such a small sample, it appears that the dichotomy presented in the terms governing rights in tangible research property are a result of the fact that universities must often enter into negotiations and/or use a separate agreement beyond the boilerplate contract when assigning these rights.

Unlike the terms for publications and rights in tangible research property, many of the terms governing university inventions are nearly uniform across the eleven universities, including: which party is awarded ownership of inventions, whether internal research licenses are offered to the nonowning party, the existence and nature of any commercial licenses, the amount of time given to elect to license (if available), the amount of time given to negotiate collective licenses, and whether the sponsor must reimburse expenses. We present an excerpt from Section 11 of the research agreement used by the Massachusetts Institute of Technology's Office of Sponsored Programs (2011) as an example of common terms presented to industrial sponsors with regard to inventions:

A. MIT INVENTIONS. MIT shall have sole title to (i) any invention conceived or first reduced to practice solely by employees and/or students of MIT in the performance of the Research (each an "MIT Invention") and (ii) any invention conceived or first reduced to practice by employees of the Sponsor with significant use of funds or facilities administered by MIT, if the invention is conceived or reduced to practice other than in the performance of the Research. The Sponsor shall be notified of any MIT Invention promptly after a disclosure is received by MIT's Technology Licensing Office. MIT may (a) file a patent application at its own discretion or (b) shall do so at the request of the Sponsor and at the Sponsor's expense.

B. LICENSING OPTIONS. For each MIT Invention on which a patent application is filed by MIT, MIT hereby grants the Sponsor a non-exclusive,

37. The eleven universities in alphabetical order are Georgia Tech, Harvard, Johns Hopkins University, Massachusetts Institute of Technology, Stanford, University of Arizona, University of California at Berkeley, University of Texas at Austin, University of Washington, University of Wisconsin, and Washington University.

non-transferable, royalty-free license for internal research purposes. The Sponsor shall further be entitled to elect one of the following alternatives by notice in writing to MIT within six (6) months after MIT's notification to the Sponsor that a patent application has been filed:

1. a non-exclusive, non-transferable, world-wide, royalty-free license (in a designated field of use, where appropriate) to the Sponsor, without the right to sublicense, in the United States and/or any foreign country elected by the Sponsor pursuant to Section 11.C. below, to make, have made, use, lease, sell and import products embodying or produced through the use of such invention, provided that the Sponsor agrees to (a) demonstrate reasonable efforts to commercialize the technology in the public interest, (b) reimburse MIT for the costs of patent prosecution and maintenance in the United States and any elected foreign country, and (c) indemnify MIT for any liability arising from Company's use or sale of the invention; or
2. a royalty-bearing, limited-term, exclusive license (subject to third party rights, if any, and in a designated field of use, where appropriate) to the Sponsor, including the right to sublicense, in the United States and/or any foreign country elected by the Sponsor pursuant to Section 11.C. below, to make, have made, use, lease, sell and import products embodying or produced through the use of such invention, provided that this option to elect an exclusive license is (a) subject to MIT's concurrence and the negotiation of commercially reasonable terms and conditions and (b) conditioned upon Sponsor's agreement to reimburse MIT for the costs of patent prosecution and maintenance in the United States and any elected foreign country and to cause any products produced pursuant to this license that will be used or sold in the United States to be substantially manufactured in the United States.

If the Sponsor and MIT do not enter into a license agreement within three (3) months after Sponsor's election to proceed under paragraph 11.B.1. or 11.B.2. above, the Sponsor's rights under paragraphs 11.B.1. and 11.B.2. will expire.

As observed in MIT's agreement, the university retains ownership of all project inventions in each case and can therefore disclose the knowledge via patent filing. In addition, almost all universities examined automatically offer the sponsor a license for internal research use and none explicitly deny such a license. With regard to commercial licenses, the terms range from an option to negotiate a nonexclusive royalty-free license (NERF) to giving a royalty-bearing sublicense will contract. However, the majority of universities offer both nonsublicensable NERFs and royalty-bearing sublicensable contracts. Harvard is the only outlier, offering a NERF for blocking intellectual property, which is sublicensable if the license for dominating intellectual property is also granted, and options for royalty-bearing licenses that are either exclusive and sublicensable or nonexclusive and nonsublicensable. As with university project inventions, the terms governing the ownership and licensing of copyrightable software and databases are consistent across the ten universities we examined.[38]

Taken together, the university-industry contracts suggest that the nature of the disclosure terms that prevail when university academics seek out private-sector funding are more complex than those used under conditions of public-sector federal funding. We have been led to believe in our informal conversations with university Offices of Sponsored Research that in recent years public funding coming from philanthropic sources is increasingly the subject of more stringent disclosure conditions. Rather than attempting to limit disclosure and enable secrecy (albeit time limited), philanthropic foundations are hoping to force more rapid disclosure by shifting the burden on publication from a norm or expectation toward a requirement. Likewise, they hope to shift ownership or licensing terms related to patents in a way that ensures that commercial rights still enable the development of useful products and services for underserved communities and nations (Furman, Murray, and Stern 2010). These trends, which deserve further scrutiny, highlight the critical role of disclosure requirements in shaping scientists' preferences for funding from different sources.

In the model that follows, we combine our understanding of both the selection and disclosure requirements of funds and their interaction with scientists' preferences to offer a window into the role of public versus private funding of R&D in academia.

1.4 Selection, Commercialization, and Disclosure in a Model of Private-Public Funding

The two previous sections illustrated the selection intentions as well as the conditions that public funders place on the disclosure and commercialization of research. For example, funders usually select projects on the basis of scientific merit rather than capacity for immediate application. In addition, for the most part, funders do not explicitly consider whether other sources of funding might be forthcoming for projects within their selection set. Nonetheless, funders do display an active concern about what might become of the outcomes of research projects. They often impose disclosure requirements—through publication and other means—and can also limit commercialization options.

In this section, we provide a model of private and public funding of scientific projects and the ways in which funding criteria (both in selection and disclosure) made by these types of funders interact and shape the portfolio of funded projects. This modeling approach allows us to examine whether

38. Harvard's standard research agreement does not address copyrightable works.

and how funding conditions impact the number, mix, and openness of projects that are funded. We see this theoretical exercise as a critical first step toward identifying the first-order trade-offs that arise when publicly funded projects interact with privately funded ones. This will provide a basis for hypotheses that may be tested empirically in the future, as well as important considerations in identifying the causal impact of changes in funding policy (such as those that arose as a result of the Bayh-Dole Act).

To this end, the focus of our model is on the public funder's conditions regarding commercialization and patenting rather than on selection and disclosure per se (although those conditions have important consequences for these). With regard to selection, we assume that it is difficult for the funder to observe immediate applicability, while it can more readily evaluate scientific merit. We do, however, discuss what happens when funders can observe aspects beyond pure scientific merit. With regard to disclosure, the aforementioned evidence suggests that we can take as a given that disclosure rights are preserved and, indeed, compelled as a condition for the receipt of public funds. We will demonstrate that this requirement, however, has an important impact on the decisions of scientists and potential commercial funders to accept such funds.

1.4.1 Key Assumptions and Setup

We assume that there is a $[0,1] \times [0,1]$ space of research projects that can potentially be funded. The cost of funding each project is a constant amount, k. Projects also require a scientist to perform the research.[39] Projects differ in terms of their potential immediate social benefit, v, and their potential present value of future scientific benefits, b. The b and v are independently and identically distributed, uniformly on $[0,1]$.[40]

For a project with potential benefits (b, v) there are constraints on realizing this scientific and social value. With regard to immediate social (and economic) value, v is realized if the results of the research project are commercialized by competitive firms; otherwise, a fraction of the value, δ, is lost under monopoly production. We assume that competition can be fully provided by two firms who each capture β of immediate value while a monopolist captures a fraction $\mu \in [2\beta, 1-\delta]$.

With regard to scientific benefit, b is realized if, and only if, research outcomes are publicly disclosed (i.e., the scientist engages in disclosure via publishing). Otherwise, there are no scientific benefits. It is assumed that the scientist appropriates b in "kudos" if the project proceeds and its results are disclosed in a scientific publication.

Taken together, these conditions assure that maximum social value is realized if there is both competitive commercialization and scientific publication

39. It is assumed that scientists are suitable for, at most, one potential project.
40. We examine the consequences of nonindependence of b and v later.

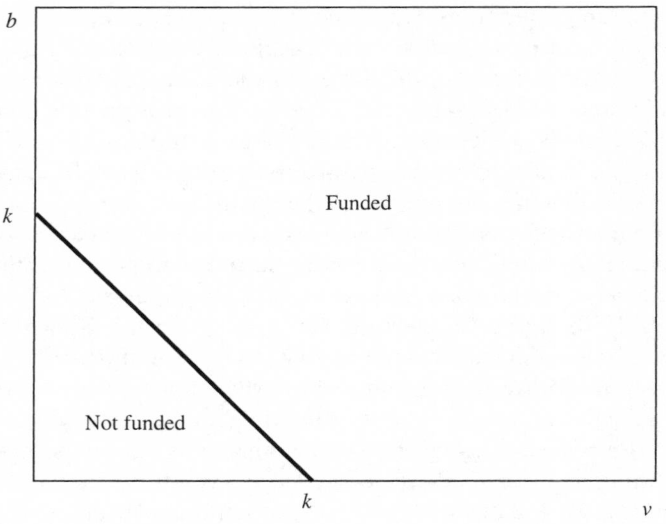

Fig. 1.5 Optimal funding

under conditions where all projects for which $v + b \geq k$ are funded while those with $v + b < k$ do not proceed (figure 1.5).

1.4.2 Intellectual Property and Competition

For simplicity, we assume that at most two firms can commercialize the outcome of a given research project.[41] Commercialization of a project carries no cost for the firm who funds a project but a cost, θ, for a rival firm engaging in parallel commercialization. This cost is distributed uniformly on [0,1]. However, if there is a publication, these costs are reduced by a fixed amount, $d < 1 - \beta v$.[42]

If permitted by the funder, the research outcome from a project may include a patent that is conferred on one firm. The existence of a patent generates a probability that entry may be blocked. There are many ways this might be modeled. Here we assume that, if there is a patent, then with probability $1 - \rho$, entry is possible; otherwise, it is not. Specifically, if not blocked by a patent, an entrant will only enter if $\beta v + d \geq \theta$ if there is a publication or $\beta v \geq \theta$, if there is not. This means that, if a firm controls the intellectual property of a research project, its expected profits are

41. If more firms can commercialize the research, then this only intensifies the gap between competition and monopoly in terms of profits and social value.

42. Later we consider what happens if commercialization requires the scientist's cooperation to transfer key knowledge (other than that done through publication). This will raise the possibility that commercialization is not a certain outcome when the scientist does not have a commercial interest.

$\mu v - (1 - \rho)(\beta v + d)(\mu - \beta)v$ if there is disclosure of scientific knowledge and $\mu v - (1 - \rho)\beta v(\mu - \beta)v$ otherwise.[43] In what follows, we use a variable, i, to indicate whether a firm as a patent ($i = 1$) or not ($i = 0$).

1.4.3 Scientist-Firm Negotiations

Firms provide the project capital, while scientists provide the labor. In this model, it is clear that while scientists may benefit from publication, firms do not.[44] However, publication may increase joint surplus if $b > (1 - i\rho)d(\mu - \beta)v$. In this case, if profits are still nonnegative, a firm would find it profit maximizing to allow publication, as this would allow them to reduce payments to the scientist to ensure they participated in the project (Stern 2004).

For many projects, there will be a surplus (or rents) created. The division of the surplus is determined by the relative bargaining power of scientists and firms. In Gans, Murray, and Stern (2010), negotiations over whether to disclose research results are modeled using a Nash bargaining solution with arbitrary bargaining power. Here, for expositional ease, it is assumed that scientists have all of the bargaining power. Specifically, it is assumed that the private supply of capital is perfectly elastic and consequently, firms will receive enough surplus (net of payments to scientists or license fees to scientist employers) to ensure that profits cover their capital costs.

1.4.4 Pure Private Funding

We begin by examining outcomes when only private funding is available. In this case, there will be no constraints placed on the ability to patent or earn commercial returns. However, disclosures through publication may still arise if this raises total surplus generated by the research project.

It is useful to define the threshold values of v that will allow a project to be commercially viable; that is, how high does v have to be to ensure that the commercial profits cover capital costs? This defines the set of projects capable of commercial funding and in the case the only projects funded in a regime of pure private funding. First, we define $\underline{v}$ as the minimum level of immediate value that would allow the net profits from any project with $v \geq \underline{v}$ to cover capital costs. That is,

$$(1) \qquad \mu\underline{v} - (1 - \rho)\beta\underline{v}(\mu - \beta)\underline{v} = k.$$

Second, we define $\underline{v}_{d,1}$ as the minimum level of immediate value that would allow the net profits from any project with publication and a patent and with $v \geq \underline{v}_{d,1}$ to cover capital costs. That is,

43. Note that it is always profit maximizing for the firm to choose to patent if it is permitted to do so. In reality, patents have their own disclosure requirements and other transactional costs that may make this decision more nuanced.

44. This is an extreme assumption. Firms may benefit from funding in terms of marketing benefits, attracting talent, reputation and also defensive publishing to influence patent race outcomes.

(2) $$\mu \underline{v}_{d,1} - (1-\rho)(\beta \underline{v}_{d,1} + d)(\mu - \beta)\underline{v}_{d,1} = k.$$

Third, we define $\underline{v}_{d,0}$ as the minimum level of immediate value that would allow the net profits from any project with publication but no patent and with $v \geq \underline{v}_{d,0}$ to cover capital costs. That is,

(3) $$\mu \underline{v}_{d,0} - (\beta \underline{v}_{d,0} + d)(\mu - \beta)\underline{v}_{d,0} = k.$$

Note that $\underline{v} < \underline{v}_{d,1} < \underline{v}_{d,0}$ as a publication diminishes commercial returns. This implies that all projects with $v \geq \underline{v}$ will be funded. This is because, even without publication, the profits from those projects will enable the project to cover capital and scientist costs.

The following proposition characterizes the equilibrium outcomes:

PROPOSITION 1. *A research project* (b, v) *is privately funded with no publication if* $v \geq \underline{v}$ *and (i)* $b < d(1-\rho)(\mu-\beta)v$ *or (ii)* $b \geq d(1-\rho)(\mu-\beta)v$ *and* $v < \underline{v}_{d,1}$. *A research project* (b, v) *is privately funded with publication if and only if* $b \geq d(1-\rho)(\mu-\beta)v$ *and* $v \geq \underline{v}_{d,1}$.

The proof involves a straightforward comparison of the conditions that maximize total surplus. Figure 1.6 depicts the equilibrium outcome. Importantly, projects that have both a high future and immediate value are more likely to be funded and are also more likely to be disclosed through publication. These projects lie squarely in Pasteur's Quadrant. Because the scientist is liquidity constrained, some projects whereby $b \geq d(1-\rho)(\mu-\beta)v$ are funded but do not involve a publication.

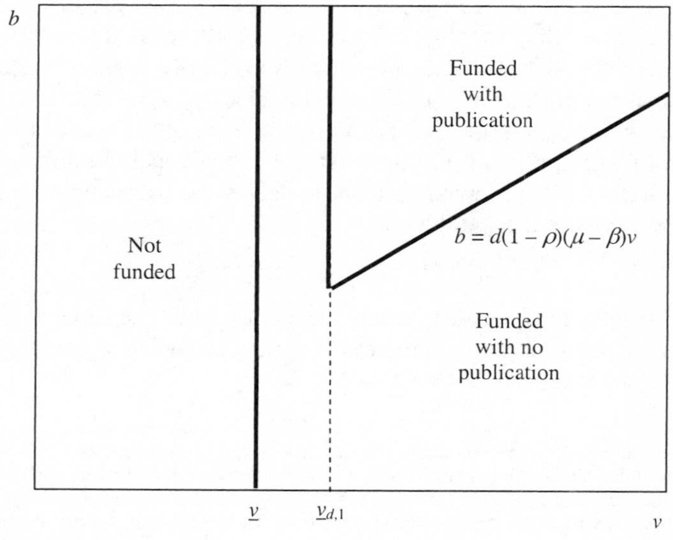

Fig. 1.6 Pure private funding

At this point, it is useful to note the impact of stronger intellectual property protection, as measured by ρ, on the equilibrium outcome. Notice that an increase in ρ will increase both $\underline{v}$ and $\underline{v}_{d,1}$ but will also impact on the margin between publishing and not. The former comparative static comes from the pure increment to commercial returns accompanying stronger patent protection. The latter arises because stronger patents protect the firm from the consequences of published disclosure, thereby reducing the costs of such disclosure. This means that more projects will be funded and, in addition, a larger number of projects will be funded that permit publication. As Gans, Murray, and Stern (2010) demonstrate, this is not a consequence of scientists having all of the bargaining power and can arise simply because firms wish to economize on scientist labor costs.

1.4.5 Public Funding

We now turn to examine what happens to the mix and disclosure of projects when there is a public funder who is interested in providing maximizing social value ($b + v$). Under these conditions, we assume that the public funder is constrained in its ability to assess and consequently select projects for funding. Specifically, we assume that the public funder can only observe b and cannot observe v. The idea is that b is something that is subject to possible peer review in such a way that it can be properly assessed, whereas v is somewhat harder to extract as information from the marketplace. Maurer and Scotchmer (2004) tie this specifically to published outputs that can serve as a signal of scientific value being met and also likely to be met in the future through a reputational mechanism. We later examine what happens when more symmetric information acquisition across project dimensions is possible.

The public funder is assumed to be liquidity constrained (in contrast to private funders). It has total funds available of K ($< k$) so it can only fund at most K/k projects. This implies that there exists some threshold, $\underline{b}$, such that it would fund all proposals with $b > \underline{b}$.[45] Note that, as some projects satisfying this constraint may choose not to apply for public funding but be purely privately funded, $\underline{b}$ depends on the equilibrium outcome in terms of each project's opt-in decisions.

The key focus of our analysis is on the restrictions the public funder attaches to funds received. One obvious restriction is a requirement to publish without which future value cannot be generated. Consequently, it will

45. It is possible that the funder could also have a maximum cut off that did not fund projects with very high scientific value. This might arise if many such projects would be funded anyway and so the funder was willing to sacrifice not funding those with high scientific value that would not otherwise be funded. As this possibility does not fit the description of any known funding agency, we implicitly assume that is not the case here. However, strictly speaking this would only apply under certain distributional assumptions on the space of projects as well as the availability of public funds.

be assumed throughout that the public funder always requires this in return for accepting any funds.

The other restrictions we consider are as follows: First, the scientist cannot profit from commercialization, and no patent can be applied for and granted. This is a common requirement from funding by government sources. Second, the scientist can profit from commercialization, but patenting is not permitted. Finally, that there are no commercialization restrictions and patenting is permitted without any conditions on how patent rights are used. We examine each in turn.

No Commercial Payments or Patent

When scientists (or their institutions) cannot receive commercial payments, their decision as to whether to accept public funding (if offered) will compare the kudos they receive, b, with the potential surplus otherwise.

PROPOSITION 2. *When public funding prohibits commercial payments to the scientist, such funding will only be accepted by a research project* (b, v) *if:*

(i) $v < \underline{v}$*; or*

(ii) $v \in \{\underline{v}, \underline{v}_{d,1}\}$ *and* $b \geq \mu v - (1-\rho)\beta v(\mu - \beta)v - k$.

A research project (b, v) *will be privately funded with publication if* $v \geq \underline{v}_{d,1}$ *and* $b > d(1-\rho)(\mu-\beta)v$. *A research project* (b, v) *will be privately funded without publication if* $v \geq \underline{v}$ *and* $b < \mu v - (1-\rho)\beta v(\mu-\beta)v - k$.

The proof is straightforward once it is noted that:

$$\mu v - (1-\rho)\beta v(\mu - \beta)v - k > (1-\rho)d(\mu - \beta)v \Leftrightarrow v > \underline{v}_{d,1}.$$

A possible outcome is depicted in figure 1.7. There are three things of interest. First, if a project was privately funded with publication prior to the existence of a public funder, it remains privately funded. This is because the scientist can earn profits as well as kudos with private funding. Second, public funding does crowd out some private funding but where it does so it generates a publication. Thus, more projects are funded and overall openness has increased compared to a purely private system. Finally, there may be projects the public funder would like to fund in order to generate scientific benefits from publication, but these projects remain privately funded and unpublished. This is because the funding conditions restricting commercial payment cause too many projects to opt out of receiving public funding.

Interestingly, in this regime, the total level of public funding available has no impact on whether projects with $v \geq \underline{v}_{d,1}$ are funded and what type of funding those projects would receive; those projects remain private. That is, *the addition of public funding with restrictions on profiting from commercialization and patenting does not change the set of privately funded projects that are disclosed.*

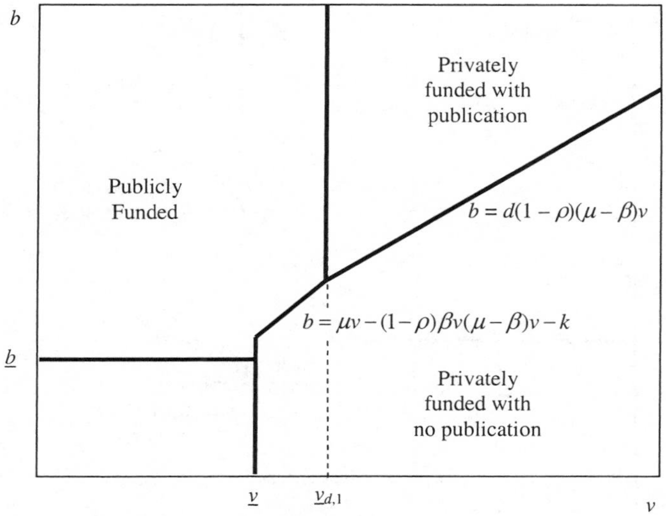

Fig. 1.7 Public funding (no commerce/no patent)

Commercial Payment but No Patent

Suppose now that the scientist is permitted to have a commercial interest in the project, but if it accepts public funds, no patent can be taken out. Consequently, imitative entry can proceed in an uninhibited manner.[46] The following proposition summarizes the resulting equilibrium:

PROPOSITION 3. *When public funding prohibits patenting, such funding will only be accepted by a research project (b, v) if:*

(*i*) $v < \underline{v}$; *or*

(*ii*) $v \in \left\{ \underline{v}, \frac{1}{2\beta}\left(\sqrt{d^2 + \frac{4k\beta}{(\mu - \beta)\rho}} - d \right) \right\}$ *and* $b \geq (\rho\beta v + d)(\mu - \beta)v - k$.

A research project (b, v) will be privately funded with publication if $v \geq (1/[2\beta])(\{d^2 + [4k\beta/(\mu - \beta)\rho]\}^{1/2} - d)$ *and* $b > d(1 - \rho)(\mu - \beta)v$. *A research project (b, v) will be privately funded without publication if* $v \geq \underline{v}$ *and* $b < (\rho\beta v + d)(\mu - \beta)v - k$.

The proof follows from that fact that:

$$(\rho\beta v + d)(\mu - \beta)v - k > (1 - \rho)d(\mu - \beta)v \Leftrightarrow v > \frac{1}{2\beta}\left(\sqrt{d^2 + \frac{4k\beta}{(\mu - \beta)\rho}} - d \right).$$

46. In addition, no license revenue can be generated; something we discuss later.

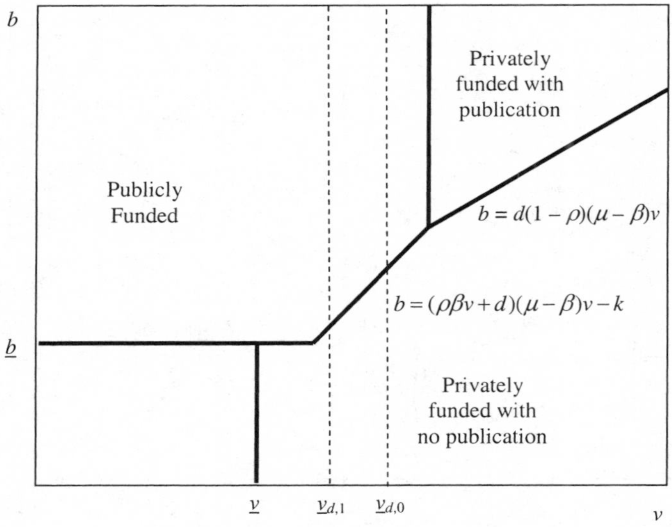

Fig. 1.8 Public funding (commerce/no patent)

A possible outcome is depicted in figure 1.8. In comparison to the no commercial payment case, observe first that there is more crowding out of privately funded projects and consequently, the total number of projects funded falls. This means that the marginal project receiving public funding has a higher b. Moreover, some of those projects crowded out are those that received private funding but involved disclosure. Nonetheless, some additional projects are disclosed. These projects, however, are of relatively low b (our proxy for scientific and potential future value). Finally, the additional projects receiving public funding have a higher chance of resulting in competition and so the realized immediate value for those projects is likely to be higher.

It is useful to compare this outcome to a weaker restriction—that a patent can be taken out, but it should be licensed openly, as proposed in Furman, Murray, and Stern (2010) and elsewhere. The idea here is to increase the probability that there is competition and that the immediate value of the innovation is socially realized. The question is whether this actually adds value to the firm relative to the no patent case.

If a patent is licensed to rivals, this allows the firm to earn more revenue in the event such rivals should enter. Indeed, if there were no restrictions on the fee that could be offered to a potential competitor, the firm could appropriate all of the competitor's profits; that is, $\beta v + d - \theta$ (assuming the fixed cost is realized and observable prior to license negotiations taking place). In that case, the firm's expected profits from accepting public funding become $\mu v - (\beta v + d)((\mu - v)v - 1/2(\beta v + d))$. This makes it more likely that the firm would accept public funding but significantly makes the firm less concerned about the impact of disclosure requirements on its profits.

Of course, this assumes that the firm can charge a lump-sum license fee but not otherwise control ex post competition through a license agreement; for example, by setting a license fee that preserves monopoly. A public funder would unlikely find much value in open licensing if it did not increase realized social value.

In addition, open licensing could give rivals a significant degree of bargaining power; especially if the onus was on the patent holder to ensure that licensing takes place. In this case, the fee may end up being close to some minimum amount as required by the funder and the outcomes may not be very different from the case where a patent is simply prohibited.

No Restrictions

Finally, we consider what happens when the public funder places no restrictions on how the research project might be commercialized. Previously, public funding may not be accepted because of a desire to appropriate commercial profits and take out a patent. In this case, the only restriction is that the project outcome has to be published. If $b < d(1-\rho)(\mu-\beta)v-k$, this may result in a project choosing to opt out of public funding. Otherwise, such funding will be accepted if it is available. Figure 1.9 depicts a possible outcome.

The first thing to note is that every project that might have been privately funded with publication will opt to take out public funds if they are available.

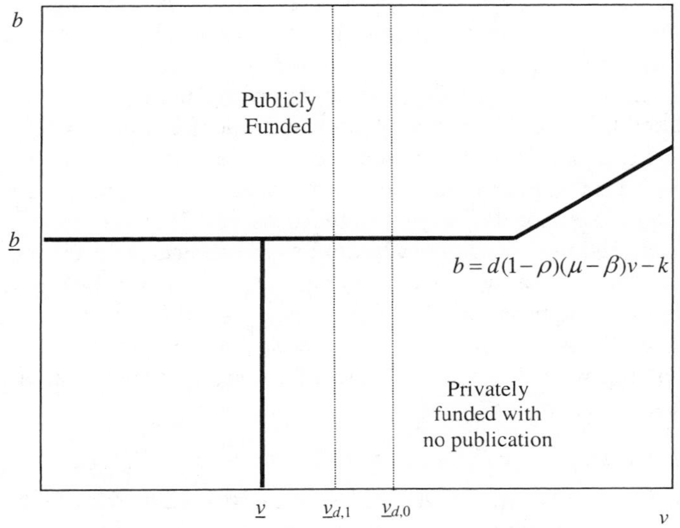

Fig. 1.9 Public funding (no restrictions)

Compared to the situation where the public funder allowed a commercial interest but no patent, this is a pure crowding out effect, with no benefits in terms of disclosure or increase in likely competition. Second, there are some privately funded projects without publication that do not receive public funding. However, there are also those for which the reverse might be the case. However, these are of lower b and hence, the shift in publications is socially more valuable.

1.4.6 Impact of the Bayh-Dole Act

This analysis gives some insight into the possible impact of the Bayh-Dole Act of 1980. That legislation removed restrictions on the patenting of government-funded research performed within universities. While it is not necessarily the case that scientists themselves appropriated commercial returns in the period that followed, their employers did, with a likely sharing of benefits in nonmonetary form. Thus, it was akin to a move from the no commercial interest, no patent case to the no restriction case.

The likely impact of the Act was, first, to have caused projects that might otherwise have been privately funded to become publicly funded. Moreover, the analysis demonstrates that this may not necessarily increase the degree of openness by the same amount, as many of the high scientific value projects would likely have been disclosed anyway.

There is little evidence that the Bayh-Dole Act had a significant impact on the number of research projects funded and performed within universities (Mowery and Sampat 2001) or on the mix of those projects (Mowery and Ziedonis 2002). While there was an increase in patenting, there is evidence that this was stimulated by other factors and, in fact, the quality of the patents was, on average, lower than prior to 1980 (Henderson, Jaffe, and Trajtenberg 1998).

Our analysis here is consistent with empirical findings that the quality of patented research from universities was reduced by the Bayh-Dole Act. Note that the marginal projects both encouraged and now patented as a result of the change in funding conditions are all at the lower end in terms of commercial prospects—arguably, the measure of quality associated with patent citation rates. Consequently, our model predicts precisely the decline in average quality that was observed empirically. Nonetheless, our analysis also identifies the broader role of university-based researchers in private innovative efforts as being relevant to consider when evaluating the full impact of the Bayh-Dole Act. To our knowledge, no such evaluation has yet been conducted.

Interdependence between Immediate Value and Scientific Merit

So far, we have assumed that b and v are independently distributed. What happens if they are interdependent? Specifically, how does this change the importance of imposing funding conditions on crowding out of private funding? If b and v are negatively correlated, then even in the absence of funding restrictions, very few high b projects would be available to opt for public funding and consequently, the crowding out effect will be lower. In this case, funders can more freely offer funding without restrictions. On the other hand, positive correlation of b and v implies that the reverse is true. In this case, public funders will want to be more diligent regarding conditions on commercialization and patenting to minimize crowding out.

What if Scientists Receive Kudos for Obtaining Grants?

In the previous analysis, scientists care about two things—kudos from publication and potential earnings from commercialization. In many higher education institutions, scientists also receive prestige from obtaining grants from public funders. The model here demonstrates that such prestige is likely to have negative consequences. In particular, it means that scientists may opt for public funding even in cases where they might have been able to privately fund projects with publication. This increases the crowding out effect, even in situations where public funders impose many restrictions on commercialization and patenting. The clear implication is that when crowding out is an issue, prestige associated with obtaining grants has negative consequences. Practically, however, it is difficult to separate out the prestige associated with grant awards, especially competitive grant awards, with the kudos likely to be generated from the outcomes of such grants.

Scientist Effort in Commercialization

Of course, expanding the funding base and assisting openness were not the primary rationales behind the Bayh-Dole Act. Instead, it was to unlock university research for commercialization by giving universities the ability to clarify commercial ownership and an obligation to facilitate commercialization and appropriate commercial returns. The idea behind this is quite consistent with economic theory: in the absence of a commercial stake, universities and academics would not expend much energy in trying to find commercial partners and communicate their innovations and research outcomes widely. Indeed, there is evidence that the Bayh-Dole Act did stimulate university level activities in technology transfer (Mowery and Ziedonis 2002).

In other words, when comparing a no commercial payment situation to a pure privately funded situation, some research projects would accept public funds but at the same time be commercialized at a lower rate than they would have been if they had been privately funded. As we move to a situation where public funding is granted unconditionally, then projects that receive some funding are more likely to be commercialized. This may include some low v projects. However, selection again plays a role. If we expect that it is high v projects that are more likely to be commercialized, we can also observe that those projects would have likely received private funding prior to the

Bayh-Dole Act. Thus, mere observations that more projects are being commercialized after 1980 may mask the true impact of the Bayh-Dole Act on commercialization—which is likely to be lower. This suggests considerable caution in the interpretation of such results.

The other implication is that proposals to improve the transactional efficiency of the commercialization process should receive additional attention, as these will impact on university-based research across the board. Kenney and Patton (2009) argue that ownership of patents should be vested with scientists, and Litan, Mitchell, and Reedy (2007) argue that universities should not have an exclusive option on commercializing research that is federally funded but performed in their home institutions. Instead, each emphasizes the role of competition in promoting more efficient search and commercialization from Universities.

Placing Weight on Immediate Value in Selection

So far, we have assumed that the public funder can only observe the future value of a research project and not its immediate value. Consequently, it could only use future value as a selection criterion. However, if the funder could also observe immediate application value, then it could reject funding of projects that had both high scientific and immediate value and could allocate those funds to other projects. Thus, perfect information would allow the funder—even operating alongside a private system—to more closely approximate the socially optimal outcome. As noted earlier, there was a sense in which the Gates Foundation undertook this practice by emphasizing projects of immediate value that, for some reason, were subject to difficulties in private appropriability that limited their ability to attract private funding.

More realistic is the possibility that public funders could use more sophisticated mechanisms to reveal whether a project would otherwise be of high immediate value. For example, Maurer and Scotchmer (2004) argue that matching funds assist public funders in selecting projects with high social prospects and not those with low prospects. They argue that a pure capital subsidy means that public funders may end up funding some low value projects. Instead, suppose that all projects required a minimum capital contribution from private funders before receiving an additional subsidy. In that situation, for projects with low social value, the minimum capital contribution screens them out, as even with the subsidy such projects will not earn a return for their private backers.

Here, the concern is with projects that might otherwise have received private funding and not require public funds. In this case, minimum capital requirements would not screen out those projects. Instead, matching funds could be tied to funding conditions. For instance, restricted grants that prevented commercialization or patenting might receive the full capital costs whereas unrestricted grants may only receive partial funding. Of course, these latter grants would still require disclosure through publication. In this

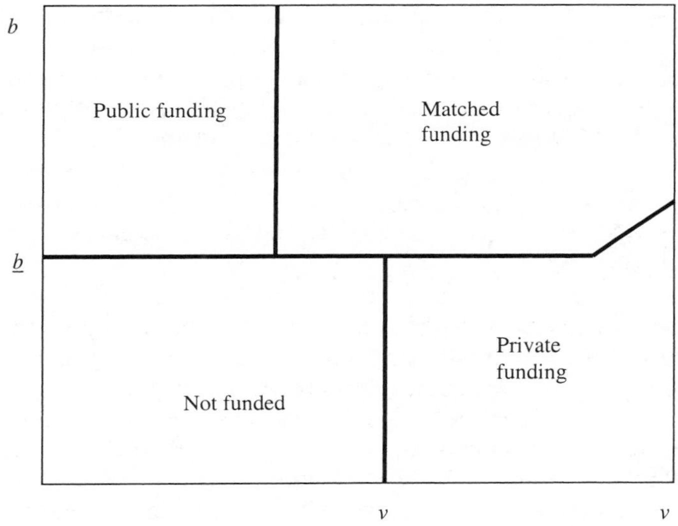

Fig. 1.10 Mixed funding rules

case, public funders would offer researchers a menu of options. A possible outcome of this is depicted in figure 1.10.

In figure 1.10, note that some projects choose open science with full public funding rather than the matching grant option. Note also that the matching grant makes public funding more attractive to some projects that switch from no publication to publication. However, it is clear that this outcome is superior for the public funder compared with the unrestricted funding case, as more projects receive funding and high scientific merit but low commercial return projects operate under open science. This suggests a rationale for tying a lack of restrictions on patenting and commercial exploitation of research with shared capital contributions for that research.

This mixed system overcomes some of the difficulties identified with matching grant systems. That occurs here, but by also providing restricted funding without matching grants, those projects with high scientific merit can be funded regardless.

1.5 Discussion and Agenda for Research

The design of research contracts by public or publicly spirited funders is an issue that has been understudied. Some prior formal models have examined the role of funding conditions on individual projects and their performance. Most notably, Aghion, Dewatripont, and Stein (2009) examine the interplay between an academic's choice of project (which comes with public funding) and ceding that right to private commercial interests. Their concern was that research effort be optimally allocated between exploration and exploitation of promising paths (see also Banal-Estañol and Macho-Stadler 2010). Importantly, they emphasized the importance of conditions (to select research direction) attached to public funding and contrasted these with conditions that would be imposed by private funders. With regard to openness, Mukherjee and Stern (2009) and Gans, Murray, and Stern (2010) examined the disclosure rights afforded research scientists. None of these investigations, however, analyzed how public funding conditions affect the mix of private-public projects and with it the level of disclosures across the whole system.

Our approach, in contrast, allows us to explore several of the more contentious issues associated with research funding. Specifically, we shed light on the arguments of some scholars who, noting the variability in the amount of profit that can be appropriated from inventive activity (see Romer 1990; Maurer and Scotchmer 2004), raise concerns that private funding may be concentrated among highly appropriable projects. Others claim that blanket public support may also fail to select the most socially valuable projects, and more sophisticated mechanisms should be employed to screen projects and also to ensure quality.

This chapter highlights a number of critical trade-offs that public funders must confront when supporting research projects. Our chief finding is a surprising one; even in the absence of public funding, many projects with high scientific merit and immediate applications will indeed be funded and, in fact, disclosed in an open manner. Public support, offered with conditions attached that shape commercialization (e.g., patents), will not be attractive to projects that are commercially valuable, and so a natural screen occurs. However, unrestricted public funds will ensure that those projects will take public funding thus leading to fewer projects funded overall without consequent gains in openness. This has implications as to the way funding organizations should think about the conditions they impose. Even where their support is directed toward projects with high scientific value, the funder's choice of disclosure requirements and commercialization restrictions affect the portfolio of projects that will be attracted by the support. Research scientists often have a range of funding choices, including private sector support, and this contours the final set of projects available to and selected by the public sector. Specifically, we noted that while lifting commercialization restrictions may increase the number of projects with immediate application to seek public funds, this comes at the expense of projects that might both have been privately funded and, in even in that environment, generated high levels of disclosure. The end result may be a significant crowding out effect, with limited gains in terms of the quality of scientific discourse and disclosure.

Supporting this notion, we observed that, while public funding organizations have paid attention to the impact of funding conditions on the outcomes of specific projects they fund, very little attention is paid to broader outcomes on the innovation system per se. Our survey notes that selection criteria tend to have common claims based on measurable scientific outcomes across funding organizations but are less explicit in their acknowledgement of wider impacts. In contrast, the growing not-for-profit foundation sector, in an attempt to differentiate themselves from purely public funders, has increased their emphasis on social impact. The broad implications of this transformation are not yet understood, nor do we have the systematic information we need to assess the influence of foundations on the public-private R&D complex. We noted also that disclosure requirements, while acknowledged, were not necessarily a key condition of funding, although they may play a role in reputational mechanisms to ensure future grants. This trend is changing in the context of foundations that are also becoming more aggressive regarding their disclosure and commercialization conditions but work within a limited framework of analysis in enforcing these requirements. Finally, we observed that commercialization outcomes have been considered with explicit concern for conflicts of interest as well as their effects in facilitating the diffusion of scientific ideas. However, little attention has been paid to whether these restrictions have adversely affected the distribution of public funds or generated real improvements overall in the openness in science.

These concerns suggest the need for future research to understand these trade-offs. In our opinion, future research should be directed at the following questions:

1. How do *stated* selection and disclosure criteria translate into *realized* selection and disclosure outcomes? There is a need to examine the mix of projects actually funded by public organizations and to see where, in fact, they lie along the scientific merit/immediate application space as identified by Stokes (1997). In addition, are there indeed systematic differences in the level of disclosure achieved in this space conditioned on the source of funding (private vs. public)?
2. Do changes in commercialization opportunities affect the mix of projects funded and their level of disclosure? Taking, for example, the Bayh-Dole Act as an experiment, what was the impact of this reform on the mix of projects claiming public funds? Did projects that might have otherwise been privately funded end up involving higher levels of disclosure through academic routes?
3. How do scientists actually match their desired research projects to particular funding sources? Our model has identified the key role that scientists play in shaping the demand for research funding associated with different terms and conditions. They also shape their particular projects to meet the selection criteria at hand from different funders. To date, however, our analysis of research funding has focused almost exclusively on the supply-side, with little or no insight into demand-side issues.
4. Do mechanisms such as matching grants, university-industry alliance funding, or other joint mechanisms reduce crowding out while promoting

high level of scientific openness? Matching grants are designed to allow self-selection away from projects that might be inefficiently funded. However, they increase the need for commercial returns in order to be viable. Such motivations may conflict with goals of scientific openness.

5. Do open licensing requirements stimulate scientific openness? The chapter identifies a complementarity between the strength and effectiveness of intellectual property protection and commercial interests to permit scientific disclosure. Open licensing requirements may promote greater use of scientific outputs, but at the same time they weaken intellectual property protection's role in facilitating scientific openness. In an area where open licensing emerged as a new requirement, this would provide an empirical environment to test such claims.

6. Do foundations play a complementary role in the research-funding complex? How does their stated social mission interact with their emphasis on funding projects of high scientific merit? This chapter provides a framework within which to analyze the implications of foundations' growing commitment to rapid and full disclosure, alternative commercialization rights, and public-private collaborations.

These questions are central to analyzing the effectiveness of current mechanisms and processes attached to public funding of research and development. As noted in the introduction, significant, ongoing, and unresolved issues remain in the arena of the public support of science with regard to the efficiency whereby capital funds are directed. We believe that this agenda is necessary to understand some of the new trade-offs explored in this chapter.

References

Aghion, P., M. Dewatripont, and J. Stein. 2009. "Academic Freedom, Private-sector Focus and the Process of Innovation." *RAND Journal of Economics* 39 (3): 617–35.

ARPA-E. 2010a. ARPA-E Broad Funding Announcement. http://arpa-e.energy.gov/.

ARPA-E. 2010b. ARPA-E Mission. http://arpa-e.energy.gov/About/Mission.aspx.

ARPA-E. 2010c. ARPA-E Programs Main Overview. http://arpa-e.energy.gov/ProgramsProjects/Programs.aspx.

Arrow, K. 1962. "Economic Welfare and the Allocation of Resources for Invention." In *The Rate and Direction of Inventive Activity: Economic and Social Factors,* Universities-National Bureau Committee for Economic Research and the Committee on Economic Growth of the Social Science Research Councils, 609–25. Princeton, NJ: Princeton University Press.

Azoulay, P., J. Graff Zivin, and G. Manso. 2010. "Incentives and Creativity: Evidence from the Howard Hughes Medical Investigator Program." Working Paper.

Banal-Estañol, A., and I. Macho-Stadler. 2010. "Scientific and Commercial Incen-

tives in R&D: Research versus Development?" *Journal of Economics and Management Strategy* 19 (1): 185–221.
BBSRC (Biotechnology and Biological Sciences Research Council). 2011. Cross Council Research Grant Terms and Conditions. www.bbsrc.ac.uk/web/FILES/.../research-grants-terms-conditions.pdf.
Biagioli, M. 2000. "Replication or Monopoly? The Economies of Invention and Discovery in Galileo's Observations of 1610." *Science in Context* 13 (3–4): 547–90.
Blumenthal, D., E. Campbell, N. Causino, and K. Seashore Louis. 1996. "Participation of Life-Science Faculty in Research Relationships with Industry." *New England Journal of Medicine* 335:1734–9.
Blumenthal, D., E. G. Campbell, M. Gokhale, R. Yucel, B. Clarridge, S. Hilgartner, and N. A. Holtzman. 2006. "Data Withholding in Genetics and the Other Life Sciences: Prevalence and Predictors." *Academic Medicine* 81 (2): 137–45.
Bush, V. 1945. "Science: The Endless Frontier." A Report to the President. Washington, DC: US Government Printing Office.
Clemins, P. J. 2010. "Historical Trends in Federal R&D." Chap. 2 in *American Association for the Advancement of Science Report XXXIV: Research and Development FY2010.* Washington, DC: American Association for the Advancement of Science.
Dasgupta, P., and P. A. David. 1994. "Towards a New Economics of Science." *Research Policy* 23:487–521.
David, P. A. 2008. "The Historical Origins of 'Open Science': An Essay on Patronage, Reputation and Common Agency Contracting in the Scientific Revolution." *Capitalism and Society* 3 (2): Article 5.
Furman, J., F. Murray, and S. Stern. 2010. "More for the Research Dollar." *Nature* 468:475–8.
Gans, J. S., F. Murray, and S. Stern. 2010. "Contracting Over the Disclosure of Scientific Knowledge: Intellectual Property and Academic Publication." MIT Working Paper.
Groopman, J. 2001. "The Thirty Years' War." *Annals of Medicine, The New Yorker* June 4: 52.
Haack, S. 2006. "Scientific Secrecy and Spin: The Sad, Sleazy Saga of the Trials of Remune." *Law and Contemporary Problems,* Vol. 69. University of Miami Legal Studies Research Paper no. 2007-02. Available at: http://ssrn.com/abstract=938485.
Henderson, R., A. B. Jaffe, and M. Trajtenberg. 1998. "Universities as a Source of Commercial Technology: A Detailed Analysis of University Patenting, 1965–1988." *Review of Economics and Statistics* 80 (1): 119–27.
Huang, K., and F. Murray. 2009. "Does Patent Strategy Shape The Long-Run Supply Of Public Knowledge? Evidence from the Human Genome." *Academy of Management Journal* 52 (6): 1193–221.
Judson, H. F. 1979. *The Eighth Day of Creation: The Makers of the Revolution in Biology.* New York: Cold Spring Harbor Press.
Kenney, M., and D. Patton. 2009. "Reconsidering the Bayh-Dole Act and the Current University Invention Ownership Model." *Research Policy* 38:1407–22.
Kitch, E. W. 1977. "The Nature and Function of the Patent System." *Journal of Law & Economics* 265:274–5.
Litan, Robert E., Lesa Mitchell, and E. J. Reedy. 2007. "Commercializing University Innovations: Alternative Approaches." Available at: http://ssrn.com/abstract=976005.
Machlup, F., and E. Penrose. 1950. "The Patent Controversy in the Nineteenth Century." *Journal of Economic History* 10 (1): 1–29.

Maurer, S., and Suzanne Scotchmer. 2004. "Profit Neutrality in Licensing: The Boundary between Antitrust Law and Patent Law." NBER Working Paper no. 10546. Cambridge, MA: National Bureau of Economic Research, June.
Merton, R. K. 1957. "Priorities in Scientific Discovery: A Chapter in the Sociology of Science." *American Sociological Review* 22 (6): 635–59.
Mokyr, J. 2004. *The Gifts of Athena.* Princeton, NJ: Princeton University Press.
Mowery, D., R. R. Nelson, B. Sampat, and A. Ziedonis. 2004. *Ivory Tower and Industrial Innovation—University-Industry Technology Transfer.* Palo Alto, CA: Stanford University Press.
Mowery, D.C., and B. N. Sampat. 2001. "Patenting and Licensing University Inventions: Lessons from the History of the Research Corporation." *Industrial and Corporate Change* 10 (2): 317–55.
Mowery, D.C., and A. A. Ziedonis. 2002. "Academic Patent Quality and Quantity Before and After the Bayh-Dole Act in the United States." *Research Policy* 31: 399–418.
Mukherjee, A., and S. Stern. 2009. "Disclosure or Secrecy: The Dynamics of Open Science." *International Journal of Industrial Organization* 27:449–62.
Murray, F. 2002. "Innovation as Co-evolution of Scientific and Technological Networks: Exploring Tissue Engineering." *Research Policy* 31 (8–9): 1389–1403.
Murray, F., and S. Stern. 2007. "Do Formal Intellectual Property Rights Hinder the Free Flow of Scientific Knowledge? An Empirical Test of the Anti-commons Hypothesis." *Journal of Economic Behavior and Organization* 63 (4): 648–87.
Nathan, D. G., and D. J. Weatherall. 2002. "Academic Freedom in Clinical Research." *New England Journal of Medicine* 347:1368–71.
National Academy of Sciences. 2007. *Rising Above the Gathering Storm: Energizing and Employing America for a Brighter Economic Future.* Washington, DC: National Academies Press.
Nelson, R. R. 1959. "The Simple Economics of Basic Scientific Research." *Journal of Political Economy* 67 (3): 297–306.
OECD. 2002. *Frascati Manual: Proposed Standard Practice for Surveys on Research and Experimental Development.* Paris: OECD.
Office of Sponsored Programs, MIT. 2011. MIT Template Research Agreement. http://osp.mit.edu/sites/osp/files/u9/mit_research_agreement_for_us_sponsors_050111_website_version.pdf.
Olivieri, N. F., G. M. Brittenham, D. Matsui, M. Berkovitch, L. M. Blendis, R. G. Cameron, R. A. McClelland, P. P. Liu, D. M. Templeton, and G. Koren. 1995. "Iron-Chelation Therapy with Oral Deferiprone in Patients with Thalassemia Major. *New England Journal of Medicine* 332:918–22.
Owen-Smith, J. 2005. "Dockets, Deals, and Sagas: Commensuration and the Rationalization of Experience in University Licensing." *Social Studies of Science* 35 (1): 69–97.
Romer, P. M. 1990. "Endogenous Technological Change." *Journal of Political Economy* 98 (5): S71–102.
Schiebinger, L., and C. Swan, eds. 2005. *Colonial Botany: Science, Commerce, and Politics in the Early Modern World.* Philadelphia: University of Pennsylvania Press.
Scotchmer, S., and J. Green. 1990. "Novelty and Disclosure in Patent Law." *Rand Journal of Economics* 21 (1): 131–40.
Sloan Foundation. 2008. Apply for Grants. http://www.sloan.org/apply/page/4.
Sponsored Projects Office, University of California, Berkeley. 2011. http://www.spo.berkeley.edu/Forms/UCForms.html.
Stern, S. 2004. "Do Scientists Pay to be Scientists?" *Management Science* 50 (6): 835–53.

Stokes, D. 1997. *Pasteur's Quadrant: Basic Science and Technological Innovation.* Washington, DC: The Brookings Institution.
Stroup, A. 1990. *A Company of Scientists: Botany, Patronage, and Community at the Seventeenth-Century Parisian Royal Academy of Sciences.* Berkeley: University of California Press.
Williams, H. 2010. "Intellectual Property Rights and Innovation: Evidence from the Human Genome." Harvard Working Paper.

Comment Suzanne Scotchmer

The Role of Disclosure in R&D

Political and economic debates about innovation policy tend to center on intellectual property, and its defects as an incentive mechanism. This is because intellectual property involves a complex set of rules and objectives that interact and are hard to evaluate, and also because intellectual property is a well-defined body of law in law school curriculums. However, the complexity of intellectual property law pales beside the complexity of the public funding system. A nice contribution of the Gans and Murray chapter is that it illuminates the complexity of the public funding system.

The focus of the chapter is on disclosure requirements. The chapter begins with a survey of the rules that are imposed by various funding agencies. These requirements have apparently accreted over time without a well-articulated objective. The rules consequently seem fragmented. My take-away from this hodge-podge is that the purposes of disclosure are not well understood.

There is a very immediate purpose for disclosure in patent law, namely, notice. Without disclosure, what is protected? Notice is clearly important, but does not leave much room for economists to think strategically about why patent applicants want to minimize what is disclosed, or why disclosure is good for society as a whole. There are clearly other issues involved, else patent applicants would not seek to minimize their disclosures.

For example, an industrial context where not much disclosure is required is computer software. Patent practice has evolved such that very little useful knowledge needs to be disclosed by the applicant (see Lemley et al. 2002, 204–205). For copyrighted works, disclosure ought to be automatic because copyright protects "expression." However, it is not quite clear what is expressive in computer software, especially since software can be distributed in compiled form. Oddly enough, for copyrighted source code, US Copyright Circular 61 contains an explicit exemption from full disclosure, rather than a requirement for full disclosure. This raises more questions than it answers.

Suzanne Scotchmer is professor of economics, law, and public policy at the University of California, Berkeley, and a research associate of the National Bureau of Economic Research.

Is there anything different about software than other industrial products that would demand different disclosure rules? Gans's and Murray's survey suggests that the public funding system has similar inconsistencies throughout, again calling for a theory.

The chapter is not focused on theories of disclosure *per se,* but rather on how disclosure requirements can induce firms to choose a proprietary, unsponsored mode of development in order to avoid the disclosure rules. The first best is for all projects to be disclosed and competitively supplied. That cannot be accomplished without public funding, because competitive prices cannot support innovation. If all innovations were publicly funded, the first best would be to require disclosure, and the resulting knowledge should enter the public domain.

However, the point of the Gans and Murray chapter is to illuminate that it is counterproductive for public sponsors to choose rules that try to implement the first best. Requirements for disclosure and nonexclusive use may only cause innovators to eschew public funds in favor of an unrestricted right to protect their discoveries with intellectual property. Disclosure rules and other details of public funding should be chosen with an eye to how they affect the funding choices of innovators.

The authors assume that innovators dislike disclosure because disclosure lowers the cost of rivals who want to enter the protected market. This is a credible story, but perhaps it is useful to close by listing some other ways that disclosure can be socially useful. Disclosure has had less attention from

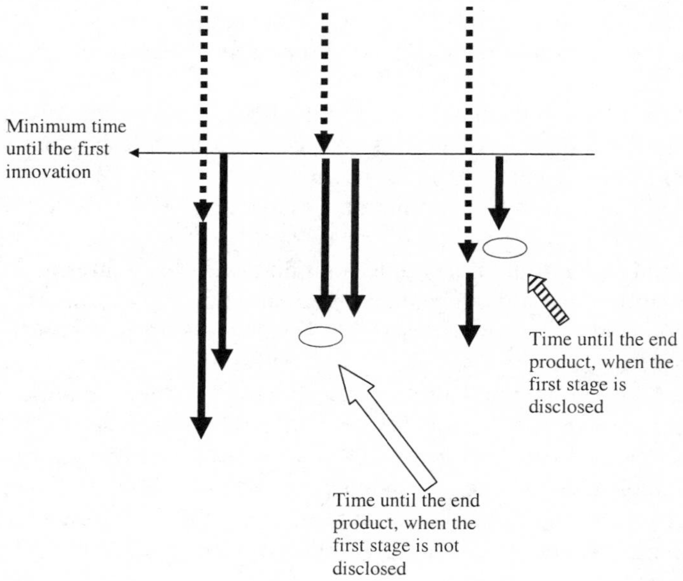

Fig. 1C.1

economists than in the public policy literature; for example, the contribution by Paul David (2003).

- In patent law, disclosure gives notice of what is protected.
- Disclosure reduces the costs of entry into the protected market (Gans and Murray).
- Disclosure can reduce the costs of rivals trying to make further cumulative progress, and can thus accelerate innovation for the economy as a whole (Scotchmer and Green 1990).
- Disclosure can stimulate imagination in the sense of allowing other firms to think of new investment opportunities.

The third bullet point occurs through what I call the "concatenation of order statistics." This is shown in figure 1C.1, where an innovation that is useful for end users requires two stages of progress. Time is measured vertically. It is assumed that the time required for each firm to accomplish each task is random, either because innovators think of research ideas at random times (Erkal and Scotchmer 2009) or because the R&D process is stochastic. There are three potential innovators. The dotted arrow (the top arrow) shows a realization of how long the first discovery takes for each of the three firms. The solid arrows (the bottom arrows) show a realization of how long the second (final) discovery takes. If the firm that achieves the first stage does not disclose, so that the others keep working on the first stage when they could alternatively be working on the second stage, the expected time to discovery is longer.

References

David, P. 2003. "The Economic Logic of 'Open Science' and the Balance between Private Property Rights and the Public Domain in Scientific Data and Information: A Primer." In *The Role of the Public Domain in Scientific and Technical Data and Information,* National Research Council, 19–34. Washington, DC: National Academies Press.

Erkal, N., and S. Scotchmer. 2009 "Scarcity of Ideas and R&D Options: Use it, Lose it, or Bank it." NBER Working Paper no. 14940. Cambridge, MA: National Bureau of Economic Research, May.

Lemley, M., P. Menell, R. Merges, and P. Samuelson. 2002. *Software and Internet Law,* 2nd ed. New York: Aspen Law and Business.

Scotchmer, S., and J. Green. 1990. "Novelty and Disclosure in Patent Law." RAND *Journal of Economics* 21:131–46.

2

The Diffusion of Scientific Knowledge across Time and Space

Evidence from Professional Transitions for the Superstars of Medicine

Pierre Azoulay, Joshua S. Graff Zivin, and Bhaven N. Sampat

If Whitehead's characterization of modern philosophy as "a series of footnotes to Plato" is perhaps a slight exaggeration, then the claim that contemporary scholarship on the economics of innovation is largely an extension of themes laid out in the 1962 *Rate and Direction* volume is no more of one. The contributors' prescience about the potential economic importance of academic science is particularly impressive, since at the time the conference was held (in 1960), the post-Sputnik transformation of the academic enterprise into the behemoth we know today had only just begun. The volume laid out a belief that basic research was important for innovation, marshalling theory, case studies, and data to support the assertions about the economic payoffs from basic research made in Vannevar Bush's "Science: the Endless Frontier" just fifteen years before. However, the conference volume was very much a call for more research, emphasizing the need for more data, and deeper understanding. In this chapter we attempt to rise to this challenge by examining the diffusion of knowledge across time and space within the life sciences. This endeavor remains as important at the beginning of this century as it was in the middle of the last one, given perennial calls for

Pierre Azoulay is associate professor at the Sloan School of Management, Massachusetts Institute of Technology, and a faculty research fellow of the National Bureau of Economic Research. Joshua S. Graff Zivin is associate professor of economics at the School of International Relations and Pacific Studies at the University of California, San Diego, and a research associate of the National Bureau of Economic Research. Bhaven N. Sampat is assistant professor in the Department of Health Policy and Management at the Mailman School of Public Health at Columbia University.

Send correspondence to pazoulay@mit.edu. We gratefully acknowledge the financial support of the National Science Foundation through its SciSIP Program (Award SBE-0738142). We thank the conference audience, our discussant Adam Jaffe, as well as Scott Stern and Manuel Trajtenberg, for useful comments and suggestions. The usual disclaimer applies.

justification of substantial public funds for biomedical research (especially during periods of fiscal austerity) and current attempts to ground "science of science policy" on stronger theoretical and empirical footing (Marburger 2005).

Our analyses share a main motivation with the original conference, to understand how nonmarket controls and incentives at universities operate, and affect innovation. (The subtitle of the *Rate and Direction* volume is, after all, "Economic and Social Factors.") Over the past five decades, a voluminous literature on the workings of academic science has emerged in economics, sociology, and other disciplines (Stephan 2010; Dasgupta and David 1994; Merton 1973). Similarly, the rise of endogenous growth theory (Romer 1990; Aghion and Howitt 1992) and its emphasis on spillovers has focused attention on how knowledge flows across individuals, locations, and institutional settings. A particular focus has been on the extent to which knowledge flows are geographically localized (see, *inter alia,* Jaffe, Trajtenberg, and Hendeson [1993]; Thompson and Fox-Kean [2005]; and the response by Henderson, Jaffe, and Trajtenberg [2005]). Location was not a central concern in the 1962 volume (with the exception of the chapter by Wilbur Thompson). However, it has become an important policy issue since. The extent to which knowledge flows are geographically mediated is relevant to local and national policymakers, in deciding whether the benefits of the research they fund will accrue to those that fund it, or diffuse more generally.

A second theme in the volume is the difficulty in measuring economic activity. Several chapters explored the utility of patent data as indicators of innovation, and also emphasized that patent data alone may paint a distorted picture of the rate and direction of innovation (Kuznets 1962). Measuring knowledge flows is perhaps even more difficult than measuring innovation, since these flows leave few footprints (Krugman 1991). Nonetheless, a long literature in sociology and bibliometrics has attempted to measure knowledge flows among academics, using publication-to-publication citations. More recently, economists have employed patent-to-patent citations to examine knowledge flows from academics to industry (Jaffe and Trajtenberg 1999). A few papers (Branstetter 2005; Belenzon and Schankerman 2010) also use patent-publication citations.

Our study joins a small but distinguished literature relating patterns of citations to individual mobility. Almeida and Kogut (1999) use a sample of highly cited semiconductor patents, and information on citations to these patents (and a control sample of other patents in the same class as citing patents) to examine the extent and determinants of citation localization in this industry. They also identify the set of inventors on these patents who had moved previously, constructing career paths using patent records. The authors use these data to distinguish between regions with high intra- and interregional mobility, and find that patents from regions with high intraregional mobility are more likely to have citations that are local, and patents from regions with high interregional mobility are less likely to have local citations.[1]

Using a similar research design, but one more closely related to our own, Agrawal, Cockburn, and McHale (2006) examine all US patents applied for in 1989 and 1990 by movers, operationalized as individuals with the same names who had previously patented in the same patent class. Their analysis shows that the citations to postmove patents emanating from the inventors' prior location are disproportionately high, estimating that 50 percent more of the citations to postmove patents come from the prior location than would have if the inventor had not previously lived there. Since this citation premium to postmove patents is unlikely to reflect low communication costs or direct interaction (variables often invoked in explaining why geography matters), they interpret these results as evidence of the enduring importance of social relationships.

Our analysis also departs from these previous analyses in important ways: we identify movers from scientists' vitae (rather than patent data); we examine cited and citing knowledge longitudinally, exploiting detailed information on the timing of the move; and we look at three distinct measures of knowledge flows. The use of multiple indicators allows us to assess not only whether knowledge flows from academe are geographically mediated, but also to probe some of the mechanisms that might underlie this relationship—in short, to deepen our understanding of knowledge diffusion and its implications for the level and rate of technological innovation within the economy.

We examine these issues using a novel identification strategy that exploits labor mobility in a sample of 9,483 elite academic life scientists to examine the impact of moving on the citation trajectories associated with individual articles (respectively patents) published (respectively granted) *before* the scientist moved to a new institution. This longitudinal contrast purges our estimates of most sources of omitted variable bias that can plague cross-sectional comparisons. However, the timing of mobility itself could be endogenous. To address this concern, we pair each moving scientist/article dyad (respectively scientist/patent dyad) with a carefully chosen control article or patent associated with a scientist who does not transition to a new position. In addition to providing a very close match based on time-invariant characteristics, these controls also share very similar citation trends prior to the mobility event. By analyzing the data at the matched-pair level of analysis, this simple difference-in-difference framework provides a flexible and nonparametric methodology to evaluate the effects of labor mobility on knowledge flows.

1. In some analyses, Almeida and Kogut also explore individual (rather than regional) level mobility, finding that inventors who move within a region tend to have citations that are geographically local.

Indeed, conditional on the assumption that the matching algorithm we employ successfully pairs articles and patents of comparable quality, we are able to present the findings in a straightforward, graphical form.

The results reveal a nuanced story. We find that article-to-article citations from a scientist's origin location are barely affected by their departure. In contrast, patent-to-article citations, and especially patent-to-patent citations, decline at the origin location following a superstar's departure, suggesting that spillovers from academia to industry are not completely disembodied. We also find that article-to-article citations from a scientist's destination location markedly increase after they move. To the extent that academic scientists do not internalize the effect of their location decisions on the circulation of ideas, our results raise the intriguing possibility that barriers to labor mobility in academic science limit the recombination of individual bits of knowledge, resulting in a suboptimal rate of scientific exploration.

The chapter proceeds as follows. The next section discusses the construction of our multilevel panel data set and presents relevant descriptive statistics. Section 2.2 discusses our econometric approach and identification strategy. Section 2.3 reports the results. The final section includes a discussion of policy implications, caveats, and directions for future research.

2.1 Data and Sample Characteristics

The setting for our empirical work is the academic life sciences. This sector is an important one to study for several reasons. First, there are large public subsidies for biomedical research in the United States. With an annual budget of $29.5 billion in 2008, support for the National Institutes of Health (NIH) dwarfs that of other national funding agencies in developed countries (Cech 2005). Deepening our understanding of how the knowledge generated by these expenditures diffuses across time, space, and institutional settings will allow us to better assess the return to these public investments.

Second, technological change has been enormously important in the growth of the health care economy, which accounts for roughly 15 percent of US gross domestic product (GDP). Much biomedical innovation is science-based (Henderson, Orsenigo, and Pisano 1999), and interactions between academic researchers and their counterparts in industry appear to be an important determinant of research productivity in the pharmaceutical industry (Cockburn and Henderson 1998; Zucker, Darby, and Brewer 1998).

Lastly, the existence of geographic research clusters in the life sciences has been extensively documented, raising the possibility that scientific knowledge diffuses only slowly and with a lag from areas richly endowed with academic research institutions to others. To the extent that scientist labor mobility is needed to support the circulation of ideas to the periphery, a dearth of mobility events might be one of the centripetal forces leading to the persistence of such clusters.

In the next section, we provide a detailed description of the process through which the matched scientist/article (resp. scientist/patent) data set used in the econometric analysis was assembled. We begin by describing the criteria used to select our sample of superstar life scientists, along with basic demographic information. Next, we explore the prevalence and characteristics of mobility events; the set of products (i.e., journal articles and patents) generated by these elite scientists along with the citations they accrue. Finally, we discuss the matching procedure implemented to identify control articles and patents associated with scientists who do not change their location.

2.1.1 Superstar Sample

Our basic approach is to rely on professional transitions in a sample of "superstar" scientists in the United States to estimate the extent to which citation flows to individual pieces of knowledge are constrained by their producers' geographic location.

The study's focus on the scientific elite can be justified both on substantive and pragmatic grounds. The distribution of publications, funding, and citations at the individual level is extremely skewed (Lotka 1926; de Solla Price 1963) and only a tiny minority of scientists contribute through their published research to the advancement of science (Cole and Cole 1972). Furthermore, analyzing the determinants of citations flowing to the ideas of elite scientists is arguably more interesting than conducting the same exercise for a sample of less distinguished scientists, since superstars presumably produce knowledge that is more important to diffuse.

From a practical standpoint, it is also more feasible to trace back the careers of eminent scientists than to perform a similar exercise for less eminent ones. We began by delineating a set of 10,450 "elite" life scientists (roughly 5 percent of the entire relevant labor market) who are so classified if they satisfy at least one of the following criteria for cumulative scientific achievement: they are (a) highly funded scientists; (b) highly cited scientists; (c) top patenters; or (d) members of the National Academy of Sciences.

These four criteria naturally select seasoned scientists, since they correspond to extraordinary achievement over an entire scientific career. We combine these measures with three others that capture individuals who show great promise at the early and middle stages of their scientific careers, whether or not these episodes of productivity endure for long periods of time: scientists who are (e) NIH MERIT awardees; (f) Howard Hughes Medical Investigators; or (g) early career prize winners. Appendix A provides additional details regarding these seven indices of "superstardom."

We trace back these scientists' careers from the time they obtained their first position as independent investigators (typically after a postdoctoral fellowship) until 2006. We do so through a combination of curricula vitæ, NIH biosketches, *Who's Who* profiles, accolades/obituaries in medical journals, National Academy of Sciences biographical memoirs, and Google searches. For each one of these individuals, we record employment history, degree held, date of degree, gender, and up to three departmental affiliations. We also cross-reference the list with alternative measures of scientific eminence. For example, the elite subsample contains every US-based Nobel Prize winner in Medicine and Physiology since 1975, and a plurality of the Nobel Prize winners in Chemistry over the same time period.[2]

The 9,483 scientists who are the focus of this chapter constitute a subset of this larger pool of 10,450. We impose several additional criteria to derive the final list. First, we eliminate from the sample scientists who transition from academic positions to jobs in industry; second, we eliminate scientists who move to foreign institutions, since we have less ability to track knowledge flows to these locations; third, we eliminate scientists who move twice in quick succession, since these cases make it difficult to assign to these individuals unique origin and destination locations. Finally, we eliminate scientists who moved to new institutions prior to 1975, the beginning of our observation window.

Turning to patterns of labor mobility, we find that 2,894 scientists (30 percent) in the sample transitioned between two academic institutions between 1975 and 2004. Our mobility data is tabulated precisely from biographical records, rather than inferred from affiliation information in papers or patents (cf., Almeida and Kogut 1999; Fallick, Fleischmann, and Rebitzer 2006; Marx, Strumsky, and Fleming 2009). In particular, we observe the exact timing of professional transitions even in the cases in which a scientist has ceased to be active in research; for example, because she or he has moved into an administrative position. Because the overwhelming majority of mobility events take place in the summer, we adopt the following convention: a scientist is said to move from institution A to institution B in year t whenever the actual timing of his or her move coincided with the summer of year $t-1$. Incorporating a lag is necessary, since life scientists need to move entire laboratories rather than simply books and computer equipment. Anecdotal evidence suggests that mobility disrupts the pace of these scientists' research activities, if only temporarily.

We focus on transitions between distant institutions; that is, those separated by at least fifty miles. This limitation can be justified on both substantive and pragmatic grounds. First, many of the social impediments to labor mobility (such as dual-career concerns or disruption in the lives of these scientists' children) are less salient for professional transitions that do not compel an individual to change his place of residence. Second, our ability

2. Though we apply the term of superstar to the entire group, there is substantial heterogeneity in intellectual stature within the elite sample (see table 2.1).

Table 2.1 **Superstar scientists' cumulative output by 2006 or career end**

	Mean	Median	Std. dev.	Min.	Max.
Stayers (N = 6,589)					
NIH funding	$17,491,538	$11,261,535	$25,598,484	$0	$588,753,152
Publications	171	142	125	2	1,167
Patents	3.29	0	9.79	0	258
Paper cites [to papers]	10,639	7,332	11,248	15	139,872
Patent cites [to papers]	117	67	166	0	1,728
Patent cites [to patents]	91	19	240	0	5,596
Movers (N = 2,894)					
NIH funding	$16,256,723	$12,373,582	$16,243,082	$0	$195,611,552
Publications	174	144	121	1	1,631
Patents	3.15	0	8.30	0	117
Paper cites [to papers]	10,878	7,455	10,533	2	83,301
Patent cites [to papers]	120	69	159	0	1,821
Patent cites [to patents]	67	15	164	0	2,079

Notes: Sample consists of 9,483 elite academic life scientists. Movement is defined by a change in academic institution with at least fifty miles separating origin and destination.

Table 2.2 **Demographic characteristics**

	Degree year	Female	MD	PhD	MD/PhD
Stayers (N = 6,589)	1970.3	0.14	0.33	0.58	0.10
Movers (N = 2,894)	1972.7	0.14	0.30	0.61	0.10
Total (N = 9,483)	1971.0	0.14	0.32	0.59	0.10

to assign precisely the institutional affiliation of citing authors and inventors is limited. Therefore, we define an elite scientist's location by drawing a twenty-five-mile radius circle centered around the middle of the zip code in which his employer is located. Combined with our emphasis on moves between institutions separated by at least fifty miles, this ensures that origin and destination locations never overlap in the subsample of scientists that move.

Tables 2.1 and 2.2 provide descriptive statistics for the superstar sample. The gender composition of the sample is heavily skewed, no doubt because our metrics of superstardom favor more seasoned scientists, who came of age before female scientists had made significant inroads in the professoriate. The average degree year is 1971, and MDs account for a third of the sample. On the output side, the stars received an average of roughly seventeen million dollars in NIH grants and published 172 papers that garnered close to 11,000 citations as of early 2008. The number of patents per scientist is considerably smaller, and close to 40 percent of the sample scientists have no patent at all. While patents and papers can each appear as prior art cited in subsequent patents, the number of such citations is quite modest compared

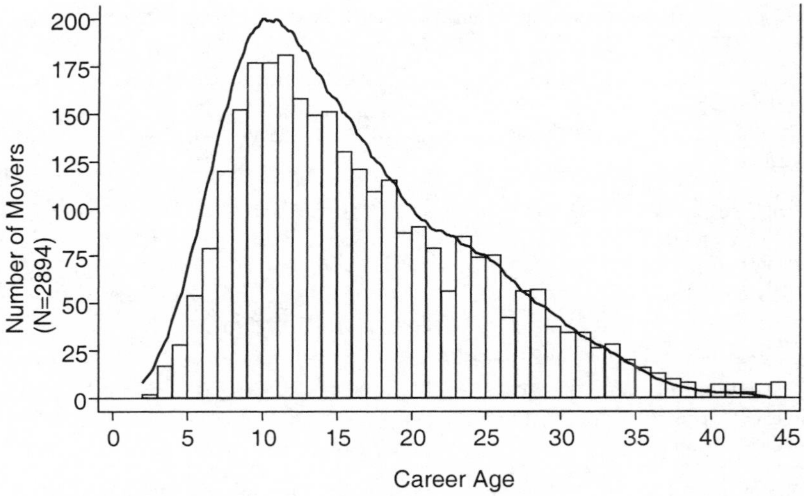

Fig. 2.1 Career age at time of move
Note: Nine observations between 46 and 54 years omitted.

to the number of article-to-article citations.[3] Achievement and demographic characteristics appear broadly similar between "moving" (i.e., treated) and "staying" (i.e., control) stars.

Figure 2.1 displays the distribution of career age at the time of move in the subsample of movers. The likelihood of a mobility event peaks at about twelve years (career age is measured as the number of years that elapsed since the receipt of one's highest degree). Figure 2.2 displays the distribution of distance moved, conditional on a move. That the shape of this distribution is strongly bimodal is not surprising, given the existence of life sciences research clusters on both coasts of the United States. Finally, figure 2.3 examines whether our elite scientists systematically drift from areas rich in the relevant type of intellectual capital to areas less well endowed (or vice versa). We compute total NIH funding flowing to scientists' origin and destination areas (panel A) and repeat the same exercise with the number of patents issued to inventors located in these same areas (panel B). While not symmetric in a strict statistical sense, these histograms make clear that most of the transitions in the sample involve relatively little difference in the resource endowments of the relevant locations, while a few are big moves in the sense of taking a scientist away from a less prestigious institution into a more intellectually vibrant climate (or vice versa).

3. Nonetheless, it is striking that the mean number of citations to these scientists' papers is larger than those to their patents. This difference (even more pronounced when considering the medians) is consistent with the results of Cohen, Nelson, and Walsh (2002), who find that the bulk of knowledge flows from academe to industry occur via open science channels.

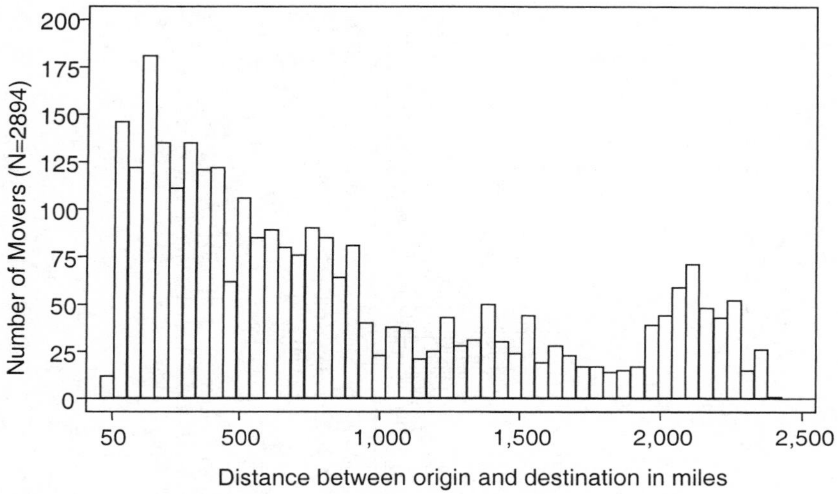

Fig. 2.2 Distance moved
Note: Five observations between 2,500 and 4,500 miles omitted.

2.1.2 Matching Scientists with Their Output

The second step in the construction of our data set is to link scientists with the knowledge they generate in tangible form, namely journal articles and patents. A useful metaphor for this exercise is that of linking producers with their products. Past scholarship in the field of the economics of science has generated numerous studies that rely on variation between individual producers, either cross-sectionally (Zucker, Darby, and Brewer 1998), or over time (Azoulay, Ding, and Stuart 2009; Azoulay, Graff Zivin, and Wang 2010), while paying scant attention to the detailed characteristics of the products involved. Conversely, a more recent and vibrant strand of the literature has exploited the availability of citations to individual products over time, for the most part abstracting away from the characteristics of their producers (Furman and Stern, forthcoming; Aghion et al. 2009).[4]

A major innovation in our study is to link detailed producer and product characteristics to create a multilevel panel data set.[5] Social scientists face difficult practical constraints when attempting to attribute individual products to particular producers. When the products involved are journal articles, there are thorny issues of name uniqueness: common names make it difficult to distinguish between scientists, and even scientists with relatively

4. In what follows, the use of the word "product" will also be useful whenever we want to refer to the output of our elite scientists in a generic way so that our statements apply equally well to journal articles and to patented inventions.

5. Recent efforts along the same line include Agarwal and Singh (forthcoming) and Azoulay, Stuart and Wang (2010).

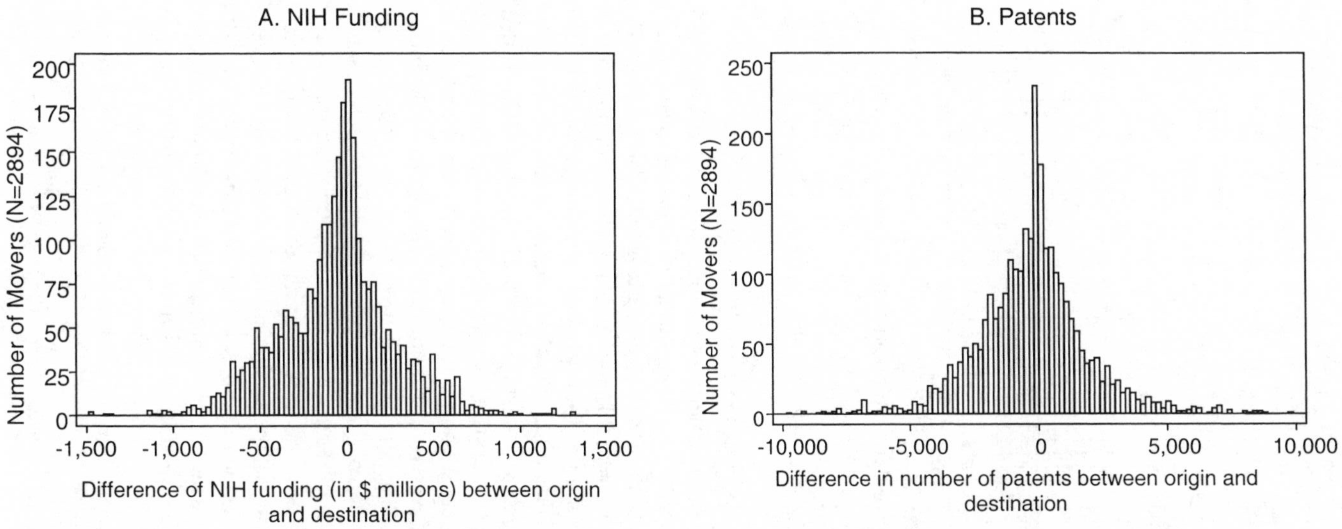

Fig. 2.3 Similarity between origin and destination locations

Note: The preceding histograms map the extent to which professional transitions in our sample take elite scientists to destinations that differ from, or are similar to, the areas from which they originate, along two dimensions: NIH funding accruing to institutions located in 25-mile radius centered on the origin and destination institution (panel A); and the number of patents applied for by inventors located in 25-mile radius centered on the origin and destination institution (panel B).

rare names sometimes are inconsistent in their use of publication names. By adopting the labor-intensive practice of designing customized search queries for each scientist in the sample, we ensured the accuracy of their bibliomes. Further details on the linking process are provided in appendix B. Linking scientists with their patented inventions is considerably easier, since the United States Patent and Trademark Office (USPTO) data records inventors' full names (as opposed to first and middle initials), and we can further make use of assignee information to distinguish between the patents of inventors with frequent names. Further details on the linking process are provided in appendix C.

We select from these publication and patent data to construct the final sample. For journal articles, we eliminate from the consideration set letters, comments, and editorials. Second, we eliminate all articles published eleven or more years prior to the date of the earliest move in the sample (1976); similarly, we eliminate all articles published in 2004 (the latest move year we observe) or in subsequent years. Third, we delete from the sample all articles published by moving scientists after they moved. We proceed similarly for patents. To account for potential truncation, we assume an average grant lag of three years, and we ignore all patents applied for after the year 2001.

2.1.3 Three Measures of Knowledge Flows

As noted by many authors, beginning with the seminal work of Jaffe, Trajtenberg, and Henderson (1993), knowledge flows sometimes leave a paper trail, in the form of citations in either patents, or journal articles. The innovation in the present study is that we present evidence pertaining to three distinct measures of knowledge flows: citations to articles authored by our elite scientists in the open science literature; citations to articles authored by our elite scientists listed in the prior art section of patents issued by the US Patent and Trademark Office (USPTO); and citations to patents granted to our elite scientists in patents subsequently granted to other inventors by the USPTO. Each of these measures exhibits a particular set of strengths and weaknesses. We describe them in turn.

Patent-to-Patent Citations. The bulk of the voluminous research on knowledge spillovers has relied on patent citations in other patents to infer patterns of knowledge diffusion (cf. Jaffe and Trajtenberg 1999). The difficulties involved in interpreting these citations as evidence of knowledge flows—mostly because of the high share of citations added by examiners, rather than assignees—have been explored in detail (Alcácer and Gittelman 2006; Alcácer, Gittelman, and Sampat 2009) and need not be repeated here. Despite these acknowledged problems, survey results confirm that roughly 50 percent of patent-to-patent citations represent some sort of knowledge flow (Jaffe, Trajtenberg, and Fogarty 2002). Moreover, the prevalence of examiner-added citations is much smaller in the life sciences than in other fields (Sampat 2010).

Article-to-Article Citations. Beyond the low "signal-to-noise" ratio associated with patent citations, a more serious limitation for our purposes is that the bulk of the output of the academics we study is in publications, rather than patents. Fully 60 percent of the scientists in our superstar sample never apply for a patent, and the great majority of those who do patent have only one or two inventions to their credit. Therefore, we also collect the number of citations in subsequent journal articles that flow to each of the papers generated by our superstars, over time. A great advantage of these citations is that they are numerous, making it possible to parse these data in ever finer slices to tease out the underlying mechanisms that support the diffusion of scientific knowledge. Their main drawback is that 95 percent of citations flowing to the articles in our sample come from other academics. These data are therefore less useful to track the flow of ideas across the boundary between academia and for-profit firms.

Patent-to-Article Citations. These limitations lead us to introduce a novel measure of knowledge flows, namely, references to the open science literature found in the nonpatent prior art section of patents granted by the USPTO. This is appealing both because publications rather than patents are the main output of scientific researchers (Agrawal and Henderson 2002), but also because the vast majority of patent-to-paper citations, over 90 percent, come from applicants rather than examiners, and are thus more plausible indicators of real knowledge flows than patent-to-patent citations (Lemley and Sampat 2010). Another advantage of these data comes from the greater diversity of citing institution types, relative to the patterns exhibited by the more traditional data sources mentioned earlier. In previous work, systematic analyses of these nonpatent references has been limited, since they are free-form text and difficult to link to other data. Our work relies on a novel match between nonpatent references and biomedical articles indexed in PubMed, described in detail in appendix D. While programming improvements and computing speed have enabled us to mine this source of data, only 12 percent of the published output of the scientists in our sample is ever cited in patents. For this reason, the bulk of our analyses will focus on citation flows inferred from article-to-article citations.

After collecting the citation data, we further process it in order to make it amenable to statistical analysis. First, we eliminate all self-citations since these do not correspond to knowledge flows in the traditional sense.[6] Second, we parse the address fields in both the citing patents and citing publications to associate each citing product with a set of zip codes (for US addresses) or country names (for foreign addresses). Third, we parse the citing assignee names and citing institution names and tag these fields with an

6. In the case of patents, we infer self-citation from overlap between the names of inventors in the cited and citing patents, rather than overlap in assignee names.

indicator variable denoting an industrial affiliation, making use of suffixes such as Inc., Corp., Ltd. (or their international variants). In a final step, we aggregate the data from the cited product-citing product pair level up to the cited product-year level of analysis. In other words, we can track the flow of citations from birth to 2006 for each producer/product tuple in the sample.[7]

We can further separate those citations that accrue to a scientist's origin location, to his or her destination, or to all other locations. A complication arises because it is not clear what destination means for the sample of superstars who do not transition to a new location. Ideally, we would select as a counterfactual location the institution that provides the highest degree of fit for these scientists outside of their actual home institution. In practice, it is very difficult to model the determinants of fit, and we select a location at random from the set of locations that moving scientists transition to, provided they are separated by at least fifty miles from the stayers' actual locations.

2.1.4 From Control Producers to Control Products: A Nonparametric Matching Procedure

A perennial challenge in the literature on the localization of knowledge flows is whether citing and cited producers' locations can be credibly assumed to be exogenous. Henderson, Jaffe, and Trajtenberg (2005) describe this thorny issue:

> Professor Robert Langer of MIT, for example, is one of the world's leading experts in tissue engineering, and is the author of over 120 patents in the area. A large fraction of the citations to these patents are geographically localized. Are they local just because the authors of the citing patents lived in the same city and hence were more likely to learn about Langer's work (i.e., knowledge spillovers)? Or because Boston is one of the world's centers for tissue engineering, and so people working in the area are disproportionately likely to live in Boston (i.e., geographic collocation due to other common factors)? Or perhaps it is the case that Boston is one of the world's centers for tissue engineering precisely because firms locate in the area in order to be able to take advantage of spillovers from people like Robert Langer?

Previous scholars faced severe data constraints in their attempts to divine whether a particular citation would have taken place, if contrary to the fact, either the citing or the cited producer had been located elsewhere (Jaffe, Trajtenberg, and Henderson 1993; Jaffe and Trajtenberg 1999). In this study,

7. Since the latest year in which a scientist moves is 2004, and the latest product vintage we include in the sample is 2003, the postmove observation period will always extend for a minimum of three years.

we can relax these constraints and design more credible counterfactuals, since we can "unbundle" producers from their products, and we are able to observe two different locations for a significant subset of the producers in the sample.

Yet, relying on labor mobility to generate variation in the geographic distance separating the source and potential recipients of knowledge is not a panacea for two reasons. First, producer mobility might influence the quality of the underlying products, for instance, because the scientist finds himself or herself located in an institution for which she or he is a better match. We deal with the threat of unobserved heterogeneity of this type by narrowing our focus to products generated by scientists *prior* to their move. It is difficult to imagine a mechanism through which the quality of these products could have been affected by the characteristics of the destination location.

Second, it is possible that job transitions for academic scientists are partly driven by expectations of interactions with academic peers in their home institution, or with the local industrial base. To generate a set of estimates that can be given a causal interpretation, we create the matched sample of "staying" producers described earlier, which we link to their products following the exact same techniques.

Coarse Exact Matching Procedure. We design a procedure to cull from the universe of products associated with "control" producers (i.e., scientists who do not change locations) a subset that provides a very close match with the products of "treated" producers (i.e., those scientists who do move to another institution at some point during the observation period). The goal of the construction of this matched sample is to create for the nonmovers a counterfactual set of products that mimic the citation trajectories associated with movers' papers and patents.

What makes a good control? Control and treated products should be well matched on time-invariant characteristics that have an important impact on the magnitude of citation flows. For journal articles, such characteristics might include the journal in which the article appeared, the exact time of publication, the number of scientists on the article's authorship list, and so forth. For patents, finding a control such that application year, issue year, number of inventors, assignee type, and patent classes/subclasses coincide would be valuable. More importantly, there should be no differential citation trends that affect treated products, relative to control products, in the period that precedes the move. Finally, in an ideal world, the match would operate at the producer/product pair level, such that focal producer characteristics (age, gender, and eminence) would also be comparable between treated and control observations.

In practice, identifying close matches is difficult. Because we are interested in the fate of individual products, but the shock we observe (mobility) operates at the scientist-level of analysis, semiparametric matching techniques (such as the propensity score and its variants) are of limited use in our context. We propose instead a nonparametric matching approach, a so-called "coarse exact matching" (CEM) procedure (Blackwell et al. 2009).

The selection of controls proceeds in a series of sequential steps. The first task is to select a relatively small set of covariates on which we would like to guarantee balance between the treatment and control group. The second step is to create a large number of strata to cover the entire support of the joint distribution of the covariates selected in the previous step. Next, each observation is allocated to a unique strata; any strata that either has no product associated with a mover, or that has less than five potential control products, is then dropped from the data. In a fourth and final step, we select in each strata a unique control product such that the sum of squared differences in citation flows between the treated and control product from the year of publication/issue up to the year preceding the move year is minimized. We break ties at random when there are several candidate products that minimize this distance metric.

Internal versus External Validity. The procedure is coarse because we do not attempt to precisely match on covariate values; rather, we coarsen the support of the joint distribution of the covariates into a finite number of strata, and we match a treated observation if and only if a control observation can be recruited from this strata. An important advantage of CEM is that the analyst can guarantee the degree of covariate balance ex ante, but this comes at a cost: the more fine-grained the partition of the support for the joint distribution (i.e., the higher the number of strata), the larger the number of unmatched treated observations. In general, the analyst must trade off the quality of the matches with external validity: the longer the list of matching covariates, the more difficult it is to identify an "identical twin" for each article or patent in the treatment group.

We illustrate the essence of the matching procedure in figures 2.4 (for articles) and 2.5 (for patents). Implementation details can be found in appendix E. In the case of article-to-article citations, we start from a universe of 40,023 papers corresponding to the published output of movers in the 10 years that precede their change in location. We match 10,249 out of these 40,023 tuples (25.61 percent). This relatively low match rate is not surprising. Nonparametric matching procedures such as CEM are prone to a version of the "curse of dimensionality" whereby the proportion of matched units decreases rapidly with the number of strata. For instance, requiring a match on an additional indicator variable (e.g., matching on focal scientist gender in addition to the covariates mentioned earlier) would result in a match rate of about 10 percent. Conversely, failing to impose that control and treated articles are drawn from the same scientific journal would increase the match rate to 70 percent, but doing so might threaten the internal validity of our empirical exercise. In the case of article-to-patent citations, we match 2,435 articles out of a potential 6,492 (37.51 percent). In the case of

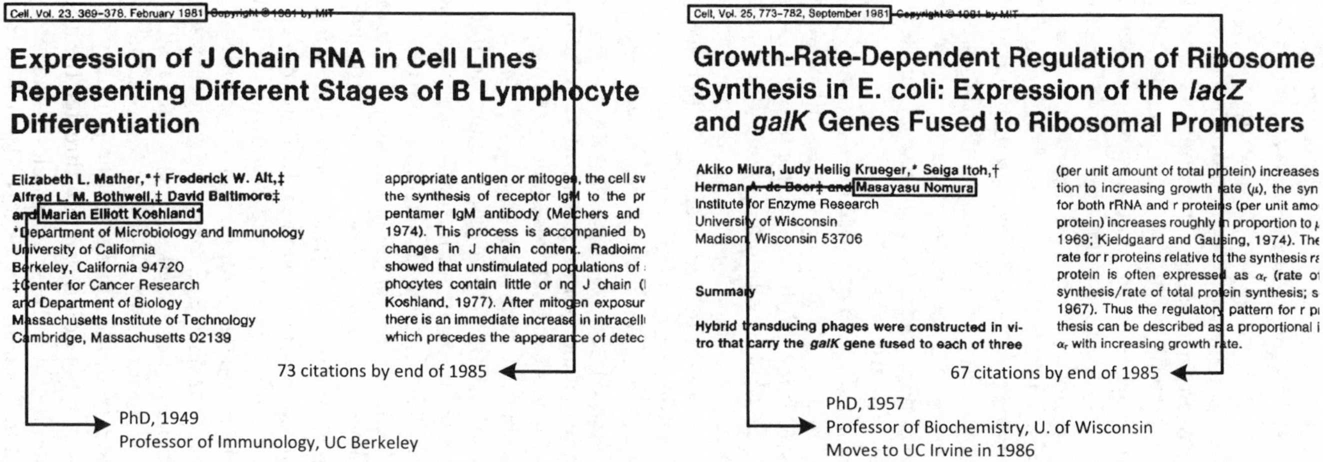

Fig. 2.4 Article-level match

Note: The two articles illustrate the essence of the coarse exact matching procedure. These two articles appeared in the journal *Cell* in 1981. They received a very similar number of citations up to 1985: 73 citations for Mather et al.; 67 citations for Miura et al. Masayasu Nomura, the PI on the article on the right-hand side, moved from the University of Wisconsin to UC Irvine in 1986.

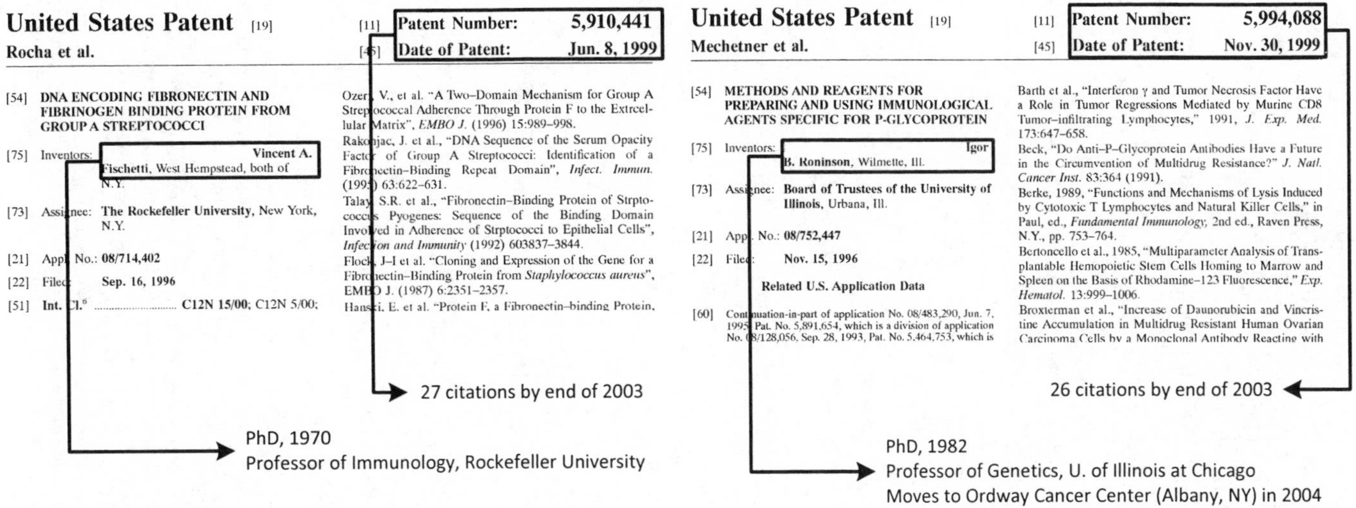

Fig. 2.5 Patent-level match

Note: The two patents illustrate the essence of the coarse exact matching procedure. These two patents were issued in 1999 and applied for in 1996. They both belong to patent class 435 (Molecular Biology & Microbiology). They received a very similar number of citations up to 2003: 27 citations for Fischetti's (Richa et al.); 26 citations for Roninson's (Mechetner et al.). Igor Roninson—the focal inventor on patent 5,994,088—moved from the University of Illinois at Chicago to the Ordway Cancer Center in Albany, New York, in 2004.

patent-to-patent citations, the match rate is higher still: 41.36 percent (1,417 matched patents out of a potential 3,426 matches).

Descriptive Statistics. We present univariate statistics at baseline—that is, in the year preceding the (possibly counterfactual) move year—for the matched product data sets in tables 2.3, 2.4, and 2.5. Examining the raw data across these three panel data sets, a number of stylized facts emerge.

First, in all three cases, the match is "product-centric" rather than "producer-centric." That is, product-level attributes exhibit a high level of

Table 2.3 Article-to-article citation flows: Descriptive statistics ($n = 2 \times 10{,}249$), articles published *before* the move

	Mean	Median	Std. dev.	Min.	Max.
Journal Articles by Stayers					
Number of authors	4.463	4	2.980	1	129
Focal author is last	0.653	1	0.476	0	1
Article age at baseline	2.483	2	2.055	1	10
Focal author gender	0.098	0	0.297	0	1
Focal author graduation year	1967.491	1968	10.893	1931	2001
Article baseline stock of article citations	27.666	3	66.750	0	2399
Article baseline stock of article citations from industry	1.023	0	3.731	0	135
Article baseline stock of article citations at origin	1.952	0	6.550	0	135
Article baseline stock of article citations at destination	0.355	0	2.210	0	80
Journal Articles by Movers					
Number of authors	4.489	4	3.238	1	180
Focal author is last	0.653	1	0.476	0	1
Article age at baseline	2.483	2	2.055	1	10
Focal author gender	0.084	0	0.277	0	1
Focal author graduation year	1972.603	1973	9.289	1940	1997
Article baseline stock of citations	27.824	3	63.855	0	1226
Article baseline stock of article citations from industry	1.036	0	3.477	0	103
Article baseline stock of article citations at origin	1.834	0	6.284	0	149
Article baseline stock of article citations at destination	0.624	0	3.249	0	131

Notes: The match is article centric; that is, the control article is always chosen from the same journal in the same publication year. The control article is coarsely matched on the number of authors (exact match for one, two, and three authors; four or five authors; between six and nine authors; and more than nine authors). We also match on focal scientist's position in the authorship roster (first author; last author; middle author). For articles published one year before appointment, we also match on the month of publication. For articles published two years before appointment, we also match on the quarter of publication. In addition, the articles in the control and treatment groups are matched on article citation dynamics up to the year before the (possibly counterfactual) transition year. The cost of a very close, nonparametric match on article characteristics is that author characteristics do not match closely. Imposing a close match on focal scientist age, gender, and overall productivity at baseline would result in a match rate which is unacceptably low.

Table 2.4 **Patent-to-article citation flows: Descriptive statistics ($n = 2 \times 2{,}435$), articles published *before* the move**

	Mean	Median	Std. dev.	Min.	Max.
Journal articles by stayers					
Number of authors	5.062	5	2.596	1	38
Focal author is last	0.598	1	0.490	0	1
Article age at baseline	3.118	2	2.333	1	10
Focal author gender	0.083	0	0.276	0	1
Focal author graduation year	1965.539	1967	12.022	1931	1999
Article baseline stock of patent citations	0.499	0	1.649	0	29
Article baseline stock of patent citations from industry	0.352	0	1.375	0	24
Article baseline stock of patent citations at origin	0.040	0	0.449	0	16
Article baseline stock of patent citations at destination	0.012	0	0.306	0	14
Journal articles by movers					
Number of authors	5.049	5	2.433	1	26
Focal author is last	0.598	1	0.490	0	1
Article age at baseline	3.118	2	2.333	1	10
Focal author gender	0.086	0	0.281	0	1
Focal author graduation year	1974.161	1975	8.709	1940	1995
Article baseline stock of patent citations	0.540	0	1.889	0	46
Article baseline stock of patent citations from industry	0.367	0	1.652	0	46
Article baseline stock of patent citations at origin	0.029	0	0.284	0	6
Article baseline stock of patent citations at destination	0.019	0	0.236	0	7

Notes: The match is article centric; that is, the control article is always chosen from the same journal in the same publication year. The control article is coarsely matched on the number of authors (exact match for one, two, and three authors; four or five authors; between six and nine authors; and more than nine authors). We also match on focal scientist's position in the authorship roster (first author; last author; middle author). For articles published one year before appointment, we also match on the month of publication. For articles published two years before appointment, we also match on the quarter of publication. In addition, the articles in the control and treatment groups are matched on patent citation dynamics up to the year before the (possibly counterfactual) transition year. The cost of a very close, nonparametric match on article characteristics is that author characteristics do not match closely. Imposing a close match on focal scientist age, gender, and overall productivity at baseline would result in a match rate which is unacceptably low.

covariate balance between treated and control products, whether these characteristics are time-invariant (such as number of authors or focal scientist position on the authorship roster) or time-varying (such as the stock of overall citations, whose distributions we display graphically in figure 2.6). In contrast, producer characteristics do not match as well, as can be seen by examining the distribution of covariates such as degree year or gender.

Second, most citations do not accrue in the areas corresponding to these

Table 2.5 **Patent-to-patent citation flows: Descriptive statistics ($n = 2 \times 1{,}417$), patents issued *before* the move**

	Mean	Median	Std. dev.	Min.	Max.
Patents by stayers					
Patent age at baseline	4.579	4	2.610	1	10
Focal author gender	0.056	0	0.231	0	1
Focal author graduation year	1969.762	1970	10.806	1932	1996
Patent baseline stock of patent citations	7.076	1	14.770	0	135
Patent baseline stock of patent citations from industry	5.880	0	12.830	0	98
Patent baseline stock of patent citations at origin	0.563	0	2.899	0	48
Patent baseline stock of patent citations at destination	0.167	0	1.439	0	37
Patents by movers					
Patent age at baseline	4.579	4	2.610	1	10
Focal author gender	0.047	0	0.212	0	1
Focal author graduation year	1976.711	1978	8.678	1950	1996
Patent baseline stock of patent citations	7.198	1	15.608	0	148
Patent baseline stock of patent citations from industry	5.787	0	13.239	0	137
Patent baseline stock of patent citations at origin	0.370	0	1.714	0	34
Patent baseline stock of patent citations at destination	0.231	0	1.966	0	53

Notes: The match is patent centric; that is, the control patent is always chosen from the same application year and the same issue year. In addition, control and treatment patents are matched on patent citation dynamics up to the year before the (possibly counterfactual) transition year. The cost of a very close, nonparametric match on patent characteristics is that author characteristics do not match closely. Imposing a close match on focal scientist age, gender, and overall productivity at baseline would result in a match rate which is unacceptably low.

scientists' location. As an example, only 6.82 percent of citations up to the baseline year have accrued at the origin location; the figure is 1.77 percent in the destination location.

Third, whereas citations at the origin location are well matched at baseline, this is not the case for citations at destination. In all cases, movers have accrued many more citations in the area they will soon transition to, relative to the citations that have accrued to the products of stayers in a location picked at random. This is consistent with the view that mobility events are jointly determined with expected spillovers of knowledge; for instance, because scientists who know your work are more likely to win the competition to lure you away. These baseline differences further justify our emphasis on identifying a closely matched set of control products.

Finally, the salience of industrial citers varies greatly across our measures of knowledge flows, accounting for only 3.61 percent of article-to-article

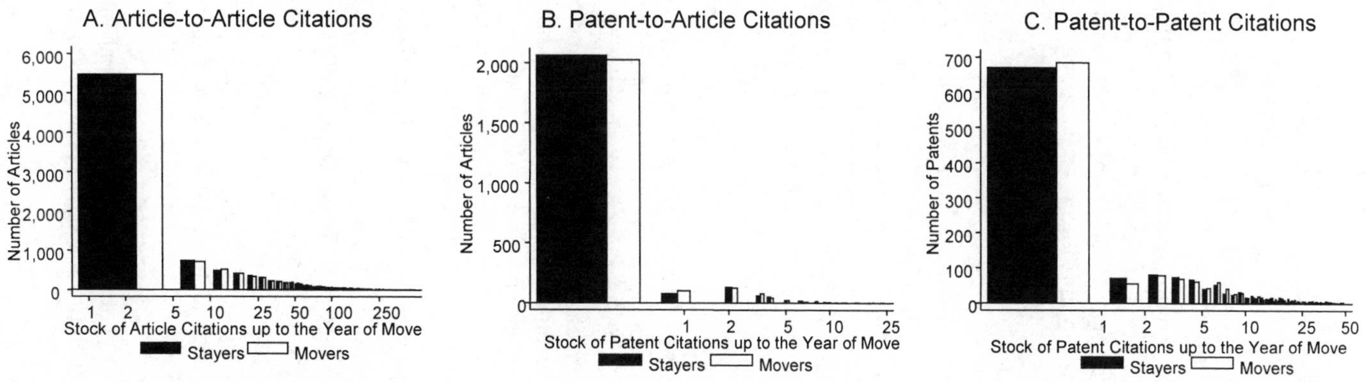

Fig. 2.6 Covariate balance at baseline

Note: We compute the cumulative number of citations for treatment and control articles/patents, respectively, up to the year that immediately precedes that of the professional transition for the superstar.

cites, but 80.72 percent of article-to-patent cites, and 83.04 percent of patent-to-patent citations.

2.2 Econometric Considerations

A natural starting point for a difference-in-difference (DD) analysis of the causal effect of labor mobility on knowledge flows is to conduct the statistical analysis using all product-year observations (treated and control) as the estimation sample. Since the mobility effect is mechanically correlated with the passage of time, as well as with an article's age, it is necessary to include life cycle and period effects, as is the norm in studies of scientific productivity (Levin and Stephan 1991).

In this framework, the control group that pins down the counterfactual vintage and calendar time effects for the products that were generated by scientists currently transitioning to new positions contains three categories of products: (a) those generated by movers who transitioned in earlier periods, (b) those generated by scientists who will move in the future, and (c) those generated by stayers. This approach is problematic insofar as products that appeared after a scientist has moved are not appropriate controls if the mobility event negatively affects the trend in their citations. If this is the case, fixed effects may underestimate the true effect of mobility.

To produce an analysis in which the control group consists solely of products associated with stayers, we instead perform the statistical analysis at the *product-pair* level. Specifically, the outcome variable is the *difference* between the citations received in a given year by a treated product and its associated control identified in the matching procedure previously described. Let i denote an article associated with a mover and let i' index the corresponding control product. Then our estimating equation relates $\Delta\text{CITES}_{ii't} = \text{CITES}_{it} - \text{CITES}_{i't}$ with the timing of mobility in the following way:

$$(1) \quad E[\Delta\text{CITES}_{ii't} \mid X_{ijt}] = \beta_0 + \beta_1\text{AFTER\_MOVE}_{jt} + f(\text{AGE}_{jt}) + \gamma_{ii'},$$

where AFTER_MOVE denotes an indicator variable that switches to one in the year focal scientist j moves, $f(\text{AGE})$ corresponds to a flexible function of the scientist's age, and the $\gamma_{ii'}$ correspond to product-pair fixed effects, consistent with our approach to analyze *changes* in the pair's citation rate following the move of investigator j.[8] We also run slight variations of this specification in which the dependent variable has been parsed so that we can break down citation flows by location or by citer type (i.e., industrial vs. academic citers).

There is another benefit to conducting the analysis at the product-pair level: since treated and control products always originate in the same year,

8. We do not need to include product vintage or year effects in the specification, since both products in the pair appeared in the same year, by construction.

experimental time and calendar time coincide, making it simple to display the results of the analysis graphically. The graphical approach is advantageous because it makes the essence of the empirical exercise transparent. The regression analysis, however, will prove useful when exploring interactions between the treatment effect and various star or product characteristics.

2.3 Results

2.3.1 Effect of Mobility on Citation Rates to Articles Published *After* the Move

As explained earlier, the bulk of our analysis focuses on citation flows to articles (respectively to patents) published (respectively issued) before the move so that we can separately identify the effect of mobility from that of correlated influences that might have an impact on the quality of the research itself. For example, mobility events such as those analyzed in this chapter might be driven by the availability of resources in the destination location, including laboratory equipment, trainees, or potential collaborators. From a descriptive standpoint, it is still interesting to examine the geographic spread of citations that accrue to products that postdate the mobility event, and these results are reported in figure 2.7. For the sake of brevity, we examine this for article-to-article citation flows only.[9]

We pair articles written by superstar movers with articles written by superstar stayers who are observationally quite similar at the time of the mobility event, so that the match is both "article-centric" and "scientist-centric." The scientist-level covariates used to create the match are (a) year of highest degree (coarsened in three-year intervals); (b) gender; (c) NIH funding status (funded vs. not funded at the time of the move); and (d) the total number of citations having accrued by 2006 to all premove publications. This ensures that the scientists being compared are not only demographically similar, but also of comparable renown at the time of the (possibly counterfactual) move. In addition, we match on article characteristics, including the journal, the length of the authorship roster, the focal author's position, and the publication year. Descriptive statistics for the resulting sample of $2 \times 26{,}254 = 52{,}508$ articles are displayed in table 2.6.

In the three panels of figure 2.7, we display the difference in average citation trends for the article pairs in the sample (the solid line), along with a 95th confidence interval (the dashed lines). Panel A focuses on differential citation patterns at the origin location. Relative to articles by stayers, it appears that postmove research is cited less in the area the moving scientist departed from; this citation discount is small (less than one citation per year

9. Our discussant Adam Jaffe uses the metaphor of carefully examining the dirty bath water before throwing it out to focus on the (hopefully clean) baby.

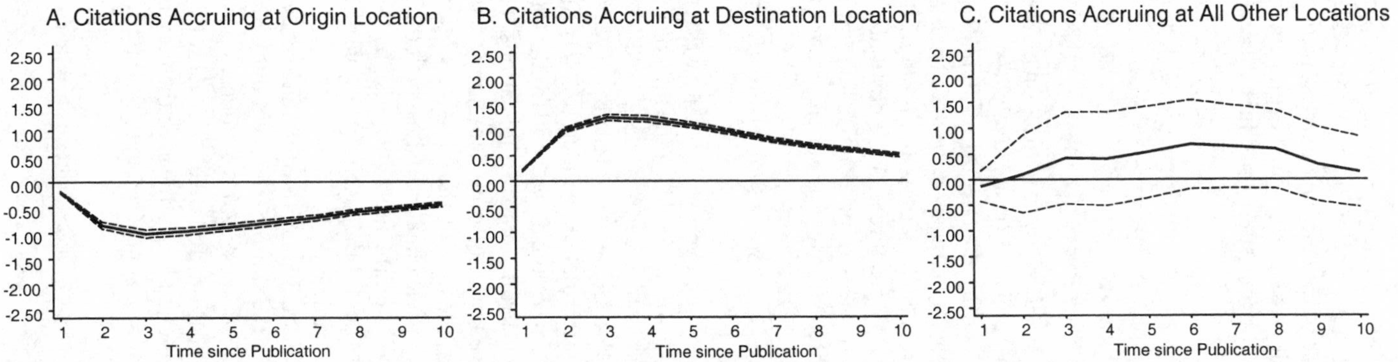

Fig. 2.7 Effect of professional transitions on article-to-article citation rates, by location (articles published *after* the move)

Note: Dynamics for the difference in yearly citations between movers' and stayers' matched articles written in the postmove period. Articles in each pair appeared in the same year and journal, and are also matched on focal scientist position on the authorship list, as well as overall number of authors. Further, the superstar authors are matched on gender, year of highest degree (in three-year bins), NIH funding at the time of the (possibly counterfactual) move, and cumulative number of citations for all articles published up to (and including) the year of the move.

In panel A, only citations accruing at the origin location are tallied. In panel B, only citations accruing at the destination location are tallied. For stayers, the destination location is chosen at random from among the set of locations that movers move to and that are separated by at least fifty miles from the staying star's actual location. In panel C, only citations accruing at all other locations are tallied.

Table 2.6 **Article-to-article citation flows: Descriptive statistics ($n = 2 \times 26{,}254$), articles published *after* the move**

	Mean	Median	Std. dev.	Min.	Max.
Journal articles by stayers					
Number of authors	4.915	4	4.077	1	255
Focal author is last	0.661	1	0.473	0	1
Article stock of citations up to 2006	273.818	133	542.514	1	22,336
Article publication year	1992.271	1992	6.208	1977	2003
Move year	1986.912	1987	6.212	1976	2002
Focal author graduation year	1970.270	1970	8.198	1931	1996
Focal author gender	0.023	0	0.149	0	1
Scientist citations at baseline	5,283	3,623	5,215	0	60,496
Scientist NIH funding at baseline	$3,828,267	$2,412,251	$5,297,164	$0	$101,678,352
Journal Articles by movers					
Number of authors	4.887	4	3.843	1	255
Focal author is last	0.661	1	0.473	0	1
Article stock of citations up to 2006	279.845	134	576.462	0	22,298
Article publication year	1992.271	1992	6.208	1977	2003
Move year	1986.912	1987	6.212	1976	2002
Focal author graduation year	1970.422	1970	7.990	1940	1996
Focal author gender	0.023	0	0.149	0	1
Scientist citations at baseline	5,248	3,584	5,157	0	51,174
Scientist NIH funding at baseline	$3,563,252	$2,306,315	$4,381,859	$0	$118,257,904

Notes: The match is both scientist centric and article centric. The control article is always chosen from the same journal in the same publication year. The control article is coarsely matched on the number of authors (exact match for one, two, and three authors; four or five authors; between six and nine authors; and more than nine authors). We also match on focal scientist's position in the authorship roster (first author; last author; middle author). In addition, the following individual covariates for the moving and staying stars match: gender, year of highest degree (in three-year bins), NIH funding status as of the moving year (funded vs. not); and total number of citations having accrued by 2006 to all premove publications (below the 10th percentile; between the 10th and 25th percentile; between the 25th percentile and the median; between the median and the 75th percentile; between the 75th and 95th percentile; between the 95th and 99th percentile; and above the 99th percentile).

on average), but it is enduring. Panel B repeats the same analysis for the destination location; we find the opposite pattern, in that postmove articles benefit from a lasting citation premium equal to less than one citation per year in the new location, relative to the number of citations accruing to the matched articles of stayers in a random location. Finally, Panel C examines citation outcomes in all other locations. Though the articles of movers appear to benefit from more "buzz" than those of stayers, this effect is both very small and imprecisely estimated.

From these results, it would appear that scientist mobility slightly shifts the allocation of citations across scientific areas without much of an impact on the diffusion process in the aggregate. Of course, because our controls for scientist-level and article-level quality are imperfect, we should resist the temptation to overinterpret these patterns. For instance, a citation discount at origin could mean that the superstar's former colleagues are quick to forget his or her research after the mobility event. But she or he may have moved to a new location precisely because his or her research was delving into areas that appealed less to his or her old peers. In this case, the causality would flow from (expected) impact to job mobility, rather than in the direction we hypothesize. Similarly, at destination, the citation premium might reflect the interest of colleagues who extended an offer to the mover precisely in the expectation of deeper intellectual connections.

For these reasons, the rest of the chapter will focus on changes in citation rates following mobility events (and their allocation across geographic areas) for articles published before the move. This research design will enables us to better isolate the effect of mobility per se from that of correlated and competing influences.

2.3.2 Effect of Mobility on Citation Rates to Articles and Patents Published *Before* the Move

Our primary results are presented in figures 2.8 through 2.13. Table 2.7 presents estimates from simple ordinary least squares (OLS) regressions with article-pair fixed effects, corresponding to the earlier estimating equation. Robust standard errors, clustered at the scientist level, appear below the coefficient estimates in parentheses.

Article-to-Article Citation Flows. Panel A of figure 2.8 displays the citation dynamics corresponding to article-to-article flows, without disaggregating these flows by citer location or institutional type. It is clear from the picture that our matching procedure succeeded in identifying good control articles, since there is no evidence of deviation from zero in the years preceding the move. Moreover, there is a clear uptick in the rate of citations after the move, though it is modest in magnitude and relatively short-lived,

Table 2.7 **Effects of professional move on citation rates, by location**

	Article-to-article citations		Patent-to-article citations		Patent-to-patent citations	
	Origin (1a)	Destination (1b)	Origin (2a)	Destination (2b)	Origin (3a)	Destination (3b)
After appointment	0.026	0.069***	–0.026	0.007	–0.121***	0.041**
	(0.026)	(0.015)	(0.012)	(0.006)	(0.036)	(0.017)
Nb. of observations	175,715	175,715	41,114	41,114	21,221	21,221
Nb. of article pairs	10,249	10,249	2,435	2,435	1,417	1,417
Nb. of scientists	2,106	2,106	928	928	426	426
Adjusted R^2	0.295	0.323	0.157	0.125	0.215	0.214

Notes: Standard errors in parentheses, clustered by scientists. All specifications are estimated by OLS; the models include article-pair fixed effects.

***Significant at the 1 percent level.

**Significant at the 5 percent level.

*Significant at the 10 percent level.

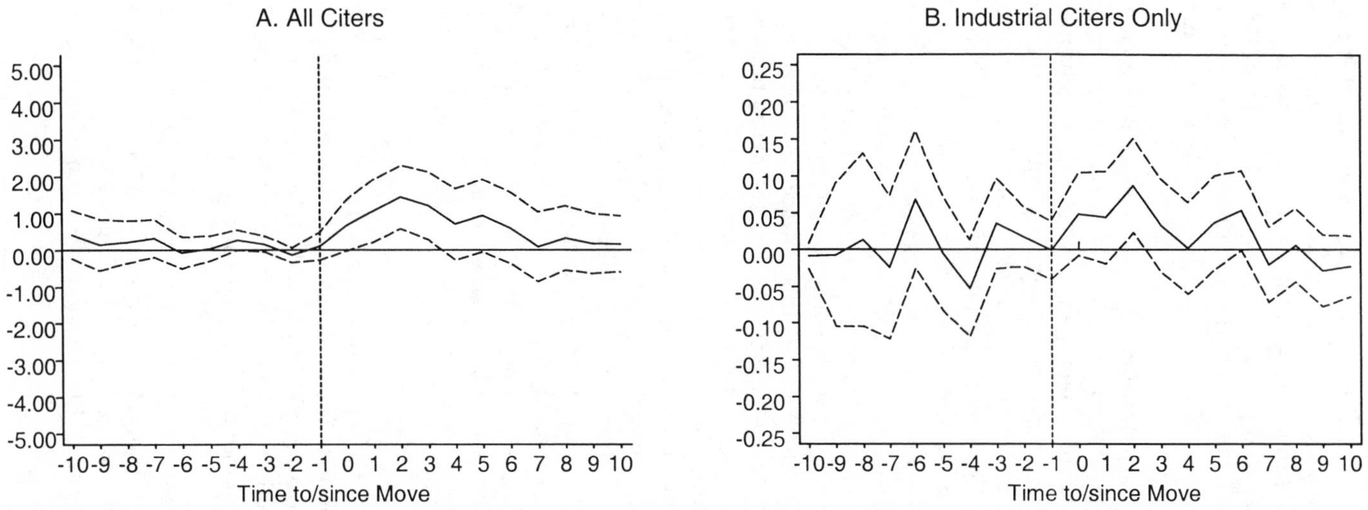

Fig. 2.8 Effect of professional transitions on article-to-article citation rates, by citing institution type (articles published *before* the move)

Notes: Dynamics for the difference in yearly citations between movers' and stayers' matched articles written in the premove period. Articles in each pair appeared in the same year and journal, and are also matched on focal scientist position on the authorship list, as well as overall number of authors. Further, control articles are selected such that the sum of squared differences in citations between control and treated article up to year $t_0 - 1$ is minimized—where t_0 is the year of (possibly counterfactual) move. In addition, when the year of publication is in the year prior to the move, the articles in each pair appeared not only in the same year, but also in the same month. Similarly, when the year of publication is in the penultimate year prior to the move, the articles in each pair appeared not only in the same year, but also in the same quarter.

fading out completely seven years later. Panel B examines whether the same patterns can be observed when restricting the outcome variable to article citations from industrial firms. The scale of the vertical axis is different, since these industrial cites account for a relatively tiny fraction of the total. Due to the paucity of the industrial citations, the results are very imprecise, though there is a very modest upward deviation from trend one year after the move.

Figure 2.9 display the results for citation flows disaggregated by citer location. Perhaps surprisingly, citations at the origin location do not appear to decline upon a star's departure (panel A). This lack of forgetting on the part of academics points to a capacity to absorb scientific knowledge that is disembodied from the producer of a particular idea. However, this view needs to be tempered in light of the results displayed in panel B, which focuses on citations accruing at the destination location. Relative to the flows in a random—but distant—location for the stayer, the level of flows is higher for movers at destination even before the move, with an upward trend starting two years before the move is effective. This provides strong evidence that academic superstars are, at least in part, "recruited for ideas" (Agarwal and Singh, forthcoming). Furthermore, this upward trend becomes more pronounced after the move, peaking two years later, but fading out only slowly over time. In other words, there is clear evidence that itinerant scientists circulate their old ideas in their new locations. The magnitude of this effect is not trivial: by the end of the observation period, movers have accrued more than twice as many citations to their old ideas at destination than stayers have in their counterfactual, random location.

Panel C examines citation dynamics in all locations, save for the origin and destination. One can discern a slight increase in citations after the move, though it is neither large nor precisely estimated. Yet, this should not be surprising if we think that mobility events give scientists looking for a new position an opportunity to give their ideas—old and new—a boost in exposure.

The asymmetry between the citation dynamics at location and origin strikes us as noteworthy, since it provides clear evidence that labor mobility increases the circulation of scientific ideas. If one espouses the view that knowledge flows are economically and socially valuable, then our results raise the intriguing possibility that scientists move too little, relative to what would lead to an optimal rate of scientific exploration. We return to this point in the discussion.

Tables 2.8 and 2.9 explore whether the magnitude of the treatment effect is affected by a number of article and scientist characteristics, at the origin and destination locations, respectively.[10] We do not discuss these in detail, since they tend to be quite noisy. Furthermore, with an unlimited number of

10. We do not repeat these analyses for patent-to-patent and patent-to-article citations, since they are sparse as is, and analyses that separate them into bins would be very noisy.

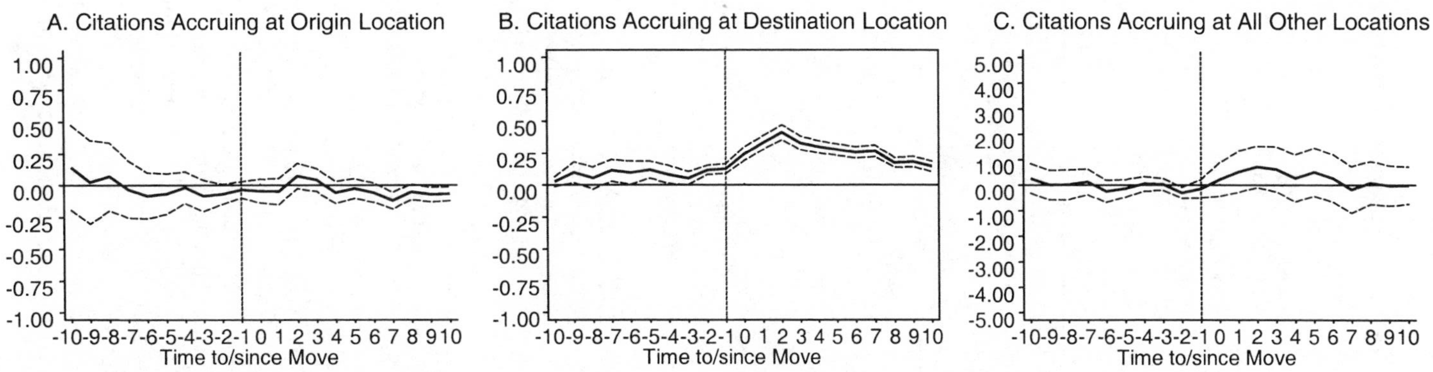

Fig. 2.9 Effect of professional transitions on article-to-article citation rates, by location (articles published *before* the move)

Note: Dynamics for the difference in yearly citations between movers' and stayers' matched articles written in the premove period. Articles in each pair appeared in the same year and journal, and are also matched on focal scientist position on the authorship list, as well as overall number of authors. Further, control articles are selected such that the sum of squared differences in citations between control and treated article up to year $t_0 - 1$ is minimized—where t_0 is the year of (possibly counterfactual) move. In addition, when the year of publication is in the year prior to the move, the articles in each pair appeared not only in the same year, but also in the same month. Similarly, when the year of publication is in the penultimate year prior to the move, the articles in each pair appeared not only in the same year, but also in the same quarter.

In panel A, only citations accruing at the origin location are tallied. In panel B, only citations accruing at the destination location are tallied. For stayers, the destination location is chosen at random from among the set of locations that movers move to and that are separated by at least fifty miles from the staying star's actual location. In panel C, only citations accruing at all other locations are tallied.

Table 2.8 **Effects of professional move on article-to-article citation rates at origin location**

	Novel vs. not		Young vs. old		Journal prestige	
	Novel (1a)	Not (1b)	Young (2a)	Old (2b)	Low JIF (3a)	High JIF (3b)
After appointment	–0.054	0.083**	–0.000	0.045	0.032	0.022
	(0.039)	(0.034)	(0.041)	(0.033)	(0.028)	(0.040)
Nb. of observations	80,165	95,550	82,580	93,135	84,114	91,601
Nb. of article pairs	3,713	6,536	4,524	5,725	4,884	5,365
Nb. of scientists	1,273	1,648	1,192	914	1,698	1,489
Adjusted R^2	0.243	0.320	0.290	0.299	0.269	0.305

	Pre- vs. post-Internet		Big vs. small status change		PI vs. non-PI pubs	
	1975–1994 (4a)	1995–2003 (4b)	Big (5a)	Small (5b)	First or last position (6a)	Middle position (6b)
After appointment	0.023	0.038	–0.014	0.037	0.045*	–0.026
	(0.028)	(0.067)	(0.057)	(0.029)	(0.025)	(0.066)
Nb. of observations	150,880	24,835	34,414	141,301	130,230	45,485
Nb. of article pairs	7,456	2,793	2,049	8,200	7,315	2,934
Nb. of scientists	1,782	564	417	1,689	1,872	1,200
Adjusted R^2	0.251	0.361	0.322	0.289	0.253	0.334

	Well-cited at baseline		Well-funded at baseline		Prolific patenter at baseline	
	No (7a)	Yes (7b)	No (8a)	Yes (8b)	No (9a)	Yes (9b)
After appointment	0.011	0.043	0.021	0.044	0.016	0.054
	(0.032)	(0.040)	(0.030)	(0.052)	(0.028)	(0.057)
Nb. of observations	88,823	86,892	131,548	44,167	135,818	39,897
Nb. of article pairs	5,240	5,009	7,787	2,462	7,477	2,772
Nb. of scientists	1,406	700	1,708	398	1,732	374
Adjusted R^2	0.276	0.306	0.285	0.322	0.275	0.328

Note: Standard errors in parentheses, clustered by scientists. All specifications are estimated by OLS; the models include article-pair fixed effects.

***Significant at the 1 percent level.

**Significant at the 5 percent level.

*Significant at the 10 percent level.

potential contingencies, pure luck would dictate that at least some interaction effects would be statistically significant. In table 2.8, we find almost all interaction effects to be imprecisely estimated zeros.

New results, some reassuring, others more puzzling, emerge when focusing on citation flows at destination (table 2.9). We examine whether the mobility premium at destination varies with authorship credit for the focal

Table 2.9 **Effects of professional move on article-to-article citation rates at destination location**

	Novel vs. not		Young vs. old		Journal prestige	
	Novel (1a)	Not (1b)	Young (2a)	Old (2b)	Low JIF (3a)	High JIF (3b)
After appointment	0.036*	0.093***	0.035	0.094***	0.078***	0.063***
	(0.021)	(0.020)	(0.025)	(0.018)	(0.014)	(0.024)
Nb. of observations	80,165	95,550	82,580	93,135	84,114	91,601
Nb. of article pairs	3,713	6,536	4,524	5,725	4,884	5,365
Nb. of scientists	1,273	1,648	1,192	914	1,698	1,489
Adjusted R^2	0.237	0.360	0.343	0.305	0.256	0.345
	Pre- vs. post-Internet		Big vs. small status change		PI vs. non-PI pubs	
	1975–1994 (4a)	1995–2003 (4b)	Big (5a)	Small (5b)	First or last Position (6a)	Middle Position (6b)
After appointment	0.046***	0.164***	0.039	0.077***	0.077***	0.047
	(0.015)	(0.043)	(0.038)	(0.016)	(0.016)	(0.030)
Nb. of observations	150,880	24,835	34,414	141,301	130,230	45,485
Nb. of article pairs	7,456	2,793	2,049	8,200	7,315	2,934
Nb. of scientists	1,782	564	417	1,689	1,872	1,200
Adjusted R^2	0.295	0.361	0.355	0.315	0.313	0.342
	Well-cited at baseline		Well-funded at baseline		Prolific patenter at baseline	
	No (7a)	Yes (7b)	No (8a)	Yes (8b)	No (9a)	Yes (9b)
After appointment	0.077***	0.061**	0.078***	0.043**	0.066***	0.078**
	(0.016)	(0.025)	(0.018)	(0.026)	(0.016)	(0.034)
Nb. of observations	88,823	86,892	131,548	44,167	135,818	39,897
Nb. of article pairs	5,240	5,009	7,787	2,462	7,477	2,772
Nb. of scientists	1,406	700	1,708	398	1,732	374
Adjusted R^2	0.253	0.350	0.331	0.297	0.309	0.340

Notes: Standard errors in parentheses, clustered by scientists. All specifications are estimated by OLS; the models include article-pair fixed effects.

***Significant at the 1 percent level.

**Significant at the 5 percent level.

*Significant at the 10 percent level.

scientists. For this purpose, we exploit a robust social norm in the natural and physical sciences, whereby last authorship is systematically assigned to the principal investigator of a laboratory, first authorship is generally assigned to the junior author who was responsible for the actual conduct of the investigation (or, more rarely, to the principal investigator (PI) of a collaborating lab), and the remaining credit is apportioned to authors in the middle of the authorship list, generally as a decreasing function of the distance from the extremities (Riesenberg and Lundberg 1990). We split the cited-article sample in two by consolidating the first and last authorship categories, and contrasting it with those article-pairs in which the focal scientists appear in the middle of the authorship list. We find clear evidence of a more pronounced mobility effect for article pairs in which the departing scientist is either first or last author. The evidence for middle-position authors is much smaller in magnitude. This is reassuring because the level of contribution of middle authors is often sufficiently small that one would not expect these old, marginal articles (from the point of view of the mover's overall corpus of work) to gain significant exposure at the new destination.

Second, we fail to detect a mobility premium of larger magnitude for the citations to the papers of superstars who shine particularly bright, regardless of the ways in which we seek to distinguish the elite from others who might be less accomplished (models 7a through 9b of table 2.9).

The anomalous result that bears mention pertains to the sample split corresponding to articles of recent versus older vintage. We separate the analysis for papers that appeared prior to and after 1995, a date that we pick as a marker for the Internet becoming ubiquitous in academia. We find that the mobility premium is four times higher for papers written in the Internet era than for papers published in the pre-Internet times. These results are inconsistent with the widespread belief that the diffusion of the Internet led to the "death of distance," though they should be interpreted cautiously since they may also reflect other changes over time.

Patent-to-Article Citation Flows. Figure 2.10 and 2.11 present the evidence on the second measure of knowledge flows, citations made to articles published in the open science literature in patents granted by the USPTO. In panel A of figure 2.10, we cannot detect any differential citation trend for the overall citations flowing to treated, rather than control articles. In fact, there is only the faintest evidence of a decline after the move. Panel B, which focuses on citations from industrial assignees alone, similarly shows no clear result.

The evidence on localization, presented in figure 2.11, is also relatively weak. This time, we observe a meaningful decline of citations at the origin location following the departure of a superstar, but this temporary dip is not pinned down precisely. Table 2.7, column (2a) presents the same analysis in regression form, but uses a longer postmove observation period, and constrains the mobility effect to be constant over time. In this case, we can detect a statistically significant decline equal to a quarter of a citation per year on average. Similarly, we observe a small increase in citations for treated articles at destination, relative to controls, but we cannot reject the hypothesis of a mobility premium equal to zero.

Patent-to-Patent Citation Flows. We employ the more traditional measure of knowledge flows—patent-to-patent citations—in the next batch of analyses, presented in figures 2.12 and 2.13. Once again, premove citation

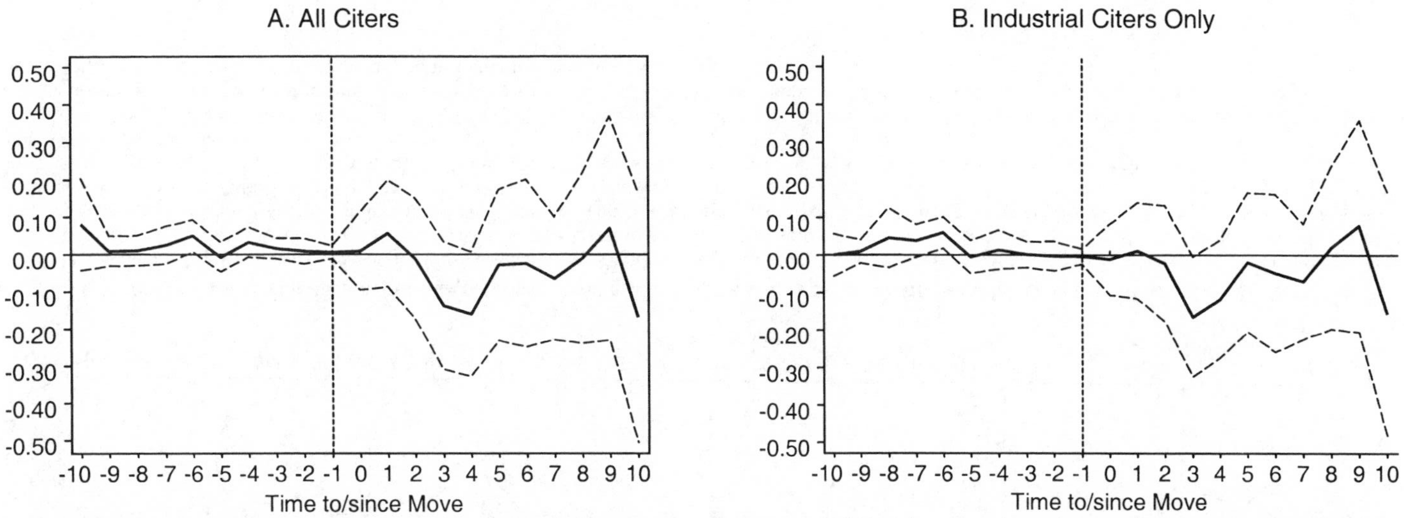

Fig. 2.10 Effect of professional transitions on patent-to-article citation rates, by citing institution type (articles published *before* the move)

Notes: Dynamics for the difference in yearly citations between movers' and stayers' matched articles written in the premove period. Articles in each pair appeared in the same year and journal, and are also matched on focal scientist position on the authorship list, as well as overall number of authors. Further, control articles are selected such that the sum of squared differences in citations between control and treated article up to year $t_0 - 1$ is minimized—where t_0 is the year of (possibly counterfactual) move. In addition, when the year of publication is in the year prior to the move, the articles in each pair appeared not only in the same year, but also in the same month. Similarly, when the year of publication is in the penultimate year prior to the move, the articles in each pair appeared not only in the same year, but also in the same quarter.

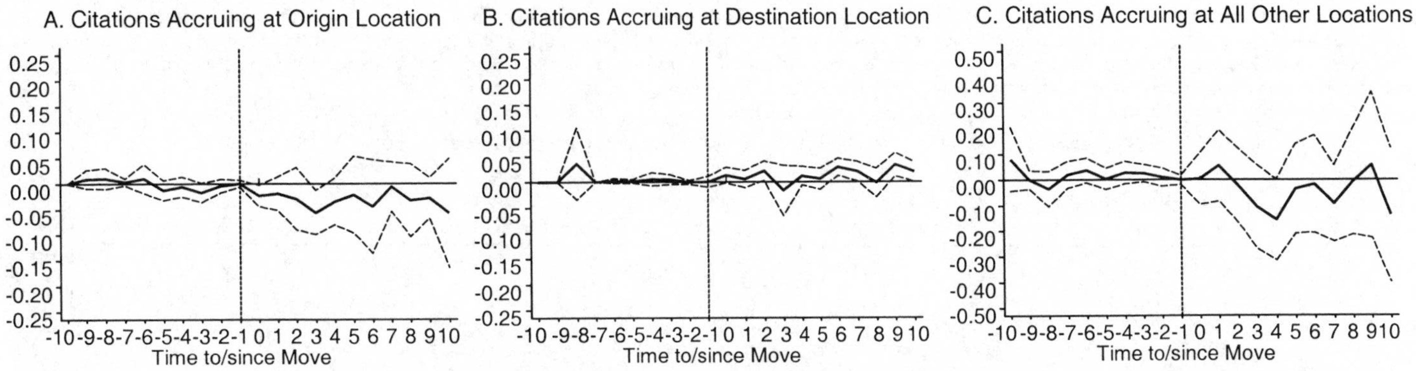

Fig. 2.11 Effect of professional transitions on patent-to-article citation rates, by location (articles published *before* the move)

Note: Dynamics for the difference in yearly citations between movers' and stayers' matched articles written in the premove period. Articles in each pair appeared in the same year and journal, and are also matched on focal scientist position on the authorship list, as well as overall number of authors. Further, control articles are selected such that the sum of squared differences in citations between control and treated article up to year $t_0 - 1$ is minimized—where t_0 is the year of (possibly counterfactual) move. In addition, when the year of publication is in the year prior to the move, the articles in each pair appeared not only in the same year, but also in the same month. Similarly, when the year of publication is in the penultimate year prior to the move, the articles in each pair appeared not only in the same year, but also in the same quarter.

In panel A, only citations accruing at the origin location are tallied. In panel B, only citations accruing at the destination location are tallied. For stayers, the destination location is chosen at random from among the set of locations that movers move to and that are separated by at least fifty miles from the staying star's actual location. In panel C, only citations accruing at all other locations are tallied.

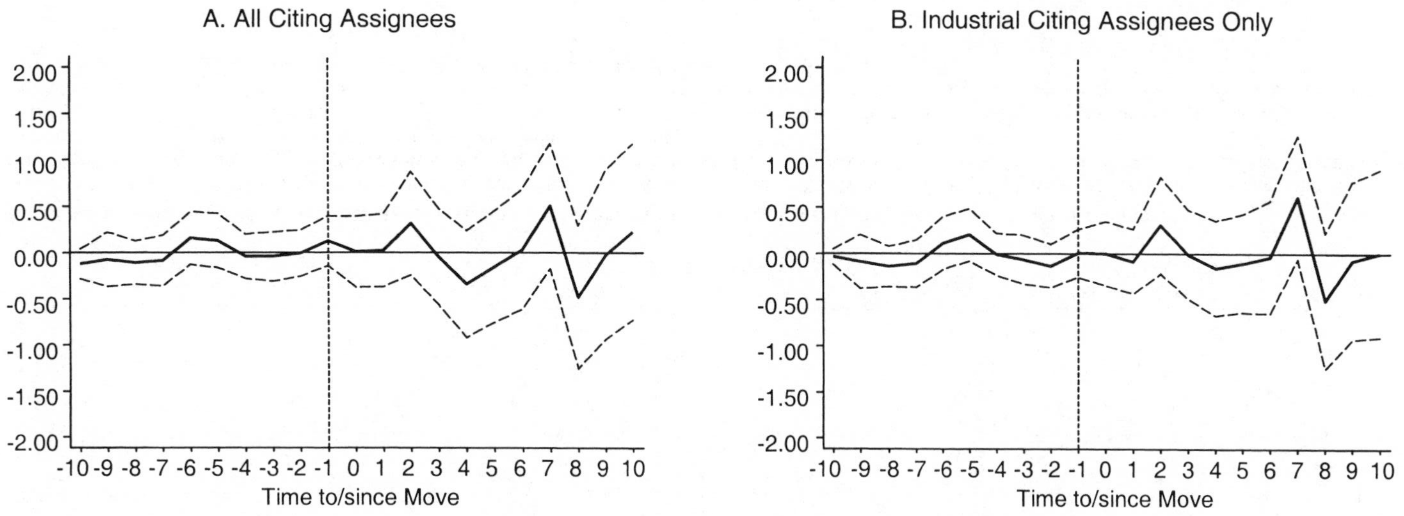

Fig. 2.12 Effect of professional transitions on patent-to-patent citation rates, by citing assignee type (patents issued *before* the move)

Notes: Dynamics for the difference in yearly citations between movers' and stayers' matched patents issued in the premove period. Patents in each pair share the same application and issue years. Further, control patents are selected such that the sum of squared differences in citations between control and treated patents up to year $t_0 - 1$ is minimized—where t_0 is the year of (possibly counterfactual) move.

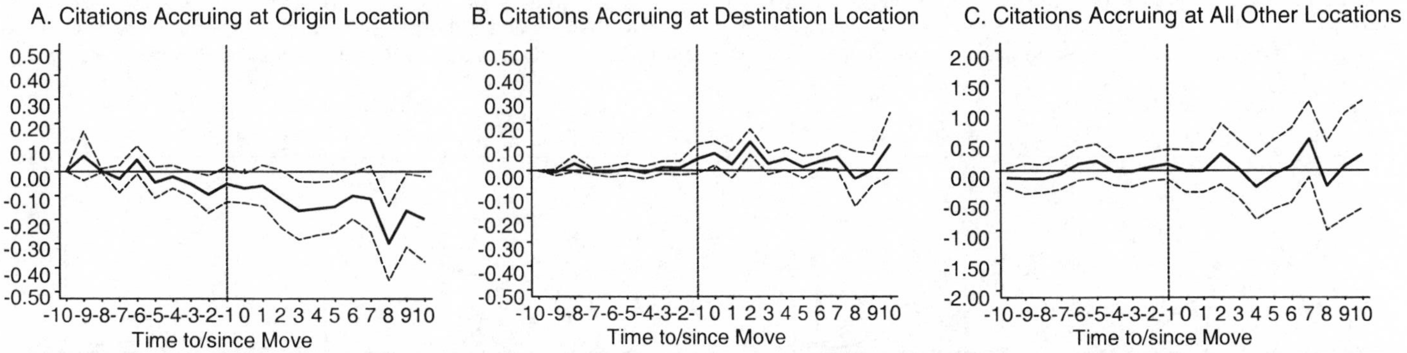

Fig. 2.13 Effect of professional transitions on patent-to-patent citation rates, by location (patents issued *before* the move)

Note: Dynamics for the difference in yearly citations between movers' and stayers' matched patents patents in the premove period. Patents in each pair share the same application and issue years. Further, control patents are selected such that the sum of squared differences in citations between control and treated patents up to year $t_0 - 1$ is minimized—where t_0 is the year of (possibly counterfactual) move.

In panel A, only citations accruing at the origin location are tallied. In panel B, only citations accruing at the destination location are tallied. For stayers, the destination location is chosen at random from among the set of locations that movers move to and that are separated by at least fifty miles from the staying star's actual location. In panel C, only citations accruing at all other locations are tallied.

dynamics appear very similar up until the year of the move, which is expected given the extensive efforts we deployed in our search for appropriate control patents. There is no evidence that mobility increases citation flows overall (figure 2.12).

The localization effects presented in figure 2.13 are much more dramatic. First, there is a decline in the rate of citations in the location of origin, which becomes more pronounced over time and shows no sign of abating even ten years after the scientist has departed (panel A). This may reflect the importance of physical proximity to university laboratories for helping industrial firms develop the inventions of academic entrepreneurs (Zucker, Darby, and Brewer 1998; Audretsch and Stephan 1996). However, this interpretation is undermined by evidence that the onset of this decline precedes the move by almost four years (though this preexisting downward trend is small in magnitude and imprecisely estimated).

The upward trend at destination (panel B) is not quite as dramatic, but clear. Here again, there is some weak evidence of anticipation, with citations being slightly higher for movers in the baseline year at destination, relative to stayers. It is therefore difficult to distinguish between the view that physical proximity to academic entrepreneurs begets absorptive capacity, from the alternative perspective that a scientist's assessment that the local industrial base has grown stale (or at least less receptive to his/her ideas) triggers mobility.

2.4 Discussion

In this chapter, we examine the impact of geography on knowledge transfer by exploiting professional transitions within the academic life sciences coupled with publication and patent citation data over time. The results reveal a rather nuanced story. Consistent with models of localized knowledge diffusion, we find strong evidence that publication-to-publication citations (to papers published before the move) rise at destination locations after the move takes place. We also find, however, persuasive evidence of a legacy effect at the origin institution—citation rates do not decline after the scientist departs. While the findings on the patent side are less conclusive than those on publications alone, they reveal a slightly different role for geography. Here again citations at the destination location rise (or at least remain the same) after the move, while citations at the origin location appear to fall, particularly for patent-to-patent citations.

The normative implications of our findings are not straightforward, especially since there may be first-order effects of job mobility we do not observe. Nonetheless, we offer some broader speculations here. Let's begin with a deeper look at the publication-to-publication citation results. A surge in citations at the new location with little drop off at the old location underscores the importance of scientist interactions, but also makes clear that these interactions are not easily forgotten. Since the sharing and recombining of existing ideas is viewed as an essential component in the innovation process (Weitzman 1998; Burt 2004; Simonton 2004), might our evidence suggest that scientists are moving too little?

The answer to this will, of course, depend upon the degree to which scientists internalize the impacts of their location decisions, but suboptimal levels of mobility seem likely. Nearly all of the costs of moving are borne privately, yet much of the credit associated with new scientific discoveries is apportioned out narrowly to the lead scientists on that project, leaving researchers with incentives that appear too weak from a societal perspective. While the best way to address this limited mobility is unclear, it has potentially large and important implications for the rate, and especially the direction of technological innovation within the economy, and eventually for economic growth.

The analysis of patent citations—most of which are generated by biomedical firms—suggests a distinct knowledge production process within industry. The output of local talent is most influential when it remains local. That ideas are quickly forgotten after a scientist departs suggests an important role for face-to-face interactions. One possible explanation for this finding is that the limited absorptive capacity within most firms necessitates a substantive dialogue with academic scientists in order to translate scientific output into something more useful for organizations concerned with its translation into marketable products. Such dialogues are clearly less costly with local talent, especially if the fruitful search for ideas is not one that is narrowly circumscribed around a well-defined issue. The opportunities that are lost when a scientist departs, however, are not entirely clear. Even if firms are abandoning science that the academy believes is still useful, what is the proper benchmark here? The academy and industry may simply value different types of ideas. Even still, some ideas that firms should value are likely to fall off the radar screen when scientists depart, offering at least some temperance to the idea that the innovative costs of scientist mobility are negligible.

These conjectures assume the construct validity of our measures: that publication-publication citations actually measure knowledge flows among academics, and that patent-patent and patent-publication citations actually measure academic industry spillovers. In the spirit of recognizing measurement difficulties (see e.g., Kuznets and Schmookler in the 1962 volume) we acknowledge these are assumptions. For example, numerous scholars of bibliometrics have noted the ceremonial function of publication citations (Merton 1968; MacRoberts and MacRoberts 1996). While we have interpreted the finding that there is little forgetting of superstars research after a move as evidence that face-to-face interaction may not be so necessary for knowledge flows, it could instead reflect that the scientists continue to be cited for ceremonial reasons. A related explanation: if citations are less about intellectual influence than just knowing about research (MacRoberts and MacRoberts 1996), we may not expect any decay after professional transitions.

Similar concerns could be raised about citations in patents. As Jaffe and Trajtenberg and others have emphasized, the claim that these citations reflect real knowledge flows, or spillovers, is only an assumption. Survey work (Jaffe, Trajtenberg, and Fogarty 2002) suggests they are noisy measures. Recent analyses (Alcácer, Gittelman, and Sampat 2009; Sampat 2010; Hegde and Sampat 2009) on the importance of patent examiners in generating these citations may undermine the notion that they are true knowledge flows. One of the reasons for using patent-to-publication citations is that these are less affected by examiner influence (Lemley and Sampat 2010) and potentially better measures of knowledge flows (Roach and Cohen 2010), though here too there are questions of whether applicants have incentives to disclose all relevant knowledge, and only relevant knowledge (Cotropia, Lemley, and Sampat 2010). All this granted, it is difficult to construct an explanation of our "forgetting" result for patent-to-patent and patent-to-publication citations that is driven only by incentives to cite (or citation practices).

Appendix A

Criteria for Delineating the Set of 10,450 "Superstars"

We present additional details regarding the criteria used to construct the sample of 10,450 superstars.

Highly Funded Scientists. Our first data source is the Consolidated Grant/Applicant File (CGAF) from the US National Institutes of Health (NIH). This data set records information about grants awarded to extramural researchers funded by the NIH since 1938. Using the CGAF and focusing only on direct costs associated with research grants, we compute individual cumulative totals for the decades 1977 to 1986, 1987 to 1996, and 1997 to 2006, deflating the earlier years by the Biomedical Research Producer Price Index.[11] We also recompute these totals excluding large center grants that usually fund groups of investigators (M01 and P01 grants). Scientists whose totals lie in the top ventile (i.e., above the 95th percentile) of either distribution constitute our first group of superstars. In this group, the least well-funded investigator garnered $10.5 million in career NIH funding, and the most well-funded $462.6 million.[12]

11. http://officeofbudget.od.nih.gov/UI/GDPFromGenBudget.htm.

12. We perform a similar exercise for scientists employed by the intramural campus of the NIH. These scientists are not eligible for extramural funding, but the NIH keeps records of

Highly Cited Scientists. Despite the preeminent role of the NIH in the funding of public biomedical research, the previous indicator of superstardom biases the sample toward scientists conducting relatively expensive research. We complement this first group with a second composed of highly cited scientists identified by the Institute for Scientific Information. A Highly Cited listing means that an individual was among the 250 most cited researchers for their published articles between 1981 and 1999, within a broad scientific field.[13]

Top Patenters. We add to these groups academic life scientists who belong in the top percentile of the patent distribution among academics—those who were granted 17 patents or more between 1976 and 2004.

Members of the National Academy of Sciences. We add to these groups academic life scientists who were elected to the National Academy of Science between 1975 and 2007.

MERIT Awardees of the NIH. Initiated in the mid-1980s, the MERIT Award program extends funding for up to five years (but typically three years) to a select number of NIH-funded investigators "who have demonstrated superior competence, outstanding productivity during their previous research endeavors and are leaders in their field with paradigm-shifting ideas." The specific details governing selection vary across the component institutes of the NIH, but the essential feature of the program is that only researchers holding an R01 grant in its second or later cycle are eligible. Further, the application must be scored in the top percentile in a given funding cycle.

Former and Current Howard Hughes Medical Investigators. Every three years, the Howard Hughes Medical Institute selects a small cohort of midcareer biomedical scientists with the potential to revolutionize their respective subfields. Once selected, HHMIs continue to be based at their institutions, typically leading a research group of ten to twenty-five students, postdoctoral associates, and technicians. Their appointment is reviewed every five years, based solely on their most important contributions during the cycle.[14]

Early Career Prize Winners. We also included winners of the Pew, Searle, Beckman, Rita Allen, and Packard scholarships for the years 1981 through 2000. Every year, these charitable foundations provide seed funding to between twenty and forty young academic life scientists. These scholarships

the number of internal projects each intramural scientist leads. We include in the elite sample the top ventile of intramural scientists according to this metric.

13. The relevant scientific fields in the life sciences are microbiology, biochemistry, psychiatry/psychology, neuroscience, molecular biology and genetics, immunology, pharmacology, and clinical medicine.

14. See Azoulay, Graff Zivin, and Manso (2011) for more details and an evaluation of this program.

are the most prestigious accolades that young researchers can receive in the first two years of their careers as independent investigators.

Appendix B
Linking Scientists with Their Journal Articles

The source of our publication data is PubMed, a bibliographic database maintained by the US National Library of Medicine that is searchable on the web at no cost.[15] PubMed contains over 14 million citations from 4,800 journals published in the United States and more than 70 other countries from 1950 to the present. The subject scope of this database is biomedicine and health, broadly defined to encompass those areas of the life sciences, behavioral sciences, chemical sciences, and bioengineering that inform research in health-related fields. In order to effectively mine this publicly available data source, we designed Publication Harvester, an open-source software tool that automates the process of gathering publication information for individual life scientists (see Azoulay, Stellman, and Graff Zivin 2006 for a complete description of the software). Publication Harvester is fast, simple to use, and reliable. Its output consists of a series of reports that can be easily imported by statistical software packages.

This software tool does not obviate the two challenges faced by empirical researchers when attempting to link accurately individual scientists with their published output. The first relates to what one might term "Type I error," whereby we mistakenly attribute to a scientist a journal article actually authored by a namesake; the second relates to "Type II error," whereby we conservatively exclude from a scientist's publication roster legitimate articles.

Namesakes and Popular Names. PubMed does not assign unique identifiers to the authors of the publications they index. They identify authors simply by their last name, up to two initials, and an optional suffix. This makes it difficult to unambiguously assign publication output to individual scientists, especially when their last name is relatively common.

Inconsistent Publication Names. The opposite danger, that of recording too few publications, also looms large, since scientists are often inconsistent in the choice of names they choose to publish under. By far the most common source of error is the haphazard use of a middle initial. Other errors stem from inconsistent use of suffixes (Jr., Sr., 2nd, etc.), or from multiple patronyms due to changes in spousal status.

To deal with these serious measurement problems, we opted for a labor-

15. http://www.pubmed.gov/.

intensive approach: the design of individual search queries that relies on relevant scientific keywords, the names of frequent collaborators, journal names, as well as institutional affiliations. We are aided in the time-consuming process of query design by the availability of a reliable archival data source, namely, these scientists' curriculum vitaes (CVs) and biosketches. PublicationHarvester provides the option to use such custom queries in lieu of a completely generic query (e.g., "azoulay p" [au] or "sampat bn" [au]). As an example, one can examine the publications of Scott A. Waldman, an eminent pharmacologist located in Philadelphia, PA, at Thomas Jefferson University. Waldman is a relatively frequent name in the United States (with 208 researchers with an identical patronym in the Association of American Medical Colleges (AAMC) faculty roster); the combination "waldman s" is common to three researchers in the same database. A simple search query for "waldman sa" [au] OR "waldman s" [au] returns 302 publications at the time of this writing. However, a more refined query, based on Professor Waldman's biosketch returns only 210 publications.[16]

The previous example also makes clear how we deal with the issue of inconsistent publication names. PublicationHarvester gives the end-user the option to choose up to four PubMed-formatted names under which publications can be found for a given researcher. For example, Louis J. Tobian, Jr. publishes under "tobian 1," "tobian 1 jr," and "tobian 1j," and all three names need to be provided as inputs to generate a complete publication listing. Furthermore, even though Tobian is a relatively rare name, the search query needs to be modified to account for these name variations, as in ("tobian l" [au] OR "tobian 1j" [au])

We are confident that this labor-intensive customization ensures the accuracy of our superstar scientists' bibliomes.

Appendix C

Linking Scientists with Their Patents

A number of recent efforts have been devoted to assigning unique identifiers to inventors in the US Patent Data (Trajtenberg, Shiff, and Mclamed 2006; Marx, Strumsky, and Fleming 2009). Rather than relying on recursive algorithms that help group together patents issued to the same inventors, we make use of the richness of our data to improve the quality of the matched inventor/invention links.

In a first step, we eliminate from the set of potential patents all patents

16. ((("waldman sa" [au] NOT (ether OR anesthesia)) OR ("waldman s" [au] AND (murad OR philadelphia [ad] OR west point [ad] OR wong p [au] OR lasseter kc [au] OR colorectal))) AND 1980:2010 [dp])

issued in classes that appear unrelated to the life sciences, writ large. Second, we focus on the set of superstars with relatively rare names, and automate the match with the patent data by declaring as valid any link in which (a) the inventor's full name matches, and (b) at least one patent assignee matches with one of the scientist's employer, past or present. We then relax these constraints one at a time, examining potential matches by hand. Using knowledge about the research of these scientists stemming from their biographical records, we then pass judgement on the validity of these more uncertain matches. The same procedure is repeated for the set of inventors with common names, though these records often require the inspection of each potential patent to ascertain whether they correspond to legitimate or spurious matches.

Following Thursby, Fuller, and Thursby (2009), we find that many patents associated with the elite scientists in our sample are not assigned to their employer, but rather unassigned, or assigned solely to an industrial firm. As a result, we are very careful to inspect manually records for which the inventor name matches that of one of our superstars, but there is no assignee information to match with the available biographical record for this individual.

One objection to this linking procedure is that it is ad hoc, and difficult to replicate across different empirical contexts. Moreover, it is very labor intensive, and therefore would not scale up to a much larger sample of inventors. Yet, we suspect that using prior knowledge about the direction of an inventor's research to link them precisely with their patented inventions results in higher-quality matches.

Appendix D

Linking PubMed References to USPTO Patents

Determining whether patents cite publications is more difficult than tracing patent citations: while the cited patents are unique seven-digit numbers, cited publications are free-form text (Callaert et al. 2006). Moreover, the USPTO does not require that applicants submit references to literature in a standard format. For example, Harold Varmus's 1988 *Science* article "Retroviruses" is cited in twenty-nine distinct patents, but in numerous different formats, including Varmus; "Retroviruses" *Science* 240:1427–1435 (1988) (in patent 6794141) and Varmus et al., 1988, *Science* 240:1427–1439 (in patent 6805882). As this example illustrates, there can be errors in author lists and page numbers. Even more problematic, in some cases certain fields (e.g., author name) are included, in others they are not. Journal names may be abbreviated in some patents, but not in others.

To address these difficulties, we developed a matching algorithm that compared each of several PubMed fields—first author, page numbers, volume, and the beginning of the title, publication year, or journal name—to all references in all biomedical and chemical patents issued by the USPTO since 1976. Biomedical patents are identified by technology class, using the patent class-field concordance developed by the National Bureau of Economic Research (Jaffe and Trajtenberg 2005). We considered a dyad to be a match if four of the fields from PubMed were listed in a USPTO reference.

Overall, the algorithm returned 558,982 distinct PMIDs (unique article identifiers in PubMed) cited in distinct 172,815 patents. Since it necessarily relied on probabilistic rather than exact matches, we also tested it across a sample of references where we were confident the match to the PubMed data was accurate. Specifically, we sampled 200 references from the biomedical/chemical patents, and two research assistants and one of the authors (Sampat) manually investigated whether the references had associated PMIDs. Sampat carefully reviewed and adjudicated any cases where there was disagreement among the three coders.

Manual matching, while cumbersome, provides an extremely reliable match, a gold standard against which we can gauge the algorithm. The algorithm returned the correct PMID information for 86 percent of the references. There were no false positives: if our manual match returned no PMID, neither did our algorithm. And in almost all cases, if the algorithm generated a PMID, it was the correct one. But for 14 percent of the references there were false negatives; that is, a PMID was found via the manual match, but none was found via the algorithm. While these errors are unlikely to be related to any variables of interest, we can also test robustness of any results obtained using these data using matches from a more liberal implementation of the algorithm (based on matching three rather than four elements of the PubMed record to the patent references), which returns fewer false negatives but more false positives.

Choosing between the loose and strict algorithms involves making tradeoffs between the Type I and Type II errors. In the analyses following, we rely primarily on the strict algorithm, erring on the side of understating the extent to which patents cite the biomedical literature.

Appendix E

Construction of the Product Control Group

We detail the "coarse exact matching" (CEM) procedure implemented to identify the sample of control products from among the universe of products associated with stayers. As opposed to methods that rely on the estimation of a propensity score, CEM is a nonparametric procedure.[17]

In its basic outline, the matching procedure is very similar across the three measures of knowledge flows; whether we are focused on journal articles or patents, the sample of control products is constructed such that the following two conditions are met:

1. Treated articles/patents exhibit no differential citation trends relative to control products up to the time of mobility.
2. Treated and control articles/patents match on a number of time-invariant article characteristics.

However, implementation details vary with cited and citing product type, as explained later.

Journal Articles. We identify controls based on the following set of covariates: (1) year of publication; (2) specific journal (e.g., *Cell* or the *New England Journal of Medicine*); (3) number of authors (the distribution is coarsened into six bins: one, two, three, four or five, between six and nine, and ten or more authors); (4) focal-scientist position on the authorship list (first author, middle author, or last author). In the case of articles published in the year immediately preceding appointment, the list of matching covariates is expanded to also include the month of publication. In the case of articles published two years before appointment, the list of matching covariates is expanded to also include the quarter of publication. To ensure that premove citation trends are similar, we proceed in two steps. First, we also match on cumulative number of citations at baseline, coarsened into 7 strata (0 to 10th; 10th to 25th; 25th to 50th; 50th to 75th; 75th to 95th; 95th to 99th; and above the 99th percentile). However, we have found that this is not enough to eliminate premove citation trends. As a result, we select all control articles that match according to the previous covariates, and pick among those potential matches a single article that further minimizes the sum of squared differences in the number of citations up until the year before the year of move.

Patents. We identify controls based on the following set of time-invariant covariates: (1) year of issue; (2) year of application; and (3) main patent class. To ensure that premove citation trends are similar, we match on cumulative number of citations at baseline, coarsened into 4 strata (0 to 50th; 50th to 95th; 95th to 99th; and above the 99th percentile).

17. A propensity score approach would entail estimating the probability that the scientists in the data move in a given year, and then using the inverse of this estimated probability to weight the data in a second stage analysis of the effect of mobility on subsequent citation rates. However, because citations occur at the article level, achieving covariate balance by weighting the data by the scientist-level likelihood of moving, even if the determinants of mobility were observable, would not resolve the problem of controlling for article-level quality.

Coarse Exact Matching. We create a large number of strata to cover the entire support of the joint distribution of the covariates mentioned earlier. Each observation is allocated to a unique strata. We then drop from the data all observations corresponding to strata in which there is no treated article and all observations corresponding to strata in which there are less than five potential controls.

The procedure is coarse because we do not attempt to precisely match on covariate values; rather, we coarsen the support of the joint distribution of the covariates into a finite number of strata, and we match a treated observation if and only if a control observation can be recruited from this strata. An important advantage of CEM is that the analyst can guarantee the degree of covariate balance ex ante, but this comes at a cost: the more fine-grained the partition of the support for the joint distribution (i.e., the higher the number of strata), the larger the number of unmatched treated observations.

We implement the CEM procedure year by year, without replacement. Specifically, in move year t, $1976 \leq t \leq 2004$, we do the following:

1. Eliminate from the set of potential controls all products published by stayers who have collaborated with movers prior to year t
2. For each year of publication/issue $t - k$, $1 \leq k \leq 10$
   a. Create the strata
   b. Identify within strata a control for each treated unit; break ties at random
   c. Repeat these steps for year of publication/issue $t - (k + 1)$
3. Repeat these steps for year of appointment $t + 1$

Sensitivity Analyses. The analyst's judgement matters for the outcome of the CEM procedure insofar as he must draw a list of reasonable covariates to match on, as well as decide on the degree of coarsening to impose. Therefore, it is reasonable to ask whether seemingly small changes in the details have consequences for how one should interpret our results.

Nonparametric matching procedures such as CEM are prone to a version of the "curse of dimensionality" whereby the proportion of matched units decreases rapidly with the number of strata. For instance, requiring scientist-level characteristics to match in addition to article-level characteristics would result in a match rate below 10 percent, which seems to us unacceptably low.

However, we have verified that slight variations in the details of the implementation (e.g., varying slightly the number of cutoff points for the stock of citations) have little impact on the basic results we present. To conclude, we feel that CEM enables us to identify a population of control products appropriate to guard against the specific threats to identification mentioned in section 2.1.4.

References

Aghion, Philippe, Mathias Dewatripont, Fiona Murray, Julian Kolev, and Scott Stern. 2009. "Of Mice and Academics: Examining the Effect of Openness on Innovation." NBER Working Paper no. 14819. Cambridge, MA: National Bureau of Economic Research, March.

Aghion, Philippe, and Peter Howitt. 1992. "A Model of Growth through Creative Destruction." *Econometrica* 60 (2): 323–51.

Agrawal, Ajay, Iain Cockburn, and John McHale. 2006. "Gone But Not Forgotten: Labor Flows, Knowledge Spillovers and Enduring Social Capital." *Journal of Economic Geography* 6 (5): 571–91.

Agrawal, Ajay, and Rebecca Henderson. 2002. "Putting Patents in Context: Exploring Knowledge Transfer from MIT." *Management Science* 48 (1): 44–60.

Agrawal, Ajay, and Jasjit Singh. 2011. "Recruiting for Ideas: How Firms Exploit the Prior Inventions of New Hires." *Management Science* 57 (1): 129–50.

Alcácer, Juan, and Michelle Gittelman. 2006. "How Do I Know What You Know? Patent Examiners and the Generation of Patent Citations." *Review of Economics and Statistics* 88 (4): 774–79.

Alcácer, Juan, Michelle Gittelman, and Bhaven Sampat. 2009. "Applicant and Examiner Citations in U.S. Patents: An Overview and Analysis." *Research Policy* 38 (2): 415–27.

Almeida, Paul, and Bruce Kogut. 1999. "Localization of Knowledge and the Mobility of Engineers in Regional Networks." *Management Science* 45 (7): 905–17.

Audretsch, David B., and Paula E. Stephan. 1996. "Company-Scientist Locational Links: The Case of Biotechnology." *American Economic Review* 86 (3): 641–52.

Azoulay, Pierre, Waverly Ding, and Toby Stuart. 2009. "The Effect of Academic Patenting on the Rate, Quality, and Direction of (Public) Research Output." *Journal of Industrial Economics* 57 (4): 637–76.

Azoulay, Pierre, Joshua Graff Zivin, and Gustavo Manso. 2011. "Incentives and Creativity: Evidence from the Academic Life Sciences." *RAND Journal of Economics* 42 (3): 527–54.

Azoulay, Pierre, Joshua Graff Zivin, and Jialan Wang. 2010. "Superstar Extinction." *Quarterly Journal of Economics* 125 (2): 549–89.

Azoulay, Pierre, Andrew Stellman, and Joshua Graff Zivin. 2006. "PublicationHarvester: An Open-Source Software Tool for Science Policy Research." *Research Policy* 35 (7): 970–4.

Azoulay, Pierre, Toby Stuart, and Yanbo Wang. 2011. "Matthew: Effect or Fable?" Massachusetts Institute of Technology, Working Paper.

Belenzon, Sharon, and Mark Schankerman. 2010. "Spreading the Word: Geography, Policy and University Knowledge Diffusion." Center for Economic and Policy Research. Discussion Paper no. 8002.

Blackwell, Matthew, Stefano Iacus, Gary King, and Giuseppe Porro. 2009. "CEM: Coarsened Exact Matching in Stata." *The Stata Journal* 9 (4): 524–46.

Branstetter, Lee. 2005. "Exploring the Link Between Academic Science and Industrial Innovation." *Annales d'Economie et de Statistique* 79–80 (Suppl): 119–42.

Burt, Ronald S. 2004. "Structural Holes and Good Ideas." *American Journal of Sociology* 110 (2): 349–99.

Callaert, Julie, Bart Van Looy, Arnold Verbeek, Koenraad Debackere, and Bart Thijs. 2006. "Traces of Prior Art: An Analysis of Non-Patent References Found in Patent Documents." *Scientometrics* 69 (1): 3–20.

Cech, Thomas R. 2005. "Fostering Innovation and Discovery in Biomedical Research." *Journal of the American Medical Association* 294 (11): 1390–3.

Cockburn, Iain M., and Rebecca M. Henderson. 1998. "Absorptive Capacity, Coauthoring Behavior, and the Organization of Research in Drug Discovery." *Journal of Industrial Economics* 46 (2): 157–82.

Cohen, Wesley M., Richard R. Nelson, and John P. Walsh. 2002. "Links and Impacts: The Influence of Public Research on Industrial R&D." *Management Science* 48 (1): 1–23.

Cole, Jonathan R., and Stephen Cole. 1972. "The Ortega Hypothesis." *Science* 178 (4059): 368–75.

Cotropia, Christopher A., Mark Lemley, and Bhaven Sampat. 2010. "Do Applicant Citations Matter? Implications for the Presumption of Validity." Columbia University. Working Paper.

Dasgupta, Partha, and Paul David. 1994. "Towards a New Economics of Science." *Research Policy* 23 (5): 487–521.

de Solla Price, Derek J. 1963. *Little Science, Big Science.* New York: Columbia University Press.

Fallick, Bruce, Charles A. Fleischmann, and James B. Rebitzer. 2006. "Job Hopping in Silicon Valley: Some Evidence Concerning the Micro-foundations of a High Technology Cluster." *Review of Economics and Statistics* 88 (3): 472–81.

Furman, Jeffrey, and Scott Stern. 2011. "Climbing Atop the Shoulders of Giants: The Impact of Institutions on Cumulative Knowledge Production." *American Economic Review* 101 (5): 1933–63.

Hegde, Deepak, and Bhaven Sampat. 2009. "Applicant Citations, Examiner Citations, and the Private Value of Patents." *Economics Letters* 5 (3): 287–9.

Henderson, Rebecca, Adam Jaffe, and Manuel Trajtenberg. 2005. "Patent Citations and the Geography of Knowledge Spillovers: A Reassessment: Comment." *American Economic Review* 95 (1): 461–4.

Henderson, Rebecca, Luigi Orsenigo, and Gary P. Pisano. 1999. "The Pharmaceutical Industry and the Revolution in Molecular Biology: Interactions Among Scientific, Institutional, and Organizational Change." In *Sources of Industrial Leadership,* edited by David C. Mowery and Richard R. Nelson, 267–311. New York: Cambridge University Press.

Jaffe, Adam B., and Manuel Trajtenberg. 1999. "International Knowledge Flows: Evidence from Patent Citations." *Economics of Innovation and New Technology* 8 (1): 105–36.

Jaffe, Adam B., and Manuel Trajtenberg. 2005. *Patents, Citations, and Innovations.* Cambridge, MA: MIT Press.

Jaffe, Adam B., Manuel Trajtenberg, and Michael S. Fogarty. 2002. "The Meaning of Patent Citations: Report on the NBER/Case-Western Reserve Survey of Patentees." In *Patents, Citations, and Innovations,* edited by Adam B. Jaffe and Manuel Trajtenberg, 379–401. Cambridge, MA: MIT Press.

Jaffe, Adam B., Manuel Trajtenberg, and Rebecca Henderson. 1993. "Geographic Localization of Knowledge Spillovers as Evidenced by Patent Citations." *Quarterly Journal of Economics* 108 (3): 577–98.

Krugman, Paul. 1991. "Increasing Returns and Economic Geography." *Journal of Political Economy* 99 (3): 483–99.

Kuznets, Simon. 1962. "Inventive Activity: Problems of Definition and Measurement." In *The Rate and Direction of Economic Activity: Economic and Social Factors,* Universities-National Bureau Committee for Economic Research and the Committee on Economic Growth of the Social Science Research Councils, 19–52. Princeton, NJ: Princeton University Press.

Lemley, Mark, and Bhaven Sampat. 2010. "Examiner Experience and Patent Office Outcomes." Columbia University. Working Paper.

Levin, Sharon G., and Paula E. Stephan. 1991. "Research Productivity Over the Life Cycle: Evidence for Academic Scientists." *American Economic Review* 81 (1): 114–32.

Lotka, Alfred J. 1926. "The Frequency Distribution of Scientific Productivity." *Journal of the Washington Academy of Sciences* 16 (12): 317–23.

MacRoberts, M. H., and Barbara MacRoberts. 1996. "Problems of Citation Analysis." *Scientometrics* 36 (3): 435–44.

Marburger, John H. 2005. "Wanted: Better Benchmarks." *Science* 308 (5725): 1087.

Marx, Matthew, Debbie Strumsky, and Lee Fleming. 2009. "Mobility, Skills, and the Michigan Non-compete Experiment." *Management Science* 55 (6): 875–99.

Merton, Robert K. 1968. "The Matthew Effect in Science." *Science* 159 (3810): 56–63.

Merton, Robert K. 1973. *The Sociology of Science: Theoretical and Empirical Investigation.* Chicago: University of Chicago Press.

Riesenberg, Don, and George D. Lundberg. 1990. "The Order of Authorship: Who's on First?" *Journal of the American Medical Association* 264 (14): 1857.

Roach, Michael, and Wesley M. Cohen. 2010. "Patent Citations as Measures of Knowledge Flows from Public Research." University of North Carolina. Working Paper.

Romer, Paul M. 1990. "Endogenous Technological Change." *Journal of Political Economy* 98 (5): S71–S102.

Sampat, Bhaven. 2010. "When Do Applicants Search for Prior Art?" *Journal of Law and Economics* 53 (2): 399–416.

Simonton, Dean Keith. 2004. *Creativity in Science: Chance, Logic, Genius, and Zeitgeist.* New York: Cambridge University Press.

Stephan, Paula E. 2010. "The Economics of Science." In *Handbook of The Economics of Innovation,* edited by Bronwyn H. Hall and Nathan Rosenberg, 217–73. Amsterdam: North-Holland.

Thompson, Peter, and Melanie Fox-Kean. 2005. "Patent Citations and the Geography of Knowledge Spillovers: A Reassessment." *American Economic Review* 95 (1): 450–60.

Thursby, Jerry, Anne W. Fuller, and Marie Thursby. 2009. "US Faculty Patenting: Inside and Outside the University." *Research Policy* 38 (1): 14–25.

Trajtenberg, Manuel, Gil Shiff, and Ran Melamed. 2006. "The 'Names Game': Harnessing Inventors' Patent Data for Economic Research." NBER Working Paper no. 12479. Cambridge, MA: National Bureau of Economic Research, September.

Weitzman, Martin L. 1998. "Recombinant Growth." *Quarterly Journal of Economics* 113 (2): 331–60.

Zucker, Lynne G., Michael R. Darby, and Jeff Armstrong. 1999. "Intellectual Capital and the Firm: The Technology of Geographically Localized Knowledge Spillovers." NBER Working Paper no. 4946. Cambridge, MA: National Bureau of Economic Research, April.

Zucker, Lynne G., Michael R. Darby, and Marilynn B. Brewer. 1998. "Intellectual Human Capital and the Birth of U.S. Biotechnology Enterprises." *American Economic Review* 88 (1): 290–306.

Comment Adam B. Jaffe

I am reminded of President Kennedy's quip about how when he had accumulated his brain trust, it was the largest accumulation of brain power in the White House since Jefferson dined alone.

I feel like this is the largest concentration of knowledge and insight about technical change since Zvi Griliches opened his mail at the lunch seminar.

So quickly, what did they do? They built this new data set, 10,000 so-called superstar scientists, and then they tested this issue of the geographic localization of knowledge flows as proxied by these citations from articles and from patents, to both articles and patents. For those of you who are small-minded and wondering where is the fourth element of the pair, there are almost no citations from articles to patents. There are a few, but not very many, so we don't bother.

In looking at this, there is this identification problem, which he used the quote from my paper with Manuel and Rebecca to illustrate. We do not know whether the apparent localization is due to the fact that proximity facilitates communication or whether it is just due to the fact that there is already a geographic concentration of interest in a given topic. And so that is something we would like to tease out. So, there are solutions you could think of in this language of difference-in-difference estimation. We are going to look at scientists who move. That is the difference. But, we are not just going to look at scientists that move.

We are going to compare them to scientists who did not move. So, that is the difference-in-difference structure to this project. For the citations from articles, they actually do some regressions that look at interaction effects with article and scientist attributes to try to see if they can tease out more about what is going on here. And then the last thing they did very briefly is they have some speculative normative inferences about scientists moving, and I'll comment on that.

Figure 2C.1 is my summary of the chapter. There are three kinds of citations—article-to-article, patent-to-article, and patent-to-patent. After the move, we are only looking at citations to the output of the scientists from before the move. We are not looking at the dynamic of the new work that the scientist is doing after the move, because again, that is a more complicated question about exactly what is going on there. We are really trying to do this very clean test about just the localization through communication. We are looking at citations from the time period after the move to the work, the output, be it articles or patents, from before the move. We look at citations

Adam B. Jaffe is the Fred C. Hecht Professor in Economics and dean of the College of Arts and Sciences at Brandeis University and a research associate of the National Bureau of Economic Research.

	From Old Location	From New Location
Article to article	No change	UP
Patent to article	Weakly Down	Weakly Up
Patent to patent	Down	Weakly Up

Fig. 2C.1 Effects of move on citations to premove output

coming from the old location and from the new location. And basically what we find is for these article-to-article citations, they are up. For the patent-to-patent citations there is pretty clear evidence at the old location of what they call forgetting. And for the others, there are some weaker effects where weaker basically means it goes in that direction but it is not statistically significant in the difference-in-differences formulation.

So, what I like about this chapter. First of all, it is a very important and interesting problem, in my view, but of course my saying that communicates absolutely nothing new because I have worked on this problem a lot myself; obviously, I think it is important and interesting. You can make your own judgment about whether it actually is important and interesting, but I think it is. Second, this is an incredible data construction effort, one that as a dean, I would say is probably foolhardy for junior faculty to undertake. But I mean that as a compliment. This is the kind of work that our profession underrewards. It really should reward it more. That is why it might be foolhardy, but it really is incredibly important work. Where they were faced with a choice about how to do something, they always chose the very labor-intensive but better approach over the easier but not as good approach. So this is really an incredible data set, and I think there are going to be enormous spillovers as we go, as this field evolves to other work.

The chapter very clearly explains everything they did. It is very well done. And this difference-in-difference approach is about as clean a causal test as you can get. There was some discussion of this the other day, about how one of the problems in this area generally is that everything is always correlated with everything and it is very hard to test causality. This is about as good as you can get.

It is the job of a discussant to make some additional suggestions. I am not going to worry about which of these things you might actually do in this chapter and which of these things you might do some other time, but these are just thoughts I have about things you might do. First of all, the first two are very small points. The word superstar seems inappropriate to me. We have 10,000 people here, so I would call them productive scientists. If you want to call them stars, I would probably buy that. But they are not superstars.

There is another small thing. There is a paper by Almeida and Kogut, that is conceptually similar. They look at the semiconductor industry and the effect of mobility of engineers on citations. So you should connect to that.

Another obvious suggestion is that you can look at other things beside just the total number of citations. Manuel and Rebecca and I had this measure of "generality," which captures the extent to which citations are broadly distributed rather than concentrated technologically. That would be interesting. You might conjecture that the less closely technologically related people are less geographically sensitive, but that is something in your data that you could actually look at.

Another thing to do would be to look at the citations made by the scientists who move. In the chapter, you say you threw them out. I hope you did not really throw them out. You just meant you were not using them in this chapter. I am assuming that MIT recruited Scott back to Cambridge for the benefit that his work would have on Pierre, but presumably Scott moved back in part for the benefit that Pierre is going to have on him. So that is just as interesting. It is a different issue, but it is just as interesting.

This next point is probably the biggest one I want to make. I started to say that you threw the baby out with the bathwater, and then when I thought about it, realized that is not quite the right metaphor. I think the metaphor here is you did not throw the baby out, but the bathwater itself is actually pretty interesting. What I mean by that is I would not have just reported difference-in-difference results. I would have actually reported some of the results before you do the difference-in-difference. So for example, I would have liked to have seen the picture represented hypothetically in figure 2C.2.

There is a solid line and a dotted line. I made this up. This is not data. But I am guessing that something like this is going on, that if we look at the whole pattern of citations over time from a work at the new location, they are getting more citations than they were getting at the old location. But we don't know that it looks like this. It might look like figure 2C.3. It may just be that you get a very rapid diffusion, which then fades out. And there are lots of other issues that one would like to understand. Now the causal interpretation of this is more complicated than the difference-in-difference, but before we go trying to get a really pure causal story, I think we should try to have a better sense of what it is we are explaining. What is actually

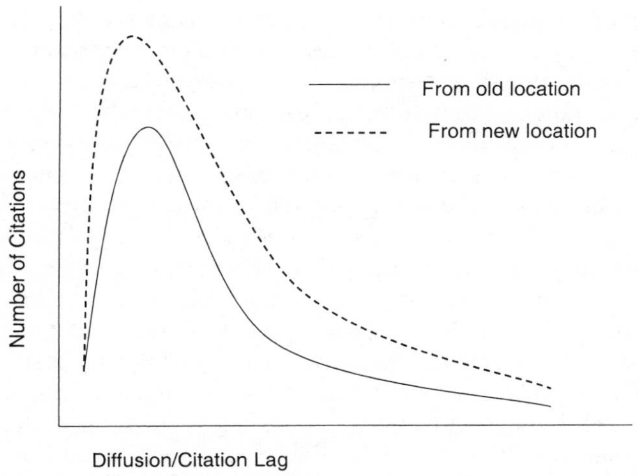

Fig. 2C.2 Postmove citations to premove output

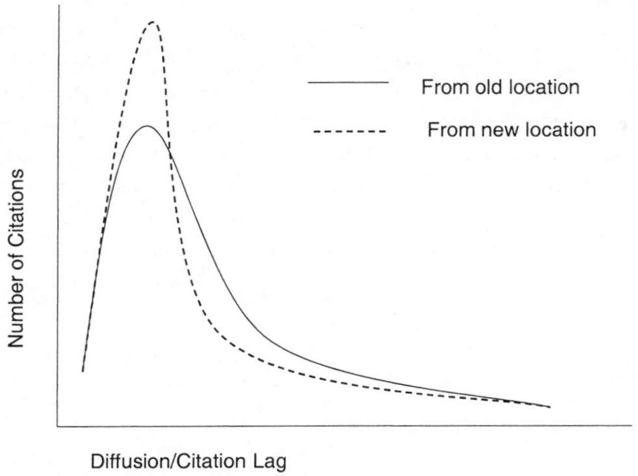

Fig. 2C.3 Postmove citations to premove output—alternative time path

going on here? And that is lost when we start by looking at the difference-in-difference result. So I think the chapter and the whole line of research would be much more interesting if you let us see the first order effects before we go to the comparison, because after all, it is already one difference. You do have something changing in terms of the scientist moving and I think that that is worth knowing something about.

So just a couple of final points. I think the normative speculations about mobility are really pushing it, because in some sense, what you are looking at are second order effects of what actually is affected both privately and publicly when somebody moves. So yes, you said they were speculative, so in that sense I cannot really convict you. But still, I found that very uncompelling. And then the last thing I would like to suggest is that you should put these data up on the web analogously to the NBER patent data set. And since one of the themes of this conference is a little bit of kind of history of the development of this field, I will tell you when Manuel and Rebecca and Bronwyn and I were first thinking about accumulating these data in the early 1990s, we actually had some extended discussions from a private return perspective in terms of our own careers. Should we hold on to this and write as many papers as we could or should we make it public so that other people could use it? I don't remember who took which side in the debate.

But the fact of the matter is, we put these data up, and I think this was before we, at least, were thinking about open source versus walled gardens or any of that stuff. We put all of the data on the web. I looked last night on Google Scholar. The paper that is the sort of handbook for using these data has 997 citations. So clearly from a private perspective, if our objective function is sort of prestige and so forth as measured by citations, we benefited professionally by making these data public. And so I would urge you to do the same. Google Scholar is doing some very similar work about massaging these various data. It seems to me it is socially wasteful for people to do that twice. So in some sense, maybe you guys should talk to them about some kind of joint venture where you would share the efforts to clean these data, to organize them in a way that would be useful for research.

3

The Effects of the Foreign Fulbright Program on Knowledge Creation in Science and Engineering

Shulamit Kahn and Megan MacGarvie

3.1 Introduction

The science and engineering workforce is becoming increasingly global. The share of science and engineering (S&E) doctoral degrees produced outside the United States has grown in recent years (National Science Foundation [NSF] *Science and Engineering Indicators* 2010), and some countries have increased their efforts to attract star scientists.[1] International migration of the highly skilled has become a hotly debated topic, with some experts pointing to "brain drain" (whereby the most talented citizens of a lower-income country are lured away by opportunities in countries like the United States) and others highlighting "brain circulation" (whereby individuals trained in the United States disseminate knowledge back to their home countries).[2] Many countries with relatively low levels of scientific activity subsidize the costs of doctoral education for their citizens in countries with cutting-edge research environments. Historically these investments have had limited success in the sense that many PhDs have not returned to their home countries. Some governments counter this tendency by requiring funded students to return home post-PhD. Alternatively, students may be encour-

Shulamit Kahn is associate professor at Boston University School of Management. Megan MacGarvie is associate professor at Boston University School of Management and a faculty research fellow of the National Bureau of Economic Research.

We thank the Institute for International Education and Jerry Murphy for the Fulbright directories. We thank Richard Freeman, Rodrigo Canales, Jenny Hunt, Carlos Serrano, Paula Stephan, Scott Stern, and participants in the NBER Rate and Direction preconference for helpful comments. This project is funded by National Science Foundation Grant SBE-0738371.

1. The Canada Research Chairs program and the Australian Research Council's Federation Fellowships offer incentives to attract researchers to these countries.

2. See Saxenian (2002).

aged to study under the US Fulbright Program, which also requires students return home post-PhD.

The Fulbright Foreign Student Program, established in 1946 and primarily sponsored by the US Department of State, is the main US government program that brings students from other countries to pursue graduate study in the United States.[3] Since its inception, it has given scholarships to more than 125,000 foreign students to do graduate work in the United States. The total budget of the Fulbright program was $374.4 million in fiscal year 2008.[4] The Department of State describes the Fulbright program as "our country's premier vehicle for intellectual engagement with the rest of the world." Students who receive a Fulbright Scholarship for study in the United States come on a J-1 student visa that requires them by law to leave the United States when they finish their education and to spend at least two years in their home country before they can return to work in the United States.

Despite the long history and apparent importance of this program, we could find no formal evaluation of this program done before 2005. In 2005, SRI International was commissioned by the Department of State to survey a group of Fulbright foreign student graduates and evaluate whether receipt of Fulbright funding had indeed fostered international understanding (SRI 2005). They did not evaluate the impact of these foreign Fulbright scholars on their home countries' intellectual environment or on their contribution to global knowledge.

More generally, little is known about whether any US graduate study sponsorship requiring foreign students to return to their home countries—be it through the Fulbright Foreign Student Program or through foreign governments' programs—has been successful in improving foreign countries' research capabilities. While the program may benefit home countries by increasing return flows of highly skilled human capital, these students may have fewer opportunities to do cutting-edge work because they are required to return to countries that have less funding for research and relatively inadequate scientific infrastructure. This may lower global knowledge creation compared to a situation without these return requirements.

Given the evidence on the importance of foreign-born scientists for research in science (Levin and Stephan 1999; Stephan and Levin 2001), as well as the United States' substantial financial commitment to the Foreign Fulbright Program, it seems reasonable to ask what impact the program has on the production of scientific knowledge in the United States itself. While the main objectives of the program are the furtherance of mutual understanding and foreign policy-related goals, we can also test the hypothesis that students supported by the Fulbright program and, therefore, required to

3. Also called the Fulbright Visiting Students Program.

4. Foreign governments contributed $74.2 million to this total, and private sources (both domestic and overseas) provided $65.9 million. The number of grants to foreign students studying in the United States was approximately twice the number of grants to US students studying overseas.

leave the United States contribute less to US-based research than otherwise similar foreign students.

Alternatively, research on knowledge flows across space has shown that connections between researchers are surprisingly persistent (Agrawal, Cockburn, and McHale 2006). With growth in the potential for brain circulation and international collaboration due to faster and cheaper international communication and travel, scientists returning to home countries may find it easy to continue to access knowledge produced in the United States and at top research institutions globally. By creating links between home countries and other countries, the Fulbright program may increase rates of international collaboration and knowledge diffusion.

One of the reasons that so little empirical attention has been given to this topic is that little data is available on what happens to foreign graduate students once they leave the United States. This chapter begins to fill this void, concentrating on foreign Fulbright PhD students in science and engineering (S&E). We have collected a data set that tracks the career progression of 488 PhD scientists of foreign origin trained at US universities. Half of the scientists in our sample received fellowship funding from the Fulbright Foreign Student Program, the other half were chosen to resemble the Fulbrights as closely as possible along observable dimensions. Our data set is unique in being the only data set of which we are aware that tracks the career progression of individual US-trained PhD scientists, whether they leave the United States or not.[5] We supplement our data with descriptive statistics on the Fulbrights from the SRI (2005) study and other Fulbright Program materials.

These data allow us to address the following questions:

1. Has the Fulbright program itself attracted a foreign student body different from the population of foreign students without this funding? Has it, for instance, made it more likely for foreign students to receive US PhDs in some S&E fields or from some countries, compared to those foreigners studying in the United States without Fulbrights?
2. Do the return requirements of the Fulbright program promote mobility of US-trained PhD scientists to foreign countries?
3. Do foreign S&E Fulbright students create more or less knowledge and have more or less impact on their fields compared to other foreign students?
4. In what ways do Fulbright students contribute to their home countries' scientific environment and the US scientific environment compared to comparable foreign students?
5. Does the Fulbright Program indeed foster US-foreign scientific collaboration?

5. One can obtain information on foreign-born scientists who remain in the United States from the NSF's SESTAT database. Also, Michael G. Finn's (2007) research provides valuable information on the stay rates of PhDs of foreign origin.

To preview our findings, we find that the distribution of Fulbright students across countries of origin is substantially different from the distribution of other graduate students. We find that the Fulbright program does encourage more mobility of US-trained PhD scientists to home countries. In terms of knowledge creation and diffusion, we find that Fulbrights from richer countries have publication and citation records similar to comparable PhDs of foreign origin without return requirements, while Fulbrights from poorer countries publish less and have fewer citations. However, the most profound effect might be on the location of article production. Fulbrights produce substantially more articles listing home country authors and substantially fewer articles listing US authors. Nevertheless, the Fulbright program does seem to have achieved its goal of increasing US-home country links by increasing collaboration between these countries.

Before presenting these results in detail, we give some background on the Fulbright Foreign Student Program itself.

3.2 Background on the Fulbright Foreign Student Program

The Fulbright Program was established by Congress in 1946 to "enable the government of the United States to increase mutual understanding between the people of the United States and the people of other countries." The Fulbright Program includes not only the Foreign Student Program, but also a US Student Program that awards scholarships to US citizens for study in foreign countries and a Scholars Program that sends scholars and professionals to research and lecture in other countries, both US citizens abroad and foreign citizens to the United States. It is funded primarily by annual appropriations of the US Department of State and the Department of Education but also receives additional support from universities, foreign governments, foundations and corporations, with some of this support in kind—including tuition waivers, housing, and stipends from some universities. The annual budget of the entire Fulbright program was over $374 million in FY2008 to 2009.

The Fulbright Foreign Student Program is the primary international exchange program for graduate students in the United States. Since its inception through 2009, the Foreign Student Program has brought more than 128,146 students to US graduate programs. In the last Annual Report available (2008 to 2009), there were 3,193 foreign students receiving Fulbright support to study in the United States. This is a small number compared to the 283,329 international students who were enrolled in graduate programs in 2008 to 2009 (IIE 2009).[6] Fulbright-supported students were, however, the vast majority of international students sponsored by the US government.

6. The IIE's Open Doors Report on International Students in the United States 2009 (http://www.iie.org/en/Research-and-Publications/Open-Doors/Open-Doors-Data-Tables/2009/International-Students).

Not all of the students on Fulbrights are in doctoral programs. In fact, according to the SRI (2005) evaluation of a sample of those who received Fulbrights between 1980 and 2000, only 36 percent reported receiving a Fulbright doctoral candidate grant, although 42 percent said that they produced a doctoral thesis as a result of the Fulbright program as of the SRI 2004 survey. More than 48 percent *had* a PhD by then.

The Institute of International Education (IIE) administers the program for Fulbrights from most areas. Two organizations share responsibility with IIE for the Fulbright Foreign Student Program for the Americas and the Middle East/Northern Africa, respectively.[7]

Foreign Fulbright students came from 139 different countries in academic year 2008 to 2009. Since the Fulbright program's inception, students have come from 178 different countries. Only 31 percent of the Fulbright foreign students in recent decades studied natural sciences or engineering (excluding social science) (SRI 2005). Because we are primarily interested in the creation and diffusion of scientific knowledge, the samples that we took were limited to this 31 percent.[8]

Fulbright recipients are required to leave the United States after completing their doctorates, since the program is intended to promote understanding of the United States abroad. It is possible to apply for a waiver of the foreign residency requirement if a student falls into one of several very restrictive and quite rare categories.[9] Also, Fulbright recipients may delay their departure for a period for educational purposes; for example, for two years

7. America-Mideast Educational and Training Services, Inc. (AMIDEAST) administers the program for most students applying from the Middle East and North Africa. Latin American Academic and Professional Programs (LASPAU) shares responsibility with IIE for the Fulbright Foreign Student Program for the Americas.

8. In recent years, the Fulbright program has increased funding for science and engineering students through the International Fulbright Science and Technology Award. However, because this scholarship was introduced at the end of our sample period, we do not have any PhD recipients in our sample from this program.

9. The first route is for the student to ask his country of origin to file a "no-objection" statement. While this approach may work for students whose J-1 status arose from scholarship funding from a foreign government, it is almost never considered grounds for waiving the foreign residence for Fulbrights whose funding comes from the US government (Conversation with BU ISSO January 2008). Waivers may also be obtained if an Interested Government Agency (IGA) files a request on behalf of the student, stating that the departure of the student will be detrimental to its interest and that of the public. Our conversations with experts suggest that these waivers are obtained only in rare and special circumstances. Medical doctors may also obtain a waiver if they agree to practice in a region of the United States with a shortage of health care professionals. A third reason for a waiver of the foreign-residency requirement is the threat of persecution, in which "an exchange visitor believes that he or she will be persecuted based on his/her race, religion, or political opinion if he/she were to return to his/her home country." Finally, applications for waivers may be filed on the basis of "Exceptional hardship to a United States citizen (or legal permanent resident) spouse or child of an exchange visitor." The State department warns "Please note that mere separation from family is not considered to be sufficient to establish exceptional hardship." http://travel.state.gov/visa/temp/info/info_1288.html (accessed February 17, 2008). Finally, years working for international organizations such as the UN or World Bank are considered equivalent to returning home. This loophole affects economists and others in policy-relevant fields more than the natural scientists in our study.

of a postdoctorate and/or for up to three years of occupational or practical training (OPT) on-the-job immediately following the completion of their studies.[10] Thus, in principle, a Foreign Fulbright recipient could remain in the United States for up to five years following the receipt of a PhD before having to leave the country. Moreover, after they spend two years their home country, the Fulbright-subsidized PhD can apply for a work visa and return to the United States. The two years in their home countries need not even be 730 consecutive days, but could be a combination of summers or semester-long visits abroad or both while spending the rest of the time in a United States postdoctorate or in OPT.

Nevertheless, the enforcement of these rules is sufficiently stringent that almost all foreign Fulbright PhD recipients left the United States for some period of time following the completion of their PhDs. We discuss this in section 3.5.

In the next section, we describe how Fulbright fellowships are allocated across fields, countries, and universities and how Fulbright recipients are selected.

3.3 Has the Fulbright Program Itself Attracted a Group of Foreign Students Different from Foreign Students without This Funding?

Fulbright recipients are not a random sample of all foreign students studying in the United States. The distribution of Fulbrights across countries of origin, across US universities, and across fields is not necessarily the same as the distribution of all foreign graduate students in the United States. In this subsection, we explain the source of these differences.

Countries: Foreign students apply for Fulbright Fellowships through the Fulbright Commission/Foundation or US Embassy in their home countries. If there is no Fulbright organization in the home country, students apply through the US Embassy. Fifty-one countries presently have Fulbright Commissions. Materials on the Fulbright website assure applicants that grantees are selected through "an open, merit-based competition."[11]

Fulbright Commissions in home countries are funded jointly by the United States and partner governments and include half resident Americans and half home country citizens. The commissions plan and implement educational exchanges (both foreigners to the United States and Americans to their country, both students and scholars) and recruit and nominate candidates for fellowships as well as perform other functions such as fundraising, engaging alumni, supporting American Fulbrights in their countries, and so forth. The US-based Fulbright Foreign Scholarship Board (FSB) has

10. The OPT status allows students to work in their field of study for the purposes of obtaining on-the-job training.

11. Available at: http://fulbright.state.gov/about/frequently-asked-questions, accessed Jan. 11, 2011.

input into the process and has final responsibility for the approval of selected candidates. In countries with no Fulbright Commission, the US Embassies and FSB play a greater role in selection.

While we do not have information on the precise kinds of considerations the commissions, embassies, or the FSB presently or in the past have taken into account in their choices among candidates, we can infer some from the facts. The most recent Fulbright Annual Report lists the number of Fulbright scholars from each country for the most recent year (AY2008 to 2009) and over the entire sixty-three years since its inception. These numbers and their comparisons indicate some clear priorities. First, there is wide variation in the number from each country, ranging from 1 (from Equatorial Guinea and others) to 21,819 from Germany over the entire 63-year period.[12] The variation is clearly not random. Germany was a full 17 percent of the total number of students over the 63 years, but only 8 percent in AY2008 to 2009, and other countries in Europe also saw their proportion of the total fall proportionately. On average, Europe sent 60 percent of the foreign Fulbright students from 1946 to 2009, but by the end of that period it was sending half of that percentage.

Why so many from some countries and not from others? First, it is clear that the changing patterns by country over time reflect political relationships between the United States and the sending country. Post–World War II, US foreign policy was heavily concentrated on rebuilding Europe and strengthening ties with Western European countries. Hence, while recently Fulbrights from Europe were 30 percent of the total, over the entire 62 years (including the post–World War II years), they were 60 percent. Soviet bloc countries did not send Fulbrights at all during the period of the United Soviet Socialist Republic (USSR). Africa has become more important over time so that, in the most recent year, 7.6 percent of Fulbright foreign students came from Africa, while the 62-year average was only 4.5 percent. The same trend is evident for the Middle East. In South America, Chile, and Brazil both had notable growth percentage-wise.

Second, the United States and foreign governments share the cost of the program to varying degrees, and countries willing to put considerable resources into funding Fulbright students send more students. In 1990, Germany contributed 71.4 percent of the budget of the German binational commission, while Japan contributed 62 percent of the budget for its program. Most other higher-income countries appear to have contributed in the range of 40 to 50 percent of the budget for their country.[13] Poorer countries contribute far smaller shares of the budget, generally less than 10 percent.[14]

12. The second largest was France at 6,469.

13. The UK contributes 40 percent, France 39 percent, South Korea 39 percent, the Netherlands 55 percent, and so forth.

14. Pakistan contributed approximately 1 percent of the budget in 1990, Colombia 2 percent, and Egypt 1.6 percent. (Annual Report of the Foreign Scholarship Board [FSB], 1991.)

Interestingly, Pakistan has recently become the single largest Fulbright program, thanks to a $90 million initiative funded by the US Agency for International Development (USAID) and the Pakistani Higher Education Commission that began in 2005.[15] A similar initiative was recently launched to increase Fulbright funding for science and engineering students from Indonesia. These initiatives, reflective of current US foreign policy goals, illustrate the extent to which the geographic emphasis of the Fulbright program can vary over time.

We also find evidence that countries with commissions send more Fulbright students than countries without commissions. Two thirds (66 percent to 71 percent) of Fulbright foreign students were from countries with Fulbright commissions, yet those countries with commissions held only 16 percent of the population of all countries that had ever sent Fulbrights.[16] Of course, those countries with commissions will tend to have closer political ties to the United States as well, so it is difficult to separate the contributions of commissions. Nevertheless, the existence of an ongoing body committed to maintaining Fulbright exchanges is bound to increase those exchanges. In addition, commissions help raise funds from nongovernmental sources to support grants.

Even in countries without commissions, there is a great deal of historicity in the patterns of foreign Fulbright students by country. One reason may be that some individual professors and universities are particularly enthusiastic about the Fulbright program and are likely to encourage students to apply. In the SRI (2005) survey, a full 60 percent said that they had received encouragement from their home university or professors to apply for a Fulbright scholarship.

Our data set includes people sponsored by the Fulbright program during the 1990s, in order to allow time to track post-PhD career progressions. In our data set, the Fulbrights come from 79 different countries—similar to the number of countries in the program overall in 2008 to 2009 with 10 or more students (FSB Annual Report 2009). The distribution by country is given in table 3.1. Our sample coincides with a period during which many Fulbright doctoral students in science and engineering came from Mexico. A full 38 percent of our sample comes from Mexico, although only 3 percent of all Fulbright foreign students were from Mexico in 2008 to 2009 and only 2.4 percent were from Mexico on average over the 62 years. This also reflects variation across countries in the use of the Fulbright program to fund students in doctoral rather than master's or other programs or in their tendency

15. "The USAID, HEC Expand Fulbright Scholarship Program; Initiative Called 'Investment In Pakistan's Future'" (press release of the US Embassy in Islamabad, April 6, 2005).

16. The two-thirds applies both to 2008 and 2009 and to the entire sixty-two years from numbers in the Fulbright Annual Report. The 16.1 and 71.5 is from the population numbers for 1993 to 1997 for Fulbright. Note that these are countries with commissions at the end of this period. Some of these countries did not have commissions earlier on.

Table 3.1 **Distribution of controls and Fulbrights by country of origin**

Country of origin	Controls	Fulbrights	Total	Country of origin	Controls	Fulbrights	Total
Argentina	3	4	7	Kenya	0	2	2
Armenia	1	0	1	Korea	8	0	8
Australia	0	4	4	Lesotho	0	1	1
Austria	3	3	6	Lithuania	0	1	1
Bangladesh	2	0	2	Macedonia	1	0	1
Belgium	1	3	4	Malawi	1	1	2
Bolivia	0	1	1	Malaysia	1	0	1
Botswana	0	1	1	Mexico	9	93	102
Brazil	11	0	11	Morocco	0	2	2
Bulgaria	1	0	1	Netherlands	4	5	9
Canada	8	0	8	Nigeria	2	0	2
Chile	3	0	3	Norway	2	6	8
China	18	0	18	Pakistan	2	0	2
Colombia	4	8	12	Panama	1	1	2
Costa Rica	0	3	3	Peru	2	2	4
Cote D'Ivoire	0	2	2	Philippines	3	2	5
Croatia	1	1	2	Poland	1	1	2
Cyprus	1	0	1	Portugal	2	19	21
Czech Republic	3	1	4	Romania	5	1	6
Denmark	2	4	6	Russia	9	0	9
Ecuador	1	0	1	Singapore	1	0	1
Egypt	2	0	2	Solomon Islands	0	1	1
Ethiopia	2	2	4	South Africa	0	7	7
Finland	2	5	7	Spain	6	7	13
France	2	0	2	Sri Lanka	1	0	1
Germany	10	0	10	Swaziland	1	0	1
Ghana	0	2	2	Sweden	2	3	5
Greece	4	7	11	Switzerland	3	1	4
Guatemala	1	1	2	Taiwan	7	0	7
Haiti	0	1	1	Tanzania	1	1	2
Hungary	3	1	4	Thailand	5	5	10
Iceland	2	7	9	Togo	0	2	2
India	25	0	25	Trinidad & Tobago	1	1	2
Indonesia	4	0	4	Turkey	11	1	12
Iran	1	0	1	UK	2	4	6
Iraq	1	0	1	Uganda	1	2	3
Ireland	2	1	3	Ukraine	5	0	5
Israel	3	6	9	Venezuela	2	1	3
Italy	5	3	8	Yugoslavia	3	0	3
Japan	5	0	5	Zimbabwe	1	0	1
Jordan	1	0	1	Total	244	244	488

to send students studying S&E rather than other fields. For example, despite the fact that Germany had the largest budget for Fulbright students in 1993, all but a handful of the German Fulbrights entering PhD programs in the United States in 1994 were enrolled in nondegree programs, presumably temporary exchange programs. Of the nineteen Spanish Fulbrights entering programs in 1994, only one was pursuing a doctorate in S&E, with the others enrolled in master's or nondegree programs, mostly in nonscientific fields. By contrast, of the ninety Mexican Fulbrights arriving in 1994, sixty-four enrolled in S&E doctorates.

Universities: The Institute of International Education (IIE), headquartered in New York City, facilitates the placement of many Fulbright nominees at academic institutions and communicates with Fulbrights during their stay in the United States. In some countries (e.g., Canada, France, Germany, and Australia, and formerly the UK), students apply directly to universities, in many cases applying for Fulbright funding once they have been accepted. For students from most other countries, the IIE works with the binational commission and the student to obtain a place at a university once the student has been awarded a Fulbright. The IIE also acts as a liaison with the university and often helps students obtain additional financial support from the university. In many countries, Fulbright commissions guide the Fellows toward particular US universities and are sometimes influenced by the availability of supplementary fellowship funding from the university or the lower tuition costs of public universities or both.[17] Finally, the Fulbright Foreign Scholarship Board's policies encourage geographic diversity, stating that "Every effort will be made to affiliate grantees at institutions in all geographic areas of the United States, and at all types and sizes of institutions, provided that such affiliation is not detrimental to the goal of providing the best possible academic experience for the grantee."[18]

The SRI (2005) survey gives us a sense of how many Fulbright foreign students end up being assigned and how many choose their institutions. Of their sample of Fulbright foreign students in 1980 and 2000, 47 percent said they knew which university they wanted to attend before applying for the Fulbright, and 29 percent were either assigned to the university or were given a choice between two universities. The remaining 24 percent did not know which school they wanted to attend before applying to the Fulbright, but were not assigned.

In the data set used in this chapter, 156 students or 32 percent of the sample obtained degrees from universities in the Northeast, and 122 (25 percent) obtained degrees from Midwestern universities. There were 90 degrees (18 percent) that came from Southern universities, and the remaining 120 students or 25 percent of the sample received degrees from Western universities. A large share of the universities in our sample are publicly funded.

Fields: Within the S&E area, table 3.2 gives the distribution by fields in our sample, using the NSF major field classifications further aggregated into

17. Conversation with IIE representative, June 2009.

18. Available at: http://fulbright.state.gov/fulbright/become/programwork/program-structure-and-rules.

Table 3.2 **Distribution of controls and Fulbrights, by first-listed field of study**

	Controls	Fulbrights	Total
Agricultural sciences	30	34	64
Biological sciences	47	53	100
Engineering & computer sciences	86	82	168
Earth/air/ocean sciences	21	17	38
Mathematics & statistics	21	22	43
Physical sciences	27	23	50
Environment science	12	13	25
Total	244	244	488

seven categories because of the small size of our sample. The distribution across fields is slightly different for Fulbrights and controls because this is the first field listed in the person's (ProQuest) dissertation record. Occasionally, people listed two or more fields and we sometimes had to match Fulbrights and controls on their second field. The two distributions are not significantly different from each other (the *P*-value of a Chi-square test is 0.965). We also matched the field division to the overall distribution across S&E fields among Fulbright foreign students 1980 to 2000 (SRI 2005) and found that this was also remarkably similar ($P = .9999$). Of all PhDs in science granted in 1996 (the year closest to our median year of degree for which data were available), 45 percent were in math, computer science, or engineering, while the equivalent figure in our data set is 43 percent.[19] Of all US PhDs in 1996, 55 percent were in the natural sciences, in contrast to 57 percent of our sample.

3.4 Data Set

In order to understand whether and how Fulbrights PhD scientists' careers unfold differently from the careers of other foreign students who received their PhDs in the United States, we have collected a sample of 244 Fulbright scholars who were receiving a Fulbright foreign student fellowship to study in a PhD program in a science or engineering field between 1993 and 2005. To create this sample, we took all Fulbright scholars who completed a PhD at the institution listed in the *Foreign Fulbright Fellows: Directory of Students* for whom we could identify a location for at least half of the post-PhD period and for whom we could identify a match. We wanted to match each of these Fulbrights with a non-Fulbright foreign student who was as similar as possible to the Fulbright in terms of research potential. The characteristics

19. Data on the distribution of doctorates across fields in 1996 comes from *NSF Science and Engineering Indicators 2000.*

that we a priori believed to be most relevant for future research output while being easily identifiable include institution, advisor/field, date of graduation and, where possible, region of origin. Therefore, we used the ProQuest Dissertations and Theses database to obtain information on the year of graduation and advisor and to identify a "control" student of foreign origin who did *not* have post-PhD location restrictions, whose location could also be found on the web for at least half of their post-PhD years, and who was similar along the previous dimensions, that is, he or she graduated from the *same* program in the *same* year and, whenever such a student existed, with the same advisor and from the same region.[20] Since students who receive substantial funding from their home country's government often are required to return for some period, we searched PhD acknowledgements for evidence of foreign governmental funding and did not include the student as a control if we found any.

When several potential control students were identified for a single Fulbright fellow, we chose the student who came from the same or similar countries as those represented in the Fulbright sample. Table 3.1 lists the countries of origin of our Fulbright and control samples. It is clear that the distribution of students across countries in the treatment and control groups, while similar, is not identical. There are several reasons for this. First, the distribution of Fulbrights across countries is affected by all of those factors we discussed earlier—most notably the past and present government policies and the presence of commissions or specific individual or institutional boosters. Second, because many students from certain countries receive government funding, we were less likely to select controls from those countries. There are two cases where the differences in the numbers of Fulbrights and controls are substantial enough to be noted. There are no Fulbrights in our sample from China or India so we tried to avoid sampling controls from these countries, but when a suitable control could not be found from another country we allowed control students of Chinese and Indian origin in the sample. Also, in our sample there are many Fulbrights from Mexico but few controls since most of the Mexican students in the United States without Fulbright fellowships are subsidized by their governments. Data appendix A gives a more detailed description of how we identified control students, made sure that they were not getting major funding from their own government, searched for the locations of both the Fulbrights and their controls, and found their publication and citation information.

It is possible that our sample differs in important respects from the population of Fulbrights or foreign students in general due to our method of

20. In cases where there was no control student with the same advisor in the same year, we identified a student with the same advisor graduating within three years before or after the Fulbright. If no students met the latter criteria, we chose a student graduating in the same year in the same major field, but with a different advisor.

collecting data. Particularly, it is possible that the students for whom we are able to find location data over the Internet will be more research-active than students we were unable to find, because one of our sources for location data is the publication record itself. However, it is important to note that, because we apply the same search criteria for all the students in our database, any biases introduced by our procedure apply equally to Fulbrights and controls.

In the following sections, we use these data to compare mobility, publications, citations, and collaboration patterns for the 488 foreign students who received US doctorates in S&E. As explained earlier, the sample was constructed with the aim of choosing controls that are observationally identical to the Fulbright students. Nevertheless, in the regressions we also include control variables to account for any differences that may exist between treatment and control groups as well as differences across the 244 pairs. All of the analysis includes the following control variables:

Ranking of PhD Institution: We use the (log of the) 1995 relative ranking of the US PhD institution (by field) from the National Research Council (Goldberger, Maher, and Ebert Flattau 1995) as a control for the quality of PhD training. Note that a lower rank signifies higher quality.

Field Dummies: Fields differ widely in the number of articles published per year and even in conventions regarding citing precedents. We categorized each student by the first field listed in their (ProQuest) dissertation record. We divided fields into the seven groups listed in table 3.2.[21] Since the control was chosen from the same department as the Fulbright, the distribution across fields of study should be exactly identical. There are differences, however, since often the fields specified in ProQuest are quite narrowly defined and many dissertations list more than one field. Students of the same advisor and department may list different fields and, even if the fields listed are identical, might choose to list them in different order.

PhD Year Dummies: The PhD year is divided into 6 categories (<1995, 1995 and 1996, 1997 and 1998, 1999 and 2000, 2000, 2001 and 2002, and >2002.)[22] Table 3.3 divides our sample by PhD year and we once again see a similar but not identical distribution between Fulbrights and controls, since the control was the closest available foreign student within three years

21. Because of the limited number of observations, we could not meaningfully divide the field dummies into more categories and we were unable to converge the instrumented model for most output variables. We experimented with different field groupings and qualitative results were not affected.

22. While in principle we would have wanted to use a full set of dummies for year and years since graduation, in practice we found it difficult to estimate some of our models including a full set of dummies. We *have* estimated some regressions with dummies for each year and did not find results to differ substantially from the results using the more grouped year variables. This is likely due to the fact that our samples of controls and Fulbrights are similar in terms of PhD year.

Table 3.3 Distribution of controls and Fulbrights, by year of PhD

Year of PhD	Controls	Fulbrights	Total
1991	1	0	1
1992	2	0	2
1993	7	5	12
1994	15	17	32
1995	11	23	34
1996	31	27	58
1997	45	36	81
1998	38	40	78
1999	33	34	67
2000	28	22	50
2001	13	22	35
2002	9	10	19
2003	7	6	13
2004	2	1	3
2005	2	1	3
Total	244	244	488
Average	1997.881	1997.897	1997.889

of the Fulbright's PhD (although the mean and median year of graduation are the same.) Note that since our variables cover the span of time from PhD until 2007, PhD year also proxies for the length of the period over which the person can accumulate publications, citations, and collaborations.

Gender: We obtained data on the gender of the scientist using information from web searches (e.g., photographs, the use of personal pronouns in web bios), using a web-based algorithm for identifying the probable genders of given names when no other information was available.[23]

Log of Real GDP Per Capita of Home Country (Five Years before PhD Receipt): The gross domestic product (GDP) per capita of the scientist's country of origin may affect the quality of predoctoral training or the average financial resources available for the student's doctoral education and may also capture the standard of living in the environment of returnees.

Tables 3.2, 3.3 and 3.4 give descriptive statistics on the control variables.

3.5 Does the Fulbright Program Promote Mobility of US-trained PhDs to Foreign Countries?

Most Fulbrights return to their home country for some time post-PhD, as required. Only 12.3 percent of our Fulbright sample appeared to have remained in the United States continuously and 23.4 percent appeared never to have been in their home country post-PhD and thus to not have fulfilled

23. The gender-guessing program is found at: http://www.gpeters.com/names/baby-names.php.

their home country residency requirement, although they could have fulfilled the requirement in short segments that we did not observe. For the other 76.6 percent of the Fulbright students in our sample, we were able to find evidence that they did spend some time in their home country after receiving their PhDs, compared to only 36.1 percent of our control group of US-educated foreign-origin non-Fulbrights.

We observe our sample of 244 Fulbright scholars for a total of 2,299 person-years post-PhD. 76.4 percent of these years are spent outside the United States and 63.9 percent in the home country itself. In contrast, the 244 controls spent only 34.5 percent of their 2,359 observed person-years outside the United States and 27.9 percent in their home countries. This US stay rate of approximately 65 percent for control students is nearly identical to the average stay rate estimated in a much larger sample by Finn (2007), who found that 67 percent of foreign students who received their doctorates in 1998 (close to the average PhD year in our sample) were observed in the United States in 2003. The top row of table 3.4 documents these dramatic differences in the rates of return to home countries between Fulbrights and controls.

We have empirically modeled the number of years spent either outside of the United States or in the home country as a function of the standard control variables listed earlier, including PhD year dummies. Each dependent variable is estimated using Poisson estimation in two different specifications related to the Fulbright variable:

1. With a single Fulbright dummy variable
2. With a Fulbright dummy and an interaction term between the Fulbright and the log of GDP per capita of their home country to allow different effects for different kinds of countries

The impact on location of being a Fulbright estimated from these regressions are given in table 3.5.[24] The results in this table indicate that Fulbrights of all income per capita levels spend substantially more time outside the United States than do controls, and spend this time in their home countries. The effect is largest for Fulbrights from lower-income countries, who spend 240 percent more time outside the United States than controls. The vast majority of the time they spend outside the United States is spent in their home countries. Even Fulbrights from countries at the 90th percentile of GDP per capita spend about 49 percent more years in their home country than do controls. There is no significant difference in the number of years spent in countries that are neither the United States nor the home country, with the difference being particularly miniscule for the wealthier countries.[25]

24. Full equations available upon request from authors.
25. Differences can be seen by comparing columns (2) and (4) of table 3.5.

Table 3.4 Summary statistics on controls and Fulbrights

	Mean	Standard deviation	Min.	Max.
Location				
Proportion of post-PhD yrs spent in the US (controls) (controls)	0.655	0.476	0	1
Proportion of post-PhD years spent in US (Fulbrights)	0.236	0.425	0	1
Proportion of post-PhD years spent at home (controls)	0.279	0.449	0	1
Proportion of post-PhD years spent at home (Fulbrights)	0.639	0.48	0	1
Background characteristics				
Female gender	0.25	0.433	0	1
Rank of PhD program	37.819	34.614	1	175
ln(home country GDP per capita)	8.809	0.88	5.817	10.22
Publications and citations pre- and post-PhD				
# articles published before graduation	2.873	7.310385	0	147
# first-authored articles published before graduation	1.434	1.878169	0	15
# high-impact or first- or last-authored articles published before graduation	0.561	1.15898	0	9
Total number of articles published	10.111	20.70215	0	333
First-authored articles	3.871	5.223715	0	51
High-impact articles	4.779	17.33071	0	331
Last-authored articles	2.463	5.543062	0	48
Total forward citations	110.084	180.3952	0	655
Total forward citations to first-authored articles	45.867	74.43971	0	268
Total forward citations to last-authored articles	13.387	27.12083	0	98
Total forward citations to high-impact articles	58.607	111.321	0	402
Collaboration				
Total publications with a US author	7.494	18.612	0	333
Total publications with a home-country author	3.516	10.333	0	128
Total publications with a non-US, non-home-country author	3.240	16.118	0	333
Total publications with a home-country author excluding self	1.887	7.142	0	106
Total publications with a US author excluding self	5.031	16.963	0	333
Total publications with a non-US, non-home country author excluding self	2.969	16.005	0	333
Total publications with an author in the home country AND an author in the US	1.445	5.048	0	83
Total publications with an author in the home country AND an author in another non-US country	1.059	5.345	0	83

Table 3.5 **Proportional effect of Fulbright on location estimation method: Poisson; values given as proportional difference between Fulbrights and controls**

	(1)	(2)	(3)	(4)
Dependent variable:	Years outside the US		Years in the home country	
	Average impact of being a Fulbright			
Fulbright dummy	1.106***		1.175***	
p-value	0.0000		0.0000	
	Adding interaction with log real GDP (per capita of home country 5 yrs prior to PhD)			
25th pctile		2.423***		2.749***
p-value		0.0004		0.001
50th pctile		1.423***		1.514***
p-value		0.000		0.000
75th pctile		0.808***		0.792***
p-value		0.000		0.000
90th pctile		0.537***		0.485**
p-value		0.0018		0.019

Notes: See text for list of control variables included. Robust standard errors in parentheses. Average effect calculated as $\exp(\text{Beta}_{\text{Fulbright}}) - 1$. Effect at income levels calculated as $\exp(\text{Beta}_{\text{Fulbright}} + \text{logGDP*Beta}_{\text{FulbrightXLogGDP}})) - 1$

*Significant at the 10 percent level.

**Significant at the 5 percent level.

***Significant at the 1 percent level.

3.6 Do Foreign S&E Fulbright Students Create Less or More Knowledge and Have Less or More Impact on Their Fields Compared to Other Foreign Students?

In this section, we empirically measure whether Fulbrights publish more or less than other foreign students and whether they are cited more or less. The publication and citation data were taken from information on the Fulbright and control PhDs' publication histories from *ISI's Web of Science.*[26] From the *Web of Science,* we obtained information for the following publication-related variables.

Publication Counts: The number of articles on which the scientist is a contributing author. This may be a noisy measure of research output when articles have many authors.

First-Authored Publication Counts: The number of articles each year on which the scientist is the first author. In science, the first author is the major contributor to the research.

Last-Authored Publication Counts: The number of articles each year on which the scientist is the last author. In science, typically the last author will

26. Authors were matched to publications using information on post-PhD locations, authors' middle names, fields of research, coauthors on other work, and so forth.

be the person running the lab, who is often the Principal Investigator (PI) on the research grant funding the research. This variable is an indicator of the author's ability to secure research funding.

Publications in High-Impact Journals: The number of each year's publications in the top 50 percent of journals *in that field* as ranked by ISI's impact factors. We made this measure field-specific because different fields have very different conventions about citations. We did this by calculating impact relative to the mean impact within each field.

Forward Citation Counts: The total cumulative number of citations received *by articles published,* which proxy publication's impact on scholarship. We model citations for each of the four classes of articles previously described.[27] Table 3.4 displays the average levels of these publication and citation variables.

There are two general types of reasons why the Fulbrights and the controls might have different research productivity post-PhD. The first, and the one we are interested in testing, is that the return requirement of the Fulbright program leads otherwise identical PhD scientists to pursue different kinds of careers and to use their scientific knowledge in different ways, leading to different publication and citation patterns. The second is that non-US residents who get Fulbright funding to study in the United States are inherently different in ability or research proclivity from other non-US residents who study in the United States. The first of these reasons implies a causal impact of Fulbright on productivity while the second implies differences due to heterogeneity and selection.

We constructed our match between the Fulbright and control students with the goal of choosing controls that are as similar as possible in inherent ability and proclivity for research in order to isolate the causal impact of Fulbright scholarships. The criteria we used for matching were based on our priors about the characteristics most relevant for research output—institution, advisor/field, date of graduation, and region of origin. To the extent that US universities can observe the differences between students, the university admissions procedure may ensure that the Fulbrights and non-Fulbrights they admit to any specific department are likely to have equivalent abilities.

Moreover, whenever possible we have matched not just by institution and department but also by advisor. Faculty typically apply their own standards to the students they choose to advise and support on their grants.

Nevertheless, there may remain inherent differences between controls and Fulbrights. The sign of these differences is not obvious. Since Fulbright

27. Due to the extreme skewness of their distributions, citation counts are winsorized at the 95th percentile. Results are qualitatively similar if truncated at 99th percentile or not truncated at all.

recipients are chosen by merit, this would lead Fulbrights to have greater research potential than others studying in the United States. Similarly, as our earlier description suggested, Fulbrights may not be assigned to the best university that would have accepted them, again leading Fulbrights to be better than controls.

On the other hand, there are reasons why Fulbrights may be worse than controls. Fulbright commissions, Embassy staff, and the Fulbright Foreign Scholarship Board (FSB) may avoid funding the *most* promising students if they are believed to be less likely to spend their careers in their home country. Also, and perhaps most pertinently, many excellent students may not pursue Fulbright fellowships if they have strong preferences to remain in the US post-PhD or can afford to avoid funding that restricts their futures or both, and particularly if they receive funding directly from the universities. Finally, US departments may lower their admission standards for graduate students with outside funding.

In addition to our careful matching process, we have done several other things to remove or evaluate possible biases or both due to differing inherent research potential of Fulbrights and controls. First, we control for the GDP per capita of the home country during the doctoral program, since paired Fulbrights and controls often come from different countries. Second, in some specifications we include as control variables three measures of students' research output while in graduate school (including the year of PhD completion because of the lag between writing an article and getting it published), which we believe to be a good proxy for inherent ability. Including these pregrad publication variables may overcontrol in the sense that at least some of the Fulbright-control differences in pregrad publications may also be a result of being a Fulbright. For instance, if Fulbrights believe that they must return home to a nonresearch job, they may be less committed to getting their PhD research published. On the other hand, if Fulbrights are more concerned about having good chances of leaving their home country after two (or more) years of post-PhD residence, they may feel they need stronger credentials.

The specific pregrad publication variables included in these specifications are *total articles written while in graduate school (defined as all articles published up to and including the year following PhD receipt), first-authored publications while in graduate school, and high-impact first- or last-authored publications while in graduate school.* Note that first-authored articles are more prevalent during the PhD year than later. In fact, for the average student with any pregrad publications, 60 percent of the articles published during this graduate school time were first-authored, probably publications from their thesis work for whom the PhD student was the primary author.

Table 3.6 gives results of Poisson regressions of four measures of publications postgraduate school—total publications, first-authored publications,

Table 3.6 **Effect on Fulbright on publications and citations, coefficients and standard errors from Poisson regressions**

	(1) Total publications	(2) First-authored publications	(3) Last-authored publications	(4) High-impact publications	(5) Total (forward) citations	(6) Cites to first-authored pubs	(7) Cites to last-authored pubs	(8) Cites to high-impact pubs
Panel A: Average impact of being a Fulbright								
Fulbright	–0.253	–0.13	–0.314*	–0.479*	–0.215*	–0.096	–0.115	–0.321**
	(0.161)	(0.118)	(0.191)	(0.262)	(0.129)	(0.130)	(0.169)	(0.155)
Panel B: Adding pre-PhD publication controls								
Fulbright	–0.064	–0.064	–0.229	–0.224	–0.144	–0.035	–0.03	–0.288*
	(0.123)	(0.105)	(0.166)	(0.181)	(0.123)	(0.123)	(0.166)	(0.153)
Panel C: Adding interaction with log real GDP (per capita of home country 5 yrs prior to PhD)								
Fulbright	–2.566	–3.204**	–7.179***	–1.914	–5.105***	–4.652***	–5.110**	–6.107***
	(2.029)	(1.394)	(2.526)	(3.152)	(1.724)	(1.775)	(2.371)	(2.009)
Fulbright*GDP	0.256	0.342**	0.750***	0.157	0.537***	0.504***	0.546**	0.633***
	(0.228)	(0.154)	(0.280)	(0.354)	(0.188)	(0.193)	(0.255)	(0.219)
Panel D: Adding pre-PhD publication controls as well as interaction with log real GDP								
Fulbright	–2.054	–1.975*	–4.920***	–1.88	–3.411**	–2.787*	–3.631*	–4.274**
	(1.396)	(1.120)	(1.831)	(1.985)	(1.608)	(1.578)	(2.181)	(1.958)
Fulbright*GDP	0.221	0.213*	0.512**	0.183	0.359**	0.304*	0.394*	0.437**
	(0.152)	(0.122)	(0.199)	(0.214)	(0.175)	(0.172)	(0.234)	(0.216)

Notes: See text for list of control variables included. Robust standard errors in parentheses.
*Significant at the 10 percent level.
**Significant at the 5 percent level.
***Significant at the 1 percent level.

last-authored publications, and publications in high-impact journals—and citations to these publications. All equations include controls for field, PhD year, school rank, gender, and log of home GDP (five years before PhD receipt). The table lists only the coefficients on the Fulbright variables. Coefficients of all control variables for panel C are included as appendix B. All other results are available on request from the authors.

Panel A includes the coefficients on a single Fulbright dummy (without controls for pre-PhD publications). While the differences between Fulbrights and controls are all negative, very few of these measures are significant. At the 10 percent level of significance, Fulbrights have significantly fewer last-authored and high-impact publications and overall citations. Citations to high-impact publications, however, are significantly lower at the 5 percent level. Controlling for pregraduation research output, in panel B, we find no significant differences with the exception of cites to high-impact articles, which is now significant only at the 10 percent level. If this were all we had estimated, results would be very inconclusive.

However, a single dummy can obscure very disparate effects for Fulbrights from different backgrounds. Panel C allows the effect of the Fulbright dummy vary by GDP per capita by including an interaction term between the Fulbright dummy and GDP per capita. The interaction term is significantly positive for both first-authored and last-authored publications and for all four measures of citations. These results indicate that the impact of the Fulbright program on publications and citations differs across countries, with the effect becoming less negative (or even positive) as income increases. To measure the net effect and test its significance, in table 3.7 we report the percentage effect of being a Fulbright at four different percentiles levels of home-country GDP per capita.[28] The impacts are translated in the proportional difference between a Fulbright and a control at each income level.[29]

At very low GDP levels—the 25th percentile of all countries—the effect of being a Fulbright is significantly negative for all output measures. Fulbrights at this level have approximately 50 percent fewer total, first-authored, and highly cited publications and 82 percent fewer last-authored publications. The effect on citations is also large, with 86 percent fewer total citations and 77 percent fewer citations to high impact publications. Even at the 50th income percentile, while Fulbright-control differences fall by on average a third from their values at the 25th percentile, they remain highly significant. However, at the 75th percentile, effects are much smaller and none are significant for any publication or citation measure. Finally, Fulbrights from rich countries—at the 90th percentile of the income

28. The percentiles are taken from the Penn macroeconomic tables, for the year 1992—five years before the median PhD year in our sample.

29. These impacts are calculated as $\exp(\text{Beta}_{\text{Fulbright}} + \ln(\text{cutoffGDP})^{*}\text{Beta}_{\text{FulbrightXLogGDP}})) - 1$ from panel B table 3.6 results.

Table 3.7 **Effect of Fulbright on publications and citations at different levels of GDP per capita of home country (5 years prior to PhD)**

	(1) Total publications	(2) First-authored publications	(3) Last-authored publications	(4) High-impact publications	(5) Total (forward) citations	(6) Cites to first-authored pubs	(7) Cites to last-authored pubs	(8) Cites to high-impact pubs
25th pctile	–0.502***	–0.504***	–0.817***	–0.535*	–0.860***	–0.621***	–0.672***	–0.772***
p-value	0.009	0.000	0.000	0.059	0.000	0.000	0.000	0.000
50th pctile	–0.343***	–0.282**	–0.587***	–0.449***	–0.642***	–0.344***	–0.407**	–0.547***
p-value	0.008	0.011	0.000	0.007	0.000	0.008	0.015	0.000
75th pctile	–0.169	–0.016	–0.177	–0.363	–0.205	0.042	–0.020	–0.188
p-value	0.292	0.902	0.295	0.053	0.454	0.764	0.904	0.154
90th pctile	–0.053	0.172	0.207	–0.310	0.239	0.348	0.295	0.121
p-value	0.839	0.408	0.563	0.282	0.736	0.155	0.308	0.618

Note: Excluding pregrad pubs. Corresponds to panel C of table 3.6. Reported effects equal $\exp(\text{Beta}_{\text{Fulbright}} + \text{logGDP*Beta}_{\text{FulbrightXLogGDP}}) - 1$.

distribution—are not only significantly different from controls from similar countries for any publication or citation measure, but the point estimates of their difference are positive for six out of the eight measures of research productivity and impact.

Panel D adds measures of pregraduation publications into the regressions. This adds additional controls for heterogeneity in research ability and research proclivity, but may overcontrol if return requirements affect pre-PhD publications as well as post-PhD ones. We have calculated the effects of being a Fulbright at different income levels for this specification as well (available upon request from authors). Overall, they tell the same story as table 3.7. The magnitudes of the effects are remarkably similar, but for some dependent variables the statistical significance of the effect at the 50th percentile of GDP per capita is weaker.

Finally, as we mentioned earlier, a large number of the Fulbrights in our data set were from Mexico. This could be problematic if Fulbrights from Mexico were somehow different from other Fulbrights. To investigate this, we reestimated panel C of table 3.6 adding in an interaction term between a Mexico dummy and the Fulbright dummy (as well as the Mexico dummy itself.) For seven of the eight output measures, the Mexico interaction was insignificant, with an average p-value of 0.67.) In other words, Mexican Fulbrights were not different from other Fulbrights of similar income levels. However, for one measure, cites to first-authored articles, the interaction term with Mexico was significantly positive (5 percent level), meaning that Fulbrights from Mexico were more likely than Fulbrights from similar GDP countries to publish cited first-authored articles. We conclude that overall, the impact of the Fulbright program is similar for Mexicans and those from countries with similar GDP per capita, but that the negative impact on non-Mexican Fulbrights from middle income countries might be larger than indicated in table 3.7.[30]

To summarize results on publications and citations, research productivity and research impact of Fulbrights from poor countries is lower than that of comparable non-Fulbrights. Fulbrights differ most from controls in publishing articles in high-impact journals. Fulbrights are not significantly different from controls once income rises to the 75th percentile, with the exception of last-authored publications. Thus, even in countries at this GDP level, scientists appear to be affected by the return requirement in running their own labs (to the extent this is reflected by last-authorship). Finally, Fulbrights from the very richest countries (such as Canada and Western Europe) succeed as well as—or better than—controls from similar countries both in terms of publishing and in getting their work noticed around the world.

30. Mexico's 1992 GDP per capita was between the 50th and 75th percentile.

3.7 In What Ways do Fulbright Students Contribute to Their Home Countries' and the United States' Scientific Environments Compared to Comparable Foreign Students?

In this section, we examine the publication output of Fulbrights and controls to determine the extent to which the Fulbright program promotes knowledge production in different countries. We use information on the location(s) of the author(s) of the articles in our data set as an indicator of where papers where produced. Unfortunately, for the period under study, ISI did not link each institution with a particular coauthor, so we are limited in the kinds of collaboration variables we can calculate. We construct the following variables based on the articles authored by the people in our sample:

1. The total number of articles listing an author in the home country.
2. The total number of articles listing an author in the United States.
3. The total number of articles listing an author in a third country (not the home country and not the United States).
4. The total number of articles listing an author in the home country excluding those at the institution of the focal scientist.[31]
5. The total number of articles listing an author in the United States excluding those at the institution of focal scientist.
6. The total number of articles listing an author in a third country (not home and not the United States) excluding those at the institution of the focal scientist.
7. Total publications with an author in the home country and an author in the United States.
8. Total publications with an author in the home country and an author in a third country.

Table 3.4 gives averages for these variables. Note that collaboration variables 1, 2 and 3 are the same as 4, 5 and 6 except that the latter ones exclude the student's own institution from the count. The measures including the scientist him- or herself is a useful measure of the extent to which the Fulbright program promotes the creation of knowledge in a particular location, either through collaboration or through scientists' locations. The second set of variables allows us to ask whether Fulbright recipients are more likely to collaborate with *other* scientists in other home countries, United States or third-country institutions respectively, capturing spillover effects.

We begin, in the first panel of table 3.8, by examining the average effect of the Fulbright program on knowledge production in the home country,

31. We would have preferred to use the total number of articles coauthored by someone else from the home country, whatever institution they were at. This was not possible to calculate from *Web of Science* data from this period.

Table 3.8 **Effect of Fulbright on location of articles and collaboration, coefficients and standard errors from Poisson regressions**

	(1) Total publications with any home co. author	(2) Total publications with any US author	(3) Total publications with any 3rd co. author	(4) Total publications w. any home co. author excl self	(5) Total publications with any US coauthor excl self	(6) Total publications with any 3rd co. author excl self	(7) Total publications with authors in home AND US	(8) Total publications with authors in home AND 3rd co.
	Panel A: Average impact of being a Fulbright							
Fulbright	0.566**	–0.646***	–0.144	0.393	–0.610***	–0.159	0.190	0.394
	(0.250)	(0.177)	(0.334)	(0.316)	(0.225)	(0.352)	(0.297)	(0.400)
	Panel B: Adding pre-PhD publication controls							
Fulbright	0.787***	–0.456***	0.367**	0.717**	–0.337**	0.399**	0.502**	0.903**
	(0.244)	(0.125)	(0.181)	(0.298)	(0.145)	(0.189)	(0.211)	(0.387)
	Panel C: Adding interaction with log real GDP (per capita of home country 5 yrs prior to PhD)							
Fulbright	2.588	–2.102	0.131	2.361	–0.18	0.711	7.072*	7.411
	(3.016)	(2.306)	(3.680)	(3.445)	(2.755)	(3.958)	(4.178)	(5.433)
Fulbright*GDP	–0.221	0.161	–0.03	–0.216	–0.048	–0.096	–0.752	–0.756
	(0.334)	(0.260)	(0.419)	(0.379)	(0.313)	(0.451)	(0.467)	(0.600)
	Panel D: Adding pre-PhD publication controls as well as interaction with log real GDP							
Fulbright	2.793	–1.769	–2.003	1.681	–0.528	–1.852	5.915**	4.664
	(2.250)	(1.592)	(1.910)	(2.139)	(1.798)	(1.938)	(2.679)	(3.211)
Fulbright*GDP	–0.221	0.146	0.263	–0.107	0.021	0.25	–0.598**	–0.411
	(0.251)	(0.174)	(0.208)	(0.232)	(0.198)	(0.211)	(0.296)	(0.360)

Note: See text for list of control variables included. Robust standard errors in parentheses.
*Significant at the 10 percent level.
**Significant at the 5 percent level.
***Significant at the 1 percent level.

controlling for the GDP per capita of the home country and other covariates but not controlling for pregrad research output (panel A). We find that Fulbrights produce many more articles (76 percent) that list an author in the home country than do controls ceteris paribus (column 1), an expected result given the location restrictions of Fulbrights.[32] Also expected, Fulbrights produce significantly fewer articles with at least one US author than controls, 48 percent fewer (column 2). Fulbrights do not, on average, author significantly more articles that list an address in a third (nonhome, non-US) country (column 3). Nor do they produce more articles from the home country after excluding the author's own affiliation (column 4).

However, panel B, which controls for pre-PhD publications, tells a somewhat different story. It shows that Fulbrights are significantly different from controls across all collaboration measures and that the magnitude of Fulbright on most collaboration variables is larger than without these controls. Further investigation shows that the differences between panels A and B are primarily due to a handful of people in fields with large labs who had many publications both before and after PhD receipt, each publication having many authors due to the large lab team. Thus, the pre-PhD publication variables are serving as a control for fields with large labs and many authors per article. Moreover, the endogeneity problems caused by including pre-PhD controls is less relevant for collaboration variables than for publication variables.[33] Taken together, this suggests that the panel B results are probably a better measure of the impact of Fulbrights' return requirements on collaboration.

In panel B, controlling for pregrad publications, Fulbrights have even more additional (postgrad) home country publications than do controls (120 percent more) and this remains almost as large when the Fulbright him- or herself is excluded. Fulbrights are also significantly more likely to collaborate with third country authors whether or not the Fulbright him- or herself is excluded, with around a 50 percent difference. The only effect that is smaller in panel B than in panel A—although still significant—is the lower level of publications with a US author, which drops to between 29 percent to 37 percent depending on whether the Fulbright is excluded.[34]

Perhaps more interesting than evidence on publications by location is evidence on collaboration across countries. Controlling for pre-PhD publications, Fulbrights produce significantly more articles that list both a home-country author and a US author (column 7, 65 percent more) or a home-

32. Percentages calculated as exp(beta) – 1.

33. Thus, in the publication and citation analysis, pre-PhD publications and post-PhD publications might both be negatively affected by the return requirement of the Fulbright. However, it is more difficult to see why the possibly negative impact of return requirements on pre-PhD publications would be capturing the same factors that affect later collaboration.

34. It is not surprising that results concerning the United States or third countries do not change when excluding the Fulbrights themselves, since few Fulbrights live outside their home country.

country author and a third-country author (column 8, 147 percent more). In other words, the return requirement does lead to more collaboration between the home country and other countries including the US.

Panel C of table 3.8 adds an interaction between Fulbright and the log of real GDP per capita, similar to earlier tables. Contrary to our results on publications and citations, in no instance does the impact of collaboration differ significantly by GDP level, even at the 10 percent level.[35]

Controlling for pregraduation research (in panel D of table 3.8) does not change our qualitative results and particularly does not change our conclusion that the impact of Fulbright on the collaboration and authorship variables does not depend on GDP per capita, with one important exception. Controlling for pregrad publications, while Fulbrights overall tend to have more publications with a home-country author and a US author, this impact is limited to those from lower income home countries. Thus, the coefficient of the interaction term between GDP per capita and Fulbright column in column (7) is significantly negative. Using this coefficient, Fulbrights from median GDP countries have 144 percent more home-country US collaborations than controls. However, at the 90th percentile of per capita GDP, the difference is tiny (0.04 percent) and insignificant.

To summarize the main findings of table 3.8, we find that Fulbrights on average stimulate more articles authored in their home countries and fewer articles authored in the United States. Fulbrights also stimulate collaborations between a home-country author (presumably themselves) and a US author or a third-country author. These effects are true irrespective of GDP levels. However, it is likely that the huge increase in home-country and US collaborations is limited to those from low or middle income countries.

3.8 Conclusion

The Foreign Fulbright Program imposes a legal requirement that students funded by the program return to their home countries before applying for a work visa in the United States. The program has a major impact on the postgraduation location choices of US-trained, foreign-born scientists, with Fulbrights spending more than twice as many postgraduation years abroad. The effect is particularly large for students from countries with low per capita GDP, countries that are not otherwise attractive destinations for PhD recipients in science and engineering. This flow of highly trained human capital to lower income countries, which would not otherwise have occurred, is likely to benefit those countries substantially.

One might ask, however, what the effects are for the progress of science in general of this relocation of scientists away from the countries with the

35. We therefore do not include a table similar to table 3.7 for collaboration variables at different GDP levels.

most fertile environments for research and toward countries farther from the scientific frontier. If the environment in which one does science really matters, one might expect that Fulbright-funded scientists from less-science-rich environments and environments with fewer resources would be less productive in their subsequent careers than otherwise similar scientists whose location choices were not constrained. We find that, on average, Fulbrights from these poorer countries do typically publish less and have less of an impact on global science.

Because Fulbrights are less likely to be in the United States, they also have fewer scientific publications with US authorship. Viewed from an admittedly narrow perspective, one might conclude that the United States does not reap the full benefit of its investments in the doctoral training of Fulbright Fellows, although it must be remembered these students represent a very small percentage of total PhD degrees granted in the United States.

However, the goal of the Fulbright Program was not to increase either United States or global science, but instead to "increase mutual understanding between the people of the United States and the people of other countries." It has been quite good at achieving this objective, by stimulating 65 percent more scientific collaborations between the United States and other countries than would otherwise have occurred.

This chapter has emphasized impacts on the creation of scientific knowledge. However, the presence of Fulbright scientists in their home countries may have large benefits to home-country science in other ways—for example, through teaching and mentoring, advising governments and firms, entrepreneurship etc.—that are not measured well by the publication variables we consider here. Indeed, many of the Fulbrights we studied are working at high levels in government agencies or international NGOs and cross-governmental agencies. The impacts on future global science are likely to be far greater than manifested in their personal publication records, and we intend to investigate these contributions in future research.

Appendix A
Data Appendix

Fulbright Data

The names of Fulbrights were obtained from volumes of *Foreign Fulbright Fellows: Directory of Students* published annually by the Institute of International Education (IIE) from 1993 to 1996.

Identifying Controls and Location Search Procedure

First, we entered data from the IIE volumes on the Fulbright Student's name, graduate institution, field of study, and country of origin. Then, we searched for these students in the ProQuest database (described later) to find their date of graduation (for those who completed their studies) and advisor name. For those Fulbrights successfully completing their programs, we then performed searches on Google, Google Scholar, LinkedIn, and/or *Web of Science* to obtain as much information as possible on all the student's post-PhD locations and affiliations. The search time was limited to twenty minutes. If a student was not found at all on the web within twenty minutes, the searcher moved on to the next name.

For the students found on the web, we then searched for controls. We searched for controls obtaining PhDs in the same year, with the same advisor, at the same institution as the Fulbright. We clicked on the name of the student's advisor. If this step failed (i.e., there are no foreign students with the same advisor graduating in same year), we looked for a student with the same advisor graduating within three years of the Fulbright. When choosing controls, we alternated students graduating before the Fulbright with those graduating after the Fulbright so that on average controls graduate at the same time as Fulbrights. If this step failed, we chose a control graduating in the same year in the same field of study (e.g., biochemistry) at the same university.

We searched for the person's location on Google, Google Scholar, LinkedIn, and/or *Web of Science,* the combination of which allowed us to find both academics and nonacademics.[36] Since it tends to be easier to find academics on the web than others, we no doubt undersample nonacademics. However, this undersampling applies equally to Fulbrights and controls.

When someone at first was included in our sample but we later realized that we could not identify the location either of the Fulbright or the control for more than half of the years since PhD even after interpolating, we dropped the Fulbright-control pair. This led us to drop four pairs.

For schools listing prior degrees or biographical information in the dissertation, we used this information to infer the student's country of origin (see later). For schools that did not list prior degrees, if we found a potential control student, we looked them up on the web. If we could find their current location and evidence that they came from a foreign country (i.e., foreign undergraduate degree or biography), we recorded their name, year of PhD, current location, and estimated country of origin.

ProQuest Dissertations and Theses

The ProQuest Dissertations and Theses database is a database of almost all dissertations filed at over 700 US universities. We obtained information from this database on students' full names, advisors, fields of study, PhD

36. Many academics had CVs posted on the web. Nonacademics were more likely to be found on LinkedIn, conference or meeting programs, alumni associations, local news articles, or civic or religious organizations' websites. One person was even located via a DUI arrest. We made sure that the person we located had more than just their name in common with the student we knew (e.g., the PhD location or a previous employer might be mentioned).

completion dates, and undergraduate institution or country of birth or both. Starting in the 1990s, ProQuest began publishing online the full text of the first twenty-four pages of the dissertation.

Several universities require students to list biographical information in the front matter of the dissertation. Table 3A.1 lists these universities, which were identified by checking dissertations filed at the universities that are major producers of scientists and engineers in the United States. At some universities, the information includes a full biographical sketch (e.g., Ohio State, NC State), but in most cases, the information is limited to a list of previous degrees. Figures 3A.1 and 3A.2 present examples of this information drawn from dissertations filed at the University of Illinois and the Ohio State University.

The biographical information contained in these dissertations can be used to identify the country of origin of the student. Under the assumption that most students attend undergraduate programs in their country of origin, we treat the country of undergraduate degree as the country of origin. Using this information as a proxy for the nationality of the student will of course introduce some error, since not all students receiving undergraduate degrees do so in their country of origin. However, evidence from the NSF's *Survey of Earned Doctorates* suggests that the country of undergraduate degree is a very good proxy for the country of origin. For students completing doctorates in 2003 and 2004, the *SED* lists the country of undergraduate degree. For 84.9 percent of students, the country of undergraduate degree is the same as the country of citizenship. However, there is considerable heterogeneity across countries in the extent to which students pursue undergraduate studies outside their countries of origin. Table 3A.2 presents, for a selected

Table 3A.1 Universities listing biographic info in thesis

Auburn	Univ. California
Boston Univ.	Univ. Cincinatti
California State Univ.	Univ. Colorado
Clark	Univ. Connecticut
Cornell Univ.	Univ. Florida
Florida Institute Of Technology	Univ. Illinois
Fordham	Univ. Maine
George Washington Univ.	Univ. Massachusetts
Georgetown Univ.	Univ. Massachusetts At Amherst
Kansas State	Univ. Missouri
Louisiana State Univ.	Univ. Nevada
NC State	Univ. Oregon
OH State	Univ. Pittsburgh
OK State	Univ. South Alabama
Syracuse	Univ. South Carolina
Texas A&M	Univ. Virginia
Univ. Arkansas	

ALGORITHMS AND ARCHITECTURES FOR SOFT-DECODING REED-SOLOMON CODES

BY

ARSHAD AHMED

B.E., Regional Engineering College, Trichy, 1998
M.E., Indian Institute of Science, Bangalore, 2000

DISSERTATION

Submitted in partial fulfillment of the requirements
for the degree of Doctor of Philosophy in Electrical Engineering
in the Graduate College of the
University of Illinois at Urbana-Champaign, 2006

Urbana, Illinois

Fig. 3A.1 Sample dissertation page showing location of prior degrees
Source: ProQuest Dissertations and Theses Database.

list of countries, the share of students responding to the *SED*'s questions of who remained in their home country for undergraduate study. Students from Germany and Japan have the lowest rates of staying at home among the major producers of US graduate students (73 percent and 74 percent, respectively). However, the countries that send the most students (China, India, Taiwan, Korea, and Canada) have high stay-at-home rates for undergraduate study (98 percent, 93 percent, 89 percent, 76 percent, and 82 percent, respectively). Furthermore, counts of the number of doctoral recipients by country of origin, university, and year computed from a ProQuest sample have a correlation of 0.948 with analogous counts obtained from the *SED*.

The data on country of origin is only available beginning in the late 1990s when universities began submitting digital copies of dissertations to be posted on the web by ProQuest. However, by 1996 or 1997 almost all dissertations are available in digital format.

VITA

January 31, 1973. . . . . Born – Da-An, Jilin Province, China

September 1989 - July 1993. Bachelor of Science in Electrical Engineering, Nanjing University of Science and Technology, Nanjing, China

September 1993 ·· April 1996. . . . . .Master of Science in Electrical Engineering, Nanjing University of Science and Technology, Nanjing, China

September 2002 ··· present. . . . . .Ph.D student, Analog VLSI Laboratory, Department of Electrical and Computer Engineering, the Ohio State University, Columbus, Ohio

Since June 2006. . . . . .RFIC design engineer, Freescale Semiconductor Inc., Boca Raton, Florida

PUBLICATIONS

Research Publications

P. Zhang, and M. Ismail "A New RF Front-End and Frequency Synthesizer Architecture for 3.1–10.6 GHz MB-OFDM UWB Receivers", *Proc.* 48th *Midwest Symposium on Circuit and System.* vol.2, pp.1119–1122. August 2005.

C. Garuda, X. Cui, P. Lin, S. Doo, P. Zhang, and M. Ismail "A 3–5 GHz Fully Differerential CMOS LNA with Dual-gain Mode for Wireless UWB Applications". *Proc.* 48th *Midwest Symposium on Circuit and System.* vol.1, pp.790··793. August 2005.

Y. Yu, L. Bu, S. Shen, B. Jalali-Farahani, G. Ghiaasi, P. Zhang, and M. Ismail "A 1.8V Fully Integrated Dual-band VCO for Zero-IF WiMAX/WLNA Receiver in 0.18μm CMOS", *Proc.* 48th *Midwest Symposium on Circuit and System,* vol.1, pp. 187···190, August 2005.

vii

Fig. 3A.2 Sample dissertation page showing location of prior degrees
Source: ProQuest Dissertations and Theses Database.

Publication Data

We obtained publication histories from ISI's *Web of Science.* Authors were identified using information on post-PhD locations, authors' middle names, and fields of research. For each publication by an author, we obtained all information available on the publication record itself, including publication year, title, coauthor names, author locations, complete backward citations, counts of forward citations, publication source, abstract, specific field (for example, marine and freshwater biology), and keywords.

It should be noted that our information on the number of forward citations received by an article includes self-citations. The median backward

Table 3A.2 **Share of PhD students at US universities who received undergraduate degrees in their countries of citizenship**

Australia	85.00%
Brazil	96.02%
Canada	82.51%
China	98.35%
Egypt	96.38%
France	82.05%
Germany	73.05%
Greece	80.51%
India	92.71%
Iran	88.33%
Israel	88.46%
Japan	73.51%
Mexico	89.19%
Nigeria	60.61%
Philippines	87.23%
South Korea	76.33%
Taiwan	89.19%
Thailand	87.28%
Turkey	95.57%
UK	63.64%
Weighted average across these countries	89.50%
Weighted average across all countries	84.79%

citation lag also includes self-citations. In future work, we intend to remove these citations. However, this requires downloading bibliographic data on each specific citing article, which is a very time-consuming process.

The ISI *Web of Science* database does not cover every scientific journal published worldwide. It lists articles from 6,650 scientific journals. Among Thomson's criteria for including a journal in the index are, "The journal's basic publishing standards, its editorial content, the international diversity of its authorship, and the citation data associated with it."[37] Journals must typically publish on time, implying a substantial backlog of articles forthcoming. They must publish bibliographic information in English, and must include full bibliographic information for cited references and must list address information for each author. Thomson also looks for international diversity among contributing authors, but regionally focused journals are evaluated on the basis of their specific contribution to knowledge. The number of citations received by the journal is a key factor in evaluation for inclusion in the index, with preference going to highly cited journals or journals whose contributing authors are cited highly elsewhere.

The ISI selection procedure is designed to select the most relevant scientific journals, independent of the location of their editorial offices. Since

37. "The Thomson Scientific Journal Selection Process" Available at: http://scientific.thomson.com/free/essays/selectionofmaterial/journalselection/ (accessed March 11, 2008).

such a large share of cutting-edge science research takes place in the United States, there will inevitably be a high share of journals in this index based in the United States. Journals that do not publish bibliographic information in English are less likely to be included, so articles written abroad and published in low-profile regional journals with limited readership beyond the region (as evidenced by a failure to publish bibliographic information in English) will be excluded from our data. As a result, our publication data should be viewed as information on scientists' participation in the international scientific community, rather than raw article counts. Still, the large number of journals included, and the special consideration given to regionally focused journals means that most of the relevant journals in which our scientists publish will be included. We examined the publication records of some of our scientists located outside the United States, and found that even what might seem like relatively obscure journals (e.g., *Revista Chilena de Historia Natura, Revista Brasileira de Ciência do Solo, Acta Pharmacalogica Sinica,* etc.) were all included in the ISI index. While it is possible that ISI data is less comprehensive for articles published in non-Roman alphabets, it should be noted that only a very small number of scientists in our sample are located in Asian countries (0.36 percent of our observations are on scientists located in China, 0.55 percent in Japan, 0.87 percent in Korea, 1.03 percent in Taiwan, and 1.5 percent in Thailand). Furthermore, these are scientists who began their careers in the United States and are thus likely to continue publishing in English-language journals.

To verify more rigorously that our sample of publications is not biased toward finding articles by US-based researchers, we performed the following test. We had a research assistant collect data on the number of articles listed on scientists' CVs and the number of articles we obtained from ISI. We computed the share of a scientist's articles from the CV that were listed in the ISI database, and performed a t-test of difference in means between scientists outside the United States and those inside the United States. The average share of articles found on *Web of Science* was 0.705 for those in the United States and 0.651 for those outside the United States. We cannot reject the hypothesis of no difference in means (with a t-statistic of 0.788 and p-value of 0.433 for a two-tailed test).[38] We thus do not feel that a systematic US bias is introduced by restricting our attention to journals included in the ISI index.

We made sure to collect information on Fulbright and control publications at the same time, ideally on the same day. We did this to avoid biasing the data to include more pubs and cites for one of the groups because they were collected later and had more time to appear in the database.

38. We also tested the hypothesis that this depended on the number of years abroad by regressing the share of articles on ISI on the number of years abroad, and the coefficient on this latter variable was –0.001 with a standard error of 0.006 (insignificantly different from zero).

Appendix B

Full Regression Results for Selected Regressions (Corresponds to Panel C of table 3.6)

Table 3B.1 Full regression results for selected regressions (corresponds to panel C of table 3.6)

	Coefficients and standard errors from Poisson regressions							
	(1) Total publications	(2) First-authored publications	(3) Last-authored publications	(4) High-impact publications	(5) Total (forward) citations	(6) Cites to first-authored pubs	(7) Cites to last-authored pubs	(8) Cites to high impact pubs
Fulbright	–2.566	–3.204**	–7.179***	–1.914	–8.314*	–4.652***	–5.110**	–6.107***
	(2.029)	(1.394)	(2.526)	(3.152)	(4.756)	(1.775)	(2.371)	(2.009)
Fulbright *GDP	0.256	0.342**	0.750***	0.157	0.868	0.504***	0.546**	0.633***
	(0.228)	(0.154)	(0.280)	(0.354)	(0.536)	(0.193)	(0.255)	(0.219)
Log GDP per capita in home country 5 years before PhD	0.254	0.054	0.286**	0.458*	0.658***	0.123	0.248*	0.179
	(0.160)	(0.085)	(0.139)	(0.275)	(0.252)	(0.095)	(0.132)	(0.113)
Biological sciences	0.403	0.405*	0.572	0.254	1.488***	0.737***	0.669**	0.765***
	(0.255)	(0.239)	(0.413)	(0.368)	(0.360)	(0.215)	(0.300)	(0.260)
Engineering & computer science	–0.516**	–0.335	–0.186	–0.621	0.246	–0.431*	–0.081	–0.704**
	(0.260)	(0.227)	(0.376)	(0.379)	(0.535)	(0.254)	(0.310)	(0.321)
Earth/air/ocean sciences	–0.713**	–0.205	–0.463	–0.687*	–0.572	–0.469	0.33	–0.493
	(0.298)	(0.271)	(0.518)	(0.391)	(0.409)	(0.372)	(0.388)	(0.439)
Mathematics & statistics	–0.452	0.068	0.17	–0.003	–1.253***	–1.014**	–0.115	–0.819*
	(0.291)	(0.299)	(0.430)	(0.404)	(0.431)	(0.398)	(0.386)	(0.452)
Physical sciences	0.756**	0.36	0.312	1.254**	1.685***	0.651***	0.938***	0.983***
	(0.385)	(0.243)	(0.419)	(0.521)	(0.458)	(0.252)	(0.322)	(0.291)
Environmental science	–0.064	0.305	0.057	0.018	0.315	0.278	0.07	0.419
	(0.324)	(0.310)	(0.438)	(0.406)	(0.455)	(0.377)	(0.521)	(0.437)
Received PhD Pre-1995	0.824***	0.692***	1.812***	0.168	1.231*	0.600**	1.268***	0.554*
	(0.305)	(0.246)	(0.344)	(0.398)	(0.726)	(0.281)	(0.403)	(0.288)

(*continued*)

Table 3B.1 (continued)

	Coefficients and standard errors from Poisson regressions							
	(1) Total publications	(2) First-authored publications	(3) Last-authored publications	(4) High-impact publications	(5) Total (forward) citations	(6) Cites to first-authored pubs	(7) Cites to last-authored pubs	(8) Cites to high impact pubs
Received PhD in 1995–1996	0.761***	0.729***	1.490***	0.526	1.098*	0.584**	1.019***	0.504*
	(0.228)	(0.183)	(0.302)	(0.359)	(0.595)	(0.254)	(0.372)	(0.262)
Received PhD in 1997–1998	0.803***	0.472***	1.371***	0.670*	0.789	0.336	0.647*	0.259
	(0.257)	(0.161)	(0.292)	(0.400)	(0.629)	(0.240)	(0.360)	(0.247)
Received PhD in 1998–1999	0.107	0.128	0.648**	–0.308	–0.402	–0.266	–0.014	–0.198
	(0.230)	(0.158)	(0.313)	(0.346)	(0.582)	(0.257)	(0.394)	(0.265)
Received PhD Post-2002	–0.798***	–0.688**	–0.827*	–1.260***	–1.274**	–1.113**	–1.110**	–1.527***
	(0.298)	(0.321)	(0.444)	(0.448)	(0.632)	(0.483)	(0.565)	(0.554)
ln(Rank of PhD program)	0.05	–0.041	–0.042	0.141	–0.041	–0.083	–0.166**	–0.107
	(0.093)	(0.044)	(0.075)	(0.168)	(0.172)	(0.060)	(0.080)	(0.077)
1 if female	–0.420**	–0.298**	–1.027***	–0.351	–0.254	–0.329**	–0.827***	–0.421**
	(0.167)	(0.136)	(0.260)	(0.258)	(0.438)	(0.159)	(0.254)	(0.200)
Constant	–0.434	0.668	–2.486**	–3.109	–1.711	2.780***	0.21	2.729**
	(1.701)	(0.795)	(1.238)	(3.031)	(2.562)	(0.919)	(1.288)	(1.102)
Observations	488	488	488	488	488	488	488	488
Pseudo *R*-squared	0.23	0.11	0.21	0.25	0.4	0.23	0.21	0.27

Note: Robust standard errors in parentheses.

***Significant at the 1 percent level.

**Significant at the 5 percent level.

*Significant at the 10 percent level.

References

Agrawal, Ajay, Iain Cockburn, and John McHale. 2006. "Gone But Not Forgotten: Knowledge Flows, Labor Mobility, and Enduring Social Relationships." *Journal of Economic Geography* 6 (5): 571–91.

Finn, M. G. 2007. "Stay Rates of Foreign Doctorate Recipients from US Universities, 2005." Oak Ridge Institute for Science and Education. Working Paper.

Goldberger, Marvin L., Brendan A. Maher, and Pamela Ebert Flattau, eds. 1995. *Research-Doctorate Programs in the United States: Continuity and Change.* Washington, DC: National Research Council. National Academy of Sciences.

Institute of International Education. 1993. *Foreign Fulbright Fellows: Directory of Students 1993–94.* New York: IIE Foreign Fulbright Programs Division.

Institute of International Education. 1994. *Foreign Fulbright Fellows: Directory of Students 1994–95.* New York: IIE Foreign Fulbright Programs Division.

Institute of International Education. 1995. *Foreign Fulbright Fellows: Directory of Students 1995–96.* New York: IIE Foreign Fulbright Programs Division.

Institute of International Education. 1996. *Foreign Fulbright Fellows: Directory of Students 1996–97.* New York: IIE Foreign Fulbright Programs Division.

J. William Fulbright Foreign Scholarship Board. 1991. *Annual Report 1991–90.* Washington, DC: United States Department of State.

———. 2009. *Annual Report 2008–09.* Washington, DC: United States Department of State.

Levin, S., and P. Stephan. 1999. "Are the Foreign Born a Source of Strength for US Science?" *Science* 285 (5431): 1213–4.

National Science Foundation, Center for Science and Engineering Statistics. 2006. *Science and Engineering Indicators 2010.* Arlington, VA: National Science Board 10-01.

Saxenian, Annalee. 2002. "Brain Drain or Brain Circulation: How High-Skill Immigration Makes Everyone Better Off." *Brookings Review* 20 (1): 28–31.

Stephan, P., and S. Levin. 2001. "Exceptional Contributions to U.S. Science by the Foreign-Born and Foreign-Educated." *Population Research and Policy Review* 20:59–79.

SRI International. 2005. *Outcome Assessment of the Visiting Fulbright Student Program.* Washington, DC: United States Department of State.

Comment Paula E. Stephan

This chapter addresses an extremely important topic for this conference because of the considerable evidence that the foreign born contribute disproportionately to scientific productivity in the United States. Furthermore, it is assumed, and some anecdotal evidence exists, that if and when individuals return to their home country, the United States continues to benefit scientifically—either because of continued collaboration between the returnees

Paula E. Stephan is professor of economics at the Andrew Young School of Policy Studies at Georgia State University and a research associate of the National Bureau of Economic Research.

and US scientists or because of spillovers from the knowledge produced once the individual has left.

Moreover, it has been widely established that the policies of governments—both the sending governments and the US government—play a large role in determining who comes to the United States and who stays. It is also known that in most fields research requires resources. One reason that scientists working in the United States are arguably more productive than those working in many other countries relates to resources: compared to many other countries the United States provides considerably more resources for doing research.

This chapter matches 244 PhDs who studied in the United States on a Fulbright (FB) with 244 PhDs from foreign countries who came to the United States to study with funding that had "no strings" attached in the sense that there was no requirement that the PhD return to his or her home country for a period of time as there is with the Fulbright program. The match is performed for field, year, institution, mentor (when possible), and country of origin (when possible). The authors build the data set from ProQuest data, search for CVs on the web, and match the names to the ISI *Web of Knowledge.* It is a first-rate database that represents an extraordinary amount of work on the part of the authors. I would urge the authors to put the data in the public domain after they complete their research.

The database is not representative of foreign students in the United States. To be more specific, there are no FBs from China, Korea, Taiwan, or India. Yet these four countries are the largest source of foreign-PhD students in the United States. The authors also have a "Mexican" problem with their data: 90 of the FBs are from Mexico (37 percent); yet only 9 controls are from Mexico.

The database was initially created to study the role that resources play in scientific productivity. While scientists working in rich-resource environments are generally found to be more productive, the question of selection based on quality always haunts researchers who attempt to examine the role that resources play in scientific productivity.[1] That is, to what extent are researchers working in rich resource environments more productive because they are better researchers; to what extent is their higher productivity due to their having access to better resources? In other work Kahn and MacGarvie

1. It is not only that scientists working in rich-resource environments outside the United States have access to better resources; they also have the resources to come back and forth to the United States. The 2006 Survey of Doctorate Recipients (SDR) asked U.S.-based researchers whether they have a foreign collaborator. Conditional upon having a foreign collaborator, the SDR then asked whether the collaborator came to the United States to work with the respondent. The survey found that over 50 percent of those who had a foreign collaborator replied that their foreign collaborator comes to the United States to work with them. Moreover, the respondent was more likely to host the collaborator in the United States than to travel abroad to work with the collaborator (National Science Board, Science and Engineering Indicators 2010, Appendix, Tables 5–22).

argue that this question can be studied by matching Fulbrights, who are required to return home for at least two years, with a sample who do not face the return home requirement. To the degree they are randomly assigned, one should be able to isolate the effects of resources from quality.

It turns out, however, as Kahn and MacGarvie discuss in this chapter, that it does not appear that Fulbrights are randomly assigned. The argument can be made that they are of lower quality than the control group because high quality students decline the Fulbright (or do not apply). They may do so precisely because of the return requirement or the fact that in some countries they have little say regarding their destination university in the United States. On the other hand, the argument can be made that the FBs are better than the controls, being chosen on merit. They may also be underplaced, given the way FBs are assigned, and thus better than the controls they are matched to.

In the chapter prepared for this conference, Kahn and MacGarvie continue to focus on the productivity issue, examining the degree to which the productivity of FB scholars differs from that of controls, both for papers authored while in the United States and for papers authored outside the United States. In an effort to control for quality, they include the number of papers published as an undergraduate as a right-hand-side variable.

In addition to the resource and quality/selection hypotheses, there is an additional reason to hypothesize that Fulbrights might publish less research than the controls. For want of a better word, call this the investment hypothesis. Learning research skills while in graduate school requires an investment on the part of the student. It also requires an investment on the part of the mentor. The student-investment hypothesis is discussed by the authors. The argument is that if students know they have to return after graduate school, they may choose a different type of career path and invest less in building research skills while in graduate school. The faculty-investment hypothesis is not discussed by the authors but it is equally important. To wit, faculty select students to work in their lab, usually supporting them on their grants. If a student has other funding, faculty are less likely to invest in the student and the student may leave graduate school with fewer research skills, fewer publications, less mentoring, and a less extensive long-term network. Either variant of the investment hypothesis means that pregraduation pubs do not necessarily measure quality. Either variant also means that even if one could control for quality, one cannot use the FB program to address the resource hypothesis issue because the FBs may vary systematically from the controls in terms of level of human capital and social capital acquired in graduate school.

Kahn and MacGarvie estimate publishing equations, differentiating between Fulbrights and non-Fulbrights. They then estimate equations differentiating between FBs who are from a country that is in the top quartile of GDP per capita and FBs who are not; in an alternative specification, they differentiate between whether the FB is from a country that is in the top quartile in terms of the number of scientific articles produced versus in the lower 75 percent. In the revised version of the chapter they draw finer lines, distinguishing between the 25th, 50th, 75th and 90th percentile. They also examine the degree to which the Mexican FBs differ from other FBs and find that for seven of the eight output measures Mexican FBs are not different from other FBs of similar income level.

In future research the authors may wish to test to see if the FB effects are statistically different for those from different levels of GDP. In the conference version of the chapter and the revised version, the authors compare coefficients without testing to see if the coefficients are significantly different from each other.

More importantly, I would urge the authors to consider alternative, nonpublication-based measures of the contribution a PhD makes after graduate school. Which is more valuable in a poor country: publishing four or five articles (which are likely to be in B journals) or contributing to the quality of life in the home country by helping to diffuse knowledge learned in graduate school that can contribute to better health outcomes, greater agricultural productivity, and a more highly educated workforce? The answer, I think, is fairly obvious.

A different measure of contribution would also more accurately reflect the goals of the FB program, which, as stated by the authors, are to "Enable the government of the U.S. to increase mutual understanding between the people of the U.S. and the People of other countries." It is not to enhance scientific productivity of either the United States or of the home country. If it were, there are far better policy levers to use than the FB program.

III

Market Structure and Innovation

4

Schumpeterian Competition and Diseconomies of Scope
Illustrations from the Histories of Microsoft and IBM

Timothy F. Bresnahan, Shane Greenstein, and Rebecca M. Henderson

4.1 Introduction

Schumpeterian "waves of creative destruction" are bursts of innovative activity that threaten to overwhelm established dominant firms. Schumpeter argued that such waves renew markets and strike fear in even the most entrenched monopolists, motivating them to innovate. Despite the strength of that incentive, established dominant firms often fail to dominate in the new technological era. This fact has had great influence on the literature in organizational theory and technology management, and has also taken deep hold in the business press and in the popular imagination.[1]

Within economics the theoretical basis for explaining an incumbent's difficulty in responding to radical or discontinuous innovation focuses on the potential for cannibalization as drag on incumbent investment in the new

Timothy F. Bresnahan is the Landau Professor in Technology and the Economy and professor, by courtesy, of economics in the Graduate School of Business at Stanford University and a research associate of the National Bureau of Economic Research. Shane Greenstein is the Elinor and Wendell Hobbs Professor of Management and Strategy at the Kellogg School of Management, Northwestern University, and a research associate of the National Bureau of Economic Research. Rebecca M. Henderson is the Senator John Heinz Professor of Environmental Management at Harvard Business School and a research associate of the National Bureau of Economic Research.

We are all affiliated with the NBER and also with, respectively, Department of Economics, Stanford University; Kellogg School of Management, Northwestern University; and Harvard Business School, Harvard University. We thank Bill Aspray, James Cortada, Robert Gibbons, Brent Goldfarb, Tom Haigh, Bronwyn Hall, Bill Lowe, Cary Sherburne, Kristina Steffensen McElheran, Alicia Shems, Ben Slivka, Scott Stern, Catherine Tucker, and many seminar audiences for comments. We are responsible for any errors.

1. See, for example, Dosi and Mazzucato (2006), Gerstner (2004), Henderson and Clark (1990), Utterback (1994), Christensen (1993, 1997), among many others. A related literature in evolutionary economics has also taken up this problem, summarized in Dosi and Nelson (2010).

technology, and more broadly on the ways in which potential for strategic interaction between the old and new businesses constrains the incumbent's response to new opportunities.[2] When cannibalization does not constrain the incumbent, however, the mainstream economics literature remains underdeveloped. Economics crashes up against two puzzles. It has little to say about why incumbents should not be able to simply duplicate the behavior of successful entrants—or even to do much better. Incumbent firms, after all, usually have important sources of advantage through existing assets that might yield economies of scope. In those cases in which incumbents responding to creative destruction can take advantage of existing assets—assets such as brands, channels, manufacturing capability, knowledge of the market, and so forth—why should incumbents not have an advantage over entrants? Indeed, antitrust and innovation policy often implicitly assumes that "anything an entrant can do an incumbent can do better."[3]

One possibility is that radical technological change generates uncertainty and thus produces discontinuities.[4] If any single firm, including the incumbent, has only a probability of introducing the right product or having the right capabilities in the midst of a Schumpeterian wave, incumbents might be replaced simply because they are unlucky. Such an argument, while clearly compelling in some cases, does not explain why incumbents do not more often become successful strong seconds—duplicating the successful entrant's technology and leveraging their existing assets to gain the market. Indeed, Schumpeter himself leaves open the question about whether incumbent and entrant firms face similar costs in a new market, treating it as one of several unknown factors that market events will reveal as circumstances unfold.[5]

Another possibility that has been extensively explored by organizational scholars is that the firm's existing incentives, organizational routines and ways of seeing the world, or embedded cognitive frames, may be inappropriately imposed on new units, leading them to act in suboptimal ways.[6] This literature suggests that senior management at incumbent firms may become complacent and inward looking, leading them to neglect new opportunities or to frame them as extensions of the existing business, and that even when senior management understands the nature of the new market they may be forced to rely on organizational competencies developed to serve the old business that are ill suited to the new.

2. See, for example, Arrow (1962), Gilbert and Newberry (1982), Henderson (1993, 1995), Gawer and Henderson (2007). One key question is whether the incumbent should see through to the equilibrium outcome and thus cannibalize rather than be replaced by an entrant.

3. For example, see Davis, MacCrisken, and Murphy (2002).

4. See Klepper (1997), Stein (1997), Jovanovic (1982), Adner and Zemsky (2005), or Cassiman and Ueda (2006).

5. See Schumpeter (1942) for a number of the arguments we have cited.

6. Henderson and Clark (1990), Henderson (1993), O'Reilly and Tushman (2008), Tripsas and Gavetti (2000), Kaplan and Henderson (2005), Daft and Weick (1984), and Kaplan (2008).

Even accepting its premises, this line of research seems in many circumstances too restrictive in its assumptions about what is possible in an organization. One question for any model based on the limitations of organizational process or cognition is why firms cannot simply create a firm within a firm that replicates the organizational structure and competences of a new entrant. Moreover, we have several examples of firms that have succeeded in recreating themselves quite effectively, even in circumstances where existing ideas were quite strong and senior management felt the powerful temptation to complacency.

While this stream of research is compelling as one potential explanation of incumbent difficulties, the view that it is the explanation has led to a false dichotomy. Continued success by a firm is identified with an outbreak of foresight and good judgment, while declines of a formerly dominant firm are identified with suboptimal choices.[7] Our goal in this chapter is to break out of this identification of the explanation with the phenomenon to be explained.

Here we propose a third source for the difficulty incumbents experience in mimicking entrant behavior, stressing that the replacement of the old by the new never occurs instantaneously. We argue that *diseconomies of scope* may play an essential role during the interval when old still thrives and new first appears. We suggest that such diseconomies are not a function of any market distortion or any disequilibrium, but are, rather, a systematic factor in many Schumpeterian waves.

In broad outline, we argue that diseconomies of scope may arise from the presence of necessarily shared assets. These are assets—such as a firm's reputation for reliability or for conforming to closed or open standards—that inevitably adhere to the firm, rather than to the operating units, no matter how organizationally distinct the units may be, whenever two businesses are sufficiently close. It is the necessity of sharing the asset across business units that leads to the possibility of scope diseconomies.

Of course, the most usual case is that assets shared between related businesses will be useful in both. However, it need not always be so. First, there is the possibility that specific features of the asset built up in the old business will be mismatched to the market reality of the new one. When the features of the shared asset that would be desirable in each business are adequately distinct, sharing creates diseconomies of scope. If the asset is necessarily shared, no reorganization short of divestiture permits the firm

7. See, for example, Teece et al. (2000) who argue the goal of research is to "understand how firms get to be good, how they sometimes stay that way, why and how they improve, and why they sometimes decline" or Dosi and Nelson (2010) who relate that "In these and other cases when a radically new technology has replaced an older mature one, as we have noted, old dominant firms often have difficulty in making the adjustments. In such circumstances, technological change has been what Tushman and Anderson (1986) have called 'competence destroying.' The industry may experience a renewal of energy and progress, but often under the drive of a new set of firms." The latter definition captures the idea of a competence that works in a particular market environment.

to escape the scope diseconomies. Further, any such mismatch also creates costly organizational conflict between the two lines of business. We know from recent research in organizational economics that it is not possible to give conflict-free incentives to the managers of potentially competing divisions, in the sense of giving them both incentives to simply maximize firm value, and that, in our application, the managers of the established division will therefore fight with the management of the new division over how best to use or develop shared assets or both.[8]

Scope diseconomies can offer the incumbent firm a difficult choice. In the extreme, particularly if there are also significant strategic interdependences between the businesses, the firm may have to choose between not supplying the new business at all or assigning control rights over the shared asset either to the old or to the new business. If either the control rights are assigned to the old business (which, after all, built the asset) or there is joint control of the asset, the new business will be managed very differently from the entrants with whom it must compete. We do not argue that such an outcome represents suboptimal behavior on the part of the firm. Rather, we suggest that these kinds of organizational diseconomies of scope explain why the investments and behavior of the incumbent firm are likely to be very different from those of entrants in the new markets.

We do not suggest that operating two lines of business when an asset must be shared presents problems in every circumstance, or inevitably leads to failure at incumbent firms. Instead, we suggest that it makes failure more likely if the costs of organizational conflict are considerable and if the marketplace does not value the benefits of increased coordination.

Our analysis also highlights the consequences of those cases in which the firm *chooses* to share an asset across the old and new line of business. We show that this decision can also lead to significant organizational conflict and can impose real costs on one or both of the businesses—but that since choosing to share an asset implies avoiding the added cost of duplicating it for the new business, it is difficult to assert that this is a plausible cause of incumbent replacement at times of technological transition.

We focus on two well-known cases of incumbent firms attempting to react to major Schumpeterian waves, International Business Machines (IBM) to the Personal computer (PC) in the early 1980s and Microsoft to the widespread use of the Internet in the late 1990s, in order to make the case that diseconomies of scope have competitive implications during Schumpeterian competition. In each case we present a detailed historical account that both explores the changing strategic incentives facing each firm and the organizational conflicts that emerged within each firm.

While many economists think of Microsoft and IBM as highly distinct, we

8. See, for example, Hart and Holmstrom (2002), Baker, Gibbons, and Murphy (2002), Anand and Galetovic (2000), and Anton and Yao (1995).

shall see that looking at each of them at the height of its dominance reveals firms that were far more similar than different. Each was a highly successful established dominant firm with powerful technology marketing capabilities and proven ability as a strong second. Each used vertical integration to some degree as a structure to limit entry into its core markets. Faced with a new wave of potentially transformative importance, each firm at first missed but soon saw the importance. Both set up separate units within the firm to invest in the new technology—IBM created an entirely new operating division, while Microsoft created a separate engineering group that eventually grew to more than 4,000 people. Both firms eventually rolled these new units back into the existing organization, effectively ending the effort to be a dynamic competitor in the new area. There are, of course, important differences, which we shall revisit in detail in the history.

In both cases, we shall show that the firm encountered difficulties in attempting to respond to the Schumpeterian wave in both old and new business. In IBM's case, they forced the firm to exit the competition for control over standard setting in PC business and, years later, to effectively exit the business. In Microsoft's case, while they left the firm as dominant in one new Internet technology, the browser, they forced the firm to pursue a very different strategy with respect to the Internet than those pursued by successful new entrants—at, we believe, significant long-run cost to the firm.

We pick these two examples with three broad methodological points in mind. First, their market circumstances and their internal organization are well documented in the key eras. We are convinced historical methods revolving around the deep investigation of the specifics of organization and market alignment in specific examples are the right way to pursue an initial investigation of theories like these. The depth of our account allows us to explore the complex interplay that unfolded between the strategic incentives facing the firms and the need to share assets across businesses and the internal organizational dynamics that resulted and that in turn shaped investment decisions.

Second, both firms were extremely well managed. It is a common anachronistic error to think of Microsoft as better managed than IBM: rather, both were excellently managed firms at the moment we study them. Neither was inert, neither was a "dinosaur," neither failed to come to an understanding of what was required for market success in the new era, and neither lacked the implementation skills needed for the new market. In neither case did the established firm lack the necessary technical skills nor did it fail to (if not immediately, soon enough) recognize the importance of the oncoming wave or fail to make substantial investments in response. Indeed, IBM built a $4 billion PC business—one that had it been a freestanding firm would have been the third largest computer company in the world. While there are undoubtedly cases in which incumbents were unable to build the organizational capabilities required to address the new market, this is not the case here. In both cases, outside innovators demonstrated a market opportunity that appeared attractive to many entrants, including the leading firm. In both cases, the leading firm was a commercial organization contemporaries regarded as an extraordinarily effective strong second. There is something deeper to explain here.

Perhaps most importantly, each of these firms appears to have had the kind of well-developed firm level assets that could create tremendous scope *economies* between its old and its new business. That each was unable to achieve this, instead bearing large scope *diseconomies,* speaks to the importance of looking at the details of the economics of the organization.

Finally, these are very important firms and very important transitions, linked not only to shareholders' wealth but to the growth of the national and world economies. Studying Schumpeterian waves in such cases gets us closer to the ultimate purpose of Schumpeterian economics.

Our analysis also stresses that diseconomies of scope are not the same as cannibalization. In both cases there were (eventually, in the case of IBM and immediately, in the case of Microsoft) important strategic interdependencies between the old and new businesses that created very significant tension between the managers of the two units. In both cases there were also critical, necessarily shared firm-wide assets whose forced use imposed costs on both businesses and that also created organizational tension. In IBM's case this forced sharing created significant costs even before the strategic interdependencies between the old and new businesses emerged, and we suspect that this is a general result.

We also depart from a large strand of prior writing about Schumpeterian waves in which competitors take advantage of an established firm's weakness. Rather, in our view organizational diseconomies of scope arise in the area of the greatest strength of established firms, not in any area of weakness. These firms can deploy their inherited strengths; however, a problem can arise when the inherited strength has uses in both the old and the new market and the two market settings call for very different deployments, so much so that realizing goals in one market impedes realizing them in the other.

Finally, we provide an explanation that avoids a common error in methodology. There is a strong but erroneous tradition of seeking to classify firm organizations as good or bad and of discovering that the most recently successful firm in an industry has good organizations. We emphasize that instead organizational diseconomies of scope explain a large number of events. We are most careful to discuss outcomes, since the anachronistic error is often linked to outcomes data like profits or market share. In the case of the IBM PC, we argue that organizational diseconomies not only *could,* but, in fact, *did* shape the market outcome in the PC market. IBM's loss of standard-setting leadership in that market followed, in the context of that difficult competitive market, from strategic errors forced upon the

IBM PC division as a result of internal conflicts with mainframe divisions. Nonetheless, IBM remained well-organized for its existing mainframe business, and stayed, for a time, the world's largest and most profitable computer and software company. In the case of Microsoft and the browser, we note that Microsoft is still the leading firm in its old businesses and is also the leading market share firm in the browser market. Nonetheless, Microsoft gave up real opportunities for profitable business in Internet-based industries at the end of the browser war. Microsoft remained well-organized to be the dominant PC software firm, an extremely profitable business, but scope economies have left the firm with little role in the development of mass market computing on the Internet. In short, rather than effectively pursuing the new business, in both cases long-run decisions led the firm to focus on its old business.

Section 4.2 provides a review of our framework. Section 4.3 illustrates its application to IBM's behavior in the PC markets. Section 4.4 explores Microsoft's behavior in the browser markets. Section 4.5 identifies a number of implications and outlines some directions for further research.

Our analysis is of the firm, but of the firm faced with a challenge from the market. On the policy front, our analysis lends further credence to the idea that incumbent firms, alone, are unlikely to be able to duplicate the technological diversity characteristic of the market. That suggests that vigorous entry, and not only incumbent dominant firms' incentives in response to entry, may be a key contributor to the innovativeness of an industry or an economy.

4.2 Sketching a Model

Here we outline a brief presentation of our framework. A more complete explanation lies in our companion paper (Bresnahan, Greenstein, and Henderson 2009).

Our analysis will not assume that economies or diseconomies of scope are automatic or that, when diseconomies arise, market transition is a foregone conclusion. Instead, we consider the question open ex ante before the diffusion of a new technology. This model has four stages, labeled as: (1) Search; (2) Institute investment; (3) Organizational Experiment; and (4) Assess and Resolve.

We model stage (1) minimally, and say that an outside entrant opens a new market at that time. We take the technical and marketing aspects of this new market as exogenous. Incumbent firms enter the new market in stage (2) with assets that possess attributes already determined in their established markets. While the incumbent firm can create new assets at this stage, our key assumption (borne out in our examples) is that some existing assets must be shared with the new business. Since we are writing about industries with rapid technical change, we endow firms at stage (2) with rational expectations but not perfect foresight. A firm might, for example, enter a new market not fully knowing its costs in that market. Stage (3) serves to inform managers about (unanticipated) conflicts, or, what will often be equivalent, about (unanticipated) costs from attributes of inherited and necessarily shared assets. We also model stage (4) minimally, arguing that incumbent firms then invest in firm assets and in the division of organizational responsibilities in an attempt to obtain resolution to prior conflicts.

4.2.1 Modeling Shared Assets

Consider two markets: an established market, "A" and a new market "B." In market A customers place a high value on product attributes a_1, a_2, while in market B customers place a high value on attributes b_1 and b_2. As a first step, assume that firms can choose whether to serve the two markets with a single shared asset, F, or with two separate assets, F_1 and F_2. Under these circumstances the firm's decision as to whether to use a single asset to serve both markets or to develop an entirely new asset to serve the new market is, of course, a function of the cost of the asset and the degree to which a single asset can serve both markets.

In general, firms will choose to use a single asset the more the preferences across the two markets are similar and the more flexible the asset. Thus, for example, Coca Cola's reputation for quality and excitement is valuable in many markets, so the firm uses a single brand to serve many niches, despite the fact that in each niche the nature of the drink—sweet, fruity, low calorie, and so forth—is quite different. Similarly, Unilever uses a single distribution channel to sell both a wide range of food products (ice cream, tea, rice) and a wide range of personal and home care products (deodorants, laundry soap). These are examples of the classic economies of scope identified by scholars such as Sutton (1991, 1998) as so central to long-term incumbent advantage and by those exploring diversification as central to related diversification; for example, Wernerfelt (1988).

Notice that choosing to share an asset may not be costless. Sharing an asset that may not be optimally matched to either market may create conflict between divisional management, and may put either or both divisions at a disadvantage. But since in many cases it is likely to be considerably cheaper than recreating the asset, it may nonetheless be rational and may lead to significant economies of scope.

Of course when preferences across the two markets are sufficiently different, firms may choose to invest in two assets rather than attempting to share a single asset across markets. In the extreme, the assets supporting General Electric (GE)'s locomotive business are almost entirely different from those supporting GE's financial service or media businesses, for example.[9] A less

9. Whether this type of "unrelated" diversification ever makes sense if the two businesses share no assets at all is a long-standing topic of debate in the literature. The argument has been made, for example, that GE shares assets such as access to the credit markets and a unique ability to develop managerial talent across its businesses.

extreme example would be that of Corning Glass's medical equipment and visual display businesses. Both rely on highly sophisticated glass technology and they both make use of the same advanced research and development (R&D) facilities, but they also rely on quite different manufacturing plants and sales and distribution channels.

This line of analysis is standard in the literature, and is the source of the intuition that, in general, incumbents should be advantaged in entering new markets. In the best case they can make use of existing assets and take advantage of economies of scope; in the worst they can build new assets and compete with entrants on their own terms. Here we argue, however, that if the incumbent firm *cannot* choose to develop a new asset to serve the new market—if an asset is "necessarily shared," then the incumbent may be at a significant disadvantage in serving new markets or at the very least constrained to act in very different ways from de novo entrants.

What kinds of assets might be necessarily shared? What attributes adhere to the firm, per se, rather than to the operating units? Here we do not attempt to develop a comprehensive theory of the *causes* of necessary sharing, focusing instead on its consequences. However we suspect them to be relatively common, and in our empirical analysis we begin to sketch out some possible explanations for the existence. One plausible candidate, for example, is the firm's credit rating.[10] As the recent financial crisis so vividly demonstrated, the divisions of a firm cannot isolate themselves from other divisions in accessing the capital markets. American International Group (AIG), for example, was effectively destroyed by the actions of a single (small) unit. Until that unit was sold the other divisions, no matter how profitable and well run, could not access credit of any kind.

Another plausible candidate is the firm's reputation, or in some circumstances the reputation of the firm's senior management. In the case of IBM, for example, before the advent of the PC the mainframe business had an enviably strong reputation for quality and reliability and for close engagement with its customers. It also had a reputation for being a strong second—the firm was very rarely first to market with a new technology—and for developing closed proprietary systems. The PC business, in contrast, initially developed a reputation for speed and for using an open system approach, and was simultaneously able to take advantage of IBM's historical reputation for quality and reliability to develop a very strong position in the market place. It was a very successful business—if it had been freestanding it would have been the third largest computer company in the world—and it appeared that the company had been able to take advantage of classic economies of scope.

As the PC market developed, however, this "separation of reputations" became increasingly problematic. In our discussion we explore the reasons for this in some detail, but in essence it appears to have been the case that

10. We are indebted to Claudine Madras for this example.

as the PC business grew, and as PCs were increasingly sold to traditional mainframe customers, these customers became increasingly concerned that the design and quality problems that emerged in the PC business were indicative of design and quality problems in IBM as a whole. Increasingly IBM's reputation across the two markets could not be differentiated, and as a result it became increasingly mismatched with both.

In both IBM's and Microsoft's cases, the firm's reputation for supporting proprietary standards also became an asset that was necessarily shared, largely became of the potential for strategic interaction between the two businesses. In the case of IBM, the management of the mainframe business came to believe that a PC business based on proprietary standards could be a powerful strategic complement to the mainframe business.[11] In the case of Microsoft, the managers of the Windows business not only wished to manage the browser as a strategic asset to the Windows business, but also early on became aware that a browser based on open standards might weaken Window's proprietary position substantially. In both cases managers of the existing, legacy business thus had strong incentives to manage the new business *in the interests of* the existing business. We cannot assert that ex ante these managers were mistaken—indeed in the Microsoft case it is not at all clear that they were wrong. But what we can say is that the existence of these incentives made it impossible for the new businesses to develop a credible reputation for "openness." Such a reputation was of considerable value in both markets, but in both cases customers and eco system partners were very much aware that IBM's and Microsoft's strategic incentives were not—and *could not*—be the same as those of a de novo entrant.

This necessary sharing imposes two costs. The first order cost is the obvious one: the firm is forced to use a single asset in two markets that is not ideally suited to either. In IBM's case the value of IBM's reputation in the mainframe business was severely impacted, and in Microsoft's case the firm's ability to compete effectively in the Internet space was greatly compromised. The second order cost is more subtle and may be both longer lasting and most costly. As assets must be shared between divisions, very considerable organizational conflict emerges. This is illustrated in figure 4.1.

In the figure, the vertical axis is a common sense of product quality, like performance on a set task. The horizontal axis is the distinction between speed and engagement. We show the indifference curves of two sets of customers; while both like quality, those in one market like "engagement" and those in the other market like "speed." As a result, the manager of the old business prefers one product market reputation and the manager of the new business prefers another. There is divisional concord about the quality part

11. Another potential source of strategic interaction—namely that a PC industry based on open standards could trigger substitutability away from IBM's mainframe business—did not become clear until considerably later in our period.

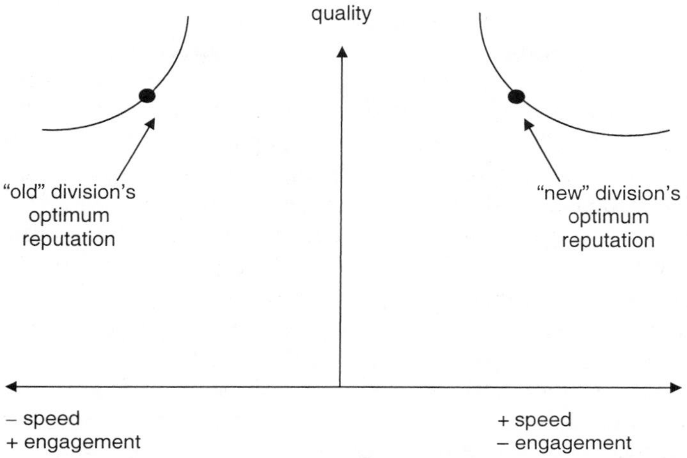

Fig. 4.1 Divisional concord and conflict: Product development reputation optima

of the fixed asset, but potential divisional conflict over its speed/engagement attributes. One can imagine a similar diagram for the attributes of "open" and "proprietary."

This potential for conflict may not be apparent at the earliest stages of experimentation with a new business. The optimum attributes for *F* are presumably known for the old business at stage (2), but may very well be unknown for the new business at that stage, and only learned after experience with stage (3). In this model *F* is chosen at stage (2) for one set of reasons and at stage 4 after experiencing competition.

The presence of conflict arises from the combination of (a) the indivisibility of *F* with (b) the inability of senior managers to write a contract that can give the managers of the two businesses "perfect" incentives to maximize total firm value. Conflict will arise both if the attributes of *F* are a choice variable and if the determination of *F*'s attributes is something that is endogenously determined by operational decisions. A reputation for speedy product introductions, for example, could arise from investment by one division, while a reputation for engagement with customers to determine product design could arise from investment from the other division. In this model, stages (1) and (2) take place in the shadow of precedent and stages (3) and (4) may take place in anticipation of future conflict. The manager of product A will then care about the operational behavior of division B and vice versa.

Standard principles in organizational economics suggest that this conflict cannot be costlessly resolved since within a firm, effective action involves effort that cannot be effectively monitored and outcomes that cannot be specified in such a way that top management could write enforceable contracts around them. In the absence of contractible measures, managers must rely on second-best contracts. Said another way, under many circumstances top managers cannot give perfect high-powered incentives that maximize the value of the entire firm to everyone in an organization at once. In essence, even when managers can put in place "relational contracts," incentive issues cannot be perfectly resolved. See, for example, Hart and Holmstrom (2002), Baker, Gibbons, and Murphy (2002), Anand and Galetovic (2000), and Anton and Yao (1995). Thus, even under optimally designed incentive contracts the incentives of the two divisions will differ, and as a result both will advocate for different characteristics of the shared asset.

An emerging literature considers the problem of optimal organizational design when there are dependencies of a form related to this between business units. These show the circumstances, in stylized models somewhat related to the problem we model, in which there will be a control structure that then gives operational and strategic control over one business to the managers of another business, to centralize control, or to create a firm within a firm.[12] These models are quite interesting in that they show that none of these structures is costless; that is, show that scope diseconomies can persist even after the optimal organizational form is adopted.

This does not imply that firms will (or should) give up on all the innovative opportunities in stage (2). Rather, for a wide set of plausible circumstances firms will rationally attempt to innovate inside their boundaries, choosing to share a single asset rather than to duplicate the asset entirely, despite the fact that the asset will not be ideally suited to either market and the organizational conflict that will inevitably result. We are agnostic about which of many types of conflicts arise, since that depends on the specifics of the shared asset and the allocation of decision rights within the firm. For example, if F has been at A's preferred point and the firm enters market B, the situation will not be entirely positive from manager A's perspective. He will be asked to compromise in the interest of the broader firm.

We are also agnostic about the allocation of control over the asset that will emerge as the two markets develop and the conflict between the managers assigned to both becomes increasingly costly. As the literature has emphasized, a variety of governance structures and incentive regimes may be optimally chosen by senior management, depending on the characteristics of the asset, the markets the firm wishes to serve, and the information structure of the problem. What is important from our perspective is that all solutions to the problem of a shared asset will lead to at least some conflict between units and to decisions that are necessarily different than those that would be made by the managers of an equivalent but freestanding business.

12. Alonso, Dessein, and Matouschek (2008) and Rantakari (2008) both explore the consequences of this incontractability for the locus of control within the firm when decisions taken by the managers of one operational unit have implications for the other.

The form of the conflict matters less than its consequences for stage (4). Conflict can take any number of forms: the managers of old and new businesses might spend time lobbying for a change in the characteristics of *F*, they may make investments in *F* that are not optimally suited to the interests of the firm as a whole, senior management may find it impossible to elicit truthful information about the benefits of different attributes for *F*, and so forth. In the case of an established firm with an established business, the costs of conflict can be so great that it may choose to spin off the new business entirely: or it may focus on its longstanding success and retreat from wholehearted competition in the new area.

In the case of both IBM and Microsoft, conflicts between the old and new units triggered both by strategic interdependencies and by the need to share key firm-level assets became so expensive that the firm chose to give control rights over the new business to the old business, and in both cases the old business—the mainframe business in IBM's case, and the Windows business in Microsoft's—began to make decisions that managed the new business as a strategic asset to the old. It is very hard to make the case, of course, that ex ante this was irrational. What we can say is that in both cases each firm faced quite different benefits and costs in entering and in operating in the new market than a de novo entrant. We now turn to our illustrations.

4.3 IBM and Personal Computing

The competitive and innovative history of the PC industry in the 1980s has a rich literature, to which we have contributed in the past.[13] The industry was a difficult environment for firm success because of rapid innovation, divided technical leadership, and frequent episodes of competition for market dominance. It is against the test posed by that difficult environment that we examine IBM's entry and later events.[14]

Following our theoretical frame, we focus on three areas of inquiry. How did the organizational sources of IBM's success in enterprise computing contribute to success in the young PC market with the participation of senior management? How did the assignment of decision making at the firm level and within the PC division contribute to IBM's success as an entrant? What were the sources of IBM's later difficulties in the PC business? It is only in this third part of our historical enquiry that the notion of scope diseconomies will emerge.

Our explanation of initial success and later problems turns on the changing role of IBM's key firm-wide assets, and its reputation with customers. At first, the existence of the firm-wide asset provided scope economies. IBM's

13. See, for example, Freiberger and Swaine (1984), Cringley (1992), Langlois (1992), Carroll (1993), Bresnahan and Greenstein (1999).

14. This case study presents only highlights from a very long sequence of events.

reputation with corporate customers aided its entry into the PC business. As the PC business grew, however, scope diseconomies emerged. The specific attributes of IBM's customer reputation became a major source of conflict between the IBM PC division and the long-established IBM mainframe business. That conflict was resolved by organizational changes that removed the conflict, and the firm choosing a high level of alignment in the old business. This necessarily implied a low level of alignment to market opportunity in the PC business.

To make this explanation plausible we need to examine the idea of alignment to a market opportunity in some detail. That detail is necessarily specific to the computer industry, even if the general idea is not. A detailed examination is also useful in discarding other theories of IBM's ultimate failure in the PC business. Some of these, including cannibalization and stupidity or inattentiveness on the part of IBM's management, are simple to discard. We take rather more time with other theories in the literature, which fall into two main classes: (a) IBM was too backward looking, focusing on hardware rather than on software, and (b) IBM was too forward looking, leaving the supply of key PC components to outside firms like Intel and Microsoft. Both of these views turn out to be wrong in interesting and productive ways.

4.3.1 IBM before the PC

IBM's capabilities and organization were aligned to a specific market opportunity, the changing and evolving enterprise computer market. IBM had dominated enterprise computing for many years.[15] The firm's long-run strategic goal was to dominate all general-purpose technologies, whether hardware, software, or networking, in enterprise computing. That had been going very well for IBM, in the first instance because of its command of distribution channels, its excellence in marketing, and its ability to incorporate innovations first made by others into its products as a strong second. Critics of IBM sometimes doubt the firm's technological innovativeness in its long era of dominance, but there is no doubt about its marketing capabilities.

While technologist-critics sometimes think of IBM's strengths as mere marketing, IBM's enterprise customers did not see it that way. IBM's emphasis on product design responding to customer concerns rather than to technologists' concerns and IBM's fabulous field support for customers gave it great advantages. Above all, IBM's field sales force dominated distribution and the flow of information to and from customers. These marketing strengths were central to IBM's emergence as the dominant supplier for enterprise computing.

15. Enterprise computing refers to the business systems, typically used in large organizations, which support key enterprise-wide functions in finance, operations, and the like. The most important technologies used in enterprise computing historically were IBM mainframes, so this segment is sometimes labeled "mainframe computing." We avoid that label because it is unhelpful for discussing the use of smaller computers, like the PC, in enterprise computing.

Having an informational link to customers through IBM's field sales force gave the firm opportunities. IBM's organization empowered the sales function to make critical decisions about the direction of technical progress. This in turn enabled the organization to pursue numerous internal technical initiatives and choose among them—commercializing some in a customer-friendly fashion, often to the great unhappiness of the technologists whose projects were not chosen. Customers came to rely on this, to IBM's tremendous competitive advantage. IBM's reputation was so strong that "nobody was ever fired for choosing IBM" became a cliché.

The Strengths Were Aligned to a Dynamic Opportunity and Were Sunk Costs

At the time of the launch of PC, IBM's strengths were not tied to a specific technology. Indeed, historically speaking, IBM had already dealt successfully with wrenching transitions in the technical basis of its core business. Among all such historical examples one stood out, the modular platform. This would support its dominant market position for decades. Introduced in 1964, the System 360 modular platform was a unified and largely proprietary architecture. It provided customers with the opportunity to mix and match larger and smaller computers, disk drives, and so forth, as long as these were within the IBM 360 compatibility sphere. This was very valuable to enterprise customers, particularly as it gave them an option to upgrade across a compatible family of computers as their needs changed and thus to preserve their investments in applications programs, data, and so on. The installed base that grew around the 360 architecture and its backward-compatible descendents provided IBM with a substantial competitive advantage. The System 360 grew to become the single-most profitable product introduction in computing, generating more revenue than any other computer product line for more than two decades.

The decision to launch the System 360 illustrates that the firm was exploiting a *dynamic* market opportunity.[16] It was a multimillion-dollar gamble for the firm, opposed by all existing computer product line managers. The firm's senior management supported the modular platform over their objections, and the sales organization directed its improvements toward strategic customer needs. The dramatic success of the 360-based mainframe business shaped the organizational capabilities of IBM thereafter in profound ways. As a direct reflection of the market-driven incentives to maintain and extend the installed base, the sales and service organization assumed a particularly strong role within the firm. Ambitious executives tried to get extensive sales experience, and in the 1970s and 1980s all the CEOs after Watson Jr. and the majority of top management had extensive sales experience.

16. It is beyond our purpose to tell this entire tale. For explanations, see, for example, Pugh (1995), Fisher, McGowan, and Greenwood (1983), Fisher, McKie, and Mancke (1983), Katz and Phillips (1982), Brock (1975), or Watson Jr. and Petre (1990).

While IBM's marketing strengths were a competitive advantage, they were also sunk costs tightly linked to the requirements of enterprise computing. The IBM sales force was structured around the existing body of customers. Compensation emphasized keeping customers and meeting and exceeding quotas for new sales. This oriented employees toward knowing their (typically corporate) customer well. In this case, customers were the information systems (IS) employees at customer firms, who operated systems, and corporate vice presidents, who controlled budgets for purchases. The sales organization was very well informed about the growth prospects in the existing enterprise computing market.

The decision-making processes inside IBM were also aligned to the dynamic market opportunity in enterprise computing. It centralized strategic decisions. A key structure was the CMC (Corporate Management Committee). By the late 1970s this process touched every aspect of strategy in IBM. This centralization shaped many incentives. "Escalating a dispute" to the CMC became a known tactic throughout IBM. Professional reputations at IBM were made or ruined from presenting well to the CMC or from wasting its time. Known for its decisive decisions (especially in the era of Watson Jr.), the CMC would spawn layers of management below it. These layers decided which disputes received attention.[17] It also became famous for its "task forces," which generated reports aimed at gaining more information in an open dispute. These structures were essential to exploiting economies of scope across multiple product lines by coordination from the center.

Consequently, IBM's top managers, in general, aggregated a wide range of customer concerns *and* coordinated large-scale product development strategies for the entire customer base. In the mainframe market, more specifically, this process gave rise to products that were, broadly speaking, high quality, backwardly compatible, technically conservative, and highly priced. Introducing products with backward compatibility (a) supported IBM's competitive position by renewing and extending the installed base and (b) kept customers happy by enabling them to preserve their large local investments.

Though IBM dominated enterprise computing, there were a large number of outside inventors of computer technologies generally. Part of IBM's strategy was to bring all new technologies with general importance to large enterprises into its platform. This called for successfully identifying such technologies and updating the platform to incorporate them. Both tasks were demanding—the first a difficult learning task as it involved both technology and complex customer demand and the second a demanding technical task. IBM could be extremely persistent and foresighted in attempting to bring new technologies into its products (though outsiders groused that IBM

17. This process continued to guide the formulation and implementation of strategy for IBM until an outsider, Lou Gerstner, became CEO in the early 1990s and eliminated it.

often chose to wait and use only the version of a new technology invented in-house).

Success at many difficult tasks contributed to IBM being serially effective at exploiting new market opportunities in enterprise computing. Major technical advances, whether invented inside the firm or not, ultimately became part of an increasingly capable IBM platform that served enterprise customers well. At least one important example arises in computer networking: As the PC wave loomed, IBM was engaged in platform improvements for electronic commerce at enterprise in support of highly valuable applications (e.g., the computerized reservation system for airlines, the automatic teller machine network for banks). These adaptations to a new environment were successful for IBM and its customers. It was with some merit, then, that IBM's employees believed they understood—in ways that others did not—the combination of organizational traits and technological features necessary for commercial success in enterprise computing.

IBM's efforts to compete *outside* its core enterprise computing market had a rather mixed record, with a substantial number of failures. This was not due to lack of experimentation. In practice, IBM relied on its own executives' judgment and its own task forces to decide what to do on the basis of steady experimentation with new technologies, overwhelmingly done in-house after soliciting heterogeneous voices reflecting a wide array of perspectives and financial incentives. Ultimately, some of these initiatives may have failed because the technology was challenging or the customer not well connected to IBM. For example, there was even a single-user computer—not remotely a PC—that did not find much of a market in the mid 1970s. Attempts to make minicomputers and other smaller systems also had long histories of commercial failure.[18]

One particular failure cast a long shadow over many early decisions regarding PCs. The minicomputer market arose outside enterprise computing, and the possibility of future entry and competition from minicomputers against IBM mainframes raised by the Digital Equipment Corporation (DEC) VAX generated a crisis within the CMC. Many in IBM forecasted, correctly, that DEC would move from its dominant position of selling to engineers to competing for IBM's primary enterprise customer base.

The IBM 4300 was the competitive response, which stumbled in the marketplace because its design and marketing were forced to partially align with IBM's existing organization and technology.[19] The IBM 4300 was a compromise between many organizational demands and market needs,

18. We will discuss some of these experiments later, but notable successful experiments included early word processors and some early small computers, such as the 1620. However, IBM's competitive difficulties responding to Wang and other providers of words processors were well known. We will also discuss some of its difficulties with general purpose minicomputers later. See Haigh (2006) for an analysis of IBM's position compared to various initiatives from other firms in office computing.

19. See, for example, Fisher, McKie, and Mancke (1983).

while DEC and other competitors simply responded to market needs. For example, the 4300 was a *partially* IBM-compatible system. At the insistence of the Mainframe Division, it respected some of IBM's existing mainframe technologies. Yet its designers gave up on full compatibility in order to embed technical advances in the system. Pricing was also a compromise, with 4300s below mainframe prices but above competitors' prices, including VAX's prices. Users largely rejected these compromises for competitive alternatives.

Many in IBM's management learned lessons from the 4300's failure that would shape future decisions about scope economies and diseconomies, particularly with regard to the PC. They concluded that IBM's decision-making process itself had led the firm to develop an ineffective product through internal compromise rather than market alignment.

This experience, and others like it, would shape the organizational response to the rise of the PC. IBM's management continued to believe that there often were legitimate issues that required coordination between different parts of IBM, but this centralized coordination process also had some readily apparent drawbacks, notably slow decisions, and the potential for influence costs. Hence, at the dawn of the PC market, there was an ongoing debate inside IBM about relying on centralized coordination for every new opportunity.

4.3.2 New Opportunities That (Soon) Appeared to Play to These Strengths

The technical and market direction of the early PC industry followed an indirect path, which at first obscured its salience to enterprise computing. Perhaps this is systematic. Every Schumpeterian wave begins with something that creates an opportunity for entrants. The PC industry was created by entrepreneurial firms exploiting unserved niches that, at first, were very far from IBM's markets and its strengths. IBM, for its part, at first ignored the PC. After a period of time, the PC began to be attractive to IBM's customers, and IBM then came quickly to view the PC as within the ambit of its long-run strategic market goals.

Before that time, however, the PC industry developed, separately from the rest of computing, a set of rapidly improving technologies and standards and a pronounced industrial organization. The PC markets were organized overwhelmingly along open-systems lines. The most important PC operating system was CP/M, which came from a vertically disintegrated supplier. While Apple produced both computers and operating systems, it encouraged outsiders to write applications. The CP/M community and the community of Apple applications developers was uncoordinated, often descended from hobbyist electronics communities. No single supplier provided the lion's share of proprietary hardware. The microchips came from Motorola, Intel, and others, while the other parts, such as disk drives and monitors, came from an assortment of low-cost standardized suppliers. There were few proprietary parts or designs. Moreover, the PC was distributed through catalogues and (at that stage) a limited number of independent retailers.

From the founding of the PC industry through 1979, IBM's managers did not have any reason to believe the PC would become a business opportunity within their enterprise computing market goals—and certainly no reason to believe that it could be a threat to the profitability of the mainframe business. Instead of corporations, the customers were hobbyists and gamers, and the largest market appeared to be in the home. From a strategic marketing perspective—as we have seen, the key perspective for long-run planning at IBM—the PC was not relevant to IBM's existing customers and thus represented, at this early stage, neither an opportunity nor a threat.

All of this changed toward the end of the 1970s as personal computers began to find a substantial market inside corporations. Suddenly, the PC was being sold to IBM's customers. This brought the PC within the scope of IBM's strategic marketing goals and raised the question of how to deal with an important, and now salient, new technology.

Just as entrepreneurs had founded the PC industry, other entrepreneurs seeing a new opportunity converted the PC from a hobbyist toy into a corporate, white-collar worker tool. Corporate users bought third-party application software such as VisiCalc, the most popular commercial application for the Apple II. Word processing started to look like a useful technology in bureaucracies, and the leading word processing supplier, WordStar, began improving itself so it resembled an emerging corporate software vendor. The PC attracted attention from programmers with a variety of backgrounds and interests, even some inside IBM.[20] The upshot was that IBM's most important firm-level asset, its marketing reputation, was now salient to the PC. The entrepreneurial creation of the corporate PC, not the earlier creation of raw PC technologies, marked the beginning of the Schumpeterian wave for IBM.

4.3.3 Seeing the New Opportunity

This is when IBM's organizational structures for perceiving new opportunities and challenges cut in. IBM's management supported forward-looking experimentation and outlook, as any firm that seeks to be a strong second should do.

IBM had a group based in Boca Raton whose primary goal was to follow small-system developments and propose responses. In the late 1970s, the managers in Boca Raton took notice of the PC industry.[21] Deliberate

20. Indeed, Lowe and Sherburne (2009, 43) note that eventually IBM CEO Frank Cary expressed concern that the creeping encroachment of the PC into corporate organizations had also infected IBM, and the Apple II has "captured the hearts and minds of IBM programmers."

21. The contemporary media also shaped perceptions. Atari and Apple computer were the darlings of the business press. See, for example, Cringley (1992) or Freiberger and Swaine (1984).

in its activities, the group became intimately familiar with the workings of every available PC, studying the technical foundations of each project and its marketing strategies, such as they were. While Boca's activities were not secret within IBM, they were also not of any importance to managers in any other existing division. Boca's was precisely the type of activity expected of a major firm that was attempting to monitor commercial activity in related markets, and, of course, most of that activity is of limited relevance most of the time.

After considering a variety of actions, Boca arranged for a presentation in front of the CMC with the active support of the CEO, Frank Carey. The leader of the Boca Raton group, Bill Lowe, made one of the most fateful presentations in the history of computing. He was able to persuade the CMC to consider making a significant investment in the PC. Because the group was already intimately familiar with the workings of every small system, both IBM's prior attempts and the PC industry, Lowe's group was able to develop a fully viable plan in a very short time, including detailed estimates for costs and time to completion.[22]

IBM saw multiple reasons for going ahead. IBM's CMC left few paper records, so most of what is known comes from many contemporary second-hand accounts[23] and one retrospective first-hand account from Bill Lowe.[24] These are among the salient issues discussed:

- The PC was about to be marketed to IBM's customers.
- PCs were already easier to use than "green screen" terminals. As an intelligent terminal, the PC potentially threatened IBM's substantial terminal revenues.
- Although PC revenues were still small, PCs were getting attention from futurists and popular trade magazines. This was especially true of the Apple II and the plans for the Apple III. Apple and others were loudly pursuing business users, gaining a hearing if not yet much in the way of sales.
- The PC industry involved a loose collection of entrepreneurial and less-established firms. Lowe argued that the introduction of professional distribution and servicing, which was IBM's traditional strength, could significantly alter the value proposition of a well-positioned design similar to what was already provided.

22. At this time Lowe was systems manager for what was called "Entry Level Systems" and he was later appointed to lab director for the site in November of 1981, before his departure. The account comes from chapter 2 of the book. Hereafter we refer to this as Lowe and Sherburne (2009).

23. This episode has been reported widely, but not the details behind managerial decision making. See, in particular, the accounts found in Chposky and Leonsis (1988) and Carroll (1993).

24. Lowe and Sherburne (2009). We thank Lowe for showing us his original presentation notes at the CMC that reveal much about IBM's thinking at the time of entry.

- Futurists forecast a computing market based on microprocessors. Left unchecked, IBM's own customers might soon ask IBM to design products that worked closely with technical standards from outsiders. As in the minicomputer market, the bulk of the revenue would flow elsewhere unless IBM acted to control standards.

We report these points as if there was significantly more clarity about the future than was possible at the time. There was clearly an element of experimentation in a very uncertain and rapidly changing area. One thing does stand out. IBM clearly understood that there was a strategic choice, not a strategic necessity, to enter the PC industry. There was no then-current competitive threat to its existing business from the PC. The competitive challenge IBM faced in its core mainframe business arose (a) a decade later and (b) much more from firms in the minicomputer or workstation markets than from PC firms.[25] Nor was there any immediate prospect of complementarity between PCs and corporate computing in 1980. Today, one of the many functions of PCs in large organizations is to access enterprise applications. Many observers, including IBM, could see that coming, and, while the timing of that complementarity relationship was uncertain, in 1980 it was clearly not in the immediate future. Instead of representing either an immediate complement to IBM mainframes or a near-term threat, the PC represented a long-run growth opportunity for IBM. Few at the time forecast as rapid growth for the PC as it has in fact had, but many observers saw that this was going to be an important technology in enterprise computing and a sizable revenue opportunity.[26]

4.3.4 New Opportunity Called for Open-Systems Approach

While entry into the PC industry was attractive to IBM, it involved important changes in strategy, enough so that there would be important organizational implications as well. In introducing the PC, IBM moved away from established processes supporting supply of existing products, making the IBM PC Division into an effective open-systems supplier. To understand why this move ultimately created scope diseconomies with the rest of IBM's business, we first examine what it called for in the PC business.

There were established standards in the PC market, like CP/M, VisiCalc, and the Intel 8088 microprocessor, but there was also clearly a window of time during which a new standard could be set for a corporate PC. As IBM began to consider entry, that window was clearly beginning to close. A number of corporate PC efforts were announced, including one from Apple

25. For an elaboration of this argument, see Bresnahan and Greenstein (1999).

26. In short, precisely because the attempt was not seen as directly related to the future success of IBM's core business, it was shielded from influence by existing organization and structure. As we argue, as soon as this perception began to shift, the division's independence came under attack, and that attack illustrates the organizational limits of economies of scope.

(the Apple III) and a new version of CP/M. Too long a delay could mean that even IBM's formidable reputation with corporate customers would be insufficient to overturn a newly established standard for a corporate PC. Timely entry would give IBM the opportunity to draw on the marketing advantage of its formidable reputation in setting an IBM PC standard.

There are a number of general observations about open-systems standard setting that mattered for IBM's entry that we shall reuse in our second case study as well, so it is worth stating them generally. First, entrepreneurial innovators are drawn to the vertical disintegration at the heart of open systems organization because (a) it permits them to specialize in one or a few technical areas, levering their resources by using technologies supplied by complementors, and (b) because the flexibility and modularity of open systems permit rapid, uncontrolled exploration to learn by market experiment which product features matter most to customers. These two features are, of course, radically different from IBM's use of a vertically integrated structure to implement a strategy of managing and controlling product improvements.

Second, while entry into a particular component market of an open system can be quite easy if done during a narrow window of time, it can also be prohibitively difficult if attempted earlier or later. This is particularly true of the "platform" components around which standards are set. At ordinary times, users and developers will tend to choose the old standards, but narrow windows of time appear in which new standards can be set. An entrant who can attract a large volume of business quickly will be particularly well favored in an effort to set a new standard. In his first book, Bill Gates summarized this part of standard-setting analysis, saying, "Both timing and marketing are key to acceptance with technology markets."[27] His analysis followed from leading industry participants' analysis of standard-setting situations, which closely parallels the economic theory of standards.[28]

Entry into a particular component market in an open system is possible at particular times. Nonetheless, even open systems can have high entry barriers for an entire de novo system, just as proprietary systems do. The difference arises because a systems entrant also needs to replace all the complementary components. Whether IBM or entrepreneur, an entrant must work with the best suppliers in all the component markets. Once again, this supply behavior contrasts sharply with IBM's traditional vertical integrated structure.

Finally, uncontrolled outside technical progress is inevitable for any firm in an open-systems industry. Rather than attempting to manage technical progress and innovation with a control system, an open-systems firm will see constant outside innovation whose form, timing, or direction it would

27. Gates, Myhrvold, Rinearson (1995, 135).
28. See David and Greenstein (1990) and Bresnahan and Yin (2006).

not necessarily have chosen. To accommodate that outside technical change, an open-systems firm makes public the information outsiders need to work with its products, cooperating with all comers without prior vetting. This, too, is in sharp contrast with IBM's traditional model of consultation with customers long in advance of bringing new technologies into its platform.

This set of market principles applied to IBM's potential entry as a strong second. Famously, IBM aligned the strategy of PC unit with the market competitive situation by adopting an open-systems strategy and organization. This had important implications for the PC's subsequent history that we return to next.

4.3.5 A Firm within a Firm

The IBM PC experiment had several novel—to IBM!—features. Among them, the CMC authorized the division in Boca Raton to use an entirely different organizational and business model than other IBM divisions, one much more aligned to open-systems industries. In addition to formal approval from the CMC, the PC group had the CEO's protection for acting in ways that did not follow "the IBM-way," as understood by IBM employees elsewhere within the company.[29] This made the IBM PC Division into a highly separate firm within a firm.

The CEO created an independent division—the term inside the company was an *independent business unit*, or IBU—with considerable autonomy. Boca Raton's managers were also given a direct reporting line to the CEO. When others in IBM tried to challenge the PC group, Carey and then Opel both backed the PC group's decision *without* calling for any presentations at the CMC, and remained committed to the schedule of review every few months.[30]

This structure also departed from a core social and procedural norm at IBM, one that supported transparent and ubiquitous internal accountability. IBM was a company where everything was inspected or potentially subject to inspection, formally and informally, at all times. Said another way, all employees expected to be held accountable for achieving targets, and

29. The protection even continued after Frank Carey stepped down as CEO in January of 1981, but remained as Chairman of the Board. John Opel became CEO and continued with the policy, though, as we shall see, after major diseconomies of scope between the division and other parts of IBM could not be controlled, began to modify it.

30. How was this commitment communicated? With a normal initiative other senior managers within IBM were allowed to raise objections and, in so doing, initiate a process to bring issues to the CMC. Frank Carey let it be known in advance that this procedure would be modified for the PC initiative—ostensibly in light of its tight deadline and importance of the initiative to the senior management. The rule was thus changed: As always, any IBM senior manager was allowed to raise an objection about the PC initiative. However, as a new condition, they would be required to travel immediately to headquarters in Armonk (potentially even the next day) to explain or defend their objection or both. Consequently, and in sharp contrast to all other major initiatives at IBM at the time, not a single objection was brought to the CMC for consideration regarding the PC over the next year. See Lowe and Sherburne (2009).

managers anticipated inspecting and controlling processes with the intent of reaching targets. Against that history, the protection for the IBU was a dramatic departure. No division had ever been given discretion to make decisions over a time period of medium length without the potential for immediate review.[31] Hence, the PC group was given a license to de facto "act like an entrant."

IBM's senior management gave the IBM PC Division time-to-market direction that departed strongly from IBM norms but was entirely aligned to the problem of a PC market entrant. Most dramatically, the managers in Boca Raton were given an executive mandate to produce a design for commercialization in less than a year—by the summer of 1981. There was no precedent for such speed at IBM: Some observers speculated that designing a PC using IBM's normal engineering approaches would involve a two- to three-year decision-making cycle.

The Boca design team made many decisions for design, development, and production that departed radically from IBM norms. Following other early PC industry firms, it used inexpensive (instead of frontier) components, even in key places such as the microprocessor.[32] IBM also sourced parts from outside suppliers for things such as memory, disk drives, and printers and, in general, used off-the-shelf parts, except in a few key places such as the ROM-BIOS, which was a proprietary IBM design. Breaking with precedent, IBM also invited other vendors to make compatible software and peripherals for the new PC. To do so, it made many technical details about its PC available to numerous other firms, which was yet another break with IBM's general practice of secrecy.[33] In short, the IBM PC Division was acting like an open-systems company, not like IBM.

Many of the preexisting parts were also chosen because they had passed marketplace tests and could easily pass internal IBM reliability standards. The rapid and incremental design was also reasonably well aligned to the needs of the PC market at that time, since it meant that the IBM PC was compatible with, or easily made compatible with, many leading components in the PC industry.

One tension arose in the early planning for production. The PC group had avoided using internal supply if the costs were not the lowest. The PC group

31. We thank Jim Cortada for pointing out how important was this particular departure from norms.

32. IBM chose the Intel 8088 over the superior and already existing 8086. It came off the shelf and permitted hardware components from existing CP/M machines to be used in IBM PCs.

33. They key word in that sentence is *invited.* By this point there was also a third-party software industry for IBM mainframes, but the relationship between those firms and IBM had emerged after numerous ups and downs in cooperation. The relationships with PC software firms looked quite different. Though IBM attempted to supply some application software, IBM took actions, such as releasing technical specifications, to overcome some of the existing mistrust. These differences were widely recognized at the time. See the accounts in Chposky and Leonsis (1988) and Carroll (1993), for example.

made many enemies at the divisions that were turned down. Even when divisions won rights to supply parts, it did not earn the PC group many friends because the group chose between internal suppliers and external suppliers based on speed and technical merit.[34]

Boca Raton—in keeping with its mission to "act like an entrant"—also did not depend on IBM's own distribution network, instead arranging for distribution through third-party retailers, Sears and Computerland. This brought the IBM PC into a distribution mode suitable for the individual end user, rather than the corporate computer department, which was closely linked to the IBM field sales force. This decision was aligned to the PC marketplace but once again departed significantly from IBM past practice.

(Unimportant) Diseconomies of Scope Emerged Quickly

Our theory is one in which shared assets can create either scope economies or scope diseconomies. At least initially, the key asset of market reputation provided considerable scope economies to IBM's PC Division. Customers in corporations turned to IBM for a PC, and application developers wrote for a platform whose success they forecast.

Meanwhile, at this early stage there were few costs—and few benefits—for existing IBM divisions from the success of the IBM PC. This followed from two things. The PC was, in the short run, neither a complement nor a substitute for IBM mainframes. Second, any internal impact was minimized by the choice to structure the PC business as an operationally distinct unit; its doings were not apparent *to other divisions* in the short run, particularly while the division was small. It appeared to the other divisions as either an irritating departure from norms or a firm-wide success or both.

What little diseconomies of scope arose were, at first, primarily a problem for the new division. Any forward-looking organization must be prepared to bear some transitory costs and these particular costs were small compared to the reputation benefit. They did, however, forecast some of the larger costs to follow. The few costs of being inside IBM that struck the new IBM PC Division were reputational costs associated with the parent companies long-time commitment to proprietary systems and to exploitation of outsiders' inventions as a strong second.

IBM sought as partners the leading suppliers of key PC complements. They succeeded in signing up the foremost makers of the microprocessor (Intel), programming tools (Microsoft), and spreadsheet (VisiCalc.) Yet IBM's reputation as a proprietary systems company led to problems negotiating with the foremost makers of the leading operating system (CP/M) and

34. This was not the norm in mainframe production: Throughout the 1970s, the mainframe group had covered everyone else's variable expenses, overhead, and cost overruns in a single company-wide profit statement. When the PC group eventually enjoyed enormous profits, several of these component groups raised questions about whether the PC Division profited by not accepting standard practice for allocating the overhead of other manufacturing units.

word processor (WordStar). The entrepreneur selling CP/M was concerned that working with IBM would simply lead to the divulgence of proprietary knowledge to IBM. The entrepreneur at WordStar saw a conflict between an IBM PC standard and a standard for writing corporate applications (much like the modern standard around Microsoft Office) that would be set by his firm. Negotiating around these conflicts, even if it were possible, would have delayed introduction of the IBM PC, which was in a race to the market.

Failing with its first choice for an operating system partner, the team from Boca Raton turned to its next choice, a clone of CP/M from Microsoft (which bought the clone for the occasion). At this stage, IBM was partnering with a motley group of PC entrepreneurs, drawn, like many firms in the industry, from the margins of the broad computer and communications industries. By traditional IBM corporate-marketing standards, Microsoft was a sketchy partner.[35] Yet this was nothing next to IBM's other second-choice compromise: the supplier of IBM's initial PC word processor was not market leader WordStar, but a quickly written (and later quickly forgotten) product from an entrepreneur previously known as "Captain Crunch," a notorious "phone phreak" (or telephone hacker).

4.3.6 Problem Was Not Not Knowing How to Enter New Markets

IBM's entry into the PC market shows that the firm—or at least the firm-within-a-firm—knew how to enter this new market. Rather than displaying the behavior of a backward-looking firm that only understood its old market, IBM adapted to the strategic requirements of its new market.

Many observers, using an ex post perspective, have said that IBM was unwise to source key components, like the OS and the microprocessor, from outsiders. To be sure, the vertically disintegrated and open PC industry was highly competitive, and IBM's participation exposed them to that competition. Yet their decision to enter as an open-systems company was essential to aligning to the new opportunity. As we shall see, IBM's competitive problems in the PC industry arose partially because it was a highly competitive environment and partially because IBM's organization retreated from the independence and alignment of the PC Division after diseconomies of scope emerged.

4.3.7 Success, Later Reversed

The launch of the IBM PC and its sales for the next few years went spectacularly well, far better than any official prediction had dared to state

35. The PC group procured their operating system from a Seattle-based company (Microsoft) consisting of a thirty-two-employee firm when IBM first called in July of 1980. Microsoft was managed by a young Harvard dropout from a local family (Bill Gates), his teenage techie buddy who would soon quit for health reasons (Paul Allen), and a Harvard friend and Stanford MBA dropout (Steve Ballmer).

prior to its launch.[36] This was an enormous accomplishment. The IBM PC became the standard design for personal computers. Complementary investment from many, many, companies flooded to the IBM PC, giving it new software, new compatible hardware components, new programming tools, a new retail sector, and a set of information institutions, from magazines to custom software houses, help users take advantage of it. That kind of complementary investment is the great benefit of open systems, and it led IBM, the dominant firm in the older segment of the computer industry, to build what would have been (if it were a stand-alone firm) the world's third-largest computer company, the "IBM PC company," in just a few years.

IBM also faced the difficulties associated with an open-systems business. There were a number of firms selling clones of the IBM PC. Since the industry had open systems, these clones could take advantage of all the complementary investments. Thus, to make its initial market success permanent, IBM would need to, at a minimum, maintain its role as the dominant firm in making the PCs themselves. Had this been accomplished, it would have given IBM a market position like Intel in microprocessors today; that is, subject to some competition from clones but continuing to earn large returns from controlling hardware architecture. IBM also could aspire to eventually making the PC less of an open-systems market; that is; taking a position where it could dictate the direction of technical and market progress to its complementors. Had *this* been accomplished, it would have given IBM a market position like Microsoft in operating systems today; controlling standards for the entire PC industry and earning enormous returns on that.

IBM did not accomplish either of those goals, as is well known. Both contemporary observers and later scholars have correctly attributed that failure to IBM's management decisions in the PC industry. IBM did not have a "market orientation"—in the language of important industry complementors. This led to a series of missteps that led to a series of setbacks. Hardware technical leadership in computer design was taken from IBM by clone manufacturers beginning in 1986. IBM attempted to move the industry to a new, superior, hardware design with proprietary elements in 1988, but could not get market acceptance. Finally, there was a successful effort to redefine the PC industry around a proprietary standard. So that goal was possible, but it is Microsoft Windows, not any IBM product, which defines the PC industry standard today and has since the early 1990s.

A natural conclusion would be that IBM was simply an old-style firm and

36. Even at this early stage, existing organizational perceptions shaped forecasting. Boca Raton's managers believed the market potential was large, but dared not say so in their first presentations to the CMC in deference to the prevailing sensibilities. The division's official forecast for sales was deliberately chosen to not exceed the total number of IBM worldwide installations at the time, just over two hundred thousand. In fact, sales of the first models eventually exceeded several million units. See Lowe and Sherburne (2009).

could not manage in this new environment. That turns out to be incorrect. IBM was, as we have seen, capable of managing in the new environment. We now turn to the sources of IBM's retreat from that competence. They lie in powerful scope diseconomies between the longstanding mainframe business and the new PC business in IBM. They created severe problems of misalignment between the IBM PC Division and the PC marketplace long before the success of the clones or the failure of IBM's efforts to install a proprietary standard. IBM's tremendous lead in the PC market after its initial introduction carried the firm for a while, but the conflict that shortly emerged between the mainframe and the new effort left it doomed.

4.3.8 Problems of Alignment to Both Old and New Business

IBM's senior management would retreat from the idea of having a division organized along open-system lines. Understanding why is the key to understanding IBM's later troubles in the industry.

We will interpret events in terms of a firm-wide problem, in light of unavoidable diseconomies of scope. Senior management faced the firm-wide costs of coordinating the use of shared assets in two divisions in two distinct market environments, where one division is well aligned to the established market, while the other serves the new market—to which it also seeks to become well aligned. Forcing the new division to coordinate with the existing imposed costs on the new, and these costs contributed to the new division's decline.[37]

We recount these events in light of many prior portrayals. IBM's PC troubles attracted considerable press attention after 1988. IBM's financial distress in the 1990s attracted attention and had huge implications for the computing marketplace. In addition, there were many arresting stories written about the seeming absurdity of IBM's managers' actions in the face of the overwhelming evidence of crisis in the early 1990s, which later culminated in a changing of CEOs. In comparison, we focus on earlier events between 1985 and 1988, which did not receive as much attention.

While the later events are certainly engaging illustrations of behavior at a formerly dominant company going through a crisis, they provide little illustration about the foundations for the organizational limits of economies of scope, which is our goal. We accordingly concentrate on earlier events. In doing so, we also shed light on what later observers missed and misunder-

37. Notice here the crucial importance of the distinction between assets that are *necessarily* shared and those that are optionally shared. Two divisions could conceivably choose to share an asset—say, a manufacturing facility—despite the fact that the decision creates organizational costs, because the benefits of sharing outweigh the costs of duplicating the asset. But we argue here that there are some assets that are necessarily shared—in the IBM case the reputation of the firm—and that the existence of these assets forces the firm to incur the costs of organizational diseconomies of scope.

stood as irrational behavior, and on the factors that made the latter events so severe.

Tensions from Aligning with Two Opportunities

The firm-within-a-firm came to an end in early 1985. Less than five years after agreeing to initiate the project, the IBM PC Division was completely brought back to the familiar IBM style of management, with no independent decision making and limited discretion for the division. How did that come about? We have already noted some small tensions within IBM over the structure and independence of the IBM PC Division. Those could easily have been overcome in the interest of having a new ongoing success in a growing market. But as the IBM PC Division grew, its behavior as an open-systems company began to influence IBM's market reputation. This led to severe scope diseconomies.

An example of the market reputation tension arose from the failure of the IBM PCjr, a smaller machine than other early IBM PCs that was aimed at the home user in an effort to increase the size of the market beyond corporations with a compatible design. This was launched in 1983, and the focus of many news stories throughout 1984. The product did not sell well and a great deal of inventory had to be written off. It was also a source of much public embarrassment for IBM.

There were many causes behind the PCjr's failure, both immediate and deep. The immediate causes included a poorly designed keyboard. Known as the "chiclet keyboard" for its diminutive size, it was ridiculed inside and outside the company. While cheaper than other IBM PCs, the PCjr was expensive for a home machine, and IBM's brand name mattered less there. To gain some market segmentation, the PCjr was not fully technically compatible with the regular IBM PC for business; both IBM and others learned a valuable lesson about open standards and universal compatibility from it.

The specifics of these product problems are less important than the inevitability of some problems given the IBM PC Division's open-systems supply stance. Like any firm in an industry like the PC, this one experimented with balancing new designs, new choices for suppliers of parts, educated guesses about the nature of demand, and compromises between cost-saving goals and desirability-enhancing features.[38] The PC group also came close to operating according to the norms of an entrepreneurial open-systems enterprise by emphasizing quick decisions, resolving disputes through verbal debate, using minimal documentation, and deliberately taking risks. Thus, *some* failure was inevitable, a byproduct of the PC group's attempt to take market risks in an open-systems market.

38. IBM was hardly alone in having some failed experiments. Apple was watching chips pop out of the Apple III's unhappy, overheating, hardware design, Microsoft's effort to write (rather than buy) an operating system flopped in the market, and so on.

The PCjr was more important as a source of internal trouble for IBM's PC group than as a marketing failure. To put it in perspective, expectations were out of scale with reality. A small firm, like most in the PC industry, with the sales of the PCjr would have considered it a success. Yet the highly publicized failure was important in creating arguments against the independence of the IBU.

As long as it succeeded, Boca Raton was safe from second-guessing. But publicized errors made it vulnerable to assessment according to established IBM norms. For example, when the PCjr did not generate large home sales, the PC group was accused of not studying and understanding its market using appropriate marketing techniques. A couple of years later, when quality problems arose at the (sole) supplier of hard drives for the PC/AT, which affected the quality of the whole product, the division was accused of violating company norms for having second sources for key components.

These disputes went beyond corporate political infighting to become a question about the key shared assets at IBM, and its reputation for reliability. The internal perception began to arise that the PC Division's failure to use IBM's existing organizational competencies was hurting its performance. At the same time, others inside IBM began to believe that the PC Division risked actively harming the core mainframe business.

In the view of the established divisions of IBM, the well-publicized errors at the PC Division diminished years of careful image building for all of IBM, hurting the firm's reputation for reliability—something that was essential to the marketing of large systems.

The specifics of these examples are less essential than their general feature. Once the division had any failures that threatened the reputation of the larger organization, senior management heard about it from other parts of the organization, including notably the profit-heavy mainframe division. Although the failures and the subsequent backlash do not make change inevitable, they do make senior management aware of the organizational costs. This meant that the management would have to (at a minimum) consider changes to the formal assignment of authority or other actions to protect its asset—its reputation.

A second set of problems arose with regard to distribution. With IBM's field sales force and the PC Division's distribution partners (Sears and Computerland) selling to the same customers, channel conflict was inevitable. It was also new. No IBM division had ever before been given the autonomy the PC Division possessed. Before this, the field sales force had been responsible for "account control."

Models of channel conflict often portray it as a form of cannibalization. In this case, cannibalization played little role at a firm-wide level. Rather, channel conflict was a grubby contest about the flow of money. By 1984, the PC Division had revenues of more than four billion dollars—making it the third-largest computer company in the world, had it been a stand-alone company. The issue arose because a significant fraction of that revenue was not contributing to sales commissions. Both the Sales Division and Sears could sell PCs, the internal IBM divisions received the PCs at a discount. The large accounts were held by the Sales Division, but smaller firms and independent buyers could purchase from Sears. Thus, IBM had an internal division competing with an external company for the sale of its product. A complex set of rules determined who could make a sale, who would get credit (and commissions) for a sale, and so on. There was even conflict over "grey market" sales; that is, authorized dealers reselling machines. To an open-systems company, to first order a sale is a sale; to a proprietary systems company, a sale without connection to the customer involves loss of control.

Once again, the specific feature of each aspect of channel conflict is less important than the general lesson behind it. IBM's distribution channel relationships were a key firm-wide asset, and the PC business and the rest of the company had powerful and misaligned incentives regarding how to use it. That does not make change inevitable, but it puts the costs in front of management, this time with the powerful Sales Division in conflict with the PC Division.

In brief, issues about changing the structure of formal authority over the firm's market reputation and over distribution were inevitable once the PC Division demonstrated any significant commercial success. The PC Division, to be an open-systems success, had used IBM's core firm-wide assets in novel ways. When that activity grew, it began to impose costs on established divisions. The situation could not persist unresolved. The scope diseconomies between old business and new did not compel any particular resolution, but they did compel some resolution.

4.3.9 Avoiding Scope Diseconomies

Senior management did react to these costs, and rather quickly. In 1983, less than two years after launching its first product, the PC Division was reformed and renamed the Entry Systems Division (ESD), and it lost its direct reporting relationship with CEO Opel. Estridge, the group's director now reported to a supervisor who reported to a CMC member who reported to Opel. While the division retained its discretion over forecasting, pricing, and servicing, this change began the integration of Boca Raton back into normal IBM operating procedures.

This was not just window dressing. It affected daily operations. Rather than running the division directly, Estridge began to spend several days a week in Armonk, taking care of internal political and operational issues, gaining approval for actions, leaving others in charge in Boca Raton of many details. He was appointed IBM vice president in 1984. Through much of 1984, he fought attempts to make the PC a part of an office automation strategy and attempts to coordinate distribution of the PC with other parts of the company.

In January of 1985, a little over three years after first selling an IBM PC, Estridge lost this broad fight, and the National Distribution Division gained control over retail dealer sales of all PC products. That officially ended the experiment with the IBU, though, as noted, many aspects of the IBU had ended some time earlier.

These formal changes involved more than just assignment of divisional responsibilities. Key personnel and geographic proximity were altered. Not long thereafter, Estridge was moved to another position.[39] The original manager for Boca Raton, William Lowe, was moved back as president of ESD.[40] Along with Lowe's reappointment came a reporting structure for the PC Division similar to those used with other IBM divisions. In June, two hundred of the top executives were moved out of Florida and to a facility near Armonk.[41]

While few written records about the CMC decision were kept, it was clearly quite controversial with employees in Boca Raton. As with the decision to initiate the project, there are several contemporary secondary sources and one primary source for understanding its change. It is clear that the conflicts among divisions were a major reason for these organizational changes, and that making them reduced scope diseconomies.

History does not record whether this was a hard-headed calculation by IBM's senior management that costs would be lower and revenues higher because the recoordinated organization was optimal for their strategic goals or whether it was the outcome of a wasteful internal political fight, or both.[42] And a counterfactual assessment of what would have happened had IBM gone down another path would be extremely difficult. Our core point is that scope diseconomies compelled some sort of compromise between IBM's new and old businesses in order to avoid internally inconsistent uses of investments in the firm's key assets.

39. Estridge was given the title Vice President, Manufacturing, and a job involving worldwide manufacturing. Most employees within the company and IBM-watchers outside the company viewed it as a demotion, though, characteristically, Estridge was good natured about it. Tragically, several months later, on their way to their first vacation in years, he and his wife were killed in an air crash at Dallas airport.

40. Lowe had spent the last few years as a General Manager of IBM's facility in Rochester, Minnesota, and then as Vice President, Systems, and later, Development, for the System Products Division in White Plains, N.Y. Prior to moving back to Boca he was Assistant Group Executive for the Information Systems and Communications Group, a position he assumed in August 1983.

41. Lowe never bought a house in Florida after arriving in March. Later, most observers inferred that Lowe took the position in Florida knowing an announcement about a move might come soon thereafter.

42. In this case, a number of historical circumstances meant that internal political power shifted to the existing business. By the mid-1980s, thanks to the macroeconomy, the mainframe business was booming and the disaster of minicomputer entry was forgotten. The mainframe organization looked great; we further note that it would have looked far worse if the conflict with the PC division came in 1978 (i.e., if the macroeconomy of 1985 had looked like it did in 1978).

4.3.10 Smothered by Support from the Parent Company

IBM's top managers imposed a structure and a planning process on the PC Division in 1985 that coordinated its decisions with other parts of the firm. As desired, it resulted in decisions screened by the CMC and fostered a consensus-building process aimed at sampling the opinions and judgments of the other parts of the company and of customers.

In this section, we shall see how the traditional IBM supply organization was stunningly misaligned to an open-systems environment like the PC market. For the next three years, from 1985 to 1987, the PC Division acted like any other division of IBM in several senses associated with preserving key firm-wide assets. New PC products were released only after internal consultation and deliberation. New products were technically reliable, priced with high margins, and introduced later than competitors. Langlois (1997) suggests that this reflected classic cognitive framing problems on the part of IBM's managers and the fact that strategic models derived from the mainframe business were inappropriately applied to the PC business. Another possibility is that the PC business suffered from exactly the kinds of costs identified by Rantakari (2008), and was simply subordinated to the strategic needs of the mainframe business. Whatever the cause, the results were dramatic.

To some degree, IBM could get away with this in the PC market. It had a very valuable brand name, and was able to sell many PCs even though there were alternative IBM PC compatible products at lower prices. As a result, initially there was only weak negative market feedback about the changes in IBM's practices, and certainly this feedback was not at all visible in PC product revenues.[43] There were no IBM actions to generate strong negative marketplace reactions until the PS/2 rolled out in 1988.

However, unfortunately for IBM's commercial prospects, potential buyers did not *need* to wait for the results of all this internal coordination because they had access to alternative compatible products with similar functionality priced at low margins. Thus, IBM could not *compel* customers to follow its technical lead. Clone hardware products began to innovate faster than IBM could (the first Intel 80386-based PC was a Compaq machine, not an IBM one).

Despite its lack of a mechanism to impose leadership on the PC industry, and despite its inability to, IBM launched a major long-term initiative: the leapfrog redesign of the PC. An important part of this was a joint venture

43. As it turned out, immediately after the changes in 1985 there were not many negative revenue events with clear association with the new strategy. The PC/AT did well in 1985 and 1986. The negotiations with Microsoft also went according to plan in 1985, and its problems later were thought to be a symptom of Bill Gate's savvy, not problems with IBM's strategy for coordination. There was one negative market event. It was the PC/XT rollout, which went badly, but it had been planned for some time, so the changes post-1985 were not held responsible.

with Microsoft for a new operating system. These initiatives failed dramatically.

The PC organization suffered under the concerns of the rest of IBM. Most critically, meeting demand elsewhere in the firm, the PC revision reverted to IBM's historical stress on proprietary products, a design decision that met with approval from senior management. The firm announced in 1988 a 386-based machine with a proprietary architecture—the IBM PS/2 with microchannel architecture (MCA). In an effort to compel the transition, it simultaneously announced that the roll out of the PS/2 would be accompanied by the discontinuance of IBM's best-selling product at the time, the PC/AT, which was based on the 80286.[44]

The PS/2 might have sold well if it had had new or different features that *users* actually wanted; MCA was not such a feature. The MCA was seen as highly valuable by internal managers from the Large Systems Division. With MCA, and related software changes, PCs could be used to access data on large systems. The use of PCs for that purpose, however, was still in the future, and not an immediate market need. Rather than undertaking changes that were aligned to the *distinct* needs of the PC market, IBM undertook changes suitable to a new vision of an all-computing market, which, unfortunately, did not yet exist. What was lost was the urgency of the competitive situation of the open-systems PC: that was something that could not be learned quickly, as we have pointed out, and it was not appreciated by an IBM with a prospering mainframe division in 1985 to 1986.

The introduction of IBM's ground-up redesigned and proprietary PC was far out of sync with the open-systems PC market. Open systems markets absorb incremental improvements in components very well, but leapfrog designs to a proprietary architecture impose switching costs on customers. By 1988, IBM's actions had fostered the perception that IBM's managers just did not understand the situation. In the summer of 1988 the clones declared independence from IBM's designs by combining to form the EISA, a 32-bit architecture that respected backward compatibility with prior IBM designs but without the MCA.[45] The announcement openly rejected IBM's stewardship in planning upgrade cycles for the IBM-PC-and-compatibles industry.[46]

44. Carroll (1993) attributes the decision to remove the PC/AT from the US market to Lowe alone. As evidence for this interpretation, he notes that just before this decision, Lowe's former boss received a promotion to head IBM-Europe, where he did not discontinue the PC/AT and it continued to sell well. Carroll's interpretation must be an overstatement. Keeping with standard practice at IBM at the time, this decision must have been reviewed by the CMC and the divisions related to distribution of products (and either party could have objected if they understood the ramifications).

45. It was sponsored by AST Research, Compaq, HP, NEC, Olivetti, Tandy, WYSE, and Zenith Data Systems.

46. The principal difference between EISA and MCA was that EISA is backward compatible with the previous bus, while MCA was not. Computers with the EISA bus could use new EISA expansion cards as well as old expansion cards. Computers with an MCA bus could use only MCA expansion cards. Ironically, this fight was largely symbolic and short-lived. A few years

The market events of the summer of 1988 are a long story and one that has been told often in the press and many books. We do not disagree with the generally well-known facts about the severity of the crisis at IBM after 1988. Contemporary observers understood its importance and newspapers commented on it. And the rise to market prominence by other PC manufacturing firms, those whose strategies were consistent with the PC market environment, is correct.

Our point is that IBM's loss of leadership in PC technology, if not its exact timing, was rendered inevitable by earlier changes in organization. IBM's earlier success in the PC industry had been contingent on the independence of its PC Division. Once that independence was gone, IBM was overtly sharing key firm assets between PC and mainframe divisions in an effort to achieve economies of scope. But this was extremely difficult; indeed, despite the close connection between the two related divisions, the effort to gain cooperation between large systems and the PC made the firm entirely misaligned to the burgeoning PC market.

It takes nothing away from the market success of the PC industry to point out that, after 1985, IBM imposed extra costs on the PC business by structuring it in a way that altered the new business to suit the established one. Managing the challenges of the market environment in PCs was already hard, as IBM's own experiences prior to 1985 illustrated. The changes after 1985 added an additional cost to the challenges at the new division—that of coordinating with the rest of IBM. This did not have to lead to failure with regard to any particular decision, but it made failure more likely if the delays caused problems and if the marketplace did not value the benefits of increased coordination. Both happened rather quickly in the event.

Recognizing the early loss of IBM's alignment to the PC industry helps understand the history in another important way. The latter part of this epoch became cemented in the popular imagination, because, for their sheer drama, there is nothing equal to the events surrounding the divorce between IBM and Microsoft—embodied in meetings between Gates and Lowe, then Gates and Cannavino, Lowe's successor. The latter meetings received enormous attention at the time.[47] They also coincided with the rollout of OS/2 and Windows 3.0, two products that would compete directly. The outcome reinforced the perception that IBM was caught between a rock and hard place.[48] Many contemporary papers treated the divorce between Microsoft

later, a new technology called the PCI bus, sponsored by Intel, came into use in combination with the old EISA bus.

47. For *all* the details, see the latter half of Carroll's (1993) book, which is a full account of what he followed in detail as the *Wall Street Journal*'s reporter.

48. That is, IBM either continued contracting for an operating system from Microsoft or it organized its own software project in-house. No option looked attractive or free from large risks. The firm's managers had vacillated for years between these options before the divorce settled it, and when it compared with Microsoft directly the market's reaction was decidedly negative.

and IBM as if it were the downfall of IBM. Many focused on the question of bad-faith bargaining on Microsoft's part.

One important implication of the IBM/Microsoft dispute is that Microsoft, unlike IBM, was ultimately able to impose a proprietary standard on the PC industry. Microsoft, unlike IBM, did not assume that it could act like a firm managing a proprietary standard until after it had succeeded in imposing one. In the 1980s, Microsoft's decision making remained attuned to the (then) open-systems nature of the PC industry.

In summary, popular reports date the beginning of the crisis to events after the clones declared their independence. We think that popular account is misleading. We see many antecedents in earlier events. Our framework offers an alternative interpretation of the likelihood, timing, and severity of these events. First, many issues had appeared far earlier than 1988.[49] Second, over the late 1980s, IBM lacked an independent manager in the PC Division who could make deals with Microsoft in real time. It also lacked a focus on the immediate market needs of the PC market. These made the division a sitting duck for a more decisive firm that was better aligned to the market (i.e., a firm with a clear view of the needs of the marketplace and the capabilities to address those needs quickly), such as Microsoft, which ultimately took control of PC standards.

IBM retained its leadership in mainframes throughout the early period we emphasize. Late in the 1980s, it began to be clear to some market participants that that position would weaken. As smaller systems began cutting into large-system demand in the early 1990s, this competition became apparent to the large-systems managers at IBM who had denied the possibility throughout the 1980s.[50] Leadership in the proprietary mainframe platform would not be lost, but it would be much less valuable. Over the years, IBM would choose an open-systems approach even for enterprise computing, becoming a leader in a profitable though inherently limited niche, providing very expensive servers, and becoming a leader in the growing and much more profitable activity of being a service firm.[51]

The later decline of IBM's traditional business takes the focus away from

49. Aside from those already mentioned, Lowe's own accounts make it clear there were tensions before 1988. For example, Lowe and Sherburne (2009) highlight initiatives by the Mainframe Division to support an open UNIX platform in an alliance with DEC, which were initiated for political appearances. These were understandably greeted by Microsoft as contrary to their interests, fomenting mistrust between Lowe and Gates in particular. They are another example of the misalignment between the PC Division's strategic interests and the strategic interests of other parts of IBM.

50. Contemporary reports that emphasize technical advance have a tendency to observe the coming of an event before commercial markets actually act on it, dating the revolution's arrival by a technology's arrival instead of a market's activity. The profitability of a company is much more sensitive to the latter. Our dating of the *actual* change in market demand is in keeping with our prior empirical studies of the competition between legacy large-system users and the emerging client-server technologies. See Bresnahan and Greenstein (1996).

51. Gerstner (2004).

the deeper lesson. The IBM example illustrates the critical role of organizational scope diseconomies in fostering misalignment. It was ultimately impossible for the firm to manage both the PC business and its existing large-system business within the same organization. Conflicts arose over the deployment of fundamental strategic assets, IBM's reputation as a firm, and its relationship to its corporate customers. The conflicts were fundamental, entailing not only the marketing, distribution, and sales functions in a narrow sense, but the engineering and product design functions of the two businesses. Where the open-systems PC business called for quick, "good enough" new products compatible with PC-market competition and innovation, the existing proprietary large-system business needed predictable product upgrades, compatibility in connection between large-systems and small-systems, and high reliability. There was no resolving this conflict.

More to the point, the scope diseconomies inside IBM reflected a fundamental conflict over key firm-level marketing assets. The PC Division's optimum arose from the pressing competitive needs of an open-standards marketplace, while the enterprise division groups' optimum arose from the pursuit of a highly profitable and dynamic proprietary standard. The optimal form of firm-wide asset differed between the old business and the new so completely that neither business could easily accommodate the other's preferred form of firm-wide asset.

There was a great irony to IBM's internal organizational resolution of this conflict. It was not that the PC business was crushed in a fight, but rather that a highly attractive companywide cooperative solution was found.[52] That internally cooperative view just happened to be entirely inconsistent with the external behavior required of an open-systems PC division at this time. Hence, the IBM PC Division died slowly in the stranglehold of cooperating with the rest of IBM.

4.4 Microsoft and Mass-Market Internet Computing

Our second example explores Microsoft's response to Netscape's introduction of the browser and the challenge posed by widespread use of the Internet. Though it appeared as an entrepreneurial entrant in our first example, by the mid-1990s Microsoft had come to dominate the most profitable and strategic segments of the PC software markets, when the widespread use of the Internet threatened a new Schumpeterian wave. As we shall see, many of the same analytical themes about old firms entering new markets arise in this history—even though the same firm changes roles.[53]

Parts of the history of this example are well known. Microsoft fended

52. See Killen (1988), whose title "IBM: The Making of the Common View" gives away the punch line for a careful insider history of this cooperative solution.

53. As with the prior case study, we present only essential highlights from a very long sequence of events.

off a threat of creative destruction by entering the web-browser market as a strong second, eventually prevailing in the "browser war." Microsoft's browser is the most widely used browser even today, although the firm is not dominant, or even particularly important, in the most innovative and profitable software markets of the mass market Internet, such as search, e-commerce, or social networking.

Less well known, but well documented in the Microsoft internal e-mails and memos brought to light by the antitrust suit, are the radical organizational changes Microsoft made in the course of responding to this wave. Finding its existing PC software development and marketing organization misaligned to the new opportunity, Microsoft created a new organizational unit to supply its browser and related software. This was a partial success, as the new organization was well-aligned to the open-systems Internet. Nonetheless, fundamental conflicts with the existing PC software business over the appropriate use of shared assets and the degree to which the browser business should support an open-standards model both caused significant organizational turmoil and imposed real costs on the Windows business. These conflicts were ultimately resolved—as they were within IBM—by ending the independence of the new, Internet-oriented, unit and managing it instead as an integral part of the legacy business.

We organize our analysis around three main eras. The first era falls before the mass-market Internet opportunity became apparent to Microsoft. We show that the firm developed organizational capabilities that were well aligned with its strategy of being the dominant firm in PC software and of being a strong second in the introduction of new technology. We also suggest that it had particularly effective strategic decision making and resource allocation processes, and that although the firm was late to enter the browser market, the timing of Microsoft's entry cannot reasonably be construed as suggesting that the firm was an unaware or incompetent or backward-looking organization.

Our second main era is the browser war, when the wave threatened to overturn Microsoft's dominance in its traditional markets. The development of the Netscape browser launched the pervasive use of the Internet and for the first time brought a widely used network to mass-market computing. Microsoft at first viewed this development as innocuous. Once the firm came to see it as a threat to the existing hierarchy of the industry, it quickly entered the browser market as a strong second, creating an independent unit within the firm and giving it both considerable strategic freedom and access to the PC distribution channel that Windows' success had secured. Microsoft had great initial success in winning the browser war.

Nonetheless, during this same era, fundamental and seemingly irreconcilable conflicts between the old and new businesses emerged. These conflicts centered on the use of the firm's most important firm-wide assets, its reputation with outsiders and its control of distribution channels, and on the strategic direction of the browser business. Managers focused on the browser as a stand-alone business wished to pursue an open-systems strategy and to distribute the browser as widely as possible. Managers focused on the Windows business wished initially to restrict sales of the browser to new PCs in order to stimulate sales of Windows and then, as the potential for the browser to become a Windows-threatening platform became apparent, to minimize this threat. In contrast with the IBM example, these conflicts emerged almost immediately upon Microsoft's entry into the browser business. In our treatment of this era, therefore, we pass back and forth repeatedly between the firm's urgent need for market and strategic alignment with the mass Internet and the equally urgent need for market and strategic alignment for the proprietary Windows business, outlining the organizational problems and very real costs that this conflict created.

Our third era covers the resolution of these conflicts. Managing both businesses simultaneously according to their own logic was imposing considerable costs on the old business, and senior management had been drawn into not only conflict resolution but also the direction of detailed operational activities. Senior management decided to deal with these costs by imposing (yet another) reorganization, this time granting control of the new business to the managers of the old. This led to cessation of conflicts and to the management of the browser business as a strategic adjunct to Windows, but it also meant, from the perspective of the pro-Internet managers in the new business, the end of the effort to exploit the new opportunity in the most effective way possible. Many of the pro-Internet managers most committed to growing the new business left Microsoft. Since our second example is more recent, we lack the long historical period after the Schumpeterian wave we could observe with IBM. Nonetheless, Microsoft's former Internet radicals appear, so far, to have been right that the organizational decision of ceding power to the old business has limited the firm's ability to compete in the most profitable and innovative new markets in mass-market computing.

4.4.1 Microsoft before the Browser

As with IBM, we start with Microsoft's existing business. Microsoft's long-run strategic goal was to either dominate or commoditize all mass-market, general purpose computer technologies, and its strategy was to enter and seek to dominate new component markets when they appeared likely to become pervasive.

Microsoft's position and strategies has similarities and differences to the IBM case. Where IBM vertically integrated into a wide variety of mainframe hardware and software technologies, Microsoft had a partial vertical integration strategy, and was the dominant supplier only of the most widely used strategic software technologies, notably the operating system (Windows) and such key business applications as word processing, spreadsheet, and presentation. Hardware and most applications software came from other firms.

Nonetheless, the "Windows PC" was a proprietary platform. The divided technical leadership of 1985 had been replaced by a proprietary dominant platform, Microsoft Windows.[54] To achieve high revenue per employee, Microsoft sought to be the dominant supplier of only those general purpose components that could not be commoditized. It sought to keep proprietary standards for itself while forcing open standards on complementors, such as hardware manufacturers. Microsoft's central position let it dictate terms to other industry suppliers, including hardware manufacturers and applications software vendors.

Microsoft's organizational strengths were not tied to a specific technology. This does not mean that the firm's capabilities were infinitely fungible to meet any new opportunity. Instead, the firm had optimized its marketing and product development capabilities, as well as its strategic information gathering and decision-making capabilities, to two aspects of its market position as the PC industry's dominant software firm. First, it was well set up to exploit the extremely profitable dynamic of improvements to the PC, and to keep the PC on a proprietary and backward-compatible Microsoft standard as technology advanced. Second, it was well set up to perceive software technical progress from outside firms and to quickly assess its strategic importance. That is, Microsoft would decide to leave the inventor to exploit its invention or to enter as a strong second.

The history of Microsoft's rise to a dominant position in the PC industry has been written frequently, and we will not reproduce it in detail here (Cusumano and Selby 1995; Cringley 1992). For our purposes, the important thing is that Microsoft had been through a number of wrenching organizational changes before this time. In each case, it had moved forward without losing its then-preexisting positions.[55]

The causes of Microsoft's success are controversial, with some authors putting more weight than others on the firm's technical capabilities. For our purposes, what is important is that there is little controversy about Microsoft's abilities as an imitator, an incremental improver of existing designs, and most especially, about Microsoft's abilities and position in marketing

54. Microsoft was in a position to dictate behavior to firms supplying complementary products. Dictating terms was not costless, but a strategic dispute Microsoft deemed important would lead it to dictate. The browser war demonstrated that Microsoft was in a position to compel many firms to take actions different from their own self-interest, including the manufacturers of PCs, the developers of software applications, microprocessor dominant firm Intel and non-Windows-PC supplier Apple.

55. For example, Microsoft had been the dominant firm in programming tools for PCs from the earliest days of the industry, and it survived entry by Borland, a firm with a far-superior product, to continue as the dominant firm. Microsoft had also moved beyond its tools business, and had frequently acted as the entrant into markets previously dominated by others (including Operating Systems, Spreadsheets, Word Processors, and Presentations).

and distributing mass-market software. Like IBM in an earlier era, Microsoft was an impressive strong second moving forward into dominance of the most strategic and profitable new technologies.

There are many historical examples of Microsoft's effectiveness as a strong second. For our analytical purposes, the key question is whether the firm still had those skills as the Internet revolution loomed. The answer to that is a resounding "yes."

By the mid-1990s many firms, including Microsoft, anticipated widespread electronic commerce, electronic entertainment, and other new mass-market online applications. Microsoft engaged in a strategy to imitate and exploit the best technologies for mass-market online applications in electronic commerce and content. The best available outside versions to imitate came from firms like AOL. Microsoft characteristically set out to enter as a strong second with a proprietary architecture. The idea was to have a proprietary Microsoft standard in place long before there was mass-market use of online services. This effort would eventually be given the name MSN, for Microsoft Network.

Microsoft expected mass-market online applications to follow the widespread distribution of broadband access, which, like many others, Microsoft predicted to be early in the new century. In other words, prior to the diffusion of the browser, Microsoft had committed itself to invest in online applications in the patient anticipation of slow user acceptance of its own and others' services, believing this gave its developers enough time to experiment with a new service and position it appropriately by the time demand by mainstream users began to grow.

In seeking to set a standard for mass-market online applications, Microsoft sought to take advantage of its dominant position in existing mass market computing; that is, the PC. At this time, almost all of mass-market computing was PCs. There were approximately 100 million users of Windows, for example, versus (they are harder to count) 4 to 6 million users connected to any wide-area network, and the networked users included very many, possibly a majority, of technical users (scientists and engineers in government, universities, etc.) rather than the kind of home and ordinary business users who would be the growth segment for mass-market online applications. To exploit its installed base advantage, Microsoft sought to distribute the user software for MSN with new PCs, beginning with Windows 95. This would immediately put the MSN user software in front of nearly two orders of magnitude more users than AOL had.

We shall return to MSN a number of times, as it played a number of different roles in our three eras of Microsoft's relationship to the Internet. For now, we note only that, while Microsoft's managers did not see the mass Internet coming, they were, nonetheless, within their information set, forward looking. They were committed to a proprietary mass-market e-commerce and content strategy in 1994, and a commitment to the future. This was not an old firm resting on its old products.

In summary, Microsoft was well organized to detect new technologies invented outside, and to quickly decide how they fit into the firm's long-run strategic plans, and ultimately to ship new products or amended products in response. The firm was an excellent imitator, incremental improver, and executor of its commercial goals. It implemented a strategy of partial vertical integration, and of proprietary standard-setting dominance. This supported profitable exploitation of noncommoditized PC technologies using a set of organizational capabilities aligned with the strategy.

Microsoft's strategies put extraordinary demands on the firm's ability to perceive outside developments and act on them. Leaving much technical development to outside firms meant that Microsoft faced the constant risk of outside invention of either strategically threatening or potentially valuable technologies. The development and success of an outside technology standard would undercut the extent to which the entire PC industry was organized around the proprietary Windows standard.[56] Senior management needed to be responsive both to a constant barrage of new information from outside and to the need to focus on implementing improvements in existing products. Much of this tension was resolved by a combination of decentralizing day-to-day authority for existing product lines and centralizing strategic direction and decision making about new initiatives, including remarkably small ones. Microsoft could be extremely patient and foresighted in the effort to expand the range of products that were its proprietary technology (though others groused that the important inventions came from outside).[57]

Microsoft was, in some very positive ways, highly centralized. The senior management team was very effective at gaining information about developments both inside and outside the company and at acting on them. Major strategic decisions were not delegated. All employees were instructed to bring their ideas for initiatives as well as their conflicts to the Strategy Team, which consisted of Gates, Ballmer, and several other high-level executives. The firm demonstrated extraordinary discipline in this, and as a result the top strategists never lacked for technical information or for heterogeneous assessments of the market potential for new technical directions. In contrast, management of the major product lines was highly decentralized. This included management of the development of new products or new versions of existing products. This combination of centralized strategic authority and decentralized implementation was quite well aligned to Microsoft's existing

56. The historical example used within the company to evoke this situation was the local area network communication standard that grew up around Netware.

57. For example, it was nearly a decade behind Apple in making a Graphical User Interface (GUI) a centerpiece of its operating system, but today by order of magnitude, more people use the Windows GUI than the Apple Macintosh GUI.

dynamic market opportunities but it also imposed a serious bottleneck on decision making. Historically, this had not been a critical issue since decision making occurred quickly, and the strategic benefits of centralization had outweighed potential costs. Nevertheless, as we shall see, it played a role in the browser wars by delaying Microsoft's response to Netscape's browser.

4.4.2 A New Opportunity, a New Schumpeterian Wave

The mass use of the Internet, triggered by the invention of the World Wide Web (WWW) and the web browser, was one of the most important technical advances of the twentieth century. However, despite the firm's strengths in perceiving outside innovations and reaching strategic decisions about them, Microsoft's decision to enter the browser market—its key strategic reaction to the Internet—was slow. Netscape's browser, not Microsoft's, was the first to obtain mass-market acceptance. Why? The established dominant firm was not ignorant of the new opportunity. Instead, it rationally (if ex post incorrectly) *decided* not to take it up.

Why did Microsoft at first leave the browser opportunity to Netscape? One logical possibility is that Microsoft did not even notice the outside developments. After all, those developments did not come from one of the many firms whose actions Microsoft monitored closely, such as Sun, IBM, Lotus, Compaq, HP, Oracle, and so on.[58] The technological and noncommercial origins of the threat also were not standard.[59]

As is the case with IBM's decision with respect to the PC, this explanation is contradicted by both broad and specific facts. Microsoft's organization was very effective at competitive intelligence. Support for third-party software firms gave its employees regular insight into the plans of other firms in the personal computer industry. Further, Microsoft employees were regular participants in the institutions of the computer industry that supported its open systems and noncommercial segments. Moreover, the process for triggering changes in response to outside developments was well-known within the firm. Requests to alter designs climbed a (comparatively flat) hierarchy directly to the Strategy Team.

In fact, Microsoft's organization functioned excellently in bringing the widespread use of the Internet and the opportunity associated with the browser to the attention of senior management. A formal presentation of

58. Though, to be sure, once the Internet began to diffuse, it did not take Oracle or Sun long to devise a strategy for "thin client and fat server," which served their interests in relation to Microsoft's. It did not commercially succeed. That is a longer story. See Bresnahan (1999).

59. The building blocks of the technology—TCP/IP, HTML, and the parts endorsed by the World Wide Web Consortium—did not come from the places where prior technological revolutions in computing science originated. The HTML came from an employee at a high-energy physics lab in Switzerland, Tim Berners-Lee, who later founded the World Wide Web Consortium. The operations for the US Internet backbone came from the recently privatized NSFNET. On these origins and their transition into commercial markets, see Abate (1999), Berners-Lee (2000), Greenstein (2008), and Mowery and Simcoe (2002).

the suggestion that Microsoft should produce a browser and other mass-market Internet technologies was made to the senior team in April of 1994. This was still early enough that the firm could have gained strategic advantage from investing in Internet applications. At that stage, however, Microsoft decided to provide only Internet "plumbing" to connect a PC—tools and processes inside the operating system to support Internet protocols, leaving the browser and other applications to outsiders.

The plumbing decision was entirely consistent with the long-run goals of the existing Windows division, who sought to encourage the adoption of Windows. Windows marketing staff saw the advantage of making it possible to connect a Windows PC to the Internet. The plumbing made it possible to connect Windows to the Internet, while leaving Microsoft cooperating with Internet-oriented firms.

The decision not to enter the browser or related applications markets reflected the assessment that a proprietary online service model a more profitable approach to the same market opportunity. In the autumn of 1994, Gates restated the then-familiar strategic analysis. He expressed considerable doubt about the potential profitability of any open-systems Internet application—for Microsoft or any another firm. Internet applications had previously been catalogued as the domain of third-party vendors and of little potential business or strategic value to Microsoft. The noncommercial and open-systems origins of the most popular browser reinforced the view that the application lacked profitability.[60] Further, Gates expressed the view that standards for PC-Internet connection would be decided by Microsoft with its (then) 100 million users. Internet plumbing connections could remain open so that data transport would be a commodity. In brief, seeing neither opportunity nor threat, the firm did not change course.

Not everyone at Microsoft agreed with management's decision. A disobedient and secret initiative was organized by Brad Silverberg in the summer and autumn of 1994. Silverberg was a comparatively senior manager who reported to members of the Strategy Team.[61] These employees ostensibly did something that was not unusual at Microsoft; examining trends aimed toward taking new initiatives after Windows 95 shipped. They were due to gain internal power and prestige later. For example, one member who reported to Silverberg, Ben Slivka, would later lead the team that built Internet Explorer (IE) 1.0, 2.0, and 3.0. At this time, however, they labored in obscurity, as do most skunk works that lack senior executive support. No one paid much attention to them, and, by the same token, they received few resources.

Their lack of status and resources was an unintended drawback to the suc-

60. The first popular browser, Mosaic, came from a team of undergraduate and staff programmers at the University of Illinois, Urbana/Champaign.

61. Ben Slivka, private communication, October 2008.

cessful execution of a centralized strategic allocation of resources—Gates and his advisors saw no value in investing in employees understanding all the various aspects of Internet technology, so deliberately none was made. Thus, Microsoft's late development of the browser began—when it did begin—without a developed internal group with intimate knowledge about all aspects of the existing capabilities for the Internet.

Just as IBM had done with the PC, Microsoft, for a time, deliberately chose not to pursue the new opportunity. For each firm, the moment of entry and changed assessment, was, of course, a time when it would have been valuable to see the new opportunity more clearly and earlier. Consideration of that value has shaped the normative business literature on firm design, with many calls for foresight and flexibility at the firm level. That is misguided, at least in the case of excellently managed firms like the ones we study here. It is inherent to high-tech industry that information changes over time, and that some new opportunities appear more important (or less!) later than they did earlier. One point of this section is that Microsoft, like IBM, made an informed deliberate decision not to enter the new business early on.

That is not to say that the decision to eschew early entry into the new market was not based on Microsoft's existing business. Indeed, the main point of this section is that the early decision to delay entry into the browser market (and hence, the severity of the competitive events hereafter) arose because Microsoft was the proprietary standards-setter in the pre-Internet PC. This, too, is parallel to the IBM case in the early stages. Each case gives us an important lesson about the incentives at early stages of Schumpeterian waves. The same new opportunities appeared profitable to entrepreneurs and unprofitable to the existing dominant firms in both cases. This interim information period left the existing dominant firm with sunk investments in firm-wide shared assets and an internal decision-making structure that were consistent with the old opportunity. It later proved to be inconsistent with the new one.

Microsoft's delay in entry gave Netscape an extraordinary commercial opportunity, which others would label an error by Microsoft. In retrospect, such an error would not—we might say, *could not*—last for very long. Microsoft was and is an organization with administrative processes designed to help it respond to market events, and to reverse past decisions by the CEO. Once it became clear that using the browser to access the Internet was as salient to mass-market computing as everyone realizes today, Microsoft reversed course.

The salience of the browser and the Internet as a threat and opportunity in mass-market computing was clear to Microsoft by the spring of 1995. Several external events had changed internal perceptions.

First, Netscape began to act like an important commercial firm in the mass-market software business. Netscape had begun to make money from sales to businesses and employed a unique distribution mode involving free downloads by households and students, anticipating revenue from business licensees.[62] Netscape had begun a program to invite third-party vendors to make applications compatible with the Netscape browser, mimicking Microsoft's practice of supporting APIs (application programming interface)—practices aimed at influencing the rate and direction of innovation. Netscape had also begun to expand its product line into complements to browsers, such as products for servers and areas of related networking.[63] This market-development activity would bring the browser and the Internet into play as an effective way to achieve mass-market e-commerce and content.

All of these developments were bolstered by an effort on Netscape's part to take advantage of the open-systems nature of the Internet. Many developers flocked to the Internet building commercial applications. While some griped that Netscape was not as committed to open systems as noncommercial entities, the reality was that mass use of the Internet was developing at the extremely rapid pace permitted by open systems. Rather than waiting for the widespread deployment of Broadband Access as under Microsoft's proprietary MSN, the market for widely used online content and commerce could (and did) develop very rapidly using dial-up capabilities.

Perhaps most importantly, the rapid rate of adoption of Netscape browsers meant that there would soon be a pervasive and strategically important software complement to Windows under the control of another firm. This marked a return to the Industrial Organization of the PC business of the 1980s. A sequel to the 1980s might have the same plot, but the roles had changed. Like IBM before it, the mature Microsoft was cast in the role of incumbent, while Netscape was playing the role of the young upstart, like Microsoft in the past.

These developments changed the outside strategic situation radically and Microsoft then quickly changed its assessment.

The Silverberg group gained attention, and conducted many wide-ranging conversations with existing stakeholders inside the firm. They established and refined a vision about the future of the marketplace and Microsoft's potential role in it, and internally publicized its views and efforts.[64] In April 1995, they organized an evening of surfing for Bill Gates, with instructions about where to go and what to look for. The demonstration succeeded in changing Gates's views. Gates spent the better part of the night surfing. A month later he issued the memo entitled "The Internet Tidal Wave," which

62. The browser was free, technically only for evaluation and educational purposes. This was a variant on a well-known practice among shareware vendors to let out software for trial use and attempt to follow up with registration during service or upgrades.

63. Cusumano and Yoffie (2000) have an extensive description of how Netscape explored the commercial potential of many complementary service markets through site visitation of lead users and interaction with many user and vendor experiments.

64. See Slivka (1995) for the fourth and final draft of this vision statement.

effectively admitted the prior oversight and announced the realignment of priorities for strategy inside the firm. The next day the skunk works issued its fourth and final version of its vision, written by Ben Slivka, entitled "The Web is the Next Platform."[65] Both Gates's and Slivka's memos show that Microsoft was now the old firm in a Schumpeterian wave. Both writers explicitly outlined scenarios that led to the loss of Microsoft's market position as a result of new competition.[66] Each also saw the potential profitability of many new long-term commercial opportunities.

The widespread use of the Internet, and the breakthrough PC software that permitted it, the browser, had three implications for Microsoft. Two of these arose immediately, an important difference from IBM's entry to the PC market. They are: (1) The browser (and the Internet resources it brought to users) was a close complement in the short run for Microsoft's PC software. Demand for PCs, and thus for Windows and Office, was about to grow very rapidly thanks to this outside innovation; (2) The browser posed an immediate threat to the established positions of Windows and Office; a Netscape browser standard could enable competition against Microsoft in much the same way a Microsoft operating system standard contributed to enabling competition against IBM earlier; and (3) In the long run, the growth of mass-market computing was going to have a strong Internet component; if Microsoft were to participate in the growth over the long haul, the firm would need an active strategy for supporting or providing new, network-oriented applications.

By far the most urgent of these three was the defensive (2); the Microsoft internal analyses recognized that the browser technology obviously held the potential to radically change the way a mass-market of users used the PC, possibly redefining the PC value chain and leaving Microsoft outside its central standard-setting position. Responding to it became a matter of competitive urgency at Microsoft. However, the delay in reaching the realization of a Schumpeterian wave was going to make dealing with the urgent competitive situation all the more difficult, and heavily influence the way the firm responded to the wave.

65. A publicly available copy of Gates (1995) is at http://www.usdoj.gov/atr/cases/ms_exhibits.htm, government exhibit 20. A publicly available copy of Slivka (1995) is government exhibit 21.

66. Gate's memo is eight pages, single spaced. Among its many themes, it stresses several different ways in which an independent browser might ultimately lead to "commodification" of the operating system. First, a browser and its extensions could accumulate the same functionality as the operating system, directly reducing the latter's market value. Second, an independent browser, combined with new technologies from Sun Microsystems called "Java," might lower entry barriers into the operating system business for Netscape or others. Third, the browser enabled something "far cheaper than a PC"—such as a network device—that might achieve sufficient capability to compete with Windows PCs. Slivka's memo, at nearly fifteen pages of text, includes many of these same scenarios, but places particular emphasis on the third.

Late Entry Proves Costly

Microsoft's early underassessment of the Internet applications platform was extremely costly in the short run. Over 1994 and most of 1995, Microsoft did little Internet-related development or marketing. As both Gates's and Slivka's memos made abundantly clear, there was no shortage of Internet-related activities relevant to Microsoft's existing businesses. Microsoft's legions of programmers had not explored the possibility of redesigning any applications, tools, or operating systems to emphasize the World Wide Web and its standards. The absence of advanced development work was a symptom of how unanticipated this threat was and how late top managers were (in comparison to entrants) in recognizing the potential.

Things got worse before they got better for Microsoft. Having recognized the possibility of a Schumpeterian wave in the Spring of 1995, Microsoft saw the importance of entering the browser market itself as a strong second. However, for the next several months (until August) the firm's first (if not only) priority would have to be the launch of Windows 95, key to ongoing dominance in its core business.

Netscape had a very substantial lead on Microsoft in a race to establish a browser standard. Microsoft's answer was to attempt to enter the browser market at the same time it launched Windows 95. Internet Explorer (IE) 1 was a hastily modified version of the Mosaic browser, originally developed at the University of Illinois, which the university was now widely licensing out through a third party.[67] However, IE 1 was not nearly as good as Netscape's browser, and there were also problems in the support network.

Users had little reason to choose IE 1. Any technical observer of both browsers could see why. While both browsers were based in noncommercial versions, the team at Netscape had reprogrammed the entire browser from scratch, tested a beta version with many users, and made numerous improvements to the browser and other programs that worked with it. Netscape's browser had nearly a year's lead time over Microsoft's. The quality gap was so large that Netscape dominated in browser usage.

Internet-oriented applications developers also had little reason to work with Microsoft's browser. Announcing support for Internet applications was not sufficient to motivate third-party developers to write software to run in Microsoft's browser when superior technologies existed elsewhere. Even developers who would have supported a Microsoft strategy in the early going did not have an opportunity to do so. Microsoft simply did not have an Internet strategy for outside developers to follow. The company did not publicly announce its strategy until early December, well after the release of Windows 95 and Netscape's IPO (both in August 1995).

67. See an account from the viewpoint of the licensor in Sink (2003). Slivka and company had arranged for the license at the end of 1994, and had only limited time to make changes oriented toward their perceptions about user needs.

The theoretically relevant conclusions we draw from the early period in which Microsoft struggled to respond to the threat posed by the Internet are necessarily limited. To state the conclusion first: Like many established dominant firms, Microsoft was not the first to see a new opportunity, and, like many other established dominant firms, bore considerable adjustment costs in the short run as it moved to enter a new business. These costs were made all the larger by the delay in perceiving the threat, by a substantial gap between its existing capabilities and those that would be aligned to the new business, and by a temporary but severe need to devote all attention, and the key asset of reputation with outside developers, to the existing business. These problems are general to established dominant firms and they were severe in this instance: they left Microsoft with no legal way to win the browser war.

Yet any such conclusion is necessarily limited by its focus on the early phase. In Microsoft's case, these adjustment costs were severe but transitory. In a few pages, we shall turn to the firm's rapid and decisive shift of attention and resources to the new business that served, over time, to reduce the importance of the short-run adjustment costs. To undertake that analysis, we first look at the details of the new business opportunity Microsoft was entering, so that we can see the goals to which it needed to realign and why these imposed nontransitory, scope diseconomies on the firm.

4.4.3 The New Opportunity

Microsoft faced a narrow window of time to enter before a Netscape browser standard would be set. Microsoft's own analyses of the browser market concluded they had a short window of time to move both users and developers over to their browser.[68] Microsoft concluded that an immediate and powerful move as a strong second might switch standard setting to its product, but a move that was either not immediate or not powerful would fail.

The decision to enter the browser market brought Microsoft into direct competition with a firm seeking to establish its own standard, Netscape. Netscape had been skillful in the way it took advantage of its long lead, working to make the browser war into an open-system, standard-setting race in which Microsoft's strengths would be devalued.

One open-systems strategy from Netscape was introducing a browser that ran on all kinds of PCs. Since almost all PCs were Windows PCs running Microsoft operating systems, this might seem like a small point. Neither the Apple Macintosh, nor desktop UNIX, nor any of the potential "thin clients" discussed at this time was likely to grow very rapidly, so in the short run, the PC was a Microsoft-dominated PC. However, Microsoft was attempting to move the Windows standard from the obsolete Windows 3.x (3.0, 3.1) to the

68. For a fully developed analysis of many market-oriented factors and their role in setting de facto standards in this case and more generally, see Bresnahan and Yin (2006).

modern Windows 95. As Netscape launched its browser, almost all PCs in use were the older standard Windows 3.x.

The effect of this was to compel Microsoft to adopt a parallel open-systems strategy for its own business, a strategy that immediately placed the browser effort in strategic tension with the Windows business, the core of the existing firm. Thus Microsoft found itself, just as IBM had earlier, a proprietary-standards company entering an open-systems market.

A second problem along the same lines arose because Netscape, like other entrepreneurial Internet firms, had developed organizational capabilities that allowed it to bring out new products rapidly and effectively. If Microsoft were to compete effectively, they would have to move away from the organizational capabilities developed by the firm during its experience prior to 1995. The firm had a long history of taking several years to commercialize software: It was demonstrably good at commercializing software that required coordinating large teams of designers, programmers, and distributors, inside and outside the firm. It was also successful at reviewing the market experience, generating lessons, and incorporating them into later versions. Those organizational capabilities were magnificently aligned to being the dominant firm in the PC industry. In a speed-based browser war, however, these capabilities had limited value.

As IBM before it, Microsoft therefore set up a firm within a firm. It was given a mandate to be fast. Most importantly, the team developing IE was situated outside the operating system group. Microsoft set up a new division, the Internet Platform and Tools Division (IPTD).

The parallel with IBM's PC Division is not complete. Microsoft's Internet division never had as much autonomy: Gates and the Strategy Team retained rights to monitor and intervene in decisions, and, from the outset, they used it frequently.[69] The IPTD did, however, have considerable independence from the existing operating systems business in Microsoft, which gave it freedom to act like an open-systems company.

The IPTD's development process, motivated by an urgent need to catch up to technological leader Netscape, departed from Microsoft norms. Rather than slowly and carefully consulting with a wide range of stakeholders in order to define users' and developers' migration path to the next major release years from now, the IPTD was quickly chasing a market leader and adding features in response to competition.

Impressively, Microsoft built the IPTD up to 4,500 people (there are considerable strategic advantages affiliated with eventually being able to deploy resources on a vast scale, as a rich dominant firm can do). Equally impressive, an elite team of programmers within the IPTD worked to improve

69. Indeed, that monitoring and intervention activity left an impressive trail of e-mail communications between various managers of this division and top management at Microsoft. For a lengthy review of much of it, see Bank (2001).

Microsoft's technology, rapidly chasing Netscape in browser quality and features. The quality gap with Netscape narrowed with each major release. By the release of IE 3 in August 1996, there was only a modest gap. The IE 4, released in September of 1997 and, for all computers, winter of 1998, had nearly caught up to the market leader. Taking two and a half years to catch up in quality was not sufficient for moving the browser standard away from Netscape, but this impressive technical effort was certainly necessary.[70]

Intending to build a large organization that played to its strategic advantage as a large software developer, Microsoft began investing simultaneously in browser technologies and the services related to supporting developers. It also let developers know about its investments and its intention to support a mass-market browser technology. These actions let developers plan for more complex applications as well as for mass-market applications for the Internet of the future, suiting users who value ease-of-use as well as network access.

The successes of the IPTD have a great deal of theoretical salience. As in the IBM example, there was no lack of learning, nor any deficiency in key capabilities. This established dominant firm learned what was necessary for success in the new market and executed its strategy. Also, we see a number of conventional scope economies here, though they were limited. The large number of extremely talented technical people inside Microsoft together with management's ability to quickly redirect resources provided a benefit in the new market, while the existing product development process and the associated reputation for slowness would be problematic. Microsoft solved this by putting great people in a new organization exempt from existing processes.

Since its technical efforts were only necessary but not sufficient for strategic success, the browser group also sought to draw on Microsoft's most important firm-wide assets in marketing and distribution. Although access to these assets gave Microsoft's browser business considerable initial advantages, they also quickly led to the imposition of significant costs on the core Windows business, tremendous organizational conflict, and increasing pressure to manage the browser business as a strategic complement to Windows. These pressures made it increasingly difficult for the browser business to "act like an entrant" and eventually led to a fundamental shift in control, just as they had done inside IBM.

Microsoft's control of the PC distribution channel and its reputation with developers were key firm-wide assets. The channel was not a necessarily shared asset—Microsoft's new browser business could and did take advantage of the channels that Netscape was using—but its availability presented the browser business with perhaps its only possible means of catching Netscape, and thus created a positive classic economy of scope for

70. See Cusumano and Yoffie (2000), Bresnahan and Yin (2006).

Microsoft. The firm's reputation with developers, in contrast, was necessarily shared—actions taken by the browser group in this regard would have immediate reverberations across the entire community, and vice versa, and the use of this asset proved to be much more problematic.

Microsoft's long-run strategy was to take advantage of growing demand over several years and undercut Netscape's initial advantage. The simplest part of this strategy was arithmetical. The existing stock of browser users overwhelmingly used Netscape. But, partly fueled by the tremendous attractiveness of Internet access, people were buying new computers at a record pace, often to get on the Internet for the first time. If Microsoft's browser were used by most new computer buyers, the rapid growth in demand meant new adopters of IE would soon outnumber the existing stock of Netscape users. Microsoft took advantage of this arithmetic—and of its control of the distribution channel—by contractually compelling computer manufacturers to distribute IE with new computers and informally banning them from distributing Netscape.[71]

This distribution strategy could not compel users who had already chosen it to stop using Netscape's browser. But it could contribute to increasing the number of users and developers dedicated to IE. Specifically, distributing only one browser to some mass-market adopters could (a) generate some adoption among users who continue with the browser that came with their computer, and (b) generate some adoption by developers who wanted to serve the users of IE. After a period of time, as the arithmetic played out, a majority and then an overwhelming majority of users would be using IE, and the standard would shift to Microsoft.

Since control of the PC distribution channel, a company-wide asset, followed from Windows' market position, control was held by the Windows division. Senior Microsoft management directed the Windows marketing organization to use this control to benefit the Microsoft browser strongly. The Windows marketing organization complied. They contractually required distribution of IE with Windows by all PC original equipment manufacturers (OEMs) whenever they shipped a new computer. Further, the Windows marketers continually let every OEM hear about Microsoft's desire not to see alternative browsers distributed with new computers, and threatened retaliation against those OEMs who did distribute Netscape. These efforts were effective, in that Netscape largely disappeared from new computers in favor of IE.[72]

71. See Fisher and Rubinfeld (2001), Rubinfeld (2004), Bresnahan and Yin (2006).

72. A parallel effort, to compel developers to favor IE over Netscape, was also implemented by the Windows organization. This was less important. The Windows organization would only give information about the next version of Windows to developers who agreed to favor IE, but in the relevant time period new versions of Windows were minor improvements like Windows 98. For longer discussion, see Rubinfeld (2004), Bresnahan (2002), and Fisher and Rubinfeld (2001).

This strategy was not without costs. Scope diseconomies connected to reputation quickly emerged.

The first problem arose in the old business. The Windows marketing organization was in a position to make take it or leave it offers to the OEMs. That did not mean the strategy was costless. The OEMs were in a competitive business and the browser their customers wanted was Netscape, not IE. This led to continuing conflicts between the Windows marketers and their primary customers, the OEMs. As the OEMs invented new ways to give their customers a choice of browsers, the Windows marketing organization in response invented more and more inefficient and constraining contractual features to prevent it. While bearing these costs was necessary for a firm-wide strategy, the Windows organization—looking narrowly at its own business—saw this as forcing increasing restrictive and inefficient contracts on their customers.

This strategy also had reputation costs for Microsoft's nascent Internet business. By foregrounding the willingness and ability of Microsoft, the dominant firm in the existing PC industry, to unilaterally force conditions on its trading partners, this strategy could only heighten the outside community's awareness that in the long run the firm might have strong incentives to move away from the browser group's claim to be an open-systems company, particularly given the close complementarity between browser and Operating System.

4.4.4 Seizing Control of Distribution in New Channels

Because Netscape was so far ahead in the browser war, and had such an effective strategy of distribution to existing PC users, Microsoft's browser division would lose if it relied only on the "arithmetic" mechanism of waiting for the stock of PCs to turn over. Thus, Microsoft was compelled to seek emergency control of the new distribution channel that emerged as the Internet developed. We cover this part of the Schumpeterian competition in this section, not so much because of its competitive logic, but because the compromises Microsoft was compelled to make in its foray into the new distribution channel—its very success in acting like a particularly effective entrant—led to tremendous internal conflicts, illuminating the depth and strength of the organizational scope diseconomies between its new and old businesses.

In 1995 most PC users, and therefore most potential browser users, were using older versions of Windows (like 3.0 or 3.1). A small minority of users wanted to access the Internet from a UNIX computer (typically in a University setting) or a Macintosh. Netscape had an open-systems strategy. It sought to distribute browsers to all existing computer users to build a mass-market quickly and turned to Internet Service Providers (ISPs) as a result.

The conversion of the Internet to a mass-market called for an industry to sell access. The rapid growth of the Internet Service Provider industry filled this need.[73] By early 1996, a wave of new ISPs offered Internet service throughout the United States. Many were local businesses organized around a bank of modems. There were also national firms: Online leader AOL (America Online) publicly switched strategies to embrace the Internet; with Web-friendly software, acquisitions, and a new pricing strategy, AOL was becoming the largest ISP in the country. As with other ISPs, AOL was introducing new Internet users to many facets of the Internet.

Netscape initially signed contracts to distribute its browser with ISPs as well as with OEMs selling new PCs. Thus, even as Microsoft cut off distribution of the Netscape browser with new PCs, people signing up for Internet access could get a Netscape browser from their ISP. This, plus Netscape's long lead time, left Microsoft with a problem: waiting for the arithmetic of exclusive distribution with new PCs would be too slow to prevent a Netscape browser standard.

Microsoft sought to plug this gap in its control of distribution by seeking exclusive distribution of IE rather than Netscape when a customer signed up for Internet access. The ISPs responded differently than OEMs to Microsoft's approach. Where Microsoft was in a position to put OEMs out of business if they did not comply, ISPs saw Microsoft as largely irrelevant to the widespread use of the Internet. With most ISPs, who were small, Microsoft overcame this problem by paying them for exclusive distribution.[74] While that sounds like a classically positive scope economy—existing dominant firms will typically have cash—the leading ISP, AOL, held out for nonmonetary and strategically important terms, which as we shall see in a moment, imposed significant costs on Microsoft's existing businesses and thus implied real scope diseconomies. However the exclusive distribution arrangements were obtained, they solved the distribution problem for Microsoft. When users signed up for Internet access, they would be given a copy of IE, not of the Netscape browser. This strategy filled the loophole: now the two effective distribution channels for browsers would both be all-IE. This distribution dominance ultimately led to the end of the browser war in Microsoft's favor.

The same strategy also dramatically increased scope diseconomies between Microsoft's new Internet business and its existing Windows business. These scope diseconomies were fundamental, a conflict between the Windows business's essential need to manage transitions in the Windows standard and the browser division's need for universal open-systems distribution.

73. Greenstein (2008) describes the regulatory and economic origins of these suppliers.

74. At this point the next largest ISPs after AOL were players with national aspirations, such as CompuServe, AT&T WorldNet, and several others. A large number of players had small market shares, but aspired to national prominence, such as MindSpring, EarthLink, and Erols. Deals with several dozen ISPs could, therefore, account for somewhere between 80 percent and 90 percent of US market share. See Greenstein (2008).

Microsoft initially distributed its new browser only with new PCs running the new Windows 95—a strategy that avoided these diseconomies of scope. The browser business gained a distribution advantage, and the Windows business gained a valuable complement for a new PC. This win-win world for Microsoft's new and old businesses would not survive the use of ISP browser distribution strategy aimed at getting Microsoft's browser into the hands of people who were *not* buying a new computer.

The ISP deals gave Microsoft's browser distribution not only to buyers of new computers but also to the users of the stock of existing computers. This was critical from a browser-market perspective, since the browser group needed distribution to the existing stock of computer users to avoid a Netscape standard, but it imposed a significant cost on the Windows business. The Windows group did not want the browser to be compatible with old versions of Windows (3.0, 3.1, and the like) so as to preserve Internet-oriented users' and application developers' incentives to upgrade to Windows 95. The Windows division sought to manage the slow backward-compatible transition from one proprietary standard (Windows 3.x) to another (Windows 95), and thus needed to ensure that the new version of Windows, rather than the old, appealed to most consumers. From this proprietary-systems perspective, all efforts should be made to have valuable new software work only with the newest version of Windows. The browser division sought to *compete* for all customers immediately, whether they used a new or an old computer. Thus the browser division was in the business of offering highly attractive Microsoft software to customers of the old operating system, creating tension between the open-systems Internet business and the proprietary standards Windows PC business.

A variant of this tension between proprietary standards and open systems showed up in connection with Microsoft's proprietary online service, MSN. Microsoft Network had been founded by Microsoft employees, many working on it as early as 1992, and they had had the commitment of top management that their effort was the future of pervasive e-commerce and online content. For many years Microsoft's strategic team had made good on its commitments: it had nurtured MSN with favored status in distribution. Microsoft had required OEMs not to alter the prominent placement of MSN's symbol on a PC's desktop. These unilateral restrictions angered assembler OEMs, who could not tailor PCs to user requests, and also firms such as AOL, who would be willing to pay considerably for a prominent place on the desktop. Microsoft's top management was unwavering in its support for MSN.

The competition with Netscape over browser distribution put MSN's special status under pressure. Microsoft wanted to strike a deal with AOL, the largest ISP, for exclusive distribution of IE. Unlike smaller ISPs, AOL would not offer an exclusive distribution deal for money but instead demanded lifting the desktop restriction on AOL's symbol—so that it could negotiate with some OEMs to have the AOL symbol visible to consumers on the Windows desktop. This would be an effective nationwide distribution strategy for AOL.

AOL's demand highlights the conflict between a proprietary strategy and Microsoft's open-source strategy in browser distribution and the degree to which the presence of Microsoft's legacy businesses implied that Microsoft faced significantly different incentives in entering the new business than de novo entrants. Microsoft's deal with AOL is arguably one that a de novo entrant would have considered, and it brought very significant benefits to the browser business, but in imposing real costs on MSN and on the Windows business it caused considerable tension within the highest managerial ranks. Indeed, Microsoft initially refused AOL's demand and attempted to bargain with other things, such as money. This initial refusal was understandable, since capitulating to AOL's demand would be reneging on the promise to MSN employees and would grievously hurt Microsoft's existing, proprietary, online effort.

The urgency of competitive events in the browser market forced a decision in favor of striking a deal with AOL.[75] AOL made IE the default browser to distribute to its ISP customers, and, in exchange, AOL was exempted from the desktop restrictions. Further deals over time supported AOL's marketing interest on the desktop and promoted Microsoft's interest in generating the use of IE by AOL's users.

The AOL deal moved many Internet users to IE. The deal was a critical part of filling loopholes in Microsoft's distribution strategy, ensuring that IE and not Netscape had widespread distribution to new users with new PCs and to existing PC users new to the Internet at the time of ISP sign-ups. This distribution strategy, together with Microsoft's eventual success at catching up to Netscape in browser quality, led to a Microsoft victory in the browser war.[76]

As anticipated, this deal's benefits came with considerable cost for Microsoft. Over the next year, many MSN employees quit as MSN lost ground to AOL, setting back MSN's development for some time.[77] It is not possible to know whether MSN would have ever achieved any of its goals without the deals with AOL, but with those deals it did not achieve much. Proprietary MSN has been relaunched as an Internet "portal" and has not achieved anything like its original goals.[78]

75. Specifically, after considerable negotiation, AOL negotiated a deal with Netscape to support Navigator for several years, but left open questions about the default browser. The contract with Netscape placed pressure on Microsoft to fish or cut bait, pressure to which Bill Gates and Steve Ballmer relented.

76. For a list of these deals, and a discussion of their controversy, see Rubinfeld (2004), Bresnahan (2002), and Fisher and Rubinfeld (2001).

77. Bank (2001).

78. While MSN has typically been number two or three in the portal and online service markets, MSN has always been a distant second or third to the leading portal in a given year,

The scope diseconomies were not limited to a conflict between Microsoft's browser and MSN. Microsoft was compelled to permit a competitor, AOL, to make use of the Windows desktop, one of Microsoft's key assets as a firm. This uncomfortable open-systems behavior was essential to buy distribution for IE from AOL, distribution that was only necessary because of the Microsoft browser's open-systems distribution problem. Microsoft, heretofore able to dictate terms about the distribution of PCs, was forced to accept the terms proposed by AOL, only because AOL had turned somewhat quicker to embrace the new Internet opportunity. Used to defining the terms of unilateral bargaining with every partner, Microsoft here was forced by the emergency period of the Schumpeterian Wave to accept an outside firm's proposed terms. While obtaining widespread exclusive distribution for its browser in an open-systems way was a strategic goal for Microsoft, the costs in the proprietary-standards parts of the company were not trivial.

4.5 Applications Software Running in the Browser

Another source of scope diseconomies arose from conflicts about the role of Microsoft as a setter of standards for applications developers. Here we see—as we did with IBM—that the existence of the legacy, proprietary business means that the incumbent may have quite different strategic incentives with respect to the new business than a de novo entrant concerned only with success in the new market. The problem began when Netscape designed its browser to permit developers to write new, network-oriented, applications that would run "in the browser." Parts of the application might also run on a server computer on the Internet, including possibly a server computer owned by an online commerce, search, or entertainment firm. This technical possibility was deeply troubling to the Windows group. The PC part of the application, by running in the browser could run on any kind of PC, not just a Windows machine.

To counter the Netscape threat, the Microsoft browser needed to provide similar facilities. New, network-oriented applications had to be able to run in the browser. With the Microsoft browser being distributed not only to new Windows computers, but also to old Windows computers and to Macintosh, the Windows group saw this open-systems strategy as highly problematic.

Meanwhile, the browser division at Microsoft needed to act like an open-systems company in achieving rapid time to market for its products and having its products work with outside technologies, whether other Microsoft businesses such as Windows were benefitted strategically or not. Thus, in

whether that is Netscape, AOL, Yahoo, or Google. It has done better than most niche businesses, but never has had a dominant position, nor have analysts ever forecast that it was imminent. MSN also has not achieved another Microsoft aspiration; that is, any notable profitability in comparison to online leaders.

December 1995, Bill Gates announced a number of different collaborative arrangements with Internet firms.

The end of divided technical leadership on the personal computer and the control of the standards for PC applications development meant that "Windows is the platform" defined the strategic view of the Windows group even as an internal technology, Microsoft IE, came more and more to embody the alternative and deeply contradictory vision, "the web is the next platform." It is hardly surprising that the conflict over platform control shifted from Windows versus outside rivals such as IBM to Windows versus IE. These were powerful internal conflicts driven by the inconsistency of the Windows proprietary standard strategy and the open-systems approach of the browser and the Internet. As we shall see, these conflicts were resolved by senior management in favor of IE for the duration of the browser war and in a very different way after the browser war ended—very much as IBM had permitted the PC business to run an open systems-strategy initially but then, as the PC became increasingly perceived as a strategic threat to the mainframe business, forced a significant change in the new unit's strategy.

4.4.6 Diseconomies of Scope Issues Resolved

The specifics of the events inside Microsoft during the Schumpeterian emergency posed by the browser war are engaging, but we do not want them to distract from the more general points they illustrate: internal conflicts between the new business and the old were deep and difficult to resolve.[79] They involved conflicts over one of the firm's most important shared assets, control of the distribution channel. These conflicts were closely linked to fundamental differences in strategic alignment to the browser versus to the proprietary businesses. In the context of the computer and software industries, this was a conflict that revolved about the open-systems browser versus proprietary MSN and proprietary Windows, but our point is the more general one that the outside market environments of the two groups made the conflict fundamental.

Furthermore, these conflicts involved deep disagreements over what the firm's reputation for steadfastness and decisiveness, one of its most important intangible assets in negotiations, meant for new decisions. Repeated attention from senior management could keep these conflicts under control for a period of time, especially with an immediate competitive threat, but ultimately they had to be resolved as the costs in senior management time and attention grew. Initially these conflicts were overwhelmingly re-

79. Our approach to a complex history has necessarily been selective; one important set of conflicts we left out was those between the open-systems browser and proprietary-standards Office (i.e., Word, Excel, etc.) applications. *These* conflicts flared up when the Office unit was enlisted in the browser war. In order to compel Apple to distribute Microsoft's browser with Macintosh computers, Microsoft threatened to end the supply of Office for Macintosh, a product highly valuable to both companies.

solved in favor of IE. This was strategically necessary; the browser war represented a competitive crisis for Microsoft, which could have lost its extremely valuable position in Windows and Office if there were an independent browser firm.

Indeed, using the variety of distributional advantages described previously, Microsoft effectively pushed its browser out to all kinds of PCs, not just new versions of Windows, and blocked similar widespread distribution of Netscape. This gave IE a growing numerical edge in usage over Netscape. Indeed, after it became clear that IE 4.0 would come close to Netscape's browser in quality and after distribution restrictions created a great deal of market momentum for IE over Netscape, contemporaries began to forecast that Microsoft's strategy would succeed. However, the end of the browser war meant that the firm could step back and make long-term decisions. We now turn to these.

The Third Era: Putting the Legacy Business in Charge

At the end of the browser war senior management faced three distinct options. Critically, only one of these would have been available to an entrant: the other two flowed from the firm's strong incumbent position. They might have (a) continued to manage the browser business as a stand-alone entity, pursuing an Internet-oriented growth business inside the firm, using the capabilities of the IPTD, the newly formed Microsoft browser standard, and the enormous growth opportunities of mass-market online content and commerce, while maintaining their position in Windows and Office and potentially using the assets of Windows and Office to advance the browser business. This is the two-business, "firm within a firm," best of both worlds, option. Alternatively, they might have (b) expanded Internet tools and applications into all aspects of the firm's business, as had been planned under competitive pressure, and for which there was considerable internal enthusiasm (especially in the IPTD). This is the "conversion to the new world" option. Or they might have (c) returned to the strategies devised for Windows years before, a continuation in the old world option.

Microsoft's managers chose option (c), continuation in the old world. Our scope-diseconomies framework explains why they chose (c) the old world, over (a) pursuing both old and new. The choice between (c) continuation in the old market, and (b) conversion to the new world, falls outside the scope of what our theory can explain. We raise it to show how a theory of diseconomies of scope sharpens questions about the choices management faced.

Absent diseconomies of scope, pursuing option (a), the best of both worlds, would have been a highly profitable one for Microsoft. With the benefit of hindsight, it is obvious why. First, there has been a great deal of profit in mass-market computing in the Internet area. Firms who have taken up Internet-oriented growth businesses, such as Google, eBay, Facebook, and many others, have made enormous fortunes. Of course, others have lost money, but that is not relevant to Microsoft's circumstances. Microsoft would have entered this era as the browser-dominant firm, and as an important maker of tools for exploiting the capabilities of the web. This would have meant expanded control over distribution of mass-market applications. It also would have reflected Microsoft's ability to enter the most profitable or strategically important markets as a strong second. Had Microsoft pursued option (a), it would have been able to expropriate the returns to some or all of the invention we have seen in mass-market computing on the Internet in the last decade, just as it expropriated many of the most valuable inventions in PC computing over the previous era.

Management made a foray into the new business, a very significant foray measured either by costs or capabilities created, but then Microsoft retreated and chose option (c). Option (c) could be denigrated as the most conservative, but what it conserved was the two largest profit streams ever created.[80] This makes it difficult to criticize as wrong. Our key point is that there was no free choice of strategy without consideration of the costs imposed (and benefits created) by both the new and the legacy business. While the firm was capable, division by division, of pursuing both the old—Windows PC, goals—and the new—Internet, goals—pursuit of multiple goals would have clearly brought substantial diseconomies of scope. An independently managed browser business might well have accelerated a "browser is the platform" or, indeed a "the web is the platform" strategy, potentially dramatically undercutting the value of the existing operating and applications businesses. It would also have meant a continuation of very high levels of organizational conflict. We cannot know whether it would have been more profitable—but we can understand why Microsoft's senior team was reluctant to try it.

The choice of option (c) was not immediate but it was final. After the browser war's outcomes began to be clear, the Windows group's standing objections to the browser effort led to proposals to restructure the organization. In this case, as it worked out, management would act rather quickly, changing the formal organizational structure not long after the release of IE 3.0. The IPTD came to an end as a separate organization, and responsibility for the browser's further development fell to the Windows group.[81]

Over time the Windows Division, managed by Jim Allchin, continued to win virtually every internal fight for supremacy over strategic direction. A number of initiatives that might be understood as bringing Microsoft into

80. Option (c) would also come with a number of proprietary strategies for the new growth opportunities, such as Microsoft operating systems for cell phones and for server computers and an online presence for Microsoft through MSN. These were ideas in place before the widespread use of the Internet.

81. Bank (2001) provides an exhaustive chronicling of these events. He emphasizes a variety of rent-seeking, career-oriented, and personally guided motives.

the new, Internet era were reversed. General internal commitments to make IE run on many other PCs or other (non-Microsoft) software and so on were also allowed to lose momentum and disappear. In short, in spite of having the capability to pursue option (a), Microsoft chose quickly and decisively not to do so.

Of course, choosing to pursue (c) implied not choosing (b) as well. Option (b) would have represented even more of a commitment to Internet-driven growth, though we also note that it would have had some advantages. It would have let Microsoft take advantage of its new opportunities (e.g., for social interaction) while deftly avoiding its new challenges (e.g., computer security.) Option (b) would, in essence, have begun a pattern of migration within mass-market computing from the PC to the Internet, with all that implied for the length of time over which revenues would continue to grow.

The decision to pursue (a) was, of course, not without costs, especially the unification of the IPTD into the Windows group. This change generated considerable acrimony and rivalry inside Microsoft. The Operating Systems Division complained about having to take in IE. The IE had been developed in a competitive race, and, out of competitive necessity, was far from elegantly designed, difficult to modify, and fraught with the potential for intentionally coding "bugs," which are unanticipated inconsistencies between different parts of the code. The browser- and Internet-oriented IPTD felt that the firm was slighting their priorities, broadly abandoning the needs for the firm in the future, and potentially giving managerial discretion to the Windows Division over many potential market opportunities in markets for web applications. This induced a large number of exits by employees who had been committed to developing new Internet businesses.[82] The direction held firm in spite of the exits. Over time, once immediate competitive pressures had lifted, the firm returned to the strategic direction and organizational practices and strategic priorities they had favored many years earlier and had proven profitable prior to the diffusion of the Internet.

It is important to understand Microsoft's decision first to act like a future-dominant firm that believed "the web is the next platform" and then to retreat from that goal in light of changing information and incentives. Senior management worked through the costs of operating both businesses as the unanticipated scope diseconomies became apparent, and apparently large. Senior management initially tried to coordinate the new opportunity with the established business. After it was apparent there would be substantial costs, management tried to minimize them with a firm-within-a-firm organization.

That organizational form was very costly because of diseconomies of

82. Eventually Silverberg and Slivka and others affiliated with promoting the Internet quit. See the extensive discussion in Bank (2001).

scope. With the dual value of exploring a new growth opportunity and preserving the profits of Windows and Office, Microsoft's management was willing to bear the organizational and opportunity costs for a transitory period.[83] But once the competitive crisis was past, one of these two values fell away and the organizational scope diseconomies led to pushing the conflict away from senior management and into a division, where it was resolved in favor of the old, familiar strategy.

The internal conflicts Microsoft encountered with its online efforts highlights the firm's innate long-run problems exploiting economies of scope within a new environment. The tension between adjusting strategic priorities and keeping existing businesses in tow is yet another example we offer of the conflict between organizational diseconomies and achieving conventional economies of scope. This outcome had important long run implications. It left the firm with serious long-run market challenges. Numerous talented programmers and managers left the firm to pursue projects and commercial opportunities more closely oriented with their interest in Internet and web technologies. Dominating Internet clients (browser, e-mail, etc.) for individual users without focusing on the Internet brought serious headaches, many of them in the security area. The existing strategy of extending Windows into low-end servers (file, print, e-mail, etc.) while reinforcing outsiders' views that Microsoft sought excessive control over complementors created a market opportunity for open source projects, such as Linux, Apache, MySQL, and others. Focus on the OS platform (and on defensive strategies such as game boxes) rather than on the Internet left vacant opportunities on the server side with mass-market appeal, including search, directory services, hosting of retail stores, social-network sharing of user-generated content, mobile electronic communication (BlackBerries and smart phones), and virtually every other notable lucrative online opportunity after the recovery from the dot-com bust except gaming.

4.4.7 Like IBM

The scope diseconomies inside Microsoft had the same root cause as those inside IBM in our earlier examples. In each case, there was fundamental conflict over key firm-level assets. In each case, the optimal form of firm-wide asset differed between the old business and the new so completely that investments by one business raised, not lowered, costs in the other. Nor could either business easily accommodate the other's preferred form of firm-wide asset. The Microsoft browser division's optimum arose from the pressing competitive needs of an open-standards marketplace, the mass-market Internet, while the Windows and other proprietary groups' optimum arose from the highly profitable logic of customer and developer migration within

83. The coordination costs may have been lowest during the height of a competitive crisis as the authority to coordinate shifted to senior management.

a dynamic proprietary standard. An important difference between the two cases arose because the browser and Windows were close complements in the late 1990s, while the PC and the mainframe were only potential future complements in demand in the 1980s. One impact of this was that Microsoft was able to use its position in Windows (and Office) to win the browser war. The market outcome was, in the short run, victory for Microsoft in holding a browser standard.

The close complementarity between browser and OS also meant that the scope diseconomies were present in the routine operations of both divisions. The Windows Group's control of the traditional distribution channel aided accommodating the needs of the browser division. However, the browser division's open-systems strategy (of widespread availability on old versions of Windows and on the Macintosh) and of innovative programming (of new applications to run in the browser) brought it into immediate and direct conflict with the main strategic goal of the Windows Division, which wanted a managed migration within the Windows standard. Strategic success for the Microsoft browser and strategic problems for Microsoft Windows were tightly linked. In contrast, the IBM divisions' conflicts, while equally irreconcilable, lacked this immediacy and strength. As a result, Microsoft had much less room to maneuver in organizational design. Where IBM might have spun off a PC company—after taking years to think about whether it was wise—Microsoft needed to resolve conflicts quickly and within the firm.

Both IBM and Microsoft, by trying to accommodate an open-systems and a proprietary-systems business selling to the same customers, had tried to build a team of horses but, once the distinctions between the old and the new markets became clear, found it had built a Pushmi-Pullyu. Neither kept that organizational form; both went back to pulling in the old direction. The scope diseconomies between old and new businesses ruled out successful pursuit of both businesses, because sharing key firm-wide assets between the two businesses (in these cases marketing reputations) led to fundamental strategic conflict (in these cases between open- and proprietary-systems market strategies).

Enough historical time has passed to see IBM's loss of PC market standards and eventual exit, not to mention the competitive crash in enterprise computing that followed later; Microsoft's future in the Internet age is unclear at this juncture, even though it staved off this first threat. Both firms avoided any short-run threat to their existing position. Again, with IBM, sufficient time has passed to see long-run threats come to fruition, whereas Microsoft today continues to dominate its historical markets, but few of the new Internet ones. Notably, it has already lost many opportunities it aspired to exploit, namely, the proprietary electronic commerce businesses it anticipated dominating as pervasive broadband and small devices diffused.

We make a broader and more general methodological point here, buttressed by our choice to use the same firm, Microsoft, first as part of the new market and then as the old dominant firm, and to use the same industry, PC hardware and software, first as the new market and then as the old. Many scholars would be tempted to conclude that Microsoft is the better organized firm by comparing it to IBM in a snapshot. Better to compare the Microsoft of today to the IBM of the 1980s, to avoid the anachronistic error of concluding that the firm organized to serve yesterday's market will also be organized to serve tomorrow's.

4.5 Conclusions: Implications and Directions for Further Research

This chapter has explored a persistent finding in the empirical literature—the observation that at moments of technological discontinuities, incumbent firms, rather than being able to take advantage of scope economies, often find themselves at a significant disadvantage relative to de novo entrants. Through detailed case of histories of IBM's response to the invention of the PC and Microsoft's response to the invention of the browser we have suggested that scope diseconomies created by the presence of necessarily shared assets have an important role to play in explaining this phenomenon.

We showed that—at least in these two cases—the two incumbent firms had no difficulty building the raw organizational capabilities necessary to compete in the new markets. Each initially created the equivalent of a firm-within-a-firm and was able to mobilize internal and external talent very effectively. However, as strategic interdependencies between the new and old markets became increasingly salient, the need to share key firm-level assets became both more critical and more difficult. Both firms saw very considerable organizational conflict emerge—and at both firms it was resolved by the decision to give the managers of the legacy business control over the new. Although we cannot say that this was per se economically irrational on an ex ante basis, in both cases it led to decisions that were quite different from those made by entrants and that, at least in retrospect, placed the new business at a considerable disadvantage.

More generally, our results suggest that organizations face limits to the exploitation of economies of scope, even where there are powerful firm-wide shared assets. Collectively these limits can add up to more than just a series of managerial inconveniences. Conflict over the optimal structure of shared assets, and conflict inherent in the difference between old and new businesses, interferes with the pursuit of new opportunities and raises their costs. While sharing existing assets with a new business seems an obvious source of scope economies, our examples show that the resulting conflict can be so costly as to reverse the gains.

Our analysis, if supported by further research, has immediate implications for both policy and managerial practice. On the policy front it lends further credence to the idea that incumbent firms, alone, are unlikely to be able to duplicate the technological diversity characteristic of the market and thus to the belief that vigorous entry may be a key contributor to the innovativeness of an industry or an economy. On the managerial front it highlights the subtle nature of the interaction between strategic and organizational conflict, suggesting that organizational conflict is often as much symptom as cause, and should be managed as such. Certainly the suggestion that an established firm should simply seek to duplicate the structure and behavior of entrants should be treated with skepticism.

We have also opened up a number of avenues for further research. Most obviously it would be useful to know if the concept of necessarily shared assets is a useful one in understanding the history of other industries and other significant discontinuities. Both IBM and Microsoft, for example, have a history of entering new markets with great success. Our preliminary analysis suggests that this was because they were able to take advantage of conventional economies of scope and because there was relatively little conflict over how necessarily shared assets should be deployed. In the case of IBM's entry into electronic computing, for example, or into software services, assets such as the firm's reputation and distribution channels could be managed to serve both assets with minimal conflict. Microsoft's early entry into applications programming or more recent entry into gaming were similarly relatively free from this particular kind of conflict.

Another important question is that of the factors that cause an asset to be necessarily shared. In the case of IBM and Microsoft, we suggested that an asset such as reputation might be necessarily shared because the firm's customers simply did not believe that the firm could develop distinctly different capabilities (reputation) or because they understood the ways in which the strategic priorities of the existing business were likely to overcome the new (open versus closed). But we suspect that the universe of necessarily shared assets is much wider than this and the range of causes correspondingly greater. We suspect, for example, that it is difficult for a firm to develop two entirely different reputations for the way in which it rewards its workforce, and that this may be another shared asset that may make it difficult to do entirely new things.[84]

Lastly, our analysis suggests that the line of research recently opened by Alonso, Dessein, and Matouschek (2008) and Rantakari (2008) is a particularly promising one that would merit much further exploration. For many years economists have dismissed accounts of organizational conflict as merely epiphenomenal, despite sustained research by organizational scholars suggesting that it has very real effects. It would be impossible to explain IBM's or Microsoft's actions without understanding the role scope diseconomies played. It would also be impossible without understanding each company's interest in continuing in one market while pursuing another.

84. On this point see Kaplan and Henderson (2005).

The essence of competitive events in both cases—timing of entry, pricing of products, distribution of market share, or even realized changes of market leadership—would be misinterpreted if viewed as solely determined by the diffusion of technology or solely by the incentives of market circumstances. It would be equally misinterpreted if seen as arising from something inherent and unchanging in the firms' capabilities or organization. Rather, the interplay between market needs and organizational diseconomies of scope shaped incumbent firm behavior and the salient features of outcomes. Our analysis thus highlights the ways in which the interaction between strategy conflict, necessarily shared assets, and conflict over the locus of control within a firm have significant economic implications. (To the degree that managers are, indeed, constrained in their decision making by cognitive frames developed through experience this problem becomes very interesting indeed.) Further empirical and theoretical research in this area is thus likely to yield significant returns.

References

Abate, Janet. 1999. *Inventing the Internet.* Cambridge, MA: MIT Press.

Adner, Ron, and Peter Zemsky. 2005. "Disruptive Technologies and the Emergence of Competition." *RAND Journal of Economics* 36 (2): 229–54.

Alonso, Ricardo, Wouter Dessein, and Niko Matouschek. 2008. "When Does Coordination Require Centralization?" *American Economic Review* 98 (1): 145–79.

Anand, B., and A. Galetovic. 2000. "Information, Non-Excludability, and Financial Market Structure." *Journal of Business* 73 (3): 357–402.

Anton, James J., and Dennis Yao. 1995. "Start-Ups, Spin-Offs, and Internal Projects." *Journal of Law, Economics and Organization* 11 (2): 362–78.

Arrow, K. 1962. "Economic Welfare and the Allocation of Resources for Invention." In *The Rate and Direction of Inventive Activity: Economic and Social Factors,* Universities-National Bureau Committee for Economic Research and the Committee on Economic Growth of the Social Science Research Councils, 609–26. Princeton, NJ: Princeton University Press.

Baker, George, Robert Gibbons, and Kevin Murphy. 2002. "Relational Contracts and the Theory of the Firm." *Quarterly Journal of Economics* 117 (1): 39–84.

Bank, David. 2001. *Breaking Windows: How Bill Gates Fumbled the Future of Microsoft.* London: The Free Press.

Berners-Lee, Tim. 2000. *Weaving the Web: The Original Design and Ultimate Destiny of the World Wide Web.* New York: HarperCollins.

Bresnahan, T. F. 1999. "New Modes of Competition: Implications for the Future Structure of the Computer Industry." In *Competition, Convergence and the Microsoft Monopoly: Antitrust in the Digital Marketplace,* edited by Jeffrey A. Eisenach and Thomas M. Lenard, 155–208. Boston: Kluwer Academic Publishers.

Bresnahan, Timothy. 2002. "The Economics of the Microsoft Antitrust Case." Stanford University. Working Paper no. 232.

Bresnahan, Timothy, and Shane Greenstein. 1996. "Technical Progress and Co-Invention in Computing and the Use of Computers." *Brookings Papers on Economic Activity: Microeconomics* 1996:1–78.

———. 1999. "Technological Competition and the Structure of the Computer Industry." *Journal of Industrial Economics* 47 (1): 1–40.

Bresnahan, Timothy, Shane Greenstein, and Rebecca Henderson. 2009. "Towards a Model of Organizational Diseconomies of Scope." Working Paper.

Bresnahan, Timothy, and Pai-Ling Yin. 2006. "Standard Setting in Markets: The Browser War." In *Standards and Public Policy,* edited by Shane Greenstein and Victor Stango, 19–59. Cambridge: Cambridge University Press.

Brock, Gerald W. 1975. *The US Computer Industry: A Study of Market Power.* Cambridge: Ballinger Publishing.

Carroll, Paul. 1993. *Big Blues, The UnMaking of IBM.* New York: Crown Publishers.

Cassiman, Bruno, and Masako Ueda. 2006. "Optimal Project Rejection and New Firm Start-ups." *Management Science* 52 (2): 262–75.

Chposky, James, and Ted Leonsis. 1988. *Blue Magic: The People, Power and Politics Behind the IBM Personal Computer.* New York: Facts on File Publications.

Christensen, Clayton M. 1993. "The Rigid Disk Drive Industry: A History of Commercial and Technological Turbulence." *Business History Review* 67 (4): 531–88.

———. 1997. *The Innovator's Dilemma.* Boston: Harvard Business School Press.

Cringley, Robert X. 1992. *Accidental Empires.* New York: HarperCollins.

Cusumano, Michael, and David Yoffie. 2000. *Competing on Internet Time: Lessons From Netscape and its Battle with Microsoft.* New York: Free Press.

Daft, R. L., and K. E. Weick. 1984. "Toward a Model of Organizations as Interpretation Systems." *Academy of Management Review* 9 (2): 284–95.

David, Paul, and Shane Greenstein. 1990. "The Economics of Compatibility of Standards: A Survey." *Economics of Innovation and New Technology* 1:3–41.

Davis, S. J., J. MacCrisken, and K. M. Murphy. 2002. "Economic Perspectives on Software Design: PC Operating Systems and Platforms." In *Microsoft, Antitrust and the New Economy: Selected Essays,* edited by D. S. Evans, 361–419. New York: Springer.

Dosi, Giovanni, and M. Mazzucato, eds. 2006. *Knowledge Accumulation and Industry Evolution.* Cambridge: Cambridge University Press.

Dosi, Giovanni, and Richard Nelson. 2010. "Technical Change and Industrial Dynamics as Evolutionary Processes." In *Handbook of the Economics of Innovation,* Vol. 1, edited by Bronwyn Hall and Nathan Rosenberg. Amsterdam: Elsevier.

Fisher, Franklin, John J. McGowan, and J. E. Greenwood. 1983. *Folded Spindled and Mutilated: Economic Analysis and U.S. vs. IBM.* Cambridge, MA: MIT Press.

Fisher, Franklin, J. W. McKie, and R. B. Mancke. 1983. *IBM and the U.S. Data Processing Industry: An Economic History.* New York: Praeger Publishers.

Fisher, Franklin, and Daniel Rubinfeld. 2001. "*U.S. v. Microsoft,* An Economic Analysis." *Antitrust Bulletin* 46:1–69.

Freiberger, P., and M. Swaine. 1984. *Fire in the Valley: The Making of the Personal Computer.* Berkeley, CA: Osborne/McGraw Hill.

Gates, Bill. 1995. "The Internet Tidal Wave." Government Exhibit 20, May 26. Available at: http://www.usdoj.gov/atr/cases/ms_exhibits.htm.

Gates, Bill, Nathan Myhrvold, and Peter Rinearson. 1995. *The Road Ahead.* New York: Viking Press.

Gawer, Annabelle, and Rebecca Henderson. 2007. "Platform Owner Entry and Innovation in Complementary Markets: Evidence From Intel." *Journal of Economics and Management Strategy* 6 (1): 1–34.

Gerstner, Louis V. 2004. *Who Says Elephants Can't Dance? Inside IBM's Historical Turnaround.* New York: Harpers Publishing.

Gilbert, Richard, and David Newberry. 1982. "Pre-Emptive Patenting and the Persistence of Monopoly." *American Economics Review* 72:514–26.
Greenstein, Shane. 2008. "The Evolution of Market Structure for Internet Access in the United States." In *The Commercialization of the Internet and its Impact on American Business,* edited by William Aspray and Paul Ceruzzi, 47–104. Cambridge, MA: MIT Press.
Haigh, Thomas. 2006. "Remembering the Office of the Future: The Origins of Word Processing and Office Automation." *IEEE Annals of the History of Computing* 28:6–31.
Hart, Oliver, and Bengt Holmstrom. 2002. "A Theory of Firm Scope." Harvard University. Unpublished manuscript.
Henderson, Rebecca. 1993. "Underinvestment and Incompetence as Responses to Radical Innovation: Evidence From the Photolithographic Alignment Equipment Industry." *Rand Journal of Economics* 24:248–70.
———. 1995. "Of Life Cycles Real and Imaginary, The Unexpectedly Long Old Age of Optical Lithography." *Research Policy* 23:631–43.
Henderson, Rebecca, and Kim Clark. 1990. "Architectural Innovation: The Reconfiguration of Existing Product Technologies and the Failure of Established Firms." *Administrative Science Quarterly* 35 (1): 9–30.
Jovanovic, Boyan. 1982. "Selection and the Evolution of Industry." *Econometrica* 50 (3): 649–70.
Kaplan, Sarah. 2008. "Framing Contests: Making Strategy Under Uncertainty." *Organization Science* 19 (5): 729–52.
Kaplan, Sarah, and Rebecca Henderson. 2005. "Inertia and Incentives: Bridging Organizational Economics and Organizational Theory." *Organization Science* 16 (5): 509–21.
Katz, B., and A. Phillips. 1982. "The Computer Industry." In *Government and Technical Progress: A Cross-Industry Analysis,* edited by R. R. Nelson, 162–232. New York: Pergamon Press.
Killen, M. 1988. *IBM–The Making of the Common View.* Boston: Harcourt Brace Jovanovich.
Klepper, S. 1997. "Industry Life Cycles." *Industrial and Corporate Change* 6 (1): 145–82. doi:10.1093/icc/6.1.145.
Langlois, Richard N. 1992. "External Economies and Economic Progress: The Case of the Microcomputer Industry." *Business History Review* 66 (1): 1–50.
———. 1997. "Cognition and Capabilities: Opportunities Seized and Missed in the History of the Computer Industry." In *Technological Innovation: Oversights and Foresights,* edited by Raghu Garud, Praveen Nayyar, and Zur Shapira, 71–94. New York: Cambridge University Press.
Lowe, William C., and Cary Sherburne. 2009. *No-Nonsense Innovation: Practical Strategies for Success.* Garden City, NJ: Morgan James.
Mowery, David, and Timothy Simcoe. 2002. "The Internet." In *Technological Innovation and Economic Performance*, edited by Benn Steil, David Victor, and Richard Nelson, 259–93. Princeton, NJ: Princeton University Press.
O'Reilly, Charles, and Michael Tushman. 2008. "Ambidexterity as a Dynamic Capability: Resolving the Innovator's Dilemma." *Research in Organizational Behavior* 28:185–206.
Pugh, Emerson W. 1995. *IBM: Shaping an Industry and It Technology.* Cambridge, MA: MIT Press.
Rantakari, Heikki. 2008. "Governing Adaptation." *Review of Economic Studies* 75 (4): 1257–85.
Rubinfeld, Daniel. 2004. "Maintenance of Monopoly, *U.S. v. Microsoft.*" In *The*

Antitrust Revolution: Economics, Competition and Policy, 4th ed., edited by John Kwoka and Lawrence White, 476–501. New York: Oxford University Press.
Schumpeter, Joseph. 1942. *Capitalism, Socialism, and Democracy.* New York: Harper Brothers.
Sink, Eric. 2003. "Memoirs from the Browser Wars." April 15. Accessed March 2007. http://biztech.ericsink.com/Browser_Wars.html.
Slivka, Ben. 1995. "The Web is the Next Platform (version 5)." May 27. Government Exhibit 21. Available at: http://www.usdoj.gov/atr/cases/ms_exhibits.ht.
Stein, Jeremy. 1997. "Waves of Creative Destruction: Learning by Doing and Dynamics of Innovation." *Review of Economic Studies* 64:265–88.
Sutton, J. 1991. *Sunk Costs and Market Structure: Price Competition, Advertising, and the Evolution of Concentration.* Cambridge, MA: MIT Press.
———. 1998. Technology and Market Structure: Theory and History. Cambridge, MA: MIT Press.
Teece, D. J. 1986. "Profiting From Technological Innovation: Implications for Integration, Collaboration, Licensing and Public Policy." *Research Policy* 15 (6): 285–305.
Tripsas, M., and G. Gavetti. 2000. "Capabilities, Cognition and Inertia: Evidence from Digital Imaging." *Strategic Management Journal* 21:1147–61.
Utterback, J. 1994. *Mastering the Dynamics of Innovation.* Boston: Harvard Business School Press.
Watson, Thomas Jr., and Peter Petre. 1990. *Father, Son and Co.: My Life at IBM and Beyond.* New York: Bantam Books.
Wernerfelt, Birger. 1988. "Umbrella Branding as a Signal of New Product Quality: An Example of Signaling by Posting a Bond." *RAND Journal of Economics* 19:458–66.

Comment Giovanni Dosi

The chapter insightfully analyzes two instances of "Schumpeterian transitions" across different technological trajectories, and the vicissitudes of the firms that were market leaders on the "old" ones. As such, it makes fascinating reading in its own right. But it is also a revealing illustration of some of the major advances made over the last half century, since the early Rate and Direction Conference, in the understanding of the nature and dynamics of technological knowledge and the conditions under which it is generated and economically exploited.[1] It is from this angle that I will offer the comments that follow.

In fact, together with the understanding of the determinants of the rates and directions of accumulation of technological knowledge, a lot of progress has been made in the understanding of business firms as major repositories

Giovanni Dosi is professor of economics at Sant'Anna School of Advanced Studies, Pisa, Italy.

1. For an overview of the state-of-the-art in the field, let me refer to Dosi and Nelson (2010).

of such knowledge. Actually, while in earlier eras much of the inventing was done by self-employed individuals, under modern capitalism business firms have become a central locus of efforts to advance technologies. Firms have long been the economic entities that employ most new technologies, produce and market the new products, and operate the new production processes.

Opening up the "organizational blackbox" has led to the acknowledgement of the (rather idiosyncratic) capabilities firms embody, not only concerning technological and manufacturing knowledge, but also marketing, interacting with users and suppliers, and the very practices of internal governance of the organization.[2] Deeply complementary to the analyses of innovative activities focused on dynamics of knowledge, artifact characteristics and input coefficients, capability-based theories of the firm have begun addressing the behavioral meaning of statements such as "firm X is good at doing Y and Z." Relatedly, one has made significant progress in the study of the mechanisms that govern how organizational knowledge is acquired, maintained, augmented, and sometimes lost.

Organizational knowledge is in fact a fundamental link between the social pool of knowledge, skills, and opportunities for discoveries on the one hand, and the microefforts, directions, and economic effectiveness of their *actual* exploration on the other.

In these respects, the work by Bresnahan, Greenstein, and Henderson adds indeed two in-depth analyses of the features of organizational capabilities and their alignment (or lack of it) with particular market requirements.

Moreover, organizations embody broad "strategic orientations"—somewhat metaphorically, the collective equivalent of "mental models"—also involving prescriptions and heuristics on how to adapt and change over time, in which markets to position, which technological trajectories to pursue, and so forth.[3]

Capabilities and organizational cognitive models contribute to shape the *coherence* of the organization also in terms of its horizontal and vertical boundaries (that is, patterns of output diversification and vertical integration).[4]

Moreover, capabilities and cognitive models map into specific (a) organizational architectures; (b) patterns of information flows, and (c) lines of command and distributions of political power within the organization. And indeed such mapping yields an ensemble of discrete combinations that may or may not be in tune with technological and market requirements. The

2. Again, for a more detailed discussion I must refer to other works (cf. Dosi, Nelson, and Winter 2000; Dosi, Marengo, and Faillo 2008).

3. All this roughly corresponds to what is referred to as the *dynamic capabilities* of a firm: cf. Teece, Pisano, and Shuen (1997) and Helfat et al. (2007).

4. For an early attempt to operationalize such notion of "coherence," cf. Teece et al. (1994). Subsequent contributions include Piscitello (2004) and Bottazzi and Pirino (2010).

two examples discussed in the chapter, especially the IBM one, are excellent illustrations of the point.

Take the IBM case. Strong technological capabilities match a commitment to incrementalism in product architectures, cumulative learning, vertical integration, proprietary standards, coordinated strategic governance (through the Corporate Management Committee) and, on the market side, a reputation for postsale service.

This IBM model, Bresnahan and colleagues insightfully show, is well aligned to market requirements under the mainframe/minicomputer trajectories, but becomes *misaligned* to the requirements of effective production and marketing of personal computers. It is not that the raw capabilities are not there. They are. And in fact IBM even proceeds to a rather successful exploration of the new *combinatorics* between elements of technological capabilities, organizational setups, and market orientation well suited to the personal computer world. However, that very success accelerates the clash between the PC organizational model and the incumbent IBM (mainframe) model. The latter wins, and by doing that IBM ultimately kills its PC line of business.

It is a story vividly illustrating the path-dependent reproduction of capabilities, shared strategic models, and specific organizational arrangements. To repeat, it is not that IBM lacks any of the single elements underlying successful, "PC-fit," combinations. It is just that capabilities, "visions," and organizational setups are better understood at least in the short term as *state* variables rather than *control* variables, in Winter's (1987) characterization. Of course, also state variables can and are indeed influenced by purposeful discretionary strategies; that is, by the explicit manipulation of control variables. However, this takes time and is tainted by initial birthmarks and subsequent historical paths the organization has followed with respect to both operational repertories and higher level collective visions concerning the very *identity* of the organization. The topical reference is Nelson and Winter (1982) on organizational routines, but a vast literature has developed since.[5] Interestingly, path-dependent reproduction of routines, strategic visions, and organizational memory might continue to be there—the IBM case in tune with the conjecture—notwithstanding turnover at the top level of management.[6]

Back to the IBM case. Was there an alternative to what actually happened?

Probably, in my view, there was, but most likely such an alternative would have massively violated the cognitive/strategic coherence of the organization: holding mainframes and PC together would have meant a sort of "IBM

5. For surveys and discussions on routines and other recurrent action patterns, cf. Becker, M. (2004), Cohen et al. (1996), and Lazaric and Lorenz (2003).

6. Some formal explorations on the features and performance implications of organizational memory are in Dosi et al. (2011).

Holding," kept together primarily in terms of ownership but not of strategic management and coordination.

Is this the story that the chapter tells? Yes and no. The interpretation of the factual story, masterfully reconstructed indeed, has two layers.

The first one is in terms of economies/discontinuities of scope.

Let me introduce a little, but important, incidental. One of the motivations of our Teece et al. (1994) was precisely to go beyond the blackboxing involved in the standard account of product diversification in terms of economies of scope. In that, two products will be produced under the same organizational roof according to the sign of the inequality

$$c(x_1) + c(x_2) \gtrless c(x_1 + x_2),$$

possibly adding fixed costs, the same possibly shared by the two activities into the $C\,(.,.)$ functions.

In Teece et al. (1994) and subsequent literature, one tries indeed to explore what is behind the foregoing inequality. The interpretation of multiproduct "coherence" runs in terms of characteristics of the technological knowledge involved in the design and manufacturing of different products, the market characteristics for the products themselves, and, dynamically, the properties of the ensuing trajectories. At the level of single firms all this, to repeat, is reflected into idiosyncratic capabilities and their links with revealed organizational strategies.

The chapter, at the theory level, in a way undertakes the opposite interpretative strategy. It masterly tells a story of capabilities, organizational memory (including biases, blind spots, and inertial visions) but then it opts to squeeze the all story back into the much smaller and darker box of economies of scope. Maybe this is as much as the contemporary representative economist is able to understand, but I am not fully convinced of how big the interpretative value added to the exercise is at the end. In fact, such an exercise is not too far from any attempt to reduce all we have learned on production knowledge and its dynamics over the last half century into more sophisticated versions of some "production function." In any case, let it be it. Or am I missing something?

Certainly my theoretical preference goes to constructive models whereby one tries to explicitly account for the problem-solving activities of organizations and their evolution over time (for still exploratory examples, among a growing number, see Levinthal [1997]; Siggelkow and Levinthal [2005]; Marengo and Dosi [2005]; and Dosi et al. [2011]). Indeed, the mapping of representations of business firms as ensembles of (cognitive and physical) problem-solving activities into a much lower dimensional space of input-output coefficients and related cost structures remains a daunting challenge, but one worth being taken up in my view.

Come as it may, I do find convincing the suggestion that the misalignment of capabilities, cognitive models, and market requirements between two lines of product—say mainframes and PCs—entailed *diseconomies of scope,* even if I do not consider that the primitive level of analysis. However, the authors push their interpretation further, and, granted the presence of such diseconomies associated with necessarily shared assets, argue that the ensuing choice of organizational arrangements facing the Schumpeterian dynamics of emergence of new products and new technological trajectories is a *genuine choice* and quite a rational one indeed. Diseconomies of scope shaped managerial incentives, it is argued, ultimately leading to the observed outcomes, which are then rationalised as equilibrium phenomena. And, of course, in such an interpretation, path-dependent organizational capabilities and mental models, as well as fuzzy intraorganizational politics, slid into the background, while the structure of incentives comes in the forefront.

Of course, both levels of analysis are important. But what are the first-order and what are the second-order levels of interpretation?

In the capability (plus politics) story, incentives are there but are second order, and vice versa, in the rational organizational design story. In fact, here rests possibly the most important divide in the analysis of organizational structures and boundaries. It is a divide already present among the interpretations of the *Rates and Directions of Innovative Activities* fifty years ago, and has been present ever since.

In my view the incentive–based equilibrium rationalization tastes far too much of Dr. Pangloss—remember Voltaire's booklet—who was going around between wars, calamities, and earthquakes, proclaiming that all that if it happened, it had to be optimal, since it had to be in the plans of the Divine Providence.

The good news is that the whole analysis of the Bresnahan, Greenstein, and Henderson work holds without putting such a rationalization on the top of it. On the contrary, I would like to enlist it as a major contribution to the analysis of the winding coevolutionary dynamics linking organizational capabilities, strategic visions, modes of intraorganizational governances, and the changing vertical and horizontal boundaries of the firms.

References

Becker, M. 2004. "Organizational Routines: A Review of the Literature." *Industrial and Corporate Change* 13 (4): 643–78.

Bottazzi, G., and D. Pirino. 2010. "Measuring Industry Relatedness and Corporate Coherence." Pisa: Sant'Anna School of Advanced Studies. LEM Working Paper Series, October.

Cohen, M. D., R. Burkhart, G. Dosi, M. Egidi, L. Marengo, M. Warglien, and S. Winter. 1996. "Routines and Other Recurring Action Patterns of Organizations: Contemporary Research Issues." *Industrial and Corporate Change* 5 (3): 653–98.

Dosi, G., L. Marengo, E. Paraskevopoulou, and Valente. 2011. "The Value and Dangers of Remembrance in Changing Worlds: A Model of Cognitive an Operational Memory of Organizations." Pisa: Sant'Anna School of Advanced Studies. LEM Working Paper, in progress.

Dosi, G., L. Marengo, and M. Faillo. 2008. "Organizational Capabilities, Patterns of Knowledge Accumulation and Governance Structures in Business Firms. An Introduction." *Organization Studies* 29 (8): 1165–85.

Dosi, G., and R. R. Nelson. 2010. "Technical Change and Industrial Dynamics as Evolutionary Processes." In *Handbook of the Economics of Innovation,* Vol. 1, edited by B. H. Hall and N. Rosenberg, 51–128. Amsterdam: Elsevier.

Dosi, G., R. R. Nelson, and S. G. Winter (eds). 2000. *The Nature and Dynamics of Organizational Capabilities.* Oxford: Oxford University Press.

Helfat, C., S. Finkelstein, W. Mitchell, M. A. Peteraf, A. Singh, D. J. Teece, and S. G. Winter. 2007. *Dynamic Capabilities: Understanding Strategic Change in Organizations.* London: Blackwell Publishing.

Lazaric, N., and E. Lorenz, eds. 2003. *Knowledge, Learning and Routines.* Cheltenham, UK: Edward Elgar.

Levinthal, D. 1997. "Adaptation on Rugged Landscapes." *Management Science* 43:934–50.

Marengo, L., and G. Dosi. 2005. "Division of Labor, Organizational Coordination and Market Mechanisms in Collective Problem-Solving." *Journal of Economic Behavior and Organization* 58:303–26.

Nelson, R., and S. Winter. 1982. *An Evolutionary Theory of Economic Change.* Cambridge, MA: The Belknap Press of Harvard University Press.

Piscitello, L. 2004. "Corporate Diversification, Coherence and Economic Performance." *Industrial and Corporate Change* 13 (4): 757–87.

Siggeltow, N., and D. Levinthal. 2005. "Escaping Real (Non-benign) Competency Traps: Linking the Dynamics of Organizational Structures to the Dynamics of Search." *Strategic Organization* 3:85–115.

Teece, D. J., G. Pisano, and A. Shuen. 1997. "Dynamic Capabilities and Strategic Management." *Strategic Management Journal* 18:509–33.

Teece, D., R. Rumelt, G. Dosi, and S. Winter. 1994. "Understanding Corporate Coherence: Theory and Evidence." *Journal of Economic Behavior and Organization* 23:1–30.

Winter, S. 1987. "Knowledge and Competence as Strategic Assets." In *The Competitive Challenge: Strategies for Industrial Innovation and Renewal,* edited by D. J. Teece, 159–84. Cambridge: Ballinger.

5

How Entrepreneurs Affect the Rate and Direction of Inventive Activity

Daniel F. Spulber

5.1 Introduction

Why does innovative entrepreneurship occur in established industries? Entrepreneurship entails costs of setting up firms and entering markets. Entrepreneurial entry also involves competing with existing firms, which dissipates economic rents and can destroy existing firms. In contrast, innovators can transfer technology to existing firms taking advantage of incumbents' assets and avoiding the costs of entrepreneurship and competition. Creative destruction therefore gives innovators and existing firms incentives to cooperate through technology transfer. Yet, innovative entrepreneurship in established industries is an important phenomenon that generates technological change, investment, employment, and economic growth. Understanding creative destruction poses a challenge to researchers, business practitioners, and public policymakers.

To examine creative destruction, I present a strategic innovation model that examines how innovators and incumbent firms choose between cooperation and competition. I show how multidimensional innovation—Schumpeter's "new combinations"—helps to explain the phenomenon of innovative entrepreneurship. I show how the transferability of product and process

Daniel F. Spulber is the Elinor Hobbs Distinguished Professor of International Business and professor of management strategy at the Kellogg School of Management, Northwestern University, and professor of law (courtesy) at Northwestern University Law School.

I gratefully acknowledge the support of a research grant from the Ewing Marion Kauffman Foundation. I thank Ken Arrow, Joshua Gans, Shane Greenstein, Josh Lerner, Bob Litan, Scott Stern, and Bob Strom for their very helpful comments. I also thank my discussant Luis Cabral for his very useful and constructive suggestions. I also thank participants at the NBER Rate and Direction of Inventive Activity 50th Anniversary conferences for their stimulating discussions.

innovations affects the mix of entrepreneurship and contracting. Innovators affect the rate and direction of inventive activity either by transferring technology to existing firms or by embodying new technology in new firms. The resulting market outcomes determine what types of firms innovate and how product and process inventions are commercialized.

I introduce a model in which inventions are multidimensional, consisting of both a new product design and a new process invention. Innovators encounter difficulties in either partial or full transfers of technology. Entrepreneurs enter the market with both a horizontally differentiated product and lower production costs. The key insight of the analysis is that product differentiation offsets the creative destruction that results from more efficient production. This generates the following main results. First, when only process innovations are transferable, greater product differentiation tends to generate entrepreneurship, helping to address the challenge of entrepreneurship. Incremental innovations tend to favor entrepreneurship, and significant innovations favor technology transfer. Greater product differentiation gives innovators greater incentives to invent than existing firms because of the incremental returns that innovators can obtain from entrepreneurship. Second, when only product design innovations are transferable, entrepreneurial entry occurs if products are sufficiently differentiated or if the production process innovation is significant. In that situation, the innovator's incentive to invent is again greater than that of an incumbent monopolist.

Third, I extend the strategic game by introducing an independent inventor with a process invention who interacts with an established firm and an independent entrepreneur. The inventor offers the new technology to the established firm and the potential entrepreneur, who in turn play a strategic technology adoption game. In the second stage, the product market outcome can consist of continued monopoly by the established firm or differentiated-products competition between the established firm and the entrepreneurial entrant. The incumbent firm's inertia, first noted by Arrow (1962), has an important new implication. The royalty that induces adoption by the incumbent firm also will induce adoption by an entrepreneurial entrant. The inventor thus will sell either to the entrepreneur or to both the entrepreneur and the incumbent firm. This means that in either situation, the inventor will transfer the process technology to an entrepreneur. This provides another answer to the challenge of entrepreneurship: Due to strategic interaction, independent inventors who do not have the option of entrepreneurship tend to license their technologies to both entrepreneurs and existing firms.

The principal contribution of the analysis is to consider product differentiation in the competition between the innovative entrant and the established firm. Sufficient product differentiation implies that industry profits can be greater than the profits of the incumbent monopolist. This contrasts with related work by Gans, Hsu, and Stern (2000), Gans and Stern (2000, 2003), and Spulber (2011). Gans and Stern (2000), for example, study an

R&D race where the winner can license the technology and faces the possibility of imitation; see also Salant (1984), Katz and Shapiro (1987), and Reinganum (1981, 1982, 1989). Gans and Stern (2000) assume that industry profits after entrepreneurial entry are less than the profits of the incumbent monopolist with the new technology, and as a result, entrepreneurial entry does not occur in equilibrium. Gans and Stern (2000) suggest that entry by a startup is "something of an economic puzzle" in the absence of noncontractible information asymmetries. Spulber (2011) considers creative destruction when the entrepreneurial entrant displaces the incumbent through Bertrand competition. It is useful to observe that standard analyses of innovation also assume homogeneous products and find that due to the effects of competition, the monopolist has a greater incentive to invent than does an entrant; see Gilbert and Newbery (1982) and Gilbert (2006). The standard assumption of homogeneous products implies that an incumbent monopolist has profits that are greater than those of the entire industry after entry. This condition is referred to as the "persistence of monopoly" and the "efficiency condition."[1] Also, in Anton and Yao's (2003) study of imitation and technology transfer, the imitative firm and the innovator are Cournot duopolists with homogeneous products.

In practice, the entry of innovative entrepreneurs demonstrates that many innovators chose to become entrepreneurs rather than to transfer their technologies to existing firms. Despite the apparent advantages of established firms, entrepreneurs have been recognized as major contributors to innovation at least since Jean-Baptiste Say (1841, 1852). Entrepreneurship is one of the main forms of commercialization of invention; see Baumol (1968, 1993, 2002, 2006), Audretsch (1995a, 1995b), Audretsch, Keilbach, and Lehmann (2006), Acs et al. (2004), Schramm (2006), and Baumol, Litan, and Schramm (2007). Schumpeter emphasizes that entrepreneurs provide a large share of the technological innovations that stimulate the growth and development of capitalist economies. Schumpeter (1934, 66) observes that "new combinations are, as a rule, embodied, as it were, in new firms which generally do not arise out of the old ones but start producing beside them." Entrepreneurs transform the economy through "gales of creative destruction," creating new firms that displace existing firms through competition. Our analysis shows why new combinations are embodied in new firms. Entrepreneurs play an important role in the economy by establishing firms that in turn create markets and organizations; see Spulber (2009). In newly established industries, entrepreneurs often flood the market applying widely different approaches and technologies, rather than relying on the initial entrants.

1. Chen and Schwartz (2009) consider vertical product differentiation where the dominant firm produces multiple goods and find that competition can yield greater returns than monopoly (see also Greenstein and Ramey 1998). This differs from my analysis in which the incumbent firm and the entrant compete on equal terms. They do not consider the question of innovation and entrepreneurship.

The chapter is organized as follows. Section 5.2 examines empirical studies of innovative entrepreneurship and technology transfer. Section 5.3 presents the game of strategic innovation played by an innovator and an incumbent firm. Section 5.4 characterizes the equilibrium outcome of the strategic innovation game. Section 5.5 considers an adoption-and-entry game with an independent innovator who chooses whether to transfer the technology to an incumbent firm, to an entrepreneur, or to both. Section 5.6 concludes the discussion.

5.2 Technology Transfer versus Entrepreneurship

There are several major modes of innovation. First, independent innovators can transfer technology by sale or licensing to existing firms or to independent entrepreneurs. Second, entrepreneurs innovate by establishing new firms that embody new products, manufacturing processes, transaction systems, and business methods. Third, existing firms can innovate by commercializing products and processes developed through their internal research and development (R&D) laboratories, collaboration with R&D partners, licensing of new technologies, and acquisition of start-ups. Innovation involves realizing new business opportunities and need not depend on scientific discoveries, as Schumpeter (1964) points out.

The theoretical analysis in the later sections examines the interaction between an innovator and an established firm, and possibly between an innovator and an independent entrepreneur. The model is designed to study the basics of cooperation and competition. In practice, there can be many innovators and incumbent firms. The problem is sufficiently complex that cross-industry studies may be needed to identify the interactive effects of product differentiation and production technologies. This section provides some industry comparisons, although additional research is needed to make these comparisons in a more systematic manner.

5.2.1 The Choice between Entrepreneurial Entry and Technology Transfers

Interaction between independent innovators and existing firms is an important determinant of the mode of innovation. Innovators and existing firms weigh the costs and benefits of transferring technology against the costs and benefits of entrepreneurial entry. Innovators may be independent inventors, scientists and engineers employed by universities and research laboratories, or specialized technology firms.

Studies of academic scientists and engineers illustrate the basic choice between entrepreneurial entry and technology transfer. These innovators engage in both entrepreneurship and technology transfers. There have been hundreds of entrepreneurial firms that are spinoffs from universities; see O'Shea et al. (2005) and the references therein. Lowe and Ziedonis (2006) consider a sample of 732 inventions at the University of California that were licensed exclusively to a firm. They distinguish between licensing to entrepreneurs and licensing to existing firms, and find that start-up firms licensed 36 percent of the inventions and existing firms licensed the remainder. The study implicitly provides evidence of the choice between licensing to a start-up and licensing to an incumbent because over 75 percent of inventions licensed to start-ups were initially reviewed by established firms that sponsored the research or through nondisclosure agreements with the opportunity to license.

Innovators in biotech who are associated with universities establish new firms or attract firms seeking technology transfers; see Prevezer (1997) and Audretsch (2001). Zucker, Darby, and Armstrong (1998) distinguish between biotech firms that are entrepreneurial entrants and those that are incumbents and consider both ownership and contractual technology transfers:

> Our telephone survey of California star scientists found that academic stars may simultaneously be linked to specific firms in a number of different ways: exclusive direct employment (often as CEO or other principal), full or part ownership, exclusive and nonexclusive consulting contracts (effectively part-time employment), and chairmanship of or membership on scientific advisory boards. (69)

Zucker, Darby, and Brewer (1998) provide indirect evidence of the choice between technology transfer and entrepreneurship, and find "strong evidence that the timing and location of initial usage by both new dedicated biotechnology firms ('entrants') and new biotech subunits of existing firms ('incumbents') are primarily explained by the presence at a particular time and place of scientists who are actively contributing to the basic science as represented by publications reporting genetic-sequence discoveries in academic journals" (290). The presence of both types of firms in the sample is suggestive of the choice between entrepreneurship and technology transfer (511 entrants, 150 incumbents, 90 unclassified), although their study does not identify whether the star scientists commercialized their technology by establishing new firms or by transferring technology to existing firms (Zucker, Darby, and Brewer 1998).

Vohora, Wright, and Lockett (2004) study nine entrepreneurial startups in the UK that were university spinouts (USOs). Academic entrepreneurs and the university examine commercialization options, essentially choosing between technology transfer and entrepreneurship. The academic entrepreneur that established the company Stem Cell attempted to transfer his technology to existing firms that had sponsored his research. He observed that: "Commercial partners and industry were not interested. It was so early stage they thought it was a bit wacky. They all had first option to acquire the patents that had been filed from the sponsored research but did not take any of them up which left the university in an interesting position with a huge patent portfolio to exploit commercially" (Vohora, Wright, and Lockett 2004, 156). Vohora and colleagues (2004, 156) observe that for those academic entrepreneurs who were not able to transfer their technology to others:

> the opportunity was re-framed in order to take account of what the academic had learnt: industry's lack of desire to license or co-develop early stage technologies in this field and a preference instead to market later stage technologies that showed a high probability of generating commercial returns. Instead of selecting licensing or co-development as routes to market, the academic entrepreneur had learnt that the best route to market was to assemble the necessary resources and develop the capabilities required to exploit the IP himself through a USO venture.

Furman and MacGarvie (2009) find that the growth of in-house R&D capabilities in large pharmaceutical firms depended heavily on technology transfer through firm-university collaborations and contract research.

Innovators also can be specialized firms who develop products and processes that are inputs to other firms. These specialized firms face the problem of entrepreneurial entry downstream or technology transfer to downstream firms. In biotech, for example, many innovators were new firms. These start-ups carried out most of the initial stages of applied research in recombinant DNA technology and molecular genetics (Galambos and Sturchio 1998). In the US biotech industry, about 5,000 small and start-up firms provided technology inputs to health care, food and agriculture, industrial processes, and environmental cleanup industries (Audretsch 2001). These biotech firms were themselves innovators who needed to decide how best to commercialize their discoveries. The small biotech firms and major pharmaceutical companies chose between cooperation and competition. The small biotech firms generally have tended to engage in technology transfer to the larger pharmaceutical companies rather than entering the market to produce and sell products based on their discoveries. Technology transfer in biotech occurred through cooperative arrangements: "The large companies exchanged financial support and established organizational capabilities in clinical research, regulatory affairs, manufacturing, and marketing for the smaller firms' technical expertise and/or patents" (Galambos and Sturchio 1998, 252).

Similar patterns of technology transfers were observed in other industries. For example, in the chemical industry, specialized engineering firms (SEFs) are examples of entrepreneurial entrants. These SEFs chose entrepreneurial entry in R&D rather than developing basic technologies for incumbent chemical companies. However, once they were established, these entrepreneurial entrants developed and marketed process technology to large oil companies and chemical companies (Arora and Gambardella 1998). Innovative entrepreneurial entry also took place in the photolithographic alignment equipment industry. Henderson (1993) examines entry of entrepreneurial firms in the period 1960 to 1985. After entry, these firms sold equipment to major semiconductor manufacturers. According to the study, single-product start-ups initially entered the industry, but as incumbent firms become large and diversified, later entrants were firms with experience in related technologies. Existing firms were displaced by later entrants who introduced innovations in photolithography rather than transferring their technology (Kato 2007).

Larger existing firms are observed to have different incentives to innovate than smaller firms including entrepreneurial entrants; see Winter (1984), Acs and Audretsch (1988), and Audretsch (1995b). This suggests opportunities for technology transfers from start-ups to existing firms. Even when existing firms have substantial in-house R&D capabilities, they often rely on independent inventors, partners, and start-ups for technology transfers. Arora, Fosfuri, and Gambardella (2001a) consider the incentives of startups to license their technology. Arora, Fosfuri, and Gambardella (2001a, 2001b) examine the evidence for the existence of international markets for technology and provide extensive analysis of the chemical industry. Blonigen and Taylor (2000) consider acquisition of start-ups by established firms in the US electronics industry. In the international context, Anand and Khanna (2000) find many licensing agreements in chemicals, electronics, and computers. Tilton (1971) and Grindley and Teece (1997) examine licensing in the international diffusion of semiconductors and electronics.

Many innovators choose entrepreneurship over licensing. For example, hundreds of companies entered the early automobile industry. Innovative entrants offered many distinct products as is shown by the significant diversity of models in early automobile manufacturing. A review of the *Standard Catalog of American Cars 1805 to 1942* (Kimes and Clark 1996) shows a vast array of product features and technologies. Additionally, automobile companies differed in terms of manufacturing technologies.[2] Innovation took the form of entrepreneurship in established industries such as retail, wholesale, airlines, computer manufacturing, Internet companies, and media.[3] Hundreds of innovative entrepreneurs entered e-commerce in the dot com boom (Lucking-Reilly and Spulber 2001). Innovators chose entrepreneurship in various types of software (Torrisi 1998), including, for example, encryption software (Giarratana 2004).

2. Bresnahan and Raff (1991) examine intraindustry heterogeneity and the partial diffusion of mass-production technology in the early automobile industry.

3. A number of studies consider entry and exit of innovative producers in the computer industry (McClellan 1984), airlines (Peterson and Glab 1994; Morrison and Winston 1995), and media companies (Maney 1995). Fein (1998) finds shakeouts in wholesaling in over a dozen industries including flowers, woodworking machinery, locksmith, specialty tools and fasteners, sporting goods, wholesale grocers, air conditioning and refrigeration, electronic components, wine and spirits, waste equipment, and periodicals. Management studies have examined competition between innovative start-ups and established firms; see Henderson and Clark (1990) and Christensen (1997).

5.2.2 Multidimensional Innovation and Technology Transfer

Innovation is typically multifaceted. Innovators rarely confine their activities to new products, new production techniques, or new business methods, because they often change many things at once. Jeff Bezos's establishment of Amazon.com involved launching a new brand, introducing new business methods, and applying new e-commerce technologies. Amazon.com provided a product that was differentiated from those of other book retailers. Amazon's business methods as an online retailer differed from traditional "bricks-and-mortar" retailers such as Barnes and Noble or Borders. Amazon.com also introduced new production methods, such as its patented invention of the "1-click" checkout system (method and system for placing a purchase order via a communications network).[4] Amazon.com subsequently licensed its ordering system to Apple for use in its iTunes online store (Kienle et al. 2004).

Schumpeter's (1934, 66) entrepreneur is an innovator who makes "new combinations," which among its elements can simultaneously include the introduction of a new good, the introduction of a new method of production, the opening of a new market, the conquest of a new source of supply of raw materials or half-manufactured goods, and the carrying out of a new organization of any industry. Alfred Chandler (1990, 597) observes that:

> The first movers—those entrepreneurs that established the first modern industrial enterprises in the new industries of the Second Industrial Revolution—had to innovate in all of these activities. They had to be aware of the potential of new technologies and then get the funds and make investments large enough to exploit fully the economies of scale and scope existing in the new technologies. They had to obtain the facilities and personnel essential to distribute and market new or improved products on a national scale and to obtain extensive sources of supply. Finally, they had to recruit and organize the managerial teams essential to maintain and integrate the investment made in the processes of production and distribution.

Kline and Rosenberg (1986, 279) point out that "There is no single, simple dimensionality to innovation. There are, rather, many sorts of dimensions covering a variety of activities."

With multidimensional innovation, technology transfer can involve a bundle of innovations. However, different types of innovations may not be equally transferable. For example, the costs of transferring manufacturing process technologies can differ from the costs of transferring new producing designs. If we lived in a frictionless world, an innovator could perfectly and costlessly transfer any technology to an incumbent firm. Also, in a friction-

4. US Patent 5,960,411; Inventors: P. Hartman, J. P. Bezos, S. Kaphan, and J. Spiegel; Assignee: Amazon.com Inc. Awarded September 28, 1999.

less world, an incumbent could absorb any type of technology and expand its operations to include new products, manufacturing processes, inputs, and transaction methods. In this ideal setting, a profit-maximizing monopolist could always outperform an industry, because profit maximization yields greater profits than competing firms that cannot coordinate their activities. In such a frictionless setting, entrepreneurship will never be observed when there are existing firms. The challenge for researchers is to explain entrepreneurship in an established industry. Clearly, some types of frictions in markets for technology are necessary for entrepreneurship.

There are many standard explanations for frictions in technology transfer. There may be *imperfect intellectual property rights* (IP) so that innovators are reluctant to reveal their technology to the existing firm; see Arrow (1962) and Anton and Yao (1994, 2003). This implies that entrepreneurship is a mechanism for protecting the innovator's intellectual property. There can be *asymmetric information* that results inefficient bargaining between the innovator and the existing firm; see Arrow (1962) and Spulber (2011). Asymmetric information implies that entrepreneurship is a mechanism for internalizing information asymmetries. Technology transfer also can be hindered by the costs of codifying and communicating the inventor's *tacit knowledge;* see Balconi, Pozzali, and Viale (2007) and the references therein. This implies that entrepreneurship is a way for the innovator to apply his tacit knowledge to establish a new firm (Spulber 2010). Technology transfer is also limited by the inability of existing firms to understand or absorb the knowledge; see Acs et al. (2004) on knowledge filters. The transaction costs of technology transfer can be due to the difficulties inherent in negotiating and writing contracts for complex scientific and technological exchanges. These transaction costs are further increased when technology transfer involves contingent contracts that depend on the performance of new technologies and market demand for new products.

In addition to frictions in the market for technology, there can also be frictions in the market for complementary assets. If either the existing firm or the potential entrepreneur has access to complementary assets, they may have an advantage in applying the new technology. These assets may include market knowledge, access to credit, access to customers, and the ability to apply new technologies. Existing firms are already in business, having cleared the regulatory hurdles and made the irreversible investments and incurred the transaction costs necessary to become established. Existing firms offer innovation efficiencies because they have complementary assets such as marketing, sales, and production capabilities; see Teece (1986, 2006).

5.2.3 Technology Transfer and Diversification by Incumbent Firms

Innovations are often bundles of different discoveries. It is likely that technology transfer costs will differ for each component of an innovation. To represent this possibility, I present a model with a two-dimensional innovation involving a new product design and a new production process. The costs of technology transfer imply that one or both components of the innovation may not be transferable to existing firms or to potential entrepreneurs.

In addition to market-related costs of technology transfer, the existing firm faces adjustment costs of adapting to new manufacturing processes and new products. Adjustment costs have traditionally applied to installation of new capital equipment. However, adopting new technologies require firms to adjust their R&D, personnel hiring and training, manufacturing, input procurement, marketing, and sales. Applying new technologies can require fundamental changes in the firm's organizational structure. These adjustment costs conceivably could be greater than the setup costs of establishing a new firm.

If the innovation involves new products, the existing firm can face adjustment costs associated with diversification. A critical determinant of the costs of diversification is the difference between the existing product and the new product. The products may be differentiated horizontally, such as Coke and Diet Coke, or the products may be differentiated vertically, such as Toyota and Lexus. Adjustment costs associated with diversification generate costs of adopting new technologies for incumbent firms that operate existing technologies.

Using illustrations from the history of Microsoft and IBM, Bresnahan, Greenstein, and Henderson (2012) suggest that firms experience diseconomies of scope because their complementary organizational assets need not be suited for multiple markets. The firm's costs of producing multiple products then would be greater than the total costs of single-product firms supplying those products. Therefore, specialized assets and diseconomies of scope imply that diversification by existing firms can be inefficient.

Offering new products, even those that are substitutes for the incumbent's initial product, can require establishing new divisions to handle the different sales channels and marketing required for the new products. This entails costs of establishing the new divisions and costs of coordination across divisions. In some industries, such diversification is feasible and incumbents tend to absorb multiple innovations by adding new products. In other industries, incumbent firms may face limitations on managerial attention that constrain the number of products they produce.

It may simply be a matter of different brands, with little differences in the products' other features. A firm offering multiple brands must adjust its marketing and sales efforts to coordinate its brand portfolio. In some cases, an existing firm diversifies its offerings by extending its brand to a variety of products. An entrepreneurial entrant may create a new brand that is difficult to transfer to an existing firm because its identity is distinct from that of the incumbent. For example, whether the sales channel is online versus bricks-and-mortar affects consumer brand loyalty for retail products (Danaher, Wilson, and Davis 2003). This suggests that a brand identified with the online retailer itself, such as Amazon.com, could be difficult to transfer to a brand identified with a bricks-and-mortar retailer. This is important for our analysis, which considers the possibility that new products are not transferable to an existing firm.

Theoretical models with "persistence of monopoly" or the "efficiency condition" often assume that the incumbent firm can diversify costlessly. Then, an incumbent monopolist can coordinate its prices across multiple differentiated products. This would generate greater profits than a competitive industry for the obvious reason that competition dissipates rents. Such an approach generates a puzzle of entrepreneurship with differentiated products. Rather than establishing a firm, an innovator would always transfer the technology to an incumbent firm who could then diversify and obtain monopoly rents with multiple goods. Again, the only explanation for entrepreneurship would then be frictions in the market for technology transfer. The problem with this approach is that the theoretical analysis implicitly assumes the incumbent can diversify without cost while the entrepreneurial entrant cannot, which is equivalent to assuming the persistence of monopoly. In this setting, the innovator will always prefer transferring the new technology to the incumbent to establishing a new firm.

The cost of developing new products is an important aspect of diversification. Our analysis assumes that the incumbent firm cannot diversify without obtaining a new product design, either through R&D or from an innovator. Klette and Kortum (2004) consider costly diversification in a model with exogenous entry of single-product firms. After entry, existing firms invest in innovation that leads to product diversification. Their discussion focuses on incumbent firm innovation without a market for technology transfer. I examine conditions under which innovators who choose between entrepreneurship and technology transfer have greater incentives to develop new products and new processes than incumbent monopolists. Incumbents diversify only by adopting a new product design, and entrants only offer a single product. A more general framework would allow for multiple products to be offered both by incumbents and by entrants.

5.3 The Strategic Innovation Game

Consider a strategic innovation game played by an innovator and an established firm. The innovator makes a two-dimensional discovery that consists of a new product design and a new production process. The game has two stages. In stage one, the innovator and the incumbent monopolist choose between cooperation and competition. If the innovator and the existing firm choose to cooperate, the innovator can transfer some aspect of the invention to an existing firm, either the new product design, the new production process, or both. Also, as a means of deterring entry, the existing firm can pay the innovator to license the discovery without necessarily adopting the new technology. If the innovator and the incumbent monopolist choose to compete, the innovator can enter the market by becoming an entrepreneur and establishing a new firm to implement the innovation.

Firms implement the innovation, engage in production, and supply products in stage two. If the innovator and the existing firm choose to cooperate in the first stage, the existing firm operates as a monopolist in the second stage. If the innovator and the existing firm do not choose to cooperate in the first stage, then in the second stage, the new firm established by the entrepreneur and the incumbent firm engage in differentiated-products Bertrand-Nash competition, with each firm supplying one good. The new firm established by the entrepreneur employs the new discovery, introducing both the new product design and the new production process.

5.3.1 The Basic Framework

The innovator's discovery consists of a new production process and a new product design. The existing firm's initial production process is represented by unit cost c_1 and the new production process is represented by unit cost c_2. For ease of presentation, assume that the new technology is superior to the existing technology, $c_2 < c_1$. The analysis can be extended readily to allow for the new technology to be inferior, in which case the existing firm would acquire the new production technology to deter entry without applying the new technology.

The existing firm initially is a single-product monopolist. The new product design is horizontally differentiated from the existing product. If the existing firm adopts the new product design, the existing firm becomes a two-product firm. If the innovator becomes an entrepreneur and establishes a firm, the entrant is a single-product firm that produces the new product. Let q_1 be the output of the good initially produced by firm 1. Let q_2 be the new good, which can be supplied by the existing firm through diversification or by the new entrant.

Market demand is derived from the preferences of a representative consumer, $U(q_1, q_2; b)$, where b represents a substitution parameter such that $0 \leq b < 1$. The consumer's utility is quadratic and symmetric in its arguments, so that products are differentiated horizontally,

$$(1) \qquad U(q_1, q_2; b) = 2q_1 + 2q_2 - (1/2)(q_1)^2 - (1/2)(q_2)^2 - bq_1q_2.$$

The representative consumer chooses consumption q_1 and q_2 to maximize surplus, $U(q_1, q_2; b) - p_1q_1 - p_2q_2$. The consumer's demand functions solve the first order conditions, $U_1(q_1, q_2; b) = p_1$ and $U_2(q_1, q_2; b) = p_2$. The consumer's demand functions are

$$q_i = D_i(p_1, p_2; b) = \frac{2 - 2b + bp_j - p_i}{1 - b^2}, \quad i \neq j, i, j = 1, 2.$$

The demand for a good is decreasing in the good's own price and, for $b > 0$, increasing in the price of the substitute good, $\partial D_i(p_1, p_2; b)/\partial p_i < 0$ and $\partial D_i(p_1, p_2; b)/\partial p_j > 0$, $i \neq j$, $i, j = 1, 2$.

To derive the existing firm's monopoly profit, let $q_2 = 0$. The representative consumer's utility function implies that $U(q_1, 0) = 2q_1 - (1/2)(q_1)^2$. The consumer's demand for the incumbent's product is $D_1(p_1) = 2 - p_1$. The monopoly price is $p^m(c_1) = (2 + c_1)/2$ and the existing monopolist's profit equals

$$(2) \qquad \Pi^m(c_1) = (p^m(c_1) - c_1)D_1(p^m(c_1)) = (2 - c_1)^2/4.$$

The incumbent monopolist is assumed to be viable with the initial technology, $c_1 < 2$, so that the monopolist also is viable with the new technology.

If the innovator transfers the new product design to the existing firm, the incumbent becomes a two-product monopolist. The profit of a two-product monopolist is given by

$$(3) \quad \Pi^m(c_1, c_2, b) = \max_{p_1, p_2} (p_1 - c_1)D_1(p_1, p_2; b) + (p_2 - c_2)D_2(p_1, p_2; b).$$

With symmetric costs, the profits from producing both goods are greater than the profits from producing only one good for all $b < 1$,

$$\Pi^m(c, c, b) = \frac{2}{1+b}\frac{(2-c)^2}{4} > \Pi^m(c).$$

When costs are symmetric, the two-product monopolist's profit is decreasing in the substitution parameter.

5.3.2 Entrepreneurial Entry and Creative Destruction

If the innovator and the existing firm choose to compete, the innovator becomes an entrepreneur by establishing a new firm that embodies the new product design and the new production technology. The existing firm continues to produce a single product with the existing technology. Designate the existing firm as firm 1 and the market entrant as firm 2. The incumbent firm and the entrepreneurial entrant engage in Bertrand-Nash price competition with differentiated products. The Bertrand-Nash equilibrium prices $p_1{}^*$ and $p_2{}^*$ solve

$$(4) \qquad \Pi_1(c_1, c_2, b) = \max_{p_1} (p_1 - c_1)D_1(p_1, p_2{}^*; b)$$

$$(5) \qquad \Pi_2(c_1, c_2, b) = \max_{p_2} (p_2 - c_2)D_2(p_1{}^*, p_2; b).$$

The equilibrium prices depend on the costs of the two firms and the product differentiation parameter, $p_1{}^*(c_1, c_2, b)$ and $p_2{}^*(c_1, c_2, b)$. We restrict attention to cost values such that outputs and profits are nonnegative for both firms. For $b = 0$, each of the firms is a monopolist.

The intensity of product-market competition depends positively on the substitution parameter b and on the difference between costs. With duopoly competition, the price functions are

(6) $p_i^*(c_1, c_2, b) = [2c_i + bc_j + 2(2 + b)(1 - b)]/(4 - b^2), \quad i \neq j, i, j = 1, 2.$

When duopoly output levels are positive they equal

$$(7) \qquad q_i^*(c_1, c_2) = \frac{(2 - b^2)(2 - c_i) - b(2 - c_j)}{(1 - b^2)(4 - b^2)}, \quad i \neq j, i, j = 1, 2.$$

The profits of the firms are

$$(8) \qquad \Pi_i(c_i, c_j, b) = \frac{[(2 - b^2)(2 - c_i) - b(2 - c_j)]^2}{(1 - b^2)(4 - b^2)^2}, \quad i \neq j, i, j = 1, 2.$$

Both firms operate profitably in equilibrium when the new technology is close to the existing technology because positive profits follows from $2 > b^2 + b$. Profits are decreasing in the firm's own cost, $\partial\Pi_i(c_i, c_j, b)/\partial c_i < 0$ and increasing in the competitor's cost, $\partial\Pi_i(c_i, c_j, b)/\partial c_j > 0, i \neq j, i = 1, 2$. For $b > 0$, the firms' costs are substitutes in the profit functions, $\partial^2\Pi_i(c_i, c_j, b)/\partial c_i\partial c_j < 0, i \neq j, i = 1, 2$.

Because the new technology is superior to the existing technology, both firms operate when the incumbent firm operates profitably. If the entrepreneurial entrant is sufficiently efficient, it drives out the incumbent firm. From equation (7), $q_1 = 0$ defines the cost threshold $c_2^0(b, c_1)$ for firm 2,

$$(9) \qquad c_2^0(b, c_1) = \frac{2b - (2 - b^2)(2 - c_1)}{b}.$$

Zanchettin (2006) shows that only the entrant operates when costs are less than or equal to the threshold, $c_2 \leq c_2^0(b, c_1)$, and both firms operate when the entrant's costs are above the threshold, $c_2 > c_2^0(b, c_1)$. The cost threshold for the new technology is less than the initial technology, $c_2^0(b, c_1) < c_1$, and is increasing in the substitution parameter, b. If the innovation is sufficiently drastic, then the entrepreneurial entrant can drive out the incumbent by offering a monopoly price, $p^m(c_2) = (2 + c_2)/2$. Driving out the incumbent with monopoly pricing occurs when the invention is sufficiently drastic. This occurs when the entrant's costs are below a lower threshold, $c_2 \leq c_2^{00}(b, c_1)$, which exists only if $c_1 + b < 2$,

$$(10) \qquad c_2^{00}(b, c_1) = \frac{2(c_1 + b - 2)}{b} < c_2(b, c_1).$$

When the innovation is below the threshold $c_2^0(b, c_1)$ but not sufficiently drastic, $2(c_1 + b - 2)/b < c_2 \leq c_2^0(b, c_1)$, the more efficient firm engages in limit pricing to deter the higher-cost firm from operating. The entrepreneurial entrant, firm 2, is the limit-pricing firm, and firm 1's output is $q_1 =$

$2(1 - b) - p_1 + bp_2 \leq 0$. Then, firm 2's reaction function becomes $p_2 = (1/b)[p_1 - 2(1 - b)]$. The incumbent firm 1 has a zero output and chooses $p_1 = c_1$. The limit-pricing entrant, firm 2, produces output greater than the monopoly output $q_2^L(c_1, c_2) = 2 - p_2 = (2 - c_2)/b > q^m(c_2) = (2 - c_2)/2$, and sets a price below the monopoly price, $p_2^L(c_1, c_2, b) = (1/b)[c_1 - 2(1 - b)] < p^m(c_2) = 1 + c_2/2$. The limit-pricing firm earns profits less than monopoly profits,

$$\Pi_2^L(c_1, c_2, b) = \frac{(2 - c_1)[b(2 - c_2) - (2 - c_1)]}{b^2} < \Pi^m(c_2) = \frac{(2 - c_2)^2}{4}.$$

The properties of the profit and price functions hold more generally. For additional discussion of the class of utility functions that yield similar properties for comparative statics analysis of a duopoly equilibrium, see Milgrom and Roberts (1990). For differentiated duopoly with symmetric costs, see Singh and Vives (1984), and for differentiated duopoly with asymmetric costs and qualities, see Zanchettin (2006). The analysis can be extended to other differentiated product settings such as Hotelling-type (1929) price competition. The results of the following analysis do not require price competition. They could be examined with the two firms engaging in Cournot quantity competition with differentiated products.

5.3.3 Cooperation versus Competition

If the innovator and the incumbent firm choose to cooperate, the incumbent firm is a monopolist with profits Π^m that will depend on what technology is transferred. If the innovator and the incumbent firm choose to compete, the incumbent firm earns duopoly profits, $\Pi_1(c_1, c_2, b)$ and the entrepreneurial entrant earns duopoly profits, $\Pi_2(c_1, c_2, b)$. The incumbent firm's net benefit from adopting the new technology offered by the innovator equals the difference between monopoly profits at the new technology and duopoly profits when the incumbent has the old technology and the entrant has the new technology. Therefore, the incumbent firm's net benefit from adopting the new technology equals the incremental returns from remaining a monopolist, $\Pi^m - \Pi_1$. This is the maximum amount that the innovator can obtain from transferring the technology to the incumbent firm.

The outcome of the strategic innovation game depends on the total returns to cooperation and competition for the innovator and the incumbent firm. The innovator and the incumbent prefer entrepreneurship to technology transfer if and only if the returns to entry are greater than the incremental returns to the incumbent firm from technology transfer,

$$\Pi_2 > \Pi^m - \Pi_1.$$

This is equivalent to the condition that total industry profits when the incumbent firm has the initial technology and the entrepreneurial firm has the new technology are greater than monopoly profits at the new technology,

$$\Pi_1 + \Pi_2 > \Pi^m.$$

If this condition holds, the innovator with a superior technology will become an entrepreneur and enter the market. If this condition does not hold, full information bargaining will result in the innovator transferring his technology to the incumbent.

For the innovator and the incumbent firm to choose competition over cooperation, the incumbent firm using the new technology must earn lower profits than the competitive industry. The possibility of entrepreneurial entry may seem counterintuitive because it may appear that the monopolist will always earn greater profits than the competitive industry. The outcome of the strategic innovation game between the innovator and the existing firm depends on the extent of the innovation. The greater the difference between costs with the new technology and costs with the initial technology, the higher the quality of the process innovation. The value of the product innovation depends on the incremental returns to diversification by the incumbent firm.

If the innovator and the established firm choose cooperation, they bargain over the royalty, R. Let the relative bargaining power of the innovator in the bargaining game be represented by the parameter, α, where $0 \leq \alpha \leq 1$. This represents the reduced form of a bargaining game between the innovator and the incumbent firm. This can represent bargaining with alternating offers and discounting of future payoffs or first-and-final offers by either party. Because there is a lump-sum royalty, bargaining is efficient and relative bargaining power does not affect the outcome of the strategic innovation game. With full information, the outcome of the strategic innovation game is efficient for the innovator and the incumbent firm. They decide whether to cooperate or to compete and if cooperation is efficient they bargain over the division of the surplus. The innovator receives a royalty from transferring the technology equal to $R = \alpha(\Pi^m - \Pi_1) + (1 - \alpha)\Pi_2$.

5.4 Equilibrium of the Strategic Innovation Game

Due to various transaction costs, the invention may be imperfectly transferable. The transferability of the invention will affect the outcome of the strategic interaction between the existing firm and the innovator. Transferability will affect the returns to licensing the invention and it will affect whether the existing firm and the innovator choose to compete or to cooperate. Because the innovation is two dimensional there are four possibilities: (1) the new technology is fully transferable, that is both the new product design and the new production process are transferable and the new production process is applicable to producing both goods; (2) the new technology is nontransferable; that is, neither the new product design nor the production technology are transferable, although the existing firm can still license the new technology as a means of deterring entry, without using the new technology; (3) the new product design is not transferable and the new production process is transferable, so the existing firm can apply the production process to the initial good; and (4) finally, if the new product design is transferable but the new production process is not transferable, then the existing firm produces both the initial product and the new product, and applies the initial production process to both products.

5.4.1 Fully Transferable Technology

With fully transferable technology, the existing firm obtains profit from producing both goods using the new production technology, $\Pi^m(c_2, c_2, b)$. If the innovator and the incumbent firm choose to compete, the incumbent firm earns duopoly profits, $\Pi_1(c_1, c_2, b)$ and the entrepreneurial entrant earns duopoly profits, $\Pi_2(c_1, c_2, b)$. Total industry profits are continuous in the new process technology c_2 and the curve representing total profits has up to three segments. If the innovation is sufficiently drastic, $c_2 \leq c_2^{00}(c_1, b)$, then a monopoly-pricing entrant eliminates the incumbent and industry profits equal single-product monopoly profits with the new process technology.

$$\Pi_1(c_1, c_2, b) + \Pi_2(c_1, c_2, b) = \Pi^m(c_2).$$

For an intermediate value of the new process technology, $c_2^{00}(c_1, b) < c_2 \leq c_2^0(c_1, b)$, the entrepreneurial entrant engages in limit pricing so that industry profits equals

$$\Pi_1(c_1, c_2, b) + \Pi_2(c_1, c_2, b) = \Pi_2^L(c_1, c_2, b) < \Pi^m(c_2).$$

These two situations correspond to creative destruction. Finally, for incremental innovations, $c_2^0(c_1, b) < c_2 < c_1$, both firms operate and total industry profits are calculated by adding the two firms' profits using equation (8). With both firms operating, industry profits are decreasing and convex in c_2. As c_2 approaches c_1, total industry profits approaches its minimum for $c_2 \leq c_1$,

$$\Pi_1(c_1, c_1, b) + \Pi_2(c_1, c_1, b) = (2 - c_1)^2 \frac{2(1 - b)}{(1 + b)(2 - b)^2} \tag{11}$$

This is the minimum for the three segments, as shown in figure 5.1.

With fully transferable technology, the returns to cooperation exceed the returns to competition. The monopolist with the new product design and the new production process earns more than industry profits with entrepreneurial entry for all $b > 0$,

$$\Pi^m(c_2, c_2, b) > \Pi_1(c_1, c_2, b) + \Pi_2(c_1, c_2, b).$$

This holds because of the rent-dissipating effects of competition and because the incumbent uses the old production process when there is entrepreneurial entry. The net returns to technology transfer, $\Pi^m(c_2, c_2, b) - \Pi_1(c_1, c_2, b)$, are

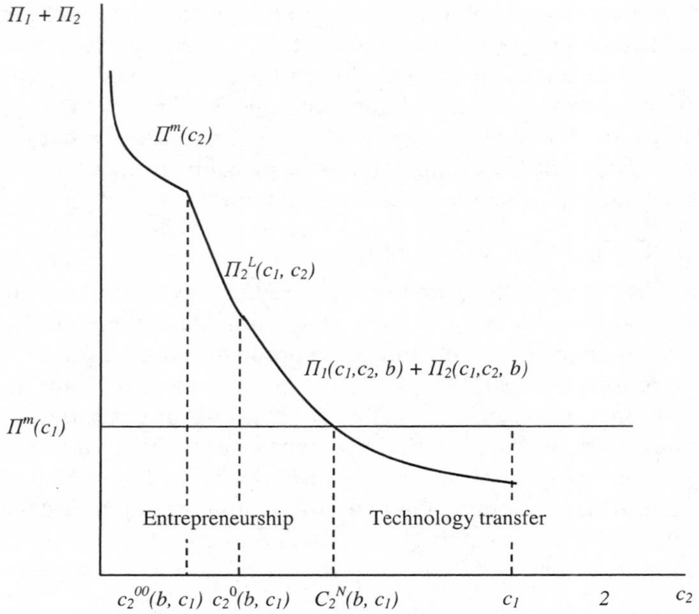

Fig. 5.1 With nontransferable technology, the outcome of the innovation game is entrepreneurship only if the new process innovation, c_2, is sufficiently below the initial cost, that is, if the new costs are less than a critical value, $C_2^N(b, c_1)$, where $C_2^N(b, c_1) \leq c_1$

greater than the returns to entrepreneurship, $\Pi_2(c_1, c_2, b)$. This immediately implies that when technology is fully transferable, the innovator and the existing firm always choose to cooperate.

PROPOSITION 1. *With fully transferable technology, entrepreneurial entry does not occur and the innovator transfers the technology to the existing firm.*

Proposition 1 yields insights into Kenneth Arrow's (1962) original investigation of the incentive to invent. The incumbent monopolist's incentive to invent equals the returns to producing both goods and applying the new process technology,

$$V^m = \Pi^m(c_2, c_2, b) - \Pi^m(c_1). \tag{12}$$

Although generalized to include diversification, the monopolist's incentive to invent reflects the inertia identified by Arrow. The firm that expects to continue to be a monopolist is concerned only about incremental profits.

Now, compare the monopolist's incentive to invent with that of the innovator. With fully transferable technology, the innovator's incentive to invent equals the royalties from technology transfer,

(13) $V^I = R = \alpha(\Pi^m(c_2, c_2, b) - \Pi_1(c_1, c_2, b)) + (1 - \alpha)\Pi_2(c_1, c_2, b).$

The innovator's incentive to invent derives from transferring the technology or from competing with the incumbent firm. If the innovator licenses the technology to the incumbent monopolist, the incumbent monopolist's willingness to pay is the difference between the incumbent's monopoly profit and the incumbent's profit after competitive entry. Due to the effects of competition, the incumbent's initial profit is greater than the incumbent's profit after entry, $\Pi^m(c_1) > \Pi_1(c_1, c_2, b)$. So, the monopolist's incentive to invent is less than the benefit of adopting the new technology,

$$V^m = \Pi^m(c_2, c_2, b) - \Pi^m(c_1) < \Pi^m(c_2, c_2, b) - \Pi_1(c_1, c_2, b).$$

The innovator's incentive to invent is greater than or equal to the returns to entrepreneurial entry and less than or equal to the incumbent's benefit from technology adoption. Define the critical value of the innovator's bargaining power by

$$(14) \qquad \alpha^* = \frac{\Pi^m(c_2, c_2, b) - \Pi^m(c_1) - \Pi_2(c_1, c_2, b)}{\Pi^m(c_2, c_2, b) - \Pi_1(c_1, c_2, b) - \Pi_2(c_1, c_2, b)}.$$

PROPOSITION 2. *With fully transferable technology, the innovator's incentive to invent is greater than that of the incumbent monopolist if and only if the innovator has sufficient bargaining power,* $\alpha \geq \alpha^*$.

With fully transferable technology and sufficient bargaining power, the possibility of entrepreneurship increases incentives to invent. Even though the innovator transfers the technology to the incumbent firm, the possibility of entrepreneurship overcomes the incumbent firm's inertia. The threat of creative destruction provides a competitive benchmark that increases the incumbent's incentive to adopt in comparison to the monopoly benchmark.

5.4.2 Nontransferable Technology

Suppose that neither the new product design nor the new production process is transferable. The innovator can still contract with the existing firm to receive a payment for not entering the market, with the incumbent licensing the technology without actually using the new product design or the new production process.[5] The existing firm that buys out the innovator would continue to operate as a single-product monopoly with profits, $\Pi^m(c_1)$. The lowest value of industry profits, $\Pi_1(c_1, c_1, b) + \Pi_2(c_1, c_1, b)$, is greater than, equal to, or less than the incumbent's profits, $\Pi^m(c_1)$ depending on the substi-

5. Rasmusen (1988) considers an entrant that seeks a buyout after entry in a homogeneous-products Cournot game with capacity constraints, although he does not consider technological change.

tution parameter. Entrepreneurial entry need not always occur because the innovator and the existing firm still have incentives to avoid competition.

For a given degree of product differentiation, entrepreneurial entry occurs if the process innovation is sufficiently large. With nontransferable technology, the incumbent and the entrant have greater incentives to cooperate to avoid creative destruction only when the innovation is incremental, as shown in figure 5.1. With nontransferable technology, a significant innovation increases the returns to entry for the entrepreneur who drives out the incumbent. The pure creative destruction effect means that the entrepreneur's returns to entry exceed the benefits to the incumbent from buying out the innovator.

With nontransferable technology, entry occurs if and only if the substitution parameter is either above or below an intermediate range, as shown in figure 5.2. With vigorous competition resulting from less product differentiation, the innovator and the existing firm have less incentive to cooperate because the entrepreneurial entrant will displace the incumbent firm. With less competition resulting from more product differentiation, the innovator and the existing firm also have less incentive to cooperate because they earn sufficient profits after entrepreneurial entry.

PROPOSITION 3. *With nontransferable technology, entrepreneurial entry occurs if and only if the substitution parameter is less than the critical value* $b^N = b^N(c_1, c_2)$ *or greater than the critical value* $b^{NN} = b^{NN}(c_1, c_2)$, *where* $b^N(c_1, c_2) < b^{NN}(c_1, c_2)$. *Also, with nontransferable technology, entrepreneurial entry occurs if and only if costs are less than the critical value,* $C_2^N(b, c_1)$, *where* $C_2^N(b, c_1) \leq c_1$, *so that significant process innovations result in entrepreneurship.*

PROOF. First, we show that the industry profits function is continuous in b with three segments. Using the quadratic formula, the critical value $0 < b^0 < 1$ that solves $c_2 = c_2^0(b^0, c_1)$ is given by

$$b^0 = \frac{-(2 - c_2) + [(2 - c_2)^2 + 8(2 - c_1)^2]^{1/2}}{2(2 - c_1)}.$$

The critical value b^{00} that solves $c_2 = c_2^{00}(b^0, c_1) = 2(c_1 + b^{00} - 2)/b^{00}$ is given by

$$b^{00} = \frac{2(2 - c_1)}{2 - c_2}.$$

For $0 \leq b < b^0$, both firms operate profitably so that industry profits equal

$$\text{(15)} \quad \Pi_1(c_1, c_2, b) + \Pi_2(c_1, c_2, b) = \frac{(4 - 5b^2 + b^4)A - (4b - 2b^3)B}{(1 - b^2)(4 - b^2)^2},$$

where $A = (2 - c_1)^2 + (2 - c_2)^2$ and $B = 2(2 - c_1)(2 - c_2)$. For $b^0 \leq b < b^{00}$, limit pricing occurs so that only firm 2 operates profitably and industry profits are equal to

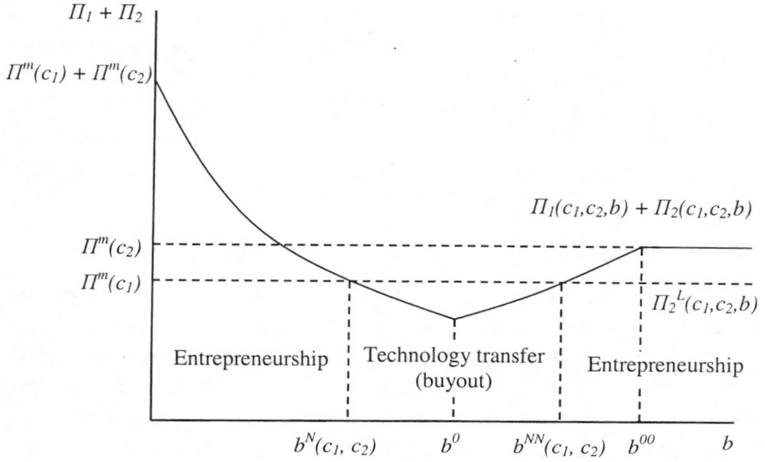

Fig. 5.2 With nontransferable technology, the outcome of the innovation game is entrepreneurship if and only if the substitution parameter is less than the critical value $b^N = b^N(c_1, c_2)$ or greater than the critical value $b^{NN} = b^{NN}(c_1, c_2)$

$$(16)\qquad \Pi_1(c_1, c_2, b) + \Pi_2(c_1, c_2, b) = \Pi_2^L(c_1, c_2, b) = \frac{(2 - c_1)[b(2 - c_2) - (2 - c_1)]}{b^2}.$$

There is a third region only if the invention is sufficiently drastic, $2(2 - c_1) < (2 - c_2)$. Then, for $b^{00} \leq b < 1$, the entrant deters the incumbent with monopoly pricing and industry profits equal the entrant's profits, $\Pi^m(c_2)$. The industry profits function is continuous at b^0, because $c_2 = c_2(b^0, c_1)$ so that from equation (16),

$$(17)\qquad \Pi_1(c_1, c_2, b^0) + \Pi_2(c_1, c_2, b^0) = \frac{(2 - c_2)^2[1 - (b^0)^2]}{[2 - (b^0)^2]^2} = \Pi_2^L(c_1, c_2, b^0).$$

The industry profits function is continuous at b^{00}, because $c_2 = 2(c_1 + b^{00} - 2)/b^{00}$ so that industry profits equal

$$(18)\qquad \Pi_2^L(c_1, c_2, b^{00}) = \frac{(2 - c_2)^2}{4} = \Pi^m(c_2).$$

For $0 \leq b < b^0$, the industry profits function in equation (15) is strictly decreasing in b. Differentiating with respect to b gives

$$\frac{\partial(\Pi_1(c_1, c_2, b) + \Pi_2(c_1, c_2, b))}{\partial b} = \frac{2[b(4 - 9b^2 + 2b^4 - b^6)A - (8 + 2b^2 - 5b^4 + 3b^6)B]}{(1 - b^2)^2(4 - b^2)^3}.$$

Note that $(8 + 2b^2 - 5b^4 + 3b^6) > 0$ for $0 \le b < 1$. If $(4 - 9b^2 + 2b^4 - b^6) \le 0$ it follows that $\partial(\Pi_1(c_1, c_2; b) + \Pi_2(c_1, c_2; b))/\partial b < 0$. Conversely, suppose that $(4 - 9b^2 + 2b^4 - b^6) > 0$. Note that when c_2 is above the threshold, it follows that $(2 - b^2)B > bA$, so that again $\partial(\Pi_1(c_1, c_2; b) + \Pi_2(c_1, c_2; b))/\partial b < 0$. For $b^0 \le b \le b^{00}$, $\Pi_2^L(c_1, c_2, b)$ is strictly increasing in b because $b < b^{00}$. The analysis shows that there exists a unique critical value of the substitution parameter, $b^N(c_1, c_2) < b^0 < 1$ that solves

$$\Pi_1(c_1, c_2, b^N) + \Pi_2(c_1, c_2, b^N) = \Pi^m(c_1). \tag{19}$$

Also, there is a critical value $b^0 < b^{NN}(c_1, c_2) < 1$ that equates industry profits with the incumbent's profits at the initial technology. So, industry profits are greater than the monopolist's profits at the new technology if and only if either $0 \le b < b^N(c_1, c_2)$ or $b^{NN}(c_1, c_2) \le b < 1$. Because the industry profits curve is downward sloping in the new process technology, and minimum industry profits are greater than, equal to or less than $\Pi^m(c_1)$ depending on the substitution parameter, it follows that entrepreneurial entry occurs if and only if costs c_2 are less than the critical value $C_2^N(b, c_1) \le c_1$. ■

With nontransferable technology, entrepreneurship takes place only if the innovation is significant. The critical cost value, $C_2^N(b, c_1)$ is less than c_1 only if industry profits in equation (11) are less than $\Pi^m(c_1)$. When the substitution parameter b is sufficiently low, competition is mitigated so that entrepreneurial entry takes place for any cost level, so that the critical value $C_2^N(b, c_1)$ equals c_1.

The incumbent monopolist can have greater incentives to invent than the innovator because nontransferable technology reduces the returns from licensing.

PROPOSITION 4. *With nontransferable technology, the incumbent monopolist has a greater incentive to invent than the innovator when products are sufficiently differentiated,*

$$b \le \frac{\Pi^m(c_2) - \Pi^m(c_1)}{\Pi^m(c_2) + \Pi^m(c_1)}.$$

PROOF. Recall that the profits of the two-product monopolist with the initial technology equals $\Pi^m(c, c; b) = 2[2/(1 + b)][(2 - c)^2/4]$. If the outcome of the innovation game is entrepreneurship, the innovator obtains $V^I = \Pi_2(c_1, c_2; b)$. Then,

$$\begin{aligned} V^m - V^I &= \Pi^m(c_2, c_2, b) - \Pi^m(c_1) - \Pi_2(c_1, c_2; b) \\ &= \{\Pi^m(c_2) - \Pi_2(c_1, c_2; b)\} + \left[\frac{1 - b}{1 + b}\Pi^m(c_2) - \Pi^m(c_1)\right] > 0. \end{aligned}$$

The first term is positive due to the effects of competition and the second term is positive from the upper limit on b. If the outcome of the innovation game is licensing, the innovator obtains $V^I = R = \alpha(\Pi^m(c_1) - \Pi_1(c_1, c_2, b)) + (1 - \alpha)\Pi_2(c_1, c_2, b)$, so that $V^I \leq \Pi^m(c_1) - \Pi_1(c_1, c_2, b)$. Then,

$$V^m - V^I \geq \Pi_1(c_1, c_2, b) + 2\{[1/(1 + b)]\Pi^m(c_2) - \Pi^m(c_1)\}.$$

The second term is positive for $b \leq [\Pi^m(c_2) - \Pi^m(c_1)]/[\Pi^m(c_1)]$, which holds from the upper limit on b, so that again $V^m > V^I$. ■

Nontransferable technology reduces incentives to invent because the innovator obtains returns from entrepreneurial entry or from a buyout to prevent entry. Greater product differentiation is sufficient for the monopolist's incentive to invent to exceed the returns from entry or from a buyout.

5.4.3 Only the New Production Process is Transferable

If the new product design is not transferable and the new production process is transferable, then with technology transfer the existing firm remains a single-product monopolist and obtains profit using the new production technology, $\Pi^m(c_2)$. Therefore, the incumbent firm's net benefit from adopting the new technology equals the incremental returns from remaining a monopolist, $\Pi^m(c_2) - \Pi_1(c_1, c_2, b)$. This is the maximum amount that the innovator can obtain from transferring the technology to the incumbent firm.

The outcome of the strategic innovation game depends on the total returns to cooperation and competition for the innovator and the incumbent firm. The innovator prefers entrepreneurship to technology transfer if and only if the returns to entry are greater than the incremental returns to the incumbent firm from technology transfer, $\Pi_2(c_1, c_2, b) > \Pi^m(c_2) - \Pi_1(c_1, c_2, b)$. This is equivalent to the condition that total industry profits when the incumbent firm has the initial technology and the entrepreneurial firm has the new technology are greater than monopoly profits at the new technology,

$$\Pi_1(c_1, c_2, b) + \Pi_2(c_1, c_2, b) > \Pi^m(c_2).$$

Product differentiation makes entrepreneurial entry possible even when the innovator can transfer only the new production process. When products are not close substitutes, the total profits of the incumbent firm and the entrant are greater than the profits of the existing firm with the new production technology. Without competition ($b = 0$), industry profits exceed the incumbent's profits evaluated at the new technology,

$$\Pi_1(c_1, c_2, b = 0) + \Pi_2(c_1, c_2, b = 0) = \Pi^m(c_1) + \Pi^m(c_2) > \Pi^m(c_2).$$

For b near zero, the threshold $c_2^0(b, c_1)$ is less than or equal to 0, so that limit pricing is ruled out for b near zero and both firms operate profitably. The threshold $c_2^0(b, c_1)$ is increasing in b and approaches c_1 as b goes to 1. When products are not close substitutes, both firms operate and the industry earns greater profits than a single-product monopolist using the new production process. As the degree of product substitution increases, industry profits decrease and eventually the lower-cost firm is able to displace the incumbent firm through limit pricing. This reduces industry profits to the profits of the entrepreneurial entrant that are less than the profits of a single-product monopolist using the new production process. With limit pricing, the lower-cost firm's profits are increasing in the degree of product substitution. When products are very close substitutes, and the invention is sufficiently drastic, the more efficient entrant with monopoly pricing can displace the incumbent using the initial technology. Then, transferring the technology generates the same profits as entrepreneurial entry.

Because the industry profits curve is downward sloping in the new process technology, there exists a unique cost threshold C_2^*, where $c_2^0(c_1, b) < C_2^*(c_1, b) \leq c_1$, such that

(20) $$\Pi_1(c_1, C_2^*, b) + \Pi_2(c_1, C_2^*, b) = \Pi^m(C_2^*).$$

The cost threshold is illustrated in figure 5.3. When the process innovation is significant, industry profits with competition are less than or equal to the profits of a single-product monopoly, thus leading to cooperation and technology transfer. The result establishes a critical threshold for technology transfer that is greater than the critical threshold for limit pricing. Below

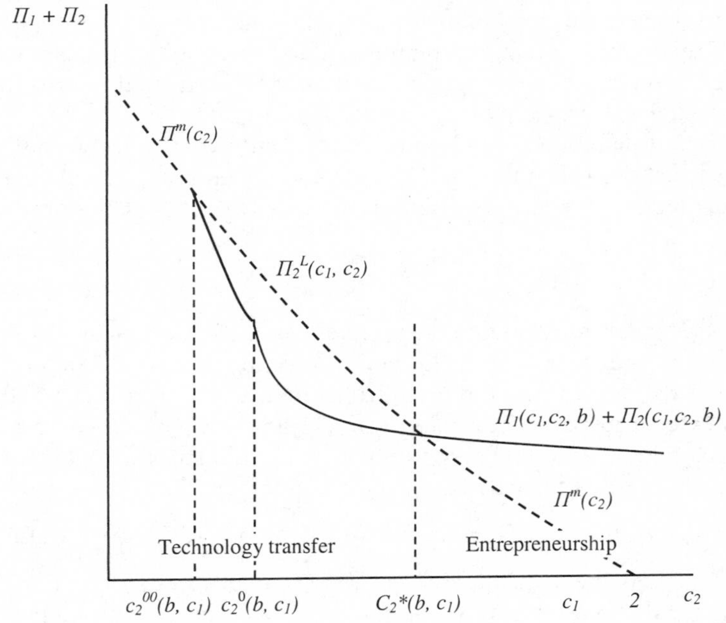

Fig. 5.3 When only the production process is transferable, the outcome of the innovation game is entrepreneurship if and only if the new process technology is incremental, $c_2 > C_2^*(c_1, b)$

that threshold, technology transfer is preferable to entrepreneurship for the innovator and the existing firm. If $c_2 \leq c_2(c_1, b)$, the returns to technology transfer outweigh the profit of the entrepreneurial entrant that drives out the incumbent, either through limit pricing, or when the invention is drastic, with a monopoly price. This implies that there is an additional range of costs, $c_2(c_1, b) < c_2 \leq C_2^*(c_1, b)$, such that the returns to technology transfer outweigh industry profits even when both firms operate after entry.

Sufficiently differentiated products or incremental innovations generate entrepreneurship when only the production process is transferable.

PROPOSITION 5. *When only the production process is transferable, entrepreneurial entry occurs when products are differentiated sufficiently,* $0 \leq b < b^*(c_1, c_2)$, *where the threshold* $b^*(c_1, c_2)$ *is unique, positive and less than one. Also, there exists a positive critical value of the new technology,* $C_2^*(c_1, b)$, *such that entrepreneurship occurs in equilibrium when the process innovation is incremental,* $c_2 > C_2^*(c_1, b)$. *The cost threshold is greater than that for limit pricing and less than or equal to the initial technology,* $c_2^0(c_1, b) < C_2^*(c_1, b) \leq c_1$.

Proposition 5 illustrates Schumpeter's observation that the entrepreneur will enter beside the existing firm. Sufficient product differentiation attenuates competition so that industry profits are greater than monopoly profits using the new production technology and the innovator obtains greater returns from entrepreneurship than from technology transfer. Because product differentiation limits product market competition, entrepreneurship also can occur when the new production technology is inferior to the incumbent's production technology.

Additionally, entrepreneurship is associated with incremental process inventions while technology transfer is associated with significant process inventions. With significant improvements in production technology, cost savings and monopoly profits outweigh the returns to product differentiation and entry so that the incumbent firm and the innovator choose cooperation over competition. With incremental improvements in technology, innovators embody their discoveries in new firms offering new products and creative destruction occurs at the margin. When entrepreneurial entry occurs in waves as Schumpeter suggested, each new entrant will introduce new products and incremental process innovations.

The industry profits function is decreasing in the substitution parameter when both firms operate profitably so that the cost threshold in Proposition 5 is increasing in the substitution parameter, $\partial C_2^*(b, c_1)/\partial b \geq 0$. This implies that with greater product differentiation, that is, with lower values of b, the cost threshold falls and the range of innovations that result in entrepreneurship increases.

COROLLARY 1. *With a transferable production process, greater product differentiation (lower b) implies an increase in the range of innovations for which entrepreneurship occurs, with the marginal process innovation at which entrepreneurship occurs becoming more significant.*

The effects of product differentiation suggest potential industry dynamics. Suppose that the substitution parameter initially takes a high value. Then, a series of innovators with superior process technologies will choose to sell their idea to the incumbent firm, which experiences technological improvements. Then, suppose that the substitution parameter declines over time. For a particular process innovation, the outcome of the innovation game would switch from technology transfer to entrepreneurial entry. In contrast, with a rising substitution parameter, the outcome of the innovation game would switch from entrepreneurial entry to technology transfer.

When only the production process is transferable, the innovator's incentive to invent both a new product and a new process technology reflects the returns from commercializing the process invention through licensing or through entrepreneurship. The innovator's incentive to invent equals

$$(21)\quad V^I = \max\{\alpha(\Pi^m(c_2) - \Pi_1(c_1, c_2, b)) + (1-\alpha)\Pi_2(c_1, c_2, b), \Pi_2(c_1, c_2, b)\}.$$

For purposes of comparison, consider the incumbent monopolist's incentive to invent only a new process technology, $V^m = \Pi^m(c_2) - \Pi^m(c_1)$. The incumbent firm using its initial technology earns more as a monopolist than with competitive entry, $\Pi^m(c_1) > \Pi_1(c_1, c_2, b)$. This implies that the monopolist's incentive to invent is less than the benefit of adopting the new technology,

$$V^m = \Pi^m(c_2) - \Pi^m(c_1) < \Pi^m(c_2) - \Pi_1(c_1, c_2, b).$$

If entrepreneurial entry is more profitable than the monopolist's returns to technology transfer, that is $\Pi^m(c_2) - \Pi_1(c_1, c_2, b) \leq \Pi_2(c_1, c_2, b)$, the entrepreneur's incentive to invent a new product and process is greater than the monopolist's incentive to invent a new production process.

PROPOSITION 6. *Consider incentives to invent when only the new production process is transferable. When products are sufficiently differentiated, $0 \leq b \leq b^*(c_1, c_2)$, or when the process innovation is incremental, $c_2 > C_2^*(c_1, b)$, the innovator's incentive to invent is greater than that of an incumbent monopolist, $V^I > V^m$.*

This result holds for all values of the bargaining power parameter. When technology transfer is the equilibrium outcome, the innovator's incentive to invent may be lower than that of the monopolist when bargaining power is low.

For any given level of product differentiation, the innovator's incentive to invent depends on the relative bargaining power of the innovator and incumbent firm. We can then define a critical value of the product differentiation parameter, $\alpha^* = \max\{0, \alpha'\}$, where

$$(22) \qquad \alpha' = \frac{\Pi^m(c_2) - \Pi^m(c_1) - \Pi_2(c_1, c_2, b)}{\Pi^m(c_2) - \Pi_1(c_1, c_2, b) - \Pi_2(c_1, c_2, b)}.$$

When the innovator has sufficient bargaining power, that is, $\alpha^* \leq \alpha \leq 1$, the innovator's incentive to invent, V^I, is greater than that of an incumbent monopolist, V^m, whether or not the new technology improves on the existing technology.[6]

The innovative monopolist experiences inertia because of initial monopoly profit. When an innovator provides an invention to the incumbent firm, the threat of entry provides a benchmark that is less than monopoly profits, which reduces the monopolist's inertia. The incumbent monopolist compares the profits from technology adoption to profit after entry of the entrepreneur. The innovator's incentive to invent reflects the returns to technology transfer and entrepreneurial entry. If the innovator becomes an entrepreneur, the return from entry must be greater than what could be obtained from transferring the technology to the incumbent. The innovator's return from being an entrepreneur is obtained by competing with the incumbent firm. Therefore, the innovator's total rents derive from the returns to differentiated products competition.

5.4.4 Only the New Product Design is Transferable

If the new product design is transferable but the new production process is not transferable, then with technology transfer the existing firm obtains profit from producing both goods using the initial technology, $\Pi^m(c_1, c_1, b)$. The innovator prefers entrepreneurship to technology transfer if and only if the returns to entry are greater than the incremental returns to the incumbent firm from technology transfer,

$$\Pi_2(c_1, c_2, b) > \Pi^m(c_1, c_1, b) - \Pi_1(c_1, c_2, b).$$

This is equivalent to the condition that total industry profits when the incumbent firm has the initial technology and the entrepreneurial firm has the new technology are greater than monopoly profits with the new product design and the initial production process,

$$\Pi_1(c_1, c_2, b) + \Pi_2(c_1, c_2, b) > \Pi^m(c_1, c_1, b).$$

6. The innovator's incentive to invent when the new technology is equivalent or inferior to that of the incumbent firm, $c_2 \geq c_1$, equals

$$V^I = \max\{\alpha(\Pi^m(c_1) - \Pi_1(c_1, c_2, b)) + (1 - \alpha)\Pi_2(c_1, c_2, b), \Pi_2(c_1, c_2, b)\}.$$

The innovator's incentive to invent is positive even with an equivalent or inferior technology. The incumbent monopolist would have an incentive to invent equal to zero if the new technology were equivalent or inferior to the existing technology, $V^m = 0$. Then, $V^I > 0 = V^m$, so the innovator's incentive to invent is always greater than that of an incumbent monopolist. This holds for all values of the substitution parameter.

When the substitution parameter equals zero, industry profits exceed the incumbent's profits evaluated at the initial production technology due to a pure efficiency effect,

$$\begin{aligned}\Pi_1(c_1, c_2, b = 0) + \Pi_2(c_1, c_2, b = 0) &= \Pi^m(c_1) + \Pi^m(c_2) \\ &> 2\Pi^m(c_1) \\ &= \Pi^m(c_1, c_2, b = 0).\end{aligned}$$

However, when products are closer substitutes, competition between the entrant and the incumbent firm diminishes the benefits of entrepreneurial entry in comparison with technology transfer. Industry profits are decreasing in the substitution parameter, although the monopolist's profits also are decreasing in the substitution parameter.

The lowest value of industry profits is less than the profit of the incumbent monopolist that produces two products with the initial process technology, for all positive b,

$$\Pi_1(c_1, c_1, b) + \Pi_2(c_1, c_1, b) = \frac{4 - 4b}{4 - 4b + b^2}\Pi^m(c_1, c_1, b) < \Pi^m(c_1, c_1, b).$$

This implies that entrepreneurship occurs if and only if the substitution parameter is outside an intermediate range.

The transferability of the new product design reverses the previous result with a transferable process technology. There is a critical cost threshold that solves

$$\Pi_1(c_1, c_2^D, b) + \Pi_2(c_1, c_2^D, b) = \Pi^m(c_1, c_1, b).$$

The lowest value of industry profits is greater than the profits of the two-product monopolist at $b = 0$. Then, the cost threshold c_2^D goes to c_1, so that all innovators choose to become entrepreneurs. For sufficiently differentiated products, the lowest value of industry profits is greater than the profits of the two-product monopolist so that the cost threshold c_2^D is strictly less than c_1. Incremental process innovations result in technology transfer and significant innovations generate entrepreneurship.

PROPOSITION 7. *When only the new product design is transferable, entrepreneurial entry occurs if and only if the substitution parameter is less than the critical value $b^D = b^D(c_1, c_2)$ or greater than the critical value $b^{DD} = b^{DD}(c_1, c_2)$. Also, entrepreneurial entry occurs if and only if $c_2 < C_2^D(c_1, b)$, so that significant process innovations result in entrepreneurship.*

Compare the innovator's incentive to invent to that of the incumbent monopolist when the invention consists of a new product design. The monopolist develops or adopts a new product design to diversify. With the initial process technology, the monopolists' incentive to develop a new product design is less than the benefit from adopting a new product design,

$$V^m = \Pi^m(c_1, c_1, b) - \Pi^m(c_1) < \Pi^m(c_1, c_1, b) - \Pi_1(c_1, c_2, b).$$

The innovator's incentive to invent the combination of a new product and a new process technology equals

$$(23) \quad V^I = \max \{\alpha(\Pi^m(c_1, c_1, b) - \Pi_1(c_1, c_2, b)) + (1 - \alpha)\Pi_2(c_1, c_2, b), \Pi_2(c_1, c_2, b)\}.$$

This implies the following result.

PROPOSITION 8. *Consider the incentive to invent when only the new product design is transferable. When either the substitution parameter is less than the critical value* $b^D = b^D(c_1, c_2)$ *or greater than the critical value* $b^{DD} = b^{DD}(c_1, c_2)$, *or when the process innovation is significant,* $c_2 < C_2^D(c_1, b)$, *the innovator's incentive to invent is greater than that of an incumbent monopolist,* $V^I > V^m$.

5.5 The Strategic Innovation Game with an Independent Inventor and a Transferable Production Process

The discussion has so far assumed that the innovator must choose between technology transfer and entrepreneurship. Suppose instead that the inventor and the prospective entrepreneur are independent actors. The inventor can offer to license the process technology both to the existing firm and to an entrepreneur. The existing firm and the entrepreneurial entrant engage in differentiated products competition. The inventor chooses the royalty for the technology license but cannot otherwise choose which firm purchases the technology. There is no need to consider the choice of licensee because if the inventor could make such a choice, the outcome would be the same as the situation in which the inventor can become an entrepreneur, which was already considered in the previous section.

5.5.1 The Entrepreneur Does Not Have the Initial Technology

By selecting the amount of royalty to charge for the license, the inventor can affect the outcome of the adoption and entry game between the incumbent firm and the entrepreneur. The existing firm chooses whether or not to adopt the new process technology. Suppose first that the entrepreneur can only enter the market by adopting the new process technology so that the entrepreneur chooses between entry with adoption and not entering. This assumption will be relaxed later in the section by allowing the entrepreneur access to the initial process technology.

The strategic adoption and entry game has four possible outcomes. The existing firm chooses between continuing with the process initial technology and adopting the new process technology. The potential entrepreneur chooses whether or not to enter the market. Let R be the lump-sum royalty offered by the inventor. If both the incumbent and the entrepreneur

Table 5.1 **The technology adoption and entrepreneurship game with payoffs (existing firm 1, entrepreneurial firm 2)**

	Entrepreneurial firm 2	
Existing firm 1	Enter	Do not enter
Adopt	$\Pi_1(c_2, c_2, b) - R, \Pi_2(c_2, c_2, b) - R$	$\Pi^m(c_2) - R, 0$
Do not adopt	$\Pi_1(c_1, c_2, b), \Pi_2(c_1, c_2, b) - R$	$\Pi^m(c_1), 0$

adopt the new technology the payoffs are symmetric, $\Pi_1(c_2, c_2, b) - R$ and $\Pi_2(c_2, c_2, b) - R$. If only the entrepreneur adopts the new process technology, the payoffs are asymmetric, with the incumbent firm earning profits $\Pi_1(c_1, c_2, b)$ and the entrepreneur earning net returns $\Pi_2(c_1, c_2, b) - R$. If only the incumbent firm adopts the new process technology, the incumbent earns $\Pi^m(c_2) - R$ and the entrepreneur's payoff is zero. If neither firm adopts the new process technology, the incumbent firm earns $\Pi^m(c_1) - R$ and the entrepreneur's payoff again is zero. Table 5.1 shows the adoption-and-entry game.

Suppose that the inventor chooses royalties that are less than or equal to the incumbent's incremental returns from adoption when there is entrepreneurial entry,

$$R \leq \Pi_1(c_2, c_2, b) - \Pi_1(c_1, c_2, b).$$

Then, the outcome (Adopt, Enter) is the unique equilibrium. To see why, first consider the incumbent firm's decisions. When $R \leq \Pi_1(c_2, c_2, b) - \Pi_1(c_1, c_2, b)$, it follows that the incumbent firm will prefer to adopt the new technology as a best response to entry by the entrepreneur because

$$\Pi_1(c_2, c_2, b) - R \geq \Pi_1(c_1, c_2, b).$$

Since $c_2 < c_1$ and $\partial\Pi_1(c_1, c_2, b)/\partial c_1 < 0$, it follows that $\Pi_1(c_2, c_2, b) > \Pi_1(c_1, c_2, b)$ and $\Pi^m(c_2) > \Pi^m(c_1)$. Also, because $\partial^2\Pi_1(c_1, c_2, b)/\partial c_1\partial c_2 < 0$, for $c_2 < c_1$,

$$\Pi_1(c_2, c_2, b) - \Pi_1(c_1, c_2, b) \leq \Pi^m(c_2) - \Pi^m(c_1).$$

This implies $R \leq \Pi_1(c_2, c_2, b) - \Pi_1(c_1, c_2, b) \leq \Pi^m(c_2) - \Pi^m(c_1)$, so that the incumbent firm will prefer to adopt the technology even if there is no entrepreneurial entry,

$$\Pi^m(c_2) - R \geq \Pi^m(c_1).$$

So, adoption is a dominant strategy for the incumbent firm.

Next, consider the decisions of the entrepreneur. If the incumbent firm adopts the technology and $R \leq \Pi_1(c_2, c_2, b) - \Pi_1(c_1, c_2, b)$, it follows that $R \leq \Pi_1(c_1, c_2, b) = \Pi_2(c_2, c_2, b)$. The entrepreneur will adopt the technology and enter the market when the incumbent also adopts the technology. Because the entrepreneur earns greater profits when the incumbent does not adopt the technology, it follows that $R \leq \Pi_2(c_2, c_2, b) \leq \Pi_2(c_1, c_2, b)$. This implies that the entrepreneur also will choose to enter the market when the incumbent does not adopt the new technology. So, entry is a dominant strategy for the entrepreneur. Therefore, if $R \leq \Pi_1(c_2, c_2, b) - \Pi_1(c_1, c_2, b)$, (Adopt, Enter) will be the unique dominant strategy equilibrium.

Now, we examine a monopoly inventor with market power who maximizes the returns from royalties. The adoption-entry game shows that if royalties induce adoption by the incumbent, they also induce entry by the entrepreneur. This is because $R \leq \Pi_1(c_2, c_2, b) - \Pi_1(c_1, c_2, b)$ implies that $R \leq \Pi_1(c_2, c_2, b) = \Pi_2(c_2, c_2, b)$. The inventor earns royalties from both the incumbent and entrant by setting

$$R^* = \Pi_1(c_2, c_2, b) - \Pi_1(c_1, c_2, b).$$

Alternatively, the inventor can raise the royalties to induce entry by the entrepreneur without adoption by the incumbent firm,

$$R^{**} = \Pi_2(c_1, c_2, b).$$

To see why the royalty that only induces adoption by the entrepreneur is greater, notice that $\partial^2\Pi_1(c_1, c_2, b)/\partial c_1 \partial c_2 < 0$ and $c_2 < c_1$ imply

$$\begin{aligned} R^* &= \Pi_1(c_2, c_2, b) - \Pi_1(c_1, c_2, b) \\ &< \Pi_1(c_2, c_1, b) - \Pi_1(c_1, c_1, b) \\ &< \Pi_1(c_2, c_1, b) = \Pi_2(c_1, c_2, b) = R^{**}. \end{aligned}$$

The incumbent firm's profit when both adopt firms adopt the technology is less than industry profits when only the entrant adopts the technology,

$$\Pi_1(c_2, c_2, b) < \Pi_1(c_1, c_2, b) + \Pi_2(c_1, c_2, b).$$

The incumbent firm has less incentive to adopt the new process technology because of the inertia generated by the initial technology, as Arrow (1962) observed. The inventor chooses the lower royalty when he earns more from both firms adopting the innovation, $2R^*$, than from adoption by the entrepreneur, R^{**}. When $2R^* \geq R^{**}$, the independent inventor induces adoption by both firms, which differs from the possible outcomes when the inventor and the potential entrepreneur are not independent. The inventor chooses to transfer the technology to both the incumbent and the entrepreneur if and only if

$$\Pi_1(c_2, c_2, b) \geq \Pi_1(c_1, c_2, b) + \Pi_2(c_1, c_2, b)/2.$$

When $2R^* < R^{**}$, the independent inventor induces adoption by only the entrepreneur, which corresponds to the equilibrium with entry when the inventor and the potential entrepreneur are not independent.

The technology transfer decision of an independent inventor has the following important implication.

PROPOSITION 9. *When the inventor is independent and the entrepreneur does not have access to the initial process technology, entrepreneurship always takes place.*

When the inventor is independent from the entrepreneur, royalties that allow technology transfer to the incumbent firm always involve also selling to the entrepreneur. The entrepreneur values the process innovation more than the incumbent because of the inertia from the initial technology. Choosing greater royalties excludes the incumbent firm so that the inventor then sells only to the entrepreneur. This result provides an additional explanation for entrepreneurship as the mechanism for innovation. It further emphasizes Schumpeter's observation that entrepreneurs operate beside incumbent firms.

The independent inventor's incentive to invent equals $V^* = \max\{2R^*, R^{**}\}$. Proposition 10 shows that an independent inventor benefits from competition for licenses between the entrepreneur and the incumbent firm in the adoption-and-entry game.

PROPOSITION 10. *The independent inventor's incentive to invent, V^*, is greater than or equal to that of nonindependent innovator, V^I, if the nonindependent inventor has limited bargaining power, $\alpha \leq \alpha^{**}$, where*

$$\alpha^{**} = \frac{2(\Pi_1(c_2, c_2, b) - \Pi_1(c_1, c_2, b)) - \Pi_2(c_1, c_2, b)}{\Pi^m(c_2) - \Pi_1(c_1, c_2, b) - \Pi_2(c_1, c_2, b)} \tag{24}$$

PROOF. The independent inventor's incentive to invent can be written as

$$V^* = \max\{2(\Pi_1(c_2, c_2, b) - \Pi_1(c_1, c_2, b)), \Pi_2(c_1, c_2, b)\}.$$

The independent inventor can raise the royalties to induce entry by the entrepreneur without adoption by the incumbent firm and obtain R^{**}. This is equivalent to entry by the nonindependent innovator, which yields $\Pi_2(c_1, c_2, b)$. So, if $\Pi_2(c_1, c_2, b) \geq \Pi^m(c_2) - \Pi_1(c_1, c_2, b)$, it follows that

$$V^* \geq R^{**} = \Pi_2(c_1, c_2, b) = V^I.$$

Conversely, if $\Pi_2(c_1, c_2, b) < \Pi^m(c_2) - \Pi_1(c_1, c_2, b)$, then $V^* \geq 2R^* \geq V^I = \alpha(\Pi^m(c_2) - \Pi_1(c_1, c_2, b)) + (1 - \alpha)\Pi_2(c_1, c_2, b)$ if $\alpha \leq \alpha^{**}$. ∎

An independent inventor is at least as well off as a nonindependent inventor who prefers to become an entrepreneur regardless of his bargaining power. An independent inventor is at least as well off as a nonindependent inventor who prefers technology transfer but has a low bargaining power. The nonindependent inventor who prefers technology transfer and has a high bargaining power can be better off than the independent inventor because he can capture the monopoly rents from transferring the technology to the incumbent. This is possible if $\Pi^m(c_2) > 2\Pi_1(c_2, c_2, b) - \Pi_1(c_1, c_2, b)$.

The independent inventor has a greater incentive to invent than the monopolist contemplating a process innovation if products are sufficiently differentiated. When only the process innovation is transferable, let b^* be the critical value of the product differentiation parameter such that industry profits increase with entry. From the definition of V^* and b^*, it follows that

$$V^* \geq \Pi_2(c_1, c_2, b) \geq \Pi^m(c_2) - \Pi_1(c_1, c_2, b) > \Pi^m(c_2) - \Pi^m(c_1) = V^m.$$

PROPOSITION 11. *The independent inventor has a greater incentive to invent, V^*, than that of the monopolist, V^m, if products are sufficiently differentiated, $0 \leq b \leq b^*$.*

The independent inventor can do better than the monopolist even if there is less product differentiation when there are returns to selling to both the incumbent and the potential entrepreneur.

5.5.2 The Entrepreneur Can Use the Initial Technology

Entrepreneurship with independent inventors does not require the potential entrepreneur's outside option to be zero. Suppose that both the incumbent and the entrant have access to the initial process technology. The entrepreneur can enter with the initial process technology that is available without cost or the entrepreneur can obtain the new process technology from the inventor. Then, both the incumbent and the entrant are subject to the same inertia. The payoffs of the adoption and entry game are symmetric, see table 5.2.

By symmetry, the inventor then sells to both the incumbent and the entrant and cannot exclude the incumbent. The innovator with market power will choose the lower royalty,

$$R^* = \Pi_1(c_2, c_2, b) - \Pi_1(c_1, c_2, b) = \Pi_2(c_2, c_2, b) - \Pi_2(c_1, c_2, b).$$

This implies that the technology adoption game has an unique dominant-strategy equilibrium. The equilibrium of the technology adoption game is for both the incumbent firm and the entrepreneur to adopt the new process technology.

Table 5.2 **The technology adoption game with payoffs (existing firm 1, entrepreneurial firm 2) when the initial process technology is available to both the incumbent firm and the entrepreneurial firm**

	Entrepreneurial firm 2	
Existing firm 1	Adopt	Do not adopt
Adopt	$\Pi_1(c_2, c_2, b) - R, \Pi_2(c_2, c_2, b) - R$	$\Pi_1(c_2, c_1, b) - R, \Pi_2(c_2, c_1, b)$
Do not adopt	$\Pi_1(c_1, c_2, b), \Pi_2(c_1, c_2, b) - R$	$\Pi_1(c_1, c_1, b), \Pi_2(c_1, c_1, b)$

Proposition 12. *When the inventor is independent and the initial process technology is available to both the incumbent firm and the entrepreneur, the inventor transfers the process technology to both the incumbent and the entrepreneur.*

5.6 Conclusion

Multidimensional innovation, with new product designs and new production processes, illustrates Schumpeter's assertion that entrepreneurs make "new combinations." The discussion extends Arrow (1962), which classifies a process innovation as being drastic or nondrastic depending upon whether the monopoly price with the new production technology is less than or greater than the unit costs under the old technology. Multidimensional innovation implies that the extent of an innovation depends both on the degree of product differentiation and on changes in production costs. The new product design and the new production process interact in an interesting way. The degree of product differentiation between the new and the existing product helps to determine the critical threshold that defines a significant process innovation. The extent of multidimensional innovation is important because it affects both the returns to technology transfer and the returns to entrepreneurial entry.

The present multidimensional innovation model provides a compelling explanation for why entrepreneurship occurs in established industries. By mitigating competition, product differentiation generates rents for entrepreneurial entrants. These rents allow innovators to pursue entrepreneurship as a profitable alternative to transferring technology to incumbent firms. By making entrepreneurship a viable option for innovators, product differentiation also means that the incumbent firm must consider how entrepreneurial entry will affect its profits. With sufficient product differentiation, industry profits with entrepreneurial entry are greater than monopoly profits for an incumbent firm. Equivalently, the returns to technology transfer from the innovator to the incumbent firm will then be less than the returns to entrepreneurial entry. When this occurs, entrepreneurship is the equilibrium outcome of the innovation game. Product differentiation sheds light on Schumpeter's concept of "creative destruction," with innovative entrepreneurs operating beside existing firms.

Transaction costs and other impediments to the transfer of discoveries make entrepreneurship a potential outcome of the innovation game. When new products and processes are fully transferable to the existing firm, entrepreneurship will not take place. However, imperfect transferability generates incentives for innovators to become entrepreneurs. When the incumbent firm can buy out the innovator but neither the new product nor the new production technology is transferable, entrepreneurship occurs when process innovations are significant. This effect is reversed when only the process innovation is transferable; incremental process innovations lead the innovator to choose entrepreneurship and significant innovations lead the innovator to transfer the technology to the incumbent firm. When only the product innovation is transferable, significant process innovations lead the innovator to choose entrepreneurship and incremental process innovations lead the innovator to transfer the technology to the incumbent firm.

The discussion extends the strategic innovation game to allow an independent inventor. The existing firm and the entrepreneurial entrant engage in differentiated-products competition. The inventor has the option of transferring the process technology to the existing firm, the entrepreneur, or to both. The inventor chooses royalties such that the existing firm and the entrepreneur decide whether or not to adopt the process technology, and entrepreneurship always occurs in equilibrium. The inventor benefits from competition between the existing firm and the entrepreneurial entrant.

The present analysis took inventions as given, following Arrow's (1962) approach. However, the model can be generalized to include endogenous R&D. Economic factors that encourage or discourage entrepreneurship will impact invention and the choice between technology transfer and entrepreneurial entry. In addition, economic factors that affect the costs of technology transfer will affect incentives to invent and the types of firms that implement innovations. Public policies such as business taxes and regulations that discourage entrepreneurship block a significant channel of innovation. Imperfect legal protections for IP that allow expropriation and imitation are likely to discourage technology transfer and encourage entrepreneurship.

Entrepreneurship stimulates inventive activity in established industries by opening multiple avenues for innovation. Innovators can commercialize inventions not only through technology transfer but also though entrepreneurship or by licensing to independent entrepreneurs. The present analysis identified conditions under which an innovator who chooses between technology transfer and entrepreneurship has a greater incentive to invent than an incumbent monopolist. This is consistent with the observed close association between innovation and entrepreneurship. Together, technology transfer to incumbents and the establishment of new firms increase the total returns to inventive activity. The outcome of the strategic innovation game and the transferability of technology also affect the mix of new products and new production processes that are commercialized. By embodying innovations in new firms, entrepreneurs profoundly influence the rate and direction of inventive activity.

References

Acs, Z. J., and D. B. Audretsch. 1988. "Innovation in Large and Small Firms: An Empirical Analysis." *American Economic Review* 78 (4): 678–90.

Acs, Z. J., D. B. Audretsch, P. Braunerhjelm, and B. Carlsson. 2004. "The Missing Link: The Knowledge Filter and Entrepreneurship in Economic Growth." Center for Economic and Policy Research. CEPR Working Paper no. 4358.

Anand, B., and T. Khanna. 2000. "The Structure of Licensing Contracts." *Journal of Industrial Economics* 48 (1): 103–35.

Anton, J. J., and D. A. Yao. 1994. "Expropriation and Inventions." *American Economic Review* 84:190–209.

———. 2003. "Patents, Invalidity, and the Strategic Transmission of Enabling Information." *Journal of Economics & Management Strategy* 12:151–78.

Arora, A., A. Fosfuri, and A. Gambardella. 2001a. *Markets for Technology: The Economics of Innovation and Corporate Strategy.* Cambridge, MA: MIT Press.

———. 2001b. "Specialized Technology Suppliers, International Spillovers and Investment: Evidence from the Chemical Industry." *Journal of Development Economics* 65:31–54.

Arora, A., and A. Gambardella. 1998. "Evolution of Industry Structure in the Chemical Industry." In *Chemicals and Long-Term Economic Growth,* edited by A. Arora and N. Rosenberg, 379–414. New York: Wiley.

Arrow, K. J. 1962. "Economic Welfare and the Allocation of Resources for Invention." In *The Rate and Direction of Inventive Activity: Economic and Social Factors,* Universities-National Bureau Committee for Economic Research and the Committee on Economic Growth of the Social Science Research Councils, 609–626. Princeton, NJ: Princeton University Press.

Audretsch, D. B. 1995a. *Innovation and Industry Evolution.* Cambridge, MA: MIT Press.

———. 1995b. "Innovation, Growth and Survival: The Post-Entry Performance of Firms." *International Journal of Industrial Organization* 13 (4): 441–57.

———. 2001. "The Role of Small Firms in U.S. Biotechnology Clusters." *Small Business Economics* 17:3–15.

Audretsch, D. B., M. C. Keilbach, and E. E. Lehmann. 2006. *Entrepreneurship and Economic Growth.* Oxford: Oxford University Press.

Balconi, M., A. Pozzali, and R. Viale. 2007. "The 'Codification Debate' Revisited: A Conceptual Framework to Analyze the Role of Tacit Knowledge in Economics." *Industrial and Corporate Change* 16 (5): 823–49.

Baumol, W. J. 1968. "Entrepreneurship in Economic Theory." *American Economic Review Papers and Proceedings* 58:64–71.

———. 1993. *Entrepreneurship, Management, and the Structure of Payoffs.* Cambridge, MA: MIT Press.

———. 2002. *The Free-Market Innovation Machine: Analyzing the Growth Miracle of Capitalism.* Princeton, NJ: Princeton University Press.

———. "Entrepreneurship and Invention: Toward Their Microeconomic Value Theory." Special Session on Entrepreneurship, Innovation and Growth I: Theoretical Approach, American Economic Association Meetings.

Baumol, W. J., R. E. Litan, and C. J. Schramm. 2007. *Good Capitalism, Bad Capitalism, and the Economics of Growth and Properity.* New Haven, CT: Yale University Press.

Blonigen, B. A., and C. T. Taylor. 2000. "R&D Activity and Acquisitions in High Technology Industries: Evidence from the US electronics Industry." *Journal of Industrial Economics* 48:47–70.

Bresnahan, T. F., and D. M. G. Raff. 1991. "Intra-Industry Heterogeneity and the Great Depression: The American Motor Vehicles Industry, 1929–1935." *Journal of Economic History* 51:317–31.

Bresnahan, T. F., S. Greenstein, and R. M. Henderson. 2012. "Schumpeterian Competition and Diseconomies of Scope: Illustrations from the Histories of Microsoft and IBM." In *The Rate and Direction of Inventive Activity Revisited,* edited by Josh Lerner and Scott Stern, 203–76. Chicago: University of Chicago Press.

Chandler, A. D. 1990. *Scale and Scope: The Dynamics of Industrial Capitalism.* Cambridge, MA: Harvard University Press.

Chen, Y., and M. Schwartz. 2009. "Product Innovation Incentives: Monopoly vs. Competition." University of Colorado. Working Paper.

Christensen, C. M. 1997. *The Innovator's Dilemma: When New Technologies Cause Great Firms to Fail.* Boston: Harvard Business School Press.

Danaher, P. J., I. W. Wilson, and R. A. Davis. 2003. "A Comparison of Online and Offline Consumer Brand Loyalty." *Marketing Science* 22 (4): 461–76.

Fein, A. J. 1998. "Understanding Evolutionary Processes in Non-Manufacturing Industries: Empirical Insights from the Shakeout in Pharmaceutical Wholesaling." *Journal of Evolutionary Economics* 8:231–70.

Furman, J. L., and M. MacGarvie. 2009. "Academic Collaboration and Organizational Innovation: The Development of Research Capabilities in the US Pharmaceutical Industry, 1927–1946." *Industrial and Corporate Change* 18 (5): 929–61.

Galambos, L., and J. L. Sturchio. 1998. "Pharmaceutical Firms and the Transition to Biotechnology: A Study in Strategic Innovation." *Business History Review* 72 (2): 250–78.

Gans, J. S., D. H. Hsu, and S. Stern. 2000. "When Does Start-Up Innovation Spur the Gale of Creative Destruction?" *Rand Journal of Economics* 33:571–86.

Gans, J. S., and S. Stern. 2000. "Incumbency and R&D Incentives: Licensing the Gale of Creative Destruction." *Journal of Economics & Management Strategy* 9:485–511.

———. 2003. "The Product Market and the Market for 'Ideas': Commercialization Strategies for Technology Entrepreneurs." *Research Policy* 32:333–50.

Giarratana, M. S. 2004. "The Birth of a New Industry: Entry by Start-ups and the Drivers of Firm Growth: The Case of Encryption Software." *Research Policy* 33 (5): 787–806.

Gilbert, R. 2006. "Looking for Mr. Schumpeter: Where Are We in the Competition-Innovation Debate?" *Innovation Policy and the Economy,* Vol. 6, edited by Adam B. Jaffe, Josh Lerner, and Scott Stern, 159–215. Cambridge, MA: MIT Press.

Gilbert, R., and D. Newbery. 1982. "Preemptive Patenting and the Persistence of Monopoly." *American Economic Review* 72:514–26.

Greenstein, S. and G. Ramey. 1998. "Market Structure, Innovation and Vertical Product Differentiation." *International Journal of Industrial Organization* 16 (3): 285–311.

Grindley, P. C., and D. J. Teece. 1997. "Managing Intellectual Capital: Licensing and Cross-Licensing in Semiconductors and Electronics." *California Management Review* 39:8–41.

Henderson, R. 1993. "Underinvestment and Incompetence as Responses to Radical Innovation—Evidence from the Photolithographic Alignment Equipment Industry." *Rand Journal of Economics* 24 (2): 248–70.

Henderson, R., and K. Clark. 1990. "Architectural Innovation: The Reconfiguration of Existing Product Technologies and the Failure of Established Firms." *Administrative Science Quarterly* 35:9–30.

Hotelling, H. 1929. "Stability in Competition." *Economic Journal* 39 (153): 41–57.

Kato, A. 2007. "Chronology of Lithography Milestones Version 0.9." Available at: http://www.lithoguru.com/scientist/litho_history/Kato_Litho_History.pdf.

Katz, M. L., and C. Shapiro. 1987. "R&D Rivalry with Licensing or Imitation." *American Economic Review* 77:402–20.

Kienle, H., D. German, S. Tilley, and H. A. Muller. 2004. "Intellectual Property Aspects of Web Publishing." In *ACM Special Interest Group for Design of Com-*

munication, Proceedings of the 22nd Annual International Conference on Design of Communication: The Engineering of Quality Documentation, 136–144. New York: Association for Computing Machinery.

Kimes, B. R., and H. A. Clark. 1996. *Standard Catalog of American Cars 1805 to 1942,* 3rd ed. Iola, WI: Krause Publications.

Klette, T. J., and S. Kortum. 2004. "Innovating Firms and Aggregate Innovation." *Journal of Political Economy* 112 (5): 986–1018.

Kline, S. J., and N. Rosenberg. 1986. "An Overview of Innovation." In *The Positive Sum Strategy: Harnessing Technology for Economic Growth,* edited by R. Landau and N. Rosenberg, 275–306. Washington, DC: National Academy Press.

Lowe, R., and A. Ziedonis. 2006. "Overoptimism and the Performance of Entrepreneurial Firms." *Management Science* 52 (2): 173–186.

Lucking-Reiley, D., and D. F. Spulber. 2001. "Business-to-Business Electronic Commerce." *Journal of Economic Perspectives* 15:55–68.

Maney, K. 1995. *Megamedia Shakeout: The Inside Story of the Leaders and the Losers in the Exploding Communications Industry.* New York: Wiley.

McClellan, S. T. 1984. *The Coming Computer Industry Shakeout: Winners, Losers, and Survivors.* New York: Wiley.

Milgrom, P., and J. Roberts. 1990. "Rationalizability, Learning, and Equilibrium in Games with Strategic Complementarities." *Econometrica* 58 (6): 1255–77.

Morrison, S. A., and C. Winston. 1995. *The Evolution of the Airline Industry.* Washington, DC: Brookings Institution.

O'Shea, R., T. Allen, A. Chevalier, and F. Roche. 2005. "Entrepreneurial Orientation, Technology Transfer and Spinoff Performance of U.S. Universities." *Research Policy* 34 (7): 994–1009.

Peterson, B. S., and J. Glab. 1994. *Rapid Descent: Deregulation and the Shakeout in the Airlines.* New York: Simon and Schuster.

Prevezer, M. 1997. "The Dynamics of Industrial Clustering in Biotechnology." *Small Business Economics* 9 (3): 255–71.

Rasmusen, E. 1988. "Entry for Buyout." *Journal of Industrial Economics* 36 (3): 281–99.

Reinganum, J. F. 1981. "Dynamic Games of Innovation." *Journal of Economic Theory* 25:1–41.

———. 1982. "A Dynamic Game of R and D: Patent Protection and Competitive Behavior." *Econometrica* 50:671–88.

———. "The Timing of Innovation: Research, Development, and Diffusion." In *Handbook of Industrial Organization,* Vol. 1, edited by R. Schmalensee and R. D. Willig, 849–908. New York: Elsevier Science Publishers.

Salant, S. W. 1984. "Preemptive Patenting and the Persistence of Monopoly: Comment." *American Economic Review* 74:247–50.

Say, J.-B. (1841) 1982. *Traité d'Économie Politique,* 6th ed. Geneva: Slatkine.

———. 1852. *Cours Complet d'Économie Politique: Pratique,* Vols. 1 and 2, 3rd ed. Paris: Guillaumin et Ce.

Schramm, C. J. 2006. *The Entrepreneurial Imperative: How American's Economic Miracle Will Reshape the World (and Change Your Life).* New York: HarperCollins.

Schumpeter, J. A. (1934) 1997. *The Theory of Economic Development.* New Brunswick, NJ: Transaction Publishers.

———. (1964) 1989 *Business Cycles: A Theoretical, Historical, and Statistical Analysis of the Capitalist Process,* (abridged version of first edition published in 1939). Philadelphia: Porcupine Press.

Singh, N., and X. Vives. 1984. "Price and Quantity Competition in a Differential Duopoly." *Rand Journal of Economics* 15:546–54.

Spulber, D. F. 2009. *The Theory of the Firm: Microeconomics with Endogenous Entrepreneurs, Firms, Markets, and Organizations.* Cambridge: Cambridge University Press.

———. 2010. "Tacit Knowledge with Innovation and Entrepreneurship." Northwestern University. Working Paper.

———. "The Innovator's Decision: Entrepreneurship versus Technology Transfer." In *Handbook of Research on Innovation and Entrepreneurship,* edited by D. Audretsch, O. Falck, S. Heblich, and A. Lederer. Northampton, MA: Edward Elgar.

Teece, D. J. 1986. "Profiting from Technological Innovation: Implications for Integration, Collaboration, Licensing, and Public Policy." *Research Policy* 15:285–305.

———. 2006. "Reflections on 'Profiting from Innovation'." *Research Policy* 35: 1131–46.

Tilton, J. E. 1971. *International Diffusion of Technology: The Case of Semiconductors.* Washington, DC: Brookings Institution.

Torrisi, S. 1998. *Industrial Organisation and Innovation: An International Study of the Software Industry.* Cheltenham, UK: Edward Elgar Publishing.

Vohora, A., M. Wright, and A. Lockett. 2004. "Critical Junctures in The Development of University High-Tech Spinout Companies." *Research Policy* 33:147–75.

Winter, S. G. 1984. "Schumpeterian Competition in Alternative Technological Regimes." *Journal of Economic Behavior and Organization* 5 (3–4): 287–320.

Zanchettin, P. 2006. "Differentiated Duopoly with Asymmetric Costs." *Journal of Economics & Management Strategy* 15 (4): 999–1015.

Zucker, L., M. Darby, and J. Armstrong. 1998. "Geographically Localized Knowledge: Spillovers or Markets?" *Economic Inquiry* 36:65–86.

Zucker, L. G., M. R. Darby, and M. B. Brewer. 1998. "Intellectual Human Capital and the Birth of U.S. Biotechnology Enterprises." *American Economic Review* 88 (1): 290–306.

Comment Luis Cabral

Let me start by saying that I enjoyed reading the chapter.

Instead of going through the details of the chapter, I thought it might be more useful to put the main results into perspective, mainly in terms of the Industrial Organization (IO) literature on innovation. Moreover, I would like to take a further step back and talk about several literatures that I think are related to this chapter (although that link has not always been explored as much as it should):

- The literature on innovation, invention, adoption, and so forth
- The productivity literature
- The literature on entry and entrepreneurship

Traditionally, the productivity literature has been largely concerned with measurement issues. The entry and entrepreneurship literature in turn has

Luis Cabral is professor of economics at the Stern School of Business, New York University.

done a lot of things, but not always focused on the issue of innovation per se. For example, a lot has been written on the determinants of entry, how entry rates vary across industries, and so forth, but normally not focusing on innovation issues.

So I think that we have three different strands of literature that really are asking for a little more bridging. (In fact, some of that bridging has been done. For example, the new growth theory provides a link between the innovation box and the productivity box. The recent work on productivity accounting provides a link between the productivity box and the entry box [e.g., when it shows that a large fraction of industry productivity increase results from firm turnover].)

Dan's chapter, I think, is a very useful addition to the effort to bridge the entry/entrepreneurship and the innovation boxes. There are many people working on entrepreneurship and entry, and there are many other people working on innovation; but the link between the two has not always been there. In addition to making this link, Dan's chapter also points to a series of interesting issues that we can and should work on so as to bring the two literatures together. I will later comment on some of these.

The chapter deals with an issue that has been studied in the IO literature extensively: the relation between incumbency, entry, and innovation incentives. I like to think of this literature in terms of two principles. The first principle is "if it ain't broke, don't fix it." This is the Arrow et al. idea that if a monopoly is not being challenged, then there is little incentive to innovate. By innovating the monopolist would just cannibalize itself. The second, opposite, principle is "fix it before it's broken." This corresponds to the idea of preemption, the idea that if there is a challenger out there (a potential entrant) then the incumbent should do what it takes to avoid competition, including innovating or buying innovation that would otherwise be acquired by the potential entrant. Which of the two principles applies depends on whether we are in a situation of uncontested monopoly ("if it ain't broke, don't fix it" applies) or contested monopoly ("fix it before it's broken" applies).

Let me give you two examples (I have been in business school for too long; you always must give examples). The video game industry is to some extent a series of uncontested monopolies, a situation when innovation entails considerable self-cannibalization. There is a case about Nintendo in the 1980s with precisely these features. As for the case of a contested monopoly, two examples that come to mind are Xerox and plain paper photocopying and a case that I think has received relatively less attention, Eli Lilly and synthetic insulin.

Dan's chapter is very much in the contested monopoly tradition. I gave you two examples of contested monopoly and only one of uncontested. I am not sure this precisely reflects the relative importance of each case in the real world. What I am sure of, however, is that we can find many examples—perhaps most examples—where there is some degree of contestability. So

I think the framework considered by Dan is a useful framework of reference. (There are a lot of papers looking at other reasons why we might have persistence or lack of persistence of monopoly; for example, organizational inertia.)

One of Dan's contributions to the innovation under contested monopoly tradition is to consider the case when there is product differentiation. In fact, it is somewhat surprising that this has not been given much attention in the previous literature. Dan also considers the distinction between product and process innovation. Finally, Dan considers various cases of possible transferability of technology and product innovation between the innovator and an incumbent firm. Together, this leads to a wealth of possible cases and results.

Although there are many cases to consider, the main result under contested monopoly is that the equilibrium solution is the one that maximizes joint profits, what Gilbert and Newbery (1982) refer to as the efficiency effect. So, in general, product differentiation favors entry to the extent that it leads to higher profits when incumbent and entrant compete in the market. In other words, the greater the degree of product differentiation, the more likely the equilibrium corresponds to entry. For the same reason, more drastic innovation tends to favor entry.

But lest you think the chapter is simply a series of trivial results, the chapter shows that the comparative statics with respect to product innovation may actually be nonmonotonic. The point is that joint profits may actually be nonmonotonic with respect to the degree of product differentiation.

In sum, there are several results in this chapter, some fairly intuitive, and some quite surprising. Ultimately, they all go back to Gilbert and Newbery's efficiency effect, though the way that works is not always obvious.

One general comment that I have is that, there being so many cases, it would be interesting to have examples to illustrate the various cases. For instance, what are good examples of situations when there is transferability and situations when there is no transferability?

Moreover, although Dan considers quite a number of different cases, there is one that is missing and I think is quite relevant: the case when the innovation has a product advantage with respect to the incumbent but a significant cost disadvantage. I suspect this is a fairly common situation, one where the assumptions of transferability are particularly important.

A more general comment is, how much of what is in this chapter is about entry, and how much of it is about entrepreneurship? I have to confess that I am not exactly sure what entrepreneurship is. This is a theory chapter, and in theory chapters you do not always make that sort of distinction. To go back to the Eli Lilly example, suppose that Eli Lilly did not buy the synthetic insulin patent from Genentech. Then several things could happen: Genentech could have entered as Genentech, or they could have sold their patent to Pfizer, or somebody who worked for Genentech could have left the firm and started a firm on his or her own. Which of these classifies as entrepreneurship and which of these classify as just entry? I'm not sure. In other words, what is so special about entrepreneurship?

I am a bit of an outsider to the literature on entrepreneurship. If you didn't know it before I started it is probably obvious by now. But being an outsider can be an advantage. What I see as an outsider is that there is a big elephant in the entrepreneurship literature room that seems to go unnoticed. There is a general perception that entrepreneurship and entry are good for innovation. Talk to any politician, policymaker, or even any academic, and they will tell you that it is obviously true. But is there a good theory for that? Let me just give you an example. Suppose you have two worlds that differ in terms of institutions that may or may not facilitate transfer technology between an entrepreneur and an incumbent. In world A, with poor technology transfer conditions, you have a lot of entrepreneurship and a lot of entry. In world B, with favorable technology transfer conditions, you have a lot less entry and entrepreneurship. Is it clear that the incentives to innovate are higher in the world where there is greater entrepreneurship and there is more entry? Not at all, because as this model suggests, entry and entrepreneurship may be precisely a response to inefficiencies, which in turn may actually reduce the innovation incentives.

Dan's chapter does not solve this issue, but it sort of forces it, which I think is an important step forward. I would be interested in seeing the results for the reasons that I just explained; that is, at a theoretical level it is not clear that more entry is associated to more innovation. And by the way, the same thing is true for the entry-productivity connection. Empirically, we know that a lot of the industry productivity increases result from firm turnover. However, it is not at all obvious that entry is generally good in terms of increasing productivity: there is good turnover and there is bad turnover. And again, if you do a comparative study across countries (as I am currently doing) in terms of barriers to entry, industry turnover and productivity growth, one finds that the relation between entry and productivity is not that clear because in some countries there's a lot of turnover for the wrong reasons (high barriers to survival), not by the right reasons (selection by productivity).

In summary, I think this is a very good chapter, an important addition to this connection between the innovation and the entrepreneurship literatures. The chapter provides a series of interesting results, but it also asks a lot of interesting questions. I look forward to the next developments in this research program, in particular the one that takes one step back and looks at innovation incentives by entrepreneurs.

References

Gilbert, R. and D. Newbery. 1982. "Preemptive Patenting and the Persistence of Monopoly." *American Economic Review* 72:514–26.

6

Diversity and Technological Progress

Daron Acemoglu

6.1 Introduction

Until the first decade of the twenty-first century, almost all research and product development efforts in the transport industry were directed toward improving the power, design, and fuel efficiency of vehicles using gasoline, even though it was widely recognized that those using alternative energy sources would have a large market in the future as oil prices increased and consumers became more environmentally conscious.[1] Investment in a variety of other alternative energy sources was similarly delayed.[2] Although many commentators now decry the delays in the development of viable alternatives to fossil fuels, it is difficult to know what the marginal rate of private and social returns to different types of research was in these sectors, and thus whether the amount of *diversity* generated by the market economy was optimal.[3]

Daron Acemoglu is the Elizabeth and James Killian Professor of Economics at the Massachusetts Institute of Technology and a research associate of the National Bureau of Economic Research.

I am grateful to Amir Reza Mohsenzadeh Kermani for excellent research assistance and for pointing out an error in a previous version, Samuel Kortum, Scott Stern, and participants at the Stanford macroeconomics seminar and The Rate and Direction of Technological Progress conference.

1. Crosby (2006) and Roberts (2005) for readable accounts of the history of research on different energy sources.

2. For example, as of 2006, more than 80 percent of all world energy consumption is from fossil fuels and less than 1 percent from geothermal, wind, and solar combined (International Energy Agency 2008).

3. In fact, this question must be answered using a theoretical framework that clarifies the margins in which the social return to diversity may exceed the private return, since even several episodes in which more diverse investments would have increased productivity (or growth) ex post would not establish that more diversity would have increased expected productivity ex ante.

As a first step in the investigation of these issues, this chapter theoretically investigates whether the market economy provides adequate incentives for research in alternative technologies—as opposed to technologies that are currently and extensively used. Put differently, I ask whether the market economy will achieve the efficient amount of *diversity* in research or whether it will tend to encourage research to be excessively concentrated in some research lines and products.

The main contributions of this chapter are twofold. The first is to develop a dynamic model of innovation that can be used to analyze the issues of equilibrium and optimal amounts of diversity of technological progress. The second is to use this model to show that there is a natural mechanism leading to too little diversity. I also suggest that a counteracting force against the potential lack of diversity in research may be the diversity of researchers: because of different competences, beliefs or preferences, researchers may choose to direct their research toward areas that are underexplored by others and this may partially redress the inefficiently low level of diversity of research in the market economy.

The mechanism at the heart of this chapter is as follows: given the patent system we have in place, an innovation creates *positive externalities* on future innovations that will build on its discoveries and advances. The patent system makes sure that no other firm can copy the current innovation (and in particular, it requires an innovation to be different from "prior art" in the area; see, for example, Scotchmer [2005]). However, provided that a certain "required inventive step" is exceeded, a new innovation, even if it builds on prior patented knowledge, would not have to make royalty payments. In fact, an important objective and a great virtue of the patent system is to make knowledge freely available to future innovators and thus some amount of building on the shoulders of past innovations is clearly both desirable and unavoidable. In addition, patent life is capped at twenty years, so even externalities created on further innovations that do not meet the inventive step requirement cannot be fully internalized. The key observation here is that this positive externality on future innovations will affect different types of innovations differentially.

Consider two potential products, a and b, which are competing in the market. Suppose that product a has higher quality, so that all else being equal, consumers will buy product a. However, at some future date, consumer tastes (or technology) will change so that product b will become more popular. We can think of product a as vehicles using fossil fuels and product b as electric cars or other clean technology vehicles. Consider two types of innovations. The first, innovation A, will lead to a higher-quality version of product a and thus the output of this innovation can be marketed immediately. Even though it creates positive externalities on future products that can build on the processes that it embeds, innovation A still generates a profit stream and this will typically encourage some amount of research. Contrast this to innovation B, which leads to a higher quality of product b and thus can only be marketed after tastes change. Improvements in product b will be useful for the society in the future (because tastes will indeed change at some point). But private incentives for innovation B are weak because the innovator is unlikely to benefit from the improvements in the quality of product b even in the future because some other innovation is likely to significantly improve over the current one before tastes change.

The previously described scenario highlights a general feature: the recognition that there will be further innovations that will discourage research in areas that will generate new products or technologies for the future relative to improving currently used products, processes, or technologies. Consequently, in equilibrium, too much research will be devoted to currently successful product and technology lines—in the aforementioned example, innovation A. I refer to this situation as *lack of diversity in research* (or alternatively as "too much conformity").

This chapter shows how these ideas can be formalized using a dynamic model of innovation. Using this model, it formalizes the ideas discussed earlier and clarifies the conditions under which there will be too little diversity in research. In particular, it shows that provided that the probability (flow rate in continuous time) of changes in tastes is sufficiently high, the market equilibrium involves too little diversity and too little growth. It should be noted that the theoretical result of lack of diversity in research is not a consequence of lack of complementarity in research effort. In particular, in the baseline model future research builds on the shoulders of past research so that there is a force pushing against too much diversity (both in equilibrium and in the socially optimal allocation). Crucially, however, private incentives are more likely to internalize the benefits resulting from this type of building on the shoulders of past giants and less likely to internalize the benefits that they create for future research by increasing diversity, which is the mechanism leading to inefficiently low diversity in the model's equilibrium.

As the discussion here illustrates, this pattern is predicated on a specific patent system. Naturally, an alternative patent system that internalizes all positive externalities created on future innovations would solve this problem. However, such a patent system is different from what we observe in practice and also difficult to implement. For example, such a patent system would require all innovations in laser technology or solid-state physics to make royalty payments to Heisenberg, Einstein, and Bohr or all steam engine innovations to make payments to Newcomen and Watts (or to their offspring).

While the baseline model here suggests that in an idealized economy there will be too little—in fact no—diversity in research even though innovations being directed at a wider set of research lines is socially optimal, in practice a society may generate a more diverse set of research output because of *diversity of researchers.* In particular, if the society has or generates a set of researchers with different competencies, preferences, and beliefs, then part of its research effort will be directed at alternative products and technologies rather than all effort being concentrated on current technology leaders. For instance, in the context of the earlier example, even though incentives to improve product *a* may be greater than those for product *b*, some researchers may have a comparative advantage in the type of research that product *b* requires or may have heterogeneous beliefs, making them more optimistic about the prospect of a change in tastes, thus strengthening their desire to undertake research for product *b*. Although this kind of researcher diversity will not restore the Pareto optimal amount of diversity in research, it will act as a countervailing force against the market incentives that imply too much homogenization. Thus the analysis here also suggests why having a more diverse set of researchers and scientists might be useful for a society's long-run technological progress and growth potential. This intuition is formalized by showing that a greater diversity in the competences of researchers increases research directed at substitute varieties and the equilibrium rate of economic growth.

Popular discussions often emphasize the importance of diversity in various settings, including in research, and also stress that nonprofit motives are important in research. The framework here offers a simple formalization of both ideas: diversity in research is important for economic growth but the market economy may not provide sufficient incentives for such diversity; diversity of researchers, in fact their nonprofit-seeking or "nerdy" behavior and responsiveness to nonmonetary rewards, may be socially beneficial as a remedy for the lack of diversity (too much conformity) in research.

The model used here is related to the endogenous technological change literature; for example, Romer (1990), Grossman and Helpman (1991), and Aghion and Howitt (1992). This literature typically does not investigate the diversity of research. In addition, the "lock-in" effects in technology choices emphasized by Nelson and Winter (1982), Arthur (1989), Dosi (1984), and the subsequent literature building on these works are closely related to the main mechanism leading to too little equilibrium diversity in the current model, though the modeling approaches are very different (the approach here builds on endogenous technological change models with forward-looking innovation decisions, while these alternative approaches rely on learning by doing externalities and organizational constraints on the type of research).[4] In this respect, our approach is also closely related to and builds on Katz and Shapiro's (1986) model of network externalities.

A smaller literature investigates the determinants of microeconomic incentives toward the direction of research. Aghion and Tirole (1994) is an

4. Cozzi (1997) provides a formalization of the technological lock-in effects proposed by Arthur (1989) and Dosi (1984) using a variant of the quality-ladder models of Grossman and Helpman (1991) and Aghion and Howitt (1992).

early contribution, focusing on incentive problems that arise in the management of innovation. More recently, Brock and Durlauf (1999) investigate equilibrium choice of research topic in scientific communities. Aghion, Dewatripont, and Stein (2007) analyze the implications of academic freedom, while Murray et al. (2008) empirically investigate the effect of scientific openness on further research. Jones (2009) argues that scientific research is becoming more difficult because there is now a larger body of existing knowledge that needs to be absorbed and shows how this can explain why major breakthroughs happen later in the lives of scientists and why scientific collaborations have become more common. Bramoullé and Saint-Paul (2008) construct a model of research cycles, where equilibrium research fluctuates between invention of new lines of research and development of existing lines. Acemoglu, Bimpikis, and Ozdaglar (2008) propose a model where firms might have incentives to delay research and copy previous successful projects rather than engage in simultaneous search. An interesting line of research pioneered by Hong and Page (2001, 2004) explicitly models problem solving by teams of heterogeneous agents and derives conditions under which diversity facilitates problem solving (see also Page [2007]; LiCalzi and Surucu [2011]). Finally, Bronfenbrenner (1966), Stephan and Levin (1992), and Sunstein (2001) emphasize the possibility of fads in academic research, and Dosi and Marengo (1993), Shy (1996), Christensen (1997), Dalle (1997), Adner and Levinthal (2001), and Malerba et al. (2007) discuss the role of diverse preferences of users on market structure and patterns of adoption of new technology. None of these works highlight or study the issues related to the role of diversity in technological progress emphasized in this chapter.

The rest of this chapter is organized as follows. Section 6.2 provides a simple example illustrating the basic idea. Section 6.3 presents the baseline environment and characterizes the equilibrium. Section 6.4 characterizes the conditions under which the equilibrium will be inefficient and technological progress will be too slow because of inefficiently low levels of diversity in research. Section 6.5 characterizes the equilibrium when there is diversity in research tastes and shows how greater diversity increases economic growth. Section 6.6 concludes, while the appendix provides an extended environment that motivates some of the simplifying assumptions in the main text. It also contains some additional derivations.

6.2 A Simple Example

In this section, I provide a simple example illustrating the main mechanism leading to inefficiently low diversity in research. Consider a two-period economy, with periods $t = 1$ and $t = 2$ and no discounting. There are two technologies j and j', both starting $t = 1$ with qualities $q_j(0) = q_{j'}(0) = 1$. A scientist can work to improve both technologies. Suppose that the scientist has a total of one unit of time. The probability of improving either of the two technologies when he devotes x units of his time to the technology is $h(x)$. Suppose that h is strictly increasing, differentiable, and concave, and satisfies the Inada condition that $\lim_{x\to 0} h'(x) = \infty$. An improvement increases the quality of the technology (j or j') to $1 + \lambda$ (with $\lambda > 0$). At $t = 1$, j is the "active" technology, so if the scientist improves technology j, he will be able to market it and receive return equal to $1 + \lambda$. Technology j' is not active, so even if the scientist improves this technology, he will not be able to market it at $t = 1$. At time $t = 2$, technology j' becomes active with probability $p > 0$, replacing technology j (and if so, technology j can no longer be marketed). Before either of the two technologies is marketed at $t = 2$, other scientists can further improve over these technologies. Suppose that this happens with (exogenous) probability $v \in (0,1]$ (and assume, for simplicity, that no such further improvements are possible if there is no innovation by the scientist at $t = 1$). In this event, the quality of the product increases by another factor $1 + \lambda$, but the original scientist receives no returns.[5]

Let us consider the problem of the scientist in choosing the optimal allocation of his time between the two research projects. When he chooses to devote $x_j \in [0,1]$ units of his time to technology j, his return can be written as

$$\pi(x_j) = h(x_j)[1 + (1 - p)(1 - v)](1 + \lambda) + h(1 - x_j)p(1 - v)(1 + \lambda). \tag{1}$$

The first line is the scientist's expected return from innovation in technology j. He is successful with probability $h(x_j)$ and receives immediate returns $1 + \lambda$. In the next period, technology j remains active with probability $1 - p$ and his innovation is not improved upon with probability $1 - v$, and in this event, he receives $1 + \lambda$ again. With probability $h(1 - x_j)$, he successfully undertakes an innovation for technology j'. Since this technology is not yet active, he receives no returns at $t = 1$, but if it becomes active at $t = 2$ (probability p) and is not improved upon (probability $1 - v$), he will receive $1 + \lambda$ at $t = 2$.

Maximizing $\pi(x_j)$ with respect to x_j gives the following simple first-order condition:

$$h'(x_j^*)[1 + (1 - p)(1 - v)] = h'(1 - x_j^*)p(1 - v). \tag{2}$$

Clearly, x_j^* is uniquely defined. It can also be verified that it is increasing in v; as the probability of further innovations increases, more of the scientist's time will be devoted to technology j. Also notably as $v \to 1$, $x_j^* \to 1$ and all research is directed to the currently active technology, j. The intuition for this result is simple. Because of future improvements, as $v \to 1$, the scientist will receive no returns from innovation in technology j'—somebody else

5. Thus there are no patents that make further innovations pay royalties to the original inventor. Patent systems and how they affect the results are discussed in the next section.

will have invented an even better version of this technology by the time it can be marketed. There will be a similar improvement over technology j if it remains active until $t = 2$, but the scientist will in the meantime receive returns from being able to market it immediately (during $t = 1$). Thus the prospect of future improvements over the current innovation disproportionately favors the currently-active technology. This intuition also explains why x_j^* is increasing in v.

For comparison, let us consider the research allocation choice of a planner wishing to maximize total value of output. This can be written as

$$\Pi(x_j) = h(x_j)[(1 + (1 - p)(1 - v)(1 + \lambda)) + (1 - p)v(1 + \lambda)^2]$$
$$+ h(1 - x_j)[p(1 - v)(1 + \lambda) + pv(1 + \lambda)^2].$$

This differs from equation (1) because the planner also benefits when there is another innovation building on the shoulders of the innovation of the scientist at $t = 1$. The allocation of time between the two technologies that would maximize $\Pi(x_j)$ is given by the following first-order condition:

$$h'(x_j^S)[(1 + (1 - p)(1 - v)) + (1 - p)v(1 + \lambda)]$$
$$= h'(1 - x_j^S)[p(1 - v) + pv(1 + \lambda)].$$

It can be verified that $x_j^S < x_j^*$, so that the social planner would always prefer to allocate more of the scientist's time to technology j' (and thus less of his time to the active technology). Interestingly, x_j^S is decreasing in v. In particular, even as $v \to 1$, $x_j^S > 0$. Intuitively, the social planner values the improvements in technology j' more than the scientist because the society will benefit from further improvements over those undertaken by the scientist at time $t = 1$. In fact, as v increases, future improvements become *more important* to the social planner relative to current gains, favoring research directed at technology j'. The scientist does not value such improvements because they deprive him of the returns from his innovation. Consequently, the choice by the scientist—relative to the allocation desired by the social planner—leads to too little diversity in the sense that the majority (or when $v \to 1$, all) of his research effort is devoted to the active technology.

Finally, it is straightforward to extend this environment by including several scientists. When all scientists have the same preferences and maximize their returns, the results are similar to those discussed here. However, when some scientists have different preferences and prefer to work on technology j', or have different beliefs and are more optimistic about a switch from technology j to technology j', then this type of diversity of researchers—and the associated nonprofit maximizing behavior—will redress some of the inefficiency due to too little diversity in research.

The next section provides a more detailed model that develops these intuitions.

6.3 Model

In this section, I introduce the baseline environment and characterize the equilibrium. The baseline environment is chosen to highlight the main economic mechanism in the most transparent manner. Subsection 6.3.4 discusses why the specific modeling assumptions were chosen. The appendix shows how similar results can be derived in a richer environment building on endogenous technological change models.

6.3.1 Description of Environment

Time is continuous and indexed by $t \in [0,\infty)$. Output is produced as an aggregate of a continuum of intermediate goods (products), with measure normalized to 1. Each intermediate $v \in [0,1]$ comes in several (countably infinite number of) varieties, denoted by $j_1(v)$, $j_2(v)$, ... Variety $j_i(v)$ of intermediate v has an endogenous quality $q_{j_i}(v,t) > 0$ (at time t). The quality of each variety is determined by the position of this product in a *quality ladder,* which has rungs equi-proportionately apart by an amount $1 + \lambda$ (where $\lambda > 0$). Thus for each $j_i(v)$, we have

$$q_{j_i}(v,t) = (1 + \lambda)^{n_{j_i}(v,t)} q_{j_i}(v,0),$$

with $n_{j_i}(v,t) \in \mathbb{Z}_+$ corresponding to the rung of this product on the quality ladder. Throughout, let us normalize $q_{j_i}(v,0) = 1$ for all $v \in [0,1]$ and $i = 1, 2, \ldots$. Product qualities increase due to technological progress driven by research, which raises the rung of the product in the quality ladder. I describe the process of technological progress later.

At any point in time, only one of the varieties of any intermediate $v \in [0,1]$ can be used in production. I use the notation j (or $j(v)$) to denote this *active* variety. Aggregate output is therefore given by

$$Y(t) = Q(t) \equiv \int_0^1 q_j(v,t)dv, \tag{3}$$

where $Q(t)$ is the average quality of active intermediates at time t. The production function (3) is a reduced-form representation of several richer endogenous growth models.[6]

Because of switches in tastes or other technological changes, the active variety of each intermediate becomes obsolete ("disappears") at the flow rate $\alpha \geq 0$ at any point. These obsolescence events are independent across intermediates and over time. The motivation for this type of obsolescence is the switch in technology induced by environmental concerns from the active technologies based on fossil fuels to substitute alternative energy sources discussed in the introduction. In particular, let us order varieties such that

6. The appendix sketches one such model, which leads to a structure identical to the reduced-form model used here.

if $j_i(v)$ is the active variety of intermediate v at t, then when it disappears the active variety becomes $j_{i+1}(v)$. With a slight abuse of notation, at any point in time I use j to denote the currently active variety and j' to denote the next variety.

There is a continuum of scientists, with measure normalized to 1. A scientist can work either on active varieties or on substitute varieties.[7] A scientist working on active varieties discovers a higher quality version of one of the intermediates at the flow rate $\eta > 0$. Which intermediate the innovation will be for is determined randomly with uniform probability. The quality ladder structure introduced earlier implies that an innovation starting from an intermediate of quality q leads to a new quality equal to $(1 + \lambda)q$.

A scientist working on substitute varieties discovers a higher quality version of the next-in-line substitute for one of the intermediates at the flow rate $\zeta\eta$, where $\zeta \geq 1$ (again chosen with uniform probability). This assumption implies that if the current active variety is $j_i(v)$ for intermediate v, then substitute research could lead to the invention of a higher quality version of $j_{i+1}(v)$. Following such a discovery, the quality of the substitute variety increases from q' to $(1 + \lambda)q'$. The presence of the term ζ allows innovation for substitute varieties to be easier than innovation for active varieties, for example, because the availability of a more advanced active variety makes some of these improvements for the related substitute variety more straightforward to discover or implement. Since improvements in the quality of substitute varieties also take the form of moving up the rungs of the quality ladder, we can summarize the quality differences between active and substitute varieties by the difference in the number of steps ("quality gap") on the ladder between the two, which I will denote by $n(v,t)$ or simply by $n(v)$ or n. Formally,

$$n(v,t) \equiv n_{j_i}(v,t) - n_{j_{i+1}}(v,t).$$

In addition to endogenous quality improvements, there are exogenous quality improvements for all substitute varieties. In particular, if variety $j_i(v)$ is the active one for intermediate v, then I assume that any $i + 1 > i$ cannot be more than N steps behind the currently active variety $j_i(v)$. In other words, $q_{j_{i+1}}(v,t)$ cannot be less than $\gamma q_{j_i}(v,t)$ when the quality of the active variety is $q_{j_i}(v,t)$, where

$$\gamma \equiv (1 + \lambda)^{-N}$$

for some $N \in \mathbb{N}$ (and thus $\gamma < 1$). The specification in particular implies that if the quality of the active variety increases from $q_{j_i}(v,t)$ to $q_{j_i}(v,t+) = (1 + \lambda)q_{j_i}(v,t)$ and we have $q_{j_{i+1}}(v,t) = \gamma q_{j_i}(v,t)$, then the quality of the substitute variety $i + 1$ also increases to $q_{j_{i+1}}(v,t+) = \gamma(1 + \lambda)q_{j_i}(v,t)$.[8] As a

7. See the appendix for a model in which research is also directed to specific intermediates.
8. The notation $q_{j_i}(v, t+)$ stands for $q_{j_i}(v,t)$ just after time t.

consequence, when a switch (from j to j') happens we always have $q_{j'}(v,t) \geq \gamma q_j(v,t)$. Furthermore, suppose throughout that $q_{j'}(v,t) \leq q_j(v,t)$ for all $v \in [0,1]$—substitute varieties cannot be more advanced than active varieties.

What about the gap between the substitute variety $j_{i+1}(v)$ and its substitute $j_{i+2}(v)$? I assume that research on substitute varieties creates a positive spillover on the quality of varieties beyond the immediate substitute (in particular, on $i + 2$), so that when be the gap between $i + 1$ and i is n so will the gap between $i + 2$ and $i + 1$; that is, $n_{j_{i+1}}(v,t) - n_{j_{i+2}}(v,t) = n_{j_i}(v,t) - n_{j_{i+1}}(v,t)$. This assumption simplifies the analysis by allowing for an explicit characterization of the stationary distribution of quality gaps.[9]

I also assume that

$$\varsigma \leq \gamma^{-1}, \tag{4}$$

so that the relative ease of innovation in substitute varieties does not exceed the productivity advantage of the active varieties.

The patent system functions as follows. A scientist who has invented a higher quality (of the active variety) of some intermediate has a perfectly enforced patent and receives a revenue equal to the contribution of its intermediate to total output. That is, a scientist with a patent on the active variety of an intermediate with quality $(1 + \lambda)q$ receives a flow revenue of λq, since the contribution of this intermediate to total output over the next highest quality, q, is $(1 + \lambda)q - q = \lambda q$.[10] Importantly, an improvement over this variety (for example, leading to quality $(1 + \lambda)q$) does not constitute a patent infringement and thus the scientist in question does not receive any revenues after another scientist improves the quality of this variety. Similarly, scientists that undertake inventions improving the quality of the substitute variety are also awarded a *perfectly enforced patent* and can receive a flow revenue of q for their product of quality q if (and after) the active variety of this intermediate disappears. Also, suppose that if there is a further innovation for the active variety, from $q_j(v,t)$ to $q_j(v,t+) = (1 + \lambda)q_j(v,t)$, then the next-in-line substitute variety of intermediate v of quality $q_{j'}(v,t+) = (1 + \lambda)\gamma q_j(v,t+)$ becomes freely available. Consequently, subsequent to such an innovation in the active variety, all substitute varieties with quality $q \leq q_{j'}(v,t+)$ would receive no revenues even if the active variety were to disap-

9. In fact, all that is necessary is the weaker assumption that $n_{j_{i+1}}(v,t) - n_{j_{i+2}}(v,t)$ has the same stochastic distribution as $n_{j_i}(v,t) - n_{j_{i+1}}(v,t)$. This will be the case, for example, under the following scenario: using the same notation as following, let p_u denote the flow rate of innovation in the active variety and p_d denote the flow rate of innovation in the next in line substitute variety; then the flow rate of innovation in the substitute of the substitute needs to be approximately p_d^2/p_u (see equation [17]).

10. This expression assumes that the current scientist is not the holder of the next highest quality. As shown later, this is without loss of any generality.

More generally, we could assume that the scientist receives a flow revenue of $\beta\lambda q$ for some $\beta \in (0,1]$, with identical results. The model presented in the appendix corresponds to the case in which $\beta \in (0,1)$.

pear. Therefore, only holders of a patent for substitute varieties of quality $q_{j'}(v,t) > \gamma q_j(v,t)$ will receive revenues when the active variety disappears.[11]

Finally, let us assume that scientists maximize the (expected) net present discounted value of their revenues with discount rate $r > 0$.

Given the earlier description, an *equilibrium* in this economy is given by a time path of research decisions by scientists that maximize their net present discounted values (in particular, they choose whether to undertake research directed at active or substitute varieties) and the distribution of technology gaps between sectors. More formally, let $\omega(t) \in [0,1]$ be the fraction of researchers at time t undertaking research in substitute varieties and $\mu_n(t) \in [0,1]$ be the fraction of intermediates where the gap between the active variety $j_i(v)$ and the next substitute variety $j_{i+1}(v)$ is $n = 0, 1, \ldots, N$ steps. An equilibrium can then be represented by time paths of $\omega(t)$ and $\mu_n(t)$ (for $n = 0, 1, \ldots, N$). A *stationary equilibrium* is an allocation in which $\omega(t) = \omega^*$ and $\mu_n(t) = \mu_n^*$ (for n $= 0, 1, \ldots, N$) for all t. I focus on stationary equilibria.

6.3.2 Equilibrium with No Diversity

In this subsection, I show that all scientists undertaking research on active varieties, that is, $\omega(t) = 0$ for all t, is a stationary equilibrium. I provide additional details on this equilibrium and conditions for this to be the unique equilibrium in the next subsection.

Consider such a candidate (stationary) equilibrium. Then the value of holding the patent to the active intermediate of quality $(1 + \lambda)q$ is

$$(5) \qquad rV(q) = \lambda q - (\alpha + \eta)V(q).$$

This is intuitive. The scientist receives a revenue of $\lambda q (= (1 + \lambda)q - q)$ until the first of two events: (a) there is a switch to the substitute technology, which takes place at the flow rate α, or (b) there is a new innovation, which happens at the flow rate η (since all scientists work to improve active varieties, the total measure of scientists is 1, and the measure of intermediates is normalized to 1).[12] Following both events, the scientist loses his patent on this product. Therefore, the right-hand side of equation (5) must be equal to the discount rate, r, times the value of the patent.[13] Note also that given the large number ("continuum") of other scientists, the likelihood that he

11. Here I am using the fact that $\gamma \equiv (1 + \lambda)^{-N}$. Without this feature, improvements in the quality of the active variety of some intermediate may reduce the potential contribution of the substitute varieties that have quality $q_{j'}(v,t) \in (\gamma q_j(v,t), (1 + \lambda)\gamma q_j(v,t))$. When $\gamma \equiv (1 + \lambda)^{-N}$, $q_{j'}(v,t) > \gamma q_j(v,t)$ we automatically have $q_{j'}(v,t) \geq \gamma(1 + \lambda)q_j(v,t)$.

12. Note that $V(q)$ refers to the value of the patent, not to the continuation value of the scientist in question; a scientist is undertaking parallel research regardless of whether this product is replaced or not. Following the disappearance of the active variety or another innovation, the value of the patent disappears, explaining the last term in equation (5).

13. More generally, $\dot{V}(q)$ should be subtracted from the left-hand side, but under this candidate stationary equilibrium, we have $\dot{V}(q) = 0$.

will be the one inventing the next highest quality is zero. This also explains why assuming that patents on the highest and the next highest qualities are never held by the same scientist is without loss of any generality.[14] Equation (5) gives the value of holding the patent for active intermediate of quality q as:

$$V(q) = \frac{\lambda q}{r + \alpha + \eta}. \tag{6}$$

Therefore, the value of directing research to active varieties can be written as

$$R^A(Q) = \eta \int_0^1 V(q(v,t))dv = \frac{\eta \lambda Q}{r + \alpha + \eta}, \tag{7}$$

where recall that $Q \equiv \int_0^1 q_j(v)dv$. In particular, such research will lead to a successful innovation at the flow rate η for one of the intermediates (chosen uniformly). When previously this intermediate had quality q, the innovation will produce a version of the same intermediate with quality $(1 + \lambda)q$ and will yield value $V(q)$, as given by equation (6), to scientists.

Under the candidate equilibrium studied here, there is no research directed to substitute varieties and thus $\omega = 0$. Then it is intuitively clear that the equilibrium will involve the same quality gap between active and substitute varieties of N steps across all intermediates; that is,

$$\mu^*_N = 1 \text{ and } \mu^*_n = 0 \text{ for } n = 0, 1, \ldots, N - 1. \tag{8}$$

Though intuitive, a formal derivation of equation (8) will be provided in the next subsection. For now, given equation (8), we can straightforwardly characterize the return to undertaking research directed at substitute varieties and obtain our main result. Suppose, in particular, that a scientist directs his research to substitute varieties. Under the candidate equilibrium (with $\omega = 0$ and thus with equation [8]), the quality of the substitute variety for intermediate v is

$$q'(v,t) = \gamma q\,(v,t)$$

when the quality of the active product is $q(v,t)$. A successful innovation on a substitute variety of quality q' leads to a product of quality $(1 + \lambda)q'(v,t) = (1 + \lambda)\gamma q(v,t)$, but this is still a substitute variety and will remain so until the active variety disappears. A patent on this product therefore has value $\tilde{V}(q')$ such that

14. If, as in the model in the appendix, we were to allow research to be directed to specific intermediates, then a standard argument based on Arrow's replacement effect (Arrow 1962) would immediately imply that scientists never wish to undertake research on the intermediate line in which they have the best product. See Acemoglu (2009) for a textbook treatment of Arrow's replacement effect.

(9) $$r\tilde{V}(q') = \alpha(V(q') - \tilde{V}(q')) - \eta\tilde{V}(q').$$

Intuitively, this patent does not provide any revenues until the active variety disappears, which takes place at the flow rate α. However, if there is an additional innovation on the active variety of this intermediate before this event, the active variety increases its quality to $(1 + \lambda)q$ and the substitute variety of quality $(1 + \lambda)\gamma q = (1 + \lambda)q'$ becomes freely available and thus the patent on this variety is no longer valuable (see also the explanation for equation [18] in the next subsection). Therefore, we have

(10) $$\tilde{V}(q') = \frac{\alpha V(q')}{r + \alpha + \eta}$$

and the return to undertaking research on the substitute varieties when the average quality of active varieties is $Q \equiv \int_0^1 q_j(v)dv$ can be written as

(11) $$\begin{aligned} R^S(Q) &= \frac{\varsigma\eta\alpha}{r + \alpha + \eta}\int_0^1 V(\gamma q(v,t))dv \\ &= \frac{\varsigma\eta\alpha}{r + \alpha + \eta} \times \frac{\lambda\gamma Q}{r + \alpha + \eta} \\ &= \frac{\varsigma\alpha\gamma}{r + \alpha + \eta}R^A(Q). \end{aligned}$$

Since $\zeta \leq \gamma^{-1}$ (from (4)) $r > 0$, $\eta > 0$, and $\alpha > 0$, comparison of equations (7) and (11) immediately establishes that $R^A(Q) > R^S(Q)$, so that the candidate equilibrium is indeed an equilibrium and no scientist undertakes research on substitute varieties. Intuitively, the fact that substitute varieties only become marketable at some future date (stochastically arriving at the flow rate α) makes research directed at them relatively unattractive compared to research on active varieties, which, when successful, will have immediate returns.[15]

Let us next compute the equilibrium growth rate. First note that for any $v \in [0,1]$ and for Δt sufficiently small, quality $q(v,t + \Delta t)$ will increase to $(1 + \lambda)q(v,t)$ with probability $\eta\Delta t + o(\Delta t)$, it will fall to $\gamma q(v,t)$ with probability $\alpha\Delta t + o(\Delta t)$, and will remain constant at $q(v,t)$ with probability $1 - \eta\Delta t - \alpha\Delta t + o(\Delta t)$, where $o(\Delta t)$ denotes second-order terms in Δt (i.e., $\lim_{\Delta t\to 0} o(\Delta t)/\Delta t = 0$). Therefore, aggregating across all intermediates, we have

$$Q(t + \Delta t) = (1 + \lambda)Q(t)\eta\Delta t + \gamma Q(t)\alpha\Delta t + Q(t)(1 - \alpha\Delta t - \eta\Delta t) + o(\Delta t).$$

15. It is also straightforward to see that this conclusion continues to be valid even if a scientist who has invented a higher-quality substitute variety maintains his patent following an exogenous improvement in quality because of an innovation for the active product (in this case, the denominator of equation (10) would be $r + \alpha$). See also the discussion of uniqueness in the next subsection.

Subtracting $Q(t)$, dividing by Δt and taking the limit as $\Delta t \to 0$, we obtain

$$g(t) = \frac{\dot{Q}(t)}{Q(t)} = g^* \equiv \lambda\eta - \alpha(1 - \gamma). \tag{12}$$

Therefore, this analysis establishes the following proposition (proof in the text).

PROPOSITION 1. *In the previously described environment, the allocation where all research is directed at the active varieties* ($\omega^* = 0$) *and all industries have a gap of N steps between active and substitute varieties* ($\mu^*_N = 1$) *is a stationary equilibrium. In this equilibrium, the economy grows at the rate* g^* *given by equation (12).*

Clearly, the growth rate of the economy is decreasing in α. A switch from the active to the substitute variety of an intermediate causes a large drop in the contribution of this intermediate to output. Aggregate output in this economy is not stochastic because there is a large number of intermediates. Instead, intermediates where the active varieties disappear (at the flow rate α) lose a fraction $1 - \gamma$ of their contribution to output. Equation (12) also shows that the equilibrium growth rate is increasing in γ: the lower is γ, the more steep is the output drop of an intermediate experiencing a switch from the active to the substitute variety.

I next provide sufficient conditions that guarantee uniqueness of this stationary equilibrium. I then discuss the reasoning for the modeling assumptions used so far and then turn to an analysis of the optimality of this equilibrium.

6.3.3 Uniqueness

Can there be stationary equilibria other than the one with $\omega^* = 0$ characterized in Proposition 1? The answer is yes because of the following mechanism: further research directed at substitute varieties increases the average quality of these varieties and makes such research more profitable. However, this mechanism is typically not strong enough to generate multiple equilibria. Moreover, there is a countervailing force pushing toward uniqueness, which is that more research directed at substitute varieties reduces the life span of each variety, thus making patents on such varieties less profitable. In this subsection, I provide sufficient conditions for uniqueness.

To investigate this issue, we need to determine the distribution of intermediates by technology gap between active and next-in-line substitute varieties (the μ_n's), which will also enable us to give a formal derivation of the intuitive result in equation (8), which we used in the previous subsection. Since we are focusing on stationary equilibria, the fraction of researchers working toward innovations in the substitute varieties is again constant at some ω (which no longer needs to be equal to zero). Given ω, I now characterize the stationary distribution of μ_n's.[16] Define $p_u \equiv \eta(1-\omega)$ and $p_d \equiv \varsigma\eta\omega$ as the flow rates of innovation of the active and substitute varieties, respectively. Then

(13) $$(p_u + p_d)\mu_n = p_u\mu_{n-1} + p_d\mu_{n+1} \quad \text{for } n = 1, \ldots, N-1.$$

Intuitively, total exits from state n (for $n = 1, 2, \ldots, N-1$) have three sources. First, there may be an innovation among the active varieties of the intermediates with gaps of n steps, which takes place at the flow rate p_u. Second, there may be an innovation among the substitute varieties of intermediates with gaps of n steps, which takes place at the flow rate p_n. Third, one of the active varieties with gaps of n steps may disappear, which takes place at the flow rate α. This makes total exits from state n equal to

$$(p_u + p_d + \alpha)\mu_n.$$

With a similar reasoning, entry into this state comes from three sources. Either there has been an innovation in the active variety in intermediates with gaps of $n-1$ (flow rate p_u times μ_{n-1}), or there has been an innovation in the substitute varieties of intermediates with gaps of $n+1$ (flow rate p_d times μ_{n+1}), or an active variety (of any gap) has disappeared. In this last case, if the active variety $j_i(v)$ of intermediate v has disappeared and been replaced by $j_{i+1}(v)$, then the relevant gap becomes the same as that between $j_{i+1}(v)$ and $j_{i+2}(v)$, but by assumption, this is the same as the gap between $j_i(v)$ and $j_{i+1}(v)$, so this last source of entry contributes $\alpha\mu_2$, to give us total entry into state n as

$$p_u\mu_{n-1} + p_d\mu_{n+1} + \alpha\mu_n.$$

Combining this with the previous expression gives equation (13).

Equation (13) does not apply at the boundaries, since the gap cannot fall below 0 and cannot increase above N. In these cases, with a similar reasoning, we have

(14) $$p_u\mu_0 = p_d\mu_1,$$

and

(15) $$p_u\mu_{N-1} = p_d\mu_N.$$

In addition, by definition

(16) $$\sum_{n=0}^{N}\mu_n = 1.$$

Equations (13) through (16) define the stationary distribution of a continuous-time Markov chain. Since this Markov chain is aperiodic and

16. The appendix characterizes the evolution of the distribution of quality gaps when $\omega(t)$ is time varying.

irreducible, it has a unique stationary distribution (e.g., Norris 1998), which can be directly computed as

$$\mu_n^* = \left(\frac{p_d}{p_u}\right)^{N-n}\left(\sum_{j=0}^{N}\left(\frac{p_d}{p_u}\right)^{N-j}\right)^{-1} \quad \text{for } n = 0, \ldots, N,$$

or written as a function of ω, as

$$\mu_n^*(\omega) = \left(\frac{\varsigma\omega}{1-\omega}\right)^{N-n}\left(\sum_{j=0}^{N}\left(\frac{\varsigma\omega}{1-\omega}\right)^{N-j}\right)^{-1} \quad \text{for } n = 0, \ldots, N. \tag{17}$$

Now consider the case we study in the previous subsection, where $\omega = 0$. Then equation (17) immediately gives equation (8) as claimed there. Next let us focus the case of interest for this subsection, where there is research directed at substitute varieties; that is, $\omega > 0$. In this case, it should be noted that we cannot simply use equation (9) to determine the value of a patent on a substitute product of quality q' because there may now be substitute varieties that are $n = 0, 1, \ldots, N$ steps behind the corresponding active variety (not just N steps behind as in the previous subsection). In that case, the exact value of n will determine the rate at which this patent may become redundant because of advances in the quality of the active variety (because q_j reaches $(1 + \lambda)\gamma^{-1}q_{j'}$). Therefore, we need to explicitly compute the value of a substitute variety of quality q' when it is n steps behind the active variety. This is given as

$$r\tilde{V}_n(q') = \alpha(V(q') - \tilde{V}_n(q')) + p_u(\tilde{V}_{n+1}(q') - \tilde{V}_n(q')) - p_d\tilde{V}_n(q'), \tag{18}$$

where $p_u \equiv \eta(1 - \omega)$ and $p_d \equiv \varsigma\eta\omega$ as before and $\tilde{V}_{N+1}(q') \equiv 0$. It can be verified that when $\omega = 0$, this equation gives (9) and (10) for $n = N$; recall that (10) applies when $\omega = 0$ and when all substitute varieties are N steps behind. More generally, equation (18) highlights that there are three sources of changes in value: (a) a switch to the active variety status (at the flow rate α giving new value $V(q')$ instead of $\tilde{V}_n(q')$); (b) a further improvement in the quality of the active variety, so that the gap increases to $n + 1$ steps (at the flow rate p_u giving new value $\tilde{V}_{n+1}(q')$ instead of $\tilde{V}_n(q')$); and (c) innovation directed at the substitute varieties replacing this product (at the flow rate p_d giving value zero).

Using the fact that $\tilde{V}_{N+1}(q') \equiv 0$ and substituting for $p_u \equiv \eta(1 - \omega)$ and $p_d \equiv \varsigma\eta\omega$, we can recursively solve equation (18) to obtain

$$\tilde{V}_n(q') = \frac{\alpha}{r + \alpha + \varsigma\eta\omega}V(q')\left[1 - \left(\frac{\eta(1-\omega)}{r + \alpha + \eta(1-\omega) + \varsigma\eta\omega}\right)^{N+1-n}\right] \tag{19}$$

for $n = 1, \ldots, N$. Note that this is equivalent to

$$\tilde{V}_N(q') = \frac{\alpha}{r + \alpha + \eta(1-\omega) + \varsigma\eta\omega}V(q').$$

For $n = 0$, the only difference is that there cannot be any further innovations in the substitute variety, thus

$$\tilde{V}_0(q') = \frac{\alpha}{r + \alpha + \varsigma\eta\omega}$$

$$\times V(q')\left[\frac{r+\alpha+\varsigma\eta\omega}{r+\alpha+\eta(1-\omega)} + \eta(1-\omega)\left(1 - \left(\frac{\eta(1-\omega)}{r+\alpha+\eta(1-\omega)+\varsigma\eta\omega}\right)^N\right)\right].$$

In a stationary allocation where a fraction ω of scientists are directing their research toward substitute varieties, the rate of replacement of active varieties will be $\eta(1-\omega)$, and thus equations (6) and (7) also need to be modified. In particular, with a similar reasoning to that in the previous subsection, these take the form

$$V(q) = \frac{\lambda q}{r + \alpha + \eta(1 - \omega)}, \tag{20}$$

and

$$R^A(Q) = n\int_0^1 V(q(v,t))dv = \frac{\eta\lambda Q}{r+\alpha+\eta(1-\omega)}. \tag{21}$$

Next, turning to the expected return to a scientist directing his research to substitute varieties, we have

$$\begin{aligned} R^S &= \varsigma\eta\sum_{n=1}^{N}\mu_n^*\tilde{V}_n(q') \\ &= \varsigma\eta\sum_{n=1}^{N}\mu_n^*\tilde{V}_n((1+\lambda)^{-n}q), \end{aligned}$$

where in the first line the summation starts from $n = 1$, since there is no possibility of successful innovation for the fraction μ_0^* of intermediates where the gap is $n = 0$. The second line expresses the values as a function of the quality of the active variety, using the identity that if there is n step gap between active and substitute varieties, then $q' = (1 + \lambda)^{-n} q$. Now using equations (17), (19), and (20), we can write

$$\begin{aligned} R^S(Q) &= \varsigma\eta\frac{\lambda Q}{r + \alpha + \eta(1 - \omega)}\frac{\alpha}{r + \alpha + \varsigma\eta\omega}\Phi(\omega) \\ &= \varsigma\frac{\alpha}{r + \alpha + \varsigma\eta\omega}\Phi(\omega)R^A(Q), \end{aligned}$$

where again $Q \equiv \int_0^1 q_j(v)dv$ and the second line uses equation (21). In this expression,

$$\Phi(\omega) \equiv \sum_{n=1}^{N}\left(\frac{\varsigma\omega}{1-\omega}\right)^{N-n}\left(\sum_{j=0}^{N}\left(\frac{\varsigma\omega}{1-\omega}\right)^{N-j}\right)^{-1} \times (1+\lambda)^{-n}\left[1-\left(\frac{n(1-\omega)}{r+\alpha+\eta(1-\omega)+\varsigma\eta\omega}\right)^{N+1-n}\right] \quad (22)$$

gives the expected quality of a substitute intermediate on which a researcher will build his innovation. It can be verified that $\Phi(0) = \gamma$ and $\Phi(\omega)$ is always strictly less than $1/(1 + \lambda)$ (since the summation starts from $n = 1$). This implies that a sufficient condition for research directed at a substitute not to be profitable is

$$\varsigma\alpha \leq (1 + \lambda)(r + \alpha). \quad (23)$$

This establishes (proof in the text):

PROPOSITION 2. *Suppose that equation (23) holds. Then all research being directed at the active varieties ($\omega^* = 0$) and all intermediates having a gap of N steps between active and substitute varieties ($\mu^*_N = 1$) is the unique stationary equilibrium.*

6.3.4 Discussion of Modeling Assumptions

The framework in this section is designed as a minimalist dynamic model for the analysis of diversity of research. It clarifies the key modeling issues and attempts to communicate the main ideas of this chapter in a transparent manner—while at the same time also providing a simple framework for the modeling of endogenously evolving technology gaps between active and substitute varieties. The appendix presents a more standard model of endogenous technological change, which leads to results similar to those presented in this and the next sections. A natural question is whether an even simpler model could have been used to highlight the key economic mechanisms. I now briefly argue why this is not possible. In particular, there are five features of the model that are important either for the results or for simplifying the exposition: (1) the quality ladder structure, (2) a continuum of intermediates, (3) continuous time, (4) the feature that research cannot be directed to specific individual intermediates, and (5) the characterization of the distribution of quality gaps between active and substitute varieties. I now explain why each of these is either necessary or greatly simplifies the analysis.

First, the quality ladder structure, for example, as in Aghion and Howitt (1992) or Grossman and Helpman (1991), is necessary for the results. This will become particularly clear in the next section, but the main idea can be discussed now. With the quality ladder structure, an innovation for the far future is not attractive because before the time to employ the innovation comes, another researcher is likely to have leapfrogged the product in question. In contrast, with a structure that incorporates horizontal innovations as in Romer (1990), following the invention of a new product (or machine), there are no further innovations replacing this product. This removes the externality that is central to the discussion here—the externality created on future versions of the same product or intermediate.

Second, the presence of a continuum of intermediates simplifies the analysis greatly by removing aggregate risk. Without this feature aggregate output would jump whenever there is an innovation or the active variety disappears. While in this case one could characterize the expected value of output, working with a continuum of intermediates simplifies the analysis both algebraically and conceptually.

Third, continuous time also simplifies the algebra. In particular, in discrete time, the relevant quantities become somewhat more involved because of the following two features: (a) the probability of success for an individual scientist depends on whether another scientist has been successful; in continuous time, the probability of two such events (success by this scientist and another) happening simultaneously vanishes, simplifying the expressions for expected returns from research; and (b) the expression for the growth rate is also similarly simplified and takes the form given in equation (12), clearly highlighting the trade-off between research on active and substitute varieties.

Fourth, research is assumed to be directed to either active or substitute varieties, but not to specific intermediates. This is because, with the current formulation, profits are proportional to quality q and all researchers would prefer to direct their research to the variety with the highest q. The general model presented in the appendix allows for a research technology that uses the final good (rather than the labor of scientists) and makes the cost of research proportional to the quality of the intermediate. With this formulation, the results do not depend on whether research can be directed to specific intermediates.

Finally, the most substantive aspect of the model is the characterization of the distribution of quality gaps between active and substitute varieties. While this introduces some amount of complication, it is necessary since the cost of lack of diversity is a large gap between the active and substitute varieties, which thus needs to be determined endogenously in equilibrium. An important modeling contribution of this chapter is to provide a tractable framework for an explicit characterization of the distribution of these gaps.

Several other features of the model are also adopted to simplify the exposition and will be relaxed in the appendix. In particular, in the appendix, I present an endogenous technological change model based on a quality ladder specification. The model in the appendix does not assume linear preferences and perfect substitutions among different intermediates. In addition, the feature that innovations receive their full marginal contribution aggregate output when used in production is replaced with an explicit derivation of the profits of monopolistically competitive firms after they innovate. Finally, as also pointed out in the previous paragraph, this extended model further allows innovations to be directed not just to the active or the substitute varieties, but also to specific intermediates.

6.4 Optimal Technological Progress

In this section, I establish that when α is sufficiently large, the equilibrium is inefficient and the growth rate is inefficiently low. I then provide the economic intuition for this result.

6.4.1 Suboptimality of Equilibrium Technological Progress

Since all agents maximize the net present discounted value of output and are risk neutral (and idiosyncratic risks can be diversified), a natural measure of the optimality of the allocation of resources in this equilibrium is the expected value of output. Let us focus on this measure. First note that if $\alpha = 0$, we can ignore research on substitute varieties and the equilibrium allocation trivially coincides with the only feasible allocation. Thus the interesting case is when $\alpha > 0$. Suppose that a planner determines the allocation of scientists between research on the active and the substitute varieties. Consider the simple scenario where a fraction ω of the scientists is allocated to undertake research on substitute varieties.

The main result of this section is the following proposition.

PROPOSITION 3. *Suppose that $\alpha > \alpha^*$, where*

$$\alpha^* \equiv \frac{\eta}{\varsigma\gamma}. \tag{24}$$

Then the stationary equilibrium in Proposition 1 is suboptimal. In particular, starting with $\omega = 0$ a small increase in ω raises long-run output growth.

This proposition states that when potential switches from active to substitute technologies are sufficiently frequent, then some amount of diversity in research, that is, research directed at both the active and the substitute varieties, is necessary to maximize steady-state equilibrium growth. Before presenting the proof of this proposition, note that it refers to long-run growth because it compares the stationary equilibrium growth rates to growth in an alternative stationary allocation. The appendix provides a comparison of the net present discounted value of output taking into account the adjustment dynamics. It shows that the same conclusion as in Proposition 3 holds provided that $\alpha > \alpha^{**} > \alpha^*$.[17] The analysis in the Appendix gives the value of α^{**} as

17. It is also clear that $\alpha > \alpha^*$ is possible while $g^* = \lambda\eta - \alpha(1 - \gamma) > 0$. For example, $\alpha = 4/3$, $\eta = 1$, $\lambda = 1.1$, $\gamma = 1/4$ and $\zeta = 4$ imply that $\alpha > \alpha^* = 1$, while $g^* = 0.1$, so that positive growth in the economy does not imply optimality.

$$(25) \qquad \alpha^{**} \equiv \frac{r+\eta}{\varsigma\gamma}.$$

As expected, when $r \to 0$, $\alpha^{**} \to \alpha^{*}$, since without discounting, the objectives of maximizing the long-run growth rate and the net present discounted value of output coincide.

To prove Proposition 3, let us first compute the relative quality gap between active and substitute varieties in a stationary allocation where a fraction ω of scientists are directing their research to substitute varieties. Let us again use Q to denote the average quality of active varieties (as defined in equation [3] and let the average quality of the substitute varieties be ΓQ. Then in a stationary distribution given by $\langle \mu_0^*(\omega), \mu_1^*(\omega), \ldots, \mu_N^*(\omega)\rangle$, this gap parameter Γ as a function of ω can be written as

$$(26) \qquad \Gamma(\omega) = \sum_{n=0}^{N}(1+\lambda)^{-n}\mu_n^*(\omega)$$
$$= \frac{\sum_{n=0}^{N}(1+\lambda)^{-n}\left(\frac{\varsigma\omega}{1-\omega}\right)^{N-n}}{\sum_{n=0}^{N}\left(\frac{\varsigma\omega}{1-\omega}\right)^{N-n}}.$$

The first line of this expression defines $\Gamma(\omega)$ as the average relative quality of substitute varieties (relative to the active varieties), simply using the fact that this is given by a weighted average of the relative qualities of the substitute varieties of intermediates where substitutes have $n = 0, 1, \ldots, N$ step gaps and the weights are given by the stationary distribution fractions of intermediates with $n = 0, 1, \ldots, N$ gaps $(\mu_0^*(\omega), \mu_1^*(\omega), \ldots, \mu_N^*(\omega))$. The second line substitutes for $\mu_n^*(\omega)$ from equation (17).

It can be verified that $\lim_{\omega \to 0}\Gamma(\omega) = \gamma \equiv (1+\lambda)^{-N}$, consistent with the derivations in the previous section. Moreover, it can also be verified that $\Gamma(\omega)$ is continuously differentiable for all $\omega \in [0, 1)$, and straightforward differentiation gives its derivative as

$$\Gamma'(\omega) = \frac{\left(\frac{1}{1-\omega}\right)^2 \varsigma\sum_{n=1}^{N-1}(N-n)(1+\lambda)^{-n}\left(\frac{\varsigma\omega}{1-\omega}\right)^{N-n-1}}{\sum_{n=0}^{N}\left(\frac{\varsigma\omega}{1-\omega}\right)^{N-n}}$$
$$- \frac{\left(\frac{1}{1-\omega}\right)^2 \varsigma\left(\sum_{n=1}^{N}(1+\lambda)^{-n}\left(\frac{\varsigma\omega}{1-\omega}\right)^{N-n}\right)\sum_{n=1}^{N-1}(N-n)\left(\frac{\varsigma\omega}{1-\omega}\right)^{N-n-1}}{\left(\sum_{n=0}^{N}\left(\frac{\varsigma\omega}{1-\omega}\right)^{N-n}\right)^2}.$$

And thus

$$\Gamma'(0) = \varsigma\lambda(1 + \lambda)^{-N} > 0.$$

With an identical argument to that in the previous section, the long-run (stationary allocation) growth rate of the economy is

$$g(\omega) = \lambda\eta(1 - \omega) - \alpha(1 - \Gamma(\omega)),$$

with the only difference from equation (12) being that the first term is multiplied by $(1 - \omega)$, reflecting the fact that not all scientists are working on active varieties, and the relative gap between active and substitute varieties is now $\Gamma(\omega)$ rather than γ. Therefore,

$$\begin{aligned} g'(0) &= -\lambda\eta + \alpha\Gamma'(0) \\ &= \alpha\varsigma\lambda(1 + \lambda)^{-N} - \lambda\eta. \end{aligned}$$

The result that whenever

$$\alpha > \alpha^* \equiv \frac{\eta(1 + \lambda)^N}{\varsigma} \equiv \frac{\eta}{\varsigma\gamma},$$

equilibrium growth is too slow then follows immediately and establishes Proposition 3.

The appendix shows that a similar result applies when we look at the adjustment of the distribution of gaps between active and substitute varieties following an increase in ω starting from $\omega = 0$.

6.4.2 Why Is the Equilibrium Suboptimal?

The externality that is not internalized in the equilibrium is the following: when a researcher undertakes an innovation either for an active or a substitute variety, it not only increases current output but also contributes to future output growth because it ensures that future innovations for this product will start from a higher base—each innovation increases existing quality by a proportional amount. However, the researcher does not capture these gains after its patent expires due to exogenous or endogenous technological change. This implies that every innovation creates positive externalities on all future innovators of the same (variety of the same) intermediate. When $\alpha = 0$, this externality does not affect the allocation of resources, since there is no choice concerning the direction of technological change and each scientist is already fully utilizing all of his capacity. However, when there is a choice between active and substitute varieties, this externality affects the relative private gains. In particular, the externality has a disproportionate effect on research directed at substitute varieties because this type of research is socially beneficial not for the immediate gains it generates but because it increases the quality of the substitute variety and creates a better platform for yet further innovation after the active variety disappears. Consequently, incentives to undertake research on such varieties are too low and there is not enough diversity in research.

This discussion also clarifies that the suboptimality identified here is a consequence of the patent system assumed in the analysis. This patent system is a stylized representation of the system of intellectual property rights used in most advanced economies, where a new product (process or technology) does not need to pay royalties to the previous innovations, provided that it improves existing technological know-how beyond a minimal required inventive step (or it improves over technologies that are more than twenty years old and are thus no longer patented).[18] Although, in practice, some innovations will need to make payments to previous patent holders, this does not change the thrust of the argument in this chapter; patent duration is capped at twenty years, and it is straightforward to extend the qualitative results presented here to a model with such limited patent payments.

In the context of the simple economy here, there exists an alternative patent system that can internalize the knowledge externalities and would prevent the inefficiency identified here. However, as discussed in the introduction, this alternative patent system is both different from actual patent systems and is difficult to implement. Let us first discuss what this alternative patent system would have to look like. Since the externality is on future innovators, the patent system would have to involve a payment (e.g., royalty) from all future innovators in a particular line to the current innovator. For example, all innovations in laser technology or solid-state physics in the twentieth century would have to pay royalties to Heisenberg, Einstein, or Bohr. In practice, patent systems do not have this feature and once a new product or procedure is deemed to pass the originality (required step) requirement, it does not have to pay royalties to the innovators of the previous leading-edge technology, let alone to all innovations that invented the technologies that preceded the previous one.

6.5 Diversity and Technological Progress

In this section, I discuss how the diversity in the preferences, competences, or beliefs of scientists affects equilibrium growth. I start with a simple variation on the model presented so far where scientists have a comparative advantage for active or substitute research. I then discuss another variation with heterogeneous beliefs.

6.5.1 Comparative Advantage

Suppose that each scientist has access to the same technology for innovating on active varieties (flow rate η), but in addition, if scientist i undertakes research on substitute varieties, then the flow rate at which he will succeed

18. See, for example, Scotchmer (2005).

is given by $\varepsilon_i\eta$, where ε_i has a distribution across scientists given by $G(\varepsilon)$.[19] The variable ε_i captures *researcher diversity*—the diversity in the abilities, interests, or beliefs of scientists concerning which research lines are likely to be successful in the future. Let us refer to ε_i as the "type" of the scientist. The model studied so far is a special case where $G(\varepsilon)$ has all of its mass at $\varepsilon = \zeta$. To ensure compatibility with the analysis in the previous section, let us assume that

$$\int_0^\infty \varepsilon dG(\varepsilon) = \varsigma.$$

Let us denote the support of G as $[\varsigma - \xi', \varsigma + \xi]$ (with $\xi', \xi > 0$). We can think of $G(\varepsilon)$ as highly concentrated around ζ if ξ' and ξ are small. Let us define the notion of *greater diversity* (of scientists or researchers) as a mean-preserving spread of G involving an increase in ξ' and ξ.

Again consider a candidate equilibrium where all scientists direct their research toward active varieties. With an identical argument to that in section 6.3, the value of undertaking research on active varieties for any scientist is given by equation (7) (since all scientists have the same productivity in research on active varieties). Similarly, the analysis leading up to equation (11) implies that the value of undertaking research toward substitute varieties for a researcher of type ε_i is

$$R^S(Q|\varepsilon_i) = \frac{\alpha\varepsilon_i\gamma}{r + \alpha + \eta} R^A(Q).$$

If G is highly concentrated around ζ, then research directed at substitute varieties will be unprofitable for all types. In particular, if

$$\varepsilon \leq \varepsilon^* \equiv \frac{r + \alpha + \eta}{\alpha\gamma} - \varsigma, \tag{27}$$

then the allocation in which no scientist undertakes research directed toward substitute varieties is once again a stationary equilibrium.

Next, consider an increase in diversity, corresponding to a mean-preserving spread of G (in particular, an increase in ξ). For a sufficiently large change in G of this form, it will become profitable for some of the researchers with high ε's to start directing their research toward substitute varieties. When this happens, the form of the equilibrium resembles that discussed in subsection 6.3.3. In particular, there will clearly exist a threshold level $\bar{\varepsilon}$ such that scientists with type greater than $\bar{\varepsilon}$ will undertake research on substitute varieties, and thus the fraction of researchers working on active varieties will be $G(\bar{\varepsilon})$. The values of undertaking research toward substitute and active varieties in this case follow from the analysis in subsection 6.3.3. In particular, the value of undertaking research toward active varieties, when average quality of such varieties is Q, becomes

19. In other words, instead of a uniform innovation rate of $\zeta\eta$ for substitute varieties as in the previous two sections, now researcher i has innovation rate of $\varepsilon_i\eta$ if he directs his research to substitute varieties.

$$R^A(Q|\bar{\varepsilon}) = \eta \frac{\lambda Q}{r + \alpha + \eta G(\bar{\varepsilon})}. \tag{28}$$

The value of research directed toward substitute varieties is characterized as in subsection 6.3.3. In particular, let us define the equivalent of $\Phi(\omega)$ in equation (22) as

$$\Phi_\xi(\bar{\varepsilon}) \equiv \sum_{n=1}^{N} \left(\frac{\int_{\bar{\varepsilon}}^{\infty} \varepsilon dG(\varepsilon)}{G(\bar{\varepsilon})} \right)^{N-n} \left(\sum_{j=0}^{N} \left(\frac{\int_{\bar{\varepsilon}}^{\infty} \varepsilon dG(\varepsilon)}{G(\bar{\varepsilon})} \right)^{N-j} \right)^{-1} (1+\lambda)^{-n} \tag{29}$$

$$\times \left[1 - \left(\frac{\eta G(\bar{\varepsilon})}{r+\alpha+\eta G(\bar{\varepsilon})+\eta \int_{\bar{\varepsilon}}^{\infty} \varepsilon dG(\varepsilon)} \right)^{N+1-n} \right],$$

which takes into account that the probability of innovation in active and substitute varieties is no longer $\eta(1 - \omega)$ and $\zeta\eta\omega$, but $\eta(1 - G(\bar{\varepsilon}))$ and $\eta\int_{\bar{\varepsilon}}^{\infty} \varepsilon dG(\varepsilon)$. This function is also subscripted by ξ to emphasize its dependence on the distribution function G, particularly on its upper support, $\zeta + \xi$. Then, the value of undertaking research toward substitute varieties for a scientist of type ε_i (when the average quality of active varieties is Q) is

$$R^S(Q|\varepsilon_i, \bar{\varepsilon}) = \eta\varepsilon_i \frac{\alpha}{r+\alpha+\eta \int_{\bar{\varepsilon}}^{\infty} \varepsilon dG(\varepsilon)} \Phi_\xi(\bar{\varepsilon}) R^A(Q|\bar{\varepsilon}). \tag{30}$$

The equilibrium value of the threshold $\bar{\varepsilon}$ is then given by the solution to

$$R^S(Q|\varepsilon_i = \bar{\varepsilon}, \bar{\varepsilon}) = R^A(Q|\bar{\varepsilon}),$$

or by $\bar{\varepsilon}$ such that

$$\eta\bar{\varepsilon} \frac{\alpha}{r+\alpha+\eta \int_{\bar{\varepsilon}}^{\infty} \varepsilon dG(\varepsilon)} \Phi_\xi(\bar{\varepsilon}) = 1.$$

In general, such $\bar{\varepsilon}$ may not be unique. Nevertheless, it is clear that if ξ is greater than ξ^*, there does not exist a stationary equilibrium with no research directed at substitute varieties. Moreover, if ξ increases just above ξ^*, by the fact that $\Phi(\bar{\varepsilon})$ is continuous and $\Phi_\xi(\bar{\varepsilon}) = \gamma$ for $\xi \leq \xi^*$, the implications of this change will be identical to those of a small increase in ω starting from $\omega = 0$ in the baseline model. This argument thus establishes the following proposition (proof in the text).

PROPOSITION 4. *In the previous environment, consider a distribution of researcher diversity G_0 such that $\xi \leq \xi^*$ (as given by equation [27]). Then all research being directed at active varieties is a stationary equilibrium. Now consider a shift to G_1 with support $[\varsigma - \xi_1', \varsigma + \xi_1]$, where $\xi_1 > \xi^*$. This will* *increase the diversity of research in equilibrium and also raise the equilibrium growth rate provided that ξ_1 is sufficiently close to ξ^*.*

Proposition 4 shows that diversity of researchers will tend to increase the extent of diversity in research—that is, with more heterogeneous competences of researchers, equilibria will involve greater research effort being directed toward substitute varieties. Since the equilibrium of the baseline model studied in the previous two sections may have too much conformity and too little diversity, diversity from researchers may improve the rate of growth and technological progress in the economy. The proposition requires that ξ_1 is close to ξ^* for the equilibrium growth rate to increase. This is natural, since an extreme mean-preserving spread can induce (close to) half of all scientists to direct their research to substitute varieties, which will not necessarily increase growth.

6.5.2 Differences in Beliefs

A related but different interpretation of the analysis of the previous subsection and of Proposition 4 is also useful. Suppose that there is no difference in the abilities of the researchers and they all have a flow rate $\zeta\eta$ of undertaking successful innovations when their research is directed at substitute varieties. Instead, scientists have either different beliefs about the likelihood of switches between active and substitute varieties or obtain additional differential utility from undertaking research directed at targets different from the majority of other researchers. Suppose that ε again has a distribution given by G, with the same definition of ξ' and ξ, and let us also adopt the same definition of "greater diversity."

With this interpretation, the equations need to change a little, since a high ε researcher working on innovations in substitute varieties is not more productive. It is straightforward to repeat the same steps as before and conclude that as long as equation (27) holds, there will be no research directed at substitute varieties. However, when this condition does not hold, the equilibrium will take a slightly different form. In particular, equation (28) remains unchanged and gives the expected return to research directed at active varieties. Expected return to research on substitute varieties is, instead, given by

$$R^S(Q|\varepsilon_i, \bar{\varepsilon}) = \varsigma\eta\varepsilon_i \frac{\alpha}{r + \alpha + \varsigma\eta(1 - G(\bar{\varepsilon}))} \hat{\Phi}_\xi(\bar{\varepsilon}) R^A(Q|\bar{\varepsilon}),$$

with

$$\hat{\Phi}_\xi(\bar{\varepsilon}) \equiv \sum_{n=1}^{N} \left(\frac{\varsigma(1-G(\bar{\varepsilon}))}{G(\bar{\varepsilon})}\right)^{N-n} \left(\sum_{j=0}^{N} \left(\frac{\varsigma(1-G(\bar{\varepsilon}))}{G(\bar{\varepsilon})}\right)^{N-j}\right)^{-1} (1+\lambda)^{-n}$$
$$\times \left[1 - \left(\frac{\eta G(\bar{\varepsilon})}{r+\alpha+\eta G(\bar{\varepsilon})+\varsigma\eta(1-G(\bar{\varepsilon}))}\right)^{N+1+n}\right].$$

An increase in diversity again has similar effects. However, this slightly different interpretation also highlights an important point: the decisions of certain scientists to direct their research to substitute varieties may be *nonprofit maximizing*. This has two implications. First, it may be precisely the nonprofit objectives of scientists that sometimes restore the diversity in research that may be socially beneficial and useful for more rapid technological progress. Second, with this interpretation, if researchers were employed in profit-maximizing organizations, there would be a conflict between the objectives of organizations (which would be to induce researchers to direct their efforts toward active varieties) and the wishes of the researchers themselves, and it would be the latter that is more useful for the society. This may then generate a justification for creating nonprofit research centers (such as universities or independent research labs), where the diversity of researchers, rather than profit incentives, can guide the direction of their research effort.

6.6 Concluding Remarks

This chapter has presented a tractable dynamic framework for the analysis of the diversity of research. Using this framework, it is shown that equilibrium technological progress may feature too little diversity. In particular, it may fail to invest in alternative technologies, even if it is known that these technologies will become used at some point in the future. The economic intuition leading to this result is simple: innovations are made for current gain—the future benefits from these innovations are not fully internalized. This externality discourages research toward technologies that will bear fruit in the future because, in these research lines, current innovations are likely to be followed by further innovations before these technologies can be profitably marketed. A social planner wishing to maximize output (the net present discounted value of output or alternatively discounted utility) would choose a more diverse research portfolio and would induce a higher growth rate than the equilibrium allocation. I also showed how diversity of researchers—in particular, the presence of researchers with different interests, competences or ideas—can induce a more diverse research portfolio and thus increase economic growth.

The broader message is that the research process may, under certain circumstances, generate too much conformity and too little diversity—with all or the majority of scientists working to develop the same research lines. The model here emphasized one mechanism for such conformity: the greater profitability of developing currently marketed products relative to technologies for the future. Other mechanisms may be equally important in practice. For example, learning from the success of others might create "herding," making the majority of the researchers follow early successes in a particular field. Or certain types of research may create greater externalities and more limited private returns, so that research becomes concentrated in low-externality fields. Depending on the exact mechanism leading to such lack of diversity in research, different types of policy and market remedies may be required.[20] If the problem is one of lack of diversity, greater diversity of preferences, beliefs, or competencies of researchers is likely to be socially useful. As discussed in the previous section, this might also suggest a justification for university-like organizations that provide nonmonetary rewards and encourage nonprofit-seeking research behavior among scientists. More detailed theoretical and empirical investigations of whether and why there may be too much conformity or too little diversity in research and how the society might respond to this challenge are interesting areas for further study.

Appendix

Characterization of Optimal Policy

I now provide a characterization of the optimal policy, which involves comparing the entire path of output rather than the more straightforward comparisons of long-run growth rates reported in the text. With an argument identical to that in the text, the growth rate of average quality of output at any t (even when we are not in a stationary allocation) is

$$g(t) = \lambda\eta(1 - \omega(t)) - \alpha(1 - \Gamma(t)), \tag{A1}$$

where

$$\Gamma(t) = \sum_{n=0}^{N}(1 + \lambda)^{-n}\mu_n(t), \tag{A2}$$

and $\mu_n(t)$ denotes the fraction of intermediates at time t with a gap of n steps between active and substitute varieties. This is similar to equation (26), and on the right-hand side we have the fractions of intermediates with different gaps (which are not necessarily the stationary equilibrium fractions). Correspondingly, with a slight abuse of notation, I use $\Gamma(t)$ rather than $\Gamma(\omega)$.

These fractions will evolve as a function of the time path of research devoted to substitute varieties, $[\omega(t)]_{t=0}^{\infty}$. In particular, with a reasoning identical to that leading to equation (13), the law of motion of these fractions is given by

$$\dot{\mu}_n(t) = \varsigma\eta\omega(t)\mu_{n+1}(t) + \eta(1 - \omega(t))\mu_{n-1}(t) - (\varsigma\eta\omega(t) + \eta(1 - \omega(t)))\mu_n(t)$$

20. And of course, if we consider a rich array of mechanisms, it is also possible that there might be too much diversity, for example, because diversity in research has greater private value than social value. This highlights that ultimately the theoretical framework used for evaluating the private and social values of diversity needs to be empirically tested and validated.

for $n = 1, \ldots, N-1$, and in addition,

$$\dot{\mu}_N(t) = \eta(1 - \omega(t))\mu_{N-1}(t) - \varsigma\eta\omega(t)\mu_N(t)$$

and

$$\dot{\mu}_0(t) = \varsigma\eta\omega(t)\mu_1(t) - \eta(1 - \omega(t))\mu_0(t).$$

However, as noted in the text, one of these differential equations for μ is redundant, and in addition we have that

$$\sum_{n=0}^{N}\mu_n(t) = 1.$$

In what follows, it is most convenient to drop the differential equation for $\mu_{N-1}(t)$ and also write

(A3) $$\mu_{N-1}(t) = 1 - \sum_{n=0}^{N-2}\mu_n(t) - \mu_N(t).$$

Then, the differential equations that will form the constraints on the optimal control problem can be written as

(A4) $$\dot{\mu}_n(t) = \varsigma\eta\omega(t)\mu_{n+1}(t) + \eta(1 - \omega(t))\mu_{n-1}(t) - (\varsigma\eta\omega(t) + \eta(1 - \omega(t)))\mu_n(t)$$

for $n = 1, \ldots, N-3$,

(A5) $$\dot{\mu}_{N-2}(t) = \varsigma\eta\omega(t)\left(1-\sum_{n=0}^{N-2}\mu_n(t)-\mu_N(t)\right) + \eta(1 - \omega(t))\mu_{N-3}(t) - (\varsigma\eta\omega(t) + \eta(1 - \omega(t)))\mu_{N-2}(t),$$

(A6) $$\dot{\mu}_N(t) = \eta(1 - \omega(t))\left(1-\sum_{n=0}^{N-2}\mu_n(t)-\mu_N(t)\right) - (\varsigma\eta\omega(t)\mu_N(t),$$

and

(A7) $$\dot{\mu}_0(t) = \varsigma\eta\omega(t)\mu_1(t) - \eta(1 - \omega(t))\mu_0(t).$$

Let us use boldface letters to denote sequences; that is, $\boldsymbol{\omega} \equiv [\omega(t)]_{t=0}^{\infty}$. Therefore, the net present discounted value of output, taking into account adjustment dynamics, is given by

$$W(\boldsymbol{\omega}) = \int_{t=0}^{\infty}\exp(-rt)Q(t)dt.$$

The optimal policy will involve choosing $\boldsymbol{\omega}$ to maximize W subject to

(A8) $$\dot{Q}(t) = g(t)Q(t),$$

with $g(t)$ given by equation (A.31), and also subject to equation (A.33), equations (A.34) through (A.37), and equation (A.38). Without loss of any generality, let us normalize $Q(0) = 1$.

Given these differential equations, the optimal policy is determined as a solution to an optimal control problem with current value Hamiltonian, with appropriately defined costate variables and Lagrange multipliers. In particular, let the multipliers on equation (A.33) be $\chi(t)$, equations (A.34) through (A.37) $\varphi_n(t)$ for $n = 0, 1, \ldots, N$, and on equation (A.38) $\kappa(t)$. Then

$$
\begin{aligned}
&H(\boldsymbol{\omega}, \mathbf{Q}, \boldsymbol{\mu}, \boldsymbol{\varphi}, \boldsymbol{\kappa}, \boldsymbol{\chi}) = \\
&\quad \exp(-rt)Q(t) \\
&\quad + \kappa(t)g(t)Q(t) \\
&\quad + \varphi_0[\varsigma\eta\omega(t)\mu_1(t) - \eta(1-\omega(t))\mu_0(t)] \\
&\quad + \sum_{n=1}^{N-3} \varphi_n(t)[\varsigma\eta\omega(t)\mu_{n+1}(t) + \eta(1-\omega(t))\mu_{n-1}(t) - (\varsigma\eta\omega(t) + \eta(1-\omega(t)))\mu_n(t)] \\
&\quad + \varphi_{N-2}\Bigg[\varsigma\eta\omega(t)\left(1 - \sum_{n=0}^{N-2}\mu_n(t) - \mu_N(t)\right) \\
&\qquad\qquad + \eta(1-\omega(t))\mu_{N-3}(t) - (\varsigma\eta\omega(t) + \eta(1-\omega(t)))\mu_{N-2}(t)\Bigg], \\
&\quad + \varphi_N(t)\left[\eta(1-\omega(t))\left(1 - \sum_{n=0}^{N-2}\mu_n(t) - \mu_N(t) - \varsigma\eta\omega(t)\mu_N(t)\right)\right] \\
&\quad + \chi(t)\left[\sum_{n=0}^{N-2}\mu_n(t) + \mu_N(t) - 1\right].
\end{aligned}
$$

Substituting from equations (A.32) and (A.33) into equation (A.31), we have

$$
\begin{aligned}
g(t) &= \lambda\eta(1-\omega(t)) \\
&\quad - \alpha\Bigg[1 - \sum_{n=0}^{N-2}(1-\lambda)^{-n}\mu_n(t) - (1+\lambda)^{-(N-1)}\left(1 - \sum_{n=0}^{N-2}\mu_n(t) - \mu_N(t)\right) \\
&\qquad\qquad - (1+\lambda)^{-N}\mu_N(t)\Bigg] \\
&= \lambda\eta(1-\omega(t)) - \alpha(1 - (1+\lambda)^{-(N-1)}) \\
&\quad + \sum_{n=0}^{N-2}((1+\lambda)^{-n} - (1+\lambda)^{-(N-1)})\mu_n(\mathrm{t}) - \alpha\lambda(1+\lambda)^{-N}\mu_N(t).
\end{aligned}
$$

Let us now write the necessary conditions for a continuous solution to this optimal control problem. We use $\mu_{N-1}(t) = 1 - \sum_{n=0}^{N-2}\mu_n(t) - \mu_N(t)$ to simplify expressions.

For $\omega(t)$, we have

$$\text{(A9)} \quad - \lambda\eta\kappa(t)Q(t) + \varphi 0(t)[\varsigma\eta\mu_1(t) + \eta\mu_0(t)] + \sum_{n=0}^{N-1} \varphi_n(t)[\varsigma\eta(\mu_{n+1}(t) - \mu_n(t)) + \eta(\mu_n(t) - \mu_{n-1}(t))] - \varphi_N(t)[\varsigma\eta\mu_N(t) + \eta\mu_{N-1}(t)] \leq 0,$$

where this condition is written as an inequality to allow for the solution to be at $\omega(t) = 0$ (and incorporating the fact that $\omega(t)$ will always be less than 1).

For $Q(t)$, we have

$$\text{(A10)} \quad -\dot{\kappa}(t) = \exp(-rt) + \kappa(t)g(t),$$

For $\mu_0(t)$, we have

$$\text{(A11)} \quad -\dot{\varphi}_0(t) = \alpha\kappa(t)[1 - (1 + \lambda)^{-(N-1)}] - \varphi_0(t)\eta(1 - \omega(t)) + \varphi_1(t)\varsigma\eta\omega(t) - \varphi_{N-2}(t)\varsigma\eta\omega(t) - \varphi_N(t)\eta(1 - \omega(t)) + \chi(t).$$

For $\mu_n(t)$ ($n = 1, \ldots N-2$), we have

$$\text{(A12)} \quad -\dot{\varphi}_n(t) = \alpha\kappa(t)((1 + \lambda)^{-n} - (1 + \lambda)^{-(N-1)}) - \varphi_n(t)[\varsigma\eta\omega(t) + \eta(1 - \omega(t))] + \varphi_{n+1}(t)\eta(1 - \omega(t)) + \varphi_{n-1}(t)\varsigma\eta\omega(t) - \varphi_{N-2}(t)\varsigma\eta\omega(t) - \varphi_N(t)\eta(1 - \omega(t)) + \chi(t).$$

For $\mu_N(t)$, we have

$$\text{(A13)} \quad -\dot{\varphi}_N(t) = -\alpha\kappa(t)\lambda(1 + \lambda)^{-N} - \varphi_{N-2}(t)\varsigma\eta\omega(t) + \varphi_N(t)[\eta(1 - \omega(t)) - \varsigma\eta\omega(t)] + \chi(t).$$

In addition, we have a set of transversality conditions corresponding to each of the state variables.

Now suppose that we start at $t = 0$ with $\mu_n(0) = 0$ for all $n = 0, 1, \ldots, N-1$, and thus naturally, $\mu_N(0) = 1$. We will now characterize the conditions under which $\omega(t) = 0$ for all t is not optimal. Suppose, to obtain a contradiction, that starting from such an allocation $\omega(t) = 0$ for all t is optimal. Let us also define (as in the text)

$$g^* \equiv \lambda\eta - \alpha(1 - \gamma).$$

Since $\mu_n(0) = 0$ for all $n = 0, 1, \ldots, N-1$, equation (A.33) is slack, thus $\chi(t) = 0$. Moreover, since $\mu_n(t) = 0$ for all t and $n = 0, 1, \ldots, N-2$, we can ignore the evolution of $\varphi_n(t)$ (for $n = 0, 1, \ldots, N-2$). Thus we can simply focus on the evolution of the two costate variables, $\kappa(t)$ and $\varphi_N(t)$. Since $\omega(t) = 0$ for all t and $\mu_n(t) = 0$ for all t and $n = 0, 1, \ldots, N-2$, their evolution is given by the following two differential equations:

$$-\dot{\kappa}(t) = \exp(-rt) + g^*\kappa(t), \tag{A14}$$

and (using also the fact that $\gamma \equiv (1 + \lambda)^{-N}$)

$$\dot{\varphi}_N(t) = \alpha\lambda\gamma\kappa(t) + \eta\varphi_N(t). \tag{A15}$$

Since equation (A.44) only depends on $\kappa(t)$, it has a unique solution of the form

$$\kappa(t) = c_K \exp(-g^*t) + \frac{\exp(-rt)}{r - g^*},$$

where c_K is a constant of integration. The transversality condition corresponding to $Q(t)$ requires that $r > g^*$ (which we assume) and that $c_K = 0$, thus

$$\kappa(t) = \frac{\exp(-rt)}{r - g^*}, \tag{A16}$$

Now using equation (A.46), the second differential equation (A.45) also has a unique solution

$$\varphi_N(t) = c_N \exp(\eta t) - r\alpha\lambda\gamma \frac{\exp(-rt)}{(r - g^*)(r + \eta)},$$

where c_N is a constant of integration, again set equal to 0 by the transversality condition. Therefore,

$$\varphi_N(t) = -\alpha\gamma\lambda \frac{\exp(-rt)}{(r - g^*)(r + \eta)}. \tag{A17}$$

Combining equations (A.46) and (A.47) with equation (A.39) and recalling the normalization that $Q(0) = 1$, we have that a necessary condition for $\omega(t) = 0$ for all t to be an optimal solution is

$$-\lambda\eta \frac{\exp(-rt)}{r - g^*} \exp(g^*t) + \varsigma\eta\alpha\lambda\gamma \frac{\exp(-rt)}{(r - g^*)(r + \eta)} \leq 0$$

for all t. Now let us look at this condition when $t = 0$, which is equivalent to

$$\zeta\gamma\alpha \leq (r + \eta).$$

Therefore, if

$$\alpha > \alpha^{**} \equiv \frac{r + \eta}{\zeta\gamma},$$

the candidate solution is not optimal and we conclude that the policy that maximizes the discounted value of income (or utility) will involve directing some research toward substitute varieties, proving the claim in the text.

General Model

I now present a more general environment building on Aghion and Howitt (1992), Grossman and Helpman (1991), and the textbook endogenous technological change model presented in Acemoglu (2009). This model generalizes the baseline environment presented in the text and shows that several assumptions used in the text are unnecessary for the results. The environment is again in continuous time and aggregate output is produced by combining a continuum of intermediates. As in the text, each intermediate v comes in a countably infinite number of varieties, denoted by $j_1(v), j_2(v), \ldots,$ again one of those being active at any point in time. Let us focus on the active variety $j(v)$, and the next-in-line (substitute) variety $j'(v)$. Qualities are again denoted by $q_j(v, t) > 0$ and $q_{j'}(v, t) > 0$, and evolve endogenously. The production function for aggregate output at time t is

$$Y(t) = \frac{1}{1-\beta}\left(\int_0^1 q_j(v,t)x_j(v,t\,|\,q)^{1-\beta}\,dv\right)L^{\beta},$$

where $x_j(v, t\,|\,q)$ is the quantity of the active variety of intermediate v (of quality $q_j(v,t)$, so that $x_j(v,t\,|\,q)$ is short for $x_j(v,t\,|\,q_j(v,t))$) purchased at time t and L is total labor, supplied inelastically. This production function exhibits constant returns to scale to intermediates and labor. As in the main text, there is a quality ladder for each intermediate (of active and substitute varieties), equidistant rung. Thus each innovation takes the machine quality up by one rung on this ladder, so that following each improvement quality increases by a proportional amount $1 + \lambda > 1$. Also as in the main text, we have that if $q_{j'}(v,t) = \gamma q_j(v,t)$ and $q_j(v,t)$ increases to $q_j(v,t+) = (1 + \lambda)q_j(v,t)$, then the quality of the substitute variety also increases to $q_{j'}(v,t+) = \gamma(1 + \lambda)q_j(v,t)$. Similarly, we also continue to assume that the quality of the next-in-line substitute variety can be no less than $\gamma q_j(v,t)$.

New machine vintages are again invented by R&D. The R&D effort can be directed to any of the different intermediates and to active or substitute varieties. Here, let us suppose that R&D uses the final good as input (rather than scientists). In particular, if $Z(v,t)$ units of the final good are spent for research to create an intermediate of quality $q(v,t)$, then it generates a flow rate

$$\frac{\eta Z(v,t)}{q(v,t)}$$

of innovation. This specification implies that one unit of R&D spending is proportionately less effective when applied to a more advanced intermediate, which ensures that research will be directed to lower quality as well as higher quality intermediates.

Suppose also that there is free entry into research, thus any firm or individual can undertake research on any of the varieties of any of the intermediates.

Once a particular machine of quality $q(v,t)$ has been invented, any quantity of this machine can be produced at marginal cost $\psi q(v,t)$. The assumption that the marginal cost is proportional to the quality of the machine is natural, because producing higher-quality machines should be more expensive. I normalize $\psi \equiv 1 - \beta$ without any loss of generality.

Let us also suppose that the consumer side of this economy admits a representative household with the standard constant relative risk aversion (CRRA) preferences, in particular, at time $t = 0$ maximizing

$$\int_0^\infty \exp(-rt)\,\frac{C(t)^{1-\theta} - 1}{1 - \theta}\,dt.$$

Finally, the resource constraint of the economy is

$$X(t) + Z(t) + C(t) \leq Y(t),$$

where $X(t) \equiv \int_0^1 x_j(v,t\,|\,q)dv$ is the total amount of the final good spent on the production of the intermediate. Thus, this constraint requires that the amounts devoted to intermediate production, R&D, and consumption should not exceed total output.

Household maximization implies the familiar Euler equation,

$$\frac{\dot{C}(t)}{C(t)} = \frac{1}{\theta}(r(t) - \rho). \tag{A18}$$

A firm that has access to the highest quality active variety of intermediate will be the monopoly supplier of intermediate and will make profits, denoted by $\pi(v, t\,|\,q)$ for intermediate $v \in [0,1]$ of quality q. The value of this firm is given by a Hamilton-Jacobi-Bellman equation similar to equation (5), in particular, taking into account possible changes in the value functions over time and denoting the endogenously determined interest rate at time t by $r(t)$, this is

$$r(t)V_j(v,t\,|\,q) - \dot{V}_j(v,t\,|\,q) = \pi(v,t\,|\,q) - (\alpha + z(v,t\,|\,q))V_j(v,t\,|\,q),$$

which again takes into account the destruction of this value due to both further innovations (at the flow rate $z(v, t\,|\,q)$) and switches away from the active variety (at the flow rate α).

Factor markets are assumed to be competitive.

Let us start with the aggregate production function for the final good producers. Straightforward maximization gives the demand for each intermediate as follows:

$$x(v,t\,|\,q) = \left(\frac{q(v,t)}{p^x(v,t\,|\,q)}\right)^{1/\beta} L \text{ for all } v \in [0,1] \text{ and } t,$$

where $p^x(v,t|q)$ refers to the price of machine of variety v of quality q at time t. This is an isoelastic demand curve and the monopoly producers of the highest quality intermediate (of the active variety) will wish to set the monopoly price that is a constant markup over marginal cost. However, we also need to ensure that this monopoly price is not so high as to make the next best vintage profitable. The following assumption is enough to ensure this:

(A19) $$\lambda \geq \left(\frac{1}{1-\beta}\right)^{(1-\beta/\beta)} - 1.$$

This then guarantees that the profit-maximizing price is

(A20) $$p^x(v,t\,|\,q) = q(v,t),$$

and thus the equilibrium involves

(A21) $$x(v,t\,|\,q) = L.$$

Consequently, the flow profits of the firm selling intermediate of quality $q(v,t)$ is

(A22) $$\pi(v,t\,|\,q) = \beta q(v,t)L.$$

Using this expression, total output in the economy is

(A23) $$Y(t) = \frac{1}{1-\beta}Q(t)L,$$

where, with the same convention that j refers to the active variety,

(A24) $$Q(t) \equiv \int_0^1 q_j(v,t)dv$$

is the average total quality of machines. This analysis thus shows that the relevant expressions here, in particular, the form of the derived production function, equation (A.53), and the returns from having access to the highest quality, equation (A.54), are very similar to those in the text, but are derived from the aggregation of profit-maximizing micro behavior. It is also important that, as in the text, the $q(v,t)$'s are stochastic, but their average $Q(t)$ is deterministic with a law of large numbers type of reasoning (since the realizations of the quality of different machine lines are independent). Total spending on intermediates can also be computed as

(A25) $$X(t) = (1-\beta)Q(t)L.$$

Finally, the equilibrium wage rate, given by the marginal product of labor, is

(A26) $$\omega(t) = \frac{\beta}{1-\beta}\,Q(t).$$

The free-entry condition for active varieties, written in complementary slackness form, is

(A27) $$\eta V_j(v,t\,|\,q) \leq q \text{ and } \eta V_j(v,t\,|\,q) = q \text{ if } Z(v,t) > 0.$$

Next, we can also write the value function for substitute varieties. To do this, let us again focus on equilibrium in which there is zero R&D toward substitute varieties. In that case, with the reasoning similar to that in the main text, we have that the value of a substitute variety of quality q' is given by

$$r(t)V_{j'}(v,t\,|\,q') - \dot{V}_{j'}(v,t\,|\,q') = \alpha(V_j(v,t\,|\,q') - V_{j'}(v,t\,|\,q')) - z^* V_{j'}(v,t\,|\,q'),$$

where z^* is the equilibrium rate of innovation in active varieties. The relevant free entry condition in this case can then be written as

$$\eta V_{j'}(v,t\,|\,q') \leq q'.$$

First, note that in the candidate equilibrium, both the value functions of active and substitute varieties will be independent of time and also of v, and can be written as $V(q)$ and $\tilde{V}(q')$. Then, an identical analysis to that in the text implies that for all $\alpha > 0$, the free entry condition for the substitute varieties of all intermediates will be slack. In this case, we have,

$$V(q) = \frac{\lambda\beta q}{r + \alpha + z}.$$

Free entry into research for active varieties requires

$$\eta V(q) \leq q,$$

or

$$\frac{\eta\beta}{r + \alpha + z} \leq 1.$$

Free entry into research for non-leading vintage can be expressed as

$$\tilde{V}(q) \leq \eta q$$

$$\frac{\alpha}{r + \alpha + z} V(q) \leq \eta q,$$

which will always be satisfied as strict inequality whenever the free entry condition for active varieties is satisfied.

With an argument similar to that in the text, the growth rate of average quality of technology is

$$\frac{\dot{Q}(t)}{Q(t)} = \lambda z^* + \alpha(\gamma - 1).$$

Moreover, in this allocation, the consumer Euler equation implies

$$r = \rho + \theta g,$$

where g is the growth rate of output and consumption.

The free entry condition then can be written as

$$\frac{\eta\lambda}{\rho + \theta(\lambda - 1)z + \theta\alpha(\gamma - 1) + z + \alpha} = 1.$$

Thus:

$$z^* = \frac{\eta\lambda - \rho - \theta\alpha(\gamma - 1) - \alpha}{1 + \theta(\lambda - 1)}.$$

$$g^* = \frac{\eta\lambda - \rho - \theta\alpha(\gamma - 1) - \alpha}{\theta + \lambda^{-1}} - \alpha(1 - \gamma).$$

Then, the growth rate of output will be positive; that is, $g^* > 0$, if

$$\eta\lambda - \rho + \theta\alpha(1 - \gamma) - \alpha > \theta\alpha(1 - \gamma) + \lambda^{-1}\alpha(1 - \gamma).$$

The rest of the analysis can be carried out in a manner similar to that in the text.

References

Acemoglu, Daron. 2009. *Introduction to Modern Economic Growth.* Princeton, NJ: Princeton University Press.

Acemoglu, Daron, Kostas Bimpikis, and Asuman Ozdaglar. 2008. "Experimentation, Patents, and Innovation." NBER Working Paper no. 14408. Cambridge, MA: National Bureau of Economic Research, October.

Adner, Ron, and Daniel Levinthal. 2001. "Demand Heterogeneity and Technological Evolution: Implications for Product and Process Innovation." *Management Science* 47:611–28.

Aghion, Philippe, Mathias Dewatripont, and Jeremy Stein. 2007. "Academic Freedom, Private Sector Focus and the Process of Innovation." Harvard University. Working Paper.

Aghion, Philippe, and Peter Howitt. 1992. "A Model of Growth Through Creative Destruction." *Econometrica* 110:323–51.

Aghion, Philippe, and Jean Tirole. 1994. "On the Management of Innovation." *Quarterly Journal of Economics* 109:1185–209.

Arrow, Kenneth J. 1962. "The Economic Implications of Learning by Doing." *Review of Economic Studies* 29:155–73.

Arthur, W. Brian. 1989. "Competing Technologies, Increasing Returns and Lock-in by Historical Events." *Economic Journal* 99:116–31.

Bramoullé, Yann, and Gilles Saint-Paul. 2008. "Research Cycles." Toulouse School of Economics. Working Paper.

Brock, William, and Steven Durlauf. 1999. "A Formal Model of Theory Choice in Science." *Economic Theory* 14:113–30.

Bronfenbrenner, Martin. 1966. "Trends, Cycles, and Fads in Economic Writing." *American Economic Review* 56:538–52.

Christensen, Clayton M. 1997. *The Innovator's Dilemma: When New Technologies Cause Great Firms to Fail.* Boston: Harvard Business School Press.

Cozzi, Guido. 1997. "Exploring Growth Trajectories." *Journal of Economic Growth* 2:385–98.
Crosby, Alfred. 2006. *The Children of the Sun: A History of Humanity's Unappeasable Appetite for Energy.* New York: W. W. Norton.
Dalle, Jean-Michel. 1997. "Heterogeneity Vs. Externalities and Technological Competition: A Tale of Possible Technological Landscapes." *Journal of Evolution Economics* 7:395–413.
Dosi, Giovanni. 1984. *Technological Change and Industrial Transformation.* London: Macmillan.
Dosi, Giovanni, and Luigi Marengo. 1993. "Some Elements of an Evolutionary Theory of Organizational Competence." In *Evolutionary Concepts in Contemporary Economics,* edited by R. W. England, 157–78. Ann Arbor: University of Michigan Press.
Grossman, Gene, and Elhanan Helpman. 1991. *Innovation and Growth in the Global Economy.* Cambridge, MA: MIT Press.
Hong, Lu, and Scott E. Page. 2001. "Problem Solving by Heterogeneous Agents." *Journal of Economic Theory* 97:123–63.
———. 2004. "Groups of Diverse Problem Solvers Can Outperform Groups of High Ability Problem Solvers." *Proceedings of the National Academy of Sciences* 101:16385–9.
International Energy Agency. 2008. *Key World Energy Statistics.* Available at: http://www.iea.org/textbase/nppdf/free/2008/key_stats_2008.pdf.
Jones, Benjamin F. 2009. "The Burden of Knowledge and the Death of the Renaissance Man: Is Innovation Getting Harder?" *Review of Economic Studies* 76 (1): 283–317.
Katz, Michael L., and Carl Shapiro. 1986. "Technology Adoption in the Presence of Network Externalities." *Journal of Political Economy* 94:822–41.
LiCalzi, Marco, and Oktay Surucu. 2011. "The Power of Diversity over Large Solution Spaces." University of Venice, Department of Applied Mathematics. Working Paper.
Malerba, Franco, Richard Nelson, Luigi Orsenigo, and Sidney Winter. 2007. "Demand, Innovation, and the Dynamics of Market Structure: The Role of Experimental Users and Diverse Preferences." *Journal of Evolutionary Economics* 17: 371–99.
Murray, Fiona, Philippe Aghion, Mathias Dewatripont, Julian Kolev, and Scott Stern. 2008. "Of Mice and Academics: Examining the Effect of Openness on Innovation." MIT Sloan School of Management. Working Paper.
Nelson, Richard, and Sidney Winter. 1982. *An Evolutionary Theory of Economic Change.* Cambridge, MA: Belknap.
Norris, J. R. 1998. *Markov Chains.* Cambridge: Cambridge University Press.
Page, Scott. 2007. *The Difference: How the Power of Diversity Creates Better Groups, Firms, Schools, and Societies.* Princeton, NJ: Princeton University Press.
Roberts, Paul. 2005. *End of Oil: On the Edge of a Perilous New World.* New York: First Mariner Books.
Romer, Paul M. 1990. "Endogenous Technological Change." *Journal of Political Economy* 98:S71–S102.
Scotchmer, Suzanne. 2005. *Innovations and Incentives.* Cambridge, MA: MIT Press.
Shy, Oz. 1996. "Technology Revolutions in the Presence of Network Externalities." *International Journal of Industrial Organization* 14:785–800.
Stephan, Paula F., and Sharon G. Levin. 1992. *Striking the Mother Lode in Science: The Importance of Age, Place, and Time.* New York: Oxford University Press.
Sunstein, Cass. 2001. "On Academic Fads and Fashions." *Michigan Law Review* 99:1251–64.

Comment Samuel Kortum

Why don't we have better electric cars by now? Daron Acemoglu formalizes an argument that there are insufficient incentives to innovate on alternative technologies. Since a mass-market for electric cars has not yet arrived, an innovation today won't generate large current profit. Nor will it generate much future profit since, by the time the market gets big, another better innovation will likely have come along.

Yet, the innovation in electric car technology that might have been made today could have a high social value. It might have become a valuable technological step on the path to future improvements. The problem is that too few steps are taken early enough in this process of getting to a better electric car. Daron's chapter turns this interesting verbal story into a mathematical model.

I want to deal with two issues in this discussion. The first is about the economic forces at work in Daron's model. I try to highlight them by introducing a simpler formulation. The second is about the economic forces missing from Daron's model. Here, I simply speculate about how they could be brought into future work on this topic.

A Simplified Model

The model in Daron's chapter builds on Grossman and Helpman (1991) in which innovations form the rungs of a "quality ladder" for each intermediate good. The arrival of a new innovation is a step up the quality ladder, leading to the depreciation of the private value, but not the social value, of the innovation left below.

Daron adds a new dimension to the model. For each of the unit continuum of intermediate goods there is also an alternative technology, not yet used in production. With a hazard rate α, this alternative becomes the new mainstream technology. When it comes into play, the innovations forming the previous mainstream quality ladder become useless. This transition implies both a private and social depreciation of the advances embodied in the old quality ladder.

Churning over quality ladders means that some level of innovation is required just to prevent technological regress. While technology improves along a given quality ladder, at some point it all becomes obsolete as a whole new approach is pursued. The idea of alternative technological trajectories captures an important aspect of reality. Not all technology builds on what came before it. I suspect this idea will itself be something that future economic models build on.

Samuel Kortum is professor of economics at the University of Chicago and a research associate of the National Bureau of Economic Research.

I thank Unnikrishnan Pillai for helpful comments.

In my stripped-down version of Daron's model, I consider a fixed arrival rate of innovations η and no aggregate technological progress. The steady-state equilibrium will feature a fixed fraction ω of research effort aimed at innovations in alternative technology and $1 - \omega$ devoted to innovations in the mainstream technology currently being used.

I follow Daron's formulation as closely as possible, but in one important respect I stick closer to Grossman and Helpman. In particular, I replace equation (3) in Daron's model with a Cobb-Douglas production function over the continuum of intermediates, so that the same amount is spent on each intermediate. Taking aggregate spending to be the numeraire, spending on each intermediate can be set to 1.

Each innovation improves the quality of an intermediate by the factor $1 + \lambda > 1$. While that innovation is in use, Bertrand competition leads to a profit flow to the innovator of $\pi = \lambda/(1 + \lambda)$, independent of the rung on the quality ladder. This profit flow comes to an end with the arrival of the next innovation on the quality ladder or with the arrival of the alternative quality ladder. The overall private obsolescence rate is therefore $\alpha + (1 - \omega)\eta$. With a discount rate r, the Bellman equation for the value V of an innovation currently in use is:

$$rV = \pi - [\alpha + (1 - \omega)\eta]V.$$

Note that this equation is nearly identical to equation (5) in the chapter, except that here we allow $\omega > 0$.

Suppose it is easier to innovate in the alternative technology. The innovation rate in alternative technologies is not $\omega\eta$ but rather $\omega\zeta\eta$, with $\zeta > 1$. Although this assumption is ad hoc, the idea is that there are more untapped opportunities in the alternative technology. The Bellman equation for the value V^A of an innovation on the alternative technology is thus:

$$rV^A = \alpha(V - V^A) - \varsigma\omega\eta V^A.$$

While there are no current returns, there is a chance of a capital gain $V - V^A$ when the alternative technology becomes mainstream. The assumption of $\zeta > 1$ gives a possible rationale for innovating in the alternative technology, since innovating there is easier. (With $\zeta \leq 1$ it would always be more profitable to innovate in the technology that is currently in use.)

Is it possible to have diversity in research ($0 < \omega < 1$), in this market equilibrium, with some innovation in the current technology and some in the alternative technology? We need ζ large enough to overcome the fact that an innovation in the alternative technology only generates revenue once it becomes the mainstream technology. Assuming $(\varsigma - 1)\alpha > r$ (i.e., for α or ζ large enough) we can solve for the allocation of research:

$$\omega = \frac{(\varsigma - 1)\alpha - r}{\varsigma\eta},$$

that is consistent with diversity; that is, $V = \varsigma V^A$.

The fraction of research devoted to alternative technologies is increasing in ζ and α while decreasing in r and η. There is an economic force lending stability to this equilibrium with diversity in research. All else equal, a higher ω would lead to more innovation on the alternative quality ladder, raising the obsolescence rate for any given innovation, and hence lowering the value of an innovation there. This equilibrating force is absent from the social planner's problem since the flow of social value, unlike the private value, is not destroyed by the arrival of the next innovation.

What are the welfare implications of this equilibrium? The flow of social surplus from an innovation in the mainstream technology is[1]

$$\pi^S = \ln(1 + \lambda) > \frac{\lambda}{1 - \lambda} = \pi.$$

Thus, the social value V^S of such an innovation solves:

$$rV^S = \pi^S - \alpha V^S.$$

Notice that the social value remains after the innovation is surpassed, but not after the quality ladder has become obsolete. The social value of an innovation in the alternative technology V^{AS} solves:

$$rV^{AS} = \alpha(V^S - V^{AS}).$$

For parameters that yield $\omega > 0$ in the market equilibrium, it is easy to show that

$$\varsigma V^{AS} > V^S.$$

The social planner would like to aim all research at the alternative technology, thus taking advantage of $\zeta > 1$ as long as α is large enough and r is small enough.

The social planner exploits the fact that it is easier to innovate in the alternative technology. Why not always innovate on the next big thing so that we are ready when it becomes mainstream? The planner therefore directs all researchers to the alternative technology. In the market equilibrium, on the other hand, research is split between alternative and mainstream technology. The bottom line of this simplified model, while not identical, is quite complementary to Daron's chapter. The market provides insufficient incentives for innovation in the alternative technology. The social planner would like to get a technologically advanced electric car sooner. On the other hand, the results on diversity are reversed from those in the chapter unless we redefine diversity to mean innovating on an alternative technology.

1. Notice that the demand curve for a single good is $q = 1/p$. Thus, the flow of social value of an innovation that lowers costs from c to $c' = c/(1 + \lambda)$ is

$$\pi^S = \int_{c'}^{c} (1/p)dp = \ln(c/c') = \ln(1 + \lambda).$$

What Is Missing?

There are several new economic forces at work in Daron's model. One is that innovations do not always improve on what came before. Occasionally we must scrap a whole line of technological advances in order to try something completely different. Another is that the divergence between the private and social returns to an innovation tilt the market away from innovation in a technology that is not currently in use. Finally, and related to the second, more innovation in a particular technology is itself a disincentive for research in that technology, since it leads to a shorter window in which to reap private returns. While the economic logic of this last effect is impeccable, one may question whether it captures an important force limiting actual research in alternative technologies.

I would conjecture, quite the opposite, that intensive research in alternative technology would tend to attract more researchers, at least up to a point. The reason is that these researchers would likely feed off each other through spillovers of knowledge and through advances in complementary technologies. For example, the reason we don't have a good electric car is likely because the battery technology is not very good. And, to make progress there you need a large talented group of researchers working on battery technology. These researchers would learn from each other, the innovations would come, and they would all make enough money to continue. In other words, the problem is not too much competition but lack of a critical mass.

Notice this logic is opposite to Daron's model. His model implies that with many people working on battery innovations, each innovation will make very little money since it will soon be surpassed by a better innovation from a competitor. But, maybe the more important force is the learning generated by that competition, with the net result that researchers are attracted by this competition. Of course, this line of argument is quite speculative. It is just another verbal story waiting to be properly formalized.

Reference

Grossman, Gene, and Elhanan Helpman. 1991. *Innovation and Growth in the Global Economy.* Cambridge, MA: MIT Press.

7

Competition and Innovation
Did Arrow Hit the Bull's Eye?

Carl Shapiro

> The only ground for arguing that monopoly may create superior incentives to invent is that appropriability may be greater under monopoly than under competition. Whatever differences may exist in this direction must, of course, still be offset against the monopolist's disincentive created by his preinvention monopoly profits.
> —Arrow (1962, 622)

> As soon as we go into details and inquire into the individual items in which progress was most conspicuous, the trail leads not to the doors of those firms that work under conditions of comparatively free competition but precisely to the doors of the large concerns . . . and a shocking suspicion dawns upon us that big business may have had more to do with creating that standard of life than with keeping it down.
> —Schumpeter (1942, 82)

7.1 Introduction

The fiftieth anniversary of the publication of NBER *Rate and Direction of Inventive Activity* volume is an opportune time to revisit what is arguably the most important question in the field of industrial organization: what organization of business activity best promotes innovation?

Carl Shapiro is the Transamerica Professor of Business Strategy at the Haas School of Business and professor of economics at the University of California at Berkeley.

The views presented here should not be attributed to any other person or organization. The author thanks Jonathan Baker, Joe Farrell, Richard Gilbert, Ken Heyer, Michael Whinston, Tor Winston, and participants in the NBER 50th Anniversary Conference on the Rate and Direction of Inventive Activity for very helpful conversations and comments on earlier drafts and presentations of this chapter.

Needless to say, this question has received intense attention by economists and other social scientists, especially since the middle of last century, when the critical importance of innovation to economic growth became more widely appreciated.[1] Hence, I wade into this topic with considerable trepidation. So, let me state at the outset that this essay is intended to be somewhat speculative: an audacious attempt to distill lessons from the huge and complex literature on competition and innovation that are simple and robust enough to inform competition policy.

My ambitious task is made somewhat more manageable because I confine myself to one specific question: how can *competition policy* best promote innovation? I do not attempt to address broader questions regarding innovation policy or competitive strategy. Within the realm of competition policy, I focus on the assessment of proposed mergers. Even in this more limited area, I am not the first to attempt to distill robust principles suitable for competition policy. To the contrary, I follow closely in the footsteps of Baker (2007), Gilbert (2006), and Katz and Shelanski (2005 and 2007), and borrow unabashedly from their work. Baker (2007) is closest in spirit to this chapter: he identifies four principles relating competition and innovation and argues strongly that antitrust fosters innovation.[2]

Before putting forward my central thesis—hypothesis, really—let us review the bidding.

Arrow (1962) famously argued that a monopolist's incentive to innovate is less than that of a competitive firm, due to the monopolist's financial interest in the status quo. This fundamental idea comports with common sense: a firm earning substantial profits has an interest in protecting the status quo and is thus less likely to be the instigator of disruptive new technology. In Arrow's words: "The preinvention monopoly power acts as a strong disincentive to further innovation."[3] Consciously oversimplifying, the Arrow position can be summarized by this principle:

Arrow: "Product market competition spurs innovation."

1. I make no attempt to survey the huge theoretical and empirical literature that explores the relationship between competition and innovation, and I apologize in advance to those whose important contributions are not explicitly cited here. I rely heavily on Gilbert (2006) and Cohen (2010). See also Sutton (1998) and (2007). Aghion and Griffith (2005) and Aghion and Howitt (2009) discuss the relationship between competition and economic growth.

2. Baker's four principles are: (1) competition among firms seeking to develop the same new product or process encourages innovation; (2) competition among firms producing an existing product encourages them to find ways to lower their costs or improve their products; (3) firms that expect to face more product market competition after innovating have less incentive to invest in R&D; and; (4) a firm will have an extra incentive to innovate if doing so discourages its rivals from investing in R&D.

3. Arrow (1962, 620). Put differently, the secure monopolist's incentive to achieve a process innovation is less than that of a competitive firm because the monopolist with lower costs will merely replace itself, while the competitive firm will (by assumption) take over the market, in which it previously earned no economic profits. Tirole (1997, 392), dubbed this the "replacement effect."

Schumpeter (1942), by contrast, even more famously emphasized that a great deal of innovation is attributable to large firms operating in oligopolistic markets, not to small firms operating in atomistic markets.

> The firm of the type that is compatible with perfect competition is in many cases inferior in internal, especially technological, efficiency. (Schumpeter 1942, 106)

While he was no fan of entrenched monopolies, Schumpeter argued that larger firms have greater incentives and ability to invest in R&D.[4] He dismissed perfect competition as the ideal market structure, stressing the importance of *temporary* market power as a reward to successful innovation:

> A system—any system, economic or other—that at *every* point in time fully utilizes its possibilities to the best advantage may yet in the long run be inferior to a system that does so at *no* given point in time, because the latter's failure to do so may be a condition for the level or speed of long-run performance. (Schumpeter 1942, 83)

Consciously oversimplifying, the Schumpeter position can be summarized in this principle:

> Schumpeter: "The prospect of market power and large scale spurs innovation."

Let the battle be joined. Arrow versus Schumpeter, in the super-heavyweight class.

Wait a minute. Are the Arrow and Schumpeter positions really incompatible? This chapter advances the claim that they are *not,* at least so far as competition policy is concerned.

What do we actually *need* to know about the relationship between competition and innovation for the purposes of competition policy? For merger enforcement, we need a framework to evaluate the effects of a proposed merger on innovation. In practice, the relevant mergers are those between two of a small number of firms who are best placed to innovate in a given area. For other areas of antitrust enforcement, we typically seek to evaluate the impact on innovation of a specific business practice, such as the package licensing of a group of patents or the decision to keep an interface proprietary rather than open. For these purposes, I argue here that we do not need a universal theory of the relationship between competition and innovation. I also argue that the Arrow and Schumpeter perspectives are fully compatible and mutually reinforcing.

Consciously oversimplifying yet again, I offer three guiding principles. These are stand-alone, ceteris paribus principles, but they work in con-

4. Schumpeter also argued that large established firms operating in oligopolistic markets are better able to finance R&D than are small firms operating in atomistic markets. In the light of today's highly developed capital markets, including venture capital markets, this argument has much less salience today.

cert, weaving together and integrating the Arrow and the Schumpeter perspectives:

> Contestability: "The prospect of gaining or protecting profitable sales by providing greater value to customers spurs innovation."

The Contestability principle focuses on the extent to which a firm can gain profitable sales from its rivals by offering greater value to customers. Sales are contestable in the relevant sense if profitable sales shift toward the successful innovator. This in turn depends on the nature of ex post product market competition. If market shares are sticky, for example, because consumers have strong brand preferences or high switching costs, relatively few sales are contestable and innovation incentives will be muted.

The Arrow effect fits well with the Contestability principle: for a given level of ex post sales, a firm with few ex ante sales has more to gain from innovation. Put differently, a firm that will make substantial sales even if it does not innovate (such as Arrow's incumbent monopolist, which faces no threat) has muted incentives to innovate.

The Schumpeter effect also fits well with the Contestability principle: companies making major innovations often are rewarded with large market shares, leading to high ex post market concentration. Conversely, a small firm that will not be able to grow much, even if it successfully innovates, has lower incentives to invest in R&D than a larger firm.

> Appropriability: "Increased appropriability spurs innovation."

The Appropriability principle operates at the level of the firm. Greater appropriability by one firm can reduce appropriability by other firms and thus retard *their* innovation.

The Appropriability principle focuses on the extent to which a successful innovator can capture the social benefits resulting from its innovation.[5] In practice, appropriability depends heavily on the extent to which a firm can protect the competitive advantage associated with its innovation. If imitation is rapid, so a firm that successfully innovates is unable to differentiate its products or achieve a significant cost advantage over its rivals, ex post profit margins will be low and innovation incentives will be muted. With rapid and effective imitation, contestability can be of limited relevance, since an innovating firm will not be able to offer superior value to customers.

The Schumpeter effect fits well with the Appropriability principle: one cannot expect substantial innovation (from commercial firms, at least) if rapid imitation causes ex post competition to be so severe that even a successful innovator earns little profit.

5. The social contribution of a firm that develops a new product before others do so independently only reflects the value of the earlier development, not the total benefits associated with the new product. See Shapiro (2007) for a more extensive discussion of appropriability in the context of multiple independent invention.

> Synergies: "Combining complementary assets enhances innovation capabilities and thus spurs innovation."

The Synergies principle emphasizes that firms typically cannot innovate in isolation. The quest for synergies is especially important in industries where value is created by systems that incorporate multiple components, as in the information and communications technology sector. The Synergies principle is directly relevant for competition policy since procompetitive mergers and business practices allow for the more efficient combination of complementary assets.

The Contestability and Appropriability principles relate to the *incentive* to innovate. The Synergies principle relates to the *ability* to innovate. *None* of these principles relates directly to product market concentration.

This chapter advances the hypothesis that the Contestability principle, the Appropriability principle, and the Synergies principle are sufficiently robust to guide competition policy. I sketch out the argument that these three principles provide the conceptual and empirical basis for a rebuttable presumption that a merger between two of a very few firms who are important, direct R&D rivals in a given area is likely to retard innovation in the area. Furthermore, I suggest, somewhat tentatively, that we have a pretty good understanding of the circumstances under which that presumption is rebutted and innovation is furthered by allowing two important, direct R&D rivals to merge. I also suggest that these three principles can usefully guide competition policy in other areas.

Perhaps you already are convinced that innovation is generally spurred by competition as reflected by the intuitive notions of contestability, appropriability, and synergies. If so, you may want to stop right here, or skip to the later discussion where I apply these principles to competition policy. But as someone actively involved in antitrust enforcement, it appears to me that a rather different, and misleading, "complexity proposition" has taken root and threatens to become the conventional wisdom, namely:

> Complexity 1: "The relationship between competition and innovation is so complex and delicate that there should be no presumption that the elimination of product market or R&D rivals will diminish innovation."

A version of this complexity proposition specific to mergers has also gained some currency:

> Complexity 2: "The relationship between competition and innovation is so complex and delicate that there should be no presumption that a merger between two of a very few firms conducting R&D in a given area is likely to diminish innovation."

These propositions echo various more general statements from the literature on competition and innovation, where it has become de rigueur to emphasize that "competition" has ambiguous effects on innovation. For example, Gilbert (2006) states that the incentives to innovate

> [D]epend upon many factors, including: the characteristics of the invention, the strength of intellectual property protection, the extent of competition before and after innovation, barriers to entry in production and R&D, and the dynamics of R&D. *Economic theory does not offer a prediction about the effects of competition on innovation that is robust to all of these different market and technological conditions.* Instead, there are many predictions and one reason why empirical studies have not generated clear conclusions about the relationship between competition and innovation is a failure of many of these studies to account for different market and technological conditions. (Gilbert 2006, 162, emphasis supplied)

In a similar vein, Motta (2004) writes:

> Both theoretical and empirical research on the link between market structure and innovation is not conclusive, even though a "middle ground" environment, where there exists some competition but also high enough market power coming from the innovative activities, might be the most conducive to R&D output. (Motta 2004, 54)

Davis (2003) is an example of the type of message that is reaching antitrust practitioners. He states that there is a "consensus or near-consensus" that "the relation of market structure to market conduct and performance in innovation is far more problematic than in the case of price competition" (695–96).

Certainly, the overall cross-sectional relationship between firm size or market structure and innovation is complex. Just think of all the variations we often see in the real world.

On the Arrow side of the ledger, that is, in praise of innovation by firms without a strong incumbency position, we have the following:

- Disruptive entrants are a potent force. They can shake up a market, bringing enormous value to customers. The mere threat of disruptive entry can stir inefficient incumbent firms from their slumber.
- Firms without a significant incumbency position may have a freer hand to innovate because they are not tied to an installed base of customers. Christenson (1997) provides an insightful and influential study along these lines.
- Firms with strong incumbency positions often resist innovations that threaten those positions. Such resistance can even take the form of exclusionary conduct that violates the antitrust laws.
- Start-up firms often play the role of disruptive entrants, introducing new products or processes.
- Firms with suitable capabilities entering from adjacent markets often play the role of disruptive entrants.

On the Schumpeterian side of the ledger, that is, in praise of innovation by large firms with an established incumbency position, we have the following:

- Some highly concentrated markets exhibit rapid innovation, and some atomistic markets seem rather stuck in their ways. One suspects that these differences are not simply the result of differences in technology opportunity.
- Larger firms often are closer to the cutting edge in technology than their smaller rivals.
- Larger firms can have greater incentives to achieve process improvements because they can apply these improvements to a larger volume of production. In contrast, a smaller firm that cannot grow significantly, even if it successfully innovates, and cannot license out its innovation, has a lower incentive to lower its costs.
- Large firms often acquire innovative start-up firms, or enter into other arrangements such as licenses or joint ventures with them, thereby accelerating the adoption and diffusion of those firms' inventions.

On top of all this, we know that appropriability matters a great deal for innovation incentives.

So, let me be clear: nothing in this chapter should be read to question the proposition that the overall relationship between product market structure and innovation is complex. The relationship between firm size and innovation is also complex. General theoretical or empirical findings about these relationships remain elusive, in part because a firm's innovation incentives depend upon the *difference* between its pre-innovation and post-innovation size. This difference depends upon the ex ante market structure and reflects the ex post market structure.

But we are not totally at sea. Yes, the world is complex, but my aim here is to suggest some general lessons for competition policy when evaluating innovation effects. Even stating these lessons requires that we be quite careful in defining our terms. Implementing them requires that one be willing and able to distinguish different settings based on a few key, observable characteristics. This approach is similar to the one advocated by Gilbert (2006), who writes:

> The many different predictions of theoretical models of R&D lead some to conclude that there is no coherent theory of the relationship between market structure and investment in innovation. That is not quite correct. The models have clear predictions, although they differ in important ways that can be related to market and technological characteristics. It is not that we don't have a model of market structure and R&D, but rather that we have many models and it is important to know which model is appropriate for each market context. (Gilbert 2006, 164–65)

The argument developed here is that competition policy can be usefully and substantially guided by the Contestability principle, the Appropriability principle, and the Synergies principle. Let me illustrate how that could work, by way of a real-world example.

In 2003 and 2004, the Federal Trade Commission (FTC) reviewed the merger between Genzyme and Novazyme, the only two firms pursuing enzyme replacement therapies to treat Pompe disease, a rare genetic disorder. The FTC Chairman Timothy Muris, explaining the Commission's decision not to challenge the merger, explicitly relied on the proposition that "economic theory and empirical investigations have not established a general causal relationship between innovation and competition."[6] This statement, taken alone, is unobjectionable. As noted before and discussed more later, much of the theoretical and empirical literature on the relationship between market structure and innovation emphasizes complexity while seeking to explain how different factors affect that relationship, recognizing that both market structure and innovation are endogenous. Nonetheless, I argue here that we *do* know enough to warrant a presumption that a merger between the only two firms pursing a specific line of research to serve a particular need is likely to diminish innovation rivalry, absent a showing that the merger will increase appropriability or generate R&D synergies that will enhance the incentive or ability of the merged firm to innovate.

Applying the Contestability, Appropriability, and Synergies principles might well have led to a different outcome in the Genzyme/Novazyme merger. Since these two companies were the only ones with research programs for enzyme replacement therapies to treat Pompe disease, the merger eliminated R&D rivalry—and thus reduced contestability—in that area. Successful innovation in this case clearly offered the prospect of gaining significant, profitable sales: the first innovator would establish a new market, and the second innovator could capture profitable sales from the first if its treatment was sufficiently superior. Invoking a presumption that a merger between the only two R&D rivals in a given area reduces competition, the merger would have been challenged absent a showing that it substantially increased appropriability or led to significant innovation synergies to offset the reduced inventive to innovate resulting from the merger. See section 7.5.2 for an extended discussion of this case.

The Genzyme and Novazyme merger is just one (prominent) example of how the "complexity perspective" on competition and innovation has taken root. As Katz and Shelanski (2007) note, some observers "argue that innovation provides a rationale for a more permissive merger policy. One argument advanced in support of this line of reasoning appeals to what is

6. Statement of Chairman Timothy J. Muris in the Matter of Genzyme Corporation/Novazyme Pharmaceuticals Inc., January 13, 2004, at http://www.ftc.gov/opa/2004/01/genzyme.shtm, citing FTC (1996) vol. I, chapter 7, at 16.

known as 'Schumpeterian competition,' in which temporary monopolists successively displace one another through innovation."[7] While not going as far as Chairman Muris, Katz and Shelanski are sufficiently swayed by these arguments to write: "In brief, we recommend that merger review proceed on a more fact-intensive, case-by-case basis where innovation is at stake, with a presumption that a merger's effects on innovation are neutral except in the case of merger to monopoly, where there would be a rebuttable presumption of harm" (6). While merger analysis tends to be highly fact-intensive, whether or not innovation effects are at issue, the standard proposed by Katz and Shelanski appears to be markedly more lenient than the one antitrust law usually applies to horizontal mergers, where there is a rebuttable presumption of harm from a merger that substantially increases concentration and leads to a highly concentrated market.[8]

Here I question whether such a lenient standard is appropriate for evaluating the impact of mergers on innovation. Yet I do not want to direct too much attention to presumptions and burdens of proof, which are more the stuff of lawyers than economists. Nor do I want to overstate the differences between my approach and that of Katz and Shelanski.[9] The key operative question is whether one can obtain reasonable accuracy in merger enforcement, in cases involving innovation, by focusing the inquiry on (1) the extent of future rivalry between the two merging firms, including consideration of the innovative abilities, efforts, and incentives of other firms, and (2) any merger-specific efficiencies that will enhance the incentive or ability of the merged firm to engage in innovation. Part (1) here asks whether the merger significantly reduces contestability; if so, part (2) asks whether the merger nonetheless enhances innovation by increasing appropriability or enabling merger-specific synergies. See section 7.5 later in the chapter.

Likewise, in evaluating the impact of specific conduct by a dominant firm on innovation, the operative question for competition policy is not whether large firms innovate more than small ones, or whether concentrated market structures are associated with more or less innovation than atomistic market structures. After all, competition policy, at least as practiced in the United States today, is not about engineering market structures or the size distri-

7. Katz and Shelanski (2007, 4, footnote omitted).

8. The strength of the "structural presumption" in antitrust law has declined in recent decades, but not nearly to the point where only mergers to monopoly are presumed to substantially lessen competition. See Baker and Shapiro (2008). The 2010 Horizontal Merger Guidelines issued by the Department of Justice and the Federal Trade Commission state in Section 5.3: "Mergers resulting in highly concentrated markets [HHI greater than 2,500] that involve an increase in the HHI of more than 200 points will be presumed to be likely to enhance market power. The presumption may be rebutted by persuasive evidence showing that the merger is unlikely to enhance market power."

9. See the later discussion of the FTC's 2009 challenge to the proposed merger between Thoratec and Heartware. Shelanski was Deputy Director of the Bureau of Economics at the time of that challenge. See also the discussion of the 2010 Horizontal Merger Guidelines. Shelanski was closely involved in developing these new guidelines (as was this author).

bution of firms. The operative question is whether the specific conduct at issue that allegedly excludes a rival, such as a refusal to open up an interface, will benefit customers by spurring innovation or harm them by retarding innovation (e.g., by excluding an innovative rival or reducing the competitive pressure placed on the dominant firm). See section 7.6 later in the chapter.

Section 7.2 shows that the emerging conventional wisdom—that there is no reliable relationship between competition and innovation—results in part from the peculiar and unhelpful way that the notion of "more competition" has been defined in the industrial organization and endogenous growth literatures. Section 7.3 gives a brief summary of the relevant empirical literature, which strongly supports the general proposition that greater competition spurs innovation, broadly defined. Section 7.4 discusses the Contestability, Appropriability, and Synergies principles and argues that they are sufficiently robust to guide competition policy. Sections 7.5 and 7.6 apply these three principles to merger enforcement policy and dominant firm conduct, respectively. Section 7.7 concludes.

7.2 Competition and Innovation: What Went Wrong?

Much of the literature on the relationship between competition and innovation has, unfortunately, given policymakers a clouded and distorted picture of what we really know about this relationship. As a result, the literature has not been as helpful to practitioners as it could be. Worse yet, the way in which the literature has been summarized and translated for policymakers is leaving a misleading impression, especially for nonspecialists. The problem stems in large part from the way the term "competition" has been used in that literature.

7.2.1 Equating "More Competition" with "Less Product Differentiation"

In the theoretical industrial organization literature on competition and innovation, "more competition" frequently is modeled as "less product differentiation." If the products offered by the various competing firms are close substitutes, price competition is more intense. So, "less product differentiation" is not an unreasonable way to define "more competitive pressure," at least in a static oligopoly setting. However, this has resulted in numerous statements in the literature that can be misleading and unhelpful for the purpose of competition policy, especially merger enforcement. In particular, while merger enforcement can directly affect the number of independent firms competing in an industry, it does not directly affect the extent of product differentiation among the products offered by those firms.

The danger can be illustrated by the discussion in Aghion and Griffith (2005). They begin in chapter 1, "A Divorce Between Theory and Empirics," with what they label as the "dominant theories of the early 1990s."

These are static models of product differentiation in which an increase in product market competition is modeled as a reduction in the extent of product differentiation, such as lower transportation costs in a model of spatial differentiation. Innovation is then measured by the equilibrium number of firms in the market, where entry involves a fixed cost. With weaker product differentiation, price/cost margins are smaller, and fewer products are supplied in the free entry equilibrium. This simple and uncontroversial proposition about product *variety* is characterized as a "Schumpeterian effect of product market competition" (11). Aghion and Griffith go on to state, "we again obtain an unambiguously negative Schumpeterian effect of product market competition on innovation" (12).[10]

I am not disputing the results in these simple models of product differentiation. Nor am I disputing that innovation incentives are low if successful innovation merely places a firm in a market where its product is only slightly differentiated from other products and where the firm has no cost advantage. What I am disputing is that such a proposition is helpful for competition policy, or innovation policy more generally. Meaningful product innovation involves the development of new products that are superior to, or at least significantly distinct from, existing products. Meaningful process innovation involves the development or adoption of production processes (broadly defined to include business methods) that significantly reduce costs. These static models of oligopoly do not involve anything I recognize or credit as innovation. They may help us understand how many brands of toothpaste will be introduced, but they cannot help us understand how firms choose to invest to develop new products that are markedly superior to current offerings. These models were never designed to study rivalry to develop new and improved products or processes. The effect of changing a parameter measuring the degree of differentiation among products is just not directly relevant to competition policy.[11]

For Aghion and Griffith, this discussion is merely a launching pad, and I do not mean to suggest that they base any of their conclusions or policy recommendations on these simple static oligopoly models. Indeed, they immediately go on to note two important and powerful forces missing from these models: "the interplay between rent dissipation and preemption incentives, and the differences between vertical (i.e., quality improving) and horizontal innovations" (13). Nonetheless, their framing of the issues is indicative of how the conversation has developed, and how research findings are trans-

10. Similarly, Aghion et al. (2005), summarizing the "main existing theories of competition and innovation," states: "The leading IO models of product differentiation and monopolization . . . deliver the prediction that more intense product market competition reduces postentry rents, and therefore reduces the equilibrium number of entrants" (710, footnoted omitted).

11. Baker (2007) puts this nicely: "antitrust is not a general-purpose competition intensifier. Rather, antitrust intervention can be focused on industry setting and categories of behavior where enforcement can promote innovation" (589, footnote omitted).

lated and conveyed to policymakers. They summarize the "early theoretical and empirical literatures" as follows: "theory pointed to a detrimental effect of competition on innovation and growth, while the empirical literature instead suggested that more competitive market structures are associated with greater innovative output, an idea that had much support in policy circles" (3–4).

These passages from Aghion and Griffith (2005) accurately reflect a strand of the theoretical literature that equates the concept of "more competition" with "less product differentiation." For much more detail on these models, see Boone (2000) and (2001), Aghion, et al. (2001), and Sacco and Schmutzler (2011). Vives (2008), "Innovation and Competitive Pressure," surveys and synthesizes this literature.[12] Schmutzler (2010) uses a generalized "competition parameter." By definition, increases in this parameter lead to lower equilibrium profit margins and a greater sensitivity of a firm's equilibrium output to that firm's cost level. Schmutzler explores the relationship between "more competition," as defined by increases in this parameter, and the level of R&D investment. While there is nothing inherently incorrect or misleading about modeling "more competitive pressure" as "less product differentiation," defining "more competition" this way can lead to statements about competition and innovation that are unhelpful or even misleading for merger enforcement policy.

In particular, the statement that "more competition discourages innovation" can be misused or misunderstood in the context of competition policy, or innovation policy more broadly. The statement, "innovation incentives are low if ex post competition is so intense that even successful innovators cannot earn profits sufficient to allow a reasonable risk-adjusted rate of return on their R&D costs" strikes me as more defensible and far more accurate, if less pithy. I doubt these conditions are common, except perhaps when appropriability is low, in which case the root problem is one of low appropriability, not excessive competition. But at least this far more precise statement is not misleading.

Clarity and precision in defining "competition" can reduce perceived complexity regarding the impact of competition on innovation.

7.2.2 Equating "More Competition" with "More Imitation"

The endogenous growth literature also explores the relationship between competition and innovation, albeit from a different perspective. See Aghion and Griffith (2005) and Aghion and Howitt (2009).[13] The paper by Aghion

12. In an oligopoly model with restricted entry, Vives also studies the relationship between the number of firms and innovation. This measure of competition is more relevant to merger enforcement policy, as discussed in section 7.5.

13. In Aghion and Howitt (2009), see especially chapter 12, "Fostering Competition and Entry," and the references therein. For a recent survey on this literature, see Scopelliti (2010).

et al. (2005), "Competition and Innovation: An Inverted-U Relationship," has been especially influential. The model used by Aghion et al. (2005) is far better for considering innovation than are the static oligopoly models just discussed, because it is a dynamic model in which firms invest to develop new and superior products.

However, as I now explain, this strand of literature typically equates "more competition" with "more imitation." This has led to the unfortunate sound bite, typically paired with a reference to Schumpeter, that "greater competition discourages innovation." Aghion et al. (2005) write:

> [I]ncreased product market competition discourages innovation by reducing postentry rents. This prediction is shared by most existing models of endogeneous growth. . . . where an increase in product market competition, or the rate of imitation, has a negative effect on productivity growth by reducing the monopoly rents that reward new innovation. (Aghion et al. 2005, 711, footnote omitted)

The standard growth-theoretic models that explore the competition/innovation relationship model "more competition" as a parameter that shifts downward the ex post demand function facing the innovator. They do not model "more competition" as an increase in contestability or appropriability. Instead, "more competition," meaning more imitation, involves *reduced* appropriability and thus lower profit margins for the innovator.

To see how this literature models competition, consider the benchmark model of innovation and productivity growth presented by Aghion and Griffith (2005).[14] In that model, "competition" is measured by the cost advantage of an innovator over a competitive fringe of imitators. I regard this as a measure of the strength of intellectual property protection, or as a measure of the spillovers associated with innovation. It is certainly not a measure of contestability or rivalry to innovate and thus win sales. Clearly, more "competition" in the sense used in this literature equates to less appropriability. It is entirely unsurprising that imitation reduces innovation incentives. Unfortunately, Aghion and Griffith (2005) interpret this finding as follows:

> However, *pro-competition policies* will tend to discourage innovation and growth by reducing χ [the cost advantage of the innovator over the imitators], thereby forcing incumbent innovators to charge a lower limit price. (Aghion and Griffith 2005, 18, emphasis supplied)

So far as I can tell, these so-called "procompetition policies" involve weaker intellectual property rights, or perhaps mandatory licensing or price controls, neither of which can properly be called "competition policies," at

14. See pp. 16–19: "This serves as a basis for the theoretical extension we will present in later chapters of this book."

least in the United States today.[15] But, unfortunately, the idea sticks: competition and procompetition policies discourage innovation and growth.

Aghion and Griffith do not rest at this point and conclude that competition discourages growth. To the contrary, they press forward, seeking to reconcile theory and evidence, emphasizing what they call the "escape competition effect." In my lexicon, this is a form of contestability: a firm that fails to innovate will find its margins squeezed, while innovating preserves these margins. However, their extension models also equate "more competition" with more complete imitation of a process innovation. For that reason, their analysis strikes me as far more relevant for policies that influence the strength of intellectual property rights than for competition policy.[16]

Let me be clear: there is nothing inherently incorrect about modeling "more competition" as "more imitation." Imitation does reduce the demand facing an innovator, and it certainly constitutes "more competition" from that firm's perspective. Furthermore, imitation can be a very important consideration when firms make R&D investment decisions, especially for product or process innovations that are difficult to protect using patents or trade secrets.[17]

Nonetheless, the statement that "more competition discourages innovation" can all too easily be misunderstood or misused in the context of competition policy, not to mention innovation policy more broadly.[18] The statement, "more rapid and complete imitation tends to discourage innovation" seems more reasonable and far more accurate.

Clarity and precision in defining "competition" can reduce perceived complexity regarding the impact of competition on innovation.

7.2.3 Equating "More Competition" with "Lower Market Concentration"

Industrial organization economists have long used product market concentration as a proxy for competition, with higher concentration indicating less competition with respect to price and output. We place less weight on this proxy than we did fifty years ago, but it certainly still has value, at least in

15. The impact of imitation on innovation and economic growth is certainly important for policies governing the design and strength of patent rights, as well as policies affecting the protection and enforcement of trade secrets. That discussion is beyond the scope of this chapter. Shapiro (2007) discusses the relationship between the reward to a patent holder and the patent holder's contribution.

16. Of course, as reflected in the Appropriability principle, imitation and spillovers can be very important in antitrust analysis. In particular, a merger that internalizes significant spillovers may promote innovation, as discussed later.

17. Patents and trade secrets are the most relevant forms of intellectual property for the product and process innovations I have in mind here. However, the same argument can be made for creative works, where copyrights typically are the applicable form of intellectual property.

18. Aghion and Griffith (2005) clearly believe their work is relevant to competition policy. In the conclusion to chapter 3, they state: "These predictions have important policy implications for the design of competition policy" (64).

properly defined relevant markets. The recently revised Horizontal Merger Guidelines continue to use Herfindahl-Hirschman Index (HHI) thresholds, with adverse competitive effects viewed as unlikely in markets with a postmerger HHI less than 1,500 and presumed likely for mergers that raise the HHI more than 200 and lead to a postmerger HHI greater than 2,500.

The link between current or recent product market concentration and R&D rivalry has always been weaker than the link between current or recent product market concentration and rivalry to win current sales. A firm's current sales may not be a good proxy for that firm's R&D incentives and abilities. Plus, R&D expenditures normally have the character of a fixed cost, leading to scale economies. If those fixed costs are large relative to sales, significant market concentration is inevitable in equilibrium, as demonstrated by Sutton (1998). Furthermore, as Schumpeter emphasized, the reward to successful innovation is some degree of market power in the technical sense—price above marginal cost—for a sufficient volume of sales to earn a risk-adjusted return on the fixed and sunk R&D costs. Plus, a highly successful innovator may come to dominate a market, in which case observing a high level ex post concentration would hardly imply a lack of ex ante competition, or a lack of innovation. In an industry where innovation has recently occurred, or is ongoing, any measurement of the current or recent market structure inevitably will be a post-innovation measurement. We should not expect to see atomistic market structures in industries that have experienced significant technological progress, and we may see high levels of concentration in markets that have recently experienced significant innovation.

The empirical literature on product market structure and competition has come to recognize all of these points, and recent work (see the following) attempts heroically to account for them. Cohen (2010) summarizes: "Regarding measures, there can be little disagreement with Gilbert's contention that the commonly employed measure of market structure, market concentration, does not accurately reflect the nature or intensity of competition" (156). Yet there remains some tendency to equate "more competition" with "lower product market concentration." Thus, a finding that unconcentrated markets (or markets where firms earn low operating profits relative to sales) are not the ones where we see the most experienced significant innovation may be interpreted—incorrectly—as "too much competition discourages innovation," or as implying that "an intermediate amount of competition is best for promoting innovation." The real lesson is that static measures of market structure can be poor metrics for assessing innovation competition.

Framing the relationship between competition and innovation as one between product market concentration and competition is not dissimilar to the view in the 1950s and 1960s that atomistic markets were the ideal and best promote (pricing and output) competition. That view gave way long ago to a more nuanced one, which recognizes that when individual firms differ greatly in their efficiency (as they normally do), and when there are significant economies of scale (as there typically are in markets where antitrust enforcement takes place), robust competition is likely to lead to a market structure in which some firms have substantial market shares. Demsetz (1973) powerfully and influentially articulated this point. This very same principle applies with even greater force to innovation: we know there are significant economies of scale, because R&D is a fixed cost, and it would be surprising indeed if firms did not differ substantially in their ability to innovate. Accounting for the inherent uncertainty associated with innovation only strengthens the point: even if several firms have comparable ex ante incentive and ability to innovate, ex post some will strike gushers and others just dry wells.

Again, there is nothing inherently wrong with observing and reporting that many highly innovative industries do not have atomistic market structures: it is helpful to know not to expect, or strive for, atomistic market structures in those industries.[19] But there is no tension between established competition policy principles and the Schumpeterian observation that successful innovators often are able to price well above marginal cost and often gain substantial market shares. The US antitrust law has understood for a very long time that the market power resulting from successful innovation is an important and inevitable part of the competitive process. As Judge Learned Hand famously observed: "the successful competitor, having been urged to compete, must not be turned upon when he wins."[20] Furthermore, of course, merger enforcement policy does not strive for atomistic markets: under the recently revised Horizontal Merger Guidelines, merger adverse competitive effects are considered unlikely if the post-merger HHI is less than 1,500, and the merger enforcement statistics show that the Department of Justice (DOJ) and the FTC often allow horizontal mergers, leading more concentrated markets to proceed without challenge.

7.3 What Does the Empirical Evidence Really Tell Us?

There is a very substantial body of empirical evidence supporting the general proposition that "more competition," meaning greater contestability of sales, spurs firms to be more efficient and to invest more in R&D. For

19. Even in concentrated industries, start-up firms can play a very positive and powerful role in spurring innovation. If they are rapidly acquired by large incumbents, or if their ideas are copied by large incumbents, their role may never be reflected in a decline in market concentration. Even if antitrust does not stand in the way of mergers that cause moderate increases in concentration, it may need still to intervene to protect customers from unilateral conduct by dominant firms that stifles disruptive innovation by start-up firms.

20. US v. Aluminum Company of America, 148 F.2d 416 (1945).

our purposes, "innovation" encompasses a wide range of improvements in efficiency, not just the development of entirely novel processes or products.

Detailed case studies of businesses operating in diverse settings almost invariably conclude that companies insulated from competition—that is, firms operating in environments in which relatively few sales are contestable—are rarely at the cutting edge in terms of efficiency and can be woefully inefficient. Porter (1990) assembles a raft of evidence showing that companies protected from international competition tend to fall behind and lose their ability to compete in export markets. Porter has long emphasized the importance of competition in spurring innovation, as reflected in this passage from Porter (2001):

> Innovation provides products and services of ever increasing consumer value, as well as ways of producing products more efficiently, both of which contribute directly to productivity. Innovation, in this broad sense, is driven by competition. While technological innovation is the result of a variety of factors, there is no doubt that healthy competition is an essential part. One need only review the dismal innovation record of countries lacking strong competition to be convinced of this fact. Vigorous competition in a supportive business environment is the only path to sustained productivity growth, and therefore to long term economic vitality. (Porter 2001, 923)

In another wide-ranging international study, Lewis (2004) finds that competitive markets are the key to economic growth. His central conclusion is that competition drives innovation:

> Most economic analysis ends up attributing most of the differences in economic performance [across countries] to differences in labor and capital markets. *This conclusion is incorrect. Differences in competition in product markets are much more important.* (Lewis 2004, 13, emphasis in original)

In discussing the relationship between competition and innovation, it is important to bear in mind the enormous differences across firms in their efficiency, even among firms in the same industry. Bartelsman and Doms (2000) survey the literature on firm-level productivity, writing:

> Of the basic findings related to productivity and productivity growth uncovered by recent research using micro-data, perhaps most significant is the degree of heterogeneity across establishments and firms in productivity in nearly all industries examined. (Bartelsman and Doms 2000, 578)

In a more recent survey, Syverson (2011) starts by stating: "Economists have shown that large and persistent differences in productivity levels across businesses are ubiquitous." He reports studies (35–48) showing how competition acts to improve productivity both through a Darwinian selection effect and by inducing firms to take costly actions to raise their productivity. He also reports studies showing how additional competition arising from trade liberalization enhances productivity. These are first-order effects that serve to remind us that the relevant notion of "innovation" is quite broad, encompassing the adoption and diffusion of best practices. Innovation is not confined to the invention of new products or new methods of production.

Leibenstein (1966) famously asked why so many firms are operated inefficiently and thus appear not to maximize profits. Economic theory has yet to fully explain why firms fail to undertake what appear to be profitable investments to improve their efficiency, but empirical evidence consistently shows that firms are more likely to make such investments when placed under competitive pressure.[21] Holmes, Levine, and Schmitz (2008) argue creatively that competition spurs innovation by reducing margins on existing products and thus reducing the opportunity cost of innovation that involves "switchover disruptions" for suppliers.

Numerous studies show specifically that increased competitive pressure resulting from lower regulatory barriers to entry generally enhances productivity and accelerates innovation. Holmes and Schmitz (2010) provide a recent review of a number of these studies, concluding:

> Nearly all the studies found that increases in competition led to increases in industry productivity. Plants that survived these increases in competition were typically found to have large productivity gains, and these gains often accounted for the majority of overall industry gains. (Holmes and Schmitz 2010, 639)

Syverson (2004) is especially instructive regarding the relationship between competitive pressure and firm-level efficiency. Studying the concrete industry, he shows that average productivity is higher, and productivity differences across firms are smaller, in local markets that are more competitive. Here "more competitive" means that the producers are more densely clustered, increasing spatial substitutability. Syverson finds that relatively inefficient firms in the concrete industry have greater difficulty operating in the more competitive local markets.

In contrast to Syverson's in-depth study of one industry, Bloom and Van Reenen (2007) examine management practices across a wide range of industries by surveying managers from over 700 medium-sized firms. They find very large differences in productivity across firms and conclude that "poor management practices are more prevalent when product market competition is weak." They explain that

> [H]igher levels of competition (measured using a variety of different proxies, such as trade openness) are strongly associated with better management practices. This competition effect could arise through a number of

21. See the survey by Holmes and Schmitz (2010), as well as the other surveys cited earlier.

> channels, including the more rapid exit of badly managed firms and/or the inducement of greater managerial effort. (Bloom and Van Reenen 2007, 1351)

Similarly, Bloom and Van Reenen (2010) observe that "firms with 'better' management practices tend to have better performance on a wide range of dimensions: they are larger, more productive, grow faster, and have higher survival rates" (204–205). They report that strong product market competition appears to boost average management practices through a combination of eliminating the tail of badly managed firms and pushing incumbents to improve their practices.

In addition to these studies, which collectively are quite convincing, there is a very large empirical literature examining the relationship between (a) firm size and innovation, and (b) product market concentration and innovation. Cohen (2010) surveys this literature.[22]

Regarding business unit size and innovation, Cohen writes:

> Thus, the robust empirical patterns relating to R&D and innovation to firm size are that R&D increases monotonically—and typically proportionately—with firm size among R&D performers within industries, the number of innovations tends to increase less than proportionately than firm size, and the share of R&D effort dedicated to more incremental and process innovation tends to increase with firm size. (Cohen 2010, 137)

As Cohen explains (138), these findings are consistent with the view that larger business units expect to be able to apply process innovations over a larger scale of output, because firms chiefly exploit their process innovations internally and often anticipate limited growth due to innovation. In contrast, Cohen writes that "the returns to more revolutionary (i.e., substitute) innovations are less tied to a firm's prior market position" (139).

Regarding the connection between market power and innovation, Cohen observes: "The empirical literature has focused principally on the effects of market concentration on innovative behavior. The literature has thus directly tested Schumpeter's conjectures about the effects of ex ante market structure" (140). Cohen further notes that "the potential for achieving ex post market power through innovation has been characterized under the general heading of appropriability conditions and measured by survey-based indicators of appropriability" (141). Cohen is thus careful to avoid conflating "more competition" with "more imitation."

Lee (2005) offers this view of a key stylized factoid that has long captured the imagination of industrial organization economists:

> The conventional wisdom from the literature postulates an inverted-U relationship between market structure, measured by seller concentration on the horizontal axis, and industry R&D intensity (i.e., R&D-to-sales

22. See Cohen and Levin (1989) and Cohen (1995) for earlier surveys of this literature.

> ratio) on the vertical axis. The inverted-U hypothesis says that moderately concentrated industries engage more intensively in R&D activity than either atomistically competitive or highly concentrated industries. (Lee 2005, 101)

This inverted-U shaped relationship between market concentration and innovation has not held up well under scrutiny, especially after correcting for industry differences in technological opportunity and for the endogeneity of product market structure. I do not intend to wade into that debate, which I do not expect to be resolved definitely one way or the other during my lifetime, either theoretically or empirically, for the reasons given earlier. Meanwhile, the message received by nonspecialists and policymakers is that we know rather little about the relationship between "competition" and innovation, notwithstanding the very powerful evidence about firm-level productivity cited before.

Lee (2005) distinguishes industries based on appropriability and emphasizes that the notions of "more competition" and "more imitation" are very different:

> [T]he concentration-R&D relationship differs depending on the strength of the link or simply the appropriability of R&D in terms of market share: A positive relationship is predicted for low-appropriability industries, where market concentration supplements low R&D appropriability, while a negative or an inverted U-shaped relationship for high-appropriability industries. An empirical analysis of data, disaggregated at the five-digit SIC level, on R&D and market concentration of Korean manufacturing industries provides supportive evidence for the predictions. (Lee 2005, 101)

Attempting to move the debate forward, and recognizing the limitations of market concentration as a proxy for the intensity of competition, the empirical literature has made progress in using measures other than market concentration as a proxy for the intensity of competition. Notably, Nickell (1996) uses a modified Lerner Index as a proxy for competition.[23] Nickell states: "I present evidence that competition, as measured by increased numbers of competitors or by lower levels of rents, is associated with a significantly higher rate of total factor productivity growth (724)."[24] More recently, Aghion et al. (2005), also using a modified Lerner index as their

23. Nickell also uses results from a one-time survey in which management was asked whether it had more than five competitors in the market for its product. He discusses the limitations of his proxies for competition (732). Nickell also uses a measure of market share, with three-digit industry sales in the denominator. Nickell notes that "the three digit industry does not represent anything like a 'market,'" and thus has little value as a cross-section measure of market power, but he argues that it is useful as a time-series measure.

24. Blundell, Griffith, and Van Reenen (1999) state: "We find a robust and positive effect of market share on observable headcounts of innovations and patents although increased product market concentration in the industry tends to stimulate innovative activity" (529). They measure innovation by counting the number of technologically significant and commercially

measure of competition, have challenged Nickell's conclusions. They find instead an inverted U-shaped relationship between product market competition and innovation.

> This paper investigates the relationship between product market competition and innovation. We find strong evidence of an inverted-U relationship using panel data. We develop a model where competition discourages laggard firms from innovating but encourages neck-and-neck firms to innovate. (Aghion et al. 2005, 701)

Aghion et al. (2005) look at two-digit Standard Industrial Classification (SIC) industries. They measure innovation using the number of citation-weighted patents. Their measure of the Lerner Index averages 4 percent, and generally falls between zero and 10 percent, with the peak of the inverted-U occurring at a Lerner index of around 5 percent. Whatever one makes of these findings, they do not challenge the extensive empirical evidence cited earlier about innovation and firm-level efficiency. Nor do they call into question the Contestability, Appropriability, and Synergies principles. In any event, they are not directly relevant to analyzing the effects of proposed mergers on innovation.

Cohen (2010) reports a number of other studies that support the general proposition that greater competitive pressure spurs firms to innovate to get ahead of their rivals. For example, he notes that "Lee (2009), using World Bank survey data for nine industries across seven countries, finds that intensity of competition may stimulate more capable firms to invest more heavily in R&D, while less capable firms may invest less" (16). Of special relevance for competition policy, Cohen reports work suggesting that entry causes innovation (144). However, this is a tricky area empirically, since high technological opportunity in an industry tends to cause both more entry and faster innovation in that industry. In summarizing the literature on market structure and innovation, Cohen (2010) states: "Moving on to our consideration of the relationship between market structure and R&D, the empirical patterns are mixed, and not terribly informative" (154). Again, this is unsurprising, given what we can measure, given the endogeneity of market structure, and given that increased market concentration may or may not go along with greater contestability.

Of particular interest here, Gilbert (2006) provides an extensive discussion of what this empirical literature implies for competition policy. As he points out, product market concentration is "a commonly used, but highly imperfect, surrogate for competition" (187). I note in particular that relevant antitrust markets do not match up well with the publicly available sales data,

---

important innovations. They define an industry at the three-digit level. Their metrics for competition are the proportion of industry sales made by the five largest domestic firms and the value of imports in proportion to home demand.

making the measurement of meaningful market shares difficult or impossible for academic researchers. Two-digit SIC industries are very far indeed from relevant antitrust markets. Likewise, academic researchers often have difficulty measuring true economic operating profits or price/cost margins using publicly available accounting data.

Gilbert concludes that these studies have failed to establish a general and robust relationship between product market concentration and innovation, once one controls for the underlying technological environment.

> Empirical studies that use market concentration as a proxy for competition fail to reach a robust conclusion about the relationship between market concentration and R&D when differences in industry characteristics, technological opportunities, and appropriability are taken into account. (Gilbert 2006, 206)

Gilbert notes several reasons for these negative results: limited data on innovative activity and market concentration, including the high level of aggregation at which market concentration is usually measured; failure to distinguish exclusive from nonexclusive property rights and between product and process innovations; differences in technological opportunities across industries and over time; and failure to control for other confounding factors.

The lack of robust results in this particular line of empirical work is understandable, given the measurement difficulties and conceptual complexities already discussed. However, given the very extensive empirical evidence showing that competitive pressure forces firms to be more efficient, and given the robust theoretical points relating innovation incentives to the contestability of future sales, the negative results in this particular area should not be interpreted as implying that "we just don't know anything about the relationship between competition and innovation." To the contrary, the empirical evidence overall gives powerful support for the proposition that heightened competitive pressure causes firms to invest more to improve their efficiency. Another advantage of having multiple firms seeking to innovate in a given area is that such decentralization supports greater innovation diversity.[25]

7.4 Competition and Innovation: Toward Robust Principles

When considering the impact of competition on innovation, rather than equating "more competition" with "less product differentiation," "more imi-

25. Even if overall profit maximization at the dominant firm entails pursuing multiple distinct approaches to developing next-generation products, organizational obstacles to doing so can be significant, especially when opinions differ greatly about which approach is most promising. Grove (1996) explains how Intel found it very difficult to pursue two distinct microprocessor architectures, CISC and RISC, at the same time. Christensen (1997) discusses the limitations of "skunk works."

tation," or "lower product market concentration," I suggest that the term "more competition" be reserved for market characteristics that correspond greater *rivalry* to serve the needs of customers. This is how the concept of "more competition" is generally applied in the area of competition policy: the competitive process is working well if there is healthy rivalry, on the merits, to win the patronage of customers by offering them superior value. Effective competition is about the *competitive process,* not the outcome. More important than terminology, assessing competition based on rivalry allows us to articulate and employ practical principles regarding innovation that are theoretically and empirically robust.

Rivalry in the current context is driven by the incentive and ability of firms to engage in innovation, broadly defined to include increased efficiency as well as the development of entirely new products and processes. The Contestability and Appropriability principles relate to innovation incentives, and the Synergies principle relates to innovation ability.

What basic factors govern an individual firm's incentive to innovate? Consider the following highly simplified model of the impact on a given firm's operating profits if that firm achieves a given product or process innovation. For simplicity, suppose the firm produces a single product, whether or not it innovates, although the firm will offer an improved product if it succeeds in achieving a product innovation. Denote the product's price by P, its output by X, and its (constant) marginal cost by C, so the profit margin on incremental units is given by $M \equiv P - C$. The firm's operating profits are $\pi = (P - C)X = MX$.[26] Whether or not the firm in question successfully innovates, it sets its price to maximize its operating profits.

Let the subscript "0" denote the situation in which the firm does not successfully innovate, and the subscript "1" denote the situation in which the firm does successfully innovate. The "no innovation" state will typically not be the pre-innovation status quo, since *other* firms may well successfully innovate even if the firm in question does not. This allows us to account for the added competitive pressure faced by the firm in question if it fails to innovate and its rivals succeed: X_0 and/or M_0 are reduced when rivals innovate. The "innovation" state incorporates rivals' reactions to the firm's innovation, including price adjustments and imitation. This setup allows us to examine the innovation incentives facing one firm, given the actions and reactions of other firms in terms of their own pricing, product offerings, efficiency, and R&D investments.

Successful innovation increases the firm's profits by $\Delta\pi = \pi_1 - \pi_0 = M_1X_1 - M_0X_0$, which can be written as

$$\Delta\pi = X_0\Delta M + M_0\Delta X + \Delta M\,\Delta X.$$

26. By operating profits I mean profits gross of R&D expenses and other costs that are fixed with respect to the firm's output level over the relevant time frame.

This expression for $\Delta\pi$ is simple, and not deep, but it does serve to remind us of the basic factors at play that govern the firm's innovation incentives.

The first term reflects the extra margin the firm earns as a result of innovating. These margins are applied to the firm's without-innovation output level, X_0. This extra margin can come from lower costs (for a process innovation) and/or from a higher price (for a product innovation). This term encompasses the "escape competition" effect in the literature.

The second term reflects the extra unit sales the firm makes by successfully innovating. These sales are valued at the firm's without-innovation margin, M_0. Other things equal, a firm that would make substantial sales *without* innovating will have a smaller sales boost from innovating, ΔX, and thus a smaller incentive to innovate. This is the Arrow replacement effect at work.

The third term is a positive interaction term between higher incremental margins and higher incremental sales. Since the firm picks its own price, the firm can choose how best to capture the rewards from innovation, as between higher margins and greater unit sales.

If successful innovation will do little to increase the firm's unit sales, ΔX is small and we have $\Delta\pi \approx X_0\Delta M$. Under these conditions, initially larger firms have greater incentives to innovate. This is a standard observation in the literature: the benefit of lowering marginal cost is proportional to output.[27] These conditions tend to apply when demand is sticky, so one firm cannot gain many sales even as a result of successful innovation, or when the innovating firm faces lasting capacity constraints. A similar situation arises for process innovations if the firm's rivals would react strongly (were the firm to lower its prices) by lowering their own prices. In that situation, the firm in question will gain few sales by lowering its own price, so the firm will tend to take the rewards from innovation in the form of higher margins on existing sales, rather than by lowering its price to expand its sales; this too implies that $\Delta\pi \approx X_0\Delta M$.

Additional insights can be obtained by examining how the firm's operating profits are boosted by incremental innovation. Denote by θ the level of innovation achieved by the firm. The innovation can involve an improvement in efficiency, or a process innovation, either of which lowers the firm's cost. To capture this, we write the firm's marginal cost as $C(\theta)$, with $C'(\theta) < 0$. The innovation also can involve an increase in the quality of the firm's product. To capture this, we write the firm's demand as $D(P,\theta,z)$, where $D_\theta(P,\theta,z) > 0$.

The variable z in $D(P,\theta,z)$ captures the attractiveness of the products

27. The simple formulation used here does not include licensing revenues. Licensing breaks the connection between the firm's own sales and the base on which higher margins can be earned.

offered by the firm's rivals, so $D_z(P,\theta,z) < 0$. Rivals can react to the firm's price and level of innovation, so $z = z(P,\theta)$. Successful innovation can weaken the firm's rivals, or even drive them from the market, so z_θ can be negative. However, we are more interested here in situations in which the rivals respond to the firm's innovation by improving their own offerings, either by lowering their prices or improving their own products (perhaps through imitation), in which case we have $z_\theta > 0$.

The firm's profits are given by $\pi(P,\theta) = D(P,\theta,z(P,\theta))(P - C(\theta))$. Applying the envelope theorem to the firm's price, achieving marginally more innovation raises operating profits by

$$\pi_\theta(P,\theta) = D(P,\theta,z)|C'(\theta)| + (P - C(\theta))[D_\theta + D_z z_\theta].$$

The first term in this expression captures the margin boost resulting from lower costs. The benefit of lower costs is proportional to the firm's output. The second term captures the sales boost resulting from product improvement. The impact of these incremental sales on profits is proportional to the gap between the firm's price and marginal cost. The sales boost consists of two terms: (1) the D_θ term reflects the increased demand given the prices and product offerings of rivals, and (2) the $D_z z_\theta$ term reflects rivals' responses to the firm's innovation.

We next show how the Contestability and Appropriability principles relate to this expression.

7.4.1 Contestability

The Contestability principle focuses on the ability of an innovating firm to gain or protect profitable sales by providing greater value to customers. This principle directs our attention to the incremental profits associated with innovation, taking as given the price and product offerings of other firms. Holding z fixed at $\bar{z}$, the incremental profits resulting from innovation are

$$\pi_\theta(P,\theta)|_{z=\bar{z}} = D(P,\theta,\bar{z})|C'(\theta)| + (P - C(\theta))D_\theta(P,\theta,\bar{z}).$$

The first term is the standard benefit to the firm from lowering its costs, which is proportional to the firm's output level. The second term is the boost in the firm's unit sales as a result of offering a better product, multiplied by the firm's price/cost margin. This second term captures the fundamental idea that a firm has greater innovation incentives if successful innovation allows the firm to gain, or protect, profitable sales. Sales are highly contestable—in the sense relevant for innovation—if a firm that provides greater value to customers gains substantial unit sales from its rivals; that is, if $D_\theta(P,\theta,\bar{z})$ is large.

An unconcentrated market is highly contestable if an innovator can gain substantial market share at a healthy margin by providing a better product or setting a lower price. In contrast, for product innovations, an unconcentrated market is not highly contestable if customers exhibit strong brand preferences, or have high switching costs, so any one firm that develops an improved product will gain few sales from its rivals.

The Arrow "replacement effect" is driven by contestability. In Arrow (1962), innovation allows a firm initially operating in a highly competitive market to take over the entire market at a margin reflecting its cost advantage. In contrast, the incumbent monopolist has far fewer sales to gain from innovation, and its without-innovation sales are not at risk since (by assumption) only the monopolist can innovate, so contestability is far lower.[28]

The robustness of the Contestability principle is nicely illustrated by seeing how it fares in the model of continual process innovation used by Aghion et al. (2005). They use this model to argue for an inverted U-shaped relationship between competition and innovation. Such a nonmonotonic relationship might appear to defy the Contestability principle. It does not.

In the Aghion et al. model, each industry is a duopoly, with no possibility of entry. The two firms sell a homogeneous product, so the only possible source of competitive advantage is a cost advantage. The duopolists can invest in R&D to lower their costs; such process innovations come in discrete steps. At any point in time, if the two firms have equal costs, the industry is said to be "neck-and-neck." Aghion et al. assume that spillovers allow a firm falling two steps behind immediately and costlessly to narrow the gap to one step, so the only other possible state of the market is for one firm to be the leader and the other the laggard, one step behind. This assumption also implies that the leader never invests in R&D, since it cannot extend its lead and since the leader's profits only depend upon the cost gap between the two firms, not on their absolute cost levels.

Aghion et al. state: "We define the degree of product market competition inversely by the degree to which the two firms in a neck-and-neck industry are able to collude" (713). A neck-and-neck firm has a stronger incentive to innovate, the greater the degree of product market competition. They call this the "escape the competition" effect, which I think of as the flip side of the Arrow replacement effect. In contrast, a laggard firm has a *weaker* incentive to innovate, the greater the degree of product market competition, since successful innovation leads to the less profitable neck-and-neck state. They call this a Schumpeterian effect. Aghion et al. cleverly exploit these mixed effects to obtain an inverted U-shaped relationship between equilibrium steady-state innovation rates (aggregated across many sectors) and the degree of product market competition (i.e., inability to collude). The model is elegant and instructive—major virtues in my view—but it is worth noting some of the strong assumptions underlying its prediction of

28. In Arrow's model, only a single firm can innovate, so the incumbent monopolist faces no danger of losing its monopoly if it is the designated innovator. If the monopolist can be dethroned, it has highly profitable sales to protect by innovating first; this is the central point in Gilbert and Newbery (1982), who allow for innovation rivalry.

the inverted U-shaped relationship between competition and innovation: there are only two firms in each industry, with no possibility of entry; the two firms sell a homogeneous product; the laggard firm cannot innovate in a different direction, for example, to differentiate its product, or take a riskier approach that might leapfrog the leader; and (due to imitation) the leader does not benefit at all from further lowering its costs.

Whether or not these conditions are realistic, the basic forces modeled by Aghion et al. (2005) fit comfortably with the Contestability principle. In particular, the inverted U-shaped relationship they uncover between "competition" and innovation does *not* correspond to a nonmonotonic relationship between contestability and innovation. In their model, "more competition" means less effective collusion when the duopolists are neck-and-neck. Their notion of "more competition" translates to more contestability when the firms are neck-and-neck: each firm has *more* to gain from pulling ahead, the more vigorously the two firms are competing. However, critically, their notion of "more competition" translates to *less* contestability when the firms are in the leader/laggard state: the laggard (the only innovator in this state) earns zero profits regardless of the degree of competition and *smaller* profits by catching up, the more vigorously the firms compete when neck-in-neck. Both states in their model are perfectly consistent with the Contestability principle.

This is a good point to elaborate on the connection between the notion of "more competition" and the operation of competition policy. Taking the Aghion et al. (2005) model at face value, it suggests that allowing some degree of collusion is desirable to spur innovation because it provides greater incentives to laggard firms to catch up so they can collude with their rival. However, in their model allowing a great deal of collusion is undesirable for innovation because the duopolists would then be more content to rest comfortably once they are neck-and-neck and effectively colluding. I am not aware of anyone actually proposing such a policy toward collusion, and for good reason. Among other problems, if the firms were given latitude to communicate and collude, they might also find a way to maximize joint profits by agreeing to stop spending money on R&D. In any event, a more relevant question for competition policy is whether reducing competition by allowing the two firms to *merge* would accelerate or retard innovation. In the Aghion et al. model, a merger between the two firms would be disastrous for innovation. Assuming that knowledge spillovers continue to limit the merged firm's competitive advantage to one step, the merged firm would immediately cease all innovation and coast along indefinitely with a one-step advantage over the imitating fringe.

7.4.2 Appropriability

Any analysis of competition and innovation needs to pay close attention to the conditions of appropriability; that is, the extent to which innovators can appropriate the social benefits their innovations have caused. The conditions of appropriability can greatly affect innovation incentives.[29] Appropriability is heavily influenced by the strength of intellectual property rights. Appropriability for a given firm is reduced by spillovers to noninnovating firms (e.g., through imitation). Some causal factors, such as low entry barriers combined with weak intellectual property rights, can lead to both more competition and more imitation. But any analysis of competition and innovation should avoid conflating "low appropriability" with "more competition."

Define the appropriability ratio as $\alpha \equiv (d\pi/d\theta)/(dW/d\theta)$, where W measures total welfare. In a model of a single firm, the appropriability ratio is less than unity under the mild condition that customers benefit from the innovation. In the special case of a single firm offering one product at a uniform price, textbook monopoly pricing theory tells us that the appropriability ratio for innovations that lower the firm's marginal cost is given by $\alpha = 1/(1 + \rho)$, where $\rho = dp/dc$ is the rate at which the firm passes cost changes through to price changes. However, analysis of the appropriation ratio becomes much more complex when the firm offers multiple products, engages in price discrimination, or faces rivals that are not price-taking firms. Fortunately, for the purposes of antitrust analysis, we typically do not need to measure the appropriability ratio; we are more interested in whether a particular merger or business practice internalizes important spillovers and thus increases appropriability.

The Appropriability principle builds on the Contestability principle by taking into account how rivals will respond to a given firm's successful innovation. In some cases, rivals respond passively by reducing their own R&D efforts or even exiting the market, adding to the rewards to the successful innovator.[30] In other cases, rivals respond aggressively by lowering their price or redoubling their own innovative efforts, either (1) improving their own efficiency, thus lowering their costs and their price, or (2) making their own product improvements, perhaps by imitating the first firm. In such cases, appropriability is reduced because the total benefits caused by the firm's innovation are larger and because that firm's rewards are reduced according to the $(P - C(\theta))D_z z_\theta$ term, which is negative if rivals improve their product offerings in response to the firm's innovation; that is, if $z_\theta > 0$.

Aggressive rivals' responses reduce appropriability by shifting the benefits of innovation to rivals and/or to customers. For example, if rivals will quickly imitate the product improvements introduced by a pioneering firm, that firm may gain little from leading the way. If that product improvement

29. Increasing appropriability for one firm can reduce it for others, especially when multiple innovating firms supply complements.

30. Responses of this type can create or bolster business-stealing effects leading to an appropriability ratio in excess of unity.

would not have been introduced without the pioneering firm taking the lead—a critical qualification—then appropriability is low in this situation. In this example, many of the benefits of innovation will flow to customers, or to suppliers of complements, not to the pioneering firm. However, one must be careful not to take this argument too far: if several firms are introducing a certain type of product improvement, little or none of the social benefits associated with that improvement are properly attributable to any one of those firms and ongoing competition to offer that improvement does not indicate any lack of appropriability.

Appropriability can be enhanced by mergers or business practices that internalize positive externalities, aka spillovers. Spillovers can occur between direct rivals through imitation, so these considerations can come into play in the analysis of horizontal mergers. Spillovers also arise between suppliers of complements, in which case the Appropriability principle reinforces the Synergies principle: combining complements can increase both innovation incentives and innovation capabilities.

7.4.3 Synergies

The Synergies principle recognizes that combining complementary assets can enhance innovation capabilities. As a classic example, in the pharmaceutical industry the process of bringing new drugs successfully to market requires an effective R&D program to identify and develop promising new compounds, the skills necessary to navigate the long and complex FDA testing and approval process, possibly demanding manufacturing capabilities, and effective marketing and distribution. Assembling these various skills, whether through contract, joint venture, strategic alliance, or integration, can lead to enhanced innovation capabilities.

7.5 Merger Enforcement

We are now ready to see what all of this implies for merger enforcement in cases where innovation effects are involved. This is no small matter, since merger enforcement is central to the work of the antitrust agencies and since many DOJ and FTC merger investigations and enforcement actions over the past fifteen years have involved innovation.[31] Here I follow in the footsteps of Katz and Shelanski (2005) and (2007), who offer an extensive

31. Katz and Shelanski (2005) and Gilbert (2006) note the growing importance of innovation in merger analysis. Katz and Shelanski (2005) also discuss a number of specific merger cases in which innovation has been an important factor. Gilbert and Tom (2001) discuss the rising importance of innovation in DOJ and FTC antitrust enforcement more generally during the 1995–2000 time period. Porter (2001) argues that antitrust treatment of mergers should focus on productivity growth. The 2010 Horizontal Merger Guidelines include, for the first time, a section devoted to innovation.

and thoughtful discussion of how merger enforcement does, and should, take account of innovation.[32]

Analysis of horizontal mergers involves predicting the effects of a specific, discrete change in industry structure, namely the joining of two former rivals under common ownership. As a practical matter, most mergers that receive serious antitrust scrutiny based on a theory of innovation effects involve two of a small number of companies with products, R&D programs, or capabilities in a given area. Usually, but not always, the two merging firms are important premerger rivals in the product market. The merger cases of greatest interest in which innovation effects are important typically fit into one of the following fact patterns:

- *Two product market rivals:* The merging firms are rivals in the relevant product market. One or both of them is investing in R&D to strengthen its position in the market.
- *Incumbent and potential entrant:* One merging firm has a strong position in the product market. The other merging firm has no current offering in the product market but is investing in R&D and will enter the product market if that R&D is successful.
- *Pure innovation rivals:* Neither merging firm has a current offering in the product market, but both are developing products to serve the market.

When examining a horizontal merger with possible innovation effects, we generally are interested in some version of this question:

> Will a merger between two rivals significantly reduce their *incentive* to innovate? If so, will the merger enhance their *ability* to innovate sufficiently to offset the reduced incentive?

The Contestability and Appropriability principles are directed at the first of these questions. The Synergy Principle applies to the second.

The overall relationship between market concentration and innovation is not especially relevant to this inquiry, especially since merger enforcement only takes place in moderately or highly concentrated markets. In particular, since merger analysis is not about a generalized increase in "competition," such as a reduction in the extent of product differentiation or an increase in imitation, the literature relating the (exogenous) degree of product differentiation to innovation is of little or no relevance to merger analysis. The Schumpeterian proposition that an ex post atomistic market structure is not conducive to innovation also is not directly relevant to merger enforcement, which involves a discrete change, usually a substantial increase in concentra-

32. Katz and Shelanski (2007) make the useful distinction between "innovation impact" and "innovation effects." My focus here is on "innovation effects."

tion, in ex ante market structure. The empirical literature on firm size and R&D is potentially more relevant, to the extent that it can inform us about the merger-specific efficiencies relating to innovation that are likely to arise when two competing business units are combined to form a larger business unit. However, the analysis of merger synergies is highly fact-specific. So far at least, general findings about firm size and innovation have not proven helpful for assessing merger-specific R&D efficiencies.

In subsection 7.5.1, I briefly explain what the recently revised Horizontal Merger Guidelines say about innovation effects. The guidelines utilize the Contestability, Appropriability, and Synergies principles. Subsections 7.5.2, 7.5.3, and 7.5.4 apply these principles to three merger cases in which innovation effects were central.

7.5.1 Innovation Effects Under the Merger Guidelines

The recently revised Horizontal Merger Guidelines contain Section 6.4, "Innovation and Product Variety." Innovation effects had not been explicitly addressed in the predecessor, 1992 Horizontal Merger Guidelines (see http://ftc.gov/os/2010/08/100819hmg.pdf). Section 6.4 begins this way:

> Competition often spurs firms to innovate. The Agencies may consider whether a merger is likely to diminish innovation competition by encouraging the merged firm to curtail its innovative efforts below the level that would prevail in the absence of the merger. That curtailment of innovation could take the form of reduced incentive to continue with an existing product-development effort or reduced incentive to initiate development of new products. The first of these effects is most likely to occur if at least one of the merging firms is engaging in efforts to introduce new products that would capture substantial revenues from the other merging firm.

This question is a direct application of the Contestability principle. Consider how the two firms are affected if Firm A introduces a new and improved product. The new product will increase Firm A's operating profits (measured gross of its R&D expenditures). If Firm B offers products that compete against Firm A's new product, the introduction of Firm A's new product will lower Firm B's operating profits. We can ask what fraction of Firm A's extra profits come at the expense of Firm B's profits. Farrell and Shapiro (2010) call this the "innovation diversion ratio."

How will this change if Firm A acquires Firm B? Applying the Contestability principle, the merger reduces the incentive to introduce this new product by more, the more profitable sales Firm A would capture from Firm B. Postmerger, sales gained at the expense of Firm B's products are no longer incremental to the merged firm: they cannibalize Firm B's profits. Put differently, the merger internalizes what had been a pecuniary negative externality. The merger turns the lost profits on Firm B's products into an opportunity cost borne by the merged firm when introducing Firm A's new product. The magnitude of the resulting "tax" on the profits from Firm A's new product is, by definition, the innovation diversion ratio.

While the innovation diversion ratio is not typically amenable to precise measurement, because it involves products not yet introduced, the marketing and financial documents of merging firms, along with other evidence, can indicate the products from which a new product is expected to gain sales. Even when the innovation diversion ratio is not amenable to measurement, it is still conceptually central to evaluating the impact of the merger on Firm A's incentive to introduce its new product. When the innovation diversion ratio is high, the merger significantly reduces the contestability associated with the new product in question.

The guidelines reflect these ideas, along with the possibility of offsetting innovation synergies:

> The Agencies evaluate the extent to which successful innovation by one merging firm is likely to take sales from the other, and the extent to which post-merger incentives for future innovation will be lower than those that would prevail in the absence of the merger. The Agencies also consider whether the merger is likely to enable innovation that would not otherwise take place, by bringing together complementary capabilities that cannot be otherwise combined or for some other merger-specific reason. (Section 6.4)

As an example of merger-specific efficiencies relating to innovation, suppose that Firm A is considering investing in R&D to develop an improved process that will lower its unit costs. Suppose also that Firm A does not expect to expand its unit sales much as a result of these lower costs.[33] If the merger will enable the process innovation to be applied to Firm B's output, and if Firm A would not license its process innovation to Firm B in the absence of the merger, the merger can enhance Firm A's incentives to develop this process innovation. Of course, any such merger synergy must be weighed against the innovation diversion effects discussed earlier. In terms of the Contestability principle, the merger can increase innovation incentives by expanding the base of sales on which lower costs can be achieved. This effect is captured by a larger value of $D(P, \theta, z)$ in the $D(P, \theta, z)|C'(\theta)|$ term that is part of the innovation reward expression. This reflects the robust idea in the literature that smaller firms have lower incentives to engage in process innovations. However, offsetting this effect is the internalization of sales captured at the expense of Firm B's product, which reduces the $D_\theta(P, \theta, z)$ term in this same expression when viewed from the perspective of the merged firm.[34]

33. As discussed before, this can occur because the firm faces binding capacity constraints or because consumers have strong brand preferences and the firm will gain relatively few sales even if it lowers its price to fully pass through its lower costs.

34. For the merged firm, this term is given by the net gain in the combined sales of the two products, weighted by their margins.

Similar ideas can be used to evaluate the longer-term impact of a merger on innovation. The guidelines state:

> The second, longer-run effect is most likely to occur if at least one of the merging firms has capabilities that are likely to lead it to develop new products in the future that would capture substantial revenues from the other merging firm. The Agencies therefore also consider whether a merger will diminish innovation competition by combining two of a very small number of firms with the strongest capabilities to successfully innovate in a specific direction.

This line of inquiry also is directly related to the Contestability principle, but applies over a longer time frame, over which the firms' durable capabilities can be more informative than are their current offerings. These effects can arise even if the merging firms are not premerger product market rivals, as in the Genzyme/Novazyme and Thoratec/HeartWare cases discussed later.

Evaluating a firm's innovation capabilities is inherently difficult, and the importance of the R&D rivalry between the merging firms can be very difficult to assess if the attributes of the products likely to result from their R&D projects are unknown. Katz and Shelanski (2005) note that many of the merger cases in which R&D rivalry was central have involved pharmaceutical mergers. The FDA approval process often makes it possible to know well in advance which firms are in the best position to introduce drugs or medical devices soon in a specific therapeutic area.

Often, the firms with the greatest ability to innovate in a given area are those that have successfully innovated in similar areas in the past, or who own the complementary assets necessary to commercialize innovations. Such firms often have a strong ex ante market position. Historical R&D successes and current market position are thus two common indicators of a firm's innovation capabilities.

The guidelines incorporate the Appropriability and Synergies principles more explicitly in Section 10, "Efficiencies."

> When evaluating the effects of a merger on innovation, the Agencies consider the ability of the merged firm to conduct research or development more effectively. Such efficiencies may spur innovation but not affect short-term pricing. The Agencies also consider the ability of the merged firm to appropriate a greater fraction of the benefits resulting from its innovations.

The guidelines specifically ask whether the merger is likely to enable merger-specific efficiencies by combining complementary capabilities within a single firm. For example, a merger can enable cross-fertilization between the research teams of the two merging firms. Likewise, a merger can enable valuable information sharing between the regular operations of one merging firm and the researchers at the other firm. Similarly, a merger can combine complementary assets such as a new product by a small start-up firm and the existing manufacturing or distribution assets of a larger, more established firm. However, merger synergies are far easier to claim than to achieve. The guidelines require that efficiencies be merger-specific and verified to be credited.

7.5.2 Genzyme/Novazyme

Genzyme Corporation acquired Novazyme Pharmaceuticals Inc. in September 2001.[35] Genzyme and Novazyme were the only companies pursuing enzyme replacement therapies for the treatment of Pompe disease, a rare and often fatal genetic disorder afflicting several thousand individuals in the United States, mostly infants and children. The FTC reviewed this merger after it was consummated but closed its investigation in January 2004, taking no action. The closing statement issued by FTC Chairman Timothy Muris stated: "The facts of this matter do not support a finding of any possible anticompetitive harm" (1). This was a striking assertion, since the merger created a monopoly in the market for Pompe enzyme replacement therapies.

The essential facts are as follows.[36] At the time of the merger, no treatments for Pompe disease had been approved by the Food and Drug Administration (FDA). Since Pompe disease is rare, under the Orphan Drug Act the first innovator to obtain FDA approval for a therapy is awarded seven years of exclusivity. By design, this regulatory structure rewards the first company to obtain FDA approval, even if patent protection is not available. However, this exclusivity may be lost if another innovator develops a superior treatment. This latter provision provides an incentive for other companies to continue their efforts to develop a superior treatment.

In the years leading up to the merger, Genzyme had invested heavily in developing a treatment for Pompe disease. At the time of the merger, Genzyme was pursing three treatments: one arising from a 1998 joint venture with Pharming, one arising from a 2000 joint venture with Synpac, and one that Genzyme had developed internally starting in 1999. The Synpac enzyme was in clinical trials and Genzyme was ramping up its own internal research program.

Novazyme had been developing its own Pompe treatment. At the time of the merger, the Novazyme treatment was not yet in clinical trials, but it had shown some promising results in mice. Novazyme was an especially aggressive innovation rival. The CEO of Novazyme, John Crowley, was

35. I rely primarily on the Federal Trade Commission (2004) for the facts of this case, but also on Anand (2006). The afterword in Anand (2006) provides an update as of October 2009.

36. I do not have access to the extensive confidential record that was available to the Federal Trade Commission. My comments here focus on the pertinent economic principles, not the FTC's enforcement decision in this case.

the father of two children with Pompe disease. His efforts to develop a treatment to save his children are documented in Anand (2006) and in the 2010 movie *Extraordinary Measures,* starring Harrison Ford. Prior to the merger, Novazyme projected that its treatment would reach clinical trials by the end of 2001. At the time of the acquisition, Genzyme announced that the Novazyme treatment would reach clinical trials in the first half of 2002.[37]

Soon after the merger, Genzyme reviewed all four treatments and decided to move forward to clinical trials with only the most promising one, which Genzyme determined to be its own internal program.[38] Anand notes, "Instead of being moved to human clinical trials, Novazyme's technology and experimental enzyme treatments were being sent back to the research labs."[39] Under Genzyme ownership, the Novazyme approach was slowed down, becoming a candidate for a superior, second-generation treatment.[40] Clinical trials for the Novazyme enzyme were substantially delayed. By the time of the FTC review in 2003, this date had been pushed back to between 2009 and 2011.[41] John Crowley left Genzyme in fall 2002. The internal Genzyme program commenced clinical trials in 2003, roughly one year after the merger with Novazyme.[42]

On its face, Genzyme's acquisition of Novazyme appears to have short-circuited a race between the two companies to be the first to obtain FDA approval of an enzyme treatment for Pompe disease. Applying the Contestability principle, all of the sales and profits accruing to the winner of this race were contestable prior to the merger. After the merger, however, far fewer sales and profits were contestable: Genzyme still had some incentive to gain FDA approval so it could begin earning profits from its treatment, but it no longer had to fear losing the race to Novazyme.

Furthermore, even if one assumes that there was no real race between the two companies, because Novazyme had no chance of gaining FDA approval before Genzyme, the merger still eliminated Novazyme as a competitor with a superior, second-generation treatment. Genzyme's incentive to develop a superior second-generation treatment would be far smaller than Novazyme's would have been, since sales of the second-generation treatment would come largely at the expense of the first-generation treatment. This is just the type of "replacement effect" identified by Arrow (1962) fifty years ago.

Application of the Contestability principle—following the approach de-

37. Federal Trade Commission (2004, 5), Dissenting Statement of Commissioner Thompson.

38. Anand (2006), chapter 23, "The Mother of All Experiments," describes Genzyme's evaluation of the four treatments.

39. Ibid., 261.

40. Ibid., 263.

41. Federal Trade Commission (2004, 5), Dissenting Statement of Commissioner Thompson.

42. The Genzyme treatment eventually gained FDA approval in spring 2006 under the brand name Myozyme. The treatment costs on average about $200,000 annually per patient. See Anand (2006, 316–17).

scribed in the 2010 Horizontal Merger Guidelines—strongly suggests that the merger had a significant adverse effect on innovation incentives. That conclusion appears to be further supported by the postmerger evidence available to the FTC at the time of its review. By 2003, it was clear that Genzyme's progress toward commercializing an enzyme treatment for Pompe disease had slowed down after the merger. As predicted by economic theory, Genzyme had delayed the development of the Novazyme treatment, pursing alternative treatments in *series* rather than in parallel.

How, then, did Chairman Muris conclude that the merger would not cause any anticompetitive harm? Muris begins by relying on "the lack of any clear theoretical or empirical link between increased concentration and reduced innovation" (2) to argue that there should be no presumption, even in a merger to monopoly such as this one, that innovation will be harmed. As discussed earlier, the overall cross-sectional relationship between market concentration and innovation is very difficult to discern for a number of reasons, including the lack of good data on concentration in relevant antitrust markets. Plus, even if one could measure this relationship, it is not directly relevant for analyzing mergers in which innovation effects are paramount, especially mergers to monopoly.

Chairman Muris does go on to examine the impact of the merger on Genzyme's incentive and ability to develop Pompe treatments. He denies that the two companies were racing for FDA approval, explaining:

> Shortly after the merger, Genzyme stated that comparative testing showed that its internal Pompe enzyme could be developed and commercialized most quickly. Genzyme also stated that the promise of the Novazyme technology was to provide a basis for an improved second-generation therapy. (Muris Statement, 12)

However, these statements, made by the merged firm itself in the face of antitrust review by the FTC, are perfectly consistent with the premerger Genzyme being spurred by the Novazyme threat to develop its treatment more quickly. In his dissenting statement, Commissioner Thompson, referring to competition between Genzyme and Novazyme states: "This competition was important because it created a race between Genzyme and Novazyme to develop Pompe ERTs, thus increasing the pace of innovation" (4). Given the inherent uncertainties associated with the new drug development process (and noting that Genzyme's treatment did not in fact gain FDA approval until 2006), it would seem hard to dismiss the possibility that, but for the merger, Genzyme would have been driven to move forward more quickly to gain FDA approval out of fear that Novazyme's treatment would gain FDA approval first.[43]

Even if one concludes that the merger did not reduce Genzyme's incen-

43. Anand (2006), chapter 20, "The Deal," offers evidence that Genzyme feared competition from Novazyme, and that these fears were a critical factor in Genzyme's decision to pay

tive to gain FDA approval for its first Pompe therapy, the merger reduced Genzyme's incentive to gain FDA approval for a *second* Pompe therapy. Chairman Muris explicitly notes this danger:

> If Genzyme has one Pompe therapy on the market, it might then have less incentive to market a second therapy than would an independent company that does not already have a product on the market. Because the second therapy would cannibalize sales of Genzyme's internal product, a merger with Novazyme could have caused Genzyme to reduce its investment in the second therapy. Moreover, Genzyme might have an incentive to delay introduction of the second therapy until the end of its initial seven years of market exclusivity in order to obtain a total of 14 years of exclusivity under the ODA. (Muris Statement, 13)

Muris dismisses this theory as well, noting that Genzyme would still have *some* incentive to develop and introduce a superior second treatment (14). However, by this argument one would never worry about the effect of a merger to monopoly on innovation because even a monopolist has *some* incentive to improve its product. Based on this dubious reasoning, Muris then states:

> In short, an analysis of Genzyme's incentives in this case does not clearly indicate whether Genzyme would have an incentive to delay the second Pompe product in the event that the first proved successful. (Muris Statement, 15)

Muris assigns a 75 percent probability to Genzyme's internal treatment gaining FDA approval, but concludes that the merger will not harm innovation to develop a superior treatment:

> There is no basis in the record for concluding that the circumstances that would give Genzyme an incentive to delay—concerns about cannibalization of sales of its internal product without sufficient offsetting expansion in demand, reduction in costs, or extension in product line—amount to anything more than a bare theoretical possibility. (Muris Statement, 19–20)

This statement appears to place no weight on Genzyme's reduced incentive to develop a superior treatment, and is peculiar given that Genzyme substantially delayed the Novazyme program during the time when the FTC was conducting its investigation.

Moving on to the Appropriability and Synergies principles, the merger does not appear to have solved an appropriability problem, or created merger-specific synergies, sufficient to offset the basic anticompetitive effects identified using the Contestability principle. Chairman Muris asserts: "By accelerating the Novazyme program, the merger may have increased its odds

$137.5 million (plus an additional $87.5 million on a contingent basis) for Novazyme, a company with no products or revenues.

of success" (17). However, as just described, the Novazyme program was greatly delayed after the merger.[44]

Muris also points to the comparative postmerger experiments conducted by Genzyme as a merger synergy. However, according to Anand (2006), Genzyme used these experiments to pick *one* Pompe treatment to pursue (its own internal program) and drop or delay the others. Without the merger, Genzyme could have performed comparative experiments among the three programs it controlled, and Novazyme could have continued with its own program, either alone or with another partner. That would have been a more innovative outcome.[45] Lastly, Anand (2006), reports that when Genzyme was bidding to acquire Novazyme in 2001, Genentech was offering to invest $22.5 million to acquire 10 percent of Novazyme and to fund the majority of the future development costs for the Novazyme Pompe treatment (224). Therefore, any benefits to Novazyme of gaining additional financing and moving forward with a major sponsor and partner were not specific to the Genzyme acquisition.

7.5.3 Thoratec/HeartWare

In February 2009, Thoratec and HeartWare signed an agreement under which Thoratec would acquire HeartWare for $282 million.[46] Thoratec was the only company offering a left ventricular assist device (LVAD) approved by the FDA for sale in the United States. According to the FTC Complaint, "LVADs are a life-sustaining technology for treating end-stage heart failure patients who have failed other courses of treatment and are likely to die while waiting for a donor heart or are ineligible for a heart transplant" (1). At the time of the proposed merger, HeartWare was developing its own LVAD, which was in the latter stages of clinical development.

The FTC challenged Thoratec's proposed acquisition of HeartWare in July 2009. According to the FTC Complaint, HeartWare was "the one company poised to seriously challenge Thoratec's monopoly of the US left ventricular assist device ('LVAD') market" (1). The FTC alleged that competition from HeartWare had already forced Thoratec to innovate and that the merger would eliminate innovation competition.

As with the Genzyme/Novazyme merger, we do not need to know about the overall cross-sectional relationship between market concentration and innovation to evaluate this merger. The Contestability principle tells us that

44. Muris later states: "it appears that the merger has accelerated the Novazyme program" (19). This assertion is difficult to reconcile with the description given in Anand (2006) and with Genzyme's public statements to investors about delays in the Novazyme program, as cited by Commissioner Thompson in his dissent (5).

45. According to Anand (2006), the Genzyme scientists had been skeptical of the Novazyme approach from the outset. This case thus also illustrates the advantages of independent ownership and competition for preserving innovation diversity when there are differences of opinion about which research tracks are the most promising.

46. I rely on the Federal Trade Commission (2009) for the facts reported here.

the merger would have substantially reduced rivalry, since many of the sales HeartWare stands to gain by obtaining FDA approval would come at the expense of Thoratec. There is no indication in the FTC complaint that the merger would have solved a substantial appropriability problem, or that the merger would have generated extraordinary merger-specific synergies.[47]

7.5.4 Ticketmaster/Live Nation

In February 2009, Ticketmaster and Live Nation announced their plans to merge.[48] For over two decades, Ticketmaster had been the dominant primary ticketing provider in the United States to major concert venues. The DOJ estimated Ticketmaster's share of primary ticketing to major concert venues at more than 80 percent, with the next closest competitor less than 4 percent.[49] Ticketmaster had also been slow to innovate and pass along lower costs to consumers:

> Ticketmaster's costs for distributing a ticket have been decreasing as consumers increasingly purchase tickets through the Internet. The cost-per-ticket to Ticketmaster for tickets sold through its website is significantly lower than the cost-per-ticket to Ticketmaster for tickets sold over the telephone or at a retail outlet. However, ticketing fees retained by Ticketmaster have not fallen as its distribution costs have declined. (DOJ Complaint, 11)

Live Nation was the largest concert promoter in the United States, also controlling over seventy-five concert venues in the United States. Live Nation had been Ticketmaster's largest primary ticketing client for a number of years. However, in 2007, Live Nation announced that it would not renew its contract with Ticketmaster and would instead become a direct competitor to Ticketmaster in primary ticketing once its Ticketmaster contract expired at the end of 2008.

In late December 2008, after nearly two years of preparation, Live Nation launched its ticketing service for its own venues and for potential third-party major concert venue clients. Live Nation represented an innovative threat to Ticketmaster's dominance in primary ticketing for major concert venues. By merging with Live Nation, Ticketmaster would have nipped that emerging threat in the bud. From the perspective of Live Nation, a large quantity of ticketing revenues were contestable, because Live Nation could capture those revenues from Ticketmaster. As initially proposed, the merger would have substantially reduced the contestability of ticketing revenues at major concert venues. However, Ticketmaster and Live Nation argued that the merger would also generate significant synergies through the vertical

47. "Any merger-specific and cognizable efficiencies resulting from the transaction will not offset the transaction's profound anticompetitive effects" (FTC Complaint, 2).

48. I rely on the Department of Justice (2010) for the facts reported here.

49. Department of Justice (2010, 10).

integration of promotion, venues, and ticketing. The Department of Justice eventually approved the merger subject to some substantial divestitures and other remedies.[50]

7.6 Exclusionary Conduct by Dominant Firms

Antitrust law in the United States has grappled for more than a century with where to draw the boundary between legitimate competition and exclusionary conduct by a dominant firm.[51] Considerable progress has been made on topics such as predatory pricing, but substantial controversy remains. Notably, the report on this topic issued by the Department of Justice in September 2008, "Competition and Monopoly: Single-Firm Conduct Under Section 2 of the Sherman Act," immediately drew sharp criticism from the Federal Trade Commission and was officially withdrawn in May 2009. My discussion here merely touches very lightly on the treatment of exclusionary conduct, focusing on innovation.

The highest-profile monopolization case in recent years, the case brought by the Department of Justice against Microsoft, centered on innovation effects. That case fit into the following general pattern: Firm M (the monopolist) is currently dominant in the market but faces the threat that Firm E (the entrant) will develop a new and improved product and overthrow Firm M as the market leader. Firm M engages in some type of conduct that impedes Firm E from developing new products, entering the market, or gaining scale. How does one determine whether Firm M's conduct is legitimate or exclusionary under the antitrust laws?

The empirical literature discussed earlier makes it clear that ongoing innovation by an incumbent is promoted if the incumbent fears that failure to improve its own product will place it at risk of being displaced as the market leader.[52] Likewise, innovation by entrants is promoted if an entrant that introduces a superior product will indeed gain substantial profitable sales, and perhaps even a dominant market position, at least for some period of time. Arrow was right that disruptive entrants with little or no financial interest in the status quo are critical to the innovative process. Schumpeter was also right that the prospect of gaining a temporary monopoly is a powerful inducement to innovate, for established firms and entrants alike.

The Contestability and Appropriability principles can go a long way—albeit at a high level—to inform the antitrust treatment of conduct by a

50. See Department of Justice (2010), Final Judgment, July 30, 2010. The author participated in this case at the DOJ.

51. For an entré to this literature that focuses on economic principles, see Kaplow and Shapiro (2007) and the references cited therein.

52. The cross-sectional relationship between market concentration and innovation is not directly relevant, especially inasmuch as the observations used to estimate that relationship involve concentration levels far lower than those associated with dominant firms facing a fringe of smaller rivals or entrants.

dominant incumbent firm in a market subject to technological change. Innovation by both incumbents and entrants is spurred if tomorrow's sales are contestable, in the sense that multiple firms are vying to win those sales and the lion's share of tomorrow's sales goes to the firm that succeeds in developing the best product. In the extreme case, one firm dominates the market at any point in time, but there is ongoing intense competition "for the market" that leads to rapid innovation. Innovation by both incumbents and entrants also is spurred if the successful innovator can appropriate a significant portion of the social benefits actually caused by its innovation.

Some have argued for a laissez faire antitrust policy in industries subject to technological change on the grounds that monopoly power in these industries is fleeting. However, this argument is seriously incomplete, since exclusionary practices (such as tying or exclusive dealing), if not checked by antitrust law, can make current monopoly power more durable by deterring innovative entrants. Others have argued for a laissez faire antitrust policy in industries subject to technological change on the grounds that such a policy would spur innovation by increasing the size of the prize won by the firm that obtains a dominant position. In a very important recent work, Segal and Whinston (2007) show that this argument also is seriously incomplete. In a model where two firms compete over time for market leadership by innovating, they provide surprisingly general conditions under which antitrust policies that protect entrants raise the rate of innovation.[53] Their analysis applies to a range of business practices by dominant firms, including long-term exclusive contracts with customers, compatibility decisions in a network industry, conduct that deters the R&D activities of entrants, and predatory activities.

7.7 Conclusions

Yes, Arrow *did* hit the bull's eye: a firm with a vested interest in the status quo has a smaller incentive than a new entrant to develop or introduce new technology that disrupts the status quo. Schumpeter was also quite correct: the prospect of obtaining market power is a necessary reward to innovation. There is no conflict whatsoever between these two fundamental insights.

The unifying principle, richly supported by the empirical literature, is that innovation, broadly defined, is spurred if the market is contestable; that is, if multiple firms are vying to win profitable future sales. This basic principle can take us a long way in evaluating the impact on innovation of horizontal mergers and of unilateral conduct by dominant firms.

53. Gans (2011) draws out some of the implications of the Segal and Whinston model for antitrust and innovation. In a related model of cumulative innovation, Raskovich and Miller (2010) provide conditions under which monopoly "extension" activities, which delay entry by the next incumbent, reduce the rate of innovation.

References

Aghion, Philippe, Nick Bloom, Richard Blundell, Rachel Griffith, and Peter Howitt. 2005. "Competition and Innovation: An Inverted-U Relationship." *Quarterly Journal of Economics* 120(2): 701–28.

Aghion, Philippe, and Rachel Griffith. 2005. *Competition and Growth: Reconciling Theory and Evidence.* Cambridge, MA: MIT Press.

Aghion, Philippe, Christopher Harris, Peter Howitt, and John Vickers. 2001. "Competition, Imitation and Growth with Step-by-Step Innovation." *Review of Economic Studies* 68:467–92.

Aghion, Philippe, and Peter Howitt. 2009. *The Economics of Growth.* Cambridge, MA: MIT Press.

Anand, Geeta. 2006. *The Cure: How a Father Raised $100 Million and Bucked the Medical Establishment in a Quest to Save His Children.* New York: HarperCollins.

Arrow, Kenneth. 1962. "Economic Welfare and the Allocation of Resources to Invention." In *The Rate and Direction of Inventive Activity: Economic and Social Factors,* edited by the Universities-National Bureau Committee for Economic Research and the Committee on Economic Growth of the Social Science Research Councils, 609–26. Princeton, NJ: Princeton University Press.

Baker, Jonathan. 2007. "Beyond Schumpeter vs. Arrow: How Antitrust Fosters Innovation." *Antitrust Law Journal* 74:575–602.

Baker, Jonathan, and Carl Shapiro. 2008. "Reinvigorating Horizontal Merger Enforcement." In *How the Chicago School Overshot the Mark: The Effect of Conservative Economic Analysis on U.S. Antitrust,* edited by Robert Pitofsky. New York: Oxford University Press.

Bartelsman, Eric, and Mark Doms. 2000. "Understanding Productivity: Lessons from Longitudinal Microdata." *Journal of Economic Literature* 38:569–94.

Bloom, Nicholas, and John Van Reenen. 2007. "Measuring and Explaining Management Practices Across Firms and Countries." *Quarterly Journal of Economics* 122:1351–408.

———. 2010. "Why Do Management Practices Differ Across Firms and Countries?" *Journal of Economic Perspectives* 24:203–24.

Blundell, Richard, Rachel Griffith, and John Van Reenen. 1999. "Market Share, Market Value and Innovation in Panel of British Manufacturing Firms." *Review of Economic Studies* 66:529–54.

Boone, Jan. 2000. "Competitive Pressure: The Effects on Investments in Product and Process Innovation." *Rand Journal of Economics* 31:549–69.

———. "Intensity of Competition and the Incentive to Innovate." *International Journal of Industrial Organization* 19:705–26.

Christensen, Clayton. 1997. *The Innovator's Dilemma.* Boston: Harvard Business School Press.

Cohen, Wesley. 1995. "Empirical Studies of Innovative Activity." In *Handbook of the Economics of Innovation and Technological Change,* edited by Paul Stoneman, 1059–1107. Basil Blackwell.

———. 2010. "Fifty Years of Empirical Studies of Innovative Activity and Performance." In *Handbook of Economics of Innovation,* vol. 1, edited by Bronwyn Hall and Nathan Rosenberg, 129–213. Amsterdam: North Holland.

Cohen, Wesley, and Richard Levin. 1989. "Empirical Studies of Innovation and Market Structure." In *Handbook of Industrial Organization,* edited by Richard Schmalensee and Robert Willig. New Holland.

Davis, Ronald. 2003. "Innovation Markets and Merger Enforcement: Current Practice in Perspective." *Antitrust Law Journal* 71:695–703.

Demsetz, Harold. 1973. "Industry Structure, Market Rivalry, and Public Policy." *Journal of Law and Economics* 16:1–9.

Department of Justice, Antitrust Division. 2008. "Competition and Monopoly: Single-Firm Conduct Under Section 2 of the Sherman Act." September. http://www.justice.gov/atr/public/reports/236681.pdf.

———. 2010. "Ticketmaster Matter Materials." http://www.justice.gov/atr/cases/ticket.htm.

Farrell, Joseph, and Carl Shapiro. 2010. "Antitrust Evaluation of Horizontal Mergers: An Economic Alternative to Market Definition." *B. E. Journal of Theoretical Economics* 10, Article 9. http://www.bepress.com/bejte/vol10/iss1/art9.

Federal Trade Commission Staff Report. 1996. *Anticipating the 21st Century: Competition Policy in the High-Tech Global Marketplace.* http://www.ftc.gov/opp/global/report/gc_v1.pdf.

Federal Trade Commission. 2004. "Genzyme/Novazyme Matter Materials." http://www.ftc.gov/opa/2004/01/genzyme.shtm.

———. 2009. "Thoratec/Heartware Matter Materials." http://www.ftc.gov/opa/2009/07/thoratec.shtm.

Gans, Joshua. 2011. "When Is Static Analysis a Sufficient Proxy for Dynamic Considerations? Reconsidering Antitrust and Innovation." In *Innovation Policy and the Economy,* vol. 11, edited by Josh Lerner and Scott Stern, 55–78. Chicago: University of Chicago Press.

Gilbert, Richard. 2006. "Looking for Mr. Schumpeter: Where Are We in the Competition-Innovation Debate." In *Innovation Policy and the Economy,* vol. 6, edited by Adam Jaffe, Josh Lerner, and Scott Stern, 159–215. Chicago: University of Chicago Press.

Gilbert, Richard, and David Newbery. 1982. "Preemptive Patenting and the Persistence of Monopoly." *American Economic Review* 72:514–26.

Gilbert, Richard, and Willard Tom. 2001. "Is Innovation King at the Antitrust Agencies? The Intellectual Property Guidelines Five Years Later." *Antitrust Law Journal* 69:43–86.

Grove, Andrew. 1996. *Only the Paranoid Survive.* New York: Random House.

Holmes, Thomas, David Levine, and James Schmitz. 2008. "Monopoly and the Incentive to Innovate When Adoption Involves Switchover Disruptions." NBER Working Paper no. 13864. Cambridge, MA: National Bureau of Economic Research, March.

Holmes, Thomas, and James Schmitz. 2010. "Competition and Productivity: A Review of Evidence." *Annual Review of Economics* 2:619–42.

Kaplow, Louis, and Carl Shapiro. 2007. "Antitrust." In *Handbook of Law and Economics,* vol. 2, edited by A. Mitchell Polinsky and Steven Shavell, 1073–225. Elsevier.

Katz, Michael, and Howard Shelanski. 2005. "Mergers Policy and Innovation: Must Enforcement Change to Account for Technological Change?" In *Innovation Policy and the Economy,* vol. 5, edited by Adam Jaffe, Josh Lerner, and Scott Stern, 109–65. Chicago: University of Chicago Press.

———. 2007. "Mergers and Innovation." *Antitrust Law Journal* 74:1–85.

Lee, Chang-Yang. 2005. "A New Perspective on Industry R&D and Market Structure." *Journal of Industrial Economics* 53:101–22.

———. 2009. "Competition Favors the Prepared Firm: Firm's R&D Response to Competitive Market Pressure." *Research Policy* 38:861–70.

Leibenstein, Harvey. 1966. "Allocative Efficiency vs. 'X-Efficiency.'" *American Economic Review* 56:392–415.

Lewis, William. 2004. *The Power of Productivity: Wealth, Poverty, and the Threat to Global Stability.* Chicago: University of Chicago Press.

Motta, Massimo. 2004. *Competition Policy: Theory and Practice.* Cambridge: Cambridge University Press.
Nickell, Stephen. 1996. "Competition and Corporate Performance." *Journal of Political Economy* 104 (4): 724–46.
Porter, Michael. 1990. *The Competitive Advantage of Nations.* New York: McMillan Press.
———. 2001. "Competition and Antitrust: Towards a Productivity-Based Approach to Evaluating Mergers and Joint Ventures." *Antitrust Bulletin* 46:919–58.
Raskovich, Alexander, and Nathan Miller. 2010. "Cumulative Innovation and Competition Policy." Antitrust Division, US Department of Justice, EAG Discussion Paper 10-5, September. http://www.justice.gov/atr/public/eag/262643.pdf.
Sacco, Dario, and Armin Schmutzler. 2011. "Is There a U-Shaped Relation Between Competition and Investment?" *International Journal of Industrial Organization* 29 (1): 65–73.
Schmutzler, Armin. 2010. "The Relation Between Competition and Innovation: Why Is It Such a Mess?" Centre for Economic Policy Research, Discussion Paper no. DP-7640, January. University of Zurich.
Schumpeter, Joseph. 1942. *Capitalism, Socialism and Democracy.* New York: Harper & Brothers. (Citations to Harper Perennial Modern Thought Edition, published 2008.)
Scopelliti, Alessandro. 2010. "Competition and Economic Growth: A Critical Survey of the Theoretical Literature." *Journal of Applied Economic Sciences* 11:70–93.
Segal, Ilya, and Michael Whinston. 2007. "Antitrust in Innovative Industries." *American Economic Review* 97:1703–30.
Shapiro, Carl. 2007. "Patent Reform: Aligning Reward and Contribution." In *Innovation Policy and the Economy,* vol. 8, edited by Adam Jaffe, Josh Lerner, and Scott Stern, 111–56. Chicago: University of Chicago Press.
Sutton, John. 1998. *Technology and Market Structure.* Cambridge, MA: MIT Press.
———. 2007, "Market Structure: Theory and Evidence." In *Handbook of Industrial Organization,* vol. 3, edited by Mark Armstrong and Robert Porter, 2301–368. Elsevier.
Syverson, Chad. 2004. "Market Structure and Productivity: A Concrete Example." *Journal of Political Economy* 112:1181–222.
———. 2011. "What Determines Productivity?" *Journal of Economic Literature* 49 (2): 326–65.
Tirole, Jean. 1997. *The Theory of Industrial Organization.* Cambridge, MA: MIT Press.
Vives, Xavier. 2008. "Innovation and Competitive Pressure." *Journal of Industrial Economics* 61:419–69.

Comment Michael D. Whinston

It is a pleasure to discuss a chapter of Carl's. The chapter focuses on an important but quite specific issue concerning innovation, namely the anti-

Michael D. Whinston is the Robert E. and Emily H. King Professor of Business Institutions at Northwestern University and a research associate of the National Bureau of Economic Research.

trust review of mergers in innovative industries. In the chapter, Carl makes two basic points: first, he argues that a merger's likely effects on innovation can often be discerned despite the seemingly negative lesson from the recent R&D and growth literatures, in which the level of innovation has no clear relation to the level of competition. Second, Carl suggests some principles that he feels can usefully guide such merger reviews. Here I will discuss these points in turn.

Let's start with the "complex relationship" between the level of competition and the rate of innovation, upon which the R&D and growth literatures have recently focused. What drives this complexity? In fact, you can see an important source of it by thinking about Arrow (1962) and Schumpeter (1942). Roughly speaking, there are two different times at which we might be concerned with market structure: ex ante (before the innovation) and ex post (after the innovation). Arrow showed that ex ante market structure is important, and that greater ex ante competition encourages innovation. The reason is simple: more ex ante competition destroys profits in the ex ante state, which gives firms a greater incentive to innovate to escape from that state. Schumpeter instead argued that competition is bad for innovation, but did so focusing on ex post market structure: destroying profits ex post reduces firms' incentives to innovate to get into that state. In essence, in the more recent models in this literature, competition is changed in *both* ex ante *and* ex post states. Because of this, things get complicated, and this tension between ex ante and ex post effects shows up in the varied effects observed in a lot of the literature.

Carl nicely illustrates this point in his discussion of the Aghion et al. (2005) paper. In that paper, the meaning of "less competition" is that there is less intense pricing rivalry when firms are in the neck-and-neck state in which they have the same technological capabilities. The neck-and-neck state is the ex post state when we look at R&D by the trailing firm when one firm is ahead and the other is behind,[1] but it is the ex ante state when we think about the R&D that occurs when the two firms are neck and neck. As a result, there are two opposing effects of more intense competition on innovation: an increase in innovation in the neck-and-neck state but a reduction in the state in which one firm is ahead. This fact then leads to an inverted U-shaped relationship between competition and innovation, where innovation is greatest at intermediate levels of competition. The reason for the inverted U is that the industry tends to spend more of its time in the state in which innovation is lowest, because that is the state firms tend not to move out of. Specifically, when there is little competition, there is little innovation in the neck-and-neck state, and a lot in the state where one firm is behind. As a result, firms are much more likely to be in the neck-and-neck state, which

1. Aghion at al. assume that a leader cannot be more than one step ahead; as a result, only the follower will do R&D in this state.

means that if we increase competition the (average) response of innovation is dominated by the response in the neck-and-neck state, which is positive. Similar reasoning implies that when competition is high in this sense, the industry is much more likely to be in the state where one firm is behind, so an increase in competition will reduce R&D on average.

While this inverted U-shaped relationship is certainly interesting and useful for understanding what we see in industry data, does it mean that we cannot predict the likely effects of a merger in an innovative industry? Carl argues no, and I agree. A key reason is that if you are thinking about mergers, the comparative statics exercise that is of interest to you—how this merger will affect the rate of innovation and welfare—differs from the comparative statics exercise that is conducted in this literature. To shamelessly plug some of my own work, a few years ago Ilya Segal and I wrote a paper (Segal and Whinston 2007) on antitrust in innovative industries. There we focused primarily on exclusionary behavior rather than on mergers, but a similar issue came up. We put the point as follows:

> The growth literature often considers how changes in various parameters will affect the rate of innovation, sometimes even calling such parameters measures of the degree of "antitrust policy". . . . Here we are much more explicit than is the growth literature about what antitrust policies toward specific practices do. This is not a minor difference, as our results differ substantially from those that might be inferred from the parameter changes considered in the growth literature. As one example, one would get exactly the wrong conclusion if one extrapolated results showing that more inelastic demand functions lead to more innovation (e.g., Aghion and Howitt 1992) to mean that allowing an incumbent to enhance its market power through long-term contracts leads to more innovation. (Segal and Whinston 2007, 1704)

Let's consider two examples to illustrate how the presence of a seemingly "complex relationship" between competition and R&D need not prevent definitive answers to specific competition policy questions. Consider first the model with Ilya. It was a quality ladder model of innovation similar to those in the growth literature. There was an entrant—if successful in its R&D, the entrant came in and competed for one period before displacing the incumbent monopolist. The entrant would then be an uncontested monopolist until he himself ultimately faced a successful new entrant and was displaced.

In this setting we asked whether allowing incumbents to deter entry through exclusive contracts with buyers would encourage or discourage innovation. (The question was motivated in part by the *Microsoft* case, where Microsoft wrote partially exclusive contracts with buyers and providers of complementary goods.) Exclusive contracts reduce the number of buyers who are free to purchase from an entrant, which tends to reduce innovative effort by prospective entrants. However, once an entrant displaces

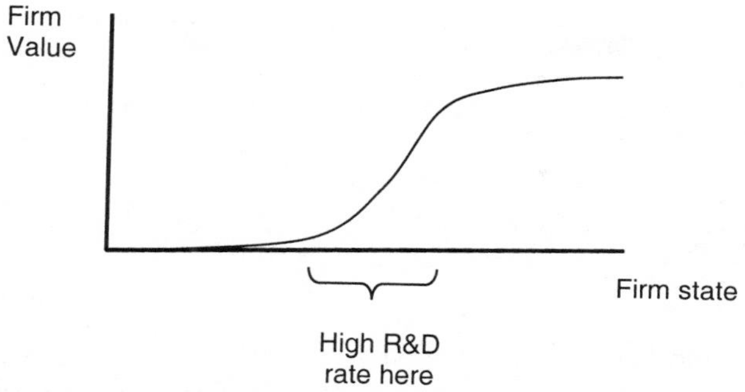

Figure 7C.1 A firm's value function in the Pakes-McGuire model

the incumbent and becomes the new monopolist, it is more profitable if it can deter entry, so allowing such deterrence could also raise the incentive to innovate. As a result, it might seem like one cannot say anything about which way the overall effect comes out. Nonetheless, we showed that fairly generally the use of exclusives lowers the rate of innovation (and both consumer and aggregate surplus).

Now consider a different dynamic model of innovation due to Pakes and McGuire (1994) (see also Ericson and Pakes 1995). In this model, there is a differentiated product oligopolistic industry in which, in each period, firms engage in price competition and can also invest in stochastic product improvement. Both entry and exit are also possible. A firm's value function in this model typically looks as in figure 7C.1, where the horizontal axis measures the firm's state (innovation can increase a firm's state, which raises its product's value to consumers) and the vertical axis measures the firm's value. The graph of the value function in the figure holds the states of the firm's rivals fixed.

As can be seen in the figure, the value function is S-shaped: relatively flat at low and high states, with a steep section in the middle. Innovation will be high when the firm is in a state at which this curve is steep (the returns to product improvement are then large). The steep section is like the neck-and-neck state in Aghion et al. (2005). Although Pakes and McGuire do not do this, I think if you actually looked at this model and had a bunch of these industries in different states, you likely would get an inverted U-shaped relationship between the rate of innovation and the intensity of competition. At the very least, the relationship would be "complex."

Nonetheless, when Pakes and McGuire simulate the effect of a merger in the Markov perfect equilibrium of their model, its impact on consumers is very clear. Table 7C.1 shows the levels of industry profit, consumer surplus, and aggregate surplus in three cases: the first best, the oligopolistic Markov perfect equilibrium, and a fully collusive outcome. The fully col-

Table 7C.1 **Profit, consumer surplus, and aggregate surplus in the Pakes-McGuire model**

	Industry profit	Consumer surplus	Aggregate surplus
First best			377
Markov perfect equilibrium	70	301	369
Collusion (industry-wide merger)	218	115	332

lusive outcome can be thought of as the result of an industry-wide merger (including all potential entrants). The first-best aggregate surplus is 377. There is a small loss in aggregate surplus in the Markov perfect equilibrium: consumer surplus is 300 and industry profit is 70. (This is an industry where, on average, three or four firms are active.) With the industry-wide merger, aggregate surplus falls 10 percent compared to the Markov perfect equilibrium and consumers do really badly: their surplus falls by almost two-thirds. (The rate of innovation also falls dramatically.) Thus, despite any general complexity of the relation between the level of competition and the rate of innovation, this merger is evidently very bad for consumers. Gowrisankaran (1995) also finds negative effects on consumers (and a reduction in R&D) in a closely-related model when he allows for (endogenous) nonindustry-wide mergers.[2]

In summary, I think Carl is completely correct in his first point: while the R&D and growth literatures that exhibit "complex" (inverted U-shaped) effects are certainly interesting and valuable contributions, they are often not on point, or only partially so, for the questions we want to ask when evaluating mergers in innovative industries.

Now to Carl's second point. Suppose a merger in an innovative industry faces antitrust review. What can we say about the merger's likely effects on innovation? Carl proposes some principles to aide such analysis. Perhaps it would be most useful if I discuss how I would think about the likely effects on innovation if I were looking at such a merger.[3] (One would also need to think about its overall effect on consumers.)

My starting point would be to assess how the merger changes the R&D incentives for the merging firms, holding fixed the R&D activities of the merging firms' rivals. Here one is assessing how the merger changes the degree to which the firms' profits respond positively to their level of inno-

2. It is worth noting that other interventions to increase "competition" need not be welfare-improving. For instance, Pakes and McGuire also simulate the effect of a rule limiting firms' market shares to be no greater than 65 percent. This rule reduces both consumer and aggregate surplus relative to the Markov perfect equilibrium.

3. Because Carl changed his statement of these principles in the revised draft of his paper, I have modified what follows somewhat from my discussion at the conference. The discussion that follows is, I think, broadly consistent with the approach Carl proposes in the final version of his chapter.

vation. Several factors go into this. The most important seems to me to be the degree to which the merger internalizes externalities arising from the merging firms' R&D. This R&D externality internalization effect of the merger could in principle be positive or negative. For example, in a quality ladder model there is an important positive externality across generations (each innovation enables later ones), so a merger could increase innovation incentives by internalizing this positive externality. On the other hand, in the Pakes and McGuire model, innovation creates only negative externalities across firms, so a merger will most likely reduce innovation incentives. But what is important to note, I think, is that this first critical factor is likely to be reasonably assessed by those reviewing the merger, and is unrelated to the factors contributing to the "complex" relationship just discussed. This is where the fact that we are focusing on the effect of a *merger,* not some other change in "competition," really matters.

Mergers also cause externalities on another set of market participants: consumers. Because the merger internalizes pricing externalities, it can alter the degree to which firms rather than consumers benefit from an innovation, and hence can alter firms' incentives to do R&D. This effect is related to the complex relationship discussed earlier, and is probably harder to assess. My own gut feeling is that in most (though not all) cases, this effect is likely to be less important than the R&D externality internalization effect.

Finally, this first step also needs to incorporate any efficiency effects in R&D production created by the merger.

A second concern is how the merging firms' rivals will react to this change. In particular, are R&D efforts strategic substitutes or strategic complements in the sense of Bulow, Geanakoplos, and Klemperer (1985)? If they are strategic complements and you dull innovation incentives for the merging firms, everyone's R&D goes down. If they are strategic substitutes, then the rivals will increase their R&D in response to the merging firms reducing theirs. In that case, it may seem that the overall effect is unclear. Typically, however, we expect that this countervailing effect does not overwhelm the direct effect—that the other firms do not expand their R&D enough to counterbalance the R&D contraction of the merging firms. Indeed, in most theoretical papers, this is just invoked as a standard assumption. Its import is that, if true, one only needs to look at the direct effect on the merging firms' R&D holding rivals' R&D efforts fixed to discern the overall effect on R&D.

Matters would be more complicated when innovative efforts are not one-dimensional. For example, a merger might enhance incentives for some types of R&D and reduce it for others. Or the R&D of the rivals may differ from that of the merging firms. Nonetheless, in many cases this way of thinking seems likely to get us fairly far in thinking about these issues.

To sum up, this is a worthwhile chapter that should help restore faith among those who need to evaluate mergers in innovative industries, and that also provides some guidance on how to do it.

References

Aghion, P., N. Bloom, R. Blundell, R. Griffith, and P. Howitt. 2005. "Competition and Innovation: An Inverted U Relationship." *Quarterly Journal of Economics* 120:701–28.

Arrow, K. 1962. "Economic Welfare and the Allocation of Resources to Invention." In *The Rate and Direction of Inventive Activity: Economic and Social Factors,* edited by Universities-National Bureau Committee for Economic Research and the Committee on Economic Growth of the Social Science Research Councils, 467–92. Princeton, NJ: Princeton University Press.

Bulow, J., J. Geanakoplos, and P. Klemperer. 1985. "Multimarket Oligopoly: Strategic Substitutes and Complements." *Journal of Political Economy* 93:488–511.

Ericson, R., and A. Pakes. 1995. "Markov-Perfect Industry Dynamics: A Framework for Empirical Analysis." *Review of Economic Studies* 62:52–82.

Gowrisankaran, G. 1995. "A Dynamic Model of Endogenous Horizontal Mergers." *RAND Journal of Economics* 30:56–83.

Pakes, A., and P. McGuire. 1994. "Computing Markov-Perfect Nash Equilibria: Numerical Implications of a Dynamic Differentiated Product Model." *RAND Journal of Economics* 25:555–89.

Schumpeter, Joseph. 1942. *Capitalism, Socialism and Democracy.* New York: Harper & Brothers.

Segal, I., and M. D. Whinston. 2007. "Antitrust in Innovative Industries." *American Economic Review* 97:1703–30.

IV
The Sources and Motivations of Innovators

8

Did Plant Patents Create the American Rose?

Petra Moser and Paul W. Rhode

In 1930, the US Congress established the first intellectual property rights (IPRs) for living organisms. With the Plant Patent Act (PPA) it created patent rights to prevent the replication of genetic materials through roots and cuttings (rather than seeds). Breeders of such "asexually-propagated" plants, including fruit trees and roses, argued that they needed IPRs to recover large development costs. By creating IPRs, the US government hoped to encourage domestic innovation and the development of a domestic plant breeding industry.

This chapter uses historical data on patents and registrations of new plant varieties to examine the effects of the Plant Patent Act on biological innovation. Evidence on a later Act, the Plant Variety Protection Act (PVPA) of 1970, is mixed. The PVPA complemented the PPA by extending IPRs to plants that reproduce "sexually" through seeds, such as wheat, soybeans, or cotton. Survey results suggest that it encouraged research expenditures and "stimulated the development of new varieties of wheat and soybeans" (Butler and Marion 1985; Perrin, Kunnings, and Ihnen 1983). Most of these increases in research investments, however, came from the public sector, and there is little evidence that crops, and specifically wheat, performed

Petra Moser is assistant professor of economics at Stanford University and a faculty research fellow of the National Bureau of Economic Research. Paul W. Rhode is professor of economics at the University of Michigan and a research associate of the National Bureau of Economic Research.

We thank Julian Alston, Jeff Furman, Eric Hilt, Josh Lerner, Philip Pardey, Scott Stern, and participants at the NBER Conference on the Rate and Direction of Technical Change for helpful comments. Ryan Lampe, Shirlee Lichtman, Kasiana McLenaghan, Jörg Ohmstedt, Fred Panier, and Tilky Xu provided outstanding research assistance. We would like to thank Helena Fitz-Patrick for helping us to secure permission to reproduce figure 8.1.

better after 1970 (Alston and Venner 2002).[1] For cotton, on the other hand, changes in acreage and in the variety of cotton crops suggest a positive effect of IPRs (Naseem, Oehmke, and Schimmelpfennig 2005).

The small number of patents for crop plants, such as fruit trees and vines, suggest that the effects of the PPA on commercial agriculture were limited: "The great hopes for agriculture have not been realized" (Daus 1967, 394). For the rose industry, however, observers noted that "the Plant Patent Act cannot be deemed unsuccessful" (Daus 1967, 389).

Nearly half of 3,010 plant patents granted between 1931 and 1970 were for roses. Large commercial nurseries, which began to operate extensive mass hybridization programs in the 1940s and 1950s, account for most of the plant patents, suggesting that the creation of IPRs may have helped to encourage the creation of a domestic US rose industry (e.g., Harkness 1985). Industry experts, however, cautioned that [p]atented roses have not lived up to expectations" (Swecker 1944, 120). A potential explanation for the discrepancy between the large number of rose patents and the disappointment about the PPA is that breeders may have used plant patents strategically to protect themselves from litigation (e.g., Kile 1934), so that increases in patenting do not reflect increases in innovation. To separate changes in strategic patenting from changes in innovation, we collect data on registrations of new rose varieties as an alternative measure of innovation.

Registration data show that US breeders created *fewer* new varieties after 1930 compared with before. European breeders continued to create most roses after 1930, and only one American breeder was among the ten breeders with the largest number of registrations. The data also show that only a small share of newly-developed roses—less than one in five—were patented.

Notably, some of the most prominent American roses were based on European roses that US nurseries had begun to license and propagate during World War II. At a time when plant patents strengthened incentives to invest in R&D, US nurseries also benefited from demand shocks as a result of World War II when European supplies were cut off and US breeders began to grow and improve roses that had been developed abroad.

8.1 The Plant Patent Act of 1930

Although Congress had discussed IPRs for plants as early as 1885, it took food shortages during World War I and demands from the farm bloc states

1. Instead of arguing that IPRs failed to encourage innovation, Alston and Venner (2002) conclude that an exemption of the PVPA, which allows farmers to copy seeds for their own use, weakened breeders' ability to appropriate the returns of R&D. Another factor is that IPRs may have limited effects on crops that can be protected through secrecy (e.g., Moser, forthcoming). Secrecy is particularly effective to protect innovations in hybrid seeds whose desirable characteristics cannot be replicated by replanting the improved seeds. Analyses of certificate data indicate that breeders of hybrid corn were reluctant to use IPRs (Janis and Kesan 2002; Dhar and Foltz 2007).

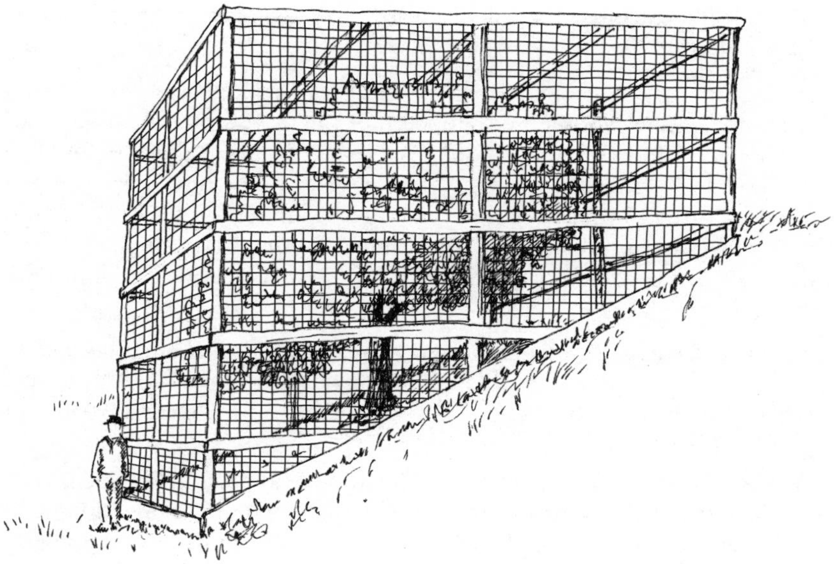

Fig. 8.1 A cage that Stark Brothers built around its *Golden Delicious* apple
Notes: The cage was built around the Stark Brother's *Golden Delicious* tree to prevent competitors from stealing shoots of the tree; it was equipped with an alarm. Drawing based on Rossman (1930, 395).

to "place agriculture on a basis of economic equality with industry" to create sufficient pressure for legislative action (Kloppenburg 2004, 132; US House 1906, 6–7; Olmstead and Rhode 2000). Breeders of roses and fruit trees, such as Paul Stark of Stark Brothers Nursery, were the driving force behind the PPA (Fowler 2000, 628–35; Kevles 2008, 210–12, Terry 1966, 30–34). In the absence of IPRs, Stark Brothers had taken desperate measures to protect agricultural innovations. In the mid-1910s it built a large cage, armed with a burglar alarm, to prevent competitors from stealing cuttings of the first *Golden Delicious* apple tree (fig. 8.1; Rossman 1930, 394–95; Terry 1966, 48). Another large nursery, Jackson and Perkins, advised Congress in May 1930 that the plant patent legislation was "of very great importance to the agricultural and horticultural interests of the United States" and would provide "wonderful stimulus" (*Congressional Record,* 71st Cong., 2nd Sess. May 12, 1930, 8751).[2] Thomas A. Edison (1847–1931) supported the Act in congressional debates:

> Nothing that Congress could do to help farming would be of greater value and permanence than to give the plant breeder the same status as

2. In the 1950s and 1960s roses accounted for 15 to 20 percent of US nursery sales, which includes other ornamental plants and fruit trees.

> the mechanical and chemical inventors now have through the patent law. (US House 1930, 2–3)

Edison had been a close friend of Luther Burbank (1849–1926) an American breeder who had developed more than new 800 plant varieties (Smith 2009, 308–309). Edison observed that at present "there are but few plant breeders" and that patents would "give us many Burbanks."[3] When Fiorello ("Little Flower") LaGuardia remarked that "Luther Burbank did very well without protection" (*Congressional Record,* 71st Cong., 2nd Sess. May 5, 1930, 8391), supporters of the Act presented a letter from Burbank to Paul Stark:

> A man can patent a mousetrap or copyright a nasty song, but if he gives to the world a new fruit that will add millions to the value of earth's annual harvest he will be fortunate if he is rewarded by so much as having his name connected with the result. (US House 1930, 11)

The Plant Patent Act passed in the House on May 13, and President Herbert Hoover signed it into law on May 23 (Allyn 1944, 13, Appendix A). In its final report, Congress emphasized the importance of intellectual property rights in the absence of alternative mechanisms:

> To-day the plant breeder has no adequate financial incentive to enter upon his work. A new variety once it has left the hands of the breeder may be reproduced in unlimited quantity by all. The originator's only hope of financial reimbursement is through high prices for the comparatively few reproductions that he may dispose of during the first two or three years. After that time, depending upon the speed with which the plant may be asexually reproduced, the breeder loses all control of his discovery. (US House 1930, 10–11)

By creating intellectual property rights the government hoped to attract private investments in R&D and support the creation of a commercially viable domestic plant breeding industry.

> To-day plant breeding and research is dependent, in large part, upon Government funds to Government experiment stations, or the limited endeavors of the amateur breeder. It is hoped that the bill will afford a sound basis for investing capital in plant breeding and consequently plant development through private funds. (US House 1930, 10)

3. Edison had entered the field of experimental plant breeding when he was trying to increase the rubber content of goldenrod, a golden yellow American flower. Edison's experiments produced a 12-foot tall plant that yielded as much as 12 percent of especially resilient and long-lasting rubber, which Edison used to build tires for his own Model T. Although Edison had turned his research over to the US government in 1930, goldenrod rubber never went beyond the experimental stage (Rossman 1930, 394–95).

8.1.1 IPRs under the Plant Patent Act of 1930

To protect the property rights of private investors, the PPA granted seventeen years of exclusive rights for new varieties of asexually propagated plants—plants that reproduce by roots, shoots, or buds. Sexually propagated plants were excluded after plant scientists of the American Society of Horticultural Sciences argued that the characteristics of new varieties would not be genetically stable. Paul Stark of Stark Brothers Nursery recalled that "it was clearly evident that no Plant Patent bill could be passed that included sexually propagated plants" (US Senate 1968, 863).[4] The Act also excluded edible tubers—such as potatoes—possibly to prevent private firms from holding monopoly rights over vital US food supplies (Allyn 1944, 34).[5]

Compared with other types of patents, plant patents are narrower in scope (Daus 1967, 392). Similar to drug patents that cover a single molecule, plant patents cover only the asexual reproduction of an individual plant grown in cultivation; they do not cover the seeds of the new plant, or other plants with the same characteristics. Grant rates, measured as patent grants over publications, are higher for plant patents than for other types of IPRs. Thus, 92 percent of applications between 1961 and 1965 were accepted by the United States Patent and Trademark Office (USPTO) (576 grants over 628 applications), compared with 59 percent for utility patents and 55 percent for design patents (Daus 1967, 392). Plants did not have to be "useful" to be patentable (Allyn 1944, 13–14).

In principle, asexually-propagated plants have to be new, distinct, and not found in the wild to be patentable; in practice, however, sports—random bud variations that can be found in a nursery, a garden, or in the wild—were frequently patented.[6] The *Briarcliff* rose, for example, which was not patented, yielded seven sports that were patented; *Talisman* yielded fourteen sports that were patented.[7] Two sports of Talisman, *Souvenir* (PP [plant patent] 25) and *Mrs. Franklin D. Roosevelt* (PP 80) produced six sports, and every one of them was patented. A sport of *Briarcliff* called *Better Times* (PP23)

4. Although the American Seed Trade Association wanted IPRs, Stark convinced them that the time was not ripe: "It seemed to be the wise thing to get established the principle that Congress recognized the rights of the plant breeder and originators. Then, in the light of experience, effort could be made to get protection also for seed propagated plants which would be much easier after this fundamental principle was established" (Fowler 1994, 82–84 citing the American Seed Trade Association, 1930 Proceedings, 66). Stark's lobbying efforts cost the American Association of Nurserymen about $12,000 in 1930 ($130,000 in 2009 purchasing power; White 1975, 132).

5. Another argument against patents for tubers was that infringements are difficult to prove for tubers, so patent rights would be difficult to enforce (US Senate 1968, 863).

6. Even though the USPTO was officially in charge of determining whether a plant was "new and distinct," the PPA allowed it to seek advice from the US Department of Agriculture (USDA).

7. *Talisman* was the offspring of *Ophelia,* introduced in 1912, which was prone to mutation and produced more than 20 sports (McFarland 1947, 191–92).

yielded thirteen sports; the USPTO patented all of them. At least one of these sports (PP452) yielded yet another generation of patented roses (Allyn 1944, 31, 50; and Fowler 1994, 86–88).

In 1954 the USPTO ruled that "mere fortuitous finds" such as mutant seedlings were not patentable, but Congress quickly amended the law to include "chance seedlings producing distinct new plants, whether found in cultivated or uncultivated states" (White 1975, 133, 256–57; Alston et al. 2010, 212).

In principle, the PPA also excluded plants that had been introduced or sold to the public more than two years before the patent application; in practice, however, most of the plants patented by 1934 were developed before 1930.[8] In 1944, the patent attorney Robert Starr Allyn observed that "many of the patents thus far issued appear to be invalid" and at least 61 of 610 plant patents granted by 1943 had been developed before 1930 (Allyn 1944, 57). Most notably, nursery stock was exempt from the rule of prior use.

Patent examiners were especially lenient in granting patents for nursery stock that Luther Burbank had developed with financing from Stark Brothers and that was owned by Stark Nurseries after his death (Allyn 1944, 54). In 1933 alone, the USPTO granted nine patents to Burbank's estate, including two for roses (PP65 and 66, *Burbank's Apple Blossom* and *Burbank's Golden Sunset*), four for plums, two for peaches (PP12, 13, 14, 15, 16, and 18), and one for a new variety of cherry (PP41). As late as 1937 and 1938, the USPTO granted PP235 for *Burbank's Golden Comet* (in 1937) and PP266, PP267, and PP269 for *Burbank's Copper Climber, Burbank's Snow White Climber,* and *Burbank's Dawn Glow* (in 1938). None of these posthumously patented roses became commercially important (Terry 1966).

8.2 Most Early Plant Patents Were Roses

On August 31, 1931, the Patent Office granted the first plant patent (PP1) to Henry F. Bosenberg, a New Jersey gardener (figure 8.2) for *New Dawn,* a continuously blooming bud variant of a disease-free and vigorous climbing rose that he selected and propagated (*Journal of Heredity,* 1931, 313–19).[9] Four additional patents were granted in 1931: two for roses, one for a dewberry, and one for a new variety of carnation.[10]

8. Allyn 1944, 55. The principle of excluding plants that had been introduced before the Act was affirmed in *Cole Nursery Co. v. Youdath Perennial Garden* (1936) over a potential infringement of PP110, the Horvath Barberry plant. Judge Paul Jones invalidated PP110 because the Horvath plant had been produced in the winter of 1923–1924. By 1943, the exclusion period had been reduced to one year.

9. *New Dawn* was nearly identical to a climbing rose that Van Fleet had discovered in his work at the USDA, but this older rose bloomed once a year (a dominant trait caused by a single gene) while *Bosenberg's New Dawn* bloomed continuously throughout the year (following the recessive trait, Kile 1934, 59–61).

10. Throughout the 1930s the average lag between application and grant was 321 days (calculated from data in "Die amerikanischen Pflanzenpatente," *Wirtschaftlicher Teil,* 1931–1939).

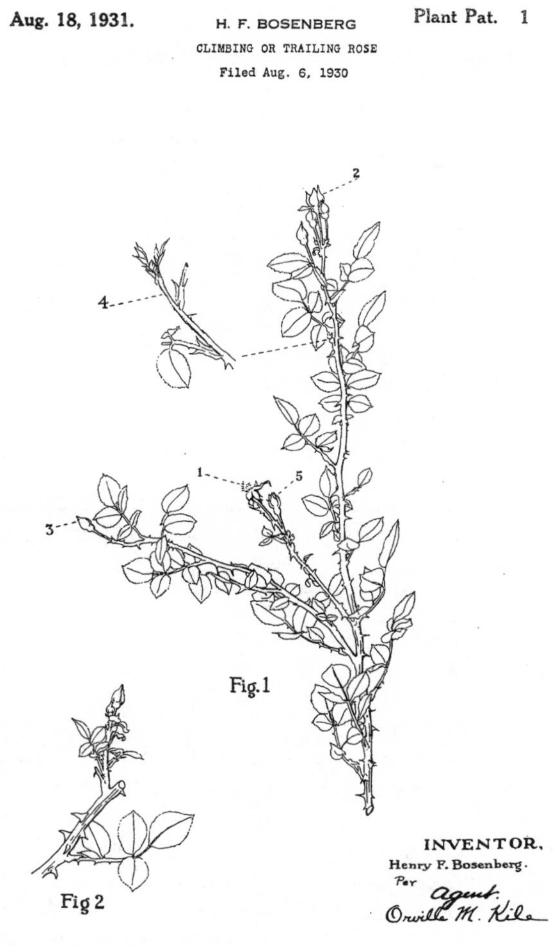

Fig. 8.2 Plant patent USPTO PP1

Notes: The first plant patent was granted to Henry F. Bosenberg on August 18, 1931, for a climbing or trailing rose that he observed in the wild. Bosenberg's rose, which became known as *New Dawn,* was a sport—a random bud variation—of another rose that Walter Van Fleet had developed before 1922. Image from the United States Patent Office (www.uspto.gov).

Between August 1931 and April 1, 2009, a total of 19,973 plant patents were granted in the United States. From 1931 to 1940 the number of plant patents per year increased from five to nearly ninety (figure 8.3); with the

More generally, the lag between a patent application and a patent grant varies with the complexity of the patent and the workload of the examiners (Popp, Juhl, and Johnson 2004). For utility patents in the chemical industry in the 1930s, the lag between patent grants and patent applications was between two and three years (Moser and Voena, forthcoming); for utility patents of sewing machines in the 1870s, the lag was 140 days (Lampe and Moser 2010).

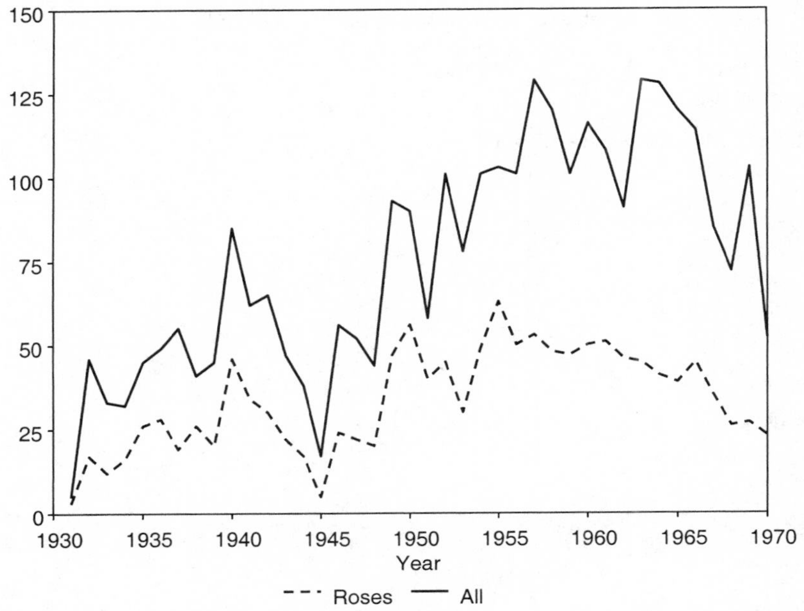

Fig. 8.3 Plant patents per year, 1931–1970

Notes: Plant patents from the USPTO *Patent Statistic Reports* (available at www.uspto.gov).

advent of World War II, patents per year fell to fewer than twenty in 1945; after the war, plant patents recovered to 120 in 1957. By 1970, the annual number of plant patents declined to fifty-two.

Nearly 45 percent of all patent grants between 1931 and 1970 were for roses. The share of rose patents was highest in the 1930s and 1940s; 295 of 592 plant patents between 1930 and December 8, 1941, were for roses (figure 8.3). During the war, rose patents declined, reaching a low of four patents in 1945. After the war rose patents recovered, reaching nearly 70 patents in 1955. After 1955, the number of rose patents per year began to decline gradually, while the number of other plant patents stayed roughly constant.

Information on the names of patentees ("originators") from the patent documents reveals that all of the top ten patentees were connected with major companies (table 8.1). Eugene S. Boerner (no. 1) was the single originator on 170 patents between 1940 and 1970; he worked for Jackson and Perkins (J&P) for his entire career from 1920 to 1973 and assigned most of his patents to J&P. Herbert C. Swim (no. 2), whom his colleagues called "the best hybridizer of them all," (McGredy and Jennett 1971, 65) appears as an originator on 115 patents, and as a sole originator on 76 patents. Swim

Table 8.1 **Breeders with the largest number of US plant patents, 1931–1970**

Breeder	Years of professional activity (years of patenting)	Nursery/common assignee	Patents		
			All	Single-authored	Weighted
Eugene S. Boerner (1893–1966)	1943–1973 (1940–1970)	Jackson & Perkins	170	170	170
Herbert C. Swim	1941–1982 (1940–1983)	Armstrong, Conard-Pyle, Weeks	115	76	95.5
Roy L. Byrum	1930–1974 (1935–1974)	Hill	54	53	53.5
Josephine D. Brownell	1940s and 1950s (1932–1955)	Brownell Nurseries	50	49	49.5
Ralph S. Moore (1907–2009)	1927–2008 (1948–2008)	Sequoia Nursery	49	49	49
Francis Meilland (1912–1958)	1912–1958 (1912–1958)	Conard-Pyle	42	42	42
Walter E. Lammerts (1904–1996)	1940–1974 (1943–1972)	Armstrong, Germains, De Vor	37	37	37
Dennison H. Morey (d. 2000)	1957–1980 (1958–1967)	Jackson & Perkins	29	29	29
Frederick H. Howard (ca. 1874–1948)	1916–1956 (1932–1949)	Howard & Smith	26	26	26
Marie Louise Meilland	1958–1994 (1958–1990)	Conard-Pyle	23	23	23

Notes: Breeders' names are collected from the full text of patent documents at www.uspto.gov. Years of professional activity are measured by the years when a breeder registered new roses according to a directory of roses at www.helpmefind.com.

changed his employer several times, which may have lowered his productivity as a breeder. "Now to leave a company . . . is a disaster for a hybridist, because the breeding stock, the roses he selected and grown to provide pollen and seed, does not belong to him and he has to leave it behind and start again" (McGredy and Jennett 1971, 65). Roy L. Byrum (no. 3) was an associate of the Joseph H. Hill Company of Richmond, Indiana. Josephine D. Brownell (no. 4) of Little Crompton, Rhode Island, one of the earliest and most prolific female patentees of plants, was married to the owner of Brownell Nursery. Brownell created two tea roses (PP347 and 458) that were continuously blooming, winter-hardy, and resistant to wilt and black rust (Stanley 1993, 37). Ralph Moore (no. 5), known as the father of miniature roses, was a co-owner of Sequoia Nursery in California; Francis and Marie-Louise Meilland (nos. 5 and 10) owned the leading French firm, which often partnered with Conard-Pyle.

8.2.1 Large Nurseries Drive the Increase in Patenting

Prolific patentees, such as Gene Boerner and Herbert Swim, assigned most of their patents to large nursery firms. For the late nineteenth century, such assignments, which typically transfer patent rights from the inventor to a firm that markets the invention, have been interpreted as a sign of improvements in markets for patented inventions (e.g., Lamoreaux and Sokoloff 1999). In the twentieth century, however, US laws effectively forced employees to assign inventions to their firm (Fisk 1998, 2001), so that assignments are a more accurate measure of the share of inventions that occurs within firms.

Assignment data indicate that commercial breeders account for a disproportionate share of rose patents. Between 1931 and 1970, 77 percent of all rose patents were assigned at issue, compared with 58 percent of other plant patents.[11] For example, Bosenberg assigned the rights to PP1 for *New Dawn* to Louis Schubert, who began to market the rose through the Somerset Rose Nursery. Similarly, Robert L. Catron assigned the rights to PP23 for *Better Times* to his employer, the Joseph H. Hill Company, which developed *Better Times* to become "the backbone of the U.S. cut rose industry until the late 1940s" (Hasek 1980, 84).

Assignment data also suggest that the increase in patenting until the mid-1950s was driven by commercial breeders. Between 1931 and 1943, the share of assigned rose patents increased from 33 to 82 percent (compared with 40 percent of other plant patents in 1943). Between 1943 and 1962, the share of assigned rose patents remained above 80 percent for most years. After

11. In comparison, assignment rates in a sample of Connecticut patents increase from only 1 in 454 patents between 1837 and 1851 to 1 in 3 patents by 1876 (Moser, forthcoming). Of 1,341 roses patented between 1931 and 1970, 1,033 were assigned at issue; 714 were assigned across state lines.

1962, the share of assigned rose patents dropped to 56 percent, while the share of other plant patents assigned at issue continued to increase.

8.3 A Brief History of Commercial Rose Breeding

The importance of patents for commercial rose breeding may be due to two characteristics that rose breeding shares with pharmaceuticals: in both industries, the costs of developing new products are high relative to the costs of imitation, and only a small number of new products become commercially successful.

The origins of commercial rose breeding date back to early nineteenth century when European merchants brought back Chinese "tea roses" from Asia. European breeders began to cross winter-hardy European roses, which produced clustered short-bloomed pink or red flowers, with Chinese tea roses, which produced stems with one large bloom in white, pink, red, and even the rare yellow for several months (Stewart 2007, 128). By the 1840s, French breeders succeeded in creating roses that bloomed repeatedly through the summer and fall (Zlesak 2007, 271–72). In 1867, Jean-Baptiste Guillot of Lyon, France, introduced *La France,* the first modern "hybrid tea rose"—a plant with a tall stature and only one large bloom per stem (Harkness 1985, 11–20; Zlesak 2007, 697). Breeders relied on pollination by wind or insects, and many new varieties originated from self-pollinating roses.

Scientific methods of rose breeding began in Stapleford, England, in 1868, when the cattle farmer Henry Bennett took pollen from one rose to fertilize the carpel (the seed-bearing receptive surface) of another rose. Bennett set up a scientific breeding station in a heated green house. Similar to Stark Brothers, Bennett relied on secrecy to protect his work: "self-interest compels me for the present to keep secret" this "entirely new mode of culture" (Harkness 1985, 24–25). Borrowing a term from cattle breeding, Bennett promoted his roses as "pedigree" hybrids of the *tea rose* (Harkness 1985, 27). In 1884 he sold the red *William Francis Bennett* for the equivalent of $109,000.[12]

Using Bennett's methods, twentieth century breeders created *polyantha,* short plants with large sprays of small blooms, *floribunda,* medium stature plants with large clusters of medium-sized blooms, and *grandiflora,* tall plants with small clusters of medium to large-sized blooms (Harkness 1985; Zlesak 2007, 699). Today, tea roses are the mainstay of the cut flower business, while roses of all types (*hybrid teas, polyantha, floribunda, grandiflora,* climbers, and miniature roses) are marketed as garden roses.

12. In 2009 purchasing power, using the GDP deflator, www.measuringworth.com.

8.3.1 Hobbyists and Public Sector Breeders Created High-Quality Roses before 1930

Prior to 1930, hobbyists and public sector researchers created a large number of new varieties in the United States. Walter Van Fleet (1857–1922), for example, improved *Rosa Rugosa* and other wild roses to create hardy climbing roses that could withstand the climate of the American Northeast. Van Fleet had left his medical practice in the late 1900s to work as a hybridizer for the US Department of Agriculture (USDA). In 1919 the Massachusetts Horticultural Society honored him with the George Robert White Medal of Honor "for advance in the hybridization of garden plants, especially of the rose"; the name "'Van Fleet' is synonymous with meritorious climbing roses of American origin" (*Journal of Heredity,* vol. XI, 1920, 95–96, also *New York Times,* January 28, 1922).

Van Fleet roses such as *Rugosa Magnifica, American Pillar, Beauty of Rosemawr,* and *Silver Moon* continue to be considered "the best in the world" (Griffin Lewis 1931, 135). *Rugosa Magnifica,* for example, is rated 9.0 out of 10 by members of the American Rose Society, placing it in the top percentile. Van Fleet's rose *Silver Moon* is rated 7.8 (in the upper range "of a very good to solid rose," compared with an average of 6).[13] Bosenberg's *New Dawn* was based on a sport of a Van Fleet rose; it is rated 8.5 ("a very good to excellent rose, recommended without hesitation," American Rose Society 1999, 3).

Van Fleet and other public sector hybridizers helped to spread scientific knowledge about rose breeding among hobbyists. Van Fleet published his "Rose Breeding Notes" in the *American Rose Annual* between 1916 and 1922. George C. Thomas, of the Society in Southern California, argued that any serious rose gardener should try to hybridize roses: "No other form of rose-culture is so intriguing as breeding new varieties. It involves but little expenses, and no more than reasonable effort . . . Anyone who has the smallest of greenhouses is foolish not to hybridize roses inside" (Thomas 1931, 33–38).

Hobbyist rose breeders shared their advances freely "over the fence" (Ross 1994). In fact, one of the main goals of the American Rose Society (ARS) was to encourage the diffusion of new roses. In the 1920s, for example, ARS began to encourage the diffusion of Van Fleet's "superb creations" (McFarland 1920, 30–31; Pyle 1921, 32–34).

Commercial nurseries continued to overlook infringements by hobbyists (Swecker 1944, 122).[14] Today, enthusiasts for "old" roses (developed

13. Ratings between 8.8 and 9.2 are granted to the top 1 percent of all roses, with "major positive features and essentially no negatives." Rankings are available at Rose Files: http://rosefile.com/Tables/xVanFleet.html.

14. The PPA includes no fair use provision, which, in the case of utility patents, allows for noncommercial applications.

before the introduction of *La France* in 1867) are especially passionate about diffusing knowledge of newly-recovered varieties. For example, Carl Cato of the Heritage Rose Society

> [B]elieves sincerely in the fellowship that this organization espouses. He's a skilled propagator, and has helped return a number of roses to the nursery trade, but when I met him he was very definite about the fact that had never sold a rose; he had given them all away.[15]

In addition to the desire to disseminate knowledge, the costs of patenting may have discouraged hobbyists from patenting. Patent fees for plant patents were around $200 in the 1930s (equivalent to $2,150 in 2009 purchasing power, using the GDP deflator), including filing and grant fees of $30 each (equivalent to $322 in 2009 purchasing power, *New York Times,* April 19, 1936; January 10, 1938). Plant patents were, however, cheaper than utility patents, with application fees around $500 a year (in 2009 dollars) in 1930 (US House Report No. 96-1307, 96th Cong., 2d Sess. (1980); Fisher 1954; Watson 1953).

8.3.2 Commercial Rose Breeding Involves High Development Costs

In contrast to hobbyists, commercial breeders had lobbied for patents and began to use them swiftly to discourage competitors from propagating new varieties (McGredy and Jennett 1971, 14, 26–27, 60–86). Infringement suits typically involved commercial growers. For example, *Cole Nursery Co. v. Youdath Perennial Garden* (1936), *Kim Bros. v. Hagler* (1958), *Pan-American Plant Co. v. Matsui* (1977), and *Imazio Nursery, Inc. v. Dania Greenhouses* (1995) were disputes among nurseries.

When lobbying for patents, commercial breeders had cited exorbitant development costs. Developing a new rose took up to twelve years, and less than 1 in 1,000 seedlings proved commercially successful (Robb 1964, 389; Stewart 2007, 131). Current methods of commercial rose breeding apply Bennett's process: breeders extract pollen from one flower to fertilize another and create a hybrid seed (de Vries and Dubous 1996, 241); after that, they propagate seedlings by budding or cuttings to create thousands of plants. Breeders, then, select plants with desirable characteristics, such as an intense color or smell, or a specific shape, and propagate them to create the next generation of roses.

This process favors large commercial nurseries that can grow many seedlings at a time.[16] Boerner, for example, created more than 250,000 crosses per year in the 1940s and 1950s as the chief breeder for J&P (Harkness 1979, 117; Harkness 1985, 74; Beales 1998, 677). By 1945, "all the large rose producers

15. Christopher (1989, 33; also see 36, 66, 84, 18, 203, and 211).

16. Selecting new plants from random bud variations would be less costly but sports with desirable properties are rare and must be noticed, selected, and systematically propagated to become commercially viable (Terry 1966, 1).

have their own research departments with a staff of scientifically trained personnel" (Sinnock 1945, 96).[17]

Large producers, such as J&P, Conard-Pyle, Stark Brothers, DeVor, Weeks, and Hill continue to dominate the domestic rose breeding industry today. Internationally, Tantau (Germany), Meilland (France), Harkness (Britain), Wilhelm Kordes Söhne (Germany), Austin (Britain), Poulsen (Denmark), Dickson (Britain), Guillot (France), and McGredy (New Zealand) are the leading firms.

8.3.3 Copying New Varieties Is Cheap

In contrast to the costly development process, replication is quick and easy. Bennett had already noted in the 1880s that the outcome of his scientific methods of breeding would be vulnerable to imitation and relied on secrecy to protect his inventions. If discovered, new roses could quickly be replicated by repeated grafting; a plant would produce 10 grafts by January, which could be used to make 100 by March, and these could be used to make 1,000 by May (Harkness 1985, 25). As a result, the price of new roses fell quickly: this was equivalent to more than a 90 percent decrease in the first year. Once discovered, "a new variety would be placed upon the market and within a year or so it would be listed in nearly all nursery catalogs" (Sinnock 1945, 95).

> The only way a grower could make a profit on a new rose before 1930 was to build up, as secretly as possible, all the stock his capital permitted, then throw it all on the market at the top prices people would pay. In a year or so, competitors would be building up their own stocks grown from the no-longer-secret variety, now widely distributed. (Kneen 1948, 363)

For example, the US firm Conard & Jones invested two years to develop *Rosa Hugonis* (aka *Father Hugo Rose*) for the American market, but lost out to other nurserymen, who had quietly propagated *Rosa Hugonis* and were able to capitalize on Conard's advertising efforts, while offering their own roses at a lower price (Moon 1920, 49–51).[18]

17. Within these research departments, star breeders play an important role. For example, Armstrong Nursery was unable to develop the nursery stock of Herbert Swim after he left (Zlesak 2007, 712; McGredy and Jennett 1971, 65–66). The rose breeding industry is also geographically concentrated, allowing firms to access a larger pool of qualified labor. In 1966 Armstrong Nurseries moved to Wasco, California, a city of 21,000 in the southern San Joaquin Valley; J&P moved its operations to Wasco when it merged with Armstrong in 1968. Over the next two decades, DeVor, Weeks, and other nurseries followed to take advantage of the 280-day growing season, sandy soil, inexpensive land, and a growing pool of workers skilled in budding roses. Today, more than half of all domestically produced roses originate from Wasco and the surrounding area (Clark 1993, 22). In the 1970s, the cut flower (as opposed to garden plants) business began to be dominated by Colombia, Ecuador, and other tropical countries with long growing seasons, cheap labor, and little regulation (Järvesoo 1983, 323–24). In 2006, domestic firms made up less than 10 percent of the value and less than 5 percent of the volume of US sales (USDA, *Floriculture and Nursery Crops Yearbook 2007,* table C-15).

18. *Rosa Hugonis* was originally bred in England in 1899, so that, had it been patented in the United States, Conard would have had to purchase the rights to it from its original breeders.

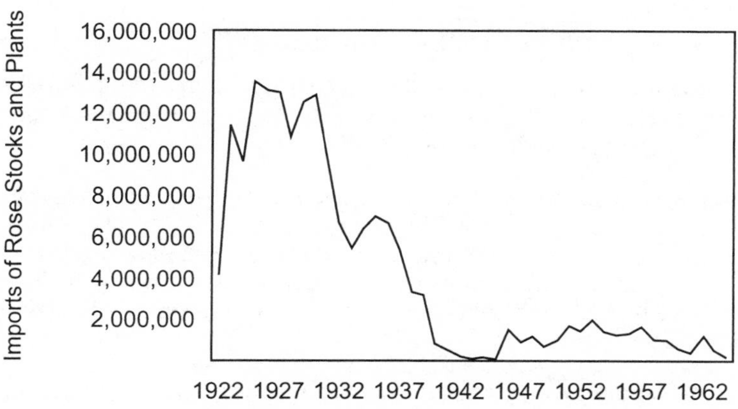

Fig. 8.4 Rose imports into the United States

Notes: Data on rose plants imported per year from US Department of Commerce, *Foreign Commerce and Navigation of the US,* various years, US Bureau of the Census, *Foreign Trade Reports* No. 110.

8.4 Did Plant Patents Create a Domestic Breeding Industry?

If high development costs and easy imitation discouraged nurseries from developing new varieties, the creation of IPRs may have encouraged innovation and facilitated the development of a domestic plant breeding industry.

> Prior to 1930, the US was not competitive in the field of plant breeding and especially of rose breeding. Most of the new roses came from second, third, and fourth generation hybridizers of Europe. Today . . . more than half the finest plant breeders and especially those breeding new varieties of roses are at work here in the US (Hart 1965, 93)

Import data, however, indicate that the US dependency on European nursery stock began to weaken prior to the Act. The number of rose plants imported into the United States declined from 12,916,461 in 1930 to 10,025,162 in 1931 and 6,715,588 in 1932 (figure 8.4). This decline was too early and too large to be due to three roses that were patented in 1931. A more plausible explanation is that the Great Depression reduced the demand for roses.[19]

19. The Smoot-Hawley Tariffs Act of June 1930, intended to protect the domestic agricultural industry (Irwin 1998; Eichengreen 1988), did not raise tariffs on roses. Rose plants, budded, grafted, or grown on their own roots were charged an import tariff of 4 cents per plant in 1913, 1922, and 1930 ("Comparison of Tariff Acts of 1913, 1922 and 1930, with Index" House, Committee on Ways and Means, Congress Session 71-3 (1930), document date 1931, 80). Tariff rates remained constant throughout the 1930s and were reduced for a select group of countries (Belgium, Netherlands, and Luxemburg) in 1948 and for the remaining countries in the 1960s (Corder and Parisi, 1959, 103–104).

8.4.1 World War II Cuts Off European Imports

When demand recovered, World War II disrupted the production of roses in Europe (Harkness 1985, 51–52, 93, 104, 141). The English rose breeder Walter Easlea II (1859–1945) deplored

> Not within living memory has there been such a shortage of rose plants for sale in Great Britain as there is in this season of 1944–45. This is mainly due to government restrictions on land that can be used for growing rose plants. Some growers who formerly produced 500,000 plants for sale have budded only 20,000 for the past two seasons. (*American Rose Annual* 1945, 46)

Unable to export grown plants, European nurseries began to export nursery stock to US firms. Meilland, for example, sent nursery stock for the *Peace* rose to be propagated by Pyle; the stock left France on the last plane before the German occupation in 1940 (Meilland 1984, 4; McGredy and Jennett 1971, 13).

American breeders made good use of the opportunity to propagate European plants and expand their own business: "WW-II left it open for the American rose industry to take off, and take off it did, with Gene Boerner and J&P as major contributors" (Cunningham 2005).

8.4.2 Gene Boerner's Mass Hybridization Program

Born to German-immigrant parents in Wisconsin in 1893, Gene Boerner joined J&P in 1920. Known as "Papa Floribunda," Boerner hybridized more than 60 *floribunda* roses, including 11 All American Rose Selections (AARS) winners (*American Rose Annual* 1945, 225; Beales 1998, 677). Boerner also acted as a "hybridizing father" to the New Zealander Sam McGredy (Harkness 1985, 77) and the younger members of the German family firm Wilhelm Kordes Söhne referred to him as "Uncle Gene."

As the chief breeder of J&P, Boerner led the company's mass hybridization program in Newark, New York, in the 1940s and 1950s. Sam McGredy argued that the existence of patent protection encouraged the creation of mass hybridization in the United States:

> The Americans were the first to have plant patents and that fact encouraged the rise of mass hybridization techniques in the States, of the techniques of the modern rose-breeding business. (McGredy and Jennett 1971, 51)

Many of J&P's most successful products, however, were based on European roses, and especially Kordes roses, which J&P began to propagate after the onset of the war. In 1939, J&P licensed Kordes' *World's Fair,* which won one of the first four AARS awards in 1940 and became a great commercial success in the United States. Its popularity allowed the J&P to capture a large market share and eliminate the middlemen by becoming a major mail order retail company.[20]

In 1942, J&P introduced *Pinocchio,* which Kordes had developed in 1940 and named after the Disney movie of the same year (Cunningham 2005). Boerner used *Pinocchio* to create *Masquerade,* of which Harkness (1985, 75–76) says: "no rose of that kind had ever been seen. The nearest to it was an old China rose, *Mutabalis,* a shrub which proceeded from buds of saffron to magenta in its old age." *Fashion,* one of the first coral-colored American roses, was Boerner's second triumph derived from *Pinocchio* (Harkness 1985, 75–76). Boerner also used *Pinocchio* to create *Lavender Pinocchio* (PP947), which continues to be prominent today. He used *Crimson Glory,* developed by Wilhelm Kordes in 1935, to create *Diamond Jubilee* (introduced in 1947).[21]

During World War I, the ability to access foreign-owned patents and produce foreign-owned inventions had encouraged domestic invention in organic chemicals (Moser and Voena, forthcoming). World War II may have had a similar effect on US roses. Under the Trading with the Enemy Act (TWEA), domestic producers were not required to pay license fees for roses that German or French firms like Kordes, Tantau, and Meilland had patented in the United States (US Office of the Alien Property Custodian 1946, 202). Boerner kept royalties for Kordes in escrow and repaid Kordes after the war to help rebuild their firm (Cunningham 2005), but it is unlikely that he could fully compensate the Kordes firm for the profits that it lost as a result of US competition.

Boerner's *floribunda* were also based on European roses; he created them by refining the small-flowered *polyantha* rose that the Danish nursery Poulsen had developed in the 1920s (McGredy and Jennett 1971, 60–61; Harkness 1985, 92). Thus, Boerner's case suggests that access to European roses was at least as important as patents to the development of US plant breeding.

8.5 Registrations of New Roses

Why did rose patents increase so quickly after the creation of IPRs? Contemporaries observed that nurseries that marketed new varieties without patents risked "having someone turn up a little later with a patent" threatening to sue for infringement (Kile 1934, 61–62). The "Plant Patent Act

20. http://www.jacksonandperkins.com/gardening/GP/gatepage/history, accessed December 28, 2010.

21. Data from www.helpmefind.com. No systematic price data are available for this period, but proponents of IPRs argue that the introduction of plant patents lowered the prices that nurseries charged to consumers. Kneen (1948, 363), for example, observed that the thornless *Festival* rose, which was introduced in 1940, sold for "much less than fancy new roses brought in pre-patent days" and that "[t]oday buyers no longer have to pay $5 or $10 for a new rose, $10 for a new iris or gladiolus bulb, $20 for a fancy dahlia."

makes it almost a necessity to take out patents on all valuable new varieties"; growers would soon learn "the necessity of handling only such new plants as have been patented" (Kile 1934, 61–62). Large nurseries, which drove the increase in rose patents, were more likely to be sued and may have used patents strategically to protect themselves from litigation.

To separate increases in strategic patents from changes in innovation, we create an alternative measure of innovation. This measure is based on the number of new varieties that were registered with the ARS between 1916 and 1970.[22] Unlike patenting, registering a new plant does not create property rights that could be enforced in court (Loscher 1986, 59–62), so that registrations cannot be used strategically in the same way as patents. Breeders register the name of new varieties for the simple purpose of naming the plant and for the prestige that it brings to them and the namesake of a rose.

Registration data include unique names for US and foreign roses.[23] An entry in the *American Rose Annual* of 1926 (188), for example, includes the name of the rose, the name of its originator, and the date of the registration:

Sarah Van Fleet, H. Rug, by the American Rose Society, June 29, 1925.[24]

Matching rose patents with registrations makes it possible to estimate the share of newly-created roses that were patented. One difficulty with this process is that plant patents typically do not list the name of a rose. To address this problem, we first appended common names to patent records, using a publication of the American Association of Nurserymen (*Plant Patents with Common Names*).[25] Ninety-six percent of all plant patents between 1931 and

22. The ARS was originally established in 1892, sixteen years after the Royal National Rose Society in Britain was formed in 1876. Although European horticulturalists had begun to discuss the establishment of an international rose register in the 1910s, World War I disrupted their efforts. The ARS, however, pushed ahead and became an early leader in rose registration. It was a "welcome candidate" in 1955 to become the International Cultivar Registration Authority (or ICRA) for the Genus, Rosa L. (Vrugtman 1986, 225–28), assuming global responsibility to register new roses. Rose societies in Australia, France, Germany, India, Italy, Japan, the Netherlands, New Zealand, South Africa, Switzerland, and the United Kingdom serve as "regional representatives." The ARS is one of seventy ICRAs currently operating under the International Code of Nomenclature for Cultivated Plants (ICNCP), charged with registering names for different groups of plants. Systems of biological registration date back to Aristotle's classification of animals and the Inquiry in Plants by his student, Theophrastus. The Swedish botanist Carl Linnaeus (1707–1778) extended these lists to create the modern taxonomy of plants.

23. Commercial breeders typically employ different trade names in different countries. For example, the French rose *Madame Ferdinand Jamin* was marketed as *American Beauty* in the United States. To create unique identifiers, rose breeders developed a parallel system of code names, which consist of a three-letter prefix that designates the breeder followed by letters or numbers that denote the specific variety. The competing systems led to disputes in the early 1980s, which ARS resolved by adjusting its classification system (Gioia 1986, 265–71).

24. In 1930, J. Horace McFarland, the *Annual*'s long-time editor, combined this information with material on foreign roses into the first edition of *Modern Roses.* We use the 12th edition of *Modern Roses* (Young, Schorr, and Baer 2007).

25. The American Association of Nurserymen was formed in 1876 and is now called the American Nursery and Landscape Association. It has administered the National Association

1970 can be matched with common names. We then use the variety's name, its originator, and the originator's location to match patents with registrations. For example, we match

> "Polar Bear," registered in 1934 by "Nicolas" with PP132, "Polar Bear" by the originator "Jean H. Nicolas" granted in 1935.

Ninety percent of patents, 1,241 between 1931 and 1970, can be matched with at least one registration. Some patents are matched with more than one registration because alternative spellings or abbreviations are recorded to create a complete record of names. For example, *Irene of Denmark* is also registered as *Irene von Dänemark* and *Doctor F. Debat* is also registered as *Dr. F. Debat.* Duplicates of this type account for 17 percent of registrations, but there is no evidence of systematic variation. To be conservative, we repeat all tests with and without duplicates.

8.5.1 Less Than One-Fifth of New Varieties Are Patented

Registration data indicate that only a minority of new varieties was patented. Including duplicates, only 18 percent of new varieties between 1931 and 1970 were patented (1,341 of 7,436, figure 8.5). Excluding duplicates, only 16 percent of new roses were patented. Low patenting rates are consistent with results in other data sets that capture innovations with and without patents. For example, roughly 20 percent of machinery innovations exhibited at the Crystal Palace World Fair of 1851 were patented. Similar to breeders of fruit and roses, nineteenth-century inventors of machinery could not depend on secrecy to protect their innovations because new machines (unlike dyes or other types of chemical innovations) could be easily copied (Moser, forthcoming).

The share of patented varieties increased as breeders learned to use the patent system and became concerned about litigation. In 1932, 11 percent of new varieties were patented; by 1954, 26 percent of new varieties were patented (figure 8.5, excluding duplicates). Patenting rates spike briefly to 31 and 33 percent in 1942 and 1952, possibly due to changes in the speed of examination. In the mid-1950s, patenting rates began to decline; by the late 1960s, only 14 percent of new varieties were patented.[26]

Changes in the number of new varieties per year closely track the conditions of the European rose breeding industry. From 1900 to 1920, registrations per year stayed relatively constant around 100, with a significant dip during World War I (figure 8.6). From the 1920s to the late 1930s, rose registrations increased to above 200 per year, with a dip during the early years of the Great Depression, when demand for roses decreased in the United

of Plant Patent Owners (NAPPO), which was organized in 1939 to address the "gross misunderstanding within the trade and in the minds of the public as to the whole concept of plant patents" (White 1975, 254).

26. This decline cannot be due to truncation: our data continue until 1978, and roses that were registered by 1970 were patented within two years of their registration date.

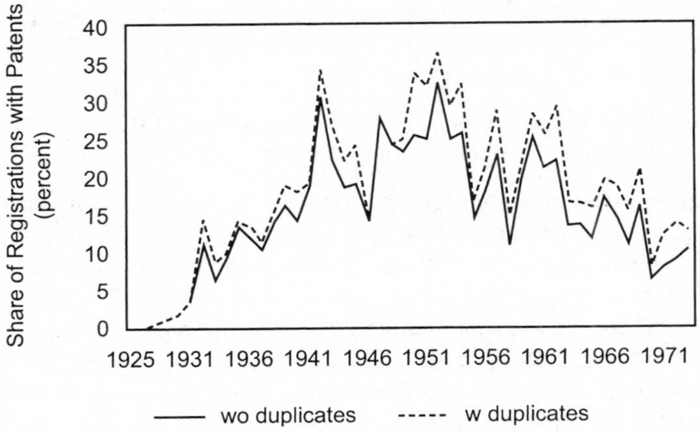

Fig. 8.5 Share of registrations with patents

Notes: Data on rose patents from American Association of Nurserymen, *Plant Patents and Common Names,* 1963, 1969, 1974. Data on rose registrations from the *American Rose Society.* Some new varieties of roses were registered more than once, using alternative abbreviations or spellings or translated names. To account for this, the line "w duplicates" includes multiple registrations for the same rose, and "wo duplicates" counts multiple registrations as one. The *x*-axis measures the year of registration.

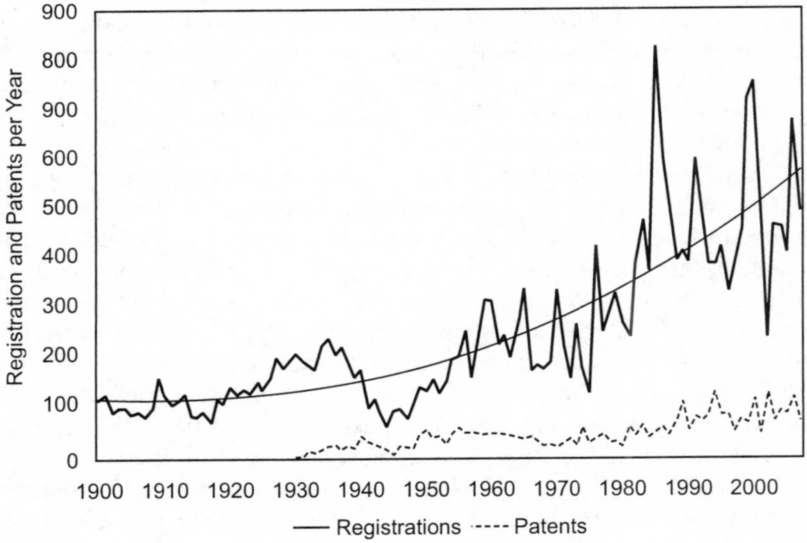

Fig. 8.6 Registrations and plant patents for roses

Notes: Data on rose registrations per year from the records of the *American Rose Society.* Patents are plant (PP) patents for roses from www.uspto.gov.

States and abroad. As World War I devastated the European rose industry, registrations declined to less than 100 per year until 1950; registrations did not go back to the prewar path of growth until the 1960s.

8.5.2 Europeans Create Most Varieties After 1931 While US Varieties Decline

Data on the national origins of breeders reveal that European breeders continued to account for the majority of new varieties. Consistent with historical accounts, the data indicate that, until the turn of the twentieth century, nearly all new roses were created by European breeders (fig. 8.7). Moreover, all except two of the top ten breeders in terms of new varieties are European (table 8.2). Wilhelm Kordes Söhne leads the list with 259 registrations. Including 133 registrations by the younger Reimer Kordes (no. 10) increases the number of Kordes registrations to nearly 400, twice the number of registrations of the French nursery Gaujard (with 201 registrations).

Eugene Boerner is the only American in the list of the top ten breeders, with 198 registrations (no. 3). Francis Meilland of the French family firm Meilland follows with 178 registrations (no. 4), then the German breeder Mathias Tantau (no. 5, 172 registrations), the Spanish breeder Pedro Dot (no. 6, 154 registrations), the French breeder C. Mallerin (a retired railway worker who acted as a mentor to the Meillands, no. 7, 153 registrations) and Delbard-Chabert (no. 8, 145 registrations). Sam McGredy, the Irishman who immigrated to New Zealand, is no. 9, with 135 registrations.

Most strikingly, the data indicate that US breeders contributed *fewer*

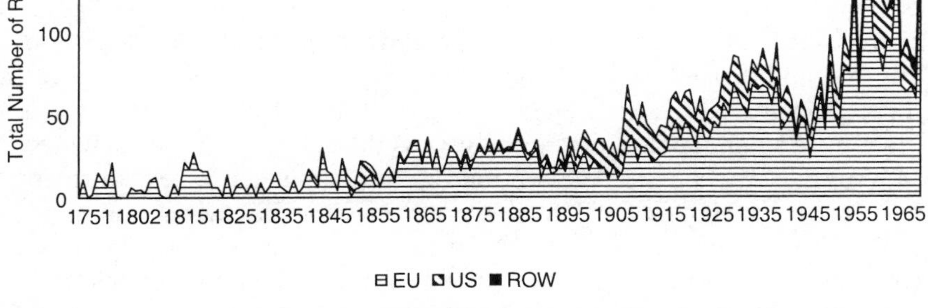

Fig. 8.7 Rose registrations by breeder's national origin: European Union (EU), United States (US), and Rest of World (ROW)

Note: Data on the number of new registrations per year from the records of the *American Rose Society*.

Table 8.2 Breeders with the largest number of rose registrations, 1931–1970

Breeder	Country of origin	Registrations
Wilhelm Kordes Söhne	Germany	259
Gaujard	France	201
Eugene Boerner	United States	198
Francis Meilland	France	178
Mathias Tantau	Germany	172
Petro Dot	Spain	154
Charles Mallerin	France	153
Delbard-Chabert	France	145
Samuel McGredy IV	New Zealand	139
Reimer Kordes	Germany	133

Source: Breeders' names were extracted from lists of registered roses in Young, Schorr, and Baer (2007).

varieties after the creation of patents in 1930. In the early decades of the twentieth century, when Van Fleet and other public sector breeders and hobbyists were active, registrations by US breeders increased to account for 39 percent of all new varieties between 1900 and 1930. After the passage of the Plant Patent Act, registrations by US breeders declined to 21 percent between 1931 and 1970, when the next Act extended patent rights to sexually-propagated plants.

8.6 Conclusions

Did the Plant Patent Act of 1930 help create the modern American rose breeding industry? Using plant patents as the sole indicator of innovation suggests that the answer is yes: large-scale breeding efforts of American firms, such as Jackson & Perkins, Armstrong, Weeks, and Conard-Pyle contributed a staggering share of US plant patents grants between 1930 and 1970, and large commercial breeders dominated the list of the top ten patentees.

A closer look, however, suggests that patents played at best a secondary role, and that US breeders mostly used patents strategically to protect themselves from litigation. Data on registrations of new varieties reveal that only a small share of new varieties, less than 20 percent, was patented. Moreover, European breeders continued to contribute the large majority of new varieties, and only one US breeder, J&P's Gene Boerner, is among the top ten breeders in terms of new varieties. In fact, the share of new varieties created by US breeders dropped after the introduction of intellectual property rights from nearly 40 percent from 1900 to 1930 to slightly over 20 percent from 1900 to 1970.

Notably, some of the most successful American roses, including Walter Van Fleet's hardy American climbers, were creations of the prepatent period.

Other prominent American roses such as Conard-Pyle's *Peace* rose, or J&P's *Pinnocchio* were originally bred by European firms. American breeders began to propagate these roses when World War II suspended European imports, leading them to improve the existing imported roses to create the American rose.

References

Allyn, Robert Starr. 1944. *The First Plant Patents. A Discussion of the New Law and Patent Office Practice, with Supplements.* Brooklyn: Educational Foundation.

Alston, Julian M., Matthew A. Andersen, Jennifer S. James, and Philip G. Pardey. 2010. *Persistence Pays: U.S. Agricultural Productivity Growth and the Benefits from Public R&D Spending.* New York: Springer.

Alston, Julian M., and Raymond J. Venner. 2002. "The Effects of the U.S. Plant Variety Protection Act on Wheat Genetic Improvement." *Research Policy* 31: 527–42.

American Association of Nurserymen. 1963. *Plant Patents with Common Names, 1 through 2207, 1931–1962.* Washington, DC: American Association of Nurserymen.

———. 1969. *Plant Patents with Common Names, 2208 through 2855, 1963–1968.* Washington, DC: American Association of Nurserymen.

———. 1974. *Plant Patents with Common Names, 2856 through 3412, 1969–1973.* Washington, DC: American Association of Nurserymen.

American Rose Society. 1945. *American Rose Annual, 1945.* Harrison, PA: American Rose Society.

———. 1999. *Handbook for Selecting Roses.* Shreveport, LA: American Rose Society.

Anderson, Neill O., ed. 2006. *Flower Breeding and Genetics: Issues, Challenges and Opportunities for the 21st Century.* Dordrecht: Springer.

Beales, Peter, ed. 1998. *Botanica's Roses: The Encyclopedia of Roses.* New York: Konemann.

Butler, L. J., and B. W. Marion. 1985. "The Impacts of Patent Protection on the U.S. Seed Industry and Public Plant Breeding." North Central Regional Research Publication 304. University of Wisconsin, Madison: College of Agricultural and Life Sciences.

Christopher, Thomas. 1989. *In Search of Lost Roses.* New York: Summit Books.

Clark, Kristi. 1993. "Why Wasco?" *American Rose Magazine,* August, 22.

Corder, Lucille, and Annette A. Parisi. 1959. *U.S. Import Duties on Agricultural Products, 1959.* USDA Agricultural Handbook no. 143. Washington, DC: GPO.

Cunningham, Ed. 2005. "Breeders of Note: Eugene Boerner." *Rhode Island Rose Review,* November. http://www.rirs.org/boerner.htm.

Daus, Donald D. 1967. "Plant Patents: A Potentially Extinct Variety." *Economic Botany* 21 (4): 388–94.

De Vries, D. P., and L. A. M. Dubois. 1996. "Rose Breeding: Past, Present, Prospects." *Acta Horticulturae* 424:241–47.

Dhar, T., and J. Foltz. 2007. "The Impact of Intellectual Property Rights in the Plant and Seed Industry." In *Agricultural Biotechnology and Intellectual Property,* edited by Jan Kesan, 161–71. Wallingford: CAB International.

Eichengreen, Barry. 1989. "The Political Economy of the Smoot-Hawley Tariff." *Research in Economic History* 12:1–43.

Fisk, Catherine L. 1998. "Removing the 'Fuel of Interest' from the 'Fire of Genius': Law and the Employee-Inventor, 1830–1930." *University of Chicago Law Review* 65 (4): 1127–98.

———. 2001. "Working Knowledge: Trade Secrets, Restrictive Covenants in Employment, and the Rise of Corporate Intellectual Property, 1800–1920." *Hastings Law Journal* 52:441–535.

Fisher, Charles. 1954. "Should Patent Office Fees Be Increased?" *Journal of the Patent Office Society* 36 (11): 827–61.

Fowler, Cary. 1994. *Unnatural Selection: Technology, Politics, and Plant Evolution.* Amsterdam: OPA.

———. 2000. "The Plant Patent Act of 1930: A Sociological History of Its Creation." *Journal of the Patent and Trademark Office* 82:621–44.

Gioia, Vincent G. 1986. "Revised Rose Name Registration System." *Acta Horticulturae, International Symposium on Taxonomy of Cultivated Plants* 182:265–71.

Griffin Lewis, George. 1931. *The Book of Roses.* R. G. Badger.

Harkness, J. L. 1979. *The World's Favorite Roses and How to Grow Them.* New York: McGraw-Hill.

———. 1985. *The Makers of Heavenly Roses.* London: Souvenir Press.

Hart, George M. 1965. "Why Patented Roses." *American Rose Annual* 50:91–94.

Hasek, Raymond F. 1980. "Roses." In *Introduction to Floriculture,* edited by Roy A Larson, 83–105. New York: Academic Press.

Irwin, Douglas. 1998. "The Smoot-Hawley Tariff: A Quantitative Assessment." *Review of Economics and Statistics* 80 (2): 326–34.

Janis, Mark, and Jay Kesan. 2002. "US Plant Variety Protection—Sound and Fury?" *Houston Law Review* 39:727–78.

Järvesoo, E. 1983. "Impact of Flower Imports on Domestic Production in the United States." *Acta Horticulturae* 135:319–26.

Journal of Heredity. 1920–1931. Washington, DC: American Genetic Association.

Kevles, Daniel J. 2008. "Protections, Privileges, and Patents: Intellectual Property in American Horticulture, the Late Nineteenth Century to 1930." *Proceedings of the American Philosophical Society* 152 (2): 207–17.

Kile, O. M. 1934. "The Plant Patent Act." *American Rose Annual* 19:57–62.

Kloppenburg, Jack Ralph, Jr. 2004. *First the Seed: The Political Economy of Plant Biotechnology,* 2nd ed. Madison: University of Wisconsin Press.

Kneen, Orville H. 1948. "Patent Plants Enrich Our World." *National Geographic Magazine* 93 (3): 357–78.

Lamoreaux, Naomi R., and Kenneth L. Sokoloff. 1999. "Inventors, Firms, and the Market for Technology in the Late Nineteenth and Early Twentieth Centuries." In *Learning By Doing in Firms, Markets, and Countries,* edited by Naomi Lamoreaux, Daniel Raff, and Peter Temin, 19–57. Chicago: University of Chicago Press.

Lampe, Ryan L., and Petra Moser. 2010. "Do Patent Pools Encourage Innovation? Evidence from the Nineteenth-Century Sewing Machine Industry." *Journal of Economic History* 70 (4): 898–920.

Llewelyn, Margaret, and Mike Adcock. 2006. *European Plant Intellectual Property.* Oxford: Hart.

Loscher, U. 1986. "Variety Denomination According to Plant Breeders' Rights," *Acta Horticulturae, International Symposium on Taxonomy of Cultivated Plants* 182:59–62.

McFarland, John Horace. 1920. "Making Dr. Van Fleet's Roses Available." *American Rose Annual* 4:30–31.

———. 1947. *Roses of the World in Color,* 2nd ed. Boston: Houghton-Mifflin.
McGredy, Sam, and Sean Jennett. 1971. *A Family of Roses.* New York: Dodd, Mead.
Meilland, Alain (in collaboration with Gilles Lambert). 1984. *Meilland: A Life in Roses.* Translated and revised by Richard C. Keating and L. Clark Keating. Carbondale: Southern Illinois University.
Moon, J. Edward. 1920. "Can We Have Plant Patents?" *American Rose Annual* 4:48–50.
Moser, Petra. Forthcoming. "Innovation Without Patents—Evidence from the World's Fairs." *Journal of Law and Economics.*
Moser, Petra, and Voena, Alessandra. Forthcoming. "Compulsory Licensing: Evidence from the Trading with the Enemy Act." *American Economic Review.*
Naseem, Anwar, James F. Oehmke, and David E. Schimmelpfennig. 2005. "Does Plant Variety Intellectual Property Protection Improve Farm Productivity? Evidence from Cotton Varieties." *AgBioForum* 8 (2/3): 100–107.
Olmstead, Alan L., and Paul W. Rhode. 2000. "The Transformation of Northern Agriculture from 1910–90." In *Cambridge Economic History of the United States, Volume III: The Twentieth Century,* edited by S. Engerman and R. Gallman, 693–742. Cambridge: Cambridge University Press.
Perrin, R. K., K. A. Kunnings, and L. A. Ihnen. 1983. "Some Effects of the US Plant Variety Protection Act of 1970." *Economics Research Report.*
Popp, David, Ted Juhl, and Daniel Johnson. 2004. "Time in Purgatory: Examining the Grant Lag for U.S. Patent Applications." *Topics in Economic Analysis & Policy* 4 (1): Article 29.
Pyle, Robert. 1921. "The Distribution of Some New Van Fleet Roses." *American Rose Annual* 5:32–34.
Robb, Harry C., Jr. 1964. "Plant Patents." In *Encyclopaedia of Patent Practice and Invention Management,* 641–55. New York: Reinhold.
Rose, George E. 1967. "The Origin of AARS." *American Rose Annual* 52:69–73.
Ross, Marty. 1994. "Rose Rustlers—Preservation of Old-Fashioned Roses." *Flower & Garden Magazine,* April–May.
Rossman, Joseph. 1930. "The Planter Breeder Becomes an Inventor." *Science News-Letter* 18 (506): 394–95.
Sinnock, Edwin P. 1945. "The Question is Patent." *American Rose Annual* 30: 95–98.
Smith, Jane S. 2009. *The Garden of Invention: Luther Burbank and the Business of Breeding Plants.* New York: Penguin Press.
Stanley, Autum. 1993. *Mothers and Daughters of Invention: Notes for a Revised History of Technology.* New Brunswick: Rutgers University Press.
Stewart, Amy. 2007. *Flower Confidential: The Good, the Bad, and the Beautiful in the Business of Flowers.* Chapel Hill: Algonquin Books of Chapel Hill.
Swecker, J. Preston. 1944. "Comments on the Plant Patent Act." *American Rose Annual* 29:120–22.
Terry, Dickson. 1966. *The Stark Story: Stark Nurseries 150th Anniversary.* St. Louis: Missouri Historical Society.
Thomas, George C. 1931. "Breeding New Roses." *American Rose Annual,* 33–38.
US Census Bureau. Census of Agriculture. *Census of Horticultural Specialties.* Washington, DC: GPO.
US Congress. 1930. *Congressional Record,* 71st Cong., 2nd Sess., Vol. LXXII, Pt 8. Washington, DC: GPO.
US Department of Agriculture. 2007. *Floriculture and Nursery Crops Yearbook, September 2007.* ERS-FLO-2007s. www.ers.usda.gov/Publications/Flo/2007/09Sep/FLO2007s.txt.

US House of Representatives, Committee on Judiciary. 1967. *General Revision of the Patent Laws. Part 1, Apr. 17, 20, 26, 27, May 4, 11, 18, 25, June 1, 8.* Washington, DC: GPO.

———. 1980. "Amending the Patent and Trademark Laws, Sept. 9, 1980." House Report 96, No. 1307, Pt. I, 96th Congress, 2nd Sess. Washington, DC: GPO.

US House of Representatives, Committee on Patents. 1906. *Arguments Before the Committee in Patents of the House of Representatives on H.R. 18851 to Amend the Laws of the United States Relating to Patents in the Interest of Originators of Horticultural Products.* May 17. Washington, DC: GPO.

———. 1930. *Plant Patents: Hearings Before the Committee on Patents, House of Representatives, Seventy-First Congress, Second Session on H. R. 11372, A Bill to Provide for Plant Patents,* April 9. Washington, DC: GPO.

US Office of the Alien Property Custodian. 1946. *Annual Report of the Alien Property Custodian for Fiscal Year Ending June 1945.* Washington, DC: GPO.

US Patent and Trademark Office, Patent Technology Monitoring Team (PTMT). 2009. *Plant Patents Report, 01/01/1977–12/31/2008.* Alexandria, VA: March.

US Senate, Committee on the Judiciary. 1967. *Promote Progress of Useful Arts, Report of President's Commission on Patent System.* Washington, DC: GPO.

US Senate, Subcommittee on Patents, Trademarks, and Copyrights, Committee on Judiciary. 1968. "Hearings on Patent Law Revision. Part 2, Jan. 30–Feb. 1, 1968." 90th Congress, 2nd Sess. Washington, DC: GPO.

Vrugtman, Freek. 1986. "The History of Cultivar Name Registration in North America." *Acta Horticulturae* 182. International Symposium on Taxonomy of Cultivated Plants, 225–28.

Watson, R. 1953. "Patent Office Fees and Expenses." *Journal of the Patent Office Society* 35 (10): 710–24.

White, Richard Peregrine. 1975. *A Century of Service: A History of the Nursery Industry Associations of the United States, American Association of Nurserymen.* Washington, DC: American Association of Nurserymen.

Wirtschaftlicher Teil. 1931–1939. "Die amerikanischen Pflanzenpatente."

Young, Marilyn A., Phillip Schorr, and Richard Baer. 2007. *Modern Roses 12.* Shreveport, LA: American Rose Society.

Zlesak, David C. 2007. "Rose." In *Flower Breeding and Genetics: Issues, Challenges and Opportunities for the 21st Century,* edited by Neil O. Anderson, 695–737. Dordrecht: Springer.

Comment Jeffrey L. Furman

I have learned many things from reading this chapter. One key lesson is that my public high school biology course was sadly inadequate to the task of understanding sexual reproduction in roses. In case there are others in the room with similar challenges in basic plant biology, I include in the talk a slightly extended primer on rose propagation. As a second note before I begin, I should also apologize that there are an embarrassing number of opportunities for word play on this project, so I ask for your tolerance if I

Jeffrey Furman is associate professor in the Strategy and Policy Department at Boston University School of Management and a research associate of the National Bureau of Economic Research.

weaken and engage in the occasional pun. If you have read the chapter, you may have noticed that the authors hide a pun in one of the footnotes. With that in mind, I would like to title this discussion, with apologies to Shakespeare, "A rose by any other IP policy."

What the authors are trying to do here is to try and understand the impact of the 1930 Patent Act on a number of outcomes. The chapter involves elements of a case study as well as elements of policy evaluation. This chapter would have fit right into the original *Rate and Direction* volume in the Case Study section of the book.

The chapter addresses one of the fundamental questions in the economics of innovation, namely, how the provision of intellectual property rights affects innovation. It considers the context of the 1930 Plant Patent Act, which established intellectual property rights for asexually propagated plants. One of the key points of context is that prior to the Act, the United States lagged behind Europe in the development of rose varieties and the production of roses. This is true to some extent with respect to the hobbyists, but especially with respect to the commercial breeders. Imports of roses are around 12 million roses per year in the 1920s and that falls following the Act.

What the authors ask, then, is, "What was the impact of the Act on innovation in roses, on the growth of the US industry?" With their approach, the authors could also ask about a number of other issues. For example, they could examine how the Act affects rose variety, how it affects rose quality, whether a market for plant ideas develops after the Patent Act. And then how did the Act change the identities of those organizations or individuals that engage in rose innovation? And do we see worries materialize about intellectual property rights stifling innovation? So Moser and Rhode's chapter addresses the classic question of what happens to innovation, and what happens to industries after IP rights are extended.

I am not sure how important the primer on plant reproduction is. I guess the key thing to remember is that plants that are propagated through sexual reproduction have variety, as a consequence of obtaining two types of DNA. Thus, you can experiment on how to create new plants through sexual reproduction in plants.

Generating new plant varieties also, however, has some properties that are similar to the process of coming up with new drugs. Approximately one out of 1,000 seedlings turn out to be successful in some way. And then the commercial firms, even in the early days, could do this in very, very large numbers.

One way that I thought about this process was similar to the way drug companies would go about developing drugs, around a similar time period. That analogy is going to break down and I think a number of other analogies may be more complete, but that is one of the things that I kept in the back of my mind, thinking about comparisons between this industry context and another.

It is relatively easy to enable asexual reproduction in plants. One can simply take a cut of a rose, replant it into the stem of another rose, and the complete DNA will transfer. The problem with this, as Paul pointed out, is if you can take one cut from anyone who has already created a new plant variety, you can completely appropriate their IP. Hence, the picture that Paul presented of the guarded apple tree. The argument on the part of the growers is therefore clear: if there is no way to prevent the theft of IP, we will not invest in innovation. This is a classical issue in agriculture innovation and begins to explain why the returns to agricultural R&D are historically so high.

I think Paul also pointed out quite well what the different varieties of intellectual property protection are for plants. Asexually produced plants are covered by the Plant Patent Act. Sexually reproducing plants are not covered until 1970. Utility patents can cover the techniques associated with creating new tools for genetic engineering, but this protection was not until recently.

Hybridization creates its own form of intellectual property protection, because the second generation of hybridized seeds does not yield as well as the first. So if you have created hybridized seeds, you can sell those, but then the folks who use them cannot use the resulting seeds from the first generation of crops to create a second generation.

Consistent with the classical tensions in the provision of IP rights, one issue we may worry about as a consequence of the 1930 Act and subsequent expansions of IP over plant innovation is whether these policies complicate and possibly restrict downstream innovation. Stated differently, should we worry about rose thickets? A current concern among agricultural economists is that patent thickets entwine some of the plant technologies. This is a concern that Brian Wright has expressed about public sector research on plants, but it seems to be a growing concern in the plant community overall.

What is the approach that Petra and Paul take? They begin by tracking rose patents. Rose patents are expressed desire to protect intellectual property over rose varieties. They also track rose registrations. By contrast, rose registrations do not confer any property rights. They are simply declarations of having developed new rose varieties. Registrations are something that hobbyists will do to demonstrate their pride and to signal that other people can come to them to talk about those varieties. They therefore confer some prestige and allow coordination among the hobbyists.

Paul and Petra engage in a matching exercise in which they link patents to the registrations to get a sense of how many of the new plant varieties end up getting intellectual property rights. They look over the long term from the 1930s to the 1970s. It is sort of like a differences and differences technique, but without some of the statistical features. They then attempt to compare at the end with carnations and fruit trees, to see how those trends differ. It seems as though some of the data that will, ultimately, be included in the chapter are still in process.

The authors suggest the following: for rose patents, about 50 percent of total plant patents are roses. That seems to reflect the enjoyment of the population in buying roses, and a lot of those are concentrated among the small commercial breeders. We may consider this as evidence that the patents' rights led to patenting—does that lead to innovation and does that lead to improvements in welfare? That question is a little bit open.

The US patent share rises following the Act, but the US share of registrations does not rise appreciably. I think there is still work that could be done to identify how the carnations and fruit trees work. I fear the numbers are a little bit too small in the data to know whether we are going to get useful leverage comparing changes in the US output of roses to changes in the US output of carnations and fruit trees. There are also some questions about whether we can get a clear counterfactual from these.

I think that the chapter generates a number of interesting questions and it is worthwhile to think about what it can best demonstrate. One key question is, what are the most important outcomes on which to focus? What are the most important things that we would worry about happening following the Plant Patent Act? It would be wonderful to get data on innovation inputs. That does not seem like it is possible. So we have mostly data on innovation outputs, some related to the plant varieties themselves, some related to how the industry grows.

We might also ask ourselves how the industry structure changes over time. Is a primary outcome of the Plant Act a great deal of consolidation among the US growers, relative to what went on in Europe? We do not know that yet from the data, although it would be interesting.

We could also ask how the Act changes the plant varieties, how the Act changes the quality, and how the firms themselves begin to change in light of the new intellectual property rights. There is only a limited amount of data available, but those seem to be some of the additional questions that we might want to get at.

The comparisons to carnations and fruit trees seem like they could be—apologies for the pun—fruitful things to do, but the number of carnations and number of fruit tree patents might not be large enough to enable pre- and post-comparisons to have sufficient leverage. As well, I am not sure whether these qualify, conceptually, as ideal counterfactuals.

One somewhat open question is whether to think of this project as a large-scale data analysis project with the typical sorts of econometric outputs, or whether we should see this more as a case study that might generate insights for modeling these questions. At the moment, it seems like this comes out as a case study that can let us think about what the key issues are in this particular context.

Some other difficulties in thinking about how to assess causality are that the US versus EU comparison is somewhat messy. World War II leads US firms to be able to appropriate German intellectual property, which—again, pardon the pun—seeds the US industry in roses. And then World War II disrupts the supply from Europe, giving another boost to the industry.

There are a number of reasons that we might think of this context as especially interesting. I think that the chapter could use these contextual factors to help motivate it and help it focus on the most interesting issues. The rose context is one with inherently weak property rights. It is extremely easy to copy innovations. There is also a very strong hobby community. As well, there is a very long development cycle and relatively low fixed costs for the innovation. Thus, it takes a long time to come up with a new rose, which is similar to the pharmaceutical industry. Unlike pharma, however, it does not require at a billion dollar investment to come up with a new rose. The other interesting feature of this context is that that these are very long-lived innovations and that very old and very new innovations compete in the marketplace. A bunch of the roses that are currently high in demand are eighty-year-old varieties.

One of the challenges, I think, for the chapter going forward is to identify the most interesting features of the rose context and to focus the analysis on those issues. One might ask about the impact of intellectual property rights in circumstances where there is a complementary hobby community. The hobbyists continue to trade their roses, often in connection with some of the commercial breeders. We might also ask about the impact of intellectual property rights on an industry with long development cycles and relatively low development costs.

Rose innovation seems to have some features of a number of other interesting contexts for innovation. Like the pharmaceutical industry, rose innovation has long development cycles and a very high experimentation-to-results ratio. There are also features of rose innovation that are similar to open source and software. Like open source software, rose innovations are easy to imitate. As well, there is a substantial amount of sharing in both contexts, and a great deal of participation in innovation from individuals who could be usefully described as hobbyists. There are other analogies to what happens in adventure sports, where there are user innovators, and hobbyists, and IP can also be protected by utility patents, although that does not occur until later on.

Overall, I think this is a case study examining the historical evolution of intellectual property rights in a specialized case, but with features that generalize to other cases, although in modestly different ways. It seems to be a pretty important case in its own right. This is not a trivial industry. It may be difficult to identify the causal impact of the Act on innovation and industry outcomes with extreme confidence. This chapter, in its current form, provides compelling and suggestive results that property rights did not necessarily lead to more progress, although they did lead to more patenting.

9

The Rate and Direction of Invention in the British Industrial Revolution
Incentives and Institutions

Ralf R. Meisenzahl and Joel Mokyr

9.1 Introduction

The Industrial Revolution was the first period in which technological progress and innovation became major factors in economic growth. There is by now general agreement that during the seventy years or so traditionally associated with the Industrial Revolution, there was little economic growth as traditionally measured in Britain, but that in large part this was to be expected.[1] The sectors in which technological progress occurred grew at a rapid rate, but they were small in 1760, and thus their effect on growth was limited at first (Mokyr 1998, 12–14). Yet progress took place in a wide range of industries and activities, not *just* in cotton and steam. A full description of the range of activities in which innovation took place or was at least attempted cannot be provided here, but inventions in some pivotal industries such as iron and mechanical engineering had backward linkages in many more traditional industries. In the words of McCloskey (1981, 118), "the Industrial Revolution was neither the age of steam, nor the age of cotton,

Ralf R. Meisenzahl is an economist in the Division of Research and Statistics at the Federal Reserve Board. Joel Mokyr is the Robert H. Strotz Professor of Arts and Sciences and professor of economics and history at Northwestern University and a member of the Board of Directors of the National Bureau of Economic Research.

Prepared for the 50th anniversary conference in honor of *The Rate and Direction of Inventive Activity*. The authors acknowledge financial support from the Kauffman Foundation and the superb research assistance of Alexandru Rus. The opinions expressed are those of the authors and do not necessarily reflect views of the Board of Governors of the Federal Reserve System.

1. The main explanations for the low level of income per capita growth during the decades of the Industrial Revolution are the unprecedented rate of population growth in this period, as well as the incidence of bad weather and war.

nor the age of iron. It was the age of progress." A similar point has been made by Temin (1997).

Outside the familiar tales of cotton textiles, wrought iron, and steam power, there were improvements in many aspects of production, such as mechanical and civil engineering, food processing, brewing, paper, glass, cement, mining, and shipbuilding. Some of the more famous advances of the time may have had a negligible direct effect on growth rates, but improved the quality of life in other ways; one thinks above all of smallpox inoculation and vaccination, the mining safety lamp, hot air and hydrogen balloons, food canning, and gas lighting (Mokyr 1990, 2009a). Britain was the world leader in innovation for a period of about a century, after which its dominance slowly dissolved. Yet Britain retained a place as one of many western nations that collaborated in a joint program to apply a rapidly growing knowledge base to economic production.

What drove British leadership, and why was Britain the most technologically advanced economy in the world for so long? The question has been attacked many times, and with many different answers.[2] In the spirit of this volume, it seems to make sense to make a distinction between the rate of technological progress and its direction, which have often been confused in the literature. In his recent influential work, Allen (2009a, 2009b) has resurrected induced innovation theory and reemphasized the role of factor prices in generating the inventions that formed the Industrial Revolution. Yet the high wages that Allen emphasized may have imparted a labor-saving direction on the innovations. However, it is hard to use them to explain the "engine of growth," which is the growing body of useful knowledge and its ever-greater accessibility in the eighteenth century. As an alternative, many scholars, led by Wrigley (2004, 2010) have emphasized the importance of the availability of coal in Britain; this may explain a bias toward fuel-intensive and perhaps the replacement of water- and animal-powered plants by steam-driven ones. Yet the improvements in coal technology point to the fact that coal production itself was subject to deeper forces.[3] Moreover, the progress in water power technology in the eighteenth century indicates that even without coal, energy-saving technological progress was feasible, and even that without coal Britain would have experienced an Industrial Revolution, albeit one that would have a somewhat different dynamic (Clark and Jacks 2007).

In what follows, we will take a closer look at one particular aspect: the importance of technological competence and the incentives of those people

2. For a slightly dated survey, see Mokyr (1998, 28–81). Recent contributions focus on institutions (North and Weingast 1989; Mokyr 2008; Acemoglu and Robinson 2012), and the roles of factor prices and coal discussed later.

3. Two examples should suffice: the pathbreaking work in using stratigraphic data to locate coal (Winchester 2001), and the "miner's friend" invented by Humphry Davy (James 2005).

who were the practical carriers of technological progress in this era.[4] Competence is defined here as the high-quality workmanship and materials needed to implement an innovation; that is, to follow the blueprint with a high level of accuracy, carry out the instructions embodied in the technique, and to have the ability to install, operate, adapt, and repair the machinery and equipment under a variety of circumstances. Beyond those, competence often involved minor improvements and refinements of a technique, which may not have qualified as a "microinvention" stricto sensu, but clearly enhanced the innovative effort in economy.[5] In principle, it is easy to see that there are deep complementarities between the small group of people who actually invent things and can be identified as such, and the somewhat larger group of skilled workmen who possessed the training and natural dexterity to actually carry out the "instructions" contained in the new recipes and blueprints that inventors wrote with a high degree of accuracy, build the parts on a routine basis with very low degrees of tolerance, and still could fill in the blanks when the instructions were inevitably incomplete.[6] We argue that Britain's industrial precocity owed a great deal to the high level of competence of those engineers and mechanics who provided the support for the inventors.

But who were they? Identifying competence falls somewhere between the two extremes of either studying a handful of heroic inventors whose names are well-known, and searching for variables that measure the overall national level of some critical input such as human capital or the supply of entrepreneurship in the population. Neither of those is satisfactory. Modern economic history has long ago distanced itself from the heroic hagiographies in which the Industrial Revolution was attributed to the genius of a few superstar inventors. On the other hand, it may seriously be doubted whether the *average* level of education of the laboring class (say, the bottom two-thirds of the income distribution) made much difference to the outcome (Mitch 1998).

Moreover, did Britain have a comparative advantage in macroinventions such as steampower and cotton spinning? While Britain did have a large number of "hall of fame" inventors, it was equally able to adopt inventions made overseas. It may be surmised that although Britain may have had an

4. In his contribution to the 1962 *Rate and Direction* volume, Fritz Machlup (1962) discussed at some length the concept of "inventive labor." Part of our purpose is to unpack that term into those "inventive workers" who are truly innovative, and those who fill in the gaps and improve the original insights, whom we refer to as tweakers. While the context here is historical, there is little doubt that this concept can readily be extended to our own time.

5. In this chapter we will be little concerned with truly epochal or *macro*inventions.

6. In another paper in the original volume, John Enos (1962) distinguishes between the "alpha" stage (the original invention) and the "beta" stage (improvement). This parallels our distinction. His finding is that most of the productivity growth in the petroleum refining industry occurred during the beta stage (319).

absolute advantage in macroinventions, its *comparative* advantage was in smaller improvements and competence—as illustrated by the large number of highly skilled technicians that Britain "exported" to the Continent. At the same time a flow of substantial continental inventions found their first applications in Britain, presumably because other factors, complementary with the innovations, were present in larger quantities.[7] But what were these complementarities? Britain provided a freer market, and overall may have had an institutional environment that was more conducive to innovation. But its human capital advantage in the form of skilled workmen is the one element that has not been sufficiently stressed.

We may distinguish between three levels of activity that drove innovation in this period. One were the macroinventions and other major breakthroughs that solved a major bottleneck and opened a new door.[8] We will refer to these inventors as major inventors, and they are, by and large, the ones that made it into economic history textbooks. Another was the myriad of small and medium cumulative microinventions that improved and debugged existing inventions, adapted them to new uses, and combined them in new applications. The people engaged in those will be referred to as *tweakers* in the sense that they improved and debugged an existing invention. Some of the more important advances among those may have been worth patenting, but clearly this was not uniformly the case. A third group, and perhaps the least recognized of Britain's advantages, was the existence of a substantial number of skilled workmen capable of building, installing, operating, and maintaining new and complex equipment. The skills needed for pure implementers were substantial, but they did not have to be creative themselves. We will refer to these as *implementers.* It goes without saying that the line between tweakers and implementers is blurry, but at the very least a patent or some prize for innovation would be a clear signal of creativity.

Some of the greatest technical minds of the Industrial Revolution clearly were good at all three, but the vast majority of highly skilled mechanics did not invent much that posterity remembers.[9] It has been argued that artisans alone, without the help of any "great inventors," could have generated much

7. Among the better-known of these inventions were the Robert continuous paper-making machine, the Jacquard loom, Berthollet's bleaching process, Leblanc's soda-making process, Lebon's gaslighting technique, De Girard's spinning machine for linen yarn, Friedrich Koenig's steam-driven printer, Appert's invention of food canning, and the Argand lamp.

8. We will use a somewhat wider definition for these major inventions than the one in Mokyr (1990a), which defines macroinventions in terms of their epistemic innovativeness and effect on the marginal product of further improvements. Here even inventions that were not dramatic new insights but had a major impact on the economy, such as the mule and the puddling and rolling process, would be classified as such.

9. A notable exception was the Dartmouth blacksmith Thomas Newcomen, who in the phrase of a recent author was "the first (or very nearly) and clearly the most important member of a tribe of a very particular, and historically original, type: the English artisan-engineer-entrepreneur" (Rosen 2010, 40).

of the technological progress of the period simply by incrementally improving and adapting existing technology.[10] Yet sophisticated artisanal economies had thrived in Europe since the late Middle Ages, and there was no reason for them to be delayed to the second half of the eighteenth century if they had been capable of generating an Industrial Revolution by themselves. At the same time, "great inventors" without the support of high-quality competence were equally doomed to create economically meaningless curiosa (of which Leonardo's myriad inventions are just one example).

The strong complementarity between the three forms of technological activity is critical to the understanding of the question of "why Britain." A nation that possessed a high level of technical competence could successfully implement major inventions wherever made. The economic success of inventors depended, among other things, on their ability to find tweakers to get the bugs out of the invention, and implementers to construct, install, and operate it. To quote a famous example, James Watt, the paradigmatic "heroic" inventor, depended for his success not only on the ability of John Wilkinson to bore the cylinders for his machine with great accuracy, but also on some of his brilliant employees such as William Murdoch (Griffiths 1992), as well as highly competent engineers such as John Southern and James Lawson (Roll 1930, 260–61).[11] Their ability to build and maintain equipment embodying new technology inevitably spilled over to small adaptations and adjustments that would have to be regarded as minor incremental innovations.

The emphasis on mechanical skills and dexterity has major implications for the assessment of the role of human capital in the British Industrial Revolution. The group to focus on is not so much the few dozen or so major inventors and scientists that can be denoted as "great inventors" (Khan 2006), nor should we concentrate on the human capital of the mass of factory workers, many of whom were still poorly educated and illiterate as late as 1850. Instead the focus ought to be the top 3 to 5 percent of the labor force in terms of skills: engineers, mechanics, millwrights, chemists, clock- and instrument makers, skilled carpenters and metal workers, wheelwrights, and similar workmen. Their numbers were in the tens of thousands, and the vast bulk of them are impossible to trace. Many of them were independent artisans and entrepreneurs; others were in the employ of others. A consider-

10. Hilaire-Pérez (2007) and Berg (2007) believe that "an economy of imitation" could lead to a self-sustaining process of improvement, driven purely by artisans. Such sequences of microinventions, without any shifts in the technological paradigm, were doomed to bog down into diminishing returns.

11. Some of the unsung heroes of the Industrial Revolution were these less-known tweakers. Thus Josias C. Gamble (1775–1848), an Irishman trained in Glasgow, was essential to James Muspratt's introduction of the Leblanc process in Britain (Musson and Robinson 1969, 187). A variety of mechanics, such as William Horrocks of Stockport and many others improved upon Cartwright's powerloom (Marsden 1895, 70–72). William Woollat was Jedediah Strutt's brother-in-law and helped him develop a mechanized stocking frame that could make ribbed hosiery (Fitton and Wadsworth 1958, 24).

able number were both or switched from one to the other. But we shall make an effort to find at least the best-known of them, although survival bias here is impossible to avoid and we can make no presumption that those who end up in our sample are representative.

9.2 Skills and Competence

What evidence is there to support Britain's advantage in tweakers and implementers? In a famous letter to his partner, John Roebuck, James Watt wrote in 1765 that "my principal hindrance in erecting engines is always smith-work" (Smiles 1874, 92) and he had considerable difficulty finding "workmen capable of fitting together the parts of a machine so complicated and of so novel a construction" (196; see also Roll [1930] 1968, 61). Yet, while competence was thus a binding constraint, Watt's engines—and those of many other machine-builders—did get built and were of high quality.[12] Foreign observers, perhaps more than local writers (who took Britain's superiority for granted) noted the comparatively high level of *competence* of British skilled workmen.[13] The flows of the kind of useful knowledge associated with workmanship are quite unambiguous. Industrial spies from the Continent converged on Britain to study the fine details of British engineering and iron-making (Harris 1998), and British technicians, mechanics, and skilled workmen left the country in droves to find employment in France, Germany, and Belgium, as well as Eastern Europe, despite the fact that such emigration was prohibited by law until 1824 and that a state of war existed between Britain and many of these countries for most of the years between 1780 and 1815 (Harris 1998; Henderson 1954). It is telling, for example, that one of the best-known eighteenth-century engineering migrants to the Continent, John Holker (1719–1786), made his career when he moved a number of highly skilled Lancashire workmen to the embryonic cotton industry in

12. A typical description of a competent British worker was provided by the engineer William Fairbairn in a book first published in 1863: "The millwright of former days was to a great extent the sole representative of mechanical art . . . a kind of jack of all trades who could with equal facility work at a lathe, the anvil, or the carpenter's bench . . . a fair arithmetician who could calculate the velocities, strength and power of machines . . . Such was the character and condition of the men who designed and carried out most of the mechanical work of this country up to the middle and end of the last century" (Fairbairn 1871, ix–x).

13. A Swiss visitor, César de Saussure, noticed in 1727 that "English workmen are everywhere renowned, and justly. They work to perfection, and though not inventive, are capable of improving and of finishing most admirably what the French and Germans have invented" (de Saussure [c. 1727] 1902, 218; letter dated May 29, 1727). Josiah Tucker, a keen contemporary observer, pointed out in 1758 that "the Number of Workmen [in Britain] and their greater Experience excite the higher Emulation, and cause them to excel the Mechanics of other Countries in these Sorts of Manufactures" (Tucker 1758, 26). The French political economist Jean-Baptiste Say noted in 1803 that "the enormous wealth of Britain is less owing to her own advances in scientific acquirements, high as she ranks in that department, as to the wonderful practical skills of her adventurers [entrepreneurs] in the useful application of knowledge and the superiority of her workmen" (Say [1803] 1821, vol. 1, 32–33).

Rouen, after which he rose to the position of "inspector-general of foreign manufactures" in 1756. His mandate in that job was, among others, to recruit more British workers.[14] After 1815, the number of British engineers and mechanics that swarmed all over the Continent increased, including especially in such early industrializers as Belgium and Switzerland. The most famous family here were William Cockerill and his sons, who set up the most successful machine-toll manufacturing plant in continental Europe in Verviers in eastern Belgium (Mokyr 1976).[15] The same was true in civil engineering. The first permanent bridge across the Danube connecting Buda and Pest was commenced in 1839 under the engineering control of William Tierney Clark. At the same time, highly original and creative minds from the European Continent found their way to Britain, in search of an environment in which their inventions could be exploited and the complementary skills that made the development of their inventions possible.[16]

On the supply side, Britain's apprenticeship system worked exceptionally well in producing highly skilled workers that could serve as implementers, despite (or perhaps because) of the weakness of British guilds (Humphries 2003).[17] The Statue of Artificers of 1563, which regulated apprenticeship, did not cover many mechanical occupations and its regulations were often ignored (Wallis 2008). All this contributed to labor markets that on the eve of the Industrial Revolution were more flexible and less encumbered than on the Continent.

The fact that millwrights were entirely produced through the apprenticeship system highlights its importance for the formation of skill and competence in Britain. In a recent paper, Karine van der Beek (2010) has shown that in the period between 1710 and 1772 at least, the English system

14. His colleague Michael Alcock modernized the famed St. Etienne ironworks in France in the 1760s with the help of skilled workmen that his wife had recruited in England. A third striking case of such migration is that of William Wilkinson, the brother of the famous Broseley ironmonger, who was charged with setting up cannon foundries and blast furnaces, at an astronomical salary of 60,000 livres per year.

15. As late as 1840, a British official informed a Parliamentary Committee that in the cotton mills in the Vienna area "the directors and foremen are chiefly Englishmen or Scotsmen from the cotton manufactories of Glasgow and Manchester" (Henderson 1954, 196). In countries with even less supplies of local skilled workmen, the importance of foreigners was even more important; much of the iron used to build St. Petersburg's famed bridges came from a local ironworks managed by Charles Baird (1766–1843), working with his son and his nephew.

16. The Swiss inventor Aimé Argand designed a new oil-burning lamp but his attempts to build and sell it in Paris failed. He went to Britain in the 1780s, where he sought and found the help of the great entrepreneur Matthew Boulton; sadly, commercial fortune eluded him here as well. More luck had the Saxon Rudolph Ackermann (1764–1834), who arrived in London in 1787 to make major contributions to the technology of coachmaking and lithography and whose firm survived until 1992.

17. The relative weakness of the guilds was in part the result of the declining power of their traditional ally, the monarchy. Second, guilds were an urban phenomenon, yet some crucial mechanical occupations such as mining engineers emerged on the countryside. Last, industry had the continuous option to produce on the countryside, which also weakened the power of the urban guilds.

produced larger numbers of apprentices in high-skilled occupations, especially in machinery-building and precision instruments, and that this took place in the industrializing midlands, where the demand for such skills was highest. At the same time the relative tuition paid to masters in high skill occupations did not increase in the long run, indicating that the apprenticeship system was sufficiently flexible to supply enough competent craftsmen. Much of the competence of these skilled workers still was in the nature of tacit knowledge, which could not be learned only from books and articles but required hands-on instruction and personal experience. The degree of tacitness varied from industry to industry, but was especially marked in the iron industry (Harris 1988, 1992).[18] Yet whether tacit or not, there can be little doubt that this strength of Britain played a central role in its success. Its skilled workers, freed from enforceable labor market restrictions, often moved from area to area, diversifying their human capital portfolios and at the same time enhancing innovation by applying ideas from one field to another, a kind of technological hybridizing.[19]

At the top of the pyramid emerged a small group of professional inventors, the kind of person of whom Smith wrote his famous lines that inventions were often made by "men of speculation, whose trade is not to do anything but to observe everything" ([1776] 1976, 14). Some of the great inventors of the Industrial Revolution, such as Crompton, Cartwright, Smeaton, and Harrison should be seen as full-time inventors, although their mechanical abilities probably exceeded their knowledge of "experimental philosophy." Others were educated part-timers who dabbled in invention and engineering; some of those were scientists such as Humphry Davy and Joseph Priestley, but gifted and obsessed amateurs also made considerable contributions.[20] Smith's inventive philosophers would, however, have had no effect on the economy had there been no dexterous and ingenious workmen to carry out and improve their designs.

How were these individuals incentivized? Britain, of course, had a patent system, which has been discussed at length in the literature (Mokyr 2009b)

18. The puddlers, an expertise that emerged quickly after Henry Cort's pathbreaking invention in 1785 were, in the words of one scholar, trained "by doing, not by talking, and developed a taciturnity that lasted all their life" (Gale 1961–62, 9).

19. Reflecting on the supply of the craftsmen he employed, Watt noted in 1794 that many of them had been trained in analogous skills "such as millwrights, architects and surveyors," with the practical skills and dexterity spilling over from occupation to occupation (cited by Jones 2008, 126–27).

20. Thus Patrick Miller (1731–1815), a wealthy Scottish banker, was a pioneer in the mechanical propulsion of boats and one of the first to experiment with steam power on a vessel, yet this was obviously more of a hobby than a serious occupation (although Miller did take out a patent on a shallow-draft vessel). Another famous amateur inventor (at least in the sense of not being motivated by financial gain) was Charles Earl of Stanhope (1753–1816), a radical member of the House of Lords who also made notable contributions to the technology of early steamship design and whose improved printing press was purchased by *The Times* and Oxford University Press.

and to which we will return later. But there were other ways in which ingenuity was rewarded. One was the awarding of prizes, set either ex ante for someone who solved a known problem, or ex post for someone whose contribution was widely recognized but who was not able to reap the rewards. The Society of Arts (f. 1754) set clear targets, such as machines that would encourage the manufacture of lace, to reduce both the dependence on French imports and encourage the employment of women (Griffiths, Hunt, and O'Brien 1992, 886). These premiums were set in advance, yet the condition for their award was that no patent was taken out. In other cases, the Society awarded medals to inventors who had little interest in taking out patents (e.g., the engineer and educational writer Richard Lovell Edgeworth, who won numerous medals). It clearly provided an alternative model to the patent system (Harrison 2006). In a few notable cases, Parliament stepped in and awarded grants or pensions to inventors of considerable merit. For others, especially those who were in business for themselves, a major form of reward was what we would call today "first-mover" advantage: by producing goods and services that were just a little better and more reliable or cheaper than their competitors,' they could make an excellent living.

Many of the most successful innovators in the Industrial Revolution were thus incentivized by multiple mechanisms: although in many cases they relied on patents or secrecy to protect the rent-generating intellectual property rights, as often they placed their knowledge in the public domain and relied on superior technology or competence. The reality on the ground was, however, that it is in many cases impractical to distinguish between those who lived off their reputation as consultants or employees and those who were in business for themselves. In the course of a career, many mechanics and engineers switched back and forth from entrepreneurial activity and self-employment to hired employees.[21]

Beyond the standard economic notions of incentives, the rate and direction of technological progress during the Industrial Revolution were affected by a zeitgeist that may be termed a *mechanical culture,* in which science and chemistry found their way to the shop floor, where entrepreneurs and engineers tried to apply them in their stubborn attempts to achieve "improvements" (Jacob 1997, 2007). Mechanical culture was part and parcel of the Industrial Enlightenment. It implied that many of the efforts to improve machinery fed on a culture that placed technological questions at the center of the social agenda. The second half of the eighteenth century witnessed

21. One well-known example is the Scottish engineer Peter Ewart (1767–1842), who worked for a time for Boulton and Watt, then went into business with Samuel Oldknow and Samuel Greg, then opened his own mill in 1811, and eventually ended up employed by the admiralty. His colleague, William Brunton (1777–1851) was also employed in Boulton and Watt's Soho work, which he left in 1808 to take another employment. Eventually he became a partner at an iron foundry in Birmingham and then moved to London where he practiced as an independent civil engineer.

the maturing of the Baconian program, which postulated that useful knowledge was the key to social improvement. In that culture, technological progress could thrive. The signs of that culture were everywhere: in which books and articles were published, in what people discussed in coffeehouses and pubs, in the establishment of scientific clubs and societies, and through all of them what happened in the workshops and factories. None of this is to deny that economic incentives were central to the story, just that they were neither "everything" nor "the only thing." The best-known people affected by this culture were the famous enlightened industrialists such as Josiah Wedgwood, Matthew Boulton, Benjamin Gott, Richard Crawshay, John Kennedy, and John Marshall. Their commitment to the culture of improvement through the application of useful knowledge to issues in manufacturing are paradigmatic examples of the Industrial Enlightenment (Jones 2008). Economic motives were not always central to the men who made the Industrial Revolution.[22] Those who came from science, such as Davy and Faraday, were probably close to the Frenchman Berthollet, the inventor of the chlorine bleaching process, who famously wrote that "[w]hen one loves science, one has little need for fortune which would only risk one's happiness" (cited by Musson and Robinson 1969, 266). But did this culture "filter down" to the layer of lesser-known people in the layer just below them?

In what follows, we try to build a database not so much of "superstar inventors" but of the layer of technically competent individuals just below them: the engineers, mechanics, chemists, and skilled craftsmen who improved and implemented the inventions of the more famous men. We show how these "tweakers" were trained, what incentives drove them (that is, how they made their living), and how deeply they were immersed in the intellectual life of the Industrial Enlightenment.

9.3 Database

Our main purpose is to shed light on the technological environment that bred technological success and innovation in the British Industrial Revo-

22. A rather striking example of this is the case of Samuel Crompton, the inventor of the mule, arguably the most productive invention of the Industrial Revolution. It was said of him that he was "of a retiring and unambitious disposition," and hence he took out no patent on his invention. His only regret was that public curiosity would "not allow him to enjoy his little invention in his garret" and to earn undisturbed the fruits of his ingenuity and perseverance (Baines 1835, 199). Yet even Crompton had to make ends meet and in the end appealed to Parliament for a reward for having made an invention that so palpably benefitted the realm. In 1812 Parliament awarded him £5,000, which he subsequently lost in a failed business venture (Farnie 2004). Another, much less famous, example is that of the Scottish plowmaker James Small (1740–1793), who redesigned the all-iron plow according to formal principles and wrote the standard text on plow design. Small insisted that this knowledge be made generally available and declined to take out a patent. He enjoyed the patronage of the two great Scottish agricultural innovators, Lord Kames and John Sinclair. His workshop in Berwickshire produced fine plows, though they were not universally popular.

lution. Rather than focus primarily on "great inventors," our argument concentrates on "competence"—that is, we look for the persons whose dexterity and training allowed them to tweak and implement the new techniques. To be in the sample, they had to have made some inventions themselves (the bulk of them would be microinventions and adaptations), but their main activity was implementation. It would be futile to distinguish between inventors and pure noninventors in a strict sense, simply because the process of innovation consists of both the new technique *and* its implementation, and during the implementation process inevitably problems are resolved and the technique is tweaked and adapted to the particular needs of the user. Most inventors spent much of their lives working on existing techniques that they or others had generated.

It must be stressed that this kind of project inevitably runs into a "tip-of-the-iceberg" problem. We have no illusions that the bulk of competent technicians who determined both rate and the direction of the Industrial Revolution in Britain simply did not leave enough of a record to become known to posterity.[23] To leave a record, an individual had to do something more than just be a competent and productive employee or artisan. The argument we make is one of continuity: if we can uncover some of the layer of competent workers below the superstars, we may be able to say something about what motivated these people and how they interacted with their institutional and cultural environments.

We are interested in the "classical" Industrial Revolution and so we use primarily sources that focus on activities before 1860. To this end we have constructed a prosopographical database that is composed of men (there is one woman in the sample) born before 1830, of a technical ability that was sufficient to make it into the literature (we excluded all persons whose role was purely entrepreneurial or commercial). We are interested in tweakers, engineers, and mechanics who made minor improvements on existing inventions. Hence for them to have taken out a patent is a sufficient condition to be included in the sample, but so would a mention of any kind of some innovation, invention, or improvement of existing technology. However, only a small subset of persons listed as having taken out any sort of patent before 1850 are included, because the majority of patentees left no other record. Our sample, then, consists of what we judge to have been successful careers at the cutting edge of technology: engineers, chemists, mechanics, clock- and instrument makers, printers, and so on.

One source is the collection of biographies of British engineers put together by Skempton (2002). It is quite detailed, and many of the essays are written by experts, but because it is focused on engineers, it is biased toward

23. Moreover, the population of known inventors consists mostly of the population of successful inventors—it stands to reason that many of the engineers and mechanics also made additional efforts in that direction that either failed, or for which they failed to receive credit. Some "failed" inventions, such as the Stirling engine, invented by clergyman Robert Stirling in 1816, have become famous, but the vast bulk of such failures will remain unknown.

road- and canal builders, contractors, architects, surveyors, military engineers, and similar occupations. While it covers some mechanical engineers, they clearly were not the main interest of the editors.[24] It leaves out many areas, most notably chemicals, paper, glass, food processing, and by and large textiles. It hence needs to be complemented with other sources. Two other biographical compendia were used. One is Day and McNeil (1996), with high-quality essays but with fairly thin coverage for Britain, since it is international in coverage. There are the various biographical studies carried out by Samuel Smiles (1865, 1884, 1889), which, despite their hagiographic character, contain a lot of useful information about minor players as well. A number of recently compiled online databases, overlapping to some extent with Skempton and Day-McNeil, were also used.[25] Finally, economic historians have carried out considerably detailed studies of a number of industries that have produced information on many relatively minor actors in the history of technological advances in the Industrial Revolution. Among the most notable and useful of these studies, we should mention Turner (1998) and Morrison-Low (2007) on scientific instruments; Burnley (1889), Heaton (1965), and Jenkins and Ponting (1982) on wool; Barlow (1878) and Chapman (1967, 1972, 1981) on textiles; Barker and Harris (1954) on paper, glass, and chemical industries; and Marshall (1978) on railroad engineers.[26] All entries were cross-checked and complemented with information from the Oxford *Dictionary of National Biography.*[27] To ensure the accuracy of the number of patents, we verified the information in the bibliographies with the *Alphabetical Index of Patentees of Inventions* by Woodcroft (1854), which includes all patents in Great Britain until the reform of the patent system in 1851.

We include people born between 1660 and 1830. For each individual we have recorded (besides the name and dates of birth and death) information about their education, their occupation, what inventions and innovation they made, what rewards and pay they received, patents they took out, publications, whether they were managers, employees, and/or self-employed (with or without partners), membership in societies, and a variety of other details and remarks recorded in the respective sources. Entries with unknown birthdates contain information when the person flourished (fl.). We subtract thirty years from this date to calculate the date of birth.

Our database consists of 759 entries: 758 men and Elenor Coade, who

24. The article on instrument maker Henry Maudslay is a page and a half, while that on civil engineer John Rennie is over fourteen pages, and the article on William Jessop is nine pages.

25. These are: http://www.steamindex.com/people/engrs.htm; http://www.steamindex.com/people/civils.htm; http://www.steamindex.com/manlocos/manulist.htm.

26. The database was augmented with information from Crouzet (1985); Henderson (1954); Honeyman (1983); Marsden (1895); Rimmer (1965); Sussman (2009); and Thornton (1959).

27. The *Dictionary of National Biography* (DNB) provides a high level of detail for some individuals, but as pointed out by MacLeod and Nuvolari (2006), there is considerable selection bias in the DNB.

Table 9.1 **Tweaker-and-implementer database, descriptive statistics**

Sector/period	Pre-1700	1700–1749	1750–1774	1775–1799	1800–1814	1815–1830	Sector total
Textiles	2.0	39.0	41.0	42.0	45.0	24.0	193.0
Ships	1.0	3.0	7.5	7.5	6.0	2.0	27.0
Road & rail & can	2.0	2.0	11.5	26.5	24.5	23.0	89.5
Other eng	11.0	19.0	32.5	44.0	27.0	14.5	148.0
Med & chem	1.0	6.0	6.0	10.0	3.0	3.5	29.5
Instruments	8.0	26.0	12.0	27.0	12.0	5.5	90.5
Iron & met	4.0	13.0	11.0	11.5	7.0	4.5	51.0
Mining	2.0	3.0	8.0	9.5	3.0	0.0	25.5
Agr & farm	2.0	7.0	2.5	4.5	3.0	2.0	21.0
Constr	0.0	10.0	11.5	15.5	5.0	0.0	42.0
Print & photo	0.0	4.0	4.5	6.5	2.5	2.0	19.5
Others	1.0	6.0	5.0	3.5	4.0	3.0	22.5
Period total	34.0	138.0	153.0	208.0	142.0	84.0	759.0
% of total	*4.5%*	*18.2%*	*20.2%*	*27.4%*	*18.7%*	*11.1%*	

invented a new process for making artificial stone, and who is the only woman included in the database. We assigned a sector to each individual by his main area of activity, which in some cases was difficult because a large number of our tweakers were polymaths who applied their ability in many distinct areas of activity and contributed materially to more than one sector. Hence thirty-five entries were assigned to two different sectors with weight 1/2, hence the fractions in table 9.1.

Table 9.1 displays the main descriptive statistics of the sample by birth-year and sector. The number of persons included (per annum) peaks in the 1800 to 1814 period, but this is largely because many of those born in the fifteen years after 1815 were active in the second half of the nineteenth century and much of what they did would not be included in many of our sources. The table reflects the rise to prominence of the textile industry in the eighteenth century, yet it also warns that even at its peak this industry did not involve more than a third of all tweakers, and for the sample as a whole they are slightly under a quarter of the "modern" (that is, technologically advanced) economy. Transportation and "other" engineering together were larger than textiles, and many other sectors were important areas for technological creativity.

9.4 Results

9.4.1 Training

One important question is the training and education of highly skilled artisans. If our argument that Britain's advantage on other European countries derived primarily from its cadres of skilled and creative tweakers, how should we explain that? How was this human capital created and how were these artisans incentivized? The origins of the highly skilled labor force in Britain have been discussed elsewhere, and need only to be briefly stated here (Mokyr 2009a). On the demand side, Britain had sectors that generated a need for a high level of skills, above all coal mining, which spawned the steam engine as well as the railroad (Cardwell 1972, 74).[28] It had, for a variety of reasons, a high number of clock- and instrument makers, optical craftsmen, millwrights, and workers involved in shipbuilding and rigging. The origins of this group of high-skill workers were at least in part due to geography; but the preexistence of a substantial British middle class with a demand for luxury goods meant a considerable market for consumer durables that required a high degree of precision and skill, such as watches, telescopes, and musical instruments. Finally, Britain was the beneficiary of the migration of Huguenots after 1685 and thus its more tolerant institutions can be seen to have paid off. All the same, the main reason for the high levels of skills in this economy were the effectiveness of its education system embedded in flexible labor markets. While the record of British schools and universities was decidedly mixed, skills were produced in the personal sphere of master-apprentice relation, where British institutions performed remarkably well (Humphries 2003; Mokyr 2009a).

The 759 persons in our sample confirm, as far as can be ascertained, this interpretation. Two-thirds of those whose educational background could be established were apprenticed. This share is the highest in textiles, but the share of those about whom we do not know their educational background is *highest* in textiles. Clearly this is the sector in which any kind of education mattered the least, largely because the mechanical issues, while often subtle and delicate, required little formal learning and success was often the result of a combination of dexterity, luck, perseverance, and focus.[29] On the other hand, a quarter of our tweakers with known background had attended university; many of these were upper-class youngsters, some of whom turned into improving landlords or the kind of amateur inventors such as Lord Stanhope mentioned earlier. It may be safely surmised that little of what they learned in English universities was of much help furthering their technical competence, although the same was probably not true for Scottish universities. Engineers, whether in shipbuilding, railroads, canals, or mining usually

28. Almost all the engineers who worked on the development of a locomotive from 1803 to 1830 were originally employed in the mining sector.

29. The two best-known inventors of the industry, Richard Arkwright and Edmund Cartwright, were trained as a wigmaker and a clergyman, respectively. But many others, insofar as we know their background, came from other sectors. Henry Houldsworth (b. 1796), the inventor of compound gear in powerlooms, was trained as a grocer. Jedediah Strutt, one of the early partners of Richard Arkwright, was trained as a wheelwright; the son of Jedediah (a successful tweaker in his own right) had a wide-ranging education and among others was active as a successful architect.

apprenticed and/or attended a university. The same can be said about instrument makers. The consistency of the high proportion of tweakers classified as engineers or instrument makers who were apprenticed leaves no doubt that this mode of skills-transmission was the dominant form of human capital accumulation of the age. Interestingly enough, the famous Statute of Apprentices and Artificers that mandated such training was repealed in 1814, but the percentages of men born after 1800 who acquired their skills in this fashion did not change and remained at about two-thirds of the entire sample of tweakers with known educational background. As a comparison of panels A and B of table 9.2 shows, there is little evidence that the role of formal education changed a lot in the training of the British technological elite: the share of people with known training who attended universities fell from 27 to 24 percent and those who only attended school only rose from 12 to 13 percent.

The apprenticeship system clearly figured highly in the creation of British competence. The modes of cultural transmission, as so often happens, can be seen in the creation of "dynasties" in which technical knowledge was passed on along vertical lines. Some famous father-and-son dynasties, such as the Darbys, the Stephensons, and the Brunels, are widely known. But there were many others.[30] Of the dynasties of master-apprentices, the best-known is the Bramah-Maudsley-Nasmyth one. Especially among coal viewers, a highly skilled and specialized branch of mining engineering, such dynasties were common: John Blenkinsop (1783–1831) was trained by Thomas Barnes (1765–1801), who himself was trained by an (unknown) viewer.

9.4.2 Incentives

How were these members of Britain's technological elite incentivized? There were essentially four different mechanisms through which these men were compensated: intellectual property rights in their knowledge, first mover advantage by independent businesses, reputation effects leading to permanent employment, and nonpecuniary rewards. We shall discuss those in turn.

Intellectual Property Rights

A standard argument in the literature has been that the patent system in Britain provided the most effective incentive toward invention. This view is not just found in the writings of modern institutionalists such as Douglass North (1981) but also in many of the contemporary writers, many of them

30. Among them the microscope-makers George Adams Sr. and Jr. were active in the second half of the eighteenth century; John Rastrick (1738–1826) and his son John Urpeth Rastrick (1780–1856), both civil engineers; the hugely inventive and versatile engineer Bryan Donkin (1768–1855) and his son and later partner John (1802–1854); the engineers William Sims (1762–1834) and James Sims (1795–1862).

Table 9.2 **Sample breakdown by education**

Sector/Education	Apprenticed	*% of sector total*	Schooled	*% of sector total*	University	*% of sector total*	None/ unknown	*% of sector total*	Sector total
				A Individuals born before 1800					
Textiles	19.5	*16*	5.0	*4*	1.5	*1*	100.5	*81*	124.0
Ships	10.0	*53*	1.0	*5*	5.5	*29*	3.5	*18*	19.0
Road & rail & can	19.0	*45*	4.0	*10*	7.0	*17*	13.0	*31*	42.0
Other eng	42.0	*39*	6.5	*6*	22.5	*21*	39.5	*37*	106.5
Med & chem	9.0	*39*	2.0	*9*	8.0	*35*	5.0	*22*	23.0
Instruments	38.0	*52*	4.5	*6*	15.5	*21*	17.0	*23*	73.0
Iron & met	17.0	*43*	4.5	*11*	4.0	*10*	15.0	*38*	39.5
Mining	13.0	*58*	1.5	*7*	3.0	*13*	6.0	*27*	22.5
Agr & farm	3.5	*22*	1.0	*6*	7.0	*44*	5.0	*31*	16.0
Constr	17.0	*46*	4.0	*11*	2.5	*7*	13.5	*36*	37.0
Print & photo	9.0	*60*	1.0	*7*	2.5	*17*	3.5	*23*	15.0
Others	5.0	*32*	2.0	*13*	2.0	*13*	6.5	*42*	15.5
Category total	202.0	*38*	37.0	*7*	81.0	*15*	228.0	*43*	533.0
				B Individuals born 1800–1830					
Textiles	14.0	*20*	1.0	*1*	0.5	*1*	54.0	*78*	69.0
Ships	4.0	*50*	2.0	*25*	2.0	*25*	0.0	*0*	8.0
Road & rail & can	36.0	*76*	3.0	*6*	4.0	*8*	6.5	*14*	47.5
Other eng	25.5	*61*	5.0	*12*	9.0	*22*	5.5	*13*	41.5
Med & chem	1.5	*23*	1.0	*15*	4.0	*62*	0.0	*0*	6.5
Instruments	6.0	*34*	2.0	*11*	6.0	*34*	5.0	*29*	17.5
Iron & met	4.5	*39*	2.0	*17*	4.0	*35*	1.0	*9*	11.5
Mining	1.0	*33*	0.0	*0*	0.0	*0*	2.0	*67*	3.0
Agr & farm	0.5	*10*	0.0	*0*	1.0	*20*	3.5	*70*	5.0
Constr	1.5	*30*	1.0	*20*	2.0	*40*	0.5	*10*	5.0
Print & photo	1.5	*33*	0.0	*0*	2.5	*56*	1.0	*22*	4.5
Others	5.0	*71*	2.0	*29*	0.0	*0*	2.0	*29*	7.0
Category total	101.0	*45*	19.0	*8*	35.0	*15*	81.0	*36*	226.0

Notes: Apprenticed + school + university > Known background due to overlaps.

hugely influential, such as Adam Smith and Goethe.[31] But the high cost of patenting in Britain before the patent reform of 1851 assured that most of the smaller inventions (and many of the larger ones) were not patented (MacLeod 1988; Griffiths, Hunt, and O'Brien 1992; Mokyr 2009b). Many inventors, especially those who were trained as scientists, were averse to the monopolistic nature of patent rights and felt that useful knowledge should be shared and that access to it and the use of it should not be limited in any way. Others were more ambivalent and circumspect about the patent system and patented some of their inventions while conspicuously failing to patent others.[32]

Given that complete patent records exist, we were able to to check how many of our sample took out patents at all. As table 9.3 indicates, for the entire period 40 percent of our tweakers never took out a patent. The interpretation of this table is rather tricky: all we can tell is that a person in our sample took out a particular patent. As Dutton (1984), MacLeod (1988), and many others have pointed out, there were major differences in the propensities to patent between different sectors, for a variety of reasons.[33] Textiles turn out to be a high-patenting sector, in part perhaps because reverse engineering was fairly easy. In fact, "one thing that all these textile machines have in common is that they satisfy Bacon's criterion for a certain kind of invention: they incorporated no principles, materials or processes that would have puzzled Archimedes" (Cardwell 1994, 185–86). Even without extensive mechanical knowledge improvements could be made and, especially in cotton, small changes in the production process led to huge improvements

31. Goethe wrote that the British patent system's great merit was that it turned invention into a "real possession, and thereby avoids all annoying disputes concerning the honor due" (cited in Klemm 1964, 173). Some modern economic historians have agreed with him, however (North and Thomas 1973, 156). In his *Lectures on Jurisprudence* ([1757] 1978), 11, 83, 472), Adam Smith argued that intellectual property rights were "actually real rights" and admitted that the patent system was the one monopoly (or "priviledge" as he called it) he could live with, because it left the decision on the merit of an invention to the market rather than to officials.

32. For a number of inventors this is well-known. For example, William Murdoch, who took out three patents for minor advances but failed to patent more important inventions. Henry Maudslay, one the great mechanical engineers of his age, had six patents to his name but did not patent his micrometer or any screw cutting invention for which he was famous. Among lesser-known people, a striking example is William Froude (1810–1879), a ship designer and inventor of the helicoidal skew arch bridge on ships, yet his only patent is a railroad valve patented in 1848; John Benjamin MacNeill (1792–1880), a road engineer who worked for Telford, and took out three patents but failed to patent his best invention, which was an instrument to be drawn along roads, to indicate their state of repair by monitoring the deflections produced by irregularities in the road surface.

33. One reason was the likely payoff. The ratio between alternative means of cashing in on an invention relative to patenting was one consideration. The cost of issuing a patent before 1851 was very substantial and may simply have been unaffordable or simply unlikely to be covered by the returns relative to keeping the invention details secret. The likelihood of a patent being upheld in court also differed substantially by sector. However, in some sectors—especially engineering—the culture of the profession was quite hostile to the patent system.

Table 9.3 **Patentees breakdown, by sector (number of patents issued)**

Sector/Patents issued	0	*% of sector total*	1	*% of sector total*	2–5	*% of sector total*	6–10	*% of sector total*	10+	*% of sector total*	Sector total
Textiles	37.0	*19*	64.0	*33*	71.0	*37*	9.0	*5*	12.0	*6*	193.0
Ships	8.0	*30*	9.0	*33*	7.5	*28*	2.5	*9*	0.0	*0*	27.0
Road & rail & can	50.0	*56*	17.5	*20*	16.5	*18*	4.0	*4*	1.5	*2*	89.5
Other eng	57.0	*39*	32.0	*22*	29.5	*20*	20.0	*14*	9.5	*6*	148.0
Med & chem	12.0	*41*	11.0	*37*	4.5	*15*	0.0	*0*	2.0	*7*	29.5
Instruments	59.0	*65*	16.0	*18*	12.0	*13*	0.5	*1*	3.0	*3*	90.5
Iron & met	15.0	*29*	11.5	*23*	20.5	*40*	2.0	*4*	2.0	*4*	51.0
Mining	15.0	*59*	7.0	*27*	2.5	*10*	1.0	*4*	0.0	*0*	25.5
Agr & farm	10.0	*48*	5.5	*26*	4.5	*21*	1.0	*5*	0.0	*0*	21.0
Constr	27.5	*65*	6.5	*15*	5.5	*13*	1.0	*2*	1.5	*4*	42.0
Print & photo	7.5	*38*	2.0	*10*	4.5	*23*	2.0	*10*	3.5	*18*	19.5
Others	6.0	*27*	10.0	*44*	6.5	*29*	0.0	*0*	0.0	*0*	22.5
Category total	304.0	*40*	192.0	*25*	185.0	*24*	43.0	*6*	35.0	*5*	759.0

in the product's quality.[34] Hence the payoff of inventing and patenting in textiles was perceived to be high. The propensity of patenting in textiles was also higher because constructing and improving textiles machinery required different but not necessarily sophisticated mechanical skills. The textiles sector therefore attracted relatively fewer people much associated with science who had been much affected with the "open-source" scientific culture that viewed knowledge to be a public good and objected to patenting as a matter of principle. As a result, only 19 percent of all tweakers active primarily in textiles never took out a single patent, compared to 40 percent for the economy as a whole.[35] Most of our tweakers are fairly minor players in the patent game, and so of the people who patented at all, 83 percent patented fewer than five inventions. All the same, our sample does include 78 individuals who had six or more patents to their name. Some of these may have been "professional inventors" but others simply were in a position to take advantage of the patent system.

None of this implies that patenting was a particularly successful ex post strategy. Securing a patent even on an economically viable invention did not ensure economic success. Patents were frequently challenged, infringed, or voided. In our data, even individuals who took out patents for some inventions failed to do so for others, and the patents they took out, especially before 1830, proved to provide little protection against infringers and challengers—especially if the invention proved profitable.[36] Judges were often unsympathetic to patentees, reflecting to a large extent the suspiciousness of the age of anything that reeked of monopoly. Tales of inventors ruined by patent suits at this time are legion, and it is reasonable to surmise that given their cost, the mean rate of return may have been negative.[37] One might

34. Different findings for textiles are not only observed for Britain, the technological leader, but also for technological followers. Becker, Hornung, and Woessmann (2011), studying the impact of literacy on technology adaption in Prussia (a technological follower), find that literacy fosters industrialization in all sectors but textiles. The authors argue that the incremental nature of technological change in textiles leads to more sector-specific knowledge that cannot be acquired through formal education.

35. As a consequence, studies that see the textile industry as a typical Industrial Revolution sector in terms of its intellectual property rights development such as Griffiths, Hunt, and O'Brien (1992) are likely to be misleading.

36. Thus the Scottish inventor George Meikle, son of the inventor of the threshing machine, took out a patent for a "scutching machine" (with his father), but the patent was repeatedly challenged and infringed upon and eventually abandoned. Nathaniel Worsdell (1809–1886) patented a device to sort mailbags in 1838, but the post office introduced a competing device that infringed on his invention; Worsdell refused to sue because his Quaker beliefs would not permit it (Birse 2004).

37. John Kay, the inventor of the "flying shuttle" was effectively ruined trying to defend his patents. Disillusioned, he moved to France in 1747 after failing to maintain patent rights in England. Similarly, Henry Fourdrinier's continuous paper-making machine was shamelessly copied and he could never recover the £60,000 he and his brother had spent on the innovation. To circumvent infringement, James Beaumont Neilson (1792–1865), the inventor of the hot blast in iron manufacture (1829), issued licenses at 1 shilling per ton. Neilson and his partners

then legitimately ask why people kept applying for patents, and a number of replies can be given, among them the "lottery effect" (a small number of highly visible successful patents may have created a false ex ante belief that they were more profitable than they were in reality) and a "signaling effect" (inventors took out patents to indicate to would-be financiers that their invention was worthwhile and secure) (Mokyr 2009b). Interestingly enough, British society realized how imperfect the patent was, and some of the big inventors who, for some reason, did not patent or whose patent failed, were compensated by Parliament or by grateful colleagues. But such grants were awarded to technological superstars, not to tweakers who made a minor improvement.

Secrecy was a viable alternative to patenting. Some tweakers relied on secrecy to secure a competitive advantage and to avoid costly legal battles. There was Sir Titus Salt (1803–1876), a textiles manufacturer, who overcame problems in utilizing alpaca wool, who never patented his processes but kept them as trade secrets. This strategy made him the richest citizen in Bradford. John Braithwaite Sr, in the business of retrieving goods from sunken shipwrecks, kept his improved diving machine, his machinery for sawing apart ships underwater, and his underwater gunpowder charges under lock and key and never took out a patent (which would have made him divulge his knowledge).[38] Joseph Gillot, a pen manufacturer and the Pen Maker to the Queen, also preferred secrecy for years before taking out patents and the masticating process—a process in the production of rubber invented by Thomas Hancock—was also never patented, but remained as a secret in the factory. For others, of course, secrecy was a risky strategy, such as the famous case of Benjamin Huntsman, the inventor of crucible steel whose secret eventually leaked out.[39]

First-Mover and Reputation Effects

Signaling quality to potential costumers and outshining the competition was crucial to ensure the economic success of the woman and men in our sample. As table 9.4 shows, most of our tweakers were at least for some part of their careers self-employed: A full 385 (51 percent of our sample and 64 percent of all those whose means of livelihood could be established) were

hoped to make the patent remunerative, but to sell it at a fee low enough to prevent widespread evasion or attacks on the patent's validity. Nevertheless the patent was disputed.

38. Of course, some patentees, such as the metal manufacturer William Champion, worded their patents in as obscure a manner as possible to try to prevent infringement.

39. Modern entrepreneurs face the same choices. Much like their counterparts during the industrial revolution, they rely on first-mover advantage, secrecy, and patents to capture the competitive advantage. Graham et al. (2009), examining entrepreneurs in the high-technology sector using the 2008 Berkeley Patent Survey, show that the only sector in which entrepreneurs find patents more important than first-mover advantages is Biotechnology—a sector that arguably did not exist during the Industrial Revolution. Secrecy is rated almost as important as patents.

Table 9.4 **Sample breakdown**

A. Ownership status											
Sector/reward	Owners (full-time)	*% of sector total*	Owners (part-time)	*% of sector total*	Managers (nonowners)	*% of sector total*	Employed (nonmanagers)	*% of sector total*	Unknown	*% of sector total*	Sector total
Textiles	58.5	*30*	5.5	*3*	3.0	*2*	6.5	*3*	119.5	*62*	193.0
Ships	17.5	*65*	3.5	*13*	0.0	*0*	5.0	*19*	1.0	*4*	27.0
Road & rail & can	36.0	*40*	26.0	*29*	21.0	*23*	5.5	*6*	1.0	*1*	89.5
Other eng	84.0	*57*	19.5	*13*	9.0	*6*	26.0	*18*	9.5	*6*	148.0
Med & chem	16.5	*56*	3.0	*10*	0.0	*0*	8.0	*27*	2.0	*7*	29.5
Instruments	54.0	*60*	7.0	*8*	0.0	*0*	17.5	*19*	12.0	*13*	90.5
Iron & met	38.5	*75*	4.5	*9*	1.0	*2*	2.0	*4*	5.0	*10*	51.0
Mining	9.5	*37*	5.0	*20*	4.0	*16*	5.0	*20*	2.0	*8*	25.5
Agr & farm	12.5	*60*	1.0	*5*	1.5	*7*	1.0	*5*	5.0	*24*	21.0
Constr	30.0	*71*	4.0	*10*	3.0	*7*	3.0	*7*	2.0	*5*	42.0
Print & photo	16.5	*85*	0.0	*0*	0.0	*0*	3.0	*15*	0.0	*0*	19.5
Others	11.5	*51*	3.0	*13*	0.5	*2*	5.5	*24*	2.0	*9*	22.5
Category total	385.0	*51*	82.0	*11*	43.0	*6*	88.0	*12*	161.0	*21*	759.0

(*continued*)

Table 9.4 (cont.)

	B. Including partnerships						
Sector	Owners (full-time)	*% of sector total*	Owners (part-time)	*% of sector total*	Partnerships	*% of owners total*	Sector total
Textiles	58.5	*30*	5.5	*3*	55.5	*87*	193.0
Ships	17.5	*65*	3.5	*13*	10.0	*48*	27.0
Road & rail & can	36.0	*40*	26.0	*29*	25.0	*40*	89.5
Other eng	84.0	*57*	19.5	*13*	54.0	*52*	148.0
Med & chem	16.5	*56*	3.0	*10*	7.0	*36*	29.5
Instruments	54.0	*60*	7.0	*8*	31.5	*52*	90.5
Iron & met	38.5	*75*	4.5	*9*	29.5	*69*	51.0
Mining	9.5	*37*	5.0	*20*	9.0	*62*	25.5
Agr & farm	12.5	*60*	1.0	*5*	6.0	*44*	21.0
Constr	30.0	*71*	4.0	*10*	11.5	*34*	42.0
Print & photo	16.5	*85*	0.0	*0*	8.5	*52*	19.5
Others	11.5	*51*	3.0	*13*	9.5	*66*	22.5
Category total	385.0	*51*	82.0	*11*	257.0	*55*	759.0

Notes: "Owners (full-time)" category includes independent contractor, entrepreneur, self-employed, manager/owner with or without partner. "Owners (part-time)" category includes inventors that were owners and managers/employees at the same time at different companies or at different points in their lifetimes.

identifiable entrepreneurs and independent operators or consultants, owning or establishing a company at some point. Another 82 (11 percent) were owners at least some of their careers.[40] A respectable 18 percent were hired engineers and managers. Again, it is striking how exceptional textiles were as an industry: for a considerable number of individuals, we were unable to establish exactly the way in which they made their living. But for the entire rest of the sample, of those for whom we could establish these facts, we found that 68 percent were owners and independent contractors throughout their careers, and another 16 percent were so through part of their career. Given that only few of those had successful patents, better quality of product and services leaning on reputation effects were central to economic success.

The centrality of first-mover advantage is hard to document in a systematic way, but examples abound. In the textile industry, first-mover advantage was common: Arkwright's patent was voided, but his technological advantage was such that he died a wealthy man. Others were able to cash in on fairly minor advantages. An example can be seen in the hosiery industry, where Jedediah Strutt came up in the 1750s with a major improvement to lace made on stocking frames, subsequently improved further by the idea of the "point net." The idea of this more efficient method was conceived by one Mr. Flint, who hired a Thomas Taylor of Nottingham to build it for him, who then acquired the invention and patented it. Years later, the point net was further improved by William Hayne, whose patent was declared invalid in 1810 (Felkin 1867, 133–41).

Many of the great clock- and instrument makers of the age, a pivotal group in the realization of the Industrial Revolution, were essentially self-employed and depended on reputation for quality and reliability.[41] John Kennedy, co-owner of M'Connel and Kennedy, one of the most successful cotton spinners in Manchester, made a number of adjustments to the fine-spinning capabilities of the mule, which allowed a much higher count (finer) yarn to be spun. Kennedy never took out a patent. In 1826 Kennedy retired from one of the best-known and prosperous enterprises in the Industrial Revolution. Another striking case was that of Joseph Aspdin, the inventor of Portland cement. Although he did take out a patent in 1824, his advantage was relatively brief. His son, William Aspdin, was the first to invent

40. Some of them were successful employees who then tried to go into business for themselves; others had the reverse career and were failed entrepreneurs who then took a job with another firm.

41. The great instrument makers of the age mostly seem to fall into that category. Thus John Bird (1709–1776) supplied instruments to Greenwich Observatory as well as to the one in Stockholm. Bird established in 1745 his own workshop in London making machine tools and small mathematical instruments. He received orders to design and make large astronomical instruments for major observatories at home and abroad. Two generations after him, Robert Bretell Bate (1782–1847) was appointed optician to King George I, an honor that was renewed on the accessions of William IV and Queen Victoria; he won government contracts with a number of government agencies. By 1820, his workshop employed twenty employees (McConnell 2004a, 2004b).

true "Portland Cement" in the early 1840s, by discovering the necessity of clinkering (grinding the product of the cement kilns and adding gypsum) but did not patent it. William's early-mover advantage did not last long because others such as Isaac Charles Johnson were following his idea on his heels. After two years, Johnson was able to develop a superior product, and yet Aspdin's advantage in time was enough to assure him financial success for a while, although in 1855 he went bankrupt and his works were sold to Johnson (Francis 1977, 116–25, 151–58).[42]

For many of our tweakers, being innovative and able to tweak technology in use was part of the job description. Innovation meant job security for employees or new commissions for the self-employed. James Watt employed a number of highly creative engineers, most of all the ingenious William Murdoch. Railway companies expected their locomotive pool managers to invent in order to cut cost, improve the quality of transportation, and deal with excessive smoke emissions. Hence for railroad engineers like Charles Markham, who adjusted fire holes in locomotives for the use of coal, innovative activity that adapted existing techniques to specific purposes was simply taken for granted and reflected in their comfortable salaries.

Innovativeness was a strong signal of competence, and competence was what people hiring consultants wanted. Self-employed engineers such as James Brindley and John Rennie, or architects like Joseph Jopling, (who won a Society of Arts gold medal for arch construction improvements), made their living by signaling their professional competence through coming up with improvements in the techniques they used. This, too, was a function of the patent office: having taken out a patent was seen, whether correctly or not, as an official imprimatur of technological expertise.[43] Reputation for expertise resulted in new commissions for their workshops.[44] Again, it is not easy to quantify this, but professional engineers, especially civil and mechanical engineers, often worked on specific commissions and consultancies.

Some of these commissions came from the government, others from overseas, but most of them were local manufacturers and colliers who needed something specific installed or built.[45] The model for this way of organizing

42. Johnson, who lived from 1811 to 1911, remained a major player in the British cement industry for much of his life, and thus perhaps exemplifies the benefits of second-mover advantage.

43. Studying the motivations for patenting of present-day entrepreneurs, Graham et al. (2009) find that enhancing the company's reputation and improving chances of securing investment or additional financing are still important reasons for entrepreneurs to take out patents.

44. It is interesting to note that for modern data hiring inventive employees seems also a good strategy to maximize the impact of innovations. Singh and Agrawal (2010) estimate (using modern US patent citation data) that when firms recruit inventors, the citation of the new recruits' prior inventions increases by more than 200 percent even if these patents are held by their previous employer. They also argue that the effect is persistent even though one might expect that the tacit knowledge of the inventor diffuses fast within a firm.

45. Thus Bryan Donkin, a prodigiously gifted tweaker, with eleven patents to his name and a reputation to match, received commissions from the excise and stamp office, the East India office, and none other than Charles Babbage (to estimate the cost of building his calculating machine).

the engineering profession was set by the great John Smeaton, who after James Watt was the most influential engineer of the eighteenth century. Smeaton took out but one patent in his life, despite a vast number of inventions and improvements, but he was in huge demand as a consulting engineer, and in fact is often said to have established engineering consultancy as a formal profession. As panel B of table 9.4 shows, more than half of the independent contractors and self-employed had partners (at some stage), although that proportion was especially high in textiles, iron, and mining and a bit lower elsewhere.

For the self-employed artisans and independent engineers who would be in the group of tweakers and implementers, the reward was first and foremost a reputation for competence that led to customers and commissions, and in some cases, the patronage of a rich or powerful person. Many of the engineers and best mechanics in the Industrial Revolution were engaged in a signaling game: in a market with imperfect information about quality, establishing a reputation for skills was a key to economic security if not perhaps to extraordinary riches. This was true for the superstar engineers in the Industrial Revolution such as John Rennie and John Smeaton, but it was equally true for lesser-known people. For many of the best mechanics and engineers, reputations meant well-paying positions in good firms or tickets for commissions and contracts. Reputation and being in very high standing among one's professional peers could lead to cash awards from the government (who relied on expert opinion in making these awards). Such cash prizes were also awarded by some private societies (such as the Society of Arts, founded in 1754). These awards were often financially significant, and with any of these rewards the reputation of an inventor grew. Awards were also associated with peer recognition and social prestige associated with mechanical achievement to a degree never before witnessed.[46] Some engineers became technological authorities and their imprimatur could make or break the career of a young engineer. Among those authorities, John Smeaton and Thomas Telford were the towering figures during the Industrial Revolution.[47]

Not all cash prizes or medals were given for meeting specified crite-

46. Consider the career of Edward John Dent (1790–1853), who won a first Premium Award at the Seventh Annual Trial of Chronometers (1829) and then won the esteem of Sir George Airy, the Astronomer Royal, who recommended him as the maker of a large clock for the tower of the new Royal Exchange. Dent later enjoyed the patronage of Queen Victoria, the Royal Navy, and the Czar of Russia. In 1852 he won the commission to make the Big Ben for the Houses of Parliament at Westminster, but he died before completing the project.

47. Telford, in his design for an all-iron bridge over the Thames to replace London Bridge (which was not built), hired a young engineer named James Douglas, whose mechanical genius earned him the epithet "the Eskdale Archimedes." Douglas was a versatile engineer who had attracted the notice of the British Ambassador in the United States, who paid his expenses home to England "so that his services might not be lost to his country." In 1799 it is known that Douglas worked for Telford, but then absconded to France in around 1802. Telford disapprovingly remarked that Douglas was "always too impatient for distinction and wealth, in the race for which in his country he found too many competitors" (Smiles 1861, 362).

ria such as the famed Board of Longitude award made to John Harrison for his marine chronometer. Cash rewards were also given to inventors in the public service, like the civil engineer and road builder John Loudon McAdam, who received £6,000 from public funds for his improvements on the British road system; to Edward Jenner, for his spectacular discovery of smallpox vaccination; to Sir Francis Pettit Smith, who was awarded £20,000 by the Admiralty for his screw propeller; and to William Symington, who received £100 from Parliament for the first steamboat. As noted, in few cases such awards were regarded as a correction to an often-malfunctioning patent system. Sir Thomas Lombe the inventor (really importer) of mechanized silk-spinning technology, was awarded £14,000 as a special dispensation in 1732 in lieu of a renewal of his patent. Of the "heroes of the Industrial Revolution," Samuel Crompton, Edmund Cartwright, and Henry Fourdrinier were among those who, after much haggling, were voted an award.

Reputation effects were often international: as noted already, many British engineers and mechanics found positions on the Continent or received commissions and assignments from overseas, as one would expect in an economy that was more richly endowed with competence than its neighbors and were often honored by them. Charles Gascoigne, the manager of the Scottish Carron ironworks in 1760, received a lucrative commission from the Russian government in 1786; ironmaster John Wilkinson's brother William was commissioned by the French government to set up the ironworks at Le Creuzot. In the nineteenth century this process continued with renewed force. Richard Roberts, perhaps the most ingenious tweaker of his generation, was invited to help install cotton-spinning machinery in Mulhouse. William Fairbairn (1789–1874), another leading engineer and one of the pioneers of the iron-hulled ships, consulted in Turkey, Switzerland, and the Netherlands. Robert Whitehead, a ship designer who made major improvements to the design of the torpedo, started his career as a naval designer working for the Austrian government and gathered a great many foreign decorations, including a French *Legion d'honneur.*

Nonpecuniary Rewards

Many of the cutting edge inventors and tweakers of the age professed to be uninterested in financial rewards. Economists are trained to regard such statements with suspicion, but that is not to say that considerations other than money did not play a role. The distinction is hard to make because prizes, medals, and other distinctions operated as signals of quality and thus enhanced reputations that themselves were correlated with patronage (steady employment) or commissions. A few "cash" prizes were also to a large extent honorary, much like book prizes today. Such rewards took a variety of forms. Some associations appointed "fellows" (the Royal Academy being the primary example), others such as the Society of Arts organized competitions and awarded medals and other distinctions for technological achievements. In Britain, of course, the highest distinction that could be awarded to someone of a working-class origin was an honorary aristocratic title. Table 9.5 summarizes the awards earned by our sample.

The data show a considerable variation in the number of medals awarded. In textiles, medals were rare, and it seems to have been the one industry in which monetary considerations were probably more or less the main incentive.[48] The categories are overlapping, so quite a few people received more than one reward. All the same, the data show that for tweakers in fields such as civil engineering, instrument-making, construction, and to a lesser extent metallurgy, such prizes were a reality, and the probability of earning such a prize was far more likely than actually cashing in on a patent (and there was no application fee). There can be little question that, as with all such prizes, personal connections and background played a role. Indeed, in a recent paper Khan (2011) has concluded that "[i]n Britain the most decisive determinants for whether the inventor received a prize were which particular university he had graduated from and membership in the Royal Society of Arts, characteristics that seem to have been somewhat uncorrelated with technological productivity. Thus, rather than being calibrated to the value of the inventor's contributions, prizes to British inventors appear to have been largely determined by noneconomic considerations" (231). One could, of course quibble with how to measure "technological productivity" (to say nothing of the distinction between economic and noneconomic considerations). But what counts here is that the probability of winning such a social recognition was nonzero and correlated with some achievement even if the correlation was not as high as one would wish in a perfect world. It stands to reason that in such distinctions, then as now, accomplishment and personal connections were complementary. As such, there can be little doubt that these institutions provided a considerable incentive for technically brilliant and industrious men. Networking counted too—but such networks by themselves held considerable technological advantages.

9.5 Were Tweakers Enlightened?

The Baconian program alluded to before was a product of the Enlightenment, and it emphasized the diffusion and dissemination of useful knowledge in addition to its creation (Mokyr 2009a). That such beliefs were held by some of the leading figures of the Industrial Revolution such as Josiah Wedgwood, Matthew Boulton, and Benjamin Gott has long been known.

48. To be sure, nine textile engineers were elevated to an aristocratic title, which, at 5 percent, is only marginally below the overall mean of 7 percent. But these were men such as Richard Arkwright, James Oldknow, and Robert Peel, who were rewarded for successful careers as entrepreneurs.

Table 9.5 **Cash prizes and nonpecuniary rewards**

Sector/reward	Medal	*% of sector total*	Cash prize	*% of sector total*	Title	*% of sector total*	Appointment	*% of sector total*	Royal Society	*% of sector total*	Sector total
					A Individuals born before 1800						
Textiles	3.0	*2*	8.0	*6*	3.0	*2*	5.0	*4*	2.0	*2*	124.0
Ships	3.5	*18*	5.5	*29*	0.5	*3*	0.5	*3*	4.5	*24*	19.0
Road & rail & can	1.0	*2*	3.0	*7*	2.0	*5*	4.5	*11*	5.5	*13*	42.0
Other eng	19.0	*18*	5.5	*5*	8.5	*8*	11.5	*11*	21.0	*20*	106.5
Med & chem	4.0	*17*	2.5	*11*	0.5	*2*	2.5	*11*	7.5	*33*	23.0
Instruments	18.5	*25*	11.5	*16*	2.0	*3*	24.0	*33*	31.0	*42*	73.0
Iron & met	1.0	*3*	1.0	*3*	3.0	*8*	3.0	*8*	5.0	*13*	39.5
Mining	2.0	*9*	1.0	*4*	0.0	*0*	2.0	*9*	3.0	*13*	22.5
Agr & farm	1.0	*6*	2.0	*13*	1.5	*9*	0.0	*0*	0.5	*3*	16.0
Constr	7.5	*20*	4.0	*11*	1.5	*4*	8.0	*22*	5.0	*14*	37.0
Print & photo	1.0	*7*	2.0	*13*	2.0	*13*	2.0	*13*	3.0	*20*	15.0
Others	3.5	*23*	1.0	*6*	1.5	*10*	4.0	*26*	3.0	*19*	15.5
Category total	65.0	*12*	47.0	*9*	26.0	*5*	67.0	*13*	91.0	*17*	533.0
					B Individuals born 1800–1830						
Textiles	3.0	*4*	0.5	*1*	6.0	*9*	3.5	*5*	0.5	*1*	69.0
Ships	1.0	*13*	0.0	*0*	2.0	*25*	1.0	*13*	2.0	*25*	8.0
Road & rail & can	1.0	*2*	0.0	*0*	3.0	*6*	5.5	*12*	5.0	*11*	47.5
Other eng	14.0	*34*	5.5	*13*	8.0	*19*	7.0	*17*	10.5	*25*	41.5
Med & chem	2.0	*31*	0.0	*0*	4.0	*62*	1.0	*15*	3.5	*54*	6.5
Instruments	7.0	*40*	0.5	*3*	2.5	*14*	8.5	*49*	3.5	*20*	17.5
Iron & met	5.0	*43*	1.0	*9*	3.0	*26*	1.0	*9*	3.0	*26*	11.5
Mining	0.0	*0*	1.0	*33*	0.0	*0*	0.0	*0*	1.0	*33*	3.0
Agr & farm	1.0	*20*	1.0	*20*	1.0	*20*	0.0	*0*	1.0	*20*	5.0
Constr	1.0	*20*	0.0	*0*	0.5	*10*	0.5	*10*	0.0	*0*	5.0
Print & photo	3.0	*67*	1.0	*22*	0.0	*0*	1.0	*22*	1.0	*22*	4.5
Others	0.0	*0*	0.0	*0*	0.0	*0*	2.0	*29*	0.0	*0*	7.0
Category total	38.0	*17*	10.5	*5*	30.0	*13*	31.0	*14*	31.0	*14*	226.0

But Robert Allen (see Allen 2009a) has questioned the degree to which such beliefs were common in the wider population of technologically relevant people. It is, of course, impossible to verify, with few exceptions, what these people believed about what they were doing. But we can see to which extent they tried to network by joining a variety of professional societies, or bring their knowledge to a wide audience by publishing. Again, such actions could be explained by other factors. Publishing, for example, served as a signal of expertise and respectability, and professional societies were social as well as professional networks.[49]

The measures are, of course, not independent. Inventions, new methods, and explanation were published in the journals edited by professional societies, such as the *Philosophical Transactions of the Royal Society* or *Transactions of the Institution of Civil Engineers.* Membership and rewards in some professional societies were granted for papers read to them. Some of our tweakers participated in public debates or provided descriptions and puzzles for the *Ladies' Diary,* an eighteenth-century journal aimed at the "fair" sex explaining improvements in the arts and sciences.[50] Beyond articles, many of our tweakers published treatises and books on matters of new technology.[51]

All the same, the fact that engineers and mechanics were networked and interacted in this fashion, if sufficiently widespread, indicates that the Industrial Revolution took place in a different cultural environment than the one that prevailed at the time of the Glorious Revolution. It should be added that the estimates presented in table 9.6 are lower bounds; the absence of evidence is not evidence of absence, and especially for some of our more obscure tweakers it has been hard to unearth all the evidence of their exploits. Many may have been members of small provincial intellectual societies and published in obscure provincial journals or anonymously. At the same time, we acknowledge that because of the way the sample was constructed, it may suffer from selection bias in the sense that engineers and inventors of the second and third tier may have been in the sample because either publication or membership left a record and thus ended up in our sample.

Again, the data show that of all sectors, textiles on which Allen relies heavily were the exception. It was the "least enlightened" and thus any inferences

49. The perhaps most striking example is the instrument maker Edward Troughton (1753–1835). Having kept one crucial method of his dividing machine secret, he later wrote a description for the *Astronomer Royal* as a "valuable present to young craftsmen." The paper was read to the Royal Society, which earned him a Copley medal and opened all doors to him.

50. The *Ladies' Diary* was edited between 1714 and 1743 by the surveyor, engineer, mathematician, and paradigmatic tweaker Henry Beighton (1683–1743).

51. For instance, Edmund Beckett Grimthorpe, who used gravity escapes in public watches, published his knowledge on watch making in *A Rudimentary Treatise on Clocks and Watchmaking,* and William Jones shared the insights he gained with his improved solar telescope in *The Description and Use of a New Portable Orrery.*

Table 9.6 **Publishers and members of societies**

Sector	Publishers only	*% of sector total*	Members of societies only	*% of sector total*	Publishers and members of societies	*% of sector total*	Sector total
Textiles	7.5	*4*	6.0	*3*	3.0	*2*	193.0
Ships	6.5	*24*	2.0	*7*	11.0	*41*	27.0
Road & rail & can	11.0	*12*	29.5	*33*	23.0	*26*	89.5
Other eng	25.0	*17*	31.0	*21*	55.0	*37*	148.0
Med & chem	4.0	*14*	3.5	*12*	13.5	*46*	29.5
Instruments	13.0	*14*	13.5	*15*	40.5	*45*	90.5
Iron & met	6.5	*13*	9.0	*18*	6.5	*13*	51.0
Mining	4.5	*18*	3.0	*12*	8.0	*31*	25.5
Agr & farm	6.5	*31*	1.5	*7*	3.5	*17*	21.0
Construction	8.0	*19*	2.5	*6*	18.0	*43*	42.0
Print & photo	3.0	*15*	2.5	*13*	4.0	*21*	19.5
Others	1.5	*7*	1.0	*4*	5.0	*22*	22.5
Category total	97.0	*13*	105.0	*14*	191.0	*25*	759.0

about the Industrial Revolution based primarily on the technological history of textiles may be misleading. Only about 10 percent of the individuals in textiles either published, belonged to a professional society, or both. For the sample as a whole, however, 52 percent of all tweakers were enlightened in the sense defined earlier. Indeed, roughly speaking, around two-thirds of all engineers in our sample either published or belonged to scientific or technical societies. The shortcoming of our sources notwithstanding, therefore, it is fair to say that an Enlightenment culture was rooted deeply in the top 3 to 5 percentile of the skill distribution—the highly competent craftsmen and engineers.

Not only did our tweakers place their knowledge in the public sphere and participated in discussions in formal societies (but although like most engineers anywhere they had limited interest in politics), quite a few were involved in liberal or progressive politics of one kind or another.[52] Some of our engineers such as Richard Reynolds, an ironmonger, can be shown to have been active in the antislavery movement. To be sure, the Enlightenment meant different things to different people, and its influence on wider British society was limited before the 1830s. However, it was an elite ideology, and

52. John Mercer (1791–1866), like many other leading figures in the technological elite, was a member of the Anti-Corn Law League. Others spent their time and money on the improvement of society, like the garden architect John Claudius Loudon, who supported a scheme for decent housing for the poor, or toolmaker and engineer Joseph Whitworth, who devoted various sums, amounting in all to £594,416, to educational and charitable purposes. Sir George Cayley (1773–1857), the famous aeronautic pioneer, was a Whig Member of Parliament for Scarborough, and strongly supported Parliamentary reform and abolition.

Table 9.7 Comparison of tweakers and stars

Education	Apprenticed		School	University	Unknown/None
Full sample	40%		7%	15%	41%
Stars	54%		10%	24%	18%
Patents	0	1	2–5	6–10	10+
Full sample	40%	25%	24%	6%	5%
Stars	19%	17%	28%	15%	21%
Employment	Owned	Managed	Employed	Unknown	Partnerships (% of owners)
Full sample	62%	6%	12%	21%	55%
Stars	79%	8%	13%	0%	54%
Rewards	Cash	Medal	Title	Appointment	Royal Society
Full sample	8%	14%	7%	13%	16%
Stars	14%	25%	18%	29%	24%
Publish/Society	Published		Membership in society		Both
Full sample	13%		14%		25%
Stars	14%		14%		35%

our tweaker sample was drawn from an elite population. The technological momentum in the Industrial Revolution was supplied by a small, elite group of highly skilled engineers, artisans, and workmen. Our sample represents the right tail of this group, the most successful and highly skilled members of an elite, yet their characteristics tell us a lot about the sources of British success.

To what extent were our tweakers different from the better-known "superstars" of the Industrial Revolution? The issue is relevant because of the assumption of "continuity" in the distribution we are making (since we are observing a highly selective sample). To test for this, we selected seventy-two members of our sample who are mentioned in two recent books on the Industrial Revolution by one of us, namely Mokyr (1990 and 2002). That yielded seventy-two names of such technological luminaries as Arkwright, Watt, Smeaton, Wedgwood, and Trevithick. We checked to what extent they resembled the rest of the sample. As they were obviously the very top of the competence distribution, more is known of them. Yet they appear to be, on the whole, much like the rest of our sample, if naturally more distinguished and more likely to be owners-entrepreneurs (see table 9.7). It is worth noting that while superstars hold, on average, more patents, a full 25 percent of the superstars did not patent all of their inventions.

9.6 Conclusions: The Rate and Direction of Technological Progress during the British Industrial Revolution

What determined the rate and direction of technological change during the Industrial Revolution? Explanations can be, very crudely, classified into demand- and supply-based explanations. In his recent book, Allen (2009a) has argued that high wages drove a search for labor-saving innovation. While we do not propose here an explanation of the macroinventions that form the backbone of usual accounts of the Industrial Revolution, we argue that a key ingredient that complemented these inventions and made them work came from human capital: it was the technical competence of the British mechanical elite that was able to tweak and implement the great ideas and turn them into economic realities. The story presented here is entirely supply-based. There is a global question, "why Europe?", and a local question, "why British leadership?" The answer is based on an unusually felicitous combination of Enlightenment culture, which characterized much of Western Europe, and technical competence, where Britain had a comparative advantage. If it had only one of those two, it seems unlikely that its economic performance would have been as spectacular.

The story, however, was not a national but by and large a local one: innovations in textiles, iron, mining, hardware, and instruments, to pick a few examples, were all local phenomena, relying largely on local resources, including talent. To be sure, our tweakers were mobile even in the prerailroad age. Moreover, there were at least two national institutions that gave a certain unity to these local developments. One was the patent office; despite the consensus view of the literature that patenting was a fairly minor source of progress, it remained in some ways a national technological institution whose presence was felt even if it was decided not to use it or if it let its users down. The other was the Royal Society and similar national institutions such as the Society of Arts, the Royal Institution, and the British Association for the Advancement of Science (f. in 1831).

Are there any policy lessons from this for our age? The one obvious conclusion to be drawn from this is that a few thousand individuals may have played a crucial role in the technological transformation of the British economy and carried the Industrial Revolution. The *average* level of human capital in Britain, as measured by mean literacy rates, school attendance, and even the number of people attending institutes of higher education, are often regarded as surprisingly low for an industrial leader. But the useful knowledge that may have mattered was obviously transmitted primarily through apprentice-master relations, and among those, what counted most were the characteristics of the top few percentiles of highly skilled and dexterous mechanics and instrument-makers, millwrights, hardware makers, and similar artisans. This may be a more general characteristic of the impact of human capital on technological creativity: we should focus neither on the mean properties of the population at large nor on the experiences of the "superstars" but on the group in between. Those who had the dexterity and competence to tweak, adapt, combine, improve, and debug existing ideas, build them according to specifications, but with the knowledge to add in what the blueprints left out were critical to the story. The policy implications of this insight are far from obvious, but clearly if the source of technological success was a small percentage of the labor force, this is something that an educational policy would have to take into account.

Finally, the supply of competence reminds us of something rather central about the direction of innovation, which seems very generally relevant. The direction is dependent on those supply factors that reflect what engineers and skilled workers actually can do regardless of what they would like to do. The drive toward improvement was quite general in the eighteenth century, but the results were highly uneven, with major productivity improvements in textiles, iron, civil engineering, and power technology, but few in farming, medicine, steel, chemicals, and communications. These reflected the difficulties on the supply side rather than any obvious demand-side bias. Competence as defined here was an integral part of the supply side, as inventors would not be able to carry out their ideas without the trained workers they employed.

References

Acemoglu, Daron, and James Robinson. 2012. *Why Nations Fail: The Origins of Power, Prosperity, and Poverty*. New York: Crown.

Allen, Robert C. 2009a. *The British Industrial Revolution in Global Perspective.* Cambridge: Cambridge University Press.

———. 2009b. "The Industrial Revolution in Miniature: The Spinning Jenny in Britain, France, and India." *Journal of Economic History* 69 (4): 901–27.

Baines, Edward. 1835. *History of the Cotton Manufacture in Great Britain.* London: H. Fisher.

Barker, T. C., and John R. Harris. 1954. *A Merseyside Town in the Industrial Revolution: St. Helens, 1750–1900.* Liverpool: Liverpool University Press.

Barlow, Alfred. 1878.*The History and Principles of Weaving by Hand and by Power*. London: Sampson, Low, Marston, Searle and Rivington.

Becker, Sascha O., Erik Hornung, and Ludger Woessmann. 2011. "Education and Catch-up in the Industrial Revolution." *American Economic Journal: Macroeconomics* 3 (3): 92–129.

Berg, Maxine. 2007. "The Genesis of 'Useful Knowledge.'" *History of Science* 45 (148) part 2: 123–34.

Birse, Ronald M. 2004. "Worsdell family (per. c. 1800–1910)." In *Oxford Dictionary of National Biography.* Oxford University Press, online edition.

Burnley, James. 1889. *The History of Wool and Woolcombing*. London: Sampson Low, Marsten, Searle and Rivington.

Cardwell, Donald S. L. 1972. *Turning Points in Western Technology.* New York: Neale Watson, Science History Publications.

———. 1994. *The Fontana History of Technology.* London: Fontana Press.

Chapman, S. D. 1967. *The Early Factory Masters: The Transition to the Factory System in the Midlands Textile Industry.* Newton Abbot: David and Charles.

———.1972. The Cotton Industry in the Industrial Revolution. London: Macmillan.

Chapman, Stanley D., and Serge Chassagne. 1981. European Textile Printers in the Eighteenth Century: A Study of Peel and Oberkampf. London: Heinemann Educational, Pasold Fund.

Clark, Gregory, and David Jacks. 2007. "Coal and the Industrial Revolution." *European Review of Economic History* 11 (1): 39–72.

Crouzet, François. 1985. *The First Industrialists: The Problems of Origins.* Cambridge: Cambridge University Press.

Day, Lance, and Ian McNeil. 1996. *Biographical Dictionary of the History of Technology.* London and New York: Routledge.

De Saussure, César. (c. 1727). 1902. *A Foreign View of England in the Reigns of George I. & George II. The Letters of Monsieur César de Saussure to His Family.* Translated and edited by Madame Van Muyden. London: J. Murray.

Dutton, H. I. 1984. *The Patent System and Inventive Activity during the Industrial Revolution 1750–1852*. Manchester: Manchester University Press.

Enos, John L. 1962. "Invention and Innovation in the Petroleum Refining Industry." In *The Rate and Direction of Inventive Activity: Economic and Social Factors,* A Conference of the Universities-National Bureau Committee for Economic Research and the Committee on Economic Growth of the Social Science Research Council, 299–321. Princeton, NJ: Princeton University Press.

Fairbairn, William. 1871. *Treatise on Mills and Millwork,* vol. 1, 3rd ed. London: Longmans, Green and Co.

Farnie, D. A. 2004. "Crompton, Samuel (1753–1827)." *Oxford Dictionary of National Biography.* Oxford: Oxford University Press.

Felkin, William. 1867. *A History of the Machine-Wrought Hosiery and Lace Manufactures.* Cambridge: Printed by W. Metcalfe.

Fitton, R. S., and A. P. Wadsworth. 1958. *The Strutts and the Arkwrights.* Manchester: Manchester University Press.

Francis, A. J. 1977. *The Cement Industry 1796–1914: A History.* Newton Abbot: David and Charles.

Gale, K. W. V. 1961–62. "Wrought Iron: A Valediction." *Transactions of the Newcomen Society* 36:1–11.

Graham, Stuart J. H., Robert P. Merger, Pam Samuelson, and Ted Sichelman. 2009. "High Technology Entrepreneurs and the Patent System: Results of the 2008 Berkeley Patent Survey." *Berkeley Technology Law Review* 24 (4): 1255–328.

Griffiths, John. 1992. *The Third Man: The Life and Times of William Murdoch.* London: André Deutsch.

Griffiths, Trevor, Philip A. Hunt, and Patrick K. O'Brien. 1992. "Inventive Active in the British Textile Industry, 1700–1800." *Journal of Economic History* 52 (4): 881–906.

Harris, John R. 1988. *The British Iron Industry, 1700–1850.* Houndmill and London: Macmillan Education Ltd.

———. 1992. "Skills, Coal and British Industry in the Eighteenth Century." In *Essays in Industry and Technology in the Eighteenth Century,* edited by John R. Harris, 67–82. Farnham and London: Ashgate Variorum.

———. 1998. *Industrial Espionage and Technology Transfer: Britain and France in the Eighteenth Century.* Aldershot: Ashgate.

Harrison, James. 2006. *Encouraging Innovation in the Eighteenth and Nineteenth Centuries.* Gunnislake, Cornwall: High View.

Heaton, Herbert. 1965. *The Yorkshire Woollen and Worsted Industries, from the Earliest Times up to the Industrial Revolution.* Oxford: Oxford University Press.

Henderson, W. O. 1954. *Britain and Industrial Europe, 1750–1870; Studies in British Influence on the Industrial Revolution in Western Europe.* Liverpool: Liverpool University Press.

Hilaire-Pérez, Liliane. 2007. "Technology As Public Culture." *History of Science* 45 (148) part 2: 135–53.

Honeyman, Katrina. 1983. *Origins of Enterprise: Business Leadership in the Industrial Revolution.* New York: St. Martin's Press.

Humphries, Jane. 2003. "English Apprenticeships: A Neglected Factor in the First Industrial Revolution." In *The Economic Future in Historical Perspective,* edited by Paul A. David and Mark Thomas, 73–102. Oxford: Oxford University Press.

Jacob, Margaret C. 1997. *Scientific Culture and the Making of the Industrial West,* 2nd ed. New York: Oxford University Press.

———. 2007. "Mechanical Science of the Factory Floor." *History of Science* 45 (148) part 2: 197–221.

James, Frank A. J. L. 2005. "How Big a Hole? The Problems of the Practical Application of Science in the Invention of the Miners' Safety Lamp by Humphry Davy and George Stephenson in Late Regency England." *Transactions of the Newcomen Society* 75:175–227.

Jenkins, D. T., and K. G. Ponting. 1982. *The British Wool Industry, 1750–1914.* London: Scolar Press.

Jones, Peter M. 2008. *Industrial Enlightenment: Science, Technology, and Culture in Birmingham and the West Midlands, 1760–1820.* Manchester and New York: Manchester University Press.

Khan, B. Zorina. 2006. "The Evolution of Useful Knowledge: Great Inventors, Science and Technology in British Economic Development, 1750–1930." Unpublished Paper. Bowdoin College.

———. 2011. "Premium Inventions: Patents and Prizes as Incentive Mechanisms in Britain and the United States, 1750–1930." In *Understanding Long Run Economic Growth: Essays in Honor of Kenneth L. Sokoloff,* edited by Dora L. Costa and Naomi R. Lamoreaux, 205–34. Chicago: University of Chicago Press.

Klemm, Friedrich. 1964. *A History of Western Technology.* Cambridge, MA: MIT Press.

Machlup, Fritz. 1962. "The Supply of Inventors and Inventions." In *The Rate and Direction of Inventive Activity: Economic and Social Factors,* A Conference of the Universities-National Bureau Committee for Economic Research and the Committee on Economic Growth of the Social Science Research Council, 143–69. Princeton, NJ: Princeton University Press.

MacLeod, Christine. 1988. *Inventing the Industrial Revolution: The English Patent System, 1660–1880.* Cambridge: Cambridge University Press.

MacLeod, Christine, and Alessandro Nuvolari. 2006. "Pitfalls of Prosopography: Inventors in the Dictionary of National Biography." *Technology and Culture* 47 (4): 757–76.

Marsden, Richard. 1895. *Cotton Weaving: Its Development, Principles, and Practice.* London: George Bell.

Marshall John. 1978. *A Biographical Dictionary of Railway Engineers.* Newton Abbot: David and Charles.

McCloskey, Deirdre N. 1981. "The Industrial Revolution: A Survey." In *The Economic History of Britain Since 1700,* 1st ed., vol. 1, edited by Roderick C. Floud and D. N. McCloskey, 103–27. Cambridge: Cambridge University Press.

McConnell, Anita. 2004a. "Bate, Robert Bretell (1782–1847)." *Oxford Dictionary of National Biography.* Oxford: Oxford University Press.

———. 2004b. "Bird, John (1709–1776)." *Oxford Dictionary of National Biography.* Oxford: Oxford University Press.

Mitch, David. 1998. "The Role of Education and Skill in the British Industrial Revolution." In *The British Industrial Revolution: An Economic Perspective,* 2nd ed., edited by Joel Mokyr, 241–79. Boulder, CO: Westview Press.

Mokyr, Joel. 1976. *Industrialization in the Low Countries, 1795–1850*. New Haven, CT: Yale University Press.

———. 1990. *The Lever of Riches: Technological Creativity and Economic Progress.* Oxford and New York: Oxford University Press.

———. 1998. "Editor's Introduction: The New Economic History and the Industrial Revolution." In *The British Industrial Revolution: An Economic Perspective,* edited by Joel Mokyr, 1–127. Boulder, CO: Westview Press.

———. 2002. *The Gifts of Athena: The Historical Origins of the Knowledge Economy*. Princeton, NJ: Princeton University Press.

———. 2008. "The Institutional Origins of the Industrial Revolution." In *Institutions and Economic Performance,* edited by Elhanan Helpman, 64–119. Cambridge, MA: Harvard University Press.

———. 2009a. *The Enlightened Economy.* New Haven and London: Yale University Press.

———. 2009b. "Intellectual Property Rights, the Industrial Revolution, and the Beginnings of Modern Economic Growth." *American Economic Review* 99 (2): 349–55.

Morrison-Low, A. L. 2007. *Making Scientific Instruments in the Industrial Revolution.* Aldershot, Hampshire: Ashgate.

Musson, A. E., and Eric Robinson. 1969. *Science and Technology in the Industrial Revolution.* Manchester: Manchester University Press.

North, Douglass C. 1981. *Structure and Change in Economic History*. New York: Norton.

North, Douglass C., and Robert P. Thomas. 1973. *The Rise of the Western World: A New Economic History*. Cambridge: Cambridge University Press.

North, Douglass C., and Barry Weingast. 1989. "Constitutions and Commitment: Evolution of Institutions Governing Public Choice in Seventeenth Century England." *Journal of Economic History* 49 (4): 803–32.

Rimmer, Gordon. 1965. *Marshalls of Leeds, Flax-Spinners, 1788–1886.* Cambridge: Cambridge University Press.

Roll, Eric. (1930). 1968. *An Early Experiment in Industrial Organization,* Reprint edition. New York: Augustus Kelley.

Rosen, William. 2010. *The Most Powerful Idea in the World.* New York: Random House.

Say, Jean-Baptiste. (1803). 1821. *A Treatise on Political Economy,* 4th ed. Boston: Wells and Lilly.

Singh, Jasjit, and Ajay K. Agrawal. 2010. "Recruiting for Ideas: How Firms Exploit the Prior Inventions of New Hires." NBER Working Paper no. 15869. Cambridge, MA: National Bureau of Economic Research, April.

Skempton, A. W., ed. 2002. *A Biographical Dictionary of Civil Engineers in Great Britain and Ireland, vol. 1: 1500–1830.* London: Thomas Telford for the Institution of Civil Engineers.

Smiles, Samuel. 1861. *Lives of the Engineers, with an Account of Their Principal Works,* vol. 2. London: John Murray.

———. 1865. *Lives of Boulton and Watt.* Philadelphia: J. B. Lippincott.

———. 1874. *Lives of the Engineers: The Steam Engine.* London: John Murray.
———. 1884. *Men of Invention and Industry.* London: J. Murray.
———. (1889). 1901. *Industrial Biography: Iron-Workers and Tool Makers.* London: John Murray (1897). http://www.fullbooks.com/Industrial-Biography6.html.
Smith, Adam. (1757). 1978. *Lectures on Jurisprudence,* edited by Ronald Meek, D. D. Raphael, and Peter Stein. Oxford: Clarendon Press.
———. (1776). 1976. *The Wealth of Nations*, edited by Edwin Cannan. Chicago: University of Chicago Press.
Sussman, Herbert L. 2009. *Victorian Technology: Invention, Innovation, and the Rise of the Machine.* Santa Barbara: Praeger Publishers.
Temin, Peter. 1997. "Two Views of the British Industrial Revolution." *Journal of Economic History* 57 (1): 63–82.
Thornton, R. H. 1959. *British Shipping*. Cambridge: Cambridge University Press.
Tucker, Josiah. 1758. *Instructions for Travellers.* Dublin: Printed for William Watson at the Poets Head in Carpel Street.
Turner, Gerard L'Estrange. 1998. *Scientific Instruments, 1800–1900: An Introduction*. Berkeley, CA: University of California Press.
van der Beek, Karine. 2010. "Technology-Skill Complementarity on the Eve of the Industrial Revolution: New Evidence from England." Presented at the Economic History Association Meetings. Evanston, Illinois, September 24–26.
Wallis, Patrick. 2008. "Apprenticeship and Training in Pre-Modern England." *Journal of Economic History* 68:832–61.
Winchester, Simon. 2001. *The Map That Changed the World.* New York: HarperCollins.
Woodcroft, Bennet. 1854. *Alphabetical Index of Patentees of Inventions (1617–1852).* London: Evelyn, Adams and McKay.
Wrigley, E. A. 2004. "The Divergence of England: The Growth of the English Economy in the Seventeenth and Eighteenth Centuries." In *Poverty, Progress, and Population,* edited by E. A. Wrigley, 44–67. Cambridge: Cambridge University Press.
———. 2010. *Energy and the English Industrial Revolution.* Cambridge: Cambridge University Press.

Comment David C. Mowery

This chapter by Meisenzahl and Mokyr addresses an important issue in the economics of technological change—the contributions of incremental innovation to technological change and economic growth. This topic was addressed in the original *Rate and Direction* volume, which included the chapter by John Enos (1962) on the contributions of incremental innovation to performance in petroleum refining during the so-called "beta phase" that followed the introduction of major innovations.

Meisenzahl and Mokyr argue that incremental innovation was an impor-

David C. Mowery holds the William A. and Betty H. Hasler Chair in New Enterprise Development at the Haas School of Business, University of California, Berkeley, and is a research associate of the National Bureau of Economic Research.

tant contributor to technical advance during the Industrial Revolution, and further assert that Great Britain enjoyed a comparative advantage in such "tweaking." Much of the evidence for their arguments draws on a novel data set describing the activities of "tweakers" during 1660 to 1830 that includes information on the sectoral distribution of these tweakers, their educational and training background, and the role of selected incentive mechanisms (prizes, patents, "first-mover advantages") in tweaking activity. The authors conclude that tweakers were active in a wide range of sectors, including textiles, the engineering industries, instruments, and so forth. The sheer breadth of incremental technological innovation during the British Industrial Revolution, the authors argue, supports a characterization of this economic transformation as one that operated on a broad front, rather than being limited to a few key sectors such as textiles or steam power.

The data set assembled by Meisenzahl and Mokyr is a rich one, and the authors should be congratulated for amassing this extensive set of measures of the activities of individuals who contributed to technical progress during the Industrial Revolution. Nevertheless, like all such data, the tweaker data set has some shortcomings that undercut the inferences of the authors. First, and most important, these data are limited to successful tweakers, those whose activities were of sufficient importance to result in entries in the *Dictionary of National Biography* and other published sources. Indeed, one can argue that the sources used by the authors mean that only the most successful tweakers are included in their database. No information exists in this data set on the size (and critically, the intersectoral distribution) of the overall population of aspirant tweakers. Among other things, a finding that tweaking was more successful in textiles or steam power (based on a comparison of the size of the aspirant and successful populations of tweakers in these and other sectors) might corroborate Allen's argument (2009) that innovation was more productive in these sectors than elsewhere, benefiting Great Britain to an unusual extent.[1] The lack of information on the relative "productivity" or success of tweaker activities in different sectors, as well as an absence of data on the contributions of such educational and training institutions as apprenticeships to tweaker productivity, mean that at least some of the conclusions in the chapter need to be qualified.

A second challenge associated with these data is the distinction between tweakers and inventors who contributed the major innovations that were the focus of the modifications and improvements undertaken by tweakers.

1. See Allen (2009), especially his concluding chapter: "It is important that the British inventions of the eighteenth century—cheap iron and the steam engine, in particular—were so transformative, because the technologies invented in France—in paper production, glass, and knitting—were not. The French innovations did not lead to general mechanization or globalization. One of the social benefits of an invention is the door it opens to further improvements. British technology in the eighteenth century had much greater possibilities in this regard than French inventions or those made anywhere else" (275).

This distinction is conceptually clear, but empirically cloudy in the data set in this chapter. The authors do not describe the specific criteria used to distinguish tweakers from inventors, making it difficult for the reader to evaluate the credibility of these distinctions and ascertain that the data set does not include inventors as well as tweakers. Indeed, the authors note that the distinction between "invention and implementation" (the latter activity presumably consisting mainly of tweaking) is not a sharp one. For example, many of the individuals included in this data set may well have made contributions as both inventor and tweaker over the course of their careers, perhaps developing important incremental improvements to their major inventions, or learning from tweaking activities in ways that eventually enabled them to undertake inventive activity. The inventive "stars" examined in table 9.7 of the chapter are all drawn from the authors' sample of tweakers, further blurring the distinctions between "great inventors" and tweakers. A clearer articulation of the criteria distinguishing tweakers from inventors and some discussion of the longitudinal stability of these distinctions would be useful. Among other things, such a discussion might support more of the cross-national comparative work that is needed to establish a key conclusion of this chapter; that is, that Great Britain enjoyed a comparative advantage in tweaking.

These empirical challenges notwithstanding, this chapter provides a fascinating portrait of innovation during the Industrial Revolution, one that underscores the importance of technological diffusion for innovation. After all, the incremental improvement of innovations that constitutes the definition of tweaking implies that tweakers had access to these major inventions. The extensive diffusion of key inventions within Great Britain therefore may have contributed to the incremental innovation that the authors examine. This interaction between diffusion and innovation, of course, is by no means limited to the Industrial Revolution or to the process innovations in petroleum refining examined by Enos (1962). For example, technological change in information technology during the last quarter of the twentieth century, especially in technologies such as desktop computers, computer networking, and Internet applications, all relied on the inventive and tweaking activities of users who benefited from easy access to a large "installed base" in the United States and other industrial economies. The contributions of tweaking to innovation thus appear to have been important in more than one historical epoch, and Meisenzahl and Mokyr deserve our thanks for highlighting these contributions in an era in which the contributions of incremental innovation all too often have been overlooked.

References

Allen, R. C. 2009. *The British Industrial Revolution in Global Perspective.* New York: Cambridge University Press.

Enos, J. L. 1962. "Invention and Innovation in the Petroleum Refining Industry." In *The Rate and Direction of Inventive Activity: Economic and Social Factors,* Universities-National Bureau Committee for Economic Research and the Committee on Economic Growth of the Social Science Research Councils, 299–321. Princeton, NJ: Princeton University Press.

10

The Confederacy of Heterogeneous Software Organizations and Heterogeneous Developers
Field Experimental Evidence on Sorting and Worker Effort

Kevin J. Boudreau and Karim R. Lakhani

10.1 Introduction

Ubiquitous yet invisible, software plays an integral role in the global economy. It is essential for the effective functioning of most modern organizations, critical to the advancement of knowledge in many fields, and often indispensible to many individuals' daily activities. The economic footprint of software is quite large. In 2007, in the United States, more than 110,000 firms engaged in the production and sale of packaged and custom-developed software and related information technology (IT) services. These firms generated in excess of $300 billion dollars in direct revenue (National Science Foundation 2010), making this one of the largest US industries. Purchased software is complemented by programs created within organizations that use it as an input for conducting business activities (Mowery 1996). The

Kevin J. Boudreau is assistant professor in the Strategy and Entrepreneurship Department at the London Business School. Karim R. Lakhani is assistant professor of business administration at Harvard Business School. Boudreau and Lakhani colead the NASA Tournament Lab at the Institute of Quantitative Social Science at Harvard University.

We are grateful to members of NASA's Space Life Sciences Directorate, including Jeff Davis, Elizabeth Richard, Jennifer Fogarty, and Bara Reyna, for assistance in identifying an appropriate computational engineering challenge. The TopCoder team, including Jack Hughes, Rob Hughes, Mike Lydon, Ira Heffan, Jessie Ford, and Lars Backstrom, provided invaluable assistance in carrying out all aspects of the experiment. This research particularly benefitted from thoughtful comments by Kenneth Arrow, Pierre Azoulay, Iain Cockburn, Peter Coles, Daniel Elfenbein, Silke Januszewski Forbes, Shane Greenstein, Nicola Lacetera, Mara Lederman, Joshua Lerner, Muriel Niederle, Gary Pisano, Al Roth, Sandra Slaughter, Scott Stern, Catherine Tucker, Eric von Hippel, Heidi Williams, and D. J. Wu. Eric Lonstein provided outstanding project management and research assistance. All errors are our own. Kevin Boudreau would like to acknowledge the financial support of the LBS M-Lab. Karim Lakhani would like to acknowledge the generous support of the HBS Division of Research and Faculty Development. A Google Faculty Research Grant supported both authors.

extent of internal software production and investment is considerable, with most firms typically spending 50 percent more for new, internally developed software than for software obtained through external vendors (Steinmueller 1996). More recently, open source software communities have emerged as viable creators of large-scale "free" software (Lerner and Tirole 2002). In the United States alone, more than three million individuals work as software developers (King et al. 2010), the majority employed by establishments that sell neither software nor software-related services (Steinmueller 1996).[1]

A striking feature of this industry (although perhaps not limited to software) is the wide variety of types of organizations in which software is produced, a veritable patchwork or confederacy of heterogeneous organizations. Software is developed by entities as diverse as small entrepreneurial firms, departments in large, multinational organizations, universities, outsourcing consultancies, collaborative endeavors like open source software communities, and the proverbial "garage" firms. Dissimilarities in these settings can extend beyond simple work rules, and relate to profound differences in institutional character. Compare, for example, the "software factories" in Japan, the "scientific" approach utilized by European electronics and technology champions, the ordered, engineering method pioneered by the US military and Software Engineering Institute, and the "slightly out of control" bootstrapped development practiced by Silicon Valley firms (Cusumano 2004). Within these different kinds of organizations, the work itself might be organized according to wildly divergent procedures (Cusumano et al. 2003). A given project might follow a "waterfall" development process that utilizes military-like hierarchical command and control structures in one department. It might, alternatively, employ small feature-teams working on delineated functions. Or it might utilize paired "agile" programming arrangements, or involve internal developers working closely with an external open source community. More recently organizations are using external innovation contests to develop the software (Boudreau and Lakhani 2009). Software-developing organizations have historically continually changed and tinkered with their development practices in search of the "silver bullet" without ever arriving at a clear resolution as to the single best approach (Brooks 1975).[2]

At least as striking as the organizational heterogeneity is the heterogeneity of workers, particularly their motivations and behavioral orientations. These issues have attracted considerable research attention on account of

1. DataMonitor, a professional market research firm, estimates global 2009 revenues of software and related services firms to be $2.3 trillion (DataMonitor Report 0199-2139), and International Data Corporation (IDC) projects the direct global software developer population to exceed 17 million individuals by 2011 (IDC Report 1517514).

2. For example, Microsoft's various changes in development process are well-chronicled by Cusumano and colleagues (Cusumano 1991; Cusumano and Selby 1995; Cusumano and Yoffie 1998) and Sinofsky and Iansiti (2010).

the importance and difficulty of motivating developers (Beecham et al. 2008; Sharp et al. 2009), resulting in a stream of work that includes more than 500 papers (Sharp et al. 2009). This large body of work from the 1950s to today identifies a range of motivators including the sheer joy of building and inventing and "solving puzzles," contributing to society through useful outputs, the continuous challenge of learning new techniques and approaches, and opportunities for growth, achievement, and career recognition (e.g., Brooks 1975; Bartol and Martin 1982).[3] Consistent across this line of research is the notion that the work is, itself, a reward, creating an overlap between the costs and benefits of software development (Weinberg 1971; Schneiderman 1980; Lakhani and Wolf 2005). As a group, software developers have tended to identify more with the profession and occupational community than with the organizations in which they toil (Couger and Zawacki 1980), and their behaviors are also swayed by norms in the profession. Crucially, Beecham et al. (2008) note that this long list of motivators should be understood as describing population averages, with individual software developers in fact influenced by complex and distinct *heterogeneous* sources of motivation. The literature also documents considerable heterogeneity in preferred social interactions during the course of software production. Although, in relation to other professions, software developers have been found to have the least need for social interaction both on and off the job (Couger and Zawacki 1980), other studies have reported that interdependent team structures improved productivity at the individual level and were better suited to tackling more complex tasks (Schneiderman 1980; Couger and Zawacki 1980).

Any number of reasons might explain the confederacy of different institutions devoted to software development. Here we speculate that one possible reason is that the heterogeneity of organizations may be closely tied to the heterogeneity of workers. We conjecture that the wide range of motivations (and concomitant social, psychological, and behavioral orientations) of workers is likely to translate to varying preferences for working in different types of organizations; that is, to an "institutional preference." In very preliminary steps toward investigating a link between organizational heterogeneity and worker heterogeneity, we report here results of a field experiment in which we test whether there might be an efficiency effect of sorting workers into institutional regimes of their preference, and particularly whether sorted workers experience higher motivation, as evidenced by their choice of exerted effort.

In our experiment, more than 1,000 workers were assigned, in groups of twenty, to virtual online "rooms" to solve the same problem. Inside the rooms, participants were organized either in team-"cooperative" or autonomous-

3. Beecham et al.'s (2008) review of the post-1980 literature on the motivations of software developers identified twenty-one sources of motivation.

"competitive" regimes. In the competitive regime, individuals competed against all others in the room; in the cooperative regime, individuals were assigned to one of four five-person teams that competed against each other. These two regimes hardly replicate the full variety of regimes we observe in the confederacy of software organizations. But they do exhibit a range of starkly opposing features that accord with different work approaches in software development; that is, software developers either work on their own or in teams. We divided participants into "sorted" and "unsorted" groups with identical skills distributions. For the sorted group, we elicited their preferences and assigned them to the regime they preferred. The unsorted (control) group was assigned without regard to their preferences, indeed they were not even asked about their institutional preferences. This group therefore constituted the population average distribution of preferences (including both those who liked and disliked the regime to which they were assigned). We were also able to compare the effects of sorting on the basis of institutional preference to the effect of formal incentives, as some groups of twenty competed for $1,000 in prizes, other groups for no prize.

We found that allocating individuals to their preferred regimes had a significant impact on choice of effort level, particularly in the autonomous competitive regime, in which sorted participants worked, on average, 14.92 hours compared to 6.60 hours, on average, for the unsorted participants. The effect was also positive and significant in the team regime, in which the sorted group worked, on average, 11.57 hours compared to 8.97 hours, on average, for the unsorted participants. We devote the bulk of the analysis to confirming the robustness of the result and investigating the nature of this sorting effect.

The rest of the chapter is organized as follows. Section 10.2 outlines the basic approach to running the sorting experiment in a way that enabled us to compare the sorted and unsorted groups on the basis of institutional preferences, with the important feature that they possess identical skills distributions. In section 10.3, we present the sample and variables. Section 10.4 reports our results, comparing mean outcomes across the sorted and unsorted groups. Concluding remarks are presented in section 10.5.

10.2 Experimental Design

In our experiment, we consider the possibility that the extraordinary heterogeneity in organizations and workers in the software industry are somehow linked. Our central goal here is to estimate the extent to which assigning individuals to work within the regime they prefer influences how hard they work. The essence of our approach is quite simple. We define two work regimes: a "cooperative" and a "competitive" regime. We assign half the participants to work within the regime they prefer and the other half without regard to their preferences. Thus, we effectively compare the effort (and underlying motivations) of a "sorted" group, in which 100 percent of participants prefer the regime to which they are assigned, to that of an "unsorted" group that exhibits the population average distribution of preferences.

10.2.1 Field Experiment Context

Given our emphasis on measuring the size of the effect in relation to how different *types* of workers behave under different circumstances, a field setting has the clear advantage of providing more meaningful estimates than a lab setting. Nonetheless, to estimate sorting effects requires an especially controlled environment. We conducted the experiment on the TopCoder open software innovation platform.[4] TopCoder is an online, two-sided platform that produces software for clients via online contests among members of its base of more than 300,000 individuals. This provided a field context with real, elite software developers that afforded an unusual ability to perform manipulations and observe relevant microeconomic variables. Over the ten-day period of the experiment, participants developed computational algorithms to optimize the Space Flight Medical Kit for NASA's Integrated Medical Model (IMM) team in the Space Life Sciences Directorate at Johnson Space Center. TopCoder provided substantial assistance in altering the platform to enable us to run a multitude of treatments concurrently and in isolation, with setting up the NASA problem on the platform, and with running the experiment.

The solution to the real, highly challenging computational-engineering problem of developing a robust software algorithm to recommend the ideal components of the space medical kit included in each space mission was to be used by NASA. The solution had to take into account that mass and volume are restricted in space flight, and that the resources in the kit needed to be sufficient to accommodate both expected and unexpected medical contingencies encountered while in space, lest the mission have to be aborted. The content of the kit also had to be attuned to the characteristics of the space flight and crew. The challenge was thus to develop an algorithm that addressed mission characteristics that traded off mass and volume against sufficient resources to minimize the likelihood of medical evacuation. The problem, being relatively focused, was expected to be solved as an integral project capable of being divided into a set of subroutines and call programs. These sorts of projects might be solved by open source or corporate development teams composed of as many as five people (Carmel 1999) and are also routinely tackled by participants in TopCoder tournaments (Boudreau, Lacetera, and Lakhani 2011).

4. Boudreau, Lacetera, and Lakhani (2011), in using the TopCoder context to analyze the impact of increasing competition on performance in software contests, provide considerable detail on the TopCoder setting.

10.2.2 An Assignment Procedure for Dividing Participants into Sorted and Unsorted Groups with Identical Skills Distributions

The potential correlation of institutional preferences with skill poses a special challenge to our experiment. In such a case, differences in behavior would reflect skills differences as well as any differences between the sorted and unsorted groups per se. So as to assure that we do not conflate skills differences with the effect of preferences per se, we devise an assignment procedure that exploits both matching and randomization, as summarized in figure 10.1. The goal of our approach is to create groups, or "virtual rooms," of twenty participants drawn from the same skills distribution (and

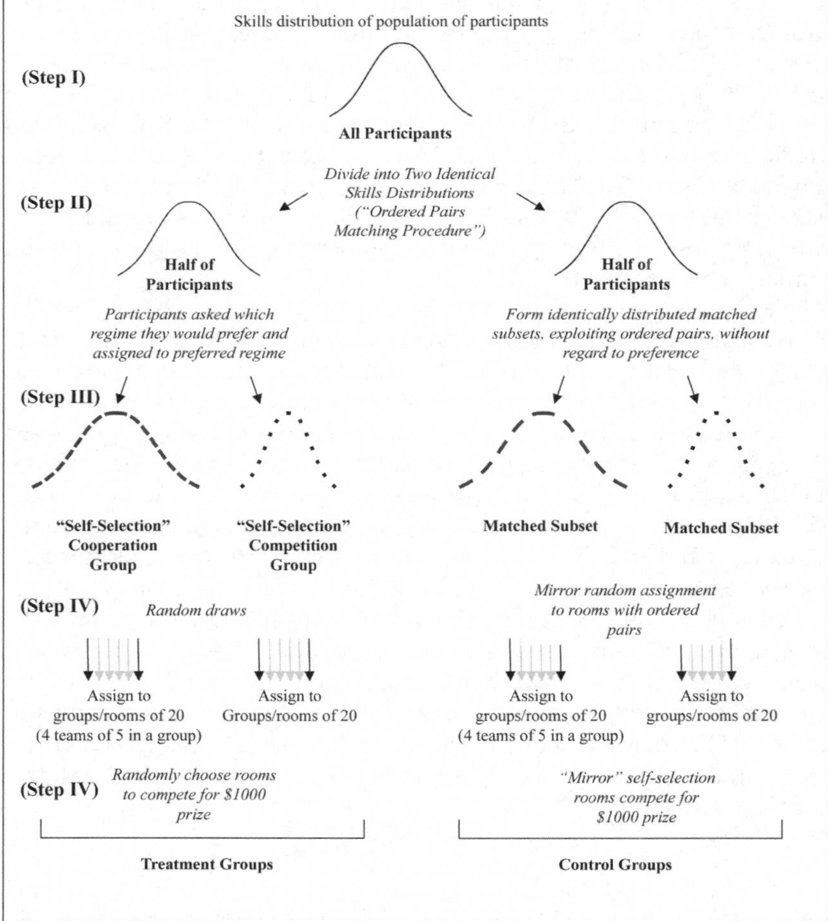

Fig. 10.1 Overview of experimental assignment

equivalent unobserved characteristics), but with different tastes for the two regimes. The construction of the sorted and unsorted groups begins by dividing the participants into two groups with identical skills distributions. This is accomplished by ordering all participants in the population from top to bottom according to their TopCoder skills rating.[5] Essentially, we created a rank order of all participants. We then divided this rank order into ordered pairs (top two highest skills, third and fourth highest skills, etc.) and randomly allocate one member of each to the sorted and the other to the unsorted group.

We then asked just the participants in the sorted group which regime they preferred. This was done in private bilateral communications between the TopCoder platform and individual participants, each of whom was asked: "Might you be interested in joining a team to compete against other teams?" Relative preference for the competitive or cooperative regime was to be indicated on a 5-point Likert scale.[6] The resulting subgroups were assigned to the cooperative and competitive regimes.

It is important to note that the groups that prefer the competitive and cooperative regimes will not have the same skills distributions if there is any correlation between skill and preference. By assigning ordered pairs of the unsorted group to the same regime as their sorted pairs, we assure that sorted and unsorted groups in both cooperative and competitive regimes have identical skills distributions. We thus constructed groups identical in skills distributions that differed systematically in terms of their preferences for regimes. The sorted group was uniformly orientated toward the regime to which it was assigned; the random-assignment group had population average preferences, with some individuals preferring, and others not, the regime in question.

The sorted groups of cooperative and competitive participants were then divided into groups of twenty individuals who competed in virtual, web-based "rooms." Cooperative rooms were formed of four teams composed (also randomly) of five individuals. We "mirror" this random assignment in the unsorted group, assigning ordered pairs to comparable groups.

5. The TopCoder skill rating is based on historical performance of the coders on the platform. It is derived from the chess grandmaster evaluation system "Elo." Boudreau, Lacetera, and Lakhani (2011) provide further detail on how it is derived.

6. Participants were first asked their preference between the regimes, then given the following options: (1) I DEFINITELY would prefer to join a team; (2) I think I MIGHT prefer to join a team; (3) I am indifferent or I am not sure; (4) I think I MIGHT prefer to compete on my own; and (5) I DEFINITELY would prefer to compete on my own. They were then provided with additional descriptive details about each of the regimes and asked the same question. We then asked them to consider the possibility that both cooperative and competitive regimes were always available on the TopCoder platform, and to indicate on a provided list of options what fraction of their time they would imagine spending in either regime. The order of responses, whether oriented toward the competitive or cooperative regime, was randomized. The second question (the one asked after clarifying the precise rules of each regime) was used as the basis for making allocation decisions.

The submitter (individual or team) of the best performing code across the entire tournament was eligible to receive a $1,000 cash prize and VIP access to one of the few remaining NASA Space Shuttle launches. We also randomized the presence of room-level incentives in our experiment by offering $1,000/room cash prizes to twenty-four rooms (twelve competition regime rooms and twelve cooperation regime rooms, equally split between sorted, and skills matched unsorted, groups). Thus, if a sorted participant was assigned to a room with a $1,000 cash prize, so was this participant's ordered pair in the unsorted group. Note that the participants did not know, ex ante, if they would be competing for room-level prizes.

10.2.3 The Cooperative and Competitive Regimes

Our primary unit of analysis of the competition regime was the twenty-person group of direct competitors. The $1,000 cash prize, if present, was divided among the top five competitors: $500 for first place, $200 for second place, $125 for third place, $100 for fourth place, and $75 for fifth place. Individuals could see the list of the other nineteen competitors on their "head-up" display with "handle" name and color code by skill. (Clicking through on a name provided a complete history of that participant's performance on the TopCoder platform and a precise breakdown of their skill rating. Scores of existing submissions by all competitors in a room appeared alongside competitor names.)

The cooperative regime also involved twenty individuals in a virtual room with five prizes. However, in this case, the twenty participants were divided into four, five-person "teams." These individuals could communicate and share code via a private discussion board. The winning team in a room was the team with the highest scoring submission (any team member could make a submission). In the cash prize treatment, the $1,000 was divided by an anonymous poll of the members of the winning team (after the competition, but before the winners were announced) regarding how each believed the prize should be shared, with prizes awarded based on average percentages. Each team could only observe other team members and the best submission at any given time by other teams.

10.3 Sample and Variables

It should also be emphasized, with regard to our research objective of measuring the selection effects of a sort, that the TopCoder membership hardly represents a random sample of individuals from the economy, or even from the software developer labor market. At the time of the experiment, some 15,000 TopCoder members regularly participated on the platform. Because the population in the experiment reflects a choice to voluntarily participate, the results should be interpreted as "treating on the treated," or assigning what is a nonrandom population to different treatments. Although there is considerable diversity in this group, which includes individuals from many countries and from industry as well as students and researchers, it remains a subset of the wider population of the global software developer labor market, and estimates of effects of sorted versus random assignment of workers should therefore be smaller than what might be possible were we to construct a more diverse sample from the broader labor market.

Our sample includes 1,040 observations (participants). Of the half of participants who were asked their preference (the sorted group), 34.9 percent expressed a clear preference for the cooperative regime, and 50.5 percent a clear preference for the competitive regime.[7] The remaining 15.6 percent of participants in the sorted group expressed uncertainty or indifference between the regimes. We assigned this latter group to the cooperative regime for two reasons. First, we interpreted this indifference to indicate some openness to the cooperative regime (TopCoder's usual regime is similar to the competitive regime). Second, we preferred to balance the numbers across regimes. (Dropping the indifferent observations from the analysis has a negligible effect on the results.)

Of the rooms formed, only twelve rooms (44 percent of the sample), six sorted and six unsorted, competed for cash prizes amounting to $1,000 per room.[8] Prizes were first assigned randomly across the sorted rooms. The "mirror" rooms of ordered pairs with corresponding assigned competitors were then also allocated $1,000 prizes.

10.3.1 Variables

We now discuss the meaning and construction of variables used in the analysis. Table 10.1 provides variable definitions and table 10.2 presents summary statistics.

Dependent Variables

We exploit both observational and self-reported survey measures of effort. The observational measure is the number of submissions made by each participant over the course of the zero-day experiment (*NumSubmissions*). This is a direct indication of the intensity of development, given that software testing and evaluation required that code be submitted to the platform so that its performance in relation to the test suite could be assessed and it could be assigned a score. (Participants' last submission became their final score.) Submitting code in this fashion was costless and resulted in virtually instantaneous feedback.

Our preferred main dependent variable records the total number of hours participants invested in the preparation of solutions throughout the course

7. We originally targeted half the entire group of 1,098, but did not receive responses from a small fraction of individuals.

8. We chose twelve simply because participation in the experiment exceeded expectations and we had not budgeted for more than twelve prizes for the competitive regime.

Table 10.1 **Variable definitions**

Variable	Definition
HoursWorked	Number of hours worked by an individual participant during the course of the experiment
NumSubmissions	Number of solutions submitted to be compiled, tested, and scored by an individual participant during the course of the experiment
SortedonPreference	Indicator switched to one for participants who were asked their preferences regarding the regimes and subsequently assigned to their preferred regime
CashPrize	Indicator switched to one for participants within a group of twenty that competed for a $1,000 cash prize
SkillRating	Measure of general problem-solving ability in algorithmic problems based on historical performance on TopCoder platform

Table 10.2 **Summary statistics**

Variable	Mean	Std. dev.	Min.	Max.
HoursWorked	10.6	18.7	0	190
NumSubmissions	2.56	5.63	0	42
SortedonPreference	.50	.49	0	1
CashPrize	0.44	.50	0	1
SkillRating	1,184	538	0	3,797

of the event. This self-reported estimate of the total number of hours worked (*HoursWorked*) was reported in a survey administered the day after the event closed.[9] (Participants were required to respond to this question electronically, as the experiment closed, in order to receive a NASA-TopCoder commemorative t-shirt imprinted with their name.) *HoursWorked* is our preferred variable, as it directly conveys meaning (and perhaps even some indication of value) and is easily interpreted. The results do not depend on which of the two measures of effort we use in the analysis.

Explanatory Variables

The key explanatory variable, *SortedonPreference,* indicates whether a competitor was in a sorted or random assignment group. A second explana-

9. Nearly all participants who submitted solutions responded. A research assistant who contacted 100 of the nonsubmitters who did not respond to the first survey found that each had devoted less than one hour to the project and had not made a submission. This enabled us to complete the nonrespondents by filling in zero hours as a relatively precise approximation. It became clear through interviews with nonsubmitters that they generally believed they would not receive a commemorative t-shirt whether they responded to the survey or not, accounting for the sharp difference in response rate between submitters and nonsubmitters. Worthy of note, however, is that a number of nonsubmitters whom we discovered had worked a nontrivial number of hours before choosing not to submit did respond to the survey.

tory variable, *CashPrize,* indicates that observations/individuals were associated with rooms for which there was a $1,000 cash prize. A third explanatory variable, *Competition,* is set to one to indicate the competitive regime, and zero to indicate the cooperative regime.

Our measure of general ability to solve algorithmic problems is TopCoder's own rating system, which essentially calculates a participant's ability to solve problems on the basis of past performance. We refer to this variable as *SkillRating.* We use specifically the rating calculated for what TopCoder terms "Algorithm" matches, software solutions to abstract and challenging problems akin to the problem in the experiment.[10]

Additional Variables

In robustness tests, we use two additional variables collected for those in the sorted group. The variable *LikertScale* captures the Likert scale responses of those asked their preferences. Recall that the numerical responses in this variable correspond to the following scale: (1) I DEFINITELY would prefer to join a team; (2) I think I MIGHT prefer to join a team; (3) I am indifferent or I am not sure; (4) I think I MIGHT prefer to compete on my own; and (5) I DEFINITELY would prefer to compete on my own. The variable *OrderofQuestion* captures whether the survey was designed to present all aspects of introducing regimes with the cooperative or competitive regime first.

10.4 Results

The average number of hours worked by participants during the ten-day experiment was 10.54 (standard deviation = 18.74 hours). Sorted individuals worked, on average, 13.27 hours (maximum 190 hours), unsorted individuals only 7.78 hours (maximum 120 hours). *NumSubmissions* was also higher for sorted participants, at 2.79 versus 2.20 for unsorted participants.

Table 10.3 breaks down the effects for the competitive and cooperative regimes. Average *HoursWorked* was only slightly higher in the competitive (10.82 hours) than in the cooperative (10.27 hours) regime.[11] In both regimes, *HoursWorked* was significantly higher for sorted participants, the starkest differences being in the competitive regime (14.92 hours for sorted participants versus 6.6 hours for unsorted participants, a 126 percent difference, compared to 11.57 and 8.97 hours, respectively, in the cooperative regime, a still large but considerably smaller 29 percent difference).

10. This has been found through the decade of operation of TopCoder to be a robust measure of skills, and is even commonly used in the software developer labor market when hiring (See Boudreau, Lacetera, and Lakhani [2011] on this measure). Nonetheless, to the extent that it might be imperfect, the randomization procedures (in particular, pair ordering and randomization of which party self-selects) should erase any possible systematic biases in estimates.

11. We found the differences in magnitudes to be surprisingly small and statistically insignificant, given the usual predictions of moral hazard in teams (Holmstrom 1982).

Table 10.3 Simple cross-tabulation comparison of means

Competitive regime						
Unsorted			Sorted			
Variable	Mean	Standard deviation	Variable	Mean	Relative to unsorted	Standard deviation
HoursWorked	6.60	13.46	*HoursWorked*	14.92	226%	24.99
NumSubmissions	1.98	5.00	*NumSubmissions*	3.77	191%	7.22

Cooperative regime						
Unsorted			Sorted			
Variable	Mean	Population std. dev.	Variable	Mean	Relative to unsorted	Population std. dev.
HoursWorked	8.97	15.70	*HoursWorked*	11.57	129%	17.61
NumSubmissions	2.44	5.53	*NumSubmissions*	1.78	73%	4.07

For *NumSubmissions,* levels were also on the order of twice as high for sorted (3.77 submissions) than for unsorted (1.98 submissions) participants. That average *NumSubmissions* was lower for sorted participants in the cooperative regime we speculate reflects greater coordination of activity across team members.[12] Given this apparent complication in using *NumSubmissions,* we take *HoursWorked* as a more direct reflection of effort exerted. (Indeed, all regression results to follow hold for *NumSubmissions,* but only for the competitive regime.) Particularities of team dynamics are beyond the scope of our analysis here.

10.4.1 Regressions

Although the earlier comparisons of means provide meaningful results, analyzing the data within a regression framework enables us to explicitly assess the experimental assumptions and better interpret results. Ordinary least squares regression results with robust standard errors are reported in table 10.4.

Assessing the Assignment Procedure

If the estimation procedure was effective and left no systematic differences across treatments, the estimates should be unchanged when we include skill controls.[13] We focus first on the results for the competitive regime. For ease of comparison, model (1) simply reiterates the two-way correlation of

12. Consistent with this interpretation, we find that sorted teams posted greater numbers of intrateam communications on the private team online bulletin board.

13. This includes differences in skill and unobservables correlated with skill.

Table 10.4 **Ordinary least squares (OLS) estimates of sorting effect**

	Competitive regime					Cooperative regime		
Explanatory variable	Model 1 Two-way correlation	Model 2 Linear skills control	Model 3 Skills-level dummies	Model 4 Ordered pair differences	Model 5 Prize control	Model 6 Two-way correlation	Model 7 Ordered pair differences	Model 8 Prize control
SortedonPreference	8.33***	8.33***	8.36***	8.71***	8.32****	2.60*	2.50*	2.48*
	(1.75)	(1.75)	(1.76)	(1.79)	(1.71)	(1.47)	(1.43)	(1.40)
CashPrize					9.14***			9.88***
					(1.85)			(1.48)
SkillRating		–1.09	–4.87		–3.60			2.01
		(1.59)	(4.30)		(4.19)			(4.22)
Skills Dummies			Yes		Yes			Yes
Constant	6.60***	8.07***				8.97***		
	(.84)	(2.28)				(.98)		
R^2	.04	.04	.05	.55	.09	.04	.55	.09

Notes: Dependent variable = *HoursWorked.* Heteroskedasticity robust standard errors reported.

***Significant at the 1 percent level.

**Significant at the 5 percent level.

*Significant at the 10 percent level.

HoursWorked with *SortedonPreference* from the competitive regime (essentially equivalent to the earlier stratified comparison of means in table 10.3). Model (2) reestimates the *SortedonPreference* coefficient with *SkillRating* included as a control. The estimated coefficient is virtually unchanged, and the coefficient on the constant, which effectively captures mean effort without sorting, changes slightly more (from 6.60 to 8.07), but the difference is statistically insignificant. To control for possible subtle nonlinearities, model (3) adds dummies for different bands of skill level to capture possible nonlinear effects, but the estimated coefficient on *SortedonPreference* is statistically identical and virtually unchanged (8.36 versus 8.33). Model (4) provides the strongest skill control by simply comparing and calculating the difference between sorted individuals and their ordered pairs (by simply including ordered pair fixed effects). The estimated effect is again statistically unchanged (although this most stringent control only yields a slightly larger coefficient). Given the random selection of rooms to receive prizes, the introduction of *CashPrize* to the model should also not have any effect on the estimated coefficient *SortedonPreference.*[14] Each of these coefficient estimates is thus statistically identical to the simple comparison of means presented in table 10.3 (14.92 – 6.6 = 8.32 hours).

Importantly, the coefficient on *CashPrize* also provides some indication of the impact of sorting relative to that of the formal incentive instrument used in this context, the $1,000 prize. The coefficient on *CashPrize,* 9.14 hours with a standard error of 1.85 hours, is statistically indistinguishable from the effect of allowing individuals to self-select to competition for cases in which competition is their preferred regime.

An analogous set of regressions performed on the cooperative regime similarly confirms estimates of the *SortedonPreference* coefficient to be insensitive to the various controls. Model (6) reiterates the two-way correlation of *HoursWorked* with *SortedonPreference* from the cooperative regime (essentially equivalent to the earlier stratified comparison of means in table 10.3), 2.6 additional hours for individuals who sorted into the cooperative regime. Reestimating the effect on the basis of directly comparing ordered pairs (model 7) or introducing *CashPrize* and controls for different levels of skills (model 8) generates similar estimates. The estimated coefficient on *SortedonPreference* is 2.60 hours. Model (6) essentially reestimates model (4) with each of the controls, but for the cooperative regime. Including each of the controls does not significantly change the coefficient on *SortedonPreference* (2.47 hours). Again, these estimates are statistically the same as those obtained from the simple comparison of means in table 10.3

14. We must go back to a model estimated on the basis of ordered pair differences given that there is no variation in CashPrize within ordered pairs because the assignment procedure assures that if one member of an ordered pair is in a group with a prize the situation will be mirrored in the other pair.

(11.57 – 8.97 = 2.60 hours). The effect of the formal cash incentive in the cooperative regime, as estimated by the coefficient on *CashPrize* (9.88 hours), is essentially the same as in the competitive regime (and the sorted effect in the competitive regime), and considerably larger than the sorted effects in the cooperative regime.[15]

An Approach to Estimating the Magnitude of Any Hawthorne Effects

Our goal was to use revealed preference as a means of allocating individuals to the regimes for which they have an inherent preference or taste. Therefore, the earlier regressions are intended to estimate the impact of this "alignment" of an individual's preference for institutional context on choice of effort. But it might still be the case that individuals made different choices simply because they were asked their preferences at all. This is a possible Hawthorne effect of sorts that should be a concern in any sorting experiment in which subjects' preferences have been directly elicited or a direct choice has been presented.

To estimate the magnitude of any such effect of eliciting preferences (as opposed to what those preferences happen to be) is challenging in an experiment in which assignments followed revealed preferences without any variation. Our approach is essentially one of detecting Hawthorne effects by comparing the subset of sorted and unsorted participants with similar preferences. If there is a Hawthorne effect, then individuals with similar institutional preferences should behave differently in sorted and unsorted groups. Results are presented in table 10.5.

Therefore, we focus on the 15 percent of sorted participants who chose a neutral response when asked to gauge their relative preferences for regimes (i.e., "I am indifferent or I am not sure"[16]). A possible limitation to this approach is that a neutral view of the cooperative regime may, in fact, imply some level of openness to an interest in this regime (given that the competitive regime is, in fact, the usual TopCoder regime).[17] To better isolate participants whose stated preferences were more likely to have been shaped by an exogenous factor than to reflect their inherent preferences, we surveyed individuals' preferences using an instrument that varied the order, sometimes presenting the competitive regime, other times the cooperative regime, first. As presented in model (1), the ordering of the question significantly affected the statement of preferences. Reestimating the model on this 15 percent of the sample (156 observations) results in a statistically identical estimate

15. As earlier noted, this result is perhaps surprising in light of the theory of moral hazard in teams (Holmstrom 1982).

16. Recall that indifferent individuals were assigned to the cooperative regime (section 10.2.2).

17. A second possible limitation is we rely on the (unobserved) preferences of ordered pairs being effectively neutral, on average.

Table 10.5 Instrumental variable (IV) estimate of Hawthorne effect

Explanatory variable	Dependent variable = *LikertScale* Model 1	Dependent variable = *HoursWorked* Model 2
SortedonPreference		–.05
		(4.40)
CashPrize	–.10	9.43***
	(.12)	(2.79)
SkillRating	.37	3.79
	(.37)	(8.20)
Skills dummies	Yes	Yes
QuestionOrder	0.28**	
	(.12)	
R^2	.05	

Note: Heteroskedasticity robust standard errors reported.
***Significant at the 1 percent level.
**Significant at the 5 percent level.
*Significant at the 10 percent level.

of the coefficient on *CashPrize,* but the coefficient on *SortedonPreference* goes to zero, suggesting zero Hawthorne effect.[18]

An Approach to Reweighting to Directly Compare the Different Sorted Groups

The skills distributions being, by design, the same across the sorted and random assignment groups, we should expect sorting to have generated differences in skills distributions across the competitive and cooperative groups. Figure 10.2, panel I presents the distribution of skills of participants who sorted themselves into the competitive and cooperative regimes (equivalently, their ordered pairs in the unsorted group). This was unavoidable in this sorting experiment, in which preferences were correlated with skill. Consequently, earlier estimates of the coefficients on *SortedonPreference* in the cooperative and competitive regimes should not be directly comparable if the magnitude of an individual sorted effect is somehow related to skill.

To more directly compare the magnitude of effects in the cooperative and competitive regimes, we reestimate effects, reweighting the data from the competitive regime to have the same skills distribution as that of the cooperative regime (as in figure 10.2, panel II). As reported in table 10.6, when the model is reestimated on competitive data, reweighted to share the

18. The estimated Hawthorne is also statistically insignificant without the use of the instrumental variable, with an estimated coefficient on *SortedonPreference* of 3.72 (s.e. = 2.61). This estimate, which is considerably larger than the instrumental variable (IV) estimate, remains statistically indistinguishable from zero, whereas the coefficient on *CashPrize,* strikingly, remains virtually unchanged in magnitude or significance in this model.

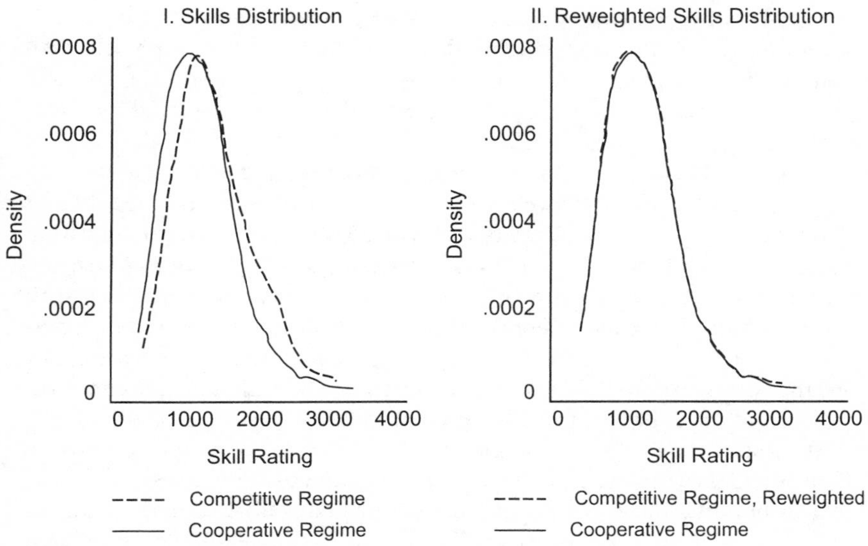

Fig. 10.2 Skills distribution in competitive and cooperative regimes

Table 10.6 Reestimated results from cooperative regime to match skills distribution of cooperative regime

Explanatory variable	Competitive regime
SortedonPreference	10.2814***
	(2.08)
CashPrize	6.7416***
	(2.20)
Skills dummies	Yes
R^2	.12

Notes: Dependent variable = *HoursWorked.* Heteroskedasticity robust standard errors reported.

***Significant at the 1 percent level.

**Significant at the 5 percent level.

*Significant at the 10 percent level.

skills distribution of the cooperative regime, the estimated coefficient on *SortedonPreference* increases from 8.32 hours to 10.28 hours. The estimated effect on *CashPrize,* by comparison, drops to 6.74.

10.5 Conclusions

Software design and development is done in very diverse organizational settings. Seemingly just as diverse and heterogeneous are the software developers who work in these organizations. This chapter takes very preliminary steps toward investigating whether there might be a link between heterogeneity of organizations and workers by assessing whether sorting software workers into their preferred regimes affected their motivations and the effort they exerted.

We devised a novel sorting experimental method that enabled us to compare a group of software developers who were sorted into a (competitive or cooperative) regime of their preference with a group of individuals who were assigned without regard to preference, assuring that both groups possessed identical distributions of raw problem-solving ability. Thus, in contrast to more conventional experimental approaches that attempt to hold the composition of groups constant while exposing them to alternative treatments, the thrust here was to hold treatments constant while allowing the composition of groups to differ in a rather precise way.

We found the effect of sorting of software developers on the basis of their preference to join the cooperative and competitive regimes in this context to be rather large. In the competitive regime, effort roughly doubled, on average. In the cooperative regime, estimates, albeit smaller, were, at a roughly 30 percent increase, still rather large. Estimates were similar across a range of specifications. We also devised a method for explicitly estimating any Hawthorne effects that may have resulted from the approach we used to elicit individuals' preferences (based on an instrumental variables estimate of a subsample of the data) and found these to be statistically indistinguishable from zero.

The present work, of course, has many limitations, and endless work remains to be done in investigating possible links between worker and organizational heterogeneity in software (and other) contexts in a competitive economy in which firms and workers match in equilibrium. With respect to the experiment conducted here, the analysis is focused on estimating mean differences rather than distributions of outcomes or associated demographic attributes of workers. Specifically, the analysis presented here emphasizes comparisons with just one type of (unsorted) control group; in considering the effect of different "types" of workers, any number of alternative and synthetic control groups might be contrived. The analysis presented here, being focused on effort, did not study effects on overall performance and productivity. There is also an indication in the results presented here that sorting may have generated subtle effects in the organization of, and patterns of collaboration in, the cooperative regime that were not further investigated here.

Our experimental results provide an opening for further investigation of how workers engaged in inventive activity might be most effectively and efficiently organized. Our work contributes to a nascent field in the economics of innovation that is utilizing microdata on scientific and technical workers and the links between incentives and creativity (Azoulay, Graff Zivin, and Manso 2011), preferences for work environments (Stern 2004), and the organization of scientific teams (Jones, Wuchty, and Uzzi 2008). As individual and team level productivity issues for creative workers become increasingly salient for organizational and national level performance (Radner 1993; Hong and Page 2001), this stream of research (and future related work) has the potential to provide relevant theoretical, empirical, and practical insights.

References

Azoulay, P., J. Graff Zivin, and G. Manso. 2011. "Incentives and Creativity: Evidence from the Academic Life Sciences." *RAND Journal of Economics* 42 (3): 527–54.

Bartol, K., and D. Martin. 1982. "Managing Information Systems Personnel: A Review of the Literature and Managerial Implications." *MIS Quarterly* 6:49–70.

Beecham, S., N. Badoo, T. Hall, and H. Robinson. 2008. "Motivation in Software Engineering: A Systematic Literature Review." *Inf. Softw. Technol.* 50 (9–10): 860–78.

Boudreau, K. J., N. Lacetera, and K. R. Lakhani. 2011. "Incentives and Problem Uncertainty in Innovation Contests: An Empirical Analysis." *Management Science* 57 (5): 843–63.

Boudreau, K. J., and K. R. Lakhani. 2009. "How to Manage Outside Innovation: Competitive Markets or Collaborative Communities?" *Sloan Management Review* 50 (4): 69–76.

Brooks, F. P. 1975. *The Mythical Man-Month: Essays on Software Engineering.* Reading: Addison-Wesley Pub. Co.

Carmel, E. 1999. *Global Software Teams: Collaborating across Borders and Time Zones.* Upper Saddle River: Prentice Hall.

Couger, J. D., and R. A. Zawacki. 1980. *Motivating and Managing Computer Personnel.* New York: Wiley.

Cusumano, M., A. MacCormack, C. F. Kemerer, and B. Crandall. 2003." Software Development Worldwide: The State of the Practice." *IEEE Softw.* 20 (6): 28–34.

Cusumano, M. A. 1991. *Japan's Software Factories: A Challenge to U.S. Management.* New York: Oxford University Press.

———. 1997. "How Microsoft Makes Large Teams Work Like Small Teams." *Sloan Management Review* 39 (1): 9–20.

———. 2004. *The Business of Software: What Every Manager, Programmer, and Entrepreneur Must Know to Thrive and Survive in Good Times and Bad.* New York: Free Press.

Cusumano, M., and R. Selby. 1995. *Microsoft Secrets: How the World's Most Powerful Software Company Creates Technology, Shapes Markets and Manages People.* New York: Free Press.

Cusumano, M. A., and D. B. Yoffie. 1998. *Competing on Internet Time: Lessons from Netscape and Its Battle with Microsoft.* New York: Free Press.

Holmstrom, B. 1982. "Moral Hazard in Teams." *The Bell Journal of Economics* 13 (2): 324–40.

Hong, L., and S. E. Page. 2001. "Problem Solving by Heterogeneous Agents." *Journal of Economic Theory* 97 (1): 123–63.
Jones, B. F., S. Wuchty, and B. Uzzi. 2008. "Multi-University Research Teams: Shifting Impact, Geography, and Stratification in Science." *Science* 322 (5905): 1259–62.
King, M., Steven Ruggles, J. Trent Alexander, Sarah Flood, Katie Genadek, Matthew B. Schroeder, Brandon Trampe, and Rebecca Vick. 2010. *Integrated Public Use Microdata Series, Current Population Survey: Version 3.0.* University of Minnesota. http://cps.ipums.org/cps.
Lakhani, K. R., and E. von Hippel. 2003. "How Open Source Software Works: Free User to User Assistance." *Research Policy* 32 (6): 923–43.
Lakhani, K. R., and R. Wolf. 2005. "Why Hackers Do What They Do: Understanding Motivation and Effort in Free/Open Source Software Projects." In *Perspectives on Free and Open Source Software,* edited by Joseph Feller, Brian Fitzgerald, Scott A. Hissam, and Karim R. Lakhani, 3–21. Cambridge, MA: MIT Press.
Lerner, J., and J. Tirole. 2002. "Some Simple Economics of Open Source." *The Journal of Industrial Economics* 50 (2): 197–234.
Mowery, D.C. 1996. *The International Computer Software Industry: A Comparative Study of Industry Evolution and Structure.* New York: Oxford University Press.
National Science Foundation. 2010. *National Patterns of R&D Resources: 2008 Data Update.* Arlington: National Science Foundation. http://www.nsf.gov/statistics/nsf10314/pdf/nsf10314.pdf.
Radner, R. 1993. "The Organization of Decentralized Information Processing." *Econometrica: Journal of the Econometric Society* 61 (5): 1109–46.
Salop, J., and S. Salop. 1976. "Self-Selection and Turnover in the Labor Market." *The Quarterly Journal of Economics* 90 (4): 619–27.
Schneiderman, B. 1980. *Software Psychology: Human Factors in Computer and Information Systems.* Boston: Little, Brown and Co.
Sharp, H., N. Badoo, S. Beecham, and T. Hall. 2009. "Models of Motivation in Software Engineering." *Information and Software* 51 (1): 219–33.
Sinofsky, S., and M. Iansiti. 2010. *One Strategy!: Organization, Planning, and Decision Making*. Hoboken, NJ: Wiley.
Steinmueller, W. E. 1996. "The U.S. Software Industry: An Analysis and Interpretive History." In *The International Computer Software Industry: A Comparative Study of Industry Evolution and Structure,* edited by David C. Mowery, 15–52. New York: Oxford University Press.
Stern, S. 2004. "Do Scientists Pay to Be Scientists?" *Management Science* 50 (6): 835–54.
Weinberg, G. M. 1971. *The Psychology of Computer Programming.* New York: Van Nostrand Reinhold.

Comment Iain M. Cockburn

The productivity of knowledge workers, particularly "high level" knowledge workers, is a first-order issue for understanding technical change, and I am

Iain M. Cockburn is professor of strategy and innovation at Boston University and a research associate of the National Bureau of Economic Research.

pleased to have the opportunity to discuss a creative and intriguing chapter on this topic. Particularly one with such a startling result: when I first read this chapter my immediate reaction was "holy cow!" Could simply giving people the opportunity to self-sort into their preferred regime of work structure and incentives really result in a doubling of effort? I suspect that most of us have probably introspected at some length on the central question raised by this chapter (how sensitive is effort by knowledge workers to their organizational context) in the context of our own work environment, and will find the magnitude of the effect intriguing. If only the Dean would just move me out of this department into that department . . . if only I were working on the same research questions, but at Google and with stock options . . . Would I really work twice as hard? Would I generate twice as much output?

Beyond idle speculation, addressing these questions empirically means confronting some quite serious problems with treatment and selection. These are, of course, difficult to deal with by looking at observational retrospective data, and I am pleased that the authors have given us a piece of experimental evidence to help us think about the problem. It is also noteworthy that this experiment is being run in the field using real people working on a real task rather than in a lab, although I am somewhat skeptical about the economic significance of the rewards and opportunity costs of participation to the programmers, as well as the significance of the output of these problem-solving teams to the "customer" (NASA). Knapsack problems are an old topic in mathematics, and NASA's engineers seem likely to have developed, refined, and implemented their own solutions to this specific problem many times over the history of the agency.

There are many things to like about this project. But I do have a few comments. The first is that the chapter focuses on measuring supply of effort, rather than on the nature of output. At least in my Dean's office, they don't appear to care much about effort. What they care about is outcomes and output. I think there is an unexploited opportunity here to look more closely at the output of the participants in the experiment. I assume that the Top Coder platform allows some quite nuanced observation of output: presumably the same mechanism that generates the quality rating for the programmer could generate a quality scoring for their solution to this knapsack problem, and there is an objective measure of the performance of each team's algorithm—fraction of wasted space. It would be very interesting to look at whether or not organizational context affects the quality of output, in the sense of better solutions, rather than just the ability to arrive at some solution. If people are allowed to self-sort into one group or another, do they produce more effective, more elegant, or more robust solutions to the problem? I'm not sure I have a prior on this, but would be very interesting to see the data.

Second, the authors focus on effort measured as self-reported hours. My guess is that self-reporting of hours could easily be biased. I am not sure which way it might be biased, but I have a feeling that this is going to be correlated, potentially in some important way, with worker type and their work context. For example, I suspect that the individuals at the top end of the skills distribution would both be more likely to always prefer to compete on an individual basis, and less likely to report truthfully that they had spent 200 hours over ten days working on the problem as opposed to claiming that they had solved it in 90 minutes. A potentially more reliable measure of effort may be the number of submissions, and, interestingly, when this measure is used; while the flavor of the results is generally the same, the magnitudes are lower.

Third, I am concerned about endogenous selection that has not been controlled for by the experimental design. One puzzling feature of these data is the substantial number of people who effectively selected themselves out of this experiment by turning in less than one hour of effort. I am not sure how we should think about this—are these the people who got randomized into a work context they did not like, or are they the ones who look at the problem and realize they have better things to do? Clearly if the selecting out is nonrandom there are substantial problems for understanding and interpreting the results from this experiment. So it would be very helpful to show us, for example, any differences in observable characteristics of those individuals who selected themselves out ex post versus inserting themselves into a work regime ex ante.

Turning from the specifics of the analysis, this chapter raises some more general questions for me. Team production may be the rule rather than the exception in knowledge work: in many activities, the scale and complexity of projects and the need to repeatedly combine highly specialized skills and knowledge may make it impossible or at least economically unattractive for individuals to work in isolation. In which case, organization, incentives, and governance of team production may be an important driver of productivity, and taken at face value the results of this chapter suggest that these may in fact be critical.

Like many other business schools, my employer emphasizes teamwork and team projects in our MBA teaching. Students are more or less randomly assigned to teams, and rewarded for the quality of their joint output. (A particularly good first assignment is to ask them to summarize Holmstrom's "Moral Hazard in Teams" article in a single Powerpoint slide.) After watching this process for a few years I am struck by several aspects of what happens over the course of the semester. Left to themselves, most such randomly assembled teams appear to quickly self-organize into an effective production unit, with clear allocation of tasks and general consensus on goals and priorities. But relatively few teams seem to be able to realize big gains from combining complementary attributes of team members without considerable effort and practice, and a small minority become dysfunctional and fall apart. By the end of the semester, however, most students have mastered the art of teamwork, and typically they report that this is one of the most useful things they learned in business school. What this suggests to me is important roles in knowledge work for both the structure and incentives of team organizations and for heterogeneity among team members in their innate or learned ability to work collaboratively.

Finally, let me focus briefly on the economic setting of this chapter, the software industry. The software sector has produced one of the most interesting new organizational forms of the contemporary economy, the open source software movement. Software is also a technology that seems to disproportionately attract distinct types of people—the Hollywood stereotype of "pale-skinned disheveled young men, slumped over a keyboard in a darkened room" may not be wholly accurate, but surely reflects some important aspects of the labor force—and software firms appear to rely disproportionately on the output of a very small minority of workers. But so do many other knowledge-intensive or creative industries, and I am less certain than the authors that the industry structure of software is uniquely different from other sectors. Nor is it obvious that software workers necessarily respond differently to opportunities to self-select into their preferred organizational structure than those in other occupations. I am provoked therefore to speculate about the results of repeating this experiment in different contexts. This would be very helpful for establishing the broader implications of the results for thinking about the organization of knowledge work, and might provide opportunities to test the robustness of the methodology. A twofold increase in output attributable to the option to self-select into one's preferred organization of work seems very large, but it is not clear what the relevant benchmark might be, and whether this effect should necessarily be larger for knowledge workers versus other workers. I would not be surprised if similar results were obtained for work tasks involving manual labor or mechanical rather than mental dexterity.

V

Panel Discussion
Innovation Incentives, Institutions, and Economic Growth

The Innovation Fetish among the *Economoi*
Introduction to the Panel on Innovation Incentives, Institutions, and Economic Growth

Paul A. David

My instructions from the organizers came with two messages: be brief and be provocative. Brief, I have heard about before. But I had to think about being provocative, because the message was opaque on the question of who it was that I was meant to provoke. In the end I decided to attempt a mass provocation.

How better to do that than introduce this panel discussion by assaulting what I take to be the very premise of the session—namely, that we all are agreed that our purpose here, and more generally, is to seek more innovation by designing stronger, more effective incentives and more appropriately supportive institutions. Rather than nod, I wish to demur and declare that I view that casual supposition as another manifestation of a widespread and rather deplorable contemporary obsession: "the innovation fetish."

Without going too deeply into ethnographic detail, much evidence has accumulated that this particular phenomenon recently has become ubiquitous among the *economoi,* that loose federation of tribal groups populating and continually extending their domain of influence within the social sciences. The innovation fetish grips its adherents—and particularly those among the *economoi* who avow special concerns with technological change and its impact upon economic growth and human welfare—with an unreasonable degree of attention to, and particular reverence for acts of commercial implementation of new processes and products, organizational practices, and business models.

Paul A. David is professor of economics emeritus at Stanford University, a senior fellow of the Stanford Institute for Economic Policy Research, a professorial fellow of the United Nations University-Maastricht Economic and Social Research Institute on Innovation and Technology, and a research associate of the Program on Innovation and Regulation in the Digital Economy at Telecom-ParisTech and l'École Polytechnique, Paris.

Worse still, the contemporary preoccupation with and excessive fixation upon innovation has spread beyond the *economoi* to national political leaders, the heads of private and public foundations that disperse funding for scholarly and proactive purposes, administrators of institutions of higher education and research, and ambitious high-school students. Possibly their behavior is only mimetic of the ecstatic obsessive practices they have witnessed on the part of the *economoi.* For the latter's engagement with innovation has taken on increasingly reverential overtones to the point that the revered object is endowed with seemingly magical or spiritual powers associated with animistic or shamanistic rituals—as in the practice of offering public policy advice that ritualistically summons up potent quasi-magical (certainly hard to measure) effects—notably in the forms of "knowledge spill-overs" and "information externalities."

The obverse side of the growing absorption of the *economoi* with such practices is their comparative indifference, if not outright reluctance, to being distracted with inquiries into the structure of incentives and institutions that may be affecting other, surrounding and related processes that along with innovation were once held to be important determinants of "the rate and direction of technological change." Here, of course, I allude to the multitude of less mentionable specifics, starting with the identification of unexplained phenomena and unmet practical needs; then to scientific discovery and invention, the implementation of inventions by product and process design and development, including production engineering and reengineering driven by producer-user interactions; then to marketing, and, last but not least, to the subsequent diffusion of novel goods and practices into widespread use, from whence flow the economic welfare gains generated in the forms of greater productivity and consumer satisfactions from the new goods' and services' enhanced qualities.

To sharpen the point of this, my first provocation, I say: we should not make the analytical mistake of discussing "innovation policy" to the exclusion of everything else, or approaching questions of science policy, or education policy, or competition policy, or regulatory policy by first asking "what will it do for innovation?" True, it would simplify the analysis and its presentation for discussion if we isolate our thinking about the innovation process from all but its most proximate determinants, such as the workings of the patent system and the licensing of inventions on one hand, and the management of the introduction of new products and processes by business enterprises on the other, and thereby remove the subject from its systemic context. The resulting simplicity, however, is a recipe for mistakes in policy and the misdirection of resources.

Instead, a systemic approach would help identify the interdependence and feedback dynamics in the relationships among what too often are treated as separable stages in the logical sequence beginning with research and invention, passing through the portal of innovation, and ending with diffusion and ubiquitous adoption. Here there are several counterintuitive observations to be considered. For example, an innovation's diffusion into more widespread use is likely to identify the need for adapting the design to accommodate unanticipated variations in conditions encountered in the field. Via that "back channel," diffusion itself can be a stimulus for further inventive activity and subsequent innovative adaptation. But, if diffusion is acknowledged to be a dynamic driver of R&D and innovations that broaden the capabilities of a novel product line, then one also should be prepared to recognize the prospect of faster innovation as a potential enemy of diffusion.

That apparent paradox is readily explained if one starts with the analysis of the determinants of the decision to adopt an innovation embodied in a durable producer-good. Viewed from that vantage point, a credible commitment of public policy to accelerating the rate of innovation in the particular class of technologies being considered for adoption is tantamount to promising the future arrival of new and superior vintages of the new capital equipment that currently is on the market. Because rational potential buyers are likely to be concerned to avoid the capital loss that the arrival of tomorrow's improved version is expected to bring some of them, at least they will defer today's acquisition of the novel equipment now available. The result of the pro-innovation policy commitment may well be the perverse slowing of adoptions, to the detriment of the innovating firm's profits and its ability to finance needed incremental technical improvements that would widen the market future vintages in its product line.

A single provocation of this kind may not be adequate to stir either the panelists or the audience. So, here is a second prod. It has become apparent that, gripped in the thrall of the innovation fetish, the *economoi* collectively have lost the ability to contemplate the possibility that enough may be enough; that a point could be reached where more innovation is worse. The near pathological impulse to push the rate of innovation to be ever-faster needs a medical psychiatric designation, and I propose to refer to it as the innovation fetish's "Imelda Marcos syndrome"—in memory of a famous instance of the uncontrollable, obsessive accumulation of more and more pairs of women's shoes (another richly documented fetish object).

The optimum rate of innovation for an economy, business entity, or social organization is a notion that rarely is discussed, except by implication, which has left it poorly defined. Yet, unless this concept somehow was implemented and thereby operationally defined, how could one claim to judge whether the pace of innovation currently prevailing in a given branch of industry or sector of the economy was too slow, rather than just right or too fast? By contrast, the optimal rate of Harrod-neutral technical change and hence the optimal steady-state rate of labor productivity growth is nicely defined, at least for certain familiar classes of growth models; and, in the literature on the economics of R&D the question whether we have too much or too little (R&D) input into the processes of research and invention is frequently asked and answered empirically. Why should not excessive innovation be acknowledged to be just as much a possibility as is excessive investment in scientific research, or in industrial R&D?

But, for all the attention and advice being offered to governments seeking to promote innovation as the key instrument responsible for economic growth, questions as to whether the prevailing rate of innovation was undesirably slow or excessively rapid barely can be posed, let alone answered. This state of affairs is not without consequences. Because one cannot say with confidence that it is or ever has been optimal, or too rapid, the judicious position for policy advisors to take regarding the innovation rate is to say in all candor that there simply are no grounds for not supposing that the pace of innovation is slower than its optimum rate. The argument from ignorance thus continues to leave full scope for policy recommendations that are justified on the ground that their effects will encourage innovation.

In confronting this, the root of the innovation fetishists' "Imelda Marcos syndrome," I shall confine myself to offering an evolutionary argument for supposing that if an optimal rate of innovation exists for any branch, industry, or economic sector, it cannot be continuously positive. Therefore its *average* rate over substantial finite durations in time must remain strictly bounded from above. This proposition in itself is not very useful as a guide for concrete policy recommendations, but, beyond serving my present provocative purposes, the "evolutionary" perspective from which I have reached it may be of some more general interest.

My argument proceeds from the observation in biogenetics that evolutionary processes that allow populations of organisms to adapt incrementally by "experimenting" with genotypic mutations—some of which have the potential to enhance aspects of the functionality (and hence inclusive fitness) in the organisms that carry them—cannot proceed continuously through time. This is to say that evolutionary dynamics in biology has to allow for finite "pauses" during which new functional traits acquire stability, in the sense of becoming "fixed" in the gene pool of the current population. By doing so, phenotypic "platforms" are created for further experiments, in which recessive mutant genes may express themselves and manage to replicate in the population, or not.

Most mutations and their associated traits, however, will give rise to nonviable "monsters" and be rapidly discarded, rather than becoming fixed in the gene pool. Analogously, it may be remarked that "inventions" in the domains of technological artifacts and financial instruments, and the innovations that seek to exploit their properties, also are most likely to result in dysfunctional monsters that are destined to be rejected as technically or commercially nonviable, or worse, actually destructive of larger systems into which they are introduced. Innovation in the technological and economic sphere is notorious as a highly dissipative process that will burn lots of resources before it finds something that is new, better, and "ecologically" sustainable enough to yield a substantial stream of quasi-rents.

Furthermore, like genetic mutations, innovations may take a considerable length of time before manifesting their full systemic consequences, and the process of selection (whether by market forces or other social mechanisms) is likely to involve many learning errors. That is the case especially when the epigenetic landscape affecting adaptive selection itself is undergoing frequent and essentially exogenous alterations—as a consequence of experiments concurrently taking place in the other inhabitants of the same ecological ("market") niche. Some of those selection errors will not be quickly sloughed off, however, and instead may persist long enough to shape the ensuing course of technological and institutional developments in ways that impose significant cumulative economic costs upon later generations.

Therefore, if one seeks the useful outcomes of a highly dissipative process, and identification of utility itself is neither straightforward nor swift, it is not unreasonable to adopt a strategy of launching as many waves of concurrent "experiments" (innovations) as can be afforded. This line of thought proffers an attractively broad and cogent rationale for even more innovation. But it should be embraced cautiously. To the extent that it is possible to partition the experimental field so that the outcomes of each trial are substantially independent of what is going on in the next field, and, by analogy, to have an economy partitioned along business and industrial lines so that linkages among them are neither very dense nor very strong, there is a case to be made that the pace at which new things are being introduced within a given sector should be left uncontrolled. To put this in more concrete terms, there are some special circumstances in which the kinds of generative, innovation-inducing externalities (of the sort whose effects that have been lauded in the endogenous economic growth literature dealing with the "general purpose technologies") safely can be expected to yield overwhelmingly beneficial systemic outcomes.

Still, it is worth pausing here to delve a little more deeply into those qualifying conditions. If the processes of diffusion, adaptation, and modification are slow-moving and only one such major "disruptive innovation" is in play, and has initial impacts that remain largely localized within one or another among the economy's major sectors, then we have conditions in which the destructive and dislocating consequences the "creative destruction" left in the Schumpeterian innovator's wake are likely to be tolerable, in the sense of being manageable at the macro-system level. This is not to ignore or minimize the adverse redistributive effects of the economic obsolescence and vanishing profitability of long-established business firms, of the displacement of workers and the lost market value and social status associated with particular human skills, or of the diminished support for certain valued social institutions and public services that were dependent upon the local tax revenues formerly generated by now destabilized and business agglomerations. Rather, it is to say simply that under certain favorable circumstances the economic damages need not assume unmanageable proportions; that such negative spill-over effects as the ramifications of creative destruction impart to other regions and agents that comprise the economy may well be offset by compensating gains in its newly emerging and rejuvenated lines of activity; and that even if no compensation can be arranged politically for the injured, at least the transition initiated by a narrowly directed burst of technological innovation in itself will not substantially degrade the performance of economy as a whole.

The situation is quite different, however, where the structure of interindustry linkages in the system renders it far from semidecomposable, or where major economic sectors are burdened by persisting structural problems, or have been seriously dislocated by foreign competition or aggregate demand shocks. One should hardly be so sanguine about policies that in *such conditions* undertake to promote disruptive innovations in order to invigorate sectors of the economy that were functionally stable, albeit technologically dormant. Unfortunately, qualifications of this sort appear sparsely if at all in the rhetoric of innovation policy that today calls for further measures to promote faster innovation, ceaselessly, and concurrently everywhere throughout the economy—taking this to be the obvious all-purpose remedy for the multiplicity of our economic difficulties.

I think I have now said enough, and perhaps more than enough to articulate the thought that there are phases in the life of economies, as in the lives of firms, where strategies of consolidation and reconfiguration of effective routines are likely to be more beneficial than those that seek to exploit opportunities for enhanced performance by "shaking up everything." If that is so, then the socially optimal rate of innovation cannot be continuously positive within industries or organizations, and it surely cannot be the maximum rate attainable. By the aggregation of diverse micro- and meso-level innovation processes whose phases are uncorrelated but similar in amplitude, a suitably diversified economy may enjoy the effects of a more or less steady average pace of innovation at the macro-level. The habit of abstracting from this more complex view of the issue in growth modeling exercises that work with single- or two-sector systems runs the risk of leading analysts and policymakers astray.

To free ourselves from the innovation fetish's grip might well lead to more thoughtful and discriminating policy advice about innovation and its role in economic growth, and it could usefully reinvigorate research on the determinants of the rate and direction of technological change. At the very least, it is likely to refresh discussions and debates among the *economoi,* hopefully on this occasion and continuing thereafter.

Innovation Process and Policy
What Do We Learn from New Growth Theory?

Philippe Aghion

What have new growth theories brought to our thinking about macro and micro issues? On the macro side, these theories (Romer 1990; Aghion and Howitt 1992) have developed frameworks where growth is driven by innovations that are motivated by the prospect of monopoly rents, and where new innovations drive out old technologies. These are frameworks where firms and industrial organization lie at the heart of the growth process. Policy and institutions/organizations affects aggregate growth by affecting entrepreneurs' incentives to innovate, their ability to finance innovations and enter new markets, and by affecting the process of competition with other firms in the market. This in turn delivers a framework that can be used to look at how institutions such as patent systems, contractual enforcement, property right protection, administrative entry costs, universities, the design of constitutions, and policies such as carbon taxes, R&D subsidies, fiscal and monetary policy, and education policy affect the growth process through affecting the economic environment faced by potential innovators.

One can also analyze how different types of policies or institutions affect growth differently for countries at different stages of development: in particular, a country where growth relies primarily upon catching up with (or imitating) more advanced technologies, does not require the same organization of education, of the financial system, of labor and product markets as more advanced countries where growth is primarily driven by frontier innovations.

Also over the past few years, one has witnessed a new wave of research on the role of culture in the growth process, which looks, for example, at the

Philippe Aghion is the Robert C. Waggoner Professor of Economics at Harvard University and a research associate of the National Bureau of Economic Research.

role of trust, social norms, and beliefs in facilitating or delaying growth and the emergence of innovation-enhancing policies and institutions.

More generally, what new growth economics brings to the analysis of how policies affect aggregate growth is the importance of interaction effects: interaction with a country's stage of development, interaction with a country's culture and beliefs, interaction with other institutional variables such as financial development or corruption. We know, for example, that a countercyclical fiscal policy may have a more growth enhancing effect on the average rate of innovation over the cycle, for firms that are more credit constrained.

There is also the interaction between fast-moving and slow-moving institutions. For example, is it good or bad for growth to increase taxes? The answer to this question hinges a lot upon whether the country is one where tax revenues end up being diverted by politicians or whether, as is the case in a country like Sweden, tax revenues are known to be well spent on higher education, infrastructure, and the like. Thus, when analyzing the effects of taxation on innovation, entry, and growth, one has to look at how taxation policy interacts with things that are slower moving—for example, corruption or government efficiency.

What have we brought to microeconomics is a more difficult question, hence my answer here is bound to be more tentative. One main thing we might have brought to the field of industrial organization is the idea of looking at composition effects or other types of general equilibrium effects to determine under which circumstances one partial equilibrium effect dominates another.

For example, in work on competition and innovation (e.g., see Aghion et al. 2001), my coauthors and I have pointed to two opposite effects of increased competition on innovation and growth: first, an escape competition effect whereby more intense competition stimulates innovation (to escape competitors), and second, a Schumpeterian effect whereby more intense competition reduces innovation rents and thereby discourages innovations. In subsequent empirical work (see Aghion et al. 2005), we have shown how the effect of more intense competition (on R&D incentives) on the equilibrium composition of sectors (which we refer to as "composition effect"), implies that starting at low levels of competition the escape competition effect dominates, whereas if starting at a high level of competition the Schumpeterian effect dominates. This in turn gives rise to an inverted U-shaped relationship between competition and innovation. Also using a similar framework, we have shown that the effect of an increased entry threat on innovation in a domestic sector depends upon the sector's distance to its world technological frontier.

Another example of growth analysis affecting our understanding of the innovation process is climate change and green innovations. There, in joint work with Acemoglu, Bursztyn, and Hemous (hereafter AABH), we show whether dirty or clean technologies are more complements or more substitutes, affect the extent to which policies aimed at avoiding environmental disasters should be temporary or permanent, or should be implemented with or without delay, and also the extent to which the fact that CO2 intensive activities deplete our oil resources is a good or a bad thing for climate change under laissez-faire. One reason is that the degree of substitutability between clean and dirty technologies impacts determines the extent to which (general equilibrium) price effects may or may nor counteract more partial equilibrium effects, whereby firms tend to innovate in activities where they already hold a comparative advantage.

Let me now build upon the earlier discussion to bring out what I consider to be three fallacies. The first fallacy is more of a "macroeconomic" nature (at least it has mostly influenced macroeconomists): namely, the idea (e.g., see Easterly 2005) that policy per se does not matter for growth, that what matters more fundamentally are institutions. Thus Easterly (2005) looks at cross-country panel regressions of growth over a whole range of policy variables (competition, black market premium, inflation, etc.). He first finds significant correlations between these policy variables and growth, but these correlations become insignificant once controlling for institutional variables such as property right protection. In other words, in the horse race between policies and institutions, the latter appear to win over the former. But what Easterly does not do, is to interact policies with institutions. Had he done so, he would have found significant effects of policies on growth, even when restricting the analysis to subset of countries with similar (slow-moving) institutions—for example, the Organization for Economic Cooperation and Development (OECD) countries. The problem with his analysis is that it averages the effects of policies across countries where such policies have very different effects. The positive effect of the policy in one subset of countries, say the more advanced countries, is likely to be offset by the effect of the same policies in other countries.

The second fallacy, which is more "micro," or at least spurred debates mainly among microeconomists, comes out of a thought-provoking book by Boldrin and Levine arguing that patents are always detrimental to competition and thereby to innovation. To provide support to their analysis these two authors built a growth model where innovation and growth can occur under perfect competition. The model is then used to argue that monopoly rents and therefore patents are not needed for innovation and growth: on the contrary, patents are detrimental to innovation because they reduce competition. That reducing competition can be detrimental to innovation is a sound idea that could not be accounted for in early innovation-based models of innovation and growth (e.g., Romer 1990, or Aghion and Howitt 1992). In these models, competition is detrimental for innovation and growth for exactly the same reason that makes patent protection (IPRs) good for innovation: namely, in these models competition reduces (post-innovation) rents whereas patent protection increases them.

However, in subsequent step-by-step innovation models (see Aghion et al. 2001, 2005), in which a laggard firm needs to catch up with the current leader in its sector (and therefore go through a neck-and-neck stage) before it can later become a leader itself, not only does competition enhance innovation as in Boldrin and Levine's model, but also and perhaps more importantly, competition and IPRs become complementary. Why? Because entrepreneurs' incentives to innovate depends on the gap between the post-innovation rent and the pre-innovation rent—call it the net innovation rent. And typically, what competition does is to lower pre-innovation rents, also maybe the post-innovation rents, although the difference between post- and pre-innovation rents will typically increase with competition, and all the more so with stronger patents that protect post-innovation rents more. In contrast, in our earlier Schumpeterian model where innovations are made by outsiders who then leap-frog incumbent firms, the pre-innovation rent is always equal to zero, thus all competition does in this case is to reduce the post-innovation rent, which is also equal to the net innovation rent. Thus, it is no wonder why higher competition reduces innovation incentives in this earlier model.

Now, an ex-student of mine, Yi Qian (Northwestern), in a recent paper published in ReStat, uses the passage of national pharmaceutical patent law as a natural experiment to test the economic impact of patent. She finds that implementation of patents stimulates innovation, mostly in countries with higher market freedom. Similarly, in current work with Peter Howitt and Susanne Prantl, we look at the effects of implementation of the single market program on R&D expenditures in countries with different degrees of IPR. Thus we look at thirteen manufacturing industries in fifteen OECD countries between 1987 and 2005, and we find that the implementation of the single market program leads to an increasing R&D expenditure in countries with strong IPR, not in others. And the positive response of R&D expenditure to the single market program in strong IPR countries is more pronounced among firms in industries whose equivalent in the United States indicate higher patent intensity. Thus, there truly seems to be a complementarity between IPRs and competition, unlike what Boldrin and Levine suggest.

A third fallacy is that industrial policy is always detrimental to competition and that they should always be precluded. A common argument is that industrial policy boils down to "picking winners," which in turn directly hurts competition. Moreover, governments are bad at picking winners, and besides they are likely to be subject to lobbying. Thus, the argument goes, any form of industrial policy should be precluded.

However, a first case in favor of sectoral policy is to redirect technical change. An example is the environment and climate change (see our discussion of AABH earlier): under laissez-faire, firms that have innovated in "dirty technologies" in the past will tend to continue innovating in these same technologies in the future (current work looking at clean versus dirty innovations in the automotive industries worldwide confirm this path-dependence in the direction of innovation). This in turn suggests a role for sectoral policies such as subsidizing clean innovation in order to redirect innovation toward clean technologies.

A second argument (see Aghion et al. 2011) in favor of sectoral policy is that it may induce firms that would otherwise differentiate themselves horizontally in order to avoid competition to locate in the same sector. Doing so would both enhance competition between firms now within the same sector, and also induce communication between these firms now that they are involved in more similar activities. This in turn may end up fostering aggregate innovation.

More generally, on the relationship between competition and industrial policy: one might think that anything that looks like a sectoral policy goes against competition. However, in current work with Ann Harrison, using a panel data set of Chinese firms, we looked at the effect of subsidies, of sectoral subsidies interacted with competition, on product innovation and total factor productivity (TFP) growth. What we find is that the higher the degree of competition in a sector, the more positive the effect of subsidies on average TFP in that sector; and the overall effect of subsidies on TFP are positive if competition is sufficiently high and/or if subsidies are sufficiently diffused among enough firms in the sector. In other words, if sectoral policy is more "competition-friendly" then it is more likely to deliver more innovation and growth.

To conclude this discussion, if I have two directions for future research on growth economics and the design of growth policies to propose, I would first suggest looking at the organization of firms and universities and their impact on the growth process. For example, we know that the incentives of academics are different from the incentives of private researchers. In particular academic researchers value openness; that is, the informal exchange of ideas with other researchers. Openness goes in fact beyond academia, for example, IBM has greatly benefited from its partnership with Linux. How does this change our views of the effects of firm boundaries and proprietary versus nonproprietary knowledge on innovation and growth? Another interesting question concerns the interplay between formal and informal contracting affecting the flow and nature of innovation. My student David Hemous has a very interesting paper explaining that informal contracting is not so good because it does not provide economic agents with the same flexibility to switch contracting partners upon innovating.

The second direction is to explore the relationship between institutions and beliefs. How much can we change beliefs through policies? How much can we transpose policy from a country to another one? For example, we tried to convert some countries in the Middle East to a Western model of values many times. It often failed because we were unable to accommodate local beliefs. This, incidentally, leads me to question the provocative idea, put forward by Paul Romer, of setting up cities (or knowledge hubs) that would be built on the same institutional model, with the expectation that the effects on innovation and growth would be the same no matter the local culture and beliefs.

References

Acemoglu, D., P. Aghion, L. Bursztyn, and D. Hemous. Forthcoming. "The Environment and Directed Technical Change." *American Economic Review*.

Aghion, P., N. Bloom, R. Blundell, R. Griffith, and P. Howitt. 2005. "Competition and Innovation: An Inverted U Relationship." *Quarterly Journal of Economics* 120:701–28.

Aghion, P., M. Dewatripont, L. Du, A. Harrison, and P. Legros. 2011. "Industrial Policy and Competition." Cambridge, MA: Harvard. mimeo.

Aghion, P., C. Harris, P. Howitt, and J. Vickers. 2001. "Competition, Imitation and Growth with Step-by-Step Innovation." *Review of Economic Studies* 68:467–92.

Aghion, P., and P. Howitt. 1992. "A Model of Growth through Creative Destruction." *Econometrica* 60:323–51.

Boldrin, M., and D. Levine. 2008. *Against Intellectual Monopoly.* Cambridge: Cambridge University Press.

Easterly, W. 2005. "National Policies and Economic Growth." In *Handbook of Economic Growth,* edited by P. Aghion and S. Durlauf. Amsterdam, Neth.: North-Holland.

Qian, Y. 2007. "Do National Patent Laws Stimulate Domestic Innovation in a Global Patenting Environment?" *Review of Economics and Statistics* 89:436–53.

Romer, P. 1990. "Endogenous Technical Change." *Journal of Political Economy* 98:71–102.

VI

The Social Impact of Innovation

11

The Consequences of Financial Innovation
A Counterfactual Research Agenda

Josh Lerner and Peter Tufano

The significance of financial innovation has been widely touted. Many leading scholars, including Miller (1986) and Merton (1992), highlight the importance of new products and services in the financial arena, sometimes characterizing these innovations as an "engine of economic growth."

At several levels, these arguments are plausible. Financial innovations can be seen as playing a role akin to that of the "general purpose technologies" delineated by Bresnahan and Trajtenberg (1995) and Helpman (1998): not only do these breakthroughs generate returns for the innovators, but they have the potential to affect the entire economic system and can lead to far-reaching changes. For instance, these innovations may have broad implications for households, enabling new choices for investment and consumption, and reducing the costs of raising and deploying funds. Similarly, financial innovations enable firms to raise capital in larger amounts and at a lower cost than they could otherwise, and in some cases (for instance, biotechnology start-ups) to obtain financing that they would otherwise simply be unable to raise. This latter idea is captured in a recent model of economic growth by

Josh Lerner is the Jacob H. Schiff Professor of Investment Banking at Harvard Business School, with a joint appointment in the Finance and the Entrepreneurial Management Units, and a research associate and codirector of the Productivity, Innovation, and Entrepreneurship Program at the National Bureau of Economic Research. Peter Tufano is the Peter Moores Dean and professor of finance at the Saïd Business School at the University of Oxford and a research associate and codirector of the Household Finance Working Group at the National Bureau of Economic Research.

We would like to thank Bob Hunt, Bill Janeway, Joel Mokyr, Antoinette Schoar, Scott Stern, and participants at the American Economic Association's 2010 Meeting, the National Bureau of Economic Research's Rate and Direction of Inventive Activity Preconference and Conference, and Brown University's Conference on Financial Innovation for their helpful comments. We thank the Division of Faculty Research and Development at the Harvard Business School for support of this project.

Michalopoulos, Laeven, and Levine (2010), who argue that growth is driven not just by profit-maximizing entrepreneurs who spring up to commercialize new technologies, but also by the financial entrepreneurs who develop new ways to screen and fund the technologists.

Moreover, it appears that financial innovation is ubiquitous. Tufano (1995, 2003) shows that far from being confined to the last few decades, financial innovation has been part of the economic landscape for centuries. Goetzmann and Rouwenhorst (2005) document nineteen major financial innovations that span the past 4,000 years, ranging from the innovation of interest to creation of Eurobonds. Not only is financial innovation an historical phenomena, it is also a widespread one. For example, Tufano (1989) shows that of all public offerings in 1987, 18 percent (on a dollar-weighted basis) consisted of securities that had not been in existence in 1974.

But at the same time, claims of the beneficial impacts of financial innovations must be approached with caution. One reason is that despite the acknowledged economic importance of financial innovation, the sources of such innovation remain poorly understood, particularly empirically. In a recent review article, Frame and White (2004) are able to identify only thirty-nine empirical studies of financial innovation. Moreover, this literature concentrates largely on the "back end" of the innovation process, focusing on the diffusion of these innovations, the characteristics of adopters, and the consequences of innovation for firm profitability and social welfare. Frame and White identify only two papers on the origins of innovation, namely, Ben-Horim and Silber (1977) and Lerner (2002).

The paucity of research in this area contrasts sharply with the abundant literature on the sources of manufacturing innovation. This neglect is particularly puzzling given the special circumstances surrounding financial innovation. Several considerations—discussed in detail in section 11.3—suggest that the dynamics of financial innovation are quite different from those in manufacturing. Together, these considerations suggest the need to examine financial innovation as a phenomenon in its own right.

The second reason for caution has been the recent crisis in the global financial system, which has shaken many economists' faith in the positive effects of financial innovation. Certainly, in many post mortems of the crisis, financial innovation was seen as far from an "engine of economic growth." For instance, Levitin characterized recent changes in retail financial services as "negative innovations," such as "opaque pricing, including billing tricks and traps . . . that encourag[e] unsafe lending practices." A similar theme was sounded by Krugman (2007) in regards to securities regulation:

> [T]he innovations of recent years—the alphabet soup of C.D.O.'s and S.I.V.'s, R.M.B.S. and A.B.C.P.—were sold on false pretenses. They were promoted as ways to spread risk, making investment safer. What they did instead—aside from making their creators a lot of money, which they didn't have to repay when it all went bust—was to spread confusion, luring investors into taking on more risk than they realized.

Given this unsettled but huge territory, it is premature to provide definitive answers regarding the causes and consequences of financial innovations and how they differ from the much better understood innovation process in the manufacturing sector. Indeed, a number of observers have pointed out recently that financial innovations are neither all bad nor all good, but contain a mixture of elements (e.g., Johnson and Kwok 2009; Litan 2010; Mishra 2010).

There are many different research approaches to understanding financial innovation, including empirical studies, theoretical models, and traditional historical descriptions. Each has advantages and disadvantages, which we discuss later. In this chapter, our goal is to lay out a complementary research agenda, which we hope will encourage subsequent scholars. After we review the definition of financial innovation, we turn to three general observations about how financial innovation is similar to and different from other forms of innovation—and which inform the limitations of standard research methods. We then consider three case studies of particular innovations and highlight both what is known and unknown about their consequences.

The original *Rate and Direction* volume was published in 1962. Just two years later, Robert W. Fogel, a future Nobel laureate in economics, published his masterpiece *Railroads and American Economic Growth.* In it, Fogel advanced a method, now used in history, political science, and economic history, to consider counterfactual histories. In a counterfactual analysis, the researcher (a) posits a set of plausible counterfactuals and how they might have come to pass; and (b) evaluates metrics to establish the implications of these alternative historical paths. We suggest how this method, while seemingly imprecise and controversial, can be used to better understand financial innovation. We also discuss the limitations of this method. In our conclusion, we suggest avenues for future exploration.

11.1 Background on Financial Innovation

Much of the theoretical and empirical work in financial economics considers a highly stylized world in which there are few types of securities (e.g., debt and equity) and a handful of simple financial institutions, such as banks or exchanges. In reality there are a vast range of different financial products, many different types of financial institutions, and a variety of processes that these institutions employ to do business. The literature on financial innovation must grapple with this real-world complexity.

Financial innovation is the act of creating and then popularizing new financial instruments, as well as new financial technologies, institutions, and markets. The innovations are sometimes divided into product or process variants, with product innovations exemplified by new derivative contracts, new corporate securities, or new forms of pooled investment products, and process improvements typified by new means of distributing securities, processing transactions, or pricing transactions. In practice, even this innocuous differentiation is not clear, as process and product innovations are often linked. Innovation includes the acts of invention and diffusion, although in point of fact these two are related, as most financial innovations are evolutionary adaptations of prior products.

As noted before, one of the major challenges associated with the study of financial innovation is the lack of data. Studies of manufacturing innovation traditionally focus on R&D spending and patenting. Given the rarity with which financial service firms report R&D spending and the fact that financial patents were used only infrequently until recently, these measures are unlikely to be satisfactory in this context. Most alternatives are also troubling. Consider, for instance, the listings of new securities compiled by Thomson Reuters' Securities Data Company (SDC), which maintains the leading database of corporate new issues. First, much of the innovation in financial services has taken place outside the realm of publicly traded securities, such as new Automatic Teller Machines and insurance products. Second, as Tufano (2003) points out, many of the "novel" securities identified in the SDC database are minor variants of existing securities, often promulgated by investment banks seeking to differentiate themselves from their peers.

Thus, saying much systematically about the variation in the rate of financial innovation across time and space is challenging. Lerner (2006) takes a first step toward addressing this gap by developing a measure of financial innovation based on news stories in the *Wall Street Journal.* The analysis finds that financial innovation is characterized by a disproportionate role of smaller firms. More specifically, a doubling in firm size is associated with less than a doubling in innovation generation. Moreover, firms that are less profitable in their respective sectors are disproportionately more innovative. These results are consistent with depictions by Silber (1975, 1983) that more marginal firms will contribute the bulk of the financial innovations. In addition, older, less leveraged firms located in regions with more financial innovation appear to be more innovative. Few patterns are seen over time, though this may reflect the fact that the analysis is confined to the years 1990 through 2002. Financial innovations seem to be disproportionately associated with US-based firms, though this may reflect the use of a US-based publication to identify the innovations.

A major focus of writings on financial innovations has been the attempt to catalog the inventions. Goetzmann and Rouwenhorst (2005) group the nineteen financial innovations they study into three categories, based on whether they (a) facilitate the transfer of value through time; (b) allow the ability to contract on future values; and (c) permit the negotiability of claims. There are almost as many schemes as authors, but many of these share the feature of looking through to the underlying functions performed by the innovations. Merton's (1992) and Crane et al.'s (1995) schemes are illustrative. In particular, they identify six functions that innovations—and more generally, economies—perform:

1. Moving funds across time and space (e.g., savings accounts)
2. The pooling of funds (e.g., mutual funds)
3. Managing risk (e.g., insurance and many derivatives products)
4. Extracting information to support decision making (e.g., markets that provide price information, such as extracting default probabilities from bonds or credit default swaps)
5. Addressing moral hazard and asymmetric information problems (e.g., contracting by venture capital firms)
6. Facilitating the sale or purchase of goods and services through a payment system (e.g., cash, debit cards, credit cards)

Not surprisingly, no classification scheme is perfect, and more importantly, given their complexity of design and use, many innovations span multiple categories in this scheme and its alternatives.

In many respects, financial innovations resemble any other kind of invention. Among the points of commonality are:

- These innovations are not easy or cheap to develop and diffuse. While the cost of developing many security innovations is considerably smaller than for manufacturing or scientific innovations, investment banks frequently retain many highly compensated PhDs and MBAs and lawyers to design new products and services. Furthermore, innovators must frequently expend considerable resources developing distribution channels for their products.
- These innovations are risky. Tufano (1989) documents that the vast majority of security discoveries do not lead to more than a handful of subsequence issuances.
- Innovation is frequently linked closely with the competitive dynamics between incumbents and entrants, as suggested by the work just cited.
- Firms have struggled, at least until recently (and perhaps temporarily), to obtain intellectual property protection, akin to many emerging industries.

But in other respects, financial innovation is quite different. It is to these dissimilarities that we turn in the next section.

11.2 What Is Different—and Challenging—about Financial Innovation?

In general, economists' thinking about financial innovation has been shaped by their experience with innovation in manufacturing industries. Assessments of the nature and consequences of innovation in the service sector are rarer. Financial innovation illustrates the limitations of our understanding of nonmanufacturing innovation in particularly sharp relief.

At first glance, it might be unclear why financial innovation should differ from other types of new product development. In the canonical accounts of financial innovation (most importantly, Ross [1976] and Allen and Gale [1994]), innovation is driven by investor demand for a particular set of cash flows. Astute intermediaries recognize this demand and engineer securities with the desired characteristics. By splitting up or combining cash flows of existing securities, the intermediaries can create profits (at least in the short run) for themselves and increase social welfare. Described in this way, the financial innovation process seems little different from Apple's decision to introduce a tablet that combined features of a laptop and a cell phone, or Tropicana's introduction of orange juice with added calcium.

But these similarities between financial and other forms of innovation can be deceptive. In this section, we posit three sets of issues that make the study of financial innovation particularly challenging:

- The financial system is highly interconnected. As a result, a financial innovation is likely to generate a complex web of externalities, both positive and negative. Therefore, assessing the social consequences of financial innovation can be very challenging.
- Financial innovations are highly dynamic. As an innovation diffuses from pioneering adopters to more general users, these products frequently change in their underlying structure, the way that they are marketed, and how they are used. These transformations mean that the consequences of an innovation may change over time.
- While certainly many forms of innovation, such as pharmaceuticals, are subject to regulation, the regulation of new financial products and services is particularly complex and dynamic, and new financial reform has an uncertain impact on the pace and direction of financial innovation.

11.2.1 The Challenge Measuring Social Welfare

Since the pioneering work of Trajtenberg (1990), economists have understood that the benefits of innovation can be empirically quantified. These studies have focused on products whose features can be reduced to a relatively modest number of attributes and price. Each innovation can then be understood as offering a different combination of attributes. Often within the context of a discrete choice model, economists then use data on actual attributes, prices, and sales to estimate the underlying demand and utility functions of the representative consumer. The benefits from an innovation can then be quantified as the increase in social welfare associated with having the new set of choices compared to the ones available in the earlier period.[1]

1. Other important papers in the literature on the quantification of the economic benefits of innovations and new goods more generally include Berry, Levinsohn, and Pakes (1995); Bresnahan (1986); Hausman (1997); and Petrin (2002).

At least in theory, such a framework would allow one to assess whether innovations tend to significantly boost social welfare, or whether much of the spending on new product development is socially wasteful, motivated instead by the rent-seeking behavior and the desire to steal market share from competitors as Dasgupta and Stiglitz (1980) suggest.

To be sure, many innovations give rise to externalities that would resist this type of straightforward analysis. For instance, the widespread diffusion of cellular telephones and text messaging has led by many accounts to an increase in automobile accidents caused by distracted drivers—and has led to regulations to prohibit these uses of the innovations. Similarly, medical advances that prolong the lives of cancer patients may have the consequence of putting greater financial pressures on Social Security and Medicare as the longevity (and associated medical costs) of senior citizens increase.

The particular challenge associated with assessing the social impact of financial innovation lies in the fact that so many of its consequences are in the form of externalities. On the positive side of the ledger, many financial innovations address broad social needs. For example, venture capitalists provide a blend of money and expertise to help young firms succeed; credit cards extend credit but also simplify the process of purchasing goods and services. Moreover, in many instances, the decisions of early adopters have important consequences for others. For instance, as the pool of mutual funds has proliferated and funds have grown, upfront and annual fees associated with these products have generally fallen. As a result, the decision to partake of a financial innovation changes the attractiveness of the innovation for others.

But at the same time, in many instances these innovations have consequences to nontransacting parties that may be less desirable. To return to the subject of Krugman's quote earlier, the collapse in the markets for many of the complex securities based on mortgages contributed to a dramatic reduction in credit availability throughout the economy. Thus, these innovations indirectly may have led to numerous small businesses facing much higher interest rates or being unable to access credit at all, even though they had no involvement with the mortgage market. Even "well-meaning" innovations, such as process innovations that reduce the costs and effort of refinancing mortgages can lead to unintended consequences in the economy, a point emphasized by Khandani, Lo, and Merton (2009).

These detrimental effects are frequently referred to as "systemic risk." One immediate challenge is that systemic risk itself is a poorly defined notion. This confusion is captured by the following quote from Alan Greenspan (1995):

> It would be useful to central banks to be able to measure systemic risk accurately, but its very definition is still somewhat unsettled. It is generally agreed that systemic risk represents a propensity for some sort of

> significant financial system disruption, . . . [but] until we have a common theoretical paradigm for the causes of systemic stress, any consensus of how to measure systemic risk will be difficult to achieve. (7)

Schwarcz (2008), after compiling the various definitions that have been used in policy circles, suggests the following definition:

> [T]he risk that (i) an economic shock such as market or institutional failure triggers (through a panic or otherwise) either (X) the failure of a chain of markets or institutions or (Y) a chain of significant losses to financial institutions, (ii) resulting in increases in the cost of capital or decreases in its availability, often evidenced by substantial financial-market price volatility. (204)

Given the interconnected nature of the financial system, it would be surprising if the most widely adopted financial innovations did not contribute to systemic risk as defined earlier, as well as "systemic benefits." When the bulk of the social impact is through positive and negative externalities, it is unclear how one should seek to assess welfare consequences of innovations.

11.2.2 The Challenge of Dynamic Impacts

The word "innovation" is used by economists to indicate a change, and financial innovation must be understood as part of a process of change. Financial innovations—especially systemically important ones—demonstrate two related dynamic features: the innovation spiral and a change in the how products are used over time.

Merton (1992) coined the term "innovation spiral" to describe the process whereby one financial innovation begets the next. Sometimes this spiral has one successful innovation providing the raw material, or building blocks, for another. For example, the innovation of a futures market in a particular commodity can allow financial engineers to build specialized and more complex over-the-counter (OTC) products using dynamic trading strategies. An innovation need not be successful, however, to be part of the innovation spiral. Tufano (1995) and Mason et al. (1995) describe a sequence of financial innovations, most of which were unsuccessful, but nonetheless provided information that led to a subsequent wave of newer products. Persons and Warther (1997) formally model this spiral process. The innovation spiral is not unique to financial innovations; elsewhere one innovation can produce follow-on effects including lowering the barriers to subsequent innovation. For example, in electronics, semiconductor innovations have made possible a host of products ranging from personal computers to industrial applications to handheld devices. Similarly, the technology developed for unsuccessful pioneering personal digital assistants, such as Go's Pen Operating System and Apple's Newton, ultimately led to the success of the BlackBerry and iPhone. Once one acknowledges the existence of an innovation spiral, one must recognize that actions that might discourage a certain innovation could have implications for the development of subsequent innovations.

Much of the research on innovation deals with the dynamics of the adoption process; that is, how a new product, process, or service is taken up, first by innovators, then early adopters, early majority, late majority, and laggards. This adoption process is typically characterized by an S-curve (or logistic function), which plots the number of adopters as a function of time. There is a substantial body of work on adoption rates, but Rogers (1962) is generally credited with codifying and advancing this literature. An S-curve adoption pattern suggests that, almost by definition, an innovation is unlikely to have economy-wide or systemic implications until it has been adopted fairly widely.

Most of the work on the diffusion of innovations deals with the characteristics of the population of potential adopters and of the actual adopters. Generally, more knowledgeable, sophisticated, and risk-taking individuals adopt innovations earlier. Generalizing across the landscape of innovations (not just financial breakthroughs), Rogers highlights five types of adopters:

- Innovators, the initial ones to take up the innovation. These are typically younger, better educated, and have higher social status than later adopters.
- Early adopters, who often serve as opinion leaders in shaping others' decision to adopt the product.
- The early majority, who adopt an innovation after a varying time lag.
- The late majority, who approach innovations with skepticism and wait until most of society has adopted the innovation.
- The laggards, who are the last to adopt an innovation, and tend to be older and of lower social status and with limited resources.

The mechanisms behind these broad patterns have attracted extensive research in subsequent years. For instance, Coleman, Katz, and Menzel (1966) highlighted how these patterns are driven by direct social ties between potential adopters; Burt (1987) has emphasized more diffuse connections with third parties; and Granovetter (1978) explained many of the differences because of differing psychological thresholds.

Not only do the identities of adopters change over time, but sometimes the way in which products are used can evolve. Early adopters may not only be more aware of the features—and limitations—of new products, but use them differently. For example, it is typically difficult to get an issuer and set of investors to be the first to issue and buy a new security. These innovation partners are often informally part of the product development process, consulted by the bankers who are trying to bring the product to market. They would typically be much more informed about the strengths and weaknesses of a product than a late majority adopter, who might take a product's widespread usage to signal its lack of flaws. For example, in litigations involving "failed" financial products, it seems anecdotally that later adopters are more likely to sue, claiming that they were unaware of the potential flaws with the product, sometimes even claiming they never even read the security documents. (Consistent with these claims, Lerner [2010] shows that those who litigate patented financial innovations are disproportionately smaller, more marginal firms, with less financial resources. Similarly, studies of litigation of new securities offerings suggest that much of the litigation is initiated by relatively unsophisticated individual investors [Alexander 1991].)

This challenge is captured in a model of financial innovation by Gennaioli, Shleifer, and Vishny (2010). The paper argues that a financial innovation can address the demand for clients for a particular set of cash flows and thus be socially beneficial. But they suggest that the risks associated with these new products' cash flows may be systematically underestimated by these investors. In this case, they show, there may be excessive issuance of novel securities by financial institutions. Once the investors suddenly realize these risks, there will be an exodus back to traditional, safer products. In this way, financial innovation can add to the fragility of the overall financial system.

Given the importance of externalities in financial innovation, the changing awareness of adopters may have broad implications. While some late adopters of smartphones might use only a portion of their newest gadget's technology, the social costs of their ignorance might be minimal. However, a late-adopting, unsophisticated investor or borrower using a new complex instrument might find himself with an exposure or liability that sophisticated earlier adopters fully appreciated. Understanding the dynamics of adoption provides some insight into the potential for financial innovations to give rise to externalities and systemic risks. We may need to understand especially the processes whereby innovations become widely accepted—by whom and for what purpose—to understand systemic risks.

An appreciation of the innovation spiral and the diffusion processes for financial innovations highlights the challenges facing much traditional empirical work on financial innovation. First, to understand social welfare, it is problematic to study a single financial innovation out of context, as any one innovation—whether successful or not—will tend to influence the path of future innovations. Second, most empirical studies, but especially structured interventions like randomized control trials, document the experiences of early adopters, and the way in which the product is used by these sophisticated adopters. However, the experiences of later adopters—and the ways in which innovations are adapted for multiple uses as they are diffused more broadly—may give greater clues as to the social welfare implications of financial innovations. Finally, the long time spans over which financial innovations diffuse and the innovation spiral that an initial innovation often engenders suggest that the researcher needs an extended time frame, or an historical approach to studying financial innovations.

11.2.3 The Interaction between Regulation and Innovation

The relationship between financial innovation and regulation is complex. There has been much written about regulation (and taxes) as being important stimuli for financial innovation. Miller (1986) expounds on this link at some length, and it is fairly easy to find financial products whose origins can be tied, at least in part, to regulations or taxes. For example, in the nineteenth century, the innovation of low-par stock was an outgrowth of state securities taxes (Tufano 1995). In the 1980s, the growth—and preferred stock form—of various adjustable rate products was stimulated by intercorporate dividend deduction rules. More recently, bank capital rules have encouraged the creation or adaptation of a variety of capital securities.

Not only does regulation give rise to certain innovations, but then regulators need to "catch up" with the products, in a cat-and-mouse process that Kane (1977) labels the regulatory dialectic. Innovators look for opportunities that exploit regulatory gaps, regulators impose new regulations, and each new regulation gives rise to new opportunities for more innovation. In this back and forth, the regulatory system can be at a disadvantage for a variety of reasons. First, many regulatory bodies have mandates that are defined by product or by institution, rather than by function. For example, consider just a few of the products that deliver equity-index exposure: baskets of stocks, index funds, exchange-traded funds (ETFs), futures contracts, index-linked annuities, indexed-linked certificates of deposit, and various structured notes. Suppose that one wanted to regulate equity exposures broadly. One would have to coordinate activities between the Securities and Exchange Commission (SEC), Commodity Futures Trading Commission, banking regulators, and state insurance regulators just for a start. Without broad mandates or functional jurisdictions, opportunities for regulatory arbitrage through innovation will occur. Second, even a well-staffed, reasonably well-paid, and highly talented regulatory agency is up against a world of potential entrepreneurs and innovators. Inevitably, regulation will tend to react to innovations, typically with a lag. From the perspective of systemic risk, this responsive approach may be appropriate, as innovations early in their S-curve adoptions are unlikely to pose economy-wide risks, and are probably bought and sold by the more sophisticated set of adopters.

11.3 A Counterfactual Approach to Studying the Social Welfare Implications of Systemic Financial Innovations

In the wake of the events of the past few years, there have been numerous calls to limit or even ban financial innovation. For example, in a 2009 *Business Week* article entitled "Financial Innovation Under Fire," Coy notes:

> [S]ome economists go further and argue that any financial innovation is guilty until proven innocent. Former International Monetary Fund chief economist Simon Johnson and James Kwak, authors of the popular Baseline Scenario blog, wrote in the summer issue of the journal *Democracy* that innovation often generates unproductive or even destructive transactions. "The presumption should be that innovation in financial products is costly . . . and should have to justify itself against those costs," they wrote.

In April 2009, Fed Chairman Bernanke, while defending financial innovation, noted its precarious state in public debates:

> The concept of financial innovation, it seems, has fallen on hard times. Subprime mortgage loans, credit default swaps, structured investment vehicles, and other more-recently developed financial products have become emblematic of our present financial crisis. Indeed, innovation, once held up as the solution, is now more often than not perceived as the problem.[2]

An interesting sign of the mood is the Security and Exchange Commission's creation of the first new division in thirty years, a Division of Risk, Strategy, and Financial Innovation, implicitly joining "financial innovation" and "risk."[3]

Against this chorus of anti-innovation rhetoric, it is important to carry out rigorous scholarly research to establish the social costs and benefits of financial innovation. Given the large number of financial innovations, it is important to come up with a research strategy that can address the important policy issues of the day. These debates seem to be of various forms: financial innovations' potential to give rise to systemic risks; financial innovations' potential to harm consumers; and "wasteful" use of private resources by financial innovators in rent-seeking behavior. Against this potential list of costs we must analyze innovation's benefits, both direct and indirect.

In this chapter, we focus on the systemic risks and benefits imposed by financial innovations. If an innovation is to have system-wide implications, it must be broadly adopted. This research strategy permits us to focus on widely adopted innovations, rather than narrowly adopted ones or others that were never or barely adopted by users. To study potentially wasteful rent-seeking or some aspects of consumer damage, one would need to include these latter innovations, but they strike us as not being the likely locus of systemic risks or benefits.

How do we define a "systemically important" or "broadly adopted" financial innovation? We use top-down data on the economy to identify these innovations. For example, if one studies the balance sheet of the US

2. http://www.federalreserve.gov/newsevents/speech/bernanke20090417a.htm.
3. http://www.sec.gov/news/press/2009/2009-199.htm.

household over the past sixty years, a number of striking trends emerge, in particular the economic importance of money market mutual funds, mutual funds more generally, and retirement plans. Clearly, these are innovations that were adopted widely in the postwar period.

Then, for a subset of these innovations, we detail the elements of their welfare implications. Using a technique of historians, we not only detail actual outcomes, but also discuss counterfactual histories: What would the economy have been like had this innovation not been invented or popularized? While this method is inherently judgmental, it frames a discussion or debate that attempts to tease out not only the direct costs and benefits, but also the externalities—both positive and negative—associated with each innovation. In the following section, we provide the logic of our selection of these case studies of systemic innovations and a brief primer on the methods of counterfactual history.

11.3.1 Methodology: Criteria for Selection of Case Studies and the Counterfactual Approach

We need a disciplined way to scan the economy to select our case studies. To do this, we consider the major changes in the way that financial functions are delivered to each of the major nongovernmental sectors in the economy. The sectors are (a) households, (b) nonfinancial corporations, (c) financial firms, and (d) public entities. As noted earlier, the functions include six activities: (a) pooling, (b) payments, (c) moving funds across time and space, (d) managing risk, (e) resolving information asymmetries, and (f) extracting information from markets. Our primary frame of reference for our exercise is the United States in the postwar period. (See table 11.1.)

We focus on three case studies: venture capital and private equity, mutual funds and exchange-traded funds, and securitization. This allows us to focus on three of the functions and three of the sectors. In addition, the selection

Table 11.1 **Typology of case studies**

	Households	Nonfinancial firms	Financial firms
Pooling	Mutual funds and exchange-traded funds	Venture capital and private equity	Securitization
Moving money across time and space			
Payments	Card products		
Managing risk	Retirement accounts	Derivatives	
Resolving information asymmetries		Venture capital and private equity	
Extracting information from markets			Derivatives

of these case studies suggests the strengths and weaknesses of a counterfactual approach, as the first two case studies are more amenable to this approach than is the third.

Most economic analyses attempt to measure outcomes of interventions relative to some alternative. We typically exploit cross-sectional and time-series variation—often with large-sample data—to tease out the relative effects of some intervention or innovation. We use control/treatment approaches or randomized control trials to minimize noise and identify phenomena. These methods work well when we have large samples or natural experiments.

Unfortunately, systemic innovations do not lend themselves well to these methods. Because they are systemic, it is difficult to find adequate "control" states. Pre- and posttests are problematic because innovations are adopted over long periods of time. These tests are also difficult because early adopters may not be representative of late adopters—and the way the product is used may vary over time. Randomized control trials do not tend to capture the systemic effects when products are broadly adopted. This is not to say that econometric methods are not useful in understanding financial impacts, but they have meaningful limits, and that complementary approaches can be valuable.

A meaningful alternative is to adopt a historical approach to understanding systemic innovations that span years or decades. There are a number of excellent studies of financial history and economic history, with a few that specialize in financial innovation. Goetzmann and Rouwenhorst's edited volume (2005) contains a set of nineteen essays on particular innovations, including the invention of interest in Sumerian Loans, the creation of Roman Shares, the origins of paper money in China, Dutch perpetuities, modern European annuities, inflation indexed bonds in early America, and the first Eurobonds in the nineteenth century. Davis' (1994) book, *A History of Money,* spans 3000 BC to the twentieth century. With this wide sweep, it covers a number of innovations in its scope. Beyond documenting the various forms of instruments created over time, Davis traces the evolution of financial institutions, for example, the working-class financial institutions of friendly societies, cooperatives, and building societies in Europe in the nineteenth century. Kindleberger (1984), Cameron et al. (1967), and Cameron (1972) are other fine examples of centuries-long, multicountry historical studies of the evolution of financial systems. Cameron (1972), studying banking in the early stages of industrialization, notes that financial innovation is "necessary for the realization of (technical innovation)" and in combination can achieve "the pooling of risks and economies of scale in finance as well as in manufacture." However, the role of some innovations in creating financial crises is highlighted in Kindleberger (1984, 270):

> Time and again in these pages it has been stressed that when the macroeconomic system is constrained by a tight supply of money, it creates more, at least for a time. Shortage of gold and silver has led to substitution of copper, pepper, salt, that is, to more primitive commodity monies, or to more sophisticated substitutes such as various forms of paper (and plastic): bank money, bank notes, bills of exchange, especially chains of bills of exchange, bank deposits, open-book credits, credit cards, certificates of deposit, Euro-currencies and so on.

In his analysis, these expansions of the money supply sometimes lead to overextension, distress, speculation, and at times panics and crashes.

While a historical approach has the advantage of intensely studying phenomena, it may not address relative performance implications, unless one adopts a comparative historical approach, for example comparing one period or country to another. Unfortunately, however, these comparisons often suffer from a great deal of endogeneity that makes interpretation difficult. For example, while we could compare economies with considerable financial innovation to those less innovative, it is highly unlikely that these comparisons would be ceteris paribus. Financial innovation, and certainly financial development more generally, is not unrelated to economic development, so these types of comparisons are problematic. For example, the adoption of mutual funds is related to a number of metrics of financial development and to the state of legal institutions (Khorana, Servaes, and Tufano 2005).

Scholars have used various approaches to deal with these inevitable issues by studying counterfactual or virtual histories. In essence, a counterfactual approach requires the analyst to posit "what would have happened if . . . had happened (or not happened)." This method has been used—and debated—by historians, economic historians, political scientists, sociologists, and philosophers. For reviews, see, for example, Ferguson (1997, chapter 1), Cowan and Foray (2002), Sylvan and Majeski (1998), Bunzl (2004), and Tetlock and Lebow (2001). While dismissed by some as a "mere parlour game" (Carr 1987), and referred to in scatological terms by others (see ref. in Ferguson 1999), the method has been used extensively.

Counterfactual reasoning seems to have been adopted most extensively in international relations and politics. For example, Ferguson (2000) is a collection of papers that study a variety of counterfactuals: "What if Charles I had avoided the Civil War? What if there had been no American Revolution? What if Germany had invaded Britain in May 1940?" Perhaps the most well-known example of the method (among economists) is Fogel's groundbreaking 1964 book *Railroad and American Economic Growth: Essays in Econometric History.* The book studies the impact of the railroads by trying to assess how the economy would have developed in their absence, as noted in Fogel's preface:

> The pages that follow contain a critical evaluation of the proposition that railroads were indispensible to American economic growth during the nineteenth century . . . [I] estimate the amount by which production possibilities of the nation would have been reduced if agricultural commodities could not have been shipped by railroads. (vii)

Fogel combines counterfactual reasoning with empirical estimates of development. He compares observed gross domestic product (GDP) increases with three counterfactuals: no railroads at all, an extension of internal navigation (canals), and the improvement of country roads. In essence, Fogel's work demonstrates the core elements of counterfactual analysis. First, he identifies an important topic where the facts do not permit the type of replicability that underscores much of scientific inquiry. Second, he identifies a set of alternative paths of history. Subsequent work has differentiated between "miracle worlds" and "plausible worlds," based on the likelihood of the alternative to have played out. In Fogel's examples, he did not posit air travel (a miracle, to be sure, in the nineteenth century), but rather quite plausible alternative transportation developments. Finally, Fogel rigorously attempts to analyze the economic implications of these alternatives using a well-defined metric.

Fogel was awarded the Nobel Prize in 1993 for having given birth to cliometrics, or new economic history. In its award, the Nobel committee made clear the importance of Fogel's pioneering of the counterfactual approach:

> Robert W. Fogel's scientific breakthrough was his book (1964) on the role of the railways in the American economy. Joseph Schumpeter and Walt W. Rostow had earlier, with general agreement, asserted that modern economic growth was due to certain important discoveries having played a vital role in development. Fogel tested this hypothesis with extraordinary exactitude, and rejected it. The sum of many specific technical changes, rather than a few great innovations, determined the economic development. We find it intuitively plausible that the great transport systems play a decisive role in development. Fogel constructed a hypothetical alternative, a so called counterfactual historiography; that is he compared the actual course of events with the hypothetical to allow a judgment of the importance of the railways. He found that they were not absolutely necessary in explaining economic development and that their effect on the growth of GNP was less than three per cent. Few books on the subject of economic history have made such an impression as Fogel's. His use of counterfactual arguments and cost-benefit analysis made him an innovator of economic historical methodology.[4]

Fogel's use of counterfactual arguments flew in the face of "common sense" and demonstrated the power of this method. Just as the innovation

4. Taken from http://nobelprize.org/nobel_prizes/economics/laureates/1993/press.html.

of railroads gave rise to some changes in the economy, but perhaps not as much as originally thought, financial innovations are long-lived phenomena that can substantially alter the economic landscape—but perhaps not as much as originally thought. We use counterfactual reasoning and methods to structure our exploration of the social consequences of these innovations. Our goal is not to definitively determine whether recent financial innovations were or were not socially valuable. Rather, we lay out an approach to make progress on this problem, and challenge others to use this approach systemically. Our three case studies provide some factual background on the innovations, then lay out—for debate—counterfactual histories and thoughts about the implications of each. A full analysis, à la Fogel, of the counterfactual history of each innovation would be beyond the scope of this chapter.

While we adopt this method as a complement to existing historical, experimental, and econometric methods, we acknowledge the many strong and legitimate criticisms of it, and of Fogel's work. There are important, and quite specific, critiques of the calculations employed by Fogel by Nerlove (1966), McClelland (1968), and David (1969), among others. In particular, David's (1969) critique focuses on problems caused by inadequate consideration of complementaries (e.g., passenger transportation or changes in inventories to reflect different transport speeds), path-dependent adoption processes (e.g., learning effects or returns to scale), finding the correct scaled metric for measuring social benefits, or the challenge of taking a partial (vs. general) equilibrium approach. This latter general point lies at the heart of the criticism—and appeal—of counterfactual analysis, as summarized by Goldin (1995, 195):

> The notion of a counterfactual was hard for many historians to swallow. It involved the hypothetical removal of the largest enterprise at the time, the first big business in America, one of the most productive sectors, and some of the wealthiest Americans, to mention just a few parts of the mental experiment. But, noted Fogel, those who were making claims about the indispensability of the railroad were implicitly invoking precisely this experiment. He was merely making the claim explicit and subjecting it to hard evidence.

In some sense, the instances where counterfactual analysis is most problematic—where an innovation is intrinsically bound up with the rest of the economy for decades—are precisely those instances where it is useful to complement existing research with this more provocative method. A full quantification of the social welfare consequences of removing railroads (or mutual funds or venture capital) from the economy is daunting, but the audacity of asking the question forces our profession to try to address the many issues that bedeviled Fogel and his critics. If this method provokes debate and criticism (and additional work) we will have achieved some of our objectives, moving the discussion beyond simplistic notions about financial innovation.

11.3.2 Venture Capital and Private Equity

A Brief History

Long before the creation of the venture capital and private equity industry, fast-growing firms were able to raise financing. Banks provided debt in the form of loans, and for more long-run, riskier investments, wealthy individuals provided equity.

But by the time of the Great Depression of the 1930s, there was a widespread perception that the existing ways of financing fast-growing young firms were inadequate. Not only were many promising companies going unfunded, but investors with high net worth frequently did not have the time or skills to work with young firms to address glaring management deficiencies. Nor were the alternatives set up by the Roosevelt administration during the New Deal—such as the Reconstruction Finance Corporation—seen as satisfactory. The rigidity of the loan evaluation criteria, the extensive red-tape associated with the award process, and the fears of political interference and regulations all suggested a need for an alternative.

The first formal venture capital firm was established with both private and social returns in mind. American Research and Development (ARD) grew out of the concerns that the United States, having been pushed out of the depression by the stimulus of wartime spending by the federal government, would soon revert to economic lethargy when the war ended. In October 1945, Ralph Flanders, then head of the Federal Reserve Bank of Boston, argued that if this danger was to be addressed, a new enterprise was needed, with the goal of financing new businesses. He argued that the enterprise would not only need to be far more systematic in "selecting the most attractive possibilities and spreading the risk" than most individual investors had been, but would need to tap into the nation's "great accumulation of fiduciary funds" (i.e., pension funds and other institutional capital) if it was to be successful in the long term.

The ARD was formed a year later to try to realize this vision. Flanders recruited a number of civic and business leaders to join in the effort, including MIT president Karl Compton. But the day-to-day management of the fund fell on the shoulders of Harvard Business School professor Georges F. Doriot. The ARD in its communications emphasized that its goal was to fund and aid new companies in order to generate "an increased standard of living for the American people."

Flanders, Doriot, and their contemporaries realized that the financing of young, growing, and restructuring companies was a risky business. Information problems made it difficult to assess these companies and permitted opportunistic behavior by entrepreneurs after the financing was received. These risks had deterred investors from providing capital to these firms.

To illustrate such problems, if the firm raises equity from outside investors, the manager has an incentive to engage in wasteful expenditures (e.g., lavish offices) because he may benefit disproportionately from these but does not bear their entire cost. Similarly, if the firm raises debt, the manager may increase risk to undesirable levels. Because providers of capital recognize these problems, outside investors demand a higher rate of return than would be the case if the funds were internally generated. Additional problems may appear in the types of more mature companies in which private equity firms invest. For instance, entrepreneurs might invest in strategies or projects that have high personal returns but low expected monetary payoffs to shareholders.

Even if the manager wants to maximize firm value, information gaps may make raising external capital more expensive or even preclude it entirely. Equity offerings of companies may be associated with a "lemons" problem: that is, if the manager is better informed about the company's investment opportunities and acts in the interest of current shareholders, then he will only issue new shares when the company's stock is overvalued. Indeed, numerous studies have documented that stock prices decline upon the announcement of equity issues, largely because of the negative signal sent to the market. This "lemons" problem leads investors to be less willing to invest at attractive valuations in young or restructuring companies, or even to invest at all.

The ARD established an approach to addressing these problems that venture capital and private equity groups have followed ever since. First, by intensively scrutinizing companies before providing capital, and only funding a small fraction of those seeking funds, they could alleviate some of the information gaps and reduce capital constraints. Second, they employed a variety of tools that allowed them to monitor and control firms after the transactions. These included the use of convertible securities with powerful control rights, the syndication and staging of investments, the provision of oversight through formal board seats and information rights, the incentivization of management through extensive equity holdings, and informal coaching of management. Finally, there was a real effort to certify the funded entrepreneurs as being different from their peers, which facilitated their ability to enter into alliances, get access to investment bankers, and so forth. The tools that venture capital and private equity investors use in this difficult environment enable companies ultimately to receive the financing that they cannot raise from other sources.

The activity in the private equity industry increased dramatically in the late 1970s and early 1980s. Industry observers attributed much of the shift to the US Department of Labor's clarification of the Employee Retirement

Income Security Act's "prudent man" rule in 1979. Prior to this year, the legislation limited the ability of pension funds to invest substantial amounts of money into venture capital or other high-risk asset classes. The Department of Labor's clarification of the rule explicitly allowed pension managers to invest in high-risk assets, including private equity. Numerous specialized funds—concentrating in areas such as leveraged buyouts, mezzanine transactions, and such hybrids as venture leasing—sprang up during these years.

The subsequent years saw both very good and trying times for private equity investors. On the one hand, the 1980s saw venture capitalists back many of the most successful high-technology companies, including Cisco Systems, Genentech, Microsoft, and Sun Microsystems. Numerous successful buyouts—such as Avis, Beatrice, Dr. Pepper, Gibson Greetings, and McCall Pattern—garnered considerable public attention during that period. At the same time, commitments to the private equity industry during this decade were very uneven. The annual flow of money into venture capital funds increased by a factor of ten during the first half of the 1980s, but steadily declined from 1987 through 1991. Buyouts underwent an even more dramatic rise through the 1980s, followed by a precipitous fall at the end of the decade.

Much of this pattern was driven by the changing fortunes of private equity investments. Returns on venture capital funds had declined sharply in the mid-1980s after being exceedingly attractive in the 1970s. This fall was apparently triggered by overinvestment in a few industries, such as computer hardware, and the entry of many inexperienced venture capitalists. Buyout returns underwent a similar decline in the late 1980s, due in large part to the increased competition between groups for transactions. Kaplan and Stein (1993) documented that of the sixty-six largest buyouts completed during the market peak (between 1986 and 1988), 38 percent experienced financial distress, which they define as default or an actual or attempted restructuring of debt obligations due to difficulties in making payments, and 27 percent actually did default on debt repayments, often in conjunction with a Chapter 11 filing. Kaplan and Schoar (2005) and other papers provide indirect supporting evidence showing that the performance of both venture and private equity funds is negatively correlated with inflows into these funds. Funds raised during periods of high capital inflows—which are typically associated with market peaks—perform far worse than their peers.

The 1990s and 2000s saw these patterns repeated on an unprecedented scale. The second half of the 1990s saw dramatic growth and excellent returns in venture capital investments; the 2000s saw tremendous growth of private equity funds. This recovery was triggered by several factors. The exit of many inexperienced investors after the earlier collapse ensured that the remaining groups faced less competition for transactions. The healthy market for initial public offerings during much of the 1990s meant that it was easier for venture funds to exit transactions, leading to high returns. Meanwhile, the extent of technological innovation—particularly in information technology-related industries—created extraordinary opportunities for venture capitalists. The mid-2000s saw unprecedented availability of debt on favorable terms, which enabled buyout groups to highly leverage firms and make high returns likely. New capital commitments to both venture and buyout funds rose in response to these changing circumstances, increasing to record levels. Once the enabling condition deteriorated, the level of fundraising and investment dropped sharply. Funds were left with large numbers of transactions that could not be exited, and investors faced the certainty of a sharp drop in returns.

The Broader Social Impact: Venture Capital

Clearly, the innovations of venture capital (VC) and private equity funds exert a major impact on the fates of individual companies. But does all this fundraising and investing influence the overall economic landscape as well? We will look at evidence regarding venture capital first, and then private equity funds. One caveat should be noted upfront: all these studies examine the last three decades, with a particular emphasis on the experience of the United States, a time and place that are certainly not representative of the entirety of economic history. There is little choice, however, given the relative youth of these intermediaries and the lack of data on earlier, pioneering funds.

To assess this question, we can look at studies of the experience of the market with the most developed and seasoned venture capital industry, the United States. Despite the fact that venture activity is particularly well-developed in this nation, the reader might be skeptical as to whether this activity would noticeably impact innovation: for most of past three decades, investments made by the entire venture capital sector totaled less than the research-and-development and capital-expenditure budgets of large, individual companies such as IBM, General Motors, or Merck.

One way to explore this question is to examine the impact of venture investing on wealth, jobs, and other financial measures across a variety of industries. Though it would be useful to track the fate of every venture capital-financed company and find out where the innovation or technology ended up, in reality only those companies that have gone public can be tracked. Consistent information on venture-backed firms that were acquired or went out of business simply does not exist. Moreover, investments in companies that eventually go public yield much higher returns than support given to firms that get acquired or remain privately held.

These firms have had an unmistakable effect on the US economy. In late 2008, 895 firms were publicly traded on US markets after receiving their private financing from venture capitalists (this does not include the firms that went public, but were subsequently acquired or delisted). One way to assess the overall impact of the venture capital industry is to look at the economic "weight" of venture-backed companies in the context of the larger economy.[5] By late 2008, venture-backed firms that had gone public made up over 13 percent of the total number of public firms in existence in the United States at that time. And of the total market value of public firms ($28 trillion), venture-backed companies came in at $2.4 trillion—8.4 percent.

Venture-funded firms also made up over 4 percent (nearly $1 trillion dollars) of total sales ($22 trillion) of all US public firms at the time. Contrary to the general perception that venture-supported companies are not profitable, operating income margins for these companies hit an average of 6.8 percent—close to the average public-company profit margin of 7.1 percent. Finally, those public firms supported by venture funding employed 6 percent of the total public-company workforce—most of these jobs were high-salaried, skilled positions in the technology sector. Clearly, venture investing fuels a substantial portion of the US economy.

This impact is quite modest in industries dominated by mature companies such as the manufacturing industries. But contrast those industries with highly innovative ones, and the picture looks completely different. For example, companies in the computer software and hardware industry that received venture backing during their gestation as private firms represented more than 75 percent of the software industry's value. Venture-financed firms also play a central role in the biotechnology, computer services, and semiconductor industries. In recent years, the scope of venture groups' activity has been expanding rapidly in the critical energy and environmental field, though the impact of these investments remains to be seen. Presumably, these are industries where the externalities generated by new activity are the greatest.

It might be thought that it would not be difficult to address the question of the impact of venture capital on innovation in a more rigorous manner. For instance, one could seek to explain across industries and time whether, controlling for R&D spending, venture capital funding has an impact on various measures of innovation. But even a simple model of the relationship between venture capital, R&D, and innovation suggests that this approach is likely to give misleading estimates.

This is because both venture funding and innovation could be positively related to a third unobserved factor, the arrival of technological opportunities. Thus, there could be more innovation at times that there was more venture capital, not because the venture capital caused the innovation, but rather because the venture capitalists reacted to some fundamental technological shock that was sure to lead to more innovation. To date, only a handful of papers have attempted to address these challenging issues.

5. This analysis is based on the authors' tabulation of unpublished data from SDC Venture Economics, with supplemental information from Compustat and the Center for Research into Securities Prices (CRSP) databases.

The first of these papers, by Hellmann and Puri (2002), examines a sample of 170 recently formed firms in Silicon Valley, including both venture-backed and nonventure firms. Using questionnaire responses, they find evidence that venture capital financing is related to product market strategies and outcomes of startups. They find that firms that are pursuing what they term an innovator strategy (a classification based on the content analysis of survey responses) are significantly more likely and faster to obtain venture capital. The presence of a venture capitalist is also associated with a significant reduction in the time taken to bring a product to market, especially for innovators (probably because these firms can focus more on innovating and less on raising money). Furthermore, firms are more likely to list obtaining venture capital as a significant milestone in the life cycle of the company as compared to other financing events. There seems to be a link between this form of financial innovation and more traditional product innovation.

The results suggest significant interrelations between investor type and product market dimensions, and a role of venture capital in encouraging innovative companies. But this does not definitively answer the question of whether venture capitalists cause innovation. For instance, we might observe personal injury lawyers at accident sites, handing out business cards in the hopes of drumming up clients. But just because the lawyer is at the scene of the car crash does not mean that he caused the crash. In a similar vein, the possibility remains that more innovative firms choose to finance themselves with venture capital, rather than venture capital causing firms to be more innovative.

Kortum and Lerner (2000) visit the same question. Here, the study looks at the aggregate level: did the participation of venture capitalists in any given industry over the past few decades lead to more or less innovation? It might be thought that such an analysis would have the same problem as the aforementioned personal injury lawyer story. Put another way, even if we see an increase in venture funding and a boost in innovation, how can we be sure that one caused the other?

The authors address these concerns about causality by looking back over the industry's history. In particular, as we discussed earlier, a major discontinuity in the recent history of the venture capital industry was the US Department of Labor's clarification of the Employee Retirement Income Security Act in the late 1970s, a policy shift that freed pensions to invest in venture capital. This shift led to a sharp increase in the funds committed to venture capital. This type of external change should allow one to figure out what the impact of venture capital was, because it is unlikely to be related to how many or how few entrepreneurial opportunities there were to be funded.

Even after addressing these causality concerns, the results suggest that venture funding does have a strong positive impact on innovation. The estimated coefficients vary according to the techniques employed, but on average a dollar of venture capital appears to be three to four times more potent in stimulating patenting than a dollar of traditional corporate R&D.

The estimates therefore suggest that venture capital, even though it averaged less than 3 percent of corporate R&D in the United States from 1983 to 1992, is responsible for a much greater share—perhaps 10 percent—of US industrial innovations in this decade.

A natural worry with the aforementioned analysis is that it looks at the relationship between venture capital and patenting, not venture capital and innovation. One possible explanation is that such funding leads entrepreneurs to protect their intellectual property with patents rather than other mechanisms such as trade secrets. For instance, it may be that the entrepreneurs can fool their venture investors by applying for large number of patents, even if the contributions of many of them are very modest. If this is true, it might be inferred that the patents of venture-backed firms would be lower quality than nonventure-backed patent filings.

How could this question of patent quality be investigated? One possibility is to check the number of patents that cite a particular patent.[6] Higher-quality patents, it has been shown, are cited by other innovators more often than lower-quality ones. Similarly, if venture-backed patents are lower quality, then companies receiving venture funding would be less likely to initiate patent-infringement litigation. (It makes no sense to pay money to engage in the costly process of patent litigation to defend low-quality patents.)

So, what happens when patent quality is measured with these criteria? As it happens, the patents of venture-backed firms are more frequently cited by other patents and are more aggressively litigated—thus it can be concluded that they are high quality. Furthermore, the venture-backed firms more frequently litigate trade secrets, suggesting that they are not simply patenting frantically in lieu of relying on trade-secret protection. These findings reinforce the notion that venture-supported firms are simply more innovative than their nonventure-supported counterparts.

Mollica and Zingales (2007), by way of contrast, focus on regional patterns: as a regional unit, they use the 179 Bureau of Economic Analysis economic areas, which are composed by counties surrounding metropolitan areas. They exploit the regional, cross-industry, and time-series variability of venture investments in the United States to study the impact of venture capital activity on innovation and the creation of new businesses. Again, they grapple with causality issues by using an instrumental variable: as an instrument for the size of VC investments, they use the size of a state pension fund's assets. The idea is that state pension funds are subject to political pressure to invest some of their funds in new businesses in the states. Hence, the size of the state pension fund triggers a shift in the local supply of VC investment, which should help identify the effect of VC on patents.

6. Patent applicants and examiners at the patent office include references to other relevant patents. These serve a legal role similar to that of property markers at the edge of a land holding.

Even with these controls, they find that VC investments have a significant positive effect both on the production of patents and on the creation of new businesses. A one standard deviation increase in VC investment per capita generates an increase in the number of patents of between 4 and 15 percent. An increase of 10 percent in the volume of VC investment increases the total number of new business by 2.5 percent.

The Broader Social Impact: Private Equity

Turning to private equity (PE), in the past decade the growth of this industry has triggered anxiety about the impact of buyouts in markets as diverse as China, Germany, South Korea, the United Kingdom, and the United States. This anxiety is not unreasonable. While the leveraged buyout transactions of the 1980s were scrutinized in a number of important academic analyses, these studies had two important limitations. First, the bulk of the older research focused on a relatively small number of transactions involving previously publicly traded firms based in the United States. But these represent only a very modest fraction of all buyouts. The second limitation of the older research relates to the fact that the industry has grown and evolved tremendously since the 1980s.

A variety of recent research has sought to assess the consequences of private equity investments over a more comprehensive sample. Each study has looked at a particular consequence of the investment process.

First, Strömberg (2008) examined the nature and outcome of the 21,397 private equity transactions worldwide between 1970 and 2007. In the most straightforward possible outcome, the author simply sought to understand the consequences of these transactions. The key findings were:

- Of the exited buyout transactions, only 6 percent end in bankruptcy or financial restructuring. This translates into an annual rate of bankruptcy or major financial distress of 1.2 percent per year. This rate is a lower default rate than for US corporate bond issuers, which has averaged 1.6 percent per year.
- Holding periods for private equity investments have increased, rather than decreased, over the years. Fifty-eight percent of the private equity funds' investments are exited more than five years after the initial transaction. So-called "quick flips" (i.e., exits within two years of investment by private equity fund) account for 12 percent of deals and have also decreased in the last few years.

This study, of course, only examines one small fraction of what would be the consequences of these transactions. It cannot answer the question of whether the bulk of the firms would be worse or better off because of these transactions.

Bloom, Sadun, and Van Reenen (2009) examine management practices across 4,000 PE-owned and other firms in a sample of medium-sized manufacturing firms in Asia, Europe, and the United States using a unique double-blind management survey to score firms across eighteen dimensions. The main goal of the study is to determine whether private equity ownership, relative to other ownership firms, is a way to achieve improved management practices within firms through the introduction of new managers and better management practices.

They find that private equity-owned firms are, on average, the best-managed ownership group. The PE-owned firms are significantly better managed across a wide range of management practices than government, family, and privately-owned firms. This is true even controlling for a range of other firm characteristics such as country, industry, size, and employee skills. The PE-owned firms are particularly strong at operations management practices, such as the adoption of modern lean manufacturing practices, using continuous improvements, and a comprehensive performance documentation process. But because the survey is only a cross-sectional one, they cannot determine whether the private equity groups turned these firms into better managed ones, or simply purchased firms that were better managed in the first place.

Lerner, Sorenson, and Stromberg (2008) examine long-run investments by firms. This work was motivated by the lively debate about the impact of private equity investors on the time horizons of the companies in their portfolios. The private status, according to some, enables managers to proceed with challenging restructurings without the pressure of catering to the market's demands for steadily growing quarterly profits, which can lead to firms focusing on short-run investments. Others have questioned whether private equity-backed firms take a longer-run perspective than their public peers, pointing to practices such as special dividends to equity investors.

In this study, one form of long-run investment was examined: investments in innovation. Innovation offers an attractive testing ground for the issues delineated earlier due to various factors. These factors include the long-run nature of R&D expenditures, their importance to the ultimate health of firms, and the extensive body of work in the economics literature that has documented that the characteristics of patents can be used to assess the nature of both publicly and privately held firms' technological innovations.

The key finding is that patenting levels before and after buyouts are largely unchanged. But firms that undergo a buyout pursue more economically important innovations, as measured by patent citations, in the years after private equity investments. In a baseline analysis, the increase in the key proxy for economic importance is 25 percent. This results from firms focusing on and improving their research in their technologies, where the firms have historically focused.

In a pair of studies, Davis et al. (2008, 2009) have examined the impact of these investments on employment and productivity. The former question has aroused considerable controversy. Critics have claimed huge job losses, while private equity associations and other groups have released several recent studies that claim positive effects of private equity on employment. While efforts to bring data to the issue are highly welcome, many of the prior studies have significant limitations, such as the reliance on surveys with incomplete responses, an inability to control for employment changes in comparable firms, the failure to distinguish cleanly between employment changes at firms backed by venture capital and firms backed by other forms of private equity, and an inability to determine in which nation jobs are being created and destroyed.

The authors constructed and analyzed a data set in order to overcome these limitations and, at the same time, encompass a much larger set of employers and private equity transactions from 1980 to 2005. The study utilizes the Longitudinal Business Database (LBD) at the US Bureau of the Census to follow employment at virtually all private equity-backed companies, before and after private equity transactions.

Among the key results were:

- Employment grows more slowly at establishments that are bought out than at the control group in the year of the private equity transaction and in the two preceding years. The average cumulative employment difference in the two years before the transaction is about 4 percent in favor of controls.
- Employment declines more rapidly in bought-out establishments than in control establishments in the wake of private equity transactions. The average cumulative two-year employment difference is 7 percent in favor of controls. In the fourth and fifth years after the transaction, employment at private equity-backed firms mirrors that of the control group.
- But firms backed by private equity have 6 percent more greenfield job creation, that is, at new facilities in the United States, than the peer group. It appears that the job losses at bought-out establishments in the wake of private equity transactions are largely offset by substantially larger job gains in the form of greenfield job creation by these firms.

In their follow-on study, the authors focus on whether and how labor productivity changed at US manufacturing firms that were targets of private equity transactions in the United States from 1980 to 2005. The interpretation of the patterns regarding employment changes needed to be cautious, because we did not examine productivity changes at these establishments.

The authors find that while firms acquired by private equity groups had higher productivity than their peers at the time of the original acquisition, they experienced in the two-year period after the transaction productivity growth 2 percentage points more than at controls. About 72 percent of this out-performance differential reflects more effective management of existing facilities, rather than the shut-down and opening of firms. (It should be noted that private equity investors are much more likely to close underperforming establishments at the firms they back, as measured by labor productivity.)

A Counterfactual Approach

As noted before, one form of analysis increasingly popular among economic historians is counterfactual reasoning. We can seek to understand the impact of venture capital and private equity by considering the possibilities that these sectors had not developed.[7]

A crucial argument offered by the functional perspective (Merton 1992) is that in the absence of a financial institution, other actors may evolve to play the same function. There are at least three alternative institutions that could have played these roles of venture capitalists and private equity investors: individual investors, governments, and integrated financial institutions. The evidence suggests that in some respects, these entities could have substituted for the missing institutions. But evidence also appears to suggest that these substitute institutions would have faced significant limitations, which are likely to have reduced their effectiveness.

As we mentioned earlier, angel investors were well-established as financiers to entrepreneurs long before the establishment of venture funds. By the last decades of the nineteenth century and the first decades of the twentieth century, wealthy families had established offices to manage their investments. Families such as the Phippes, Rockefellers, Vanderbilts, and Whitneys invested in and advised a variety of business enterprises, including the predecessor entities to AT&T, Eastern Airlines, and McDonnell Douglas.

Lamoreaux, Levenstein, and Sokoloff (2007) examine the financing of entrepreneurial ventures in Cleveland at the turn of twentieth century when, they argue, the region had a status not unlike that of Silicon Valley later in the century. They document that the entrepreneurs largely relied on personal connections to finance breakthroughs, whether through friends, family members, or mentors from earlier employment. These investors provided a bundle of services not unlike those of contemporary venture capitalists, including capital, certification of the new enterprise to strategic partners and other potential investors, and sometimes protection against exploitation by would-be opportunists.

But other evidence suggests that angels have important limitations. Hoberg et al. (2009) obtained access to a remarkable data set of entrepreneurial firms: the legal records of clients of Brobeck, Phleger & Harrison, a prestigious San Francisco law firm that filed for bankruptcy in 2003. They find that among the transactions that required a smaller amount of financ-

7. Another approach would be to identify the evolution of industries where these intermediaries were not active. Because the industries where investments took place were not randomly selected, this approach is fraught with interpretive issues.

ing (which, they argue, was largely a function of exogenous considerations such as the fundamental nature of the technology), the performance of the angel-backed and venture-backed firms were about equal: while the angel deals had a somewhat lower incidence of failure, many of these are inactive. The probability of initial public offerings and acquisitions, outcomes that are most often associated with financial success, was about the same. But among larger transactions, the venture-backed firms were more successful on all dimensions examined. The authors suggest that capital constraints may explain the differences: both types of financing can work for small deals, but the requirements of larger deals makes venture capital a superior mode of financing.

A second alternative source of financing is government funding. This substitute for traditional venture financing has been employed widely, but probably nowhere more extensively than Europe. Dozens of national and region-wide initiatives in recent decades have sought to promote funding for entrepreneurs and venture capital funds. To cite just one of many examples, in 2001, the European Commission provided more than 2 billion euros to the European Investment Fund (EIF); making it Europe's largest venture investor overnight. This amount is very significant relative to the roughly 4 billion euros that were invested by European venture funds in that year.

Through this large investment, the EIF intended to stimulate entrepreneurship. Europe had seen a low level of venture activity for many decades: when the ratio of venture investment to gross domestic product is computed for leading industrialized nations, the European nations are invariably among the lowest.[8] The lack of activity reflected the miserable returns that European venture investments have yielded. Venture Economics' calculations suggest that from the beginning of the industry through the end of 2009, the average European venture fund had an annual return of 1.6 percent: hardly a number to warm the hearts of investors![9] (The comparable number for US-based funds over the same period is 15.0 percent.) Thus, policymakers have argued, the low levels of fund-raising and low historical returns create a need for public financing.

Unfortunately, the numerous efforts launched by the European Union to encourage the financing of new firms have followed a depressingly familiar pattern. Even if the intention of the initiative is to create reasonable-sized funds, by the time every country, and every region in each country, gets its "fair share" of the government's money, the pie has been sliced in very thin pieces indeed. The European Seed Capital Fund Scheme is one telling

8. These calculations are compiled from various publications and websites of the Canadian, European, Israeli, and US (National) venture capital associations, as well as those of the *Asian Venture Capital Journal.* In some nations where venture capital investments are not clearly delineated, we employ seed and start-up investments. The GDP data are from the Central Intelligence Agency (2009).

9. Return data taken from http://banker.thomsonib.com/ta/.

example. As Gordon Murray (1998) points out, these funds (which typically had under €2 million in capital) were so undercapitalized that even if they did nothing besides pay for the salary of an investment professional and an administrative assistant, rent for a modest office, and travel, and never invested a single dollar, they would run out of capital long before their assigned ten-year life was up. Moreover, with so few euros to disperse, the investments they could make were tiny. Certainly, they were insufficient to get the typical entrepreneurial company to the point where it could go public, or even, in many cases, to the point where it would be interesting to a corporate acquirer. For a number of groups, their best hope of achieving any return from their investments was to sell the stakes back to the companies they had bought them from. This is hardly a way to achieve the European Commission's goal of providing capital to needy entrepreneurs.

A final alternative, seen particularly among latter-stage investors, are integrated financial institutions. In a number of nations, such as Japan, the bulk of the financing to rapidly growing and restructuring entities are provided by large integrated financial institutions. Even in the United States, where the independent private equity industry was founded, over one-quarter of all private equity transactions involve a bank-affiliated fund (Fang, Ivashina, and Lerner 2010).

It might be thought that these diversified financial institutions, in addition to substituting adequately for private equity groups, might actually be able to undertake investment more successfully. Such a conclusion is suggested by the literature on internal capital markets. Stein (1997), for example, sees organizational diversification across activities (in this context, banks that can engage in either underwriting or investing) as an important element of efficient capital allocation. When opportunities are poor in one industry, he argues, managers can maintain their overall capital budget (which they value in and of itself) while still making good investments in their other industries. By contrast, managers of narrowly focused firms with poor investment opportunities have no place else to invest and, in an effort to maintain their capital budgets, may end up investing in negative net present value projects.

Empirical data suggests, however, that the effectiveness of these institutionalized investors is far less effective in practice. In particular, the share of transactions affiliated with banks is procyclical, peaking at times of big capital inflows into the private equity market. Transactions done at the top of the market are most likely to experience subsequent distress, and this pattern is especially pronounced for transactions involving banks' private equity groups. This result is particularly striking because prior to the transaction, targets of bank-affiliated investments generally have significantly better operating performance than other buyout targets, though their size and other features are similar. The results suggest that incentive problems and an inability to add value to portfolio companies have limited the success of bank-affiliated funds.

These plausible counterfactual histories, in which venture and private equity investors were replaced by angels, governments, or integrated financial institutions, suggest that while important aspects of the venture capital and private equity process can be duplicated, the alternative approaches also have their own challenges, which makes it hard to duplicate the free-standing investment organizations. While we must be cautious in our interpretation, the counterfactual analysis suggests that these institutions could not have been readily replaced. Unlike the railroads, which could have been replaced by alternative transportation modes, these financial innovations may have had a larger unique contribution to economic growth.

Taking Stock

It should be noted, however, that all of these studies have important limitations. First, these studies consider venture capital and private equity in aggregate. As alluded to earlier, both industries have been characterized by highly "lumpy" fund-raising, where a few years account for the peak of the activity. These years are also characterized by poorer private returns and higher rates of bankruptcy, which might suggest that the social returns from these periods are modest as well.

These limitations are particularly acute in the case of the private equity studies. None of these studies can grapple with the consequences of the 2005 to 2008 market peak, which accounted for fully 47 percent of the private equity raised (in inflation-adjusted dollars) between 1969 and 2008.

Moreover, the findings that have been completed to date raise questions about what goes on during these boom periods. Axelson et al. (2009) document the cyclical use of leverage in buyouts. Using a sample of 1,157 transactions completed by major groups worldwide between 1985 through 2008, they show that the level of leverage is driven by the cost of debt, rather than the more industry- and firm-specific factors that affect leverage in publicly traded firms. The availability of leverage is also strongly associated with higher valuation levels in deals.

Similarly, Davis et al. (2009) find that the positive productivity growth differential at target firms (relative to controls) is not even. Rather, it is larger in periods with an unusually high interest rate spread between AAA-rated and BB-rated corporate bonds, and virtually nonexistent during periods with low spreads. One interpretation of this pattern is that private equity groups are committed to adding value to their portfolio only during periods when making money through other means (e.g., through leverage and financial engineering) is not feasible; that is, during periods when private equity activity is relative quiescent.

If firms completing buyouts at market peaks employ leverage excessively and are less likely to focus on adding value, as their findings suggest, we may expect industries with heavy buyout activity to experience more intense subsequent downturns. Moreover, the effects of this overinvestment would be exacerbated if private equity investments drive rivals not backed by private equity to aggressively invest and leverage themselves. (Chevalier [1995] shows that in regions with supermarkets receiving private equity investments, rivals responded by entering and expanding stores.)

But this claim remains unproven. A counterargument, originally proposed by Jensen (1989), is that the high levels of debt in private equity transactions force firms to respond earlier and more forcefully to negative shocks to their business. As a result, private equity-backed firms may be forced to adjust their operations earlier, at the beginning of an industry downturn, enabling them to better weather a recession. Even if some private equity-backed firms eventually end up in financial distress, their underlying operations may thus be in better shape than their peers, which facilitates an efficient restructuring of their capital structure and lowers the deadweight costs on the economy. Consistent with this argument, Andrade and Kaplan (1998) study thirty-one leveraged buyouts from the 1980s that became financially distressed, and found that the value of the firms postdistress was slightly higher than the value before the buyout, suggesting that even the leveraged buyouts that were hit most severely by adverse shocks added some economic value. Thus, the extent to which the steady-state findings are weakened and undone by the intense cyclicality in these markets remains an open question.

11.3.3 Mutual Funds and Exchange-Traded Funds

Just as venture capital and private equity have become important components of the modern US economy, mutual funds (including exchange-traded funds) have become a dominant force in the investment management arena. While there has been substantial work on mutual funds, little of it directly addresses the social welfare consequences of this innovation. To lay out the approach for studying its implications, we (a) provide a brief history of the US mutual fund industry; (b) demonstrate its economic importance; (c) highlight the areas in which funds may have positively and negatively influenced social welfare; and (d) sketch out a counterfactual history to draw out these consequences.

A Brief History of the Innovations in the US Mutual Fund Industry

While mutual funds have antecedents in nineteenth-century British Unit Investment Trusts (comparable to closed-end funds today) and earlier European structures, the "modern" open-end mutual fund was created in 1924.[10] The Massachusetts Investment Trust, launched in March 1924, was followed in quick succession by the State Street Investment Corporation in July and the Investment Corporation in November 1925. Like the investment trusts

10. For a history of the fund industry, see Fink (2008) and the references therein. For a useful list of innovations in the fund industry, see http://www.icifactbook.org/fb_appd.html. For the early predecessors of modern mutual funds, see Goetzmann and Rouwenhorst (2005), chapter 15, "The Origins of Mutual Funds" by Rouwenhorst.

that preceded them, these new funds were pooled investment vehicles offering professional active investment management services. The key innovations were the structure of the funds, as well as the manner in which redemptions were handled. Open-ended mutual funds, as they would come to be known, had a single class of investor claims in the form of equity, rather than a levered structure (still common in closed-end funds). More importantly, they allowed investors to buy or redeem shares on a daily basis at net asset value, unlike the prior investment trusts, which traded on exchanges and were (and are) typically sold at discounts or premia to net asset value. The offer of shares and redemptions was daily and continuous, as opposed to the infrequent issuance of new shares by prior investment trusts.

The next major wave of innovation in mutual funds took place in the early 1970s. Up until this time, funds had held portfolios of stocks, and, to a far lesser degree, bonds. No fund had primarily held short-term money market instruments and designed itself to maintain a stable net asset value. In September 1972, the Reserve Fund was launched, followed a few weeks later by a competing fund, the Capital Preservation Fund, and in 1974 by offerings by Dreyfus and Fidelity. The latter allowed shareholders to redeem shares through a check-writing feature. The innovation of money market funds was not the holding of short-term instruments per se, but their mechanisms to maintain stable net asset values through either rounding their net asset values (NAVs) to the nearest penny (penny rounding funds), by valuing their portfolio at amortized cost (versus market value), or by adding or subtracting realized gains and losses from accrued income on a daily basis. (See Fink (2008, 84). These practices would eventually be memorialized into regulation through section 2a7 of the 1940 Act, which would permit amortized cost accounting and penny rounding methods for money market funds.

At about the same time, in the early 1970s, the first municipal bond funds by Kemper and Fidelity were offered, expanding the asset classes in which fund shareholders could invest. In the early 1970s, institutional index funds were first offered. Rather than use active management or a completely unmanaged fixed portfolio, these investments offered investors the return of a stock index (including the occasional rebalancing due to additions/deletions by the index). The next major retail innovation would take place in 1976, with the creation of the first indexed mutual fund, Jack Bogle's Vanguard First Index Investment Trust. The First Index Investment Trust brought the indexing concept to retail investors in a mutual fund structure, wrapped around a low-cost, high-service business model that was informed by Bogle's experiences, beginning with his 1951 Princeton college thesis, "The Economic Role of Investment Companies" (see Slater 1997).

A more recent innovation, similar in spirit to index funds but with a different institutional structure, was created in 1992 by Leland O'Brien Rubinstein in the form of SuperTrust and rapidly followed by a similar offering by the American Stock Exchange in the form of SPDRs (see Tufano and Kyrillos 1994). The products, which would later morph into exchange-traded funds, had features of the old fixed-portfolio investment trusts and closed-end funds, in that they passively managed funds that were bought and sold on exchanges. The key innovation was to find a way to keep these funds trading at fundamental value or net asset value, rather than at fluctuating discounts and premia. The traditional open-end fund did so by contract form, allowing shareholders to buy and redeem shares at the NAV. The ETF innovation kept the link to NAV by allowing institutions to assemble the portfolio of underlying securities and create new ETFs (and disassemble the ETF portfolio into its underlying components). By creating a direct link between the security and its underlying components, ETFs minimize discounts or premia to NAVs. Overall, the fund industry has witnessed a high level of innovation over the past decades.

The Economic Importance of the US Mutual Fund Industry

Over the past few years, policymakers have been debating whether mutual funds, or at least money market mutual funds, are "systemically important" and should be regulated by others beyond the SEC. Regardless of the outcome of this regulatory debate, there is little question that mutual funds are one of the most successful financial innovations of the twentieth century. Whether measured by their growth rates, adoption rates, fraction of capital intermediated in the economy, or importance to household balance sheets, mutual funds are critical to the economy. Furthermore, evidencing the innovation spiral, the original actively managed stock and bond mutual fund structure has been the chassis on which we have seen innovations such as index funds, exchange-traded funds, sector funds, and money market funds.

On an absolute level, the US mutual fund industry is simply enormous. As of October 2009, industry assets (excluding ETFs) exceeded $10 trillion, as shown in table 11.2 from the Investment Company Institute's data on the 7,762 funds in operation.

These absolute numbers, while staggering in size, do not put the economic

Table 11.2 **Total net assets of US domiciled mutual funds, October 2009 (billions of dollars)**

Stock funds	4,596.2
Hybrid funds	604.5
Taxable bond funds	1,682.5
Municipal bond funds	443.9
Taxable money market funds	2,951.3
Tax-free money market funds	409.9
Total	10,688.3

Source: http://www.ici.org/research/stats/trends/trends_10_09. This total excludes exchange-traded funds, with $738 billion in assets.

Table 11.3 **Composition of US household financial market assets, 1950 and 2008**

	1950	2008	Gain/Loss
Bank-system deposits	28.1	18.2	–9.9
Money market mutual funds	0.0	4.5	4.5
Direct holdings of stocks and bonds	51.1	29.0	–22.1
Mutual funds (stock, bond, balanced)	0.7	10.0	9.3
Pension reserves (incl. DB and DC plans)	5.2	30.4	25.2
Other	14.9	7.9	–7.0
Total financial market assets	100	100	
Total mutual fund share	0.7	14.5	13.8

importance of the fund industry into context. One way to do so is to examine their adoption, in aggregate, by an important sector of the economy: households. Table 11.3 shows the breakdown of aggregate financial assets held by the US household (and nonprofit) sector in 1950 and 2008, as calculated by the Federal Reserve's Flow of Funds accounts.[11]

The pervasive impact of mutual funds can be seen in this aggregate balance sheet. First, from 1950 through 2008, households held far fewer "deposits," defined broadly, with the deposit-like share going from 28.1 percent of financial assets to 22.7 percent. Of this 22.7 percent, money market funds accounted for 4.5 percent, or nearly one-fifth. Secondly, in 1950, slightly over half of all household financial assets were in direct holdings of stocks and bonds. By 2008, this figure had dropped to 29.0 percent, but 10 percent were held in long-term stock and bond mutual funds, which increased from 0.7 percent to 10.0 percent over fifty-eight years. Finally, the decline in direct holdings of stocks and bonds was more than offset by an increase in holdings in pension reserves, which rose from 5.2 percent to 30.4 percent of all household financial assets. A large fraction of these pension assets are in defined contribution plans, which in turn are invested in mutual funds. Putting these three elements together, mutual funds have had a profound impact on the household balance sheet.

The Social Welfare Implications of Mutual Funds

While there is little question that mutual funds have not only been a financial innovation, but a successful one in terms of adoption, how can we gauge the social welfare implications of this sector? Unlike the venture capital and private equity innovations, where researchers have documented employment, business formation, product innovation, and productivity impacts, there is far less done at a macro level on the social welfare impacts of the

11. http://www.federalreserve.gov/releases/z1/ or the various data series. These numbers include financial assets, excluding equity in unincorporated businesses, to reflect financial market claims.

fund industry. In part, this may reflect the fact that funds are not typically involved with portfolio firms in the same direct way as private equity or venture capital firms. Their impact on social welfare would come from benefits to investors who seek low-cost diversified portfolios, or to capital markets, as information processors and as deep pools of capital. Our discussion focuses primarily on the former—the costs and benefits to investors.

It is clear from the past six decades of history that households' revealed preference has been to hold funds more than to hold individual securities—and to hold securities more than bank deposits. If one were to assume that these choices were the direct result of the existence of mutual funds, one could provide a crude estimate of the return differential earned by investors as a result of the mutual fund innovation, one portion of the social welfare gains from innovation. For the purpose of this thought exercise, suppose that households allocated their assets between cash (earning the risk-free rate) and the market (stocks and bonds), which earns a premium over the risk-free rate.

Define:

r_f = The risk-free rate, a proxy for the return on deposits.
RP = The equity risk premium on an unmanaged portfolio of assets.
M = The fraction of assets held in securities (market), prior to the introduction of mutual funds.
ΔM = The incremental fraction of assets held in securities (market) as a result of mutual fund introduction. Presumably, $\Delta M > 0$, based on the decrease in deposits over the postwar period.
f = The weighted average incremental fee charged by funds in excess of the embedded fees in direct holdings of equities, where the weight is given by the mix of mutual fund holdings as a fraction of all market holdings. The sign of f is unclear: while funds have explicit fees, there are implicit fees with holdings in banks (in the form of deposit-loan spreads) as well as explicit fees.

Before and after the introduction of mutual funds, the household sector's return would be

$$E(R_{\text{pre}}) = (1 - M)r_f + (M)(r_f + \text{ERP})$$
$$E(R_{\text{post}}) = (1 - M - \Delta M)r_f + (M + \Delta M)(r_f + \text{ERP-}f).$$

Taking the difference between these two and combining terms, we could calculate a net increase in return equal to

$$-Mf + \Delta M(\text{ERP-}f),$$

where the first term is the decrease in private return due to incremental weighted average fees and the second term is the net increase in return due to the increased holdings of risky market assets.

Even a quick inspection of this naïve formula makes clear some of the challenges with estimating this differential. First, an increase in returns that is accompanied by a commensurate increase in risk does not increase social welfare, unless we can show that the representative investor was better able to move closer to some optimal level of risk taking.

Second, it assumes that the introduction of funds does not affect the risk-free rate or the market risk premium. However, if in aggregate institutional and individual investors moved more funds into the market and away from banks and other low risk investments, these returns, and other market-wide elements such as liquidity, could easily be affected. The increased demand for riskier assets from the deeper pool of potential market investors could lower costs of capital for firms. The more intensive alpha-seeking behavior of funds could make prices more reflective of efficient market levels and reduce bid-ask spreads. However, both of these assertions would need to be proven.

Third, it attributes the change in deposit holdings entirely to funds and does not consider secondary influences of the innovation. For example, holdings of higher-risk portfolios would tend to increase household wealth but lead to greater fluctuations in wealth. The former would tend to increase the willingness to hold risky assets, and the latter might depress this willingness. Also, the introduction of money market funds might have led households to hold more in low-risk assets.

Fourth, while mutual funds clearly charge fees, and ample research demonstrates that funds cannot persistently beat the market, we need to calculate the incremental fees incurred by household investors. While the absolute level of mutual fund expenses is greater than zero, and while turnover is far higher than a passively managed portfolio, the relevant comparison for our purposes would be the incremental fees and turnover relative to the benchmark prefund portfolio, composed of bank deposits and direct holdings of securities. A directly held portfolio would have individual investors (or a bank trust department) managing their own investments, paying retail commissions, and implementing their own trading strategy. Most likely, this alternative would also have households less well diversified.

This simple specification makes clear some of the elements left out of this analysis. On the positive side, we would need to capture:

1. Greater development of capital and debt markets as a result of new institutions. There is extensive literature on financial development and economic development. While there are ongoing debates about the causality and magnitude of these relationships, one would have to acknowledge that mutual funds have been a substantial element of financial development.

2. Greater holding of foreign securities to counteract home bias. French (2008) documents a substantial increase in US holdings of foreign securities, which partially might be attributed directly or indirectly to mutual fund holdings.

3. Greater savings overall. While it is purely speculative, one wonders what the savings rates of individuals would have been in the absence of mutual funds.
4. Institutional competition for the fragmented and regulated banking industry. On this latter point, the development of money market funds was an explicit reaction to the interest rate caps imposed by Regulation Q.

Finally, without a mutual fund sector, would we have seen the development or widespread adoption of defined contribution (DC) pension plans, where the employee selects his or her investments from a menu largely consisting of retail funds? Technically, it would have been possible to move to this system were no retail funds in place by offering retail investors the option of investing in institutional products. However, realistically, this might have been difficult because along with the investment management aspects of mutual funds came the record-keeping systems that would support DC plans. Also, retail offerings of funds likely made it easier for firms and employees to understand and to get comfortable with workplace-based defined contribution plans. By the time DC plans were introduced (spurred by the 1974 Employee Retirement Income Security Act [ERISA] rules and the 1978 Revenue Act), consumers had extensive experience with funds, with over 10 million mutual fund accounts in America.[12]

On the negative side, this specification would not capture (a) "Excessive" rent seeking by mutual fund companies and the associated transfer of wealth from investors to the industry; (b) "Excessive" or "insufficient" savings by individuals; (c) "Excessive" risk taking by individuals; and (d) "Costly" disintermediation of the banking sector, including the relative loss of regulatory control over the money supply that bank regulators had traditionally enjoyed. All of these costs, and benefits, are difficult to measure because in many instances we lack models to determine the optimal levels of these quantities. The optimal level of risk taking in the economy, for example, depends on preferences and risk aversion, which are not exogenous.

Counterfactual Histories

Trying to untangle any of these issues is difficult enough, but the specification also makes clear that one cannot analyze the social welfare consequences of the fund industry except in context. Had mutual funds not been invented (or adopted), what counterfactual history might have emerged? Which are plausible and "miracle" alternatives? Surely investing and pooling would have continued as core functions in a financial system, but the institutional arrangements would have been different without mutual funds, index funds, and ETFs. Some possible alternatives include:

12. See http://www.icifactbook.org/fb_data.html, table 1.

1. Continuation of the prefund status quo, involving banks, bank trust departments, direct holdings of stocks and bonds, brokers and financial advisors, closed-end funds, and opaque holdings of securities through intermediaries such as insurance companies.
2. Modified status quo outcomes, where some of these institutions came to dominate others (e.g., a movement to greater intermediation but in the form of insurance-wrapped investments).
3. "Miraculous" innovations, such as fractional shares and bonds that would permit individual investors to create diversified portfolios at a small scale.

The first possibility of the prefund status quo is largely a banking and direct security holding alternative. Closed-end funds would have remained a minor player in the economy. Fink (2008) argues that closed-end funds became marginalized in the wake of the events of 1929, and direct holdings of securities—sold by brokers—were preferred as the means by which households acquired exposure to the "market." In this counterfactual world, households would hold poorly diversified, rarely rebalanced portfolios of a small number of securities. They would have been advised by bank trust departments (for the very wealthy), securities brokers, and popular periodicals. One could not assume index funds or ETFs in this counterfactual, as they were part of the innovative process we are analyzing. One may not even be able to assume low-cost brokerage models, as they too, were a relatively recent financial innovation.

While the actively managed mutual fund industry is often criticized for failing to produce reliably positive excess returns or alpha, it is less likely that investors would have performed better on their own employing this direct-ownership counterfactual. Perhaps the most complete analysis of the social welfare impacts of mutual funds, in the context of active investing, can be found in French's (2008) AFA Presidential Address. In it, he documents the perpetual, and costly, search for alpha, estimating the deadweight loss to be about 67 basis points per year relative to passive investing. French convincingly documents that actively traded mutual funds are considerably more expensive than passive portfolios, but assumes virtually zero costs for direct-held portfolios: "I assume the only expenses individuals incur when they hold shares directly are trading costs, which are included in the aggregate estimates below. I ignore, for example, the time they spend managing their portfolios and the cost of subscriptions to Value Line and Morningstar" (1543). It is unclear if he includes noncommission payments to financial advisors, bank trust departments, or others who would facilitate the direct investing activities of investors. In our counterfactual, we would need to include these costs, which were likely sizable. Furthermore, it is not clear that the direct buyers of securities would receive excellent investing advice. Recent evidence by Bergstresser, Chalmers, and Tufano (2009), for example, shows that broker-sold mutual funds consistently underperform direct-sold funds. If this is any indication, replacing thousands of fund managers with millions of even less well-informed brokers is not likely to increase household wealth. One might imagine that household portfolios might show even greater home bias and would virtually certainly not contain index-like fund holdings.

The second alternative is that an intermediated solution other than open-end funds and ETFs could have emerged. Despite their lack of popularity in the 1930s, perhaps closed-end funds might have enjoyed renewed popularity. While they provide pooling and liquidity to investors, it is unlikely that this path would have led to higher social welfare for investors. First, closed-end funds routinely trade at discounts and premia to net asset values, and investors would need to bear this additional discount risk (in addition to the risk of fluctuations in the portfolio's NAV). Second, by their nature, closed-end funds have a fixed amount of assets under management, versus an open-end fund, which can expand or contract assets in response to demand. Closed-end funds would therefore benefit less from economies of scale due to growth than would open-end funds. Closed-end funds also require incremental distribution expenses and legal expenses to start new funds to accommodate new demand, whereas open-end funds can accept new assets at virtually no administrative costs.

Another possible intermediated solution would have been that insurance-based investments would have met demand had the fund innovation not taken place. Revealed preference suggests that there is greater demand for funds than for bundled insurance-cum-investment products. As of the end of 2008, mutual funds (excluding ETFs) held \$9.6 trillion in assets; by comparison, total assets held by life insurers was \$4.6 trillion, with much of the latter backing noninvestment term insurance products.[13] Given this sizable difference in revealed demand, it is difficult to believe that a bundled insurance-investment product would have satisfied investor preferences as well as funds have. Furthermore, the bundling of these products makes them more difficult to explain and sell, likely leading to higher transaction costs (and possibly poorer matching of products to consumer needs). For a discussion of these problems and the resultant market failures that can give rise to regulation, see Campbell et al. (2010).

Another, more miraculous possibility is that an alternative functional substitute for funds would have emerged, providing low-cost pooling and investment management, small lot sizes for diversified portfolios, and liquid-

13. Data from http://www.icifactbook.org/fb_data.html (table 1) and http://www.acli.com/ACLI/Tools/Industry+Facts/Assets+and+Investments/. The mutual fund number includes \$3.8 trillion in money market funds and \$5.8 trillion in long-term investments. However, the life insurance figure includes both assets held to back term policies (with no investment element) and other policies (universal, whole life, etc.) with an investment component. In 2008, about three-quarters of all life insurance purchases were for term insurance, which does not have an investment component (http://www.acli.com/NR/rdonlyres/0BFEABCA-1E2A-4F4C-A879-95CF104238AB/22608/FB0709LifeInsurance1.pdf, table 7.2).

ity in the form of daily trading. By 2000 or so, this alternative history might not have seemed far-fetched. A number of startups offered products of this sort, allowing investors to directly buy pools of securities, including fractional shares, and provided a high level of liquidity. For example, one of the first of these innovators, folioFN permitted investors to buy folios (portfolios) of stocks (as well as mutual funds) in fractional shares. However, it would take the development of the Internet, and the adoption of Internet-based transacting, to make this counterfactual a reality. Even so, one wonders about the ultimate returns earned by direct investors. Recent behavioral finance work, by Odean (1999), Barber and Odean (2000, 2001a, 2001b, 2002, 2004), and others call into question the investing acumen of individual investors.

Overall, a more extensive consideration of these and other counterfactuals would likely suggest that the innovation of mutual funds, index funds, and ETFs likely were beneficial for investors, relative to other reasonable counterfactuals.

11.3.4 Securitization

Pooling is a timeless function of financial systems, and our first two case studies focus on pooling vehicles using different forms of intermediation. Over the past four decades, another major innovation that performs the pooling function has been securitization.[14]

Like other pooled vehicles, which assemble portfolios of assets (stakes in new companies, shares in firms, or holdings of bonds) and sell claims against them, securitization vehicles bundle a variety of financial claims, often in the form of retail IOUs (mortgages, auto loans, student loans, credit card receivables) and sell claims against them. In venture capital and private equity, there are often multiple classes of claims (general partners and limited partners), in open-end funds a single claim (equity holders), and in closed-end funds often multiple claimants (equity and debt, sometimes.) Securitized vehicles can have a single class of investors (if purely pooled vehicles) or can create multiple classes of investors. While early securitization used the former method, much of modern securitization gives different investors varying exposures to credit or prepayment risk. Even more complicated structures create tranched structures using already pooled structures (collateralized debt obligation [CDO]-squareds) or using derivatives (synthetic CDOs). For the purpose of this discussion, we will focus on "simple" securitization structures, recognizing that some of the most vociferous criticism was directed at the more complex structures.

The History and Extent of Securitization

While there was securitization of a sort in the 1920s, the practice as we know it came into widespread adoption in the 1970s and 1980s, beginning

14. For a general discussion of the pooling function, see Sirri and Tufano (1995).

with the securitization of home mortgages.[15] Before that time, most home mortgages were originated, funded, and serviced by banks and credit unions or, if they were government-insured mortgages, were bought by government-owned Fannie Mae.[16] In some instances, loans were sold from one party to another, but this whole loan market was fairly illiquid.

The first major development in securitization was the introduction of the pass-through mortgage backed security (MBS), first issued by Ginnie Mae in 1970. In a pass-through, a portfolio of mortgages are bundled together and investors receive all principal and interest payments. Pass-through MBS or participating certificates combined the sale of loans, the bundling of mortgages into a pool, and the use of an off-balance-sheet structure. Unlike later securitizations, these instruments had a single class of investors, who shared proportionally in the portfolio's risks and returns, including prepayment risks.

The next major innovation in securitization was the development of tranched structures, first used in the Collateralized Mortgage Obligation (CMO) issued by Freddie Mac in 1983. In this multiclass security, a set of rules predetermined which investors got which cash flows. A major concern in these structures was to allocate prepayment risk among investors. Because borrowers have the right to prepay their mortgages and would tend to do so when it was to their advantage (and to the disadvantage of the lenders), prepayment risk (or the embedded call option in mortgages) was an unattractive feature from the perspective of investors. Under CMO structures, certain investors willing to take on greater prepayment risk would accordingly earn higher promised returns, while other investors would be the last to be prepaid and therefore earn lower promised returns. Other structures would modify the division of prepayment risk (and credit risk) among investors in more complex ways. With the passage of the Tax Reform Act of 1986, which allowed the Real Estate Mortgage Investment Conduit (REMIC) tax vehicle, CMO issuance and securitization expanded dramatically.

The volume of securitized home mortgages grew from \$28 billion in 1976 to \$4.2 trillion in 2003.[17] Government-sponsored entities (i.e., Fannie Mae and Freddie Mac) played an important role in this process by standardizing mortgage products, pooling mortgages into mortgage-backed securities, and guaranteeing investors against losses.[18] Securitization supported the development of mortgage brokers and specialized mortgage originators who developed a new "originate-to-distribute" model, as well as third-party servicing.

15. The material in this section draws heavily upon Ryan, Trumbull, and Tufano (2010).
16. http://www.fundinguniverse.com/company-histories/Fannie-Mae-Company-History.html.
17. Loutskina and Strahan (2009).
18. Frame and White (2005).

Other lending activities also used securitization as a financing technique. Automobile loans were first securitized in 1985; credit card loans followed in 1986.[19] By 2006, approximately 55 percent of all mortgages, 45 percent of all credit card loans, and 16 percent of nonrevolving loans (many of which are auto installment loans) were securitized.[20] Over time, these networks of firms and investors displaced traditional lenders. For a more complete discussion of the history of securitization, see the definitive treatise by Frankel (2006).

Assessing the Social Welfare Implications of Securitization

Much attention has been focused on the way in which changes in financial intermediation, especially in mortgages, have influenced the national and global economy.[21] The difficulty with assessing the impacts of securitization, however, stems from the many different elements associated with this class of innovations. These elements include, but are not limited to, the following:

- The sale of a loan from the original lender to another investor(s).
- The bundling of loans from a single or multiple lenders, with subsequent sale to investors.
- The standardization of the underlying assets encouraged by parties putting together or guaranteeing pools.
- The guaranteeing of assets, fully or partly, by government or private parties.
- Other credit enhancement, for example, through overcollateralization.
- The tranching of claims to create multiple securities differentiated by credit or prepayment risk.
- The creation of stand-alone loan originators (mortgage brokers) who tended not to have an economic interest in the long-term viability of originated loans.
- The creation of stand-alone servicers with a complex set of incentives as agents of diffuse shareholders.
- The creation of securitized structures using other securitized structures (or derivatives) as underlying assets.
- The creation of securitized structures using high-risk (subprime) loans as the underlying assets.
- The use of and reliance upon credit ratings that may fail to take into account the level of risks in some of these structures.

19. *Asset Securitization Comptroller's Handbook* (1997).

20. Mortgage data from Rosen (2007). Revolving and nonrevolving debt data from Federal Reserve Statistical Release, Series G19, http://www.federalreserve.gov/releases/g19/Current/.

21. Ashcraft and Schuermann (2008); Berndt and Gupta (2008); Coval, Jurek, and Stafford (2009); Hoffman and Nitschka (2008); Mayer, Pence, and Sherlund (2009); Mian and Sufi (2008); Purnanandam (2009); and Shiller (2008).

Critiques of the innovation of "securitization" must acknowledge that a pass-through securitization of prime mortgages originated by banks is quite a different phenomenon from a CDO-squared issue where the underlying asset is a low-ranked tranche of a different CDO, whose underlying assets, in turn, are a portfolio of no-documentation subprime loans originated by mortgage brokers.

The second challenge with analyzing the welfare impacts of securitization, say of home mortgages or student loans, is to assess the appropriate outcome metric. There are a variety of legitimate measures. For example, some early studies suggest that the first decades of securitization led to lower interest rates for borrowers (see Hendershott and Shilling 1989; Sirmans and Benjamin 1990; and Jameson, Dewan, and Sirmans 1992). Others point to the wider availability of credit, leading in turn to considerably higher home ownership rates, which rose from about 62 percent in 1960 to almost 69 percent in 2004, with the strongest gains among nonwhite American households.[22] Against these positive metrics of lower rates, expanded credit availability, and broader homeownership, we must consider the cost of higher levels of foreclosure, especially among subprime borrowers, putatively the primary beneficiaries of this increased lending.

We can quantify the benefits of lower costs of financing, but how would one quantify the benefits of having an additional 1 percent of households owning homes, or the costs of 1 percent of homeowners losing their homes through foreclosure? Neither direct measurements nor a counterfactual approach can overcome the problem of multiple metrics, some of which do not lend themselves to quantitative measurement.

Identifying Counterfactual Alternatives

Which counterfactual history might we use to compare against the actual past where securitization has financed much consumer debt? Using the mortgage market as the primary research site, these alternatives might include the following:

- Depositories continue to originate and hold mostly prime loans, with limited whole loan sales to other depositories or to specialized mortgage investors.
- Depositories continue to originate mostly prime loans, but some are bundled in the form of pass-through (single class) MBS securities.
- Depositories continue to originate mostly prime loans, but some are bundled in the form of either pass-through (single class) securities or multiclass (CMO) structures—but not more complex structures (synthetic CDOs or CDO-squared structures).

22. See http://www.census.gov/hhes/www/housing/hvs/annual05/ann05t12.html for the national figures and http://www.census.gov/hhes/www/housing/hvs/annual05/ann05t20.html for the breakdowns by race.

Of course, these three alternatives are just a few of the nearly unlimited number of counterfactuals, which could be made by layering on (a) subprime lending; (b) the originate-to-distribute model using independent mortgage brokers, reimbursed through yield spread premia; (c) the existence of less-optimistic credit ratings by rating organizations. Even beyond these variants, we would need to consider even broader counterfactuals. For example, a world in which depositories originate and hold mortgages would likely operate quite differently in a setting where branching and intrastate banking were prohibited versus one in which national banking organizations could create diversified portfolios of loans by virtue of their scope.

Comparing the first (no pooling) to the second (pass-through MBS) and third (simple CMO) phases of securitization, there is some evidence that the early securitization gave rise to measurable benefits. As noted before, mortgage rates fell in the first phase, and homeownership rose from 61.9 percent to 64.4 percent from 1960 to 1980, and then to 66.2 percent in 2000. Elmer and Seelig (1998) document and study the general rise in foreclosure rates from 1950 through 1997. They examine the empirical determinants of this time series, and conclude that securitization and the ancillary activity of third-party servicing does not explain the trend in foreclosures. (Rather, they find that measures of household debt and savings are better predictors of foreclosures.) While this evidence is far from complete, it is suggestive that the roughly first three decades of securitization were not likely welfare-reducing. Indeed, having deep pools of capital to fund national mortgage markets was a likely improvement over local mortgage lenders.

The more recent history of securitization is probably a different matter. It is not clear that the economy unambiguously benefited from ever more complex structures, higher-risk underwriting of subprime borrowers, sloppier underwriting standards in general, and an increasing role for mortgage originators with few long-term incentives. In almost textbook fashion, we see an innovation more widely diffused, used by a new population (riskier borrowers) in new ways (in securitizations of securitizations), and purchased by less experienced investors (relying on ratings).

While determining social welfare implications of securitization is difficult, even establishing simpler facts about the phenomenon is not simple. A large body of papers, including a number of recent working papers, examine aspects of securitization and attempt to measure the direct impacts of the practice. For example, studies reach contradictory conclusions about whether riskier banks use securitization, whether they have lower funding costs, or whether securitization increases loan supply. (For a summary of some of these studies see Panetta and Pozzolo [2010], who study credit risk transfer in over 100 countries.) For example, a recent working paper, using propensity scoring techniques to try to determine a counterfactual (had banks not chosen to securitize) finds that after controlling for whether banks choose to securitize, there is no statistically significant impact of securitization on banks' funding costs, credit exposure, or profitability (Sarkisyan, et al. 2010). While the authors frame the work in terms of a counterfactual, it addresses a far narrower question: How would banks have performed had they not used securitization (but implicitly assuming that securitization exists and is used by other institutions)? Even so, using similar data but an instrumental variables approach using bank size as an instrument, Jiangli and Pritsker (2008) conclude that securitization played a positive role in reducing insolvency risk among banks. There are numerous papers that empirically analyze the effect of securitization on bank stability, as measured by Z-scores, systemic risk, and other measures. Not surprisingly, they, too, reach contradictory results. For a recent survey—and evidence of a negative relationship between securitization and bank financial soundness—see Michalak and Uhde (2010).

The extant literature largely attempts to address how securitization affects individual banks, but to assess the social welfare implications of this innovation, one needs a broader frame. Gorton and Metrick (2010) summarize the reasons for the growth of modern securitization (reduction in bankruptcy costs, tax advantages, reduction in moral hazard, reduced regulatory costs, transparency, and customization). They, along with Adrian and Shin (2010), highlight how securitization was part of a larger set of innovations that constitute the so-called shadow banking system, in which market-based financial intermediaries replaced traditional banks. These other elements include money market mutual funds and repo contracts. Together, these papers demonstrate another challenge with analyzing the innovation of securitization: it is closely linked to a network of innovations, so it is difficult, if not impossible, to separate their effects.

Where does this leave us? Certainly, the existing work on securitization, even if ambiguous, provides a useful first step to understanding this innovation. The precise details of securitization, in conjunction with other trends that make up the shadow banking system, will probably thwart any definitive scientific study of the phenomenon. However, one can imagine projects, similar to Fogel's, with all of the same critiques, that consider the following counterfactuals:

- What if only prime mortgages had been securitized?
- What if no "no-doc" mortgages would have been allowed to be securitized?
- What if rating agencies would have rated more poorly (or refused to rate) certain highly structured transactions?

For example, Fogel examined access to nonrail transportation modes to understand the constraints on trade had there been no railroads. In theory, one could examine the holders of various securitized products and their investment charter restrictions to determine what fraction of holdings realistically could have been placed into the market were the issues not rated.

While other institutions might have emerged with an appetite for unrated securities, the exercise would provide a meaningful boundary on the problem. Similarly, if one were to constrain the securitized pools by excluding subprime and no-doc loans, what would the pro forma default rates have been and how might they have rippled through the economy? We suspect that a thoughtful, step-by-step counterfactual approach, inspired by Fogel's 250 page masterpiece, would provide many insights not available from more traditional studies. While a counterfactual approach does not simplify matters much, it has the tangible benefit of forcing us to focus on which elements of securitization are most problematic.

11.4 Conclusions and Other Research Directions

As we have highlighted here, while existing empirical evidence and conceptual frameworks can tell us much about financial innovation, there are substantial unanswered questions. In this final section, we discuss some of the promising avenues for future research. While no method is without problems, these approaches complement one another.

The first approach is to examine settings where there are constraints on financial innovation. The exploitation of exogenous constraints is by now a well-accepted technique in empirical economic research. In particular, a classic example of such constraints that might present an opportunity for careful study is Islamic finance, particularly as practiced in Saudi Arabia and the Persian Gulf. As commonly interpreted, sharia-compliant financial structures exclude the use of debt and multiple classes of equity. Such a setting may provide a "natural experiment" for gauging impact of financial innovation or its absence. Unfortunately, while these economies may have fewer financial innovations that relate to those more common in Western economies, other differences may preclude them from providing the type of natural experiments that would sharply identify the impacts of innovation.

A second avenue may be the greater exploitation of experimental techniques. A number of efforts have attempted to gauge the consequences of new securities, with an almost exclusive focus on those geared toward the developing countries' poor. Examples of such experimental studies have included assessments of new products such as rainfall insurance (Giné, Townsend, and Vickery 2007; Cole et al. 2009), novel rules for institutions (such as Giné and Karlan's [2009] analysis of microcredit lending rules), and new institutions (for instance, Bhattamishra's 2008 study of rain banks). The focus on such innovations is easy to understand: one can gain statistically meaningful results for a very modest investment. But the methodology could be more generally applied, particularly if researchers were to work in conjunction with financial institutions. One problem with such methodologies, however, is that small-scale experiments are almost surely unable to measure the systemic costs or benefits that we just highlighted, and are likely to focus primarily on the experience of early adopters.

The same concern—an inability to assess broader externalities—is likely to be a barrier to our third suggested avenue as well: to apply the tools of structural estimation of the social impact of new products to financial innovations. While these models have assessed many classes of product innovations, financial innovations have been largely neglected. But complex dynamics just outlined may make such empirical assessments challenging.

Detailed histories or case studies of financial innovation can offer additional evidence to help uncover the social welfare implications of systemically important new products. By judicious selection of research sites, we can put appropriate attention on innovations that had major impacts on society. The historical or case study approach forces us to examine each innovation in its entirety, both in terms of the full time span of its adoption and the many ripples in the economy.

Finally, the use of counterfactuals—where we invent our own data—perversely may discipline us to be explicit about our implicit assumptions and metrics. The decades of debates over counterfactuals has sensitized us to the need to think in terms of general equilibrium rather than partial effects, to consider complementaries and path dependencies, and to carefully measure outcomes. Despite all of these problems, we believe that this less "scientific" method may add new insights into understanding financial innovation.

References

Adrian, T., and H. Shin. 2010. "The Changing Nature of Financial Intermediation and the Financial Crisis of 2007–09." Federal Reserve Bank of New York Staff Report no. 439. New York: Federal Reserve Bank of New York. http://papers.ssrn.com/so13/papers.cfm?abstract_id=1576590.

Alexander, J. 1991. "Do the Merits Matter? A Study of Settlements in Securities Class Actions." *Stanford Law Review* 43:497–598.

Allen, F., and D. Gale. 1994. *Financial Innovation and Risk Sharing.* Cambridge, MA: MIT Press.

Andrade, G., and S. Kaplan. 1998. "How Costly is Financial (Not Economic) Distress? Evidence from Highly Leveraged Transactions That Became Distressed." *Journal of Finance* 53:1443–93.

Asset Securitization Comptroller's Handbook. 1997. Washington: US Department of Treasury.

Ashcraft, A. B., and T. Schuermann. 2008. "Understanding the Securitization of Subprime Mortgage Credit." Federal Reserve Bank of New York Staff Report no. 318. New York: Federal Reserve Bank of New York.

Axelson, U., P. Strömberg, T. Jenkinson, and M. Weisbach. 2009. "Leverage and Pricing in Buyouts: An Empirical Analysis." EFA 2009 Bergen Meetings Working Paper. http://ssrn.com/abstract=1344023.

Barber, B., and T. Odean. 2000. "Trading is Hazardous to Your Wealth: The Common Stock Investment Performance of Individual Investors." *Journal of Finance* 55:773–806.

———. 2001a. "Boys will be Boys: Gender, Overconfidence, and Common Stock Investment." *Quarterly Journal of Economics* 116:261–92.

———. 2001b. "The Internet and the Investor." *Journal of Economic Perspectives* 15 (1): 41–54.

———. 2002. "Online Investors: Do the Slow Die First?" *Review of Financial Studies* 15:455–87.

———. 2004. "Are Individual Investors Tax Savvy? Evidence from Retail and Discount Brokerage Accounts." *Journal of Public Economics* 88:419–42.

Ben-Horim, M., and W. Silber. 1977. "Financial Innovation: A Linear Programming Approach." *Journal of Banking and Finance* 1:277–96.

Bergstresser, D., J. Chalmers, and P. Tufano. 2009. "Assessing the Costs and Benefits of Brokers: A Preliminary Analysis of the Mutual Fund Industry." *Review of Financial Studies* 22:4129–56.

Berndt, A., and A. Gupta. 2008. "Moral Hazard and Adverse Selection in the Originate-to-Distribute Model of Bank Credit." http://ssrn.com.ezp-prod1.hul.harvard.edu/abstract=1290312.

Berry, S., J. Levinsohn, and A. Pakes. 1995. "Automobile Prices in Market Equilibrium." *Econometrica* 63:841–90.

Bhattamishra, R. 2008. "Grain Banks: An Institutional and Impact Analysis." PhD diss., Cornell University.

Bloom, N., R. Sadun, and J. Van Reenen. 2009. "Do Private Equity-Owned Firms Have Better Management Practices?" In *Globalization of Alternative Investments Working Papers Volume 2: Global Economic Impact of Private Equity 2009,* edited by A. Gurung and J. Lerner, 1–23. New York: World Economic Forum USA.

Bresnahan, T. 1986. "Measuring the Spillovers from Technical Advance: Mainframe Computers in Financial Services." *American Economic Review* 76:742–55.

Bresnahan, T., and M. Trajtenberg. 1995. "General Purpose Technologies 'Engines of Growth'?" *Journal of Econometrics* 65:83–108.

Bunzl, M. 2004. "Counterfactual History: A User's Guide." *American Historical Review* 109:845–58.

Burt, R. 1987. "Social Contagion and Innovation: Cohesion versus Structural Equivalence." *American Journal of Sociology* 92:1287–335.

Campbell, J., H. Jackson, B. Madrian, and P. Tufano. 2010. "The Regulation of Consumer Financial Products: An Introductory Essay with Four Case Studies." http://ssrn.com/abstract=1649647.

Cameron, R., ed. 1972. *Banking and Economic Development.* New York: Oxford University Press.

Cameron, R., O. Crisp, H. Patrick, and R. Tilly. 1967. *Banking in the Early Stages of Industrialization.* New York: Oxford University Press.

Carr, E. 1987. *What is History?* London: Vintage.

Central Intelligence Agency. 2009. *CIA Factbook.* Washington, DC: Government Printing Office.

Chevalier, J. 1995. "Capital Structure and Product Market Competition: An Empirical Study of Supermarket LBOs." *American Economic Review* 85:206–56.

Cole, S., X. Giné, J. Tobacman, P. Topalova, R. Townsend, and J. Vickery. 2009. "Barriers to Household Risk Management: Evidence from India." Federal Reserve Bank of New York Staff Report no. 373. New York: Federal Reserve Bank of New York.

Coleman, J., E. Katz, and H. Menzel. 1966. *Medical Innovation: A Diffusion Study.* New York: Bobbs-Merrill.

Coval, J., J. Jurek, and E. Stafford. 2009. "The Economics of Structured Finance." *Journal of Economic Perspectives* 23:3–25.
Cowan, R., and D. Foray. 2002. "Evolutionary Economics and the Counterfactual Threat." *Journal of Evolutionary Economics* 12:539–62.
Coy, P. 2009. "Financial Innovation Under Fire." *Business Week,* September 16.
Crane, D., K. A. Froot, S. P. Mason, A. F. Perold, R. C. Merton, Z. Bodie, E. R. Sirri, and P. Tufano. 1995. *The Global Financial System.* Boston: Harvard Business School Press.
Dasgupta, P., and J. Stiglitz. 1980. "Industrial Structure and the Nature of Innovative Activity." *Economic Journal* 90:266–93.
David, P. 1969. "Transport Innovation and Economic Growth: Professor Fogel on and off the Rails." *The Economic History Review* 22 (3): 506–25.
Davis, G. 1994. *A History of Money.* Cardiff: University of Wales Press.
Davis, S., J. Haltiwanger, R. Jarmin, J. Lerner, and J. Miranda. 2008. "Private Equity and Employment." In *Globalization of Alternative Investments Working Papers Volume 1: Global Economic Impact of Private Equity 2008,* edited by A. Gurung and J. Lerner, 43–64. New York: World Economic Forum USA.
———. 2009. "Private Equity, Jobs and Productivity." In *Globalization of Alternative Investments Working Papers Volume 2: Global Economic Impact of Private Equity 2009,* edited by A. Gurung and J. Lerner, 25–44. New York: World Economic Forum USA.
Elmer, P., and S. Seelig. 1998. "The Rising Long-Term Trend of Single-Family Mortgage Foreclosure Rates." Federal Deposit Insurance Corporation Working Paper 98-2. http://ssrn.com/abstract=126128 or doi:10.2139/ssrn.126128.
Fang, L., V. Ivashina, and J. Lerner. 2010. "Unstable Equity? Combining Banking with Private Equity Investing." Unpublished Working Paper. Harvard University.
Ferguson, N., ed. 1997. *Virtual History: Alternatives and Counterfactuals.* London: Picador.
Fergusson, Niall. 2000. *Virtual History: Alternatives and Counterfactuals.* New York: Basic Books.
Fink, M. 2008. *The Rise of Mutual Funds: An Insider's View.* New York: Oxford University Press.
Fogel, R. 1964. *Railroads and American Economic Growth: Essays in Econometric History.* Baltimore, MD: Johns Hopkins Press.
Frame, S., and L. White. 2005. "Fussing and Fuming About Fannie and Freddie: How Much Smoke, How Much Fire?" *Journal of Economic Perspectives* 19: 159–84.
Frame, W., and L. White. 2004. "Empirical Studies of Financial Innovation: Mostly Talk and Not Much Action?" *Journal of Economic Literature* 42:116–44.
Frankel, T. 2006. *Securitization,* 2nd ed. New York: Fathom Publishing Company.
French, K. 2008. "Presidential Address: The Cost of Active Investing." *Journal of Finance* 63:1537–73.
Gennaioli, N., A. Shleifer, and R. Vishny. 2010. "Financial Innovation and Financial Fragility." NBER Working Paper no. 16068. Cambridge, MA: National Bureau of Economic Research, June.
Giné, X., and D. Karlan. 2009. "Group versus Individual Liability: Long Term Evidence from Philippine Microcredit Lending Groups." Unpublished Working Paper. World Bank.
Giné, X., R. Townsend, and J. Vickrey. 2007. "Patterns of Rainfall Insurance Participation in Rural India." World Bank Policy Research Working Paper 4408.
Goetzmann, W., and G. Rouwenhorst, eds. 2005. *The Origins of Value: The Financial*

Innovations That Created Modern Capital Markets. New York: Oxford University Press.

Goldin, C. 1995. "Cliometrics and the Nobel." *The Journal of Economic Perspectives* 9 (2): 191–208.

Gorton, G., and A. Metrick. 2010. "Regulating the Shadow Banking System." Yale School of Management Working Paper. http://papers.ssrn.com/sol3/papers.cfm?abstract_id=1676947.

Granovetter, M. 1978. "Threshold Models of Collective Behavior." *American Journal of Sociology* 83:420–43.

Greenspan, A. 1995. "Remarks at a Conference on Risk Measurement and Systemic Risk." Board of Governors of the Federal Reserve System, Washington, DC.

Hausman, J. 1997. "Valuing the Effect of Regulation on New Services in Telecommunications." *Brookings Papers on Economic Activity: Microeconomics* 26:1–39.

Hellmann, T., and M. Puri. 2002. "Venture Capital and the Professionalization of Start-Up Firms: Empirical Evidence." *Journal of Finance* 57:69–97.

Helpman, E., ed. 1998. *General Purpose Technologies and Economic Growth.* Cambridge, MA: MIT Press.

Hendershott, P., and J. Shilling. 1989. "The Impact of Agencies on Conventional Fixed-Rate Mortgage Yields." *Journal of Real Estate Finance and Economics* 2:101–15.

Hoberg, G., B. Goldfarb, D. Kirsch, and A. Triantis. 2009. "Does Angel Participation Matter? An Analysis of Early Venture Financing." Robert H. Smith School Research Paper no. RHS 06-072. http://ssrn.com/abstract=1024186.

Hoffman, M., and T. Nitschka. 2008. "Securitization of Mortgage Debt, Asset Prices, and International Risk Sharing." Working Paper Series, Institute for Empirical Research in Economics, University of Zurich.

Jameson, M., S. Dewan, and C. Sirmans. 1992. "Measuring Welfare Effects of 'Unbundling' Financial Innovations: The Case of Collateralized Mortgage Obligations." *Journal of Urban Economics* 31:1–13.

Jensen, M. 1989. "The Eclipse of the Public Corporation." *Harvard Business Review* 67:61–74.

Jiangli, W., and M. Pritsker. 2008. "The Impacts of Securitization on US Bank Holding Companies." SSRN Working Paper Series. http://ssrn.com/abstract=1102284.

Johnson, S., and J. Kwok. 2009. "More Financial Innovation." http://baselinescenario.com/2009/06/17/more-financial-innovation.

Kane, E. 1977. "Good Intentions and Unintended Evil: The Case Against Selective Credit Allocation." *Journal of Money, Credit and Banking* 9:55–69.

Kaplan, S., and A. Schoar. 2005. "Private Equity Performance: Returns, Persistence and Capital Flows." *Journal of Finance* 60:791–823.

Kaplan, S., and J. Stein. 1993. "The Evolution of Buyout Pricing and Financial Structure in the 1980s." *Quarterly Journal of Economics* 108:313–57.

Khandani, A., A. Lo, and R. Merton. 2009. "Systemic Risk and the Refinancing Ratchet Effect." Harvard Business School Working Paper no. 10-023.

Khorana, A., H. Servaes, and P. Tufano. 2005. "Explaining the Size of the Mutual Fund Industry Around the World." *Journal of Financial Economics* 78:145–85.

Kindleberger, C. 1984. *A Financial History of Western Europe.* London: George Allen and Unwin.

Kortum, S., and J. Lerner. 2000. "Assessing the Contribution of Venture Capital to Innovation." *Rand Journal of Economics* 31:674–92.

Krugman, P. 2007. "Innovating Our Way to Financial Crisis." *New York Times,* December 3.

Lamoreaux, N., M. Levenstein, and K. Sokoloff. 2007. "Financing Invention During the Second Industrial Revolution: Cleveland, Ohio, 1870–1920." In *Financing Innovation in the United States, 1870 to the Present,* edited by N. Lamoreaux and K. Sokoloff, 39–84. Cambridge, MA: MIT Press.
Lerner, J. 2002. "Where Does *State Street* Lead? A First Look at Finance Patents, 1971–2000." *Journal of Finance* 57:901–30.
———. 2006. "The New New Financial Thing: The Origins of Financial Innovations." *Journal of Financial Economics* 79:233–55.
———. 2010. "The Litigation of Financial Innovations." *Journal of Law and Economics* 53:807–31.
Lerner, J., M. Sorensen, and P. Stromberg. 2008. "Private Equity and Long-Run Investment: The Case of Innovation." NBER Working Paper no. 14623. Cambridge, MA: National Bureau of Economic Research, December.
Litan, R. 2010. "In Defense of Much, But Not All, Financial Innovation." Unpublished Working Paper. Brookings Institution.
Loutskina, E., and P. Strahan. 2009. "Securitization and the Declining Impact of Bank Finance on Loan Supply: Evidence from Mortgage Originations." *Journal of Finance* 64:861–89.
Mason, S., R. Merton, A. Perold, and P. Tufano. 1995. *Cases in Financial Engineering: Applied Studies of Financial Innovation.* Englewood Cliffs, NJ: Prentice Hall.
Mayer, C., K. Pence, and S. Sherlund. 2009. "The Rise in Mortgage Defaults." *Journal of Economic Perspectives* 23:27–50.
McClelland, P. 1968. "Railroads, American Growth, and the New Economic History: A Critique." *The Journal of Economic History* 28 (1): 102–23.
Merton, R. 1992. "Financial Innovation and Economic Performance." *Journal of Applied Corporate Finance* 4:12–22.
Mian, A., and A. Sufi. 2008. "The Consequences of Mortgage Credit Expansion: Evidence from the 2007 Mortgage Default Crisis." NBER Working Paper no. 13936. Cambridge, MA: National Bureau of Economic Research, April.
Michalak, T., and A. Uhde. 2010. "Credit Risk Securitization and Banking Stability: Evidence from the Micro-Level for Europe." University of Bochum Working Paper Series. http://papers.ssrn.com/sol3/papers.cfm?abstract_id=1383469.
Michalopoulos, S., L. Laeven, and R. Levine. 2010. "Financial Innovation and Endogenous Growth." Unpublished Working Paper. Brown University.
Miller, M. 1986. "Financial Innovation: The Last Twenty Years and the Next." *Journal of Financial and Quantitative Analysis* 21:459–71.
Mishra, P. 2010. "Financial Innovation in Financial Markets: A Reassessment." Unpublished Working Paper. Indian Institute of Technical Education and Research.
Mollica, M., and L. Zingales. 2007. "The Impact of Venture Capital on Innovation and the Creation of New Business." Unpublished Working Paper. University of Chicago.
Murray, G. 1998. "A Policy Response to Regional Disparities in the Supply of Risk Capital to New Technology-Based Firms in the European Union: The European Seed Capital Fund Scheme." *Regional Studies* 32:405–19.
Nerlove, M. 1966. "Review: Railroads and American Economic Growth." *The Journal of Economic History* 26 (1): 107–15.
Odean, T. 1999. "Do Investors Trade Too Much?" *American Economic Review* 89: 1279–98.
Panetta, F., and A. Pozzolo. 2010. "Why Do Banks Securitize Their Assets? Bank-Level Evidence from Over One Hundred Countries." Bank of Italy Working Paper. http://papers.ssrn.com/sol3/papers.cfm?abstract_id=1572983.

Persons, J., and V. Warther. 1997. "Boom and Bust Patterns in the Adoption of Financial Innovations." *Review of Financial Studies* 10:939–67.
Petrin, A. 2002. "Quantifying the Benefits of New Products: The Case of the Minivan." *Journal of Political Economy* 110:705–29.
Purnanandam, A. 2009. "Originate-to-Distribute Model and the Subprime Mortgage Crisis." Paper presented at the American Finance Association meeting. Atlanta, Georgia, January 3–5, 2010. http://ssrn.com.ezp-prod1.hul.harvard.edu/abstract=1167786.
Rogers, E. 1962. *Diffusion of Innovations.* New York: Free Press.
Rosen, R. 2007. "The Role of Securitization in Mortgage Lending." *Chicago Fed Letter: Essays on Issues,* no. 244, November.
Ross, S. 1976. "Options and Efficiency." *Quarterly Journal of Economics* 90:75–89.
Ryan, A., G. Trumbull, and P. Tufano. 2010. "A Brief Post-War History of Consumer Finance." Unpublished Manuscript.
Sarkisyan, A., B. Casu, A. Clare, and S. Thomas. 2010. "Securitization and Bank Performance." Sir John Cass Business School Working Paper Series, City University London. http://papers.ssrn.com/sol3/papers.cfm?abstract_id=1490925.
Schwarcz, S. 2008. "Systemic Risk." *Georgetown Law Journal* 97:193–249.
Shiller, R. 2008. *The Subprime Solution: How Today's Global Financial Crisis Happened and What to Do About It.* Princeton, NJ: Princeton University Press.
Silber, W., ed. 1975. *Financial Innovation.* Lexington: Lexington Books.
———. 1983. "The Process of Financial Innovation." *American Economic Review Papers and Proceedings* 73:89–95.
Sirmans, C., and J. Benjamin. 1990. "Pricing Fixed Rate Mortgages: Some Empirical Evidence." *Journal of Financial Services Research* 4:191–202.
Sirri, E., and P. Tufano. 1995. "The Economics of Pooling." In *The Global Financial System,* edited by D. Crane, 81–128. Boston: HBS Press.
Slater, R. 1997. *John Bogle and the Vanguard Experiment.* Chicago: Irwin.
Stein, J. 1997. "Internal Capital Markets and the Competition for Corporate Resources." *Journal of Finance* 52:11–33.
Strömberg, P. 2008. "The New Demography of Private Equity." In *Globalization of Alternative Investments Working Papers Volume 1: Global Economic Impact of Private Equity 2008,* edited by A. Gurung and J. Lerner, 3–26. New York: World Economic Forum USA.
Sylvan, D., and S. Majeski. 1998. "A Methodology for the Study of Historical Counterfactuals." *International Studies Quarterly* 42:79–108.
Tetlok, P., and R. Lebow. 2001. "Poking Counterfactual Holes in Covering Laws: Cognitive Styles and Historical Reasoning." *American Political Science Review* 95:829–43.
Trajtenberg, M. 1990. "A Penny for Your Quotes: Patent Citations and the Value of Inventions." *Rand Journal of Economics* 21:172–87.
Tufano, P. 1989. "Financial Innovation and First-Mover Advantages." *Journal of Financial Economics* 25:213–40.
———. 1995. "Securities Innovations: A Historical and Functional Perspective." *Journal of Applied Corporate Finance* 7:90–103.
———. 2003. "Financial Innovation." In *Handbook of the Economics of Finance, Volume 1a: Corporate Finance,* edited by G. Constantinides, M. Harris, and R. Stulz, 307–36. New York: Elsevier.
Tufano, P., and B. Kyrillos. 1994. "Leland O'Brien Rubinstein Associates Incorporated: SuperTrust." Case Study 294-050: Harvard Business School.

Comment Antoinette Schoar

I really enjoyed reading this chapter and as you probably already got a sense from Peter's and Josh's discussion, this is a very different empirical approach than what we normally see, especially in applied microempirical work. So what I want to do in this Comment is first outline where I think the strength of this approach comes from and then show you how it compares to more standard microempirical work that we normally do in policy evaluations, and how these two can complement each other. So I think it would be helpful to understand whether innovation in financial markets in general could be different from other product markets and why.

To me, it seems that there is this basic tension that has become very prominent in our minds about innovation in financial markets, in particular over the last three years. Of course, there are many financial innovations to share risks between households or lower the transaction costs of accessing markets—I guess we would all agree that these are useful product innovations in finance that help firms and households improve their financial decisions, such as investment and savings, and so forth. But there is this other big worry with financial innovation—they seem often to have big distributional implications or, in Peter's language, externalities. In particular, I think the two big things that worry me about the role of financial innovations is, first it looks like there is a lot of financial innovation that seems to be aimed at generating fees for the financial institutions, but that do not necessarily have much impact on helping people improve financial functions. And then the second aspect is that because of confusion of retail investors or large looming agency problems, there seems to be a lot of innovation that leads to mis-selling. Either because, as Peter says in the chapter, later adopters of these innovations do not understand them so well, or maybe because from the beginning they might be targeted to exploit the confusion of retail investors in those markets.

So why do we worry about this less in product markets and why should we be worrying about it in finance? In my mind, the answer is to a large extent that it is very difficult to learn quickly about the quality of financial investments—it takes time. It is a very noisy updating process. If you buy a computer, you do not need to know what is going on inside it. But if it does not work the way you want, you will learn this pretty quickly and from then on you will buy a competitor's product. And that will cause quick feedback loops. Here competition actually does the trick and in many situations drives out the bad product. However, in financial markets that is not so clear. For

Antoinette Schoar is the Michael Koerner '49 Professor of Entrepreneurial Finance at the Sloan School of Management, Massachusetts Institute of Technology, and a research associate of the National Bureau of Economic Research.

your retirement savings, you actually will only know in thirty years whether your broker gave you good advice or whether the broker misled you. That is obviously too late.

And I think the big debate now in finance is, especially with the new consumer financial protection agency, how to strike the right balance between allowing innovations that improve the functioning of financial markets, but at the same time curb those innovations that are mainly aimed at extracting more rents from customers. This is where a lot of the tension comes from. And so that is what I really liked about the approach that Josh and Peter propose here: thinking about counterfactual histories in financial markets is something that, if you take this as an approach, actually forces us to think about long-term implications. And to me, it seems that this could be a tool to help us set an agenda for research. That is to say, what are the comparative statics that we really want to test and what are the trends that we should do much more empirical work on? So to me, the benefits of this approach are that they can play an agenda-setting role and help us systematically map the impact of innovation, in particular on other parts of the economy such as the political, social, and regulatory context.

The second thing I wanted to mention is that one could go even further and think within this context about how current innovation affects the occurrence of future innovation, either because it affects how regulation or market entry are affected. For example, if we have innovations that need to rely on big banks, it would have completely different implications for political capture going forward than innovations that lead to a more diffused financial system.

In contrast, there are two things that I found difficult to think about in their framework. One is that in fact you are setting the bar really high because you do not only want to see causality here. You want to see causality relative to a world that never happens. It is really difficult to do, partly because we might not know what other innovations that the world could have brought about had this one thing not happened. And so you have to make a lot of judgment calls.

Now the second thing I was struggling with here is that these counterfactual histories allow you to think about systemic impact on the grand scale, but for the more practical work of regulators and financial institutions, they have to make decisions based on real data. Most regulations are actually incremental rather than designing a full counterfactual history. And so this approach is not well-suited to allow us to understand the margins that regulatory intervention can affect. In the end, I also feel that this approach does not allow us to map out the channels through which innovation actually impacts the economy. Here a more traditional, complementary approach of microempirical studies can be more useful.

So the traditional microempirical approaches allow us to understand the local impact of marginal interventions. Instead of saying should we ever have allowed CDOs to happen, or should we ever allow mutual funds to exist, the question that will help regulators is more incremental and might take the form of "should we set defaults for 401(k) plans and how should we set them"? Should we allow life cycle plans and how should they be structured? And I think these things can be answered with traditional microempirical approaches, but of course, it is the flipside of the counterfactual history.

So let me make a final suggestion; while I think that in general it is very important to understand innovation in financial markets, one dimension that is most interesting to me is to map out how innovations are either distorted or exacerbated through agency relationships and confusion of retail customers. So if we think about the consumer financial protection agency that is about to be set up, for example, we need to ask how market competition interacts with financial innovation and what is the impact of those innovations. Because the big problem that we are facing in household finance is that if indeed customers can be easily confused about the underlying quality of the financial products and services they buy it is not clear whether greater competition in these markets leads to a first best outcome. And therefore we have to think hard how regulation should work in this market.

In any case, I found it a very stimulating chapter. I think this type of approach needs to be juxtaposed with careful microempirical analysis.

12

The Adversity/Hysteresis Effect
Depression-Era Productivity Growth in the US Railroad Sector

Alexander J. Field

Throughout its history the United States has endured cycles of financial boom and bust. Boom periods have been marked by weakened or absent regulation of the financial sector and a growing willingness on the part of households, nonfinancial businesses, and financial businesses to hold riskier assets and to finance these positions with higher leverage (higher debt to equity ratios). These twin engines fuel financial sector profits and remuneration so long as asset prices continue to appreciate, but they (especially the trend toward higher leverage) render the system vulnerable when asset bubbles burst. In the boom phase, as the financial system becomes more interconnected, with narrowing capital cushions and complex webs of rights to receive from and obligations to pay to, it becomes more fragile and vulnerable. The failure of one financial institution now has the potential to bring down others like a row of dominoes, with the potential for severe impacts on the real economy as credit flows seize up (Minsky 1986).

This cycle was evident in the late 1920s (boom) going into the 1930s (bust), in the initial decade of the twenty-first century, and in a number of intervening and less severe cycles such as that associated with the Savings and Loan crisis of the late 1980s (Field 1992). In each of these instances, while the upswing of the cycle supercharged the accumulation of physical capital, particularly structures, its aftermath retarded it. The boom and bust cycle of physical accumulation has had predictable impacts on productivity growth in the short run. The upswing of the financial cycle lays the groundwork for a subsequent contraction in physical accumulation, which, amplified by multiplier effects and only partially counteracted by fiscal and monetary

Alexander J. Field is the Michel and Mary Orradre Professor of Economics at Santa Clara University and executive director of the Economic History Association.

policy, contributes to the decline in aggregate demand that induces recession, which has historically produced a short-run adverse effect on both labor productivity and total factor productivity (TFP).

This adverse effect has been reflected in growth retardation and, in many instances, outright declines in productivity measures. Why? The slowdown in physical accumulation produces a growing output gap, the result of the reduction in spending on structures and equipment amplified by multiplier effects. Productivity growth slows or declines as falling output collides with relatively inflexible costs of fixed capital, particularly structures.[1] Between 1890 and 2004, an increase in the unemployment rate of 1 percentage point was statistically associated with a reduction in the TFP growth rate for the private nonfarm economy of about 0.9 percent. This short-run cyclical effect persisted through periods characterized by both high and low trend growth rates. A weaker procyclical influence on labor productivity growth can also be identified (Field 2010).

Gordon (2010) has suggested that the historically inverse relationship between the output gap and productivity may recently have disappeared. There is increasing evidence, however, that economic downturn in the first decade of the twenty-first century will in fact be associated with weak or negative TFP growth as was the case between 1929 and 1933, and more generally throughout the entire period from 1890 to 2004. Advance between 2007 and 2008—the worst year of the Great Recession—was negative: –0.2 percent per year. There appeared to be recovery in 2010, but in spite of this, the level of TFP was lower in 2009 than it had been in 2005 (http://www.bls.gov, accessed October 20, 2011; data is for the private nonfarm economy). Even including the sharply higher index for 2010, TFP growth between 2005 and 2010 was 0.6 percent per year, barely higher than rates during the recent dark age (1973–1995) of productivity growth. All of that increase is due to the 2010 number, which may be subject to revision.

And although output per hour rose during 2009 and 2010 after declining, compared with 2007:4, in three out of the four quarters of 2008, it fell again between the first and second quarter of 2011. Recessions continue to be associated with declines in productivity or at least growth retardation.

These issues, however, involve shorter run effects since business cycles are, by definition, shorter run phenomena. What long-run effects, if any, might the financial cycle, and the cycle of physical accumulation to which it helps give rise, have on productivity growth? This requires consideration of potentially beneficial and adverse consequences of both boom and bust. The most obvious influences are clearly negative. In the later stages of a credit boom, as lending standards deteriorate, and as financial institutions

1. Although "voluntary" labor hoarding is referenced frequently in the literature as an explanation of procyclical productivity, I have argued that the involuntary "hoarding" of capital is in fact of greater significance (Field 2010).

push credit on borrowers rather than just responding to their demands for it, it becomes increasingly less likely that physical capital will be allocated to its best uses. The wrong types of capital goods may be produced, and they may be sold or leased to the wrong firms or installed or built in the wrong places. These problems are more easily remedied for equipment, because producer durables are physically moveable, and in any event, are relatively short lived.

Structures are longer lived and generally immobile and in their case a configuration decided upon in haste in the upswing may foreclose other infrastructural developmental paths. It is not always simply a problem of overbuilding, with an overhang that can be worked off in a few years. Some decisions about structural investment are irreversible, or reversible only at great cost. In growth models, more physical capital accumulation is generally preferable to less, but the reality is that in some cases the economy would have been better off (because of disposal and remediation costs) had poorly thought out prior investment not occurred at all.

Zoning and other types of planning and land use regulation can partially mitigate these effects. These were largely absent in the 1920s, and so the adverse effects on the revival of accumulation were more acute in the interwar period than they were in the 1980s or will likely be in the 2010s. During and after the Depression, and partly in response to it, and alongside the more well-known apparatus of financial sector regulation, municipalities developed a locally administered system controlling the physical accumulation of structures (both government and privately owned). The regulation of land use and construction survived the deregulatory enthusiasms of the last several decades more successfully than did the restraints on finance. Why this was so is an interesting story in itself. It had to do in part with the lower concentration of the real estate development industry, the fact that battles would have had to have been fought at the level of hundreds of local jurisdictions rather than primarily at the federal level, and the fact that land use regulation and local building codes, although sometimes perceived as an irritant, did not hinder the potential for private sector profit as much as did the legacies of New Deal regulation of the financial sector. Still, the real estate collapse that began in 2006 has been geographically specific in the severity of its impact, and it is possible some new construction may well end up evolving into blighted neighborhoods that will ultimately need to be razed.

The second adverse impact on potential output takes place during the downturn. In the bust phase of the cycle, as the financial crisis disrupts lending and other financial intermediation, physical accumulation slows down. Assuming that the speculative fever has broken, we can now expect the borrowing and lending that takes place to be more considered. But because both borrowers' and lenders' balance sheets are weaker, loan transactions are perceived as riskier, and less of them take place. So the bust imposes a purely quantitative loss to potential output in the form of accumulation not undertaken. On the expenditure side, a recession represents foregone opportunities for investment as well as consumption. Stilled productive capacity could have been used to add to the nation's physical capital stock but was not. Idle productive capacity (representing the unused service flows of both labor and capital) is like an unsold airplane seat or hotel room. The dated service flows represent potential gone forever if not used. And so some houses, warehouses, apartment buildings, or producer durables are not acquired or built that could have been.

In sum, a financial boom/bust cycle misallocates physical capital in an upswing, in some cases with irreversible or expensively reversible adverse consequences. And the downswing deprives the economy of capital formation that might have taken place in the absence of the recession. In contrast with an imagined world in which accumulation took place at steadier rates, both of these effects on aggregate supply have to be entered on the negative side in an accounting of the effect on the trend growth rate of productivity of the boom/bust financial cycle and the closely related cycle of physical capital accumulation.

The question I now pose is whether there is some compensatory effect during a recession—some positive impact on the long-run growth of potential output. In other words, is there a silver lining to depression? A subterranean theme in some economic commentary seems almost mystically to view depression as a purifying experience, not only purging balance sheets of bad investments and excessive leverage, but also refocusing economic energies on what is truly important, and perhaps stimulating creative juices in a way that expands the supply of useful innovations. This style of argument is reflected in Posner (2009) in a chapter entitled, "A Silver Lining?" and it echoes Treasury Secretary Andrew Mellon's approving Depression-era encouragement to "[l]iquidate labor, liquidate stocks, liquidate the farmers, liquidate real estate. . . . It will purge the rottenness out of the system. . . . People will work harder, live a more moral life" (Hoover 1952, 30).

Is it possible for a diet of feast then famine to toughen up the economic patient, ultimately allowing the economy to grow more rapidly, compensating for the effect on potential output of misallocated capital in the boom and foregone accumulation in the trough? The years of the Great Depression (1929–1941) were the most prolonged period in US economic history in which output remained substantially below potential. That period was also the most technologically progressive of any comparable period in US economic history (Field 2003, 2006a, 2006b, 2008, 2011a, 2011b; see also Schmookler 1966; Mensch 1979). Is there a connection? It is natural to ask whether there was and whether, because the Depression experienced such pronounced advance in this regard, we could expect some boost to longer run growth as a direct consequence of our current recession.

With respect to recent economic history, Bureau of Labor Statistics productivity data show that the decade-long information technology (IT) productivity boom ran out of steam in 2005. Although TFP for the private nonfarm economy grew at 1.57 percent per year between 1995 and 2005, it grew very slowly between 2005 and 2007 (0.4 percent per year, declined in 2008, and was lower in 2009 than it had been in 2005 [BLS Series MPU491007, accessed October 20, 2011]). We will not have determinative evidence on the longer run trajectory of TFP in the 2010s for some time, since trend growth in my view can only be reliably measured between business cycle peaks. Thus we will need to await the closing of the output gap and the economy's return to potential to get a good reading. Even then there will be a question—as there is in the case of the Great Depression—as to how much of the advance would have taken place anyway. Still, the issue of whether we can expect a "recession boost" to potential output is obviously an important one, and it is natural to turn to the Depression experience for possible indications as to whether this is likely. That long-run trajectory bears on a number of policy issues, including the adequacy of Social Security funding, our ability to address escalating health costs, and the more general question of what will happen to our material standard of living.

I offer a nuanced response to the question of whether 1929 through 1941 bred productivity improvements that might foreshadow what will happen over the next decade. The issue is best approached by thinking of TFP growth across the 1930s as resulting from the confluence of three tributaries. The first was the continuing high rate of TFP growth within manufacturing, the result of the maturing of a privately funded research and development system. The second was associated with spillovers from the buildout of the surface road network, which boosted private sector productivity, particularly in transportation and wholesale and retail distribution (Field 2011a). The third influence, which I call the adversity/hysteresis effect, reflects the ways in which crisis sometimes leads to new and innovative solutions with persistent effects. It is another name for what adherents of the silver lining thesis describe, and it is a mechanism reflected in the folk wisdom that necessity is the mother of invention.

In the absence of the economic downturn, we would probably have gotten roughly the same contribution from the first two tributaries. That is, certain scientific and technological opportunities, perhaps an unusually high number of them, were ripe for development in the 1930s, and they would have been pursued at about the same rate even in circumstances of full employment. With or without the depression Wallace Carothers would have invented nylon; Donald Douglass would have brought forth the DC3. Similarly, by the end of the 1920s, automobile and truck production and registrations had outrun the capabilities of the surface road infrastructure. Strong political alliances in favor of building more and improved roads had been formed, and issues regarding the layout of a national route system had been hashed out by the end of 1926 (Finch 1992; Paxson 1946). It is highly probable that the buildout of the surface road network would have continued at roughly the same pace in the absence of the Depression. So it is the third effect, the kick in the rear of unemployment and financial meltdown, that is most relevant in terms of a possible causal association between depression and productivity advance.

The adversity/hysteresis mechanism is familiar to households unexpectedly faced with the loss of a wage earner or suddenly cut off from easy access to credit that had been formerly available. Under such circumstances, successful families inventory their assets and focus on how they can get more out of what they already have, not just how they can get more.

Adversity does cause some people to work harder, just as it causes some people to take more risks: these are people for whom the income or wealth effects of adversity dominate the substitution effects. For others, the substitution effect leads to withdrawal from the labor force or discouragement. In more severe forms this is evident in a variety of mental and physical disorders that may show up in aggregate statistics on alcoholism, depression, suicide, and divorce. The overall effect on innovation, work effort, and risk taking is not easy to predict, given that, in economic terms, both income and substitution effects are operative, and that they pull in opposite directions (blanket opposition to tax increases based on their effects on aggregate supply typically focuses only on substitution effects). There is merit in the adage that what does not kill you makes you stronger. It's just that sometimes it kills you. Not all families or firms are resilient, and in some instances adversity destroys them. So I am skeptical overall that we can take an unqualified optimistic view of the effects of economic adversity on innovation and creativity.

These qualifications aside, there is one important sector that appears to have benefited from the silver lining effect during the Depression, and that is railroads. Railroads confronted multiple challenges. They faced adverse demand conditions specific to the industry that would have continued to plague firms with or without the Depression. The automobile was already eroding passenger traffic in the 1920s, and trucking was changing the freight business by providing strong competition in the short haul sector. For an industry faced with these challenges and characterized by heavy fixed costs, the downturn in aggregate economic activity was particularly devastating, and pushed many railroads into receivership. Access to capital was disrupted, although some ailing roads received loans from the Reconstruction Finance Corporation and, paradoxically, bankrupt rails, no longer required to meet obligations to their original creditors, could obtain credit, especially short-term financing for equipment purchases, with greater ease than lines that had not gone bankrupt. But access to cheap fifty-year mortgage money—widely available in the 1920s—was pretty much gone (Schiffman 2003). Railroads responsible for roughly one-third of US track mileage were in receivership by the late 1930s, and had their financing constraints somewhat relaxed. A corollary, however, is that railroads responsible for the remaining two-thirds were not in receivership. With generally weak balance sheets, they faced limited access to credit.

Confronted with these challenges, both labor and management took a hard look at what they had, and worked to use their hours and capital resources more effectively. The result was a substantial increase in the rate of total factor productivity growth, due to innovations in equipment, structures, and logistics. Both capital and labor inputs declined substantially.[2] Underutilized sections of track, for example, were decommissioned (see figure 12.6),[3] and the net stocks of both railroad structures and railroad equipment declined (figure 12.2) as did the number of employees (figure 12.7). Rolling stock went down by one-third, and the number of employees declined by almost that percentage.

Superimposed on this overall rationalization of the rail system were improvements in locomotives, rolling stock, and permanent way. Steam locomotives (and even some of the early electrics) began to be replaced with diesel-electrics, an almost unambiguously superior technology, particularly in comparison with steam. Diesel-electrics did not require an hour for "firing up" to deliver full power, did away with the need for rewatering stops (to replenish the boiler's source of steam), reduced or eliminated the need for refueling, and made unnecessary the locomotive position of fireman. If properly equipped, diesel-electrics could operate on both electrified or nonelectrified portions of a system, drawing power from overhead wires where available or generating their own when it was not, which made them considerably more flexible than pure electric locomotives.[4] Overall, diesel-electrics had much lower maintenance costs, produced less wear and tear on tracks, and had fuel efficency that was at least three times that of steam locomotives (Stover 1997, 213). Although diesel-electrics still represented a small fraction of the total locomotive stock in 1941, their introduction and development is testimony to the engineering advances that were being pushed forward during the Depression years.

Passenger cars also improved, with more of them constructed from lightweight aluminum and alloys; streamlining became the aesthetic hallmark

2. Posner captures the silver lining hypothesis insofar as it applies to productivity in these words: "A depression increases the efficiency with which both labor and capital inputs are used by businesses, because it creates an occasion and an imperative for reducing slack. . . . When a depression ends, a firm motivated by the recession to reduce slack in its operations will have lower average costs than before" (2009, 222–23).

3. First track mileage operated was roughly unchanged from 1919 to 1929 (263,707, declining to 262,546). But between 1929 and 1941, it dropped 5.9 percent (262,546 to 245,240) (*Statistical Abstract* 1945, table 521, 470). As first track mileage declined, however, the relative importance of secondary trackage increased (see Stover 1997, 182–83).

4. Contrary to some misconceptions, a diesel-electric does not use a diesel motor directly to power the locomotive. The diesel engine drives a generator, the electrical output of which drives an electric motor that powers the engine. It is thus closer in design philosophy to what the new Chevrolet Volt claims than say, the Toyota Prius.

for both locomotive-drawn cars and self-propelled articulated or single car (such as the Budd car) trains. Freight cars became larger. The introduction of electro-pneumatic retarders improved the efficiency of gravity switching yards. Without them "it would have been a virtual impossibility to handle war traffic through major centers" (Parmalee 1950, 43).

Complementing these improvements in equipment, investments in permanent way along with logistical innovation enabled railroads, in spite of substantial reductions in the numbers of locomotives, rolling stock, and employees, to record slightly more revenue ton miles of freight and book almost as many passenger miles in 1941 as they had in 1929. What were some of these improvements? First, more sections of the system were electrified.[5] Second, centralized traffic control systems allowed more intensive use of trackage without jeopardizing safety. Centralized traffic control was a refinement of block signaling in which the operation of trains could be monitored and controlled by a single dispatcher, who scanned a central display board providing real time location information for all trains in a division. Track mileage operated using this system increased more than sixfold between 1929 and 1941, from 341 to 2,163 miles, and then more than tripled during the war years (Stover 1997, 184). The innovation was particularly important in heavily used portions of the rail network, since it allowed substantial increases in utilization without compromising safety.

The most far-reaching and significant organizational innovation, however, was the negotiation and implementation of unlimited freight interchange. Agreements worked out during the Depression allowed the free movement of freight cars among different systems, so that, for example, a boxcar could move from one road to another without needing to break cargo. And when it reached its destination (even though outside of the system that owned it) the car could be reloaded rather than sent back empty to territory controlled by the originating road.[6] Cooperation was enabled by a standard schedule of rental payments along with agreements so that repairs and maintenance, if necessary, could be undertaken in yards owned by a railroad different from the one that owned the car.[7]

Unlimited interchange resulted in large reductions in the transactions

5. The most important Depression era project was electrification of the Pennsylvania Railroad from New York to Washington and beyond.

6. In the first half of the twentieth century most transcontinental rail passengers had to change in Chicago. As one writer put it, the city was "a phantom Chinese wall that splits America in half." After World War II the president of the Chesapeake and Ohio published advertisements announcing provocatively that "a hog could travel across the United States without changing cars but a human could not." The ads were intended to jumpstart flagging passenger traffic by showcasing the removal of Chicago as an "invisible barrier." But the copy is indirect testimony to what unlimited freight interchange had achieved during the 1930s (Stover 1997, 216–17).

7. The system eventually evolved to incorporate freight cars owned by third parties, so that today more than half of freight rolling stock is owned by entities other than railroads (Richter 2005, 35).

costs associated with moving freight long distances. It was facilitated by moves toward equipment standardization initiated during the Federal government's takeover of the railroads during World War I (Stover 1997, 175; Longman 2009), and pushed forward in the 1930s by the Association of American Railroads. The AAR, formed in October 1934 through the merger of five industry trade groups, vetted and approved, from the standpoint of both safety and efficiency, changes in freight car design, and took the lead in developing and promulgating industry standards for operations, interchange, and, ultimately, interoperability. These were and are published in its *Manual of Standards and Recommended Practices.* Because railroads are a highly interconnected network industry, standard setting takes on more importance in facilitating efficiency improvement than is the case in trucking, for example, because failure of one small part of a system can have much larger deleterious consequences.

During the Depression railroads faced strained financial circumstances, lack of easy access to financial capital, and reduced investment flows. These conditions arguably created a particular incentive to search for and implement logistical improvements, disembodied change that shows up largely in the TFP residual. If this is so, the adversity of these years can be seen as having influenced not just the rate of productivity change but also its character or direction.

The results of these and other changes were significant improvements in productivity over the course of the Depression. Kendrick's series for railroad sector output, drawn from Barger (1951), shows overall output (a weighted average of freight and passenger traffic) 5.5 percent higher in 1941 than it was in 1929. Given the big declines in inputs, this was a very impressive achievement. Other factors, largely independent of the business cycle, certainly contributed to the strong productivity performance of railroads during the Depression. For example, the buildout of the surface road network facilitated a growing complementarity between trucking and rails. But some of the productivity improvement resulted from responses internal to organizations. And whereas in households it is sometimes argued that memories are short and there is little permanent carryover of behavioral changes when times improve, institutional learning and memory particular to the corporate form probably allowed some hysteresis. Beneficial organizational innovations when times were poor persisted when times improved, and contributed to permanently higher levels of TFP, and the far superior performance of the US rail system in World War II as compared with the World War I.

In exploring this question, we need to keep the larger context in mind. If we compare total gross domestic product (GDP) in 1929 and 1941 using the Bureau of Economic Analysis's chained index number methodology, we see from the latest revisions that the aggregate grew at a continuously compounded growth rate of 2.8 percent per year over that twelve-year period

(BEA 2011, NIPA Table 1.1.6). If we make a cyclical adjustment, this rises to 2.97 per year (Field 2011b), close to the 3 percent per year often viewed as the long run "speed limit" for the US economy. The GDP surpassed its 1929 level in 1936, and was 40 percent above its 1929 level by 1941. Because private sector labor and capital inputs increased hardly at all over that period (hours were flat and net fixed assets increased at only 0.3 percent per year [http://www.bea.gov, Fixed Asset Table 1.2]), virtually all of this was TFP growth. We would like to have a sense of how much of this, if any, was the result of this adversity/hysteresis effect, relative to the other two tributaries.

If the adversity/hysteresis mechanism has some empirical punch to it, then it is possible that the storm clouds of recession/depression can have something of a silver lining. The disruption of credit availability and an increase in the cost of equity finance were both central features of the 1930s, just as their easy accessibility and cheap cost through most of the 1920s had been a feature of that decade. The boom/bust cycle was associated with declining physical capital accumulation and productivity, particularly between 1929 and 1933. At least in the case of railroads, however, there appear to have been longer run benefits to the downswing phase of the financial cycle and the closely related cycle of physical accumulation in the form of technical innovation within the context of effective organizational responses.

12.1 Railroads and the Silver Lining

In the last part of the nineteenth century, railroads dominated the US economy in a way no other economic organization ever had or ever has again. They remained a formidable presence in the 1930s, although beset with challenges from several sides. What differentiated railroads from other parts of the private economy was the scale of their enterprise, particularly the size and value of the physical capital they owned, capital whose acquisition was financed largely by borrowing. Coming out of the 1920s, railroads had huge fixed nominal debt service obligations. They did not necessarily have to worry about rolling over short-term debt, since much of their borrowing was in the form of long-term mortgages, but they still had to meet mandated payments. In the face of an economic downturn and wrenching changes in market opportunities associated with the growth of trucking and the automobile, railroads were the poster child for Irving Fisher's debt-deflation thesis. By 1935, railroads responsible for more than 30 percent of first track mileage were in receivership (figure 12.1), and this remained so for the remainder of the Depression. But the problems for the sector as a whole were in a sense less those of the roads in receivership, and more the challenges faced by those who were not. The former were actually less cash strapped than the latter. Railroad organizations were under enormous stress during the Depression, and so their productivity performance over this period is all the more remarkable.

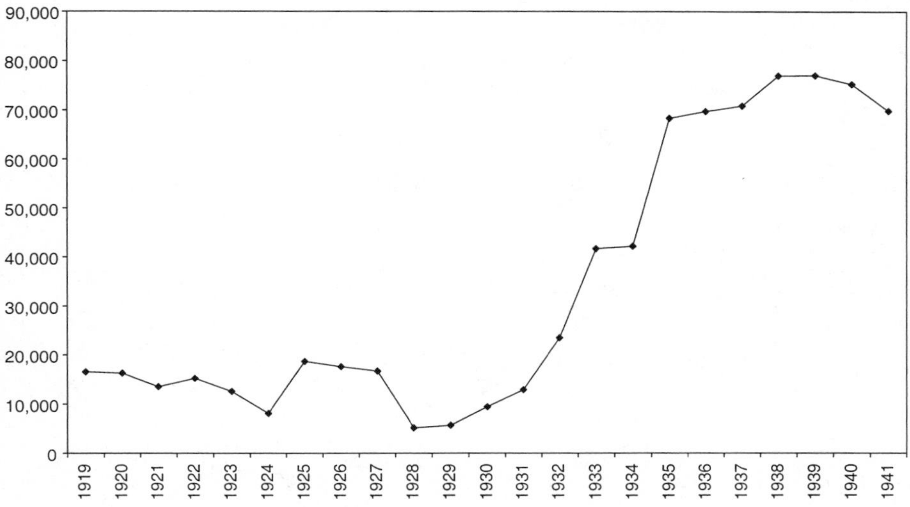

Fig. 12.1 Mileage of railroads under receivership
Source: US Bureau of the Census (1937, 1944, 1947).

If we ignore variations in income shares—which are relatively stable over time—a TFP growth rate calculation is basically a function of three numbers: the rate of growth of labor input, the rate of growth of capital input, and the rate of growth of output. Kendrick's series for railroad output are drawn from Barger (1951) and are based on data for both freight and passenger traffic, with a larger weight on freight. It shows output 5.5 percent higher in 1941 than it was in 1929. Kendrick's labor input series are also from Barger and are identical to those that continue to be listed on the BEA website (NIPA Table 6.8A, line 39). Between 1929 and 1941, the number of employees declined 30.4 percent, employee hours 31.4 percent. Kendrick's railway capital series is taken from Ulmer (1960), and shows a 1941 decline of 5.5 percent between 1929 and 1941. Putting these together, Kendrick has railway TFP rising at 2.91 percent per year over the twelve years of the Depression.

It is not possible, given currently available data, to do better than Kendrick for output and labor input. But the BEA's revised Fixed Asset Tables do give us an opportunity to update capital input. Figure 12.2 brings together NIPA data on gross investment in railroad equipment and structures. Gross investment in railroad equipment peaks in 1923 and then moves fairly steadily downward to virtually nothing in 1933. It then revives somewhat, particularly after 1935 and the big increase in railroads in receivership. Investment in railroad structures peaks in 1926 but remains high through 1930 before declining to a trough in 1933 and then recovering modestly during the remainder of the Depression, although not as sharply as equipment investment. Using the data underlying these series, I calculate that

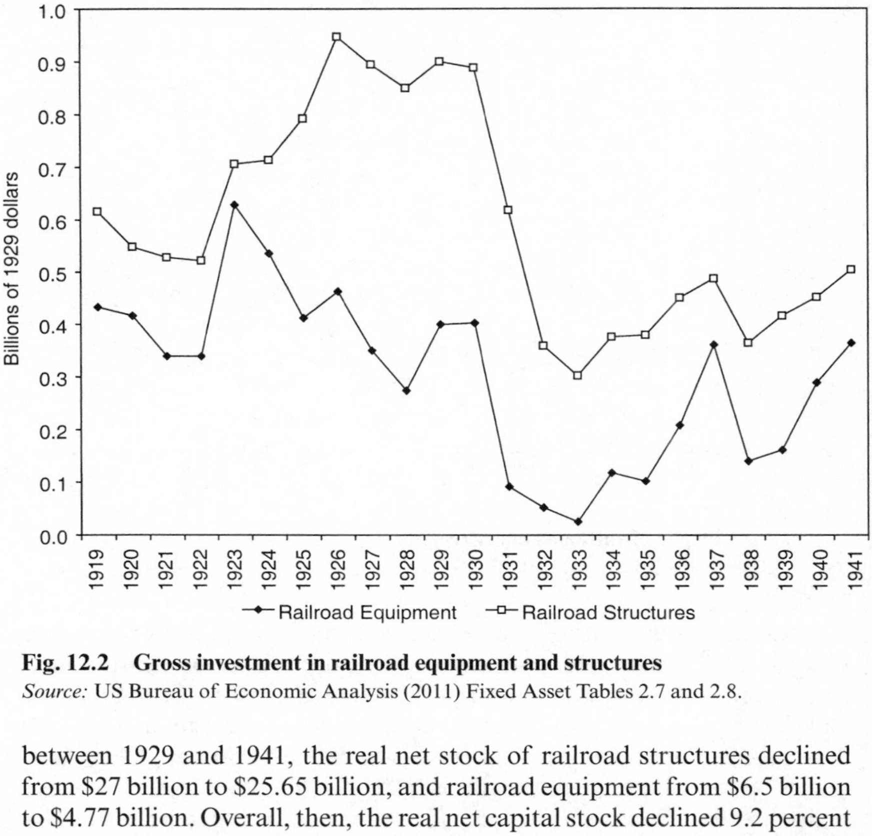

Fig. 12.2 Gross investment in railroad equipment and structures
Source: US Bureau of Economic Analysis (2011) Fixed Asset Tables 2.7 and 2.8.

between 1929 and 1941, the real net stock of railroad structures declined from $27 billion to $25.65 billion, and railroad equipment from $6.5 billion to $4.77 billion. Overall, then, the real net capital stock declined 9.2 percent over the twelve-year period, while Kendrick has it declining only 5.5 percent. (Kendrick 1961, Table G-III, 545). A more rapid decline in capital input (0.69 percent per year rather than 0.47 percent per year) would boost TFP growth in railways between 1929 and 1941 from 2.91 to 2.97 percent per year.[8]

We can get further insight into trends in railroad accumulation by looking at detailed numbers on rolling stock (Figures 12.3, 12.4, and 12.5; these data are in units, not dollars). The locomotive numbers show decumulation in 1922 and then again starting in 1925. The number of locomotives then shrinks continuously until 1941. Some of this reflects replacement of locomotives with larger, more powerful engines, but the overall trend is unmistakable. The total number of locomotives shrank from 61,257 in 1929 to 44,375 in 1941. A small but growing number of replacement engines were

8. The difference between Kendrick's capital input rate of decline of .47 and the rate of decline based on the latest BEA data (.69) is .22 percent per year, which, with a .25 weight on capital in the growth accounting equation, would add .055 percent per year to the sector's TFP growth rate.

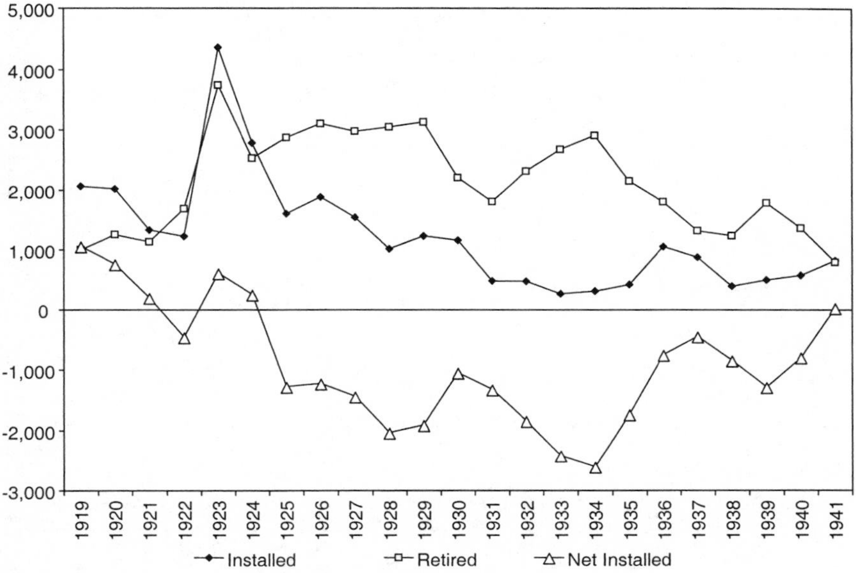

Fig. 12.3 Locomotives installed and retired, 1919–1941
Source: US Bureau of the Census (1937, 1944, 1947).

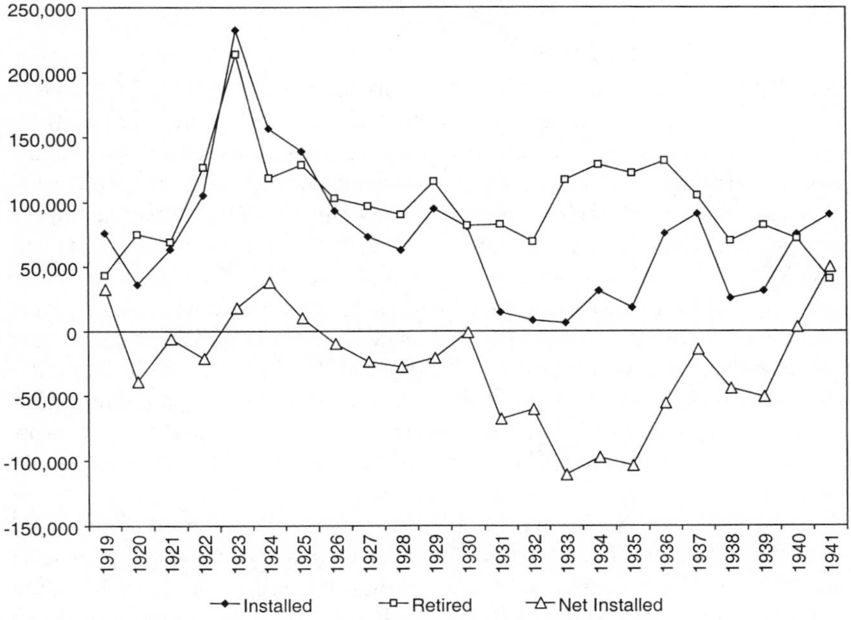

Fig. 12.4 Freight cars installed and retired, 1919–1941
Source: US Bureau of the Census (1937, 1944, 1947).

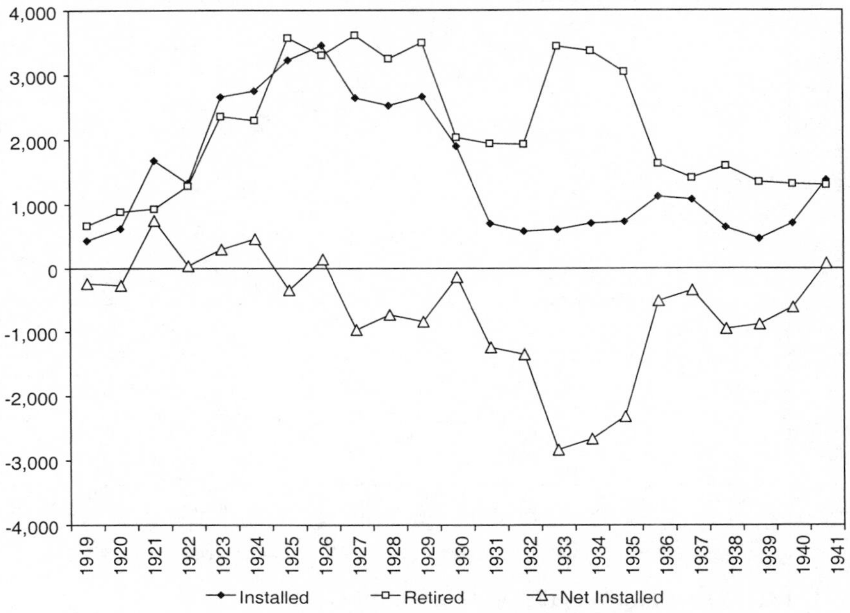

Fig. 12.5 Railroad passenger cars installed and retired, 1919–1941
Source: US Bureau of the Census (1937, 1944, 1947).

diesel-electric; the count of such locomotives rose from 621 in 1929 to 895 in 1941 (1944 *Statistical Abstract*, table 525, 473), while the average tractive power of the remaining steam engines increased from 44,801 to 51,217 pounds. Annual freight car data show continuous decumulation from 1920 through 1939, with the exception of 1924 through 1926. Over the same period, aggregate freight car capacity in kilotons shrank from 105,411 to 85,682 (1937 *Statistical Abstract*, table 427, 372; 1944 *Statistical Abstract*, table 523, 472). The replacement cars were, however, somewhat larger; average capacity rose from 46.3 to 50.3 tons between 1929 and 1941. Passenger car decumulation was modest through 1930, then increased dramatically through 1933. There was some recovery to lower rates of decumulation, particularly after 1935, but the number of passenger cars did not grow again until 1941 (figure 12.5). Numbers fell from 53,838 in 1929 to 38,344 in 1941.

Figure 12.6 is of particular interest. It reports miles of road constructed and abandoned, with abandonments taking a sharp jump to a higher level in 1932, and new construction tapering off to virtually nothing by 1934. On the labor input side (figure 12.7), the number of railroad employees declined moderately in the 1920s, then precipitously in the 1930s (figure 12.7). Bringing together all of these data on labor and capital inputs, we have a picture

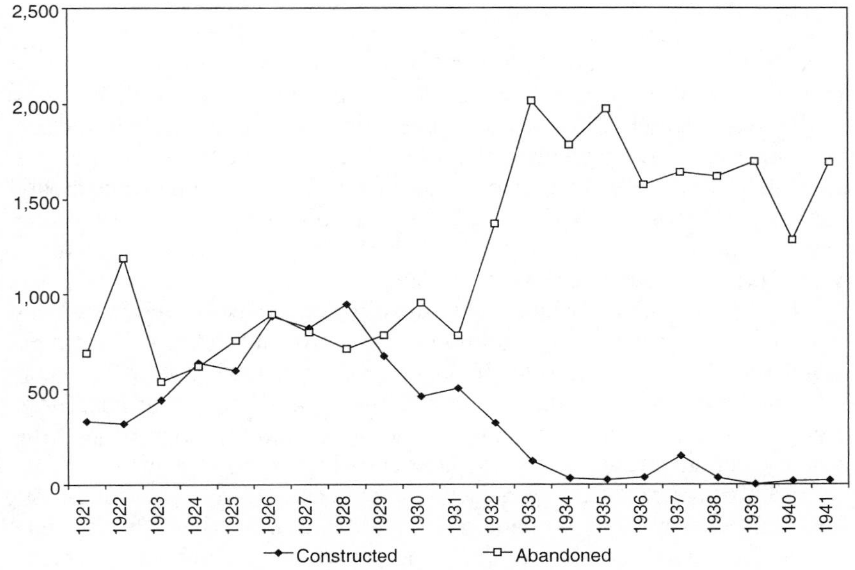

Fig. 12.6 Miles of road constructed and abandoned, all line haul steam railroads, 1921–1941
Source: Interstate Commerce Commission (1943, 14).

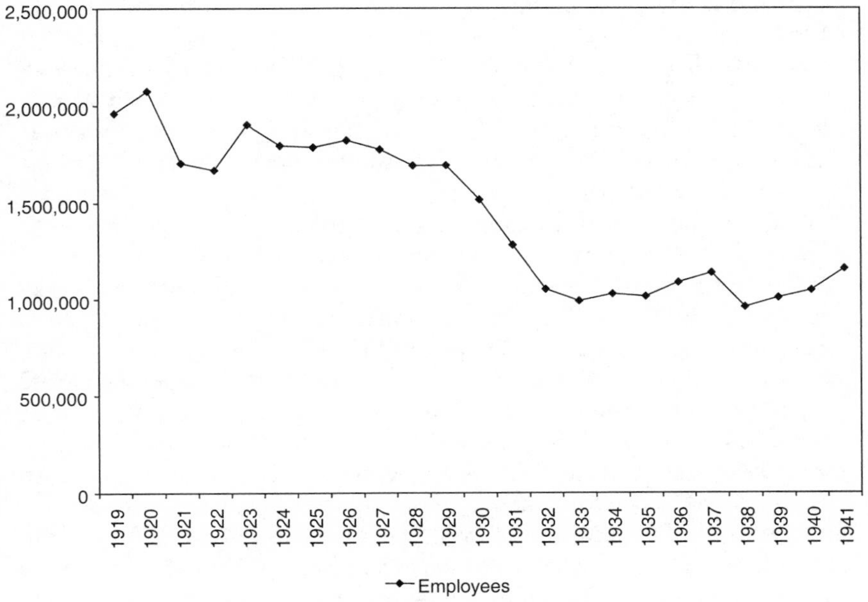

Fig. 12.7 Railroad employees, 1919–1941
Source: US Bureau of the Census (1937, 1944, 1947).

of a system undergoing wrenching rationalization, rationalization midwifed by the economic downturn and the threat or actuality of receivership.

Figures 12.8 and 12.10 provide data on freight car miles and millions of passenger miles. Despite a net stock of structures that had fallen 6 percent since its peak in 1931, in spite of a labor force that was 30 percent smaller than it had been in 1929, and in spite of the fact that the real stock of railroad capital was a full one-third lower than it had been in 1929, revenue ton miles were 6 percent greater in 1941 than 1929.

The data on passenger miles show steadily declining output by this measure throughout the 1920s, testimony to the growing threat to passenger traffic posed by the automobile, and a sharp drop to 1933. But 1941 passenger miles were within 6 percent of carriage in 1929. It is clear that since more freight was carried with many fewer freight cars, a substantial portion of the railway sector's productivity gains came from increases in freight car capacity utilization rates, which generated big increases in capital productivity. The ability to carry more freight and about the same number of passengers with much reduced numbers of locomotives, freight cars, and passenger cars also reduced the demand for railway structures: maintenance sheds, sidings, roundhouses, and so forth, which was serendipitous since the financing for expanding the stock of structures was not readily available. The US railroad system was able in 1941 to carry more freight and almost as many passengers as it had in 1929 with substantially lower inputs of labor and capital. That meant, as a matter of definition, big increases in both labor productivity and TFP. By the end of the Depression, the US rail system was in much better shape than it had been at the start of World War I, and was able to cope with huge increases in both passenger and freight traffic during World War II. Figures 12.8, 12.9, and 12.10 include data on output over the war years. If one measures from 1929 through 1942, using Kendrick's data, TFP in the sector grows by 4.48 percent per year.

Table 12.1 allows a closer examination of trends in and contributors to productivity increase. It shows the percent change in a variety of input, output, and physical productivity measures between 1919 and 1929, 1929 and 1941, and 1929 and 1942. It also reports the underlying data, as well as aggregate economic data for 1929, 1941, and 1942. The first year of full scale war mobilization is 1942, and one can see in the aggregate data the partial crowding out of consumption and investment as a result of the doubling of government expenditure. Still, civilian unemployment averaged 4.7 percent for the year, and the distortions for the economy were not as extreme as in 1943 and 1944. Therefore, there is some merit in calculating productivity growth in railroads between 1929 and 1942 as well as 1941, since the output gap in 1942 is closer to what it was in percentage terms in 1929. Also, since we are examining physical productivity measures, the distortions in pricing and valuation associated with wartime are somewhat less of a concern.

What these data show is that, overall, in spite of or perhaps in part because

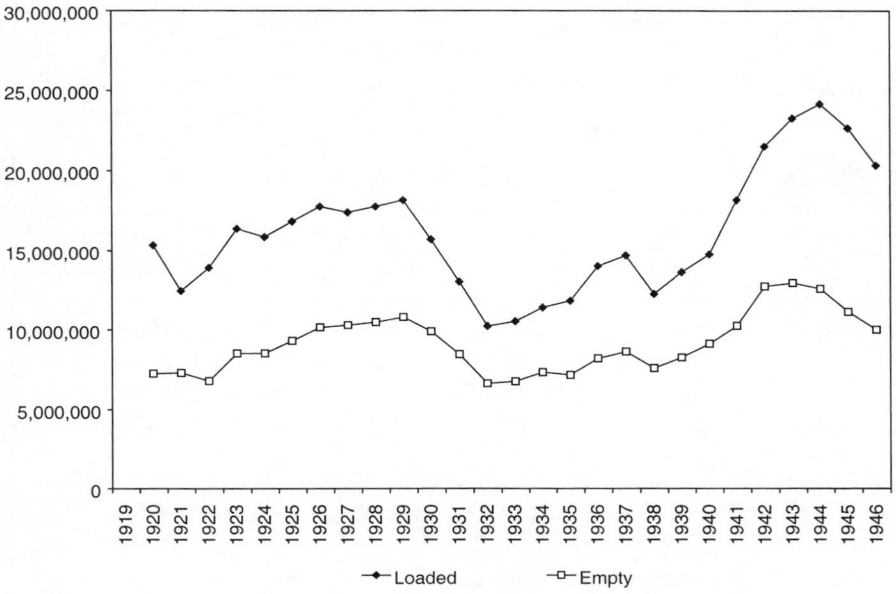

Fig. 12.8 Railroad freight car miles, 1920–1946
Source: US Bureau of the Census (1937, 1944, 1947).

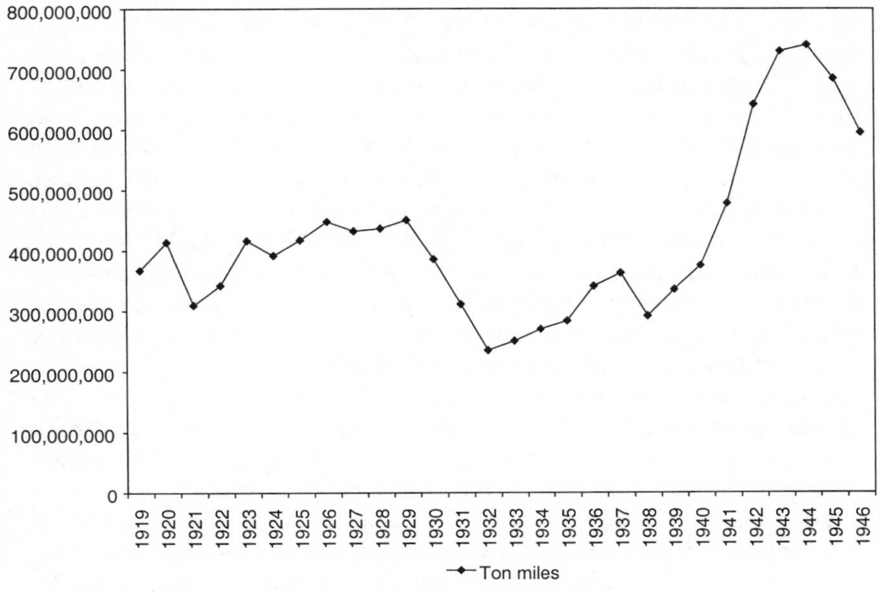

Fig. 12.9 Revenue freight ton miles, thousands, 1919–1946
Source: US Bureau of the Census (1937, 1944, 1947).

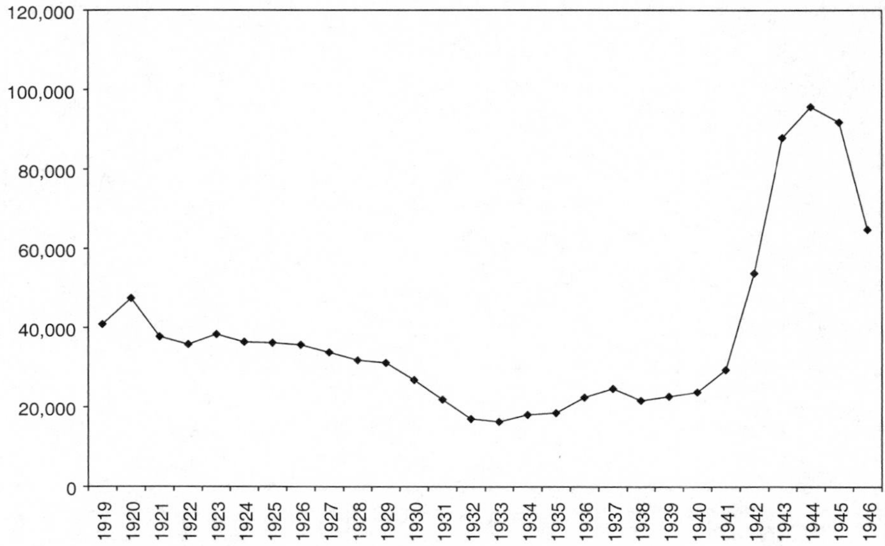

Fig. 12.10 Railroad passenger miles, millions, 1919–1946
Source: US Bureau of the Census (1937, 1944, 1947).

of the trying times, railroad productivity growth was significantly stronger across the Depression years than it had been in the 1920s. An important measure of physical productivity is revenue ton miles per freight car, which grew 28.1 percent between 1919 and 1929, 42.3 percent from 1929 to 1941, and 86.5 percent between 1929 and 1942. Let's look more closely at what underlay the Depression era increases. The total number of miles traversed by loaded freight cars in 1941 was approximately the same as it had been in 1929. The big driver of productivity improvement was that the number of cars had declined 25.6 percent. The average capacity of each car was somewhat greater—it had grown from 46.3 to 50.3 tons, making it easier to achieve a 6.1 percent increase in tons of revenue freight per loaded car. Overall, we can deduce that the average speed of each freight car (a function of average time stopped and average speed while in motion) had increased, since if it had remained the same as it had been in 1929, the 25.6 percent decline in the number of cars would have reduced total freight car miles by a comparable percentage. We also know that the number of freight car loadings in thousands declined from 52,828 in 1929 to 42,352 in 1941; freight traveled on average a longer distance, reflecting the inroads of trucking in shorter hauls.

In contrast, between 1919 and 1929, the number of cars stayed about the same, but total miles traversed by freight cars rose. Note, however, that miles booked by empty cars increased much faster than loaded miles during the 1920s, whereas between 1929 and 1941, while the total number of loaded

Table 12.1 **Percent change in inputs, outputs, and productivity, US railroad sector, 1919–1929, 1929–1941, 1929–1942**

					Percent change		
	1919	1929	1941	1942	1919–1929	1929–1941	1929–1942
Inputs							
Employees	1,960,439	1,694,042	1,159,025	1,291,000	–13.6	–31.6	–24.8
Locomotives	68,977	61,257	44,375	44,671	–11.2	–27.6	–27.1
Freight cars	2,426,889	2,323,683	1,732,673	1,773,735	–4.3	–25.5	–23.7
Passenger cars	56,920	53,888	38,334	38,445	–5.3	–28.9	–28.7
Miles of first track	263,707	262,546	245,240	242,744	–0.4	–6.6	–7.5
Outputs							
Revenue ton miles (millions)	367,161	450,189	477,576	640,992	22.6	6.1	42.4
Freight car miles (loaded) (thousands)	14,273,422	18,169,012	18,171,979	21,535,673	27.3	0.0	18.5
Freight car miles (unloaded) (thousands)	6,531,570	10,805,302	10,251,079	12,755,362	65.4	–5.1	18.0
Passenger miles (millions)	40,838	31,165	29,406	53,747	–23.7	–5.6	72.5
Physical productivity measures							
Ton miles per freight car	0.151	0.194	0.276	0.361	28.1	42.3	86.5
Tons of revenue freight per loaded car	25.72	24.78	26.28	29.76	–3.7	6.1	20.1
Average miles per car per day	23.0	32.3	40.6	46.3	40.4	25.7	43.3
Average freight car capacity (tons)	41.9	46.3	50.3	50.5	10.5	8.6	9.1
Average freight car speed (mph)	0.979	1.459	1.920	2.263	49.1	31.6	55.0
Number of freight car loadings (thousands)	41,832	52,828	42,352	42,771	26.3	–19.8	–19.0
Average haul, revenue freight (miles)	309	317	369	428	2.8	16.2	34.9
Ton miles per mile of first track	1.392	1.715	1.947	2.641	23.2	13.6	54.0
Passenger miles per passenger car	0.717	0.578	0.767	1.398	–19.4	32.6	141.7
Ton miles per employee	0.187	0.266	0.412	0.497	41.9	55.1	86.8
Passenger miles per employee	0.021	0.018	0.025	0.042	–11.7	37.9	126.3
Aggregate economic indicators							
Unemployment rate		3.2	9.9	4.7			
Real GDP (billions of chained 1937 dollars)		87.2	122.1	144.7		40.0	65.9
Real gross private domestic investment		12.2	17.6	9.3		44.3	–23.8
Real government consumption and investment		9.2	25.6	60.3		178.3	555.4
Real consumption		63.0	78.2	76.5		24.3	21.4

Sources: US Bureau of the Census (1937, 1944, 1947); NIPA Table 1.1.6A.

miles remained unchanged, unloaded miles dropped. This decline is another reflection of logistical improvement in railroad operations.

An alternate measure of the physical productivity of freight haulage is ton miles per mile of first track. This grew more strongly in the 1920s than during the Depression years, although if one measures to 1942 the reverse is true. Ton miles per employee, a rough measure of labor productivity in freight haulage, grew 41.9 percent during the 1920s, but 55.1 percent during the Depression (86.8 percent if one measures to 1942).

Passenger miles per passenger car declined 19.6 percent during the 1920s, but rose sharply across the Depression years—32.6 percent measuring to 1941, 141.7 percent measuring to 1942. Finally, passenger miles per employee, which declined almost 12 percent during the 1920s, rose 37.9 percent across the Depression years, 126.3 percent measuring through 1942.

12.2 Firm-Level Analysis

Figures 12.1 through 12.10 and table 12.1 document at the sectoral level the productivity achievements of the US railway sector during the Depression years. This last section of the chapter examines the phenomenon at the level of individual railroads. I compare the labor productivity of 128 Class I railroads in 1941 with their performance in 1929. Data are from *Statistics of Railways in the United States* (1929), a volume published annually by the Interstate Commerce Commission. During the Depression Class I railroads were those with operating revenues greater than $1 million. The 1929 edition has data on 167 Class I railroads, covering the vast majority of operations in the United States. Total 1929 employment in the sector was 1,694,042 (see figure 12.7); these 167 roads employed 1,662,095, or 98 percent of the total.

The 1941 ICC volume has data for 135 Class I railroads, employing 1,139,129 out of total sector employment of 1,159,025 (again, 98 percent). Although most railroads in existence in 1929 persisted through 1941, the total number of Class I railroads did decline by about one-fifth (19 percent).[9] In order to make meaningful comparisons between 1941 and 1929, we need to aggregate the data for some 1929 roads so that operational units are comparable to those existing in 1941. Where a number of railroads listed separately in 1929 merged or were otherwise consolidated during the Depression years, the data for the multiple 1929 operational units are pooled. Table 12.2 describes the linkages made between the railroad data in the two years.

9. The threshold to be considered a Class I railroad rose with inflation to $3 million in 1956, $5 million in 1965, $10 million in 1976, $50 million in 1978, and $250 million in 1993. Today the cutoff is $319.3 million. Whereas there were 135 Class I railroads operating in the United States in 1941, there are now only seven: Union Pacific, BNSF (Burlington Northern Santa Fe), CSX, Norfolk Southern, Kansas City Southern, Canadian Pacific, and Canadian National.

Table 12.2 **1929–1941 linkage, Class I railroads, United States**

1941		1929	
Column in 1941 ICC volume	Railroad	Column in 1929 ICC volume	Railroads
18	Erie Railway Company	17	Chicago and Erie Railway
		18	Erie Railway Company
		19	New Jersey and New York Railway
26	New York Central Railway Company	27	Michigan Central
		28	New York Central
		35	Ulster and Delaware Railway Company
		51	Cincinnati Northern
		52	Cleveland, Cincinnati, Chicago, and St. Louis
		53	Evansville, Indianapolis & Terre Haute
35	Baltimore & Ohio Railway Company	11	Buffalo, Rochester, and Pittsburgh
		39	Baltimore & Ohio Railway Company
		42	Buffalo and Susquehanna
47	Pennsylvania-Reading Seashore Lines	56	Pennsylvania System: West Jersey and Seashore Lines
		57	Reading System: Atlantic City Railroad
52	Chesapeake and Ohio	43	Chesapeake and Ohio System: Hocking Vallkey RR
		62	Chesapeake and Ohio RR
62	Atlantic Coast Line System: Louisville and Nashville RR	72	ACLS: Louisville and Nashville
		73	ACLS: Louisville, Henderson & St. Louis
68	Gulf, Mobile, and Ohio	79	Gulf, Mobile & Northern
		85	New Orleans Great Northern
		91	Mobile & Ohio

(continued)

Table 12.2 (cont.)

1941		1929	
Column in 1941 ICC volume	Railroad	Column in 1929 ICC volume	Railroads
92	Duluth, Missabe, and Iron Range	104	Duluth and Iron Range
		105	Duluth, Missabe & Northern
99	Atchison, Topeka, and Santa Fe, and Affiliated Companies	125	Santa Fe: Atchison, Topeka, and Santa Fe
		126	Santa Fe: Panhandle and Santa Fe
		138	Frisco: Ft. Worth and Rio Grande
		160	Santa Fe: Gulf, Colorado, and Santa Fe
		161	Santa Fe: Kansas City, Mexico, and Orient
		162	Santa Fe: Kansas City, Mexico, and Orient Co. of Texas
104	Chicago, Rock Island, and Pacific	122	Chicago, Rock Island, and Gulf
		123	Chicago, Rock Island, and Pacific
112	Union Pacific Railroad Co. (including its leased lines)	112	UP: Oregon Washington RR & Navigation
		130	UP: Los Angeles and Salt Lake
		131	UP: Oregon Short Line
		132	UP: St. Joseph and Grand Island
		133	UP: Union Pacific
118	Kansas City Southern Railway Co. and controlled companies	141	KS Southern: Kansas City Southern
		142	KS: Texarkana and Fort Smith
		145	Louisiana Railway and Navigation Co. of Texas
123	Missouri Kansas Texas Railroad Co. and controlled companies	148	MKT Lines: Missouri Kansas Texas
		149	MKT Lines: Missouri Kansas Texas Co. of Texas
133	St. Louis Southwestern Railway Co. and affiliated companies	158	SLSW: St. Louis Southwestern
		159	SLSW: St. Louis Southwestern Co. of Texas

Railroad history attracts interest from both professional and amateur historians and there is a wealth of information available on the web on the history of firm consolidation and corporate structure at different points in time. Using multiple searches, I have linked forty-three roads reporting in 1929 to fourteen roads in 1941, resulting on this account in a reduction of twenty-nine in the total number of Class I railroads between the two years (see table 12.2). Two other railroads, both small, drop out because they ceased operations during the interval.[10] For six other small railroads employing a total of 2,077 in 1929, I am not able to locate a successor.[11] Four small roads employing a total of 827 appear in 1941 but not 1929.[12] And I dropped two small lines, one, a small unit whose productivity numbers were an outlier, as well as a small railroad in Hawaii.[13] I end up making 1929 through 1941 comparisons for 128 linked units.

To compare labor productivity in the two years, we need a combined output measure, which requires agreement on appropriate metrics for freight and passenger operations, and on how to aggregate them. For freight output, I use revenue ton miles; for passenger traffic, revenue passenger miles. I first calculate the ratio of passenger revenue per passenger mile to freight revenue per ton mile, then use this ratio to convert passenger miles into "equivalent" freight ton miles. Adding this to freight ton miles yields, for each railroad, the output measure.

We have two basic types of output: passenger miles and freight ton miles. If cents per ton mile and per passenger mile were the same for a railroad, then passenger miles would simply be added to freight ton miles for a combined output measure. If a railroad was earning 2 cents for a passenger mile versus 1 cent for a freight ton mile, then a passenger mile for that road would be converted to a freight ton equivalent at a ratio of 2:1. This procedure is similar to what Barger (1951) used for aggregate data. In cases where consolidation took place between 1929 and 1941, I divided the total equivalent freight ton miles for the multiple 1929 units by the total employment of the 1929 roads to create a 1929 equivalent ton miles per employee that could then be compared with the 1941 measure.

The Interstate Commerce Commission (ICC) grouped Class I railroads into eight regions: New England (NE), Great Lakes (GL), Central Eastern (CE), Pocahontas (PO), Southern (SO), Northwestern (NW), Central

10. These two, with 1929 employment in parentheses, were Ft. Smith and Western (137), and Copper River and Northwestern (166).

11. These six, with their 1929 employment in parentheses, are Northern Alabama (412); Binghman and Garfield (256); Quincy, Omaha, and Kansas City (306); San Diego and Pacific (471); Wichita Valley (322); and Wichita Falls and Southern (310).

12. These four, with their 1941 employment in parentheses, are Cambria and Indiana (141); Spokane International (206); Colorado and Wyoming (413); and Oklahoma City, Ada, and Atoka (67).

13. These two roads were New York Connecting (with forty-nine employees in 1929), and Oahu Railroad and Land Company (with 407 employees in 1929).

Table 12.3 Regional output per employee, US Class I railroads, 1929 and 1941

	1929	1941	% Increase
NE	238,300	374,094	57.0
GL	320,279	469,096	46.5
CE	336,080	404,979	20.5
PO	573,978	903,237	57.4
SO	242,728	465,672	91.8
NW	298,608	437,729	46.6
CW	301,645	441,389	46.3
SW	279,799	498,331	78.1

Source: See text.

Western (CW), and Southwestern (SW). I begin by exploring regional variation in productivity levels in 1929 by regressing ton miles equivalents per employee on eight regional dummies (no constant), which essentially returns the average productivity level for railroads in each region (table 12.3).

Setting aside the Pocahontas region, which had assigned to it only four railroads, we note that in 1929 roads in the Central Eastern region tended to have somewhat higher output per employee, whereas the reverse was true for roads in the South. If we now fast forward to 1941, we see that productivity grew quite substantially in every region. There had also been some convergence, with particularly rapid growth among southern railroads and slower growth in the central eastern region. Still, the basic message conveyed by these data is that the productivity improvement in the railroad sector was a national phenomenon and aggregate advance was not driven, for example, by progress by a small number of large roads with disproportionate weight. In fact, an important negative result emerges from the statistical analysis: there is no statistically significant or economically meaningful relationship between the size of a railroad as measured by the number of its employees and its productivity level in either 1929 or 1941.

Turning now to analysis of changes between 1929 and 1941, the results are somewhat different. I define the dependent variable here as the percentage increase in output per employee between 1929 and 1941. The average increase in labor productivity over the course of the Depression for the 128 railroad sample was 56 percent, but there was substantial variation, with a standard deviation of 43 percentage points. Within the context of the general sectoral improvement, what factors particularly influenced whether a railroad performed relatively well or poorly on this dimension?

The following regression establishes several important relationships. The first right-hand side variable demonstrates that productivity improvements across the Depression years involved predominantly the movement of freight. In table 12.4, the variable %FREIGHT1941 is the share of 1941 operating revenues originating from freight. The average for all roads was 92.6 per-

Table 12.4 **Ordinary least squares (OLS) regression: Percent increase in output per employee, Class I railroads, United States, 1941 over 1929**

	Coefficient	*T*-statistic
Intercept	–0.50626	–1.51248
%FREIGHT1941	0.929605	2.677457
SOUTH	0.420113	4.983351
ΔEMPLOYMENT	–0.40371	–2.63621

Data sources: see text.
Note: $n = 128$; $R^2 = .24$.

cent, with a relatively low standard deviation of 9.8 percentage points. The measure varied from a high of 100 percent for railroads that carried no passengers to lows of 51 percent for Staten Island Rapid Transit, 64 percent for the Florida East Coast Line, and 69 percent for the New York, New Haven, and Hartford Railroad. What the positive coefficient on this variable shows is that, ceteris paribus, the greater the proportion of revenues from freight in 1941, the greater the percentage increase in productivity between 1929 and 1941. All else equal, a road with a 10 percentage point higher share of its operating revenues from freight traffic could expect a 9.2 percentage point higher increase in output per employee over the Depression. These numbers are consistent with the view that passenger carriage for American railroads was a mature business by the 1930s. Although it would experience its finest hour during World War II, it was already poised for decline. It was the freight, not the passenger side of business that was being transformed.

The second variable is a dummy for location of the railroad in the South. As table 12.3 shows, southern railroads achieved a particularly large increase in output per employee over the Depression. This reflected catch up from the relative backwardness of the region in 1929, midwifed by such New Deal programs as the Tennessee Valley Authority, as well as the more general influence of continued road building during the Depression (complementarity with the expansion of trucking, which benefited from improved roads, was a key feature in railroad productivity improvement throughout the country). The coefficient on this variable shows that, all else equal, a railroad in the South experienced a 41 percentage point higher increase in output per employee compared to a road with similar characteristics elsewhere in the country.

Finally, although the size of the railroad as measured by the number of its employees is irrelevant in accounting for levels of productivity in 1929 or 1941, the *change* in employment (ΔEMPLOYMENT) has a statistically significant and economically important influence on how much productivity grew for that railroad over the twelve-year period. The relationship was inverse: the greater the percentage decline in employment, the higher the increase in output per employee. The average reduction in employment across the 128 units was 30.4 percent, almost exactly the decline in the aggregate numbers used by Barger and Kendrick. But there was substantial variation: the standard deviation across the roads was 22 percentage points.

This result is by no means obvious, necessary, or tautological. If cutting employment in an organization were an automatic route to higher labor productivity, the road to economic progress would be a lot less obstructed. The facts are that simply firing employees or reducing employee rolls by attrition can easily cause output to fall as fast or faster than employment. After all, there was a reason the employees were hired in the first place. The trick was and is to reduce employment in a well-thought out fashion that is coordinated with changes in equipment, structures, and logistics and allows output to be sustained, or at least to decline at a slower rate than employment.

The aggregate data show that rising labor productivity coincided with declining employment. The firm-level analysis provides evidence indicative of a behavioral relationship. As noted, the average decline in employment was 30.4 percent. According to the regression results, a railroad for which employment declined an additional 10 percentage points would have enjoyed, over the twelve years of the Depression, a 4 percentage point larger increase in output per worker.

But what interpretation can we give to this result? A labor historian might say that it simply reflected speed up—the lines had become better at extracting more labor from each individual. That may have been true to some extent. But I believe we can also give it a broader and more positive spin. The ability to shrink payrolls by margins this large while at the same time sustaining and in many cases increasing output required logistical and technological innovation, not just a more effective managerial use of the whip.

Many aspects of the story suggested by the aggregate data are consistent with what the firm-level analysis tells us. Productivity improvement was a national phenomenon, affecting railroads both large and small. Innovations involved principally the logistics of moving freight, not passengers. Southern railroads, laggards on average in 1929, experienced the largest regional productivity improvements. And at the level of individual railroads, those with higher percentage declines in employment over the twelve years of the Depression reaped correspondingly higher increases in output per employee.

12.3 Conclusion

The Depression era history of the US rail system provides a compelling example of the operation of the adversity/hysteresis effect. Faced with tough times in the form of radically changing demand conditions, crushing debt burdens, and lack of access to more capital, railroad organizations reduced their main trackage, rolling stock and employees, in most cases quite dramatically. At the same time, they introduced upgraded locomotives and rolling stock as they were replaced, built more secondary trackage, changing their operating procedures as they introduced new systems for logistical control and freight interchange. In spite of these cuts, output nonetheless grew modestly to the beginning of the war and rapidly during it.

It is true that the sector faced tough times in the quarter century following the war as it struggled with the continued erosion of its passenger business and the reality that trucking also threatened its long haul freight revenues. But, after sloughing off commuter lines to state agencies and the remaining intercity passenger business to government-owned Amtrak, it emerged by the last decades of the twentieth century in relatively good shape, displaying strong productivity growth, testimony once again to the railroad sector's ability to reenergize and reinvigorate itself in the face of adversity.

References

Barger, Harold. 1951. *The Transportation Industries, 1899–1946.* New York: National Bureau of Economic Research.

Field, Alexander J. 1992. "Uncontrolled Land Development and the Duration of the Depression in the United States." *Journal of Economic History* 52:785–805.

———. 2003. "The Most Technologically Progressive Decade of the Century." *American Economic Review* 93:1399–413.

———. 2006a. "Technical Change and U.S. Economic Growth: The Interwar Period and the 1990s." In *The Global Economy in the 1990s: A Long Run Perspective,* edited by Paul Rhode and Gianni Toniolo, 89–117. Cambridge: Cambridge University Press.

———. 2006b. "Technological Change and U.S. Economic Growth in the Interwar Years." *Journal of Economic History* 66:203–36.

———. 2008. "The Impact of the Second World War on U.S. Productivity Growth." *Economic History Review* 61:672–94.

———. 2010. "The Procyclical Behavior of Total Factor Productivity in the United States, 1890–2004." *Journal of Economic History* 70:326–50.

———. 2011a. *A Great Leap Forward: 1930s Depression and U.S. Economic Growth.* New Haven, CT: Yale University Press.

———. 2011b. "Chained Index Methods and Productivity Growth During the Depression." Working Paper (May).

Finch, Christopher. 1992. *Highways to Heaven: The AUTObiography of America.* New York: HarperCollins.

Gordon, Robert J. 2010. "The Demise of Okun's Law and of Procyclical Fluctuations in Conventional and Unconventional Measures of Productivity." Paper presented at the 2010 NBER Summer Institute meetings. Cambridge, Massachusetts, July 21.

Hoover, Herbert. 1952. *The Memoirs of Herbert Hoover, vol. 3: The Great Depression 1929–1941.* New York: Macmillan.

Interstate Commerce Commission. 1929. *Statistics of Railroads in the United States, 1929.* Washington, DC: Government Printing Office.

———. 1941. *Statistics of Railroads in the United States, 1941.* Washington, DC: Government Printing Office.

———. 1943. *Statistics of Railroads in the United States, 1943.* Washington, DC: Government Printing Office.
Kendrick, John. 1961. *Productivity Trends in the United States.* Princeton, NJ: Princeton University Press.
Longman, Philip. 2009. "Washington's Turnaround Artists." *Washington Monthly,* March/April.
Mensch, Gerhard. 1979. *Stalemate in Technology: Innovations Overcome the Depression.* Cambridge: Ballinger.
Minsky, Hyman. 1986. *Stabilizing an Unstable Economy.* New Haven, CT: Yale University Press.
Parmalee, J. H. 1950. *The Railroad Situation, 1950.* Washington, DC: Association of American Railroads.
Paxson, Frederic L. 1946. "The Highway Movement, 1916–1935." *American Historical Review* 51:236–53.
Posner, Richard. 2009. *A Failure of Capitalism: The Crisis of '08 and the Descent into Depression.* Cambridge, MA: Harvard University Press.
Richter, Frank. 2005. *The Renaissance of the Railroad.* Bloomington: AuthorHouse.
Schiffman, Daniel A. 2003. "Shattered Rails, Financial Fragility, and Railroad Operations in the Great Depression." *Journal of Economic History* 63:802–25.
Schmookler, Jacob. 1966. *Invention and Economic Growth.* Cambridge, MA: Harvard University Press.
Stover, John F. 1997. *American Railroads,* 2nd ed. Chicago: University of Chicago Press.
Ulmer, Melville J. 1960. *Capital in Transportation, Communication, and Public Utilities: Its Formation and Financing.* Princeton, NJ: Princeton University Press.
US Bureau of Economic Analysis. 2011. "National Income and Product Tables: Fixed Asset Tables." http://www.bea.gov.
US Bureau of the Census. 1937. *Statistical Abstract of the United States.* Washington, DC: Government Printing Office. http://www.census.gov/prod/www/abs/statab1901-1950.htm.
———. 1944. *Statistical Abstract of the United States.* Washington, DC: Government Printing Office. http://www.census.gov/prod/www/abs/statab1901-1950.htm.
———. 1947. *Statistical Abstract of the United States.* Washington, DC: Government Printing Office. http://www.census.gov/prod/www/abs/statab1901-1950.htm.
US Bureau of Labor Statistics. 2011. "Multifactory Productivity Data." http://www.bls.gov.

Comment William Kerr

This chapter by Alexander Field is a very interesting contribution to the conference volume. Lacking a strong background in economic history, my comments are less about the specifics of the railroad industry during the Great Depression. Instead, I focus on my major takeaways from Alex's chapter and their parallels to the experiences of the US banking industry. I then apply

William Kerr is associate professor of business administration at Harvard Business School and a faculty research fellow of the National Bureau of Economic Research.

these lessons to the current position of the US auto industry, speculating on whether or not a silver lining exists for it from today's recession.

There are two moving parts in this chapter. First, Alex has an overarching discussion of the Great Depression and the substantial productivity growth that followed. There are three tributaries that he discusses: heightened R&D performance, development of the surface road network, and then specific details related to railroads and their life cycle over those twenty-five years. I focus on this third tributary, which is also where much of Alex's analysis is positioned, and we can later discuss together how these pieces all fit together.

Alex's description begins with a period of excess. Credit was easy. There was a lot of speculation and growth, resulting in some overbuilding that was not optimal or rational in the long run. We then had a period of bad times. The tide went out, and we saw who was naked. The Depression exposed fragilities and led to credit squeezing, which also potentially influenced invention or technology adoption. Ultimately, a silver lining may have existed, with surviving companies showing stronger productivity gains along the way.

My one quibble with this overall story is not about the story, but instead relates to identifying the central thesis of the chapter. There is a very broad description of everything that happened around the Great Depression, but the true emphasis here is really about the railroads. I hope to help bring sharper focus to the central questions of whether a silver lining for railroads existed due to the Depression, its relationship to the ensuing productivity boost, and ultimately to the liquidationist perspective.

Let us begin with the role of the Depression on technologies. In keeping with the conference title, did the Depression influence either the rate or the direction of technology change for railroads? Would the same technologies have been adopted anyway, but with the rate different due to the Depression? Or was the Depression centrally important in determining the types of technologies invented?

Starting with the direction question, my reading of Alex's evidence is that the direction of technical progress for the railroad industry was not centrally impacted. There does not appear evidence of directed technical change. For example, we do not see evidence of many inventions targeting the massive overcapacity in the industry. Instead, the technologies that are discussed in this chapter are things like larger car size, better logistics, and similar innovations that move freight better.

This path of technological progress does not strike one as being overly reliant on the Depression for its course. If this conclusion is in error, more discussion around the types of technologies developed would be beneficial.

Such discussion would also help identify why productivity gains were realized in one type of rail traffic more than others. Is there something about larger car sizes and logistics that especially favored freight? One can imagine that running cars faster and longer, stuffing more into them, switching them around in the middle of the night, and so forth all naturally better served freight uses than passenger uses. If true, we can more directly link up the technology that was ripe for picking with what occurred.

On the other hand, there is more evidence that the rate of technology adoption was influenced by the Depression. Because many firms faced financial difficulties, consolidation was often necessary. This may have raised the pressure to adopt technologies faster. Logistical improvements, larger car size, and so on arrived faster because of the Depression.

That is an interesting finding because—Alex briefly touched on this—the theory around the silver lining is very ambiguous. Ricardo Caballero and similar authors argue that the liquidationist perspective does not hold, and that productivity is instead hampered. Alex's findings, especially as more detail emerges, help evaluate these contrasting perspectives.

I want to turn now to the banking industry. As I thought about comparisons to the experiences of the Depression-era railroads, the strong parallels to the banking sector from the 1970s through the 1990s stood out. The banking industry also went through a period of productivity growth and declining employment, with more interesting similarities around technologies and consolidation further evident.

First, at the beginning of the 1970s, there were many new technologies (e.g., check clearing, ATM machines) that would substantially reshape the industry's economics, much like technologies that emerged for railroads. The banking sector also had massive consolidation during its period of productivity growth around crisis times. In fact, the crisis helped allow passage of regulations that facilitated the mergers.

These parallels emphasize to me the potential role of consolidations around technologies for railroads during the Depression. We know for the banking industry that the consolidations were very important for realizing economies of scale, for achieving the technology infusion that occurred, and so on. Are railroad consolidations also an essential part of the Depression story? Can we understand the technologies and the consolidations better together than as separate factors?

Alex is able to provide some detail here, and I hope that more can be developed. He has collected very detailed accounts by hand that can be exploited further. What was the output per employee of the railroads that were acquired? Do we see low labor productivity firms being acquired by high labor productivity firms? If we aggregate the data for all 1927 firms into their 1941 consolidations, we lose some of this very interesting detail that can shed light on the productivity growth.

There is a second question on the existing regression that should also be investigated further. We observe that growing firms also show declines in labor productivity. This relationship could be partly due to using labor on both sides of the estimation. Declines in labor on the right-hand side link to increases in labor productivity on the left-hand side as the denominator shrinks.

I bring this up because we are often concerned if the reallocation process in the economy is flowing toward unproductive firms or firms with declining productivity. That is not a good recipe for economic growth. So, it would be nice to check this finding against other measures of firm size and growth (e.g., track mileage). More broadly, further decomposition of these effects would be great.

To conclude, I now turn to the third industry: Does Alex's chapter offer hope for a silver lining to the auto industry today? Again, there are parallels. Both cases deal with a national champion industry past its peak. Today's automotive industry also has extreme financial distress, overcapacity, and related traits.

Alex's account outlines three questions we should ask. First, are there basic operational technologies that have yet to be adopted by the automobile industry that firms can be encouraged to adopt? Automobile firms are having harder times, and we are forcing them to reorganize to be competitive. Do technologies exist that are ripe for this effort?

Second, is consolidation possible to realize these benefits? This appears to be important in accounts for both the railroad and banking industries, but there are limits to further consolidation in the automobile industry. So, a third and related question would be: are there other organizational changes that are not dependent upon economies of scale that could help improve the efficiency of the automobile industry going forward?

My instinct from Alex's account is that these conditions are unlikely to be met, at least in a major way, in the automobile industry. The conditions that led to the silver lining for the railroad industry are not nearly as favorable for the auto industry today. But our ultimate conclusions will require further research to understand whether the conditions that Alex identified are necessary or sufficient conditions. Perhaps there are other channels through which a silver lining may emerge.

In conclusion, Alex's chapter is a very interesting account of a remarkable period of time. It is very important that we understand how and when the silver lining due to downturns emerges. Alex has made a nice contribution through his historical work and given us plenty to contemplate.

13

Generality, Recombination, and Reuse

Timothy F. Bresnahan

13.1 Motivation and Key Findings

Economists have long noted the benefits to society of recombinant technical change and of general purpose technologies.[1] Recombinant technical change is the reuse of existing innovations in new areas; Schumpeter was probably the first to point out that most technical progress is recombinant. General purpose technologies (GPT) are (a) widely used, (b) capable of ongoing technical improvement, and (c) enable complementary innovation in application sectors (AS).[2] Both recombinant technical change and GPTs involve reuse. From an ex post normative standpoint, reuse creates dynamic social increasing returns to scale and scope.[3] This chapter takes an ex ante positive standpoint and examines the economic incentives and information conditions that lead to original invention of reusable inventions. I emphasize the knowledge available to the inventor, at the time of initial invention, whose work will later be recombined or lead to the emergence of a new

Timothy F. Bresnahan is the Landau Professor in Technology and the Economy and professor, by courtesy, of economics in the Graduate School of Business at Stanford University and a research associate of the National Bureau of Economic Research.

I thank Ben Jones, Shane Greenstein, Joel Mokyr, Nathan Rosenberg, Manuel Trajtenberg, Scott Stern, and participants at the NBER Rate and Direction of Technical Change Fiftieth Anniversary preconference and conference for valuable comments.

1. See, for example, Schumpeter (1939), Nelson and Winter (1982), Weitzman (1998), Romer (1987), Bresnahan and Trajtenberg (1995), and Bresnahan (2010).

2. See Bresnahan (2010) for the more detailed definitions used in the literature.

3. I note that the language "increasing returns to scale and scope" implies a normative framework, not a positive one, and similarly that the language "social increasing returns to scale" implies a normative (cooperative) framework rather than a positive (information, incentives, and in this chapter, knowledge) framework. I note also that these benefits assessment frameworks are ex post, that is, recombination, reuse, and generality of purpose are all excellent sources of social gains if they can be achieved.

general purpose technology. Important issues, not well treated in the literature, arise when first inventors do not know of future uses because those uses depend on future invention or on the future creation of new markets and industries.

Recent investigations have deepened our understanding of the logical relationship between reuse and growth theory, and have shown the importance of GPTs in the industrial revolution, the second industrial revolution (in particularly impressive depth), and the information age.[4] Recombination and GPTs can make reuse into a powerful force for economic growth based in increasing returns. Note that this is a normative ex post perspective. Once technologies that can be widely recombined have been invented, once a GPT has been invented and is leading to the further invention of valuable applications, the economy is gaining the benefits of social increasing returns to scale.

In this chapter I focus attention on a new set of corresponding ex ante positive questions about the origins of GPTs and the origins of technologies that will later be recombined. The original invention of a technology that will be widely reused is an important economic event because of the spillovers that flow through reuse.

How, ex ante, are inventors to identify technologies that will be reused or will be general in purpose? Knowledge of what is technically feasible is not sufficient to answer these questions, for an answer depends on future complementary inventions. To make this point sharply, I distinguish between two kinds of knowledge, separating *entrepreneurial knowledge* from the more usual technical and market knowledge. Technical knowledge is a firm's knowledge of its own production possibilities. Market knowledge is what can be observed in existing markets. Entrepreneurial knowledge is, in contrast, knowledge of other firms or industries held in a particular firm or industry. The classical example of entrepreneurial knowledge comes from Hayek (1945). An inventor might know (technically) how to create a new product and yet now know (entrepreneurially) how that product will be used, by whom, and how much value that demand will create. In a decentralized economy, those are all pieces of knowledge (originally) held by others and only learned by the potential inventor at some cost. In the simplest example, a clear engineering plan to build a new mousetrap would be technical knowledge, while knowing ex ante whether the world will beat a path to your door is entrepreneurial knowledge. I extend this concept of entrepreneurial knowledge. The centerpiece of my treatment is that an inventor working in one industry may not know of potential complementary inventions in another industry ex ante.

The point of emphasizing entrepreneurial knowledge is that a market economy typically has highly distributed knowledge. If each agent knows

4. See sources in Bresnahan (2010) and also in Jovanovic and Rousseau (2005).

her own business' invention opportunities and technical needs but not those of other firms or industries—the information requirements needed for a neoclassical economy with price-taking supply—that is distributed knowledge. In this sense, the more distributed is knowledge, the scarcer is entrepreneurial knowledge. This matters for reuse when the knowledge needed to anticipate later uses is not available to an early inventor.

To analyze recombination and GPTs is to consider a world in which there are multiple potential inventors. This leads me to focus on cases in which the economy is decentralized and the resulting potential scarcity of entrepreneurial knowledge is that one potential inventor need not know another potential inventor's circumstances. The inventor of a potential general purpose technology might not, for example, know of the prospects for complementary innovation in applications sectors. Symmetrically, a potential application sector may not know of technical opportunities in what would be, if only it were to be invented, a GPT industry. This kind of scarcity of entrepreneurial knowledge can reduce the ex ante return to innovation.[5]

The second building block of my analysis concerns the way the knowledge state of the economy changes when invention occurs. Suppose once again that ex ante two potential inventors—a GPT inventor and an applications inventor, or an original inventor and a recombiner—do not know of one another's technical possibilities. If, however, one of them has invented something and commercialized it, the other can learn of it. This lessens the scarcity of entrepreneurial knowledge as the second inventor now can look at the first invention and consider whether to make a complementary invention. Of course, the search and information processing need not be costless at this stage. I assume that invention and market presence creates market knowledge, not necessarily complete and perfect market knowledge.

One mechanism by which this might work is if a potential GPT is invented and marketed "on spec," potential applications sector inventors learn of its existence. Entrepreneurial knowledge is then less scarce, and complementary innovation in the AS can be based on market knowledge of the GPT prod-

5. It is a common feature of many economic models of inventions that different inventors have different knowledge. This feature is shared by Schumpeterian models (earlier and later inventors have different knowledge, the later may creatively destroy the earlier), GPT models (GPT and AS have different knowledge needed to work together), recombinant models (ideas become more valuable when combined with other ideas), and standard models of optimal patent policy (early invention and improvement based in different knowledge). The same structure is used in models of organization; each of two agents making complementary innovations has distinct abilities and knowledge.

Another common feature of economic models of invention is the accumulation of a stock of knowledge. Early inventions pave the way for later inventions. Models of quality ladders, for example, assume that each level of quality cannot be invented until after the last level. Models of recombination assume that ideas, once made, can be combined with other ideas in potentially useful ways.

Many of these literatures have been pushed much farther than I attempt here. My goal, however, is to examine the specific problem of scarce entrepreneurial knowledge.

uct. I will call that particular mechanism a "planned initiative." Note that a planned initiative does not require much entrepreneurial knowledge after invention of the GPT. It does require, however, entrepreneurial knowledge ex ante, as the GPT innovator must know what kind of GPT product would appeal to applications sectors. I use "must know" there in an economic sense: the GPT inventor must have a good enough idea of whether AS will follow profitably to invest in a specific technical direction. I will argue that, as a historical matter, planned initiatives are scarce in white-collar work automation (WCA) precisely because this kind of broad-based entrepreneurial knowledge is typically scarce.

When the original problem was difficulties in seeing precise overlaps between technological opportunity and demand needs, early invention and commercialization can create market knowledge of a number of forms. One is that technologists' knowledge of demanders' needs can be converted from scarce entrepreneurial knowledge into widespread market knowledge. Technologists can now learn, by observing what demanders buy, knowledge of what demanders want. A body of demand, once created in a market, can be studied and thus served. An early specific technical solution, even if far from optimal (given all knowledge by both technologist and demanders) can create sufficient market knowledge to enable movement in the direction of optimality. Seeing that a demander is using technology with features G, a technologist can inquire about the marketability of features $G + \Delta g$. If such an inquiry is difficult ex ante, but feasible at the interim stage, valuable market knowledge has been created. Symmetrically, the commercialization of a specific technical product can create knowledge on the part of demanders about what is technically feasible. Demanders could then undertake experiments to see what coinvention works effectively. The results of those experiments are valuable market or technical knowledge; if the results suggest new directions to technologists, they represent an update in the market knowledge of the economy. The fact that demanders needed to undertake experiments can make it very difficult to have complete ex ante entrepreneurial knowledge. A related situation arises when demanders can only understand what a new technology can do by seeing it demonstrated. Their invention of useful applications (which was contingent on the creation of a working prototype technology) can suggest new directions by showing where the overlaps between the technically feasible and the socially desirable.

In a number of historical examples drawn from the computer industry, I examine the case, which I will argue is very important empirically for technical progress in WCA, in which entrepreneurial knowledge is scarce ex ante.[6] We shall see that in an economy with distributed knowledge, overlaps

6. In this regard I follow a long tradition in the analysis of technical change. Like Rosenberg (1996) I emphasize uncertainly and depart from the "linear" model in which science causes technology, which in turn causes application and growth. Yet I also depart from models like that of Acemoglu (2002) in which demand needs are known and directly influence inventors' choices.

between the technically feasible and the socially desirable sets of inventions can be "unknown" in the sense that no individual knows them well enough profitably to direct specific technical investments, and "unknowable" in the sense that either (a) the relevant holders of distributed information need not know one another's technical needs and capabilities with adequate specificity, or (b) detailed good faith discussions among the relevant knowledge holders need not lead to successful communications because the possibility of dual invention is too hypothetical. Initial inventive steps can make the locus of the overlap more known (and more knowable) by converting entrepreneurial knowledge into market knowledge. Since the same industry has launched a number of GPT clusters, it also permits me to examine a number of cases in which entrepreneurial knowledge was less scarce ex ante. The contrast is illuminating about the sources of some of the most important technical advances of the last half century.

13.2 Recombination Model

Economists have already recognized that recombination involves the possibility of knowledge scarcity. Weitzman (1998), in a classic model of recombinant growth, has a model in which the number of "seed" ideas is increasing over time as a result of R&D, and seed ideas can be recombined into potentially valuable inventions. Weitzman's elegant analysis shows first that the combinatorics of mixing and matching an increasing number of ideas can lead to faster- than-exponential expansion of the stock of possible useful inventions (thus easily overcoming diminishing returns). As the number of seed ideas grows, however, the information-processing costs of finding recombinant matches also grow without bound, providing a limit on the growth process. Weitzman's model has no treatment of entrepreneurial knowledge, however. A number of management scholars have taken up the question of search to create recombinant knowledge: a classic study is Fleming (2001), who notes that common knowledge of what technologies are economically related can change over time, and uses the framework of "local" knowledge as related to commercial exploitation of ideas, while "distant" search is exploratory and potentially creates hitherto unforeseen combinations.

An important related notion is that certain kinds of knowledge can come to be science, and that this has important implications for the scope of entrepreneurial knowledge in the economy. Mokyr (2002), for example, makes the important observation that the representation of technical knowledge as science during the industrial revolution in England together with the institutions of open science, lowered the costs of widespread "access" to knowledge. If the solution to the problem of scarce entrepreneurial knowledge is better representation of knowledge, then there is, as Jones (2009) points out, a "burden of knowledge." This suggests an arc of possibility (not unlike the simpler Weitzman arc) in which improving access first improves the ability of the economy to recombine different kinds of knowledge and then creates congestion.

In this section, I model the distinction between different kinds of knowledge related to an invention that may later be recombined, and how the knowledge state of the economy changes ex post its invention. Potential inventors, the only actors in the recombination model, are endowed with technical capabilities and market knowledge, which permit them to make productive inventions at a cost. Potential inventors are also endowed with knowledge about the possible productive applications of their technology. Their entrepreneurial knowledge (or its lack) arises with regard to knowledge about one another.

A simple model can illuminate the economics of entrepreneurial knowledge and recombination. The model is simple in that each potential invention can be recombined either with no other invention or with just one other invention. Potential inventors need not have perfect entrepreneurial knowledge, which in this context means that they do not necessarily know whether their invention can be recombined or, if so, with what.

Begin with a representative invention, called A. The R&D expenditure needed to invent A is r and the return to inventing A if there is no other invention complementary to it is $V(A)$. Any risk, uncertainty, and so forth related to the value of A alone is reflected in $V(A)$.[7] There are a large number of potential inventors of A so that invention will occur if the expected net return to the invention is positive. If there is no possibility of recombination or reuse for A, then the incentive to invent A is given by

$$\pi_A = V(A) - r. \quad (1)$$

Now suppose that there is another invention, B, which can be recombined with A. If both A and B are invented, they can be recombined to create, in addition to the stand-alone values $V(A)$ and $V(B)$, a further recombination value $V(A,B)$.[8] The complementarity behind this additional value is the reason technical change can be recombinant.

If first A and then B have been invented, ex post bargaining or other market transactions between their inventors give the inventor of A a share $\lambda_1 V(A, B)$ of the jointly created value. I am agnostic about how λ is determined, except that I rule out ex ante bargaining because the two complementary inventors may not have heard of one another. The inventor of A

7. I note that $V(A)$ is the return to the inventor. The mechanism by which this return is generated is in the background. If, for example, the inventor of A gets a temporary patent of monopoly on selling A, the total social surplus associated with A will exceed $V(A)$.

8. The recombinant value could arise because A and B are inventions by a supplier and a customer, or are complements in production or in demand, or because each is a multipart invention and they share a common component. My treatment abstracts away from all those different situations in order to isolate the key problem that arises when inventors of complements do not know of one another.

might get a larger share because a patent regime offers a larger claim to earlier inventors or because the first inventor gets to choose certain market institutions (such as openness) that affect information flows or market power later.[9] The inventor of *B* will get $\lambda_2 V(A,B)$.[10] Thus, if a potential inventor of *A* knows that *B* has been or is about to be invented, the incentive to invent *A* is given by

$$\pi_A = V(A) - r + C(A,B)\lambda_1. \tag{2}$$

The potential inventors of *A*, may not, however, know of the pending invention of *B* or know enough about the characteristics of invention *B* to assess the prospective increased return from joint invention. The degree to which they *do* know of such things is their entrepreneurial knowledge. I measure entrepreneurial knowledge as a probability assessment, called k, that *B* can be found by search and is an effective complement for *A*. Thus the incentive to invent *A* is

$$\pi_A = V(A) - r + V(A,B)\lambda_1 k. \tag{3}$$

I assume that the invention and marketing of *B* before the invention of *A* will improve knowledge about *B* on the part of potential inventors of *A*. That is, I assume that after *B* has been invented and marketed it becomes easier for a potential inventor of *A* to learn the technical details of *B*, to make an assessment of the degree of complementarity between *B* and *A*, or to design *A* so that it works well with the *B* that was actually invented (which may have a higher success rate than designing *A* to work with a plan of *B*). This is still entrepreneurial knowledge, but the marketing of *B* adds some market knowledge to the ex ante guessing and speculation. This higher quality knowledge is represented here by a higher probability assessment that development of *A* will lead to recombinant value $K > k$.

If there is no complementary technology for *A*, potential inventors of *A* may nonetheless think one exists, and have, as a result of this excess optimism, a higher incentive to invent. There is, however, no failure of rational expectations if $k < 1$ for all technologies that are recombinable and no agents with excess optimism. One interpretation of k is the probability that a search for a partner will succeed and an assessment of potential partners'

9. How λ is determined is also pushed to the background. It could arise, as in the models reviewed by Scotchmer (2004), as a result of ex post invention bargaining between the inventors of *A* and *B*, each of which has a patent. An alternative mechanism to determine λ is that *B* sells an input to *A* and the price of that input, in market context, determines the rent split. I treat these, and other mechanisms to determine λ, as equivalent. It is also not essential that only the synergistic part $V(A,B)$ is subject to bargaining or market division. The claims behind the bargaining reflect not only the formal patent system, but also the openness of the innovation system more generally, the value of first-mover advantages, and so on.

10. I make no assumption that *B* gets $(1 - \lambda_1)V(A,B)$. If bargaining or market power is inefficient, as one would expect generally, then the more natural assumption is that *B* gets less than that.

joint value will lead to a match. This can be less than one for all agents in search of equilibrium.[11]

In summary, k is the measure of the entrepreneurial information available to the inventor whose invention might later be recombined, while K is the measure of the entrepreneurial information of the inventor who might recombine later. After B has been invented, the incentive to invent A rises to

$$\pi_A = V(A) - r + (A,B)\lambda K. \tag{4}$$

A considerable literature has focused on the forces leading, in the language of this chapter, to $K < 1$. An elegant model by Weitzman (1998) illuminates the problem that arises when there are more and more ideas that might be recombined, so that costs of searching among them drive down K endogenously as the overall economy grows more complex and decentralized. The body of work that focuses on "recombinant search" (i.e., search by potentially recombining inventors), focuses on the difficulties in such a search because searchers must cross intellectual or industry boundaries to find and understand potential complements (Fleming 2001). The point of this chapter is that such a search can be even more difficult when the searcher is crossing intellectual or industry boundaries to find and understand potential complements before they have been invented. To search all existing technologies to see which ones offer good opportunities for complementary recombination is one thing; to extend that search to all the as-yet-uninvented technologies that might be a complement and to carefully evaluate their as-yet-undertermined features quite another. Hence my focus on the case where $k < K$.

The novel element here is a distinction between two kinds of knowledge. I distinguish between the technical knowledge of each sector and the entrepreneurial knowledge that has the possibility of creating new markets. Two points about technical knowledge are appropriate here. First, when I simply write $V(A) - r$, I am implicitly assuming good technical knowledge. Second, I am labeling knowledge about the local demand for the invention; that is, what A knows about the probability, demand, and appropriability assessments that lead to value $V(A)$ are all called "technical knowledge." The main point of this is to distinguish it from entrepreneurial knowledge; that is, knowledge about the possible future gains from trade, outside current markets, and connections. I follow Hayek (1945) in making this division between local market or technical knowledge, knowledge about one's own existing business, and entrepreneurial knowledge, knowledge of potential new connections.

The key point about entrepreneurial knowledge is that it only matters before the creation of a new connection. In my framework, once something has been invented and commercialized, knowledge of it is market knowl-

11. I am grateful to Joel Mokyr for useful discussion on this point.

Table 13.1 **Local, market, and entrepreneurial knowledge**

Agent	Local, technical K	Market K	Entrepreneurial K
Potential *A* inventor	I might invent *A*	You have invented *B*	You might invent *B*
Potential *B* inventor	I might invent *B*	You have invented *A*	You might invent *A*

edge. By that I mean that it depends on what others in the economy are doing, not what they might be doing in a hypothetical future. As a formal matter, this means that invention changes the knowledge state of the economy.

In drawing the distinction between K and k I am implicitly adding a third category of knowledge—market knowledge. If $K > k$ because B has been invented, I call the increase in knowledge about B on the part of potential inventors of A market knowledge. Market knowledge may or may not be perfect, but in table 13.1 I will typically assume that market knowledge about the same outcome is better than entrepreneurial knowledge.

Pulling this together, we have the payoffs relevant to the question of whether recombination will occur. If B has already been invented and marketed, we can focus on the incentives to invent A given market knowledge K. I label this π_{A2} because A is positioned as the second inventor:[12]

$$\pi_{A2} = V(A) - r + V(A,B)\lambda_2 K. \tag{5}$$

There is a symmetric expression for π_{B2}. An idea that is valuable in two uses might be invented first for either of them; it can then be recombined into the other. If B has not yet been invented, however, potential inventors of A will need to rely on their entrepreneurial knowledge to see any benefits of joint invention:

$$\pi_{A1} = V(A) - r + V(A,B)\lambda_1 k, \tag{6}$$

and once again there is a symmetric expression for π_{B1}.

Finally, the order of invention is set exogenously, perhaps by the date at which each stand-alone technology becomes marketable. Without loss of generality (w.l.o.g.), A goes first. One of the many potential inventors of A invents if $\pi_{A1} > 0$. Then, if A has not been invented, one of the potential inventors of B invents if $\pi_{B1} > 0$.[13] If, however, A has been invented, recombinatory technical progress occurs if $\pi_{B2} > 0$. Finally, the opportunity

12. Note that I do not assume that there is some kind of technological hierarchy in which A must be invented before B or vice versa. This assumption is common in the appropriability literature but is not suitable for my purposes. See Scotchmer (2004) for a review of a number of models with this assumption. Technological hierarchy may provide a reason to prefer stronger appropriability for earlier inventors or to oppose openness, an effect omitted from my analysis.

13. If there were only a single potential inventor of A, that inventor might find it worthwhile to wait for B; with many potential inventors, the possibility of waiting for B is irrelevant in the case $\pi_{A1} > 0$. I am examining a model with such strategic behavior by individual inventors in joint work with Iiro Makinen.

to invent A does not go away, so if B is invented and A was not invented before, that triggers a recombination if $\pi_{B2} > 0$. These conditions determine a (unique) equilibrium as a function of the economic fundamentals.

13.2.1 Social and Private Returns to Invention

For examination of the gap between the social and private rates of invention in this model, I assume

(7) $$V(A) - r < 0; \text{ and } V(B) - r < 0;$$

$$\text{but } V(A) - r + V(B) - r + V(A,B) > 0,$$

the only interesting case; that is, each stand-alone invention is unprofitable but recombination is profitable.

Consider first the familiar case with no shortage of entrepreneurial knowledge, $K = k = 1$. There is no distinction in this case between π_{A1} and π_{A2} because market and entrepreneurial knowledge are both perfect, and thus both the same; the model is also symmetric. In this case, we can interpret V as a risk-adjusted expected value and interpret (λ_1,λ_2) as the outcome of an ex post bargain between two inventors, limited by their appropriability claims and by imitation. Now, letting A be invented first, the condition for both A and B to be invented is

(8) $$\pi_{A1} = V(A) - r + V(A,B)\lambda_1 > 0$$

(9) $$\lambda_{B2} = V(B) - r + V(A,B)\lambda_2 > 0.$$

Under the assumption of perfect entrepreneurial information, only incentives (λ) matter. If market institutions or patent claims are set up so that one of the λ is too small, then the social rate of return to innovation is less than the private rate of return to innovation. If we force A to invent first (perhaps because the market yielding $V(A)$ opens a century before that yielding $V(B)$) the social return to invention will be less than the private return to invention for A if λ_1 is too small (i.e., [8] fails) and for B if λ_2 is too small ([9] fails). If bargaining is not possible, then the gap between the social and private return to innovation will prevent invention.

Under (7), nondestructive ex ante bargaining, if possible, will always lead a pair of λ, which leads to efficient invention and recombination. Since the two potential inventors know of one another ($K = k = 1$) one can easily suppose that they get together and, for example, form a single firm to internalize the externality of their two inventions; one invents first, and the other recombines into a high-value use. That does not much resemble the "recombination" discussed in the literature, which is part of my point. We now turn to a model in which the opportunity to recombine is unknown ex ante.

13.2.2 Scarce Entrepreneurial Information

Let us now consider a case with the same payoffs and the same timing; that is, joint invention is profitable and the market for A opens first. However, we consider the case with an absence of entrepreneurial information ($k = 0$) together with excellent market information ($K = 1$). Under these assumptions, the condition for both to invent is

$$\pi_{A1} = V(A) - r + V(A,B)\lambda_1 k > 0 \Leftrightarrow V(A) - r > 0$$
$$\lambda_{B2} = V(B) - r + V(A,B)\lambda_2 K > 0 \Leftrightarrow V(B) - r + V(A, B)\lambda_2 > 0.$$

The second condition, recombination by an inventor of B, will be satisfied for some admissible λ_2. The first condition, however, cannot be satisfied when only joint invention is economic (7). Reversing the order or having the potential inventors have the opportunity to invent simultaneously does not help. It is easy to see there will be no first invention under (7). The problem here is that valuable invention is not undertaken because it only becomes sufficiently valuable in the information state—unknown to an original inventor—that it will be later recombined. The fact that invention will create that information state ($K = 1$) is not helpful when the information does not exist.

Increasing original inventors' share of eventual returns by raising λ_1 does not change their incentives to invent, because λ_1 is multiplied by zero. Since the original inventor does not know about the future recombination that may create recombinant value ($k = 0$), giving them a larger share of the returns from future recombination is pushing on a rope. Changing from open innovation systems to closed, or allocating stronger patent claims to earlier innovators as a strategy to increase λ_1 is ineffective, and, to the extent it decreases λ_2, dysfunctional. The later, recombining inventor acts at a time of better information, so the decrease in their incentive to invent is far worse than the benefit to A.

This example, while extreme, reveals the importance of entrepreneurial knowledge. An invention that will gain value from later being recombined will, more generally, not have adequate invention incentives if the first inventor does not know about the potential recombination. Note that this effect does not depend on there being anything odd about the first inventor's knowledge of her own business or her own market. She can be perfectly rational, perfectly foresighted, understand all technical possibilities without regard to whether they involve a conceptual breakthrough or not, and so forth. The key assumption is one of limited entrepreneurial knowledge in the sense that knowledge is held in a distributed way (i.e., that she does not know about future technical possibilities in another business where her invention might be recombined).

In this case, the private return to innovation is below the social return to innovation if we evaluate returns using the ex post knowledge, or to put it another way, using the standard first-best assumption that we the analysts have all of the information in the economy.

This kind of scarce entrepreneurial knowledge raises the social return to innovation above the private return. Indeed, whenever we see recombination, it is reasonable to suspect that earlier entrepreneurial information about the then-future recombination was scarce. The private incentive of the original inventor to invent fell below what we now know, using ex post knowledge, was the social incentive. But this argument must be treated very carefully. The high "social return to innovation" of the first innovation can be calculated only by using all the information in the economy, not the information available to any inventor. Nor can conventional incentives (claims, market positions, etc.) raise the private return up to the social return.

Bargaining among the two inventors is not a solution. Search by potential inventors of *A* has either not led them to locate potential inventors of *B*, or has not convinced them adequately of the proposition that *B* might be a complement to act on it.

13.2.3 Comparative Statics

Each of the two first examples was extreme. More generally, even when we let both *k*, *K*, and λ be arbitrary, we get the result that, the more important is low *k* as a source of poor returns to innovation that might be recombined later, the weaker are increases in λ_1 as a mechanism to overcome it. Similarly, the larger is *K* relative to *k*, the greater is the improvement in knowledge about potential recombination, and thus the greater the advantage of giving incentives to later inventors (λ_2). Neither of these points turns on the extremity of the examples. Another comparative statics point that would arise in a more fully articulated model is that rather than not being invented at all, a first invention of a recombinant pair might be invented with too low a probability (if, e.g., *r* is a random variable) or at too late a date (if, e.g., *V* are rising because the economy is growing or *r* is falling because of technical progress elsewhere). In my historical examples, I will make obvious extensions like these without a formal model.

13.2.4 Remarks

The novel idea in this section is that the invention and commercialization of a technology depends on entrepreneurial knowledge and creates market knowledge. This puts recombination in a new light. In a decentralized economy, the ex ante perception that a particular invention might later be recombined is entrepreneurial knowledge. Scarcity of entrepreneurial knowledge ex ante, like the more familiar problems of weak appropriability or scarce technical knowledge, limits incentives to innovate. Evaluating either the private or the social rate of return to invention using all of the decentralized knowledge that exists in the economy would reveal the positive returns flowing from recombination. The problem in the case of scarce entrepreneurial knowledge is that no one knows enough to make the calculation.[14]

14. Hayek (1945, 519–21): "The peculiar character of the problem of a rational economic order is determined precisely by the fact that the knowledge of the circumstances of which

To the extent scarce entrepreneurial knowledge is a source of deviations of private from social returns to innovation, it suggests narrow patents or open systems rather than giving original inventors broader claims. Giving broad claims can be actively counterproductive (above and beyond not being productive ex ante) if the rights given to original inventors are broad enough to encompass unforeseen recombination. They limit the incentives of later inventors, who work in a better knowledge environment.

If the problem in innovation is scarce entrepreneurial knowledge, one could think that the solution is teaching everyone what everyone else knows. If that means lowering the costs of storing, retrieving, and communicating knowledge, reducing the possibility that distributed knowledge is a bottleneck, it makes excellent sense. For example, the available stock of knowledge in the economy might be partially codified into science, and access costs to that science could be lowered. This creates a widespread knowledge asset, reducing the degree to which technical knowledge is local. Of course, as the total volume of knowledge rises, the costs of information processing can make this less effective.

It is worth pointing out that all of these normative ideas, however valuable within their scope, may be of limited relevance to the economic problem of an initial invention that later is reused. Making knowledge that already exists easy to retrieve broadly is a good thing; making knowledge that does not yet exist or which is not yet known to be useful to anyone easy to retrieve risks clogging the system. Further, there are excellent reasons, related to the day-to-day functioning of the economy, why much commercial knowledge is decentralized, so it may simply not be cost-effective to have everyone know everyone else's business well enough to know exactly what everyone else might create. In short, the shortage of entrepreneurial knowledge in the economy may be a social cost.

Indeed, I shall argue in my historical section later that we should understand the entrepreneurial-knowledge shortfalls that bottlenecked some very important late twentieth-century GPTs were, in fact, social costs. My argument there is grounded in specific historical detail, of course, but the general analytical point is clear.

13.3 The Founding of GPT Clusters

I now turn to the founding of GPT clusters. A GPT cluster consists of a GPT and several applications sectors. The underlying model of a GPT

we must make use never exists in concentrated or integrated form, but solely as the dispersed bits of incomplete and frequently contradictory knowledge which all the separate individuals possess. The economic problem of society is thus not merely a problem of how to allocate 'given' resources—if 'given' is taken to mean given to a single mind which deliberately solves the problem set by these 'data.' It is rather a problem of how to secure the best use of resources known to any of the members of society, for ends whose relative importance only these individuals know. Or, to put it briefly, it is a problem of the utilization of knowledge not given to anyone in its totality."

cluster shares one crucial feature with the model of recombination in the last section: there is complementarity between invention of a GPT and invention in each applications sector. The most important difference is that a GPT has more than one potential AS partner.

Thus the simplest GPT cluster consists of three potential inventions, A_1, A_2, and G. Each of them costs r_a to invent, and each creates a stand-alone value $V(a)$, $a \in \{A_1, A_2\}$, and $V(G)$. There is also an innovative complementarity between each of the applications and G, so that a further value is created if either both A_1 and G are invented or if both A_2 and G are invented. Call this value $V(a,G)$. No (direct) innovative complementarity exists between A_1 and A_2, though as has been noted in many contexts potential inventors of these two technologies have a common interest in G.

By assembling all the distributed knowledge, we know (correctly) that one of these technologies is a GPT (G) and that the other two are potential applications sectors for it. Potential inventors, however, need not know this ex ante. The notation for who knows what is now necessarily more complex: I denote entrepreneurial knowledge once again by k; now k_a^G refers to knowledge held about G by potential inventors $a \in \{A_1, A_2\}$ while k_G^a refers to knowledge held about a by potential inventors of G. After any technology has been invented and marketed, market knowledge is created. Once again I use K to denote this, and the notation K_k^j denotes knowledge held by potential inventors of technology k about technology j after j has been invented and marketed As in the previous section, the obvious assumption is $0 \leq k_k^j \leq K_k^j \leq 1$ for all pairs j, k. Once again I will denote the share of the complementary return that go to each of the two parties (G, an a) by λ.

The market relationships between a potential GPT and potential applications sectors before and after innovation will influence k and K. In one case, G is a process component that can be used in production in a. Then we should expect k to be low and particularly so if potential inventors of G are already, preinvention, suppliers of a. If G instead is an enabling technology, such as a tool to permit inventions in a, we should expect k to be higher, and particularly so if the "coinventions" in a are itself hard to foresee. A G that primarily enables radical coinventions will have lower k than one that enables nondisruptive ones, and so on. Some cases of GPT platforms are likely to have lower k, or to call for a wider span of k. If applications share customers, and if customers must select G (one kind of platform market), a potential inventor A_1 may need entrepreneurial knowledge not only about G but about the customers A_2 may attract to G.

13.3.1 No Invention

Scarce entrepreneurial information or weak incentives can lead the private rate of return to be less than the social rate of return (the latter assessed using all the information in the economy). In particular, either low k or low λ_1 can lead to failures of the condition to invent:

(10) $$0 > V(G) + \sum_a V(a,G)\lambda_1 k_G^a - r_g$$

(11) $$0 > V(a) + V(a,G)\lambda_1 k_a^G - r_a \forall a.$$

13.3.2 Planned Initiatives

There is a natural tendency to think of GPTs in a hierarchical way. Someone invents a GPT, offers it to potential users, and induces applications sector investment in complements. The GPT inventor might also design a "local" patent or copyright regime that applies to *A* that work with *G*. In this section, I call such a path to the invention of an entire GPT cluster a "planned initiative" and point out that a successful planned initiative turns on the entrepreneurial knowledge of the firm designing the practical GPT product.

A planned initiative is the only equilibrium if a potential inventor of *G* has an incentive to invent and applications sectors have an incentive to follow but not to lead:

(12) $$V(G) + \sum_a V(a,G)\lambda_1 k_G^a - r_g > 0$$

(13) $$V(a) + V(a,G)\lambda_2 K_a^G - r_a > 0 > V(a) + V(a,G)\lambda_1 k_a^G - r_a \forall a.$$

This condition states that no potential GPT inventor has an incentive to invent as a planned initiative, anticipating follow-ons by *a*, and it succeeds in getting some complementarity value if any *a* follows, while generality is achieved if more than one *a* follows. The incentive for the GPT to be invented first need not involve contractual understandings with the *A* sectors. Instead, it may be undertaken "on spec" with the k_G^a measuring the probability assessment on the part of potential inventors of *G* that there will be an application of type *a*. For a planned initiative to succeed, the key entrepreneurial knowledge is that of the GPT or platform innovator. The innovator must have a wide enough knowledge of potential applications to assess the likelihood of success. In a planned initiative, the applications sectors come second, and thus need not have entrepreneurial knowledge of *G*, as they can see *G* in the marketplace.

When ex ante bargaining is feasible and entrepreneurial information is good, another form of planned initiative can arise in which a GPT inventor and one or more early inventors of applications set up incentives for later applications inventors.

13.3.3 Technological Convergence

The other extreme form of equilibrium in the GPT case is technological convergence (Rosenberg 1963). This denotes the case in which the *A* are invented first and only later does a general purpose technology arise. Whereas in a planned initiative, the general leads the specific, under technological convergence, specific solutions emerge first and are later generalized. The conditions for technological convergence to be the unique form of equilibrium are

(14) $$V(G)+\sum_a V(a,G)\lambda_2 K_G^a - r_g > 0 > V(G)+\sum_a V(a,G)\lambda_1 k_G^a - r_g$$

(15) $$V(a) + V(a,G)\lambda_1 k_a^G - r_a > 0 \; \forall \, a.$$

As Rosenberg (1963) points out, one attractive theory of technological convergence is that no one knows ex ante that there are common elements of the production process in A_1 and A_2. There is no technological reason for the general to be invented before the specific, especially if the specific has the goad of necessity. However, after each industry has improved its production process separately, the common elements can be seen more easily ($K_G^a > k_G^a$ in the notation of this chapter). At that point, their common technological elements can be turned into a common technological component supplied by a GPT industry. Invention of the general takes the form of abstracting from the specific.

The case of technological convergence brings out an element of GPTs that many have noted, which is the (social) increasing returns to scale that can be obtained by sharing a common, general, technical input across many applications sectors. This can be salient to the conditions that prevent emergence of a planned initiative. Consider the case in which $k_G^{A_1} > k_G^{A_2}$ and in which the profitability of a GPT turns on it being used widely; that is, on finding all the specific complementary investments in different applications. Then planned initiative might not arise because condition (12) fails, not because there is no idea that the technology inherent in a GPT is useful, but because full range of complementary investments that are necessary for a general solution to be economic are not yet visible.

Note that it is not possible to change only λ and switch conditions in which a planned initiative is the only possible equilibrium to conditions in which technological convergence is the only possible equilibrium. It is as straightforward as possible to obtain such a switch by changing k.

13.3.4 Inversion

In the simple three-inventor model, let (w.l.o.g.) $V(A_1, G) > V(A_2, G)$. In this model an inversion is the invention of A_2 first, followed by G, then followed by A_1. I call this form of equilibrium an inversion because the order of discovery of applications for the GPT is the opposite of the order suggested by valuation. The conditions for an inversion are

(16) $$0 < V(A_2) + V(A_2, G)\lambda_1 k_a^G - r_a$$

(17) $$0 > V(G) + \sum_a V(a,G)\lambda_1 k_G^a - r_g$$

(18) $$0 > V(A_1) + V(A_1, G)\lambda_1 k_a^G - r_a$$

(19) $$0 < V(G) + V(A_2,G)\lambda_2 K_G^{A_2} + V(A_1,G)\lambda_1 k_G^{A_1} - r_g$$

(20) $$0 < V(A_1) + V(A_1,G)\lambda_2 K_a^G - r_a.$$

The first two inequalities are the core distinctions between an inversion and a planned initiative or technological convergence. Inequality (16) says that an applications sector invents before any G is invented. This is like the condition for first invention in technological convergence, except that it only holds for a single sector—in the case of an inversion, a low-value sector. Inequality (17) is the opposite of the G-invention condition in a planned initiative; here, no potential inventor of a G can be adequately sure of complementary applications development to invent.

The essential feature of an inversion is thus that incomplete entrepreneurial information block joint invention of G with the most valuable application but not with other applications. This looks odd from an ex post perspective but not from an ex ante one.

To get inversion as a likely market form, we need some force that creates a negative correlation in the cross section of a sectors between $V(a, G)$ and k_a^G. There are, of course, ways to make this true. If high value applications sectors are the ones, for example, which need to experiment to take advantage of a new G capability, that would imply such a negative correlation and thus the inversion. Thinking we need a "negative correlation," however, turns on using an ex post perspective, which uses knowledge no potential inventor has ex ante. One good ex ante comparison of the conditions for inversion is to the conditions for technological convergence. If the different applications sectors are thinking about their own businesses, the key assumption behind an inversion is that only one sector invents. Neither that sector nor the applications sector that does not invent knows the relationship of complementarity between their innovation and a new technology to be invented in the future.

Another way to say this same point is that inversions tend to arise when there is a gap between social and private returns to innovation looking at the GPT and its highest value application. This also makes it clear why inversions can lead to the creation of great value. Inequality (19) holds if the invention of A_2 creates market knowledge $K_G^{A_2}$ for potential inventors in G that leads them to invent (this is much like the condition for a GPT to invent in technological convergence). Inequality (20) means that the invention of G creates market knowledge, which leads to further application.

It is that last step that I call an *acceleration.* There is an acceleration in value creation as additional sectors invent. What is going on in the acceleration is the release of the market from the bottleneck that held the private rate of return to invention below the social rate. To the extent that lack of entrepreneurial information can create a low private rate of return to invention, the acceleration in value creation is unsurprising.

The triggering event for the acceleration is the *decentralization* of invention that follows from the creation of market knowledge. In an inversion, no single agent knows enough to coordinate, and the ex ante costs of search are too high to make economic coordination possible. However, the early inventions create market knowledge, which raises the private return to other inventors. The central point here is that the decentralization of invention is part of an inversion because of the assumption of distributed knowledge.

An inversion is a market work-around to lack of entrepreneurial knowledge about the value of coordination between potential inventors of G and of A_1. The generality of G is an important assumption here. Looking only at G and of A_1's lack of entrepreneurial knowledge blocks valuable coordination of invention. The generality of use of G permits invention despite this. Of course, this is not a first-best argument. The market work-around cannot occur unless the less valuable applications are still valuable enough to pay for inventing G. Nonetheless, the possibility of accelerating value creation in the late stages of an inversion is valuable. And it is important to point out that, in conditions of limited entrepreneurial knowledge, this market work-around is feasible, where contracting to overcome the coordination problem is not feasible because of the distributed knowledge. I call this a *market* work-around to contrast it with much *antimarket* thinking about the origins of platforms and of GPT industries, focused on contracting and bargaining.

A planned initiative is not the only path to invention of a GPT. Innovation in a number of important GPTs has followed a "circuitous route." I define a circuitous route as having three characteristics: (1) inversion, (2) decentralization, and (3) acceleration. In this section, I show a model that makes definition of all three elements precise. (1) Inversion: The first invention leading to creation of a market in the GPT has a narrow and specific purpose serving a moderately valuable use. The economic motivation of the original invention does not include either generality of purpose or more valuable uses than its narrow and specific purpose. (The word "economic" here is important. Many inventors hope and anticipate that their invention will be generally useful, and it is important for causal arguments that this does not always lead to investment in their invention.) (2) Decentralization: A series of innovations, arising from a number of sources, leads to the successful exploitation of the ex post more valuable uses. Key steps in this sequence of innovations are not coordinated ex ante; instead, early innovations create knowledge about markets that informs later innovators. (3) Acceleration: Once it is known that the "GPT" is general, the positive feedback associated with social increasing returns to scale raise the returns to invention of improvements to the GPT and coinvention of applications.

13.3.5 Multiple Variants of G

Another point can be made in the standard model in which the AS are symmetrical in value—but here, various with regard to entrepreneurial information. Suppose that for each A, there are two potential ways to create new value. One is a compromise, specific to the sector and involving invention of A and $g = \gamma(a)$. The other is an efficient general to all sectors and involves invention of A and G. To capture "compromise" and "efficient" assume that $V(A,G) > V(A, \gamma(A)) > V(A, g)$ for all other g, notably including $\gamma(b)$. However, $r_G > r_{\gamma(a)}$ for all a, so the generality is expensive.

Add the assumption that entrepreneurial knowledge about $\gamma(a)$ is good, but that potential inventors of G have good entrepreneurial knowledge about applications in only ρ proportion of cases in the sense that

$$V(G) + \sum_a V(a,G)\lambda_1 k_G^a - r_g = V(G) + \rho \sum_a V(a,G)\lambda_1 - r_g.$$

Note that this condition has the advantages and the disadvantages of scope. The advantage of wide scope of applicability is that the fixed cost r_G is spread over many AS. The corresponding disadvantage arises when entrepreneurial information is scarce, for then potential GPT inventors may not know of the specific needs of their potential customers. In the case where ρ is small then the absence of entrepreneurial information about broad opportunities makes invention of a GPT on spec uneconomic. Of course, if this expression is positive, G is invented in a planned initiative and all is well. But what if it is not?

Let us assume that with an A to invent using $\gamma(A)$ (recall they have perfect entrepreneurial information) the comparable condition for invention is

$$V(a) + V(\gamma(a)) + V(a,\gamma(a)) - r_a - r_{\gamma(a)} > 0. \tag{21}$$

Assume that the proportion of applications sectors for which this will hold is Ψ and the proportion of applications sectors for which this will hold and that are entrepreneurially known to potential inventors of G is $\rho\Psi$. Then a general GPT will be invented after a first round of invention of A and $\gamma(A)$ in some sectors if

$$V(G) + \rho(1 - \Psi)\sum_a V(a,G)\lambda_1 + \Psi \sum_a V(a,G)\lambda_2 - r_g > 0. \tag{22}$$

This can be substantially larger than the condition for original invention of a GPT if there is enough opportunity to create local alternatives. It is worth noting that strong patent rights for these alternatives (enough to lower λ_2) can still prevent emergence of a general purpose technology.

13.3.6 Remarks

In this section I have constructed a model with the simplest structure that explains inversion, one built around limited entrepreneurial knowledge. Inversion is an odd enough phenomenon that it calls for adding something to the model. An added benefit is that the model predicts decentralization and acceleration. It explains why, in the case of a GPT, a market work-around is available to deal with bottlenecks caused by entrepreneurial knowledge scarcity. How important these phenomena are can only be investigated by close historical examination of the knowledge state of the economy at different stages of invention. I will show that these ideas, especially the replacement of scarce entrepreneurial knowledge with excellent market knowledge, mattered for the rate and direction of technical change.

13.4 Historical Examples

I now turn to six historical inventions of important GPTs, all within computer and information technology. Three of them are the three most important (so far!) computer GPT clusters for white-collar automation (WCA). These are (1) business data processing based on computers, (2) personal computing, and (3) the widespread use of the Internet and the World Wide Web (WWW). These three GPT clusters have included—but not begun with—a wide range of WCA applications respectively in (1) enterprise computing, (2) personal productivity computing, and (3) electronic commerce, communication, and content. The third recombined the first two (and a number of other technologies) and its applications have considerably expanded the demand for them. I also study the founding of two other important GPT clusters within the same technology category, with very different conditions of entrepreneurial knowledge. These are (4) the computer itself, (5) the minicomputer, and (6) the smartphone. At the beginning of each of those segments, an innovator had the entrepreneurial knowledge to see the overlaps between the feasible and the valuable. The contrast to my first three examples is instructive.

I study the creation of information technology GPTs for three related reasons. First, these are, particularly in their application to WCA, among the most important contemporary technologies. Second, there is a large body of careful historical studies of invention in this industry.[15] My brief treatment builds on these, and a focus on a novel historical question. Specifically, I focus on the knowledge state of the economy before markets were founded. Earlier studies have been strong on what specific firms or individuals knew and thought, laying a very strong basis for my work. Each of these reasons to study information technology GPTs is standard and simple. Each of these three began in an inversion, following, at least for a while, a circuitous route to its highest value applications.

I also turn to information technology GPTs because, at least in WCA applications, entrepreneurial knowledge has often been scarce. In particular, it has been difficult to see overlaps between the technically feasible and the

15. I draw heavily on Aspray and Campbell-Kelly (2004), Ceruzzi (1998), Freiberger and Swaine (2000), Langlois and Robertson (1992), on Usselman (1993), and on my collaborations with Shane Greenstein (1996) and Franco Malerba (1998). In some of the historical episodes I draw on new primary sources.

valuable in application. This has been noted in the past as a source of failure of cutting edge applications, a source of the slow diffusion of valuable new technologies, and an explanation of firm success based on marketing capabilities.[16] Thus I am, to a considerable degree, looking for the problem of scarce entrepreneurial knowledge where I expect to find it. That creates obvious problems, which I overcome by looking at GPT clusters based on the same broad technology area founded in conditions of better entrepreneurial knowledge.

Another advantage of these historical examples is that they help sharpen both the concept of entrepreneurial knowledge and its economic role. Conceptually, entrepreneurial knowledge must be (a) specific enough to guide investment in new technology and (b) connected enough to create a market. Grace Hopper's distinction between thinking a computer (or other new invention) was a good idea and actually building a computer that solves a problem captures much of this.[17] I would add the economist's point to that; only ideas specific enough to draw investment resources are *K*. We shall see that the distinction between broad general knowledge that some invention in a wide technological area might be useful and knowing a direction for technical progress that might well serve an identified user need is crucial for drawing investment resources.

13.4.1 Entrepreneurial Knowledge Scarcity and Market Work-Arounds at Industry Founding

Because of a scarcity of entrepreneurial knowledge linking an important technology to its most valuable use, one of the twentieth century's most valuable GPTs, business data processing, was invented in an inversion. The key shortage of entrepreneurial knowledge arose here: It was difficult to see, ex ante, the overlaps between what was technically feasible and the most valuable uses. What was clearly technically feasible was the computer; how to make a computer valuable in business was not obvious, especially not to those who best understood business data processing. The overlap between the technically feasible and the valuable in use became more visible at an interim stage, after the invention of general purpose computers to meet significant, but lesser, demand needs. To understand this more clearly, I examine the invention of the computer itself, the founding of the business data processing industry, and the founding of the minicomputer industry.

16. This has been well-documented in the writings of industry insiders (e.g. Gates 1995, see note 32). Shane Greenstein and I pointed out that the importance of marketing capabilities at the firm level has historically been far greater in the commercial (mainframe, PC, smartphone) segments than in the technical ones (minicomputer, engineering workstation). As we shall see, this is related to the relative importance of incomplete entrepreneurial knowledge in the commercial sectors.

17. Admiral Hopper was the inventer of the compiler.

13.4.2 The Computer

Much of the foundational engineering advances that constitute invention of a general purpose electronic computer were undertaken in the 1930s and 1940s, though it would take a large number of improvements and extensions over more than a half century to create all of the technologies now supporting white-collar automation. The same half century contained a looming growth bottleneck for the rich countries. Automation of physical processes and of blue-collar work in many industries (e.g., in manufacturing), was very successful but was, over the next half century or so, destined to be subject to diminishing returns. One thing clearly needed for further growth was technical progress in WCA.

Today, we all know that one group of uses of electronic computing was going to be business data processing for automation and product quality improvement in service industries and for the white-collar functions of all industries. Today, ex post it is obvious that computer-supported business data processing is a valuable overlap between technological opportunity and demand need. As ex ante entrepreneurial knowledge, it was far less obvious. To be sure, there was a great deal of excitement about the prospects for computers, largely among scientists and engineers interested in *calculation* (military or civilian).[18]

Much of the specific progress that was made in computers in the late 1930s and in the 1940s was to make machines that could compute; that is, do arithmetic calculations. Specifically, they were invented by scientists and engineers to support scientific and engineering calculations, frequently supported by military funding. Very important examples include the work, funded by the Army, of Eckert and Mauchly at Penn, and the work of physicists and mathematicians recruited to work on atomic weapons projects, notably John von Neumann. The scientific and engineering calculations they wanted to undertake included some that were numerically difficult, such as making artillery tables, and others that were both conceptually deep and numerically difficult, such as the calculations needed to design the H-Bomb, which involved understanding some of the deepest mathematics and physics ever conceived. From the perspective of entrepreneurial knowledge, however, it is entirely correct to assume a large k_a^G—the *relationship* of the desired calculations to a machine that could do calculations was, unlike the calculations themselves, not complex. That relationship is *entrepreneurial knowledge.* This is how the inversion started. One potential group of *A*s, scientific computing, had very good entrepreneurial knowledge.

It is also helpful to locate technical knowledge and entrepreneurial knowledge together. Scientists and engineers were also well set up to understand

18. There were also widespread forecasts that computers would be useful for everything. This is not the same as entrepreneurial knowledge that guided investment.

the technical requirements of an electronic calculating machine itself. They could see, once the problem of creating a machine to undertake calculations was set, paths to making such a machine. Of course, it was extremely helpful that some of the goals of calculations were obviously beneficial in a military sense, so the scientists and engineers were often well-funded. This was an example of particularly good entrepreneurial knowledge about the value of a new tool, electronic computers, held by people with the knowledge to make it—physical scientists and engineers.[19]

Many, many inventors have claimed to be the first in some aspect of the electronic computer, the stored program computer, and so forth. This includes a claim from IBM, later to be the most successful electronic data processing firm using electronic computers, related to their joint work with Howard Aiken of Harvard in the late 1930s and during the war. This claim is important to the present inquiry because IBM was (like others) already engaged in business data processing in the 1930s. However, IBM did not have the requisite entrepreneurial information to invest in electronic computing for business data processing. Like its competitors, IBM was investing overwhelmingly in research and development of mechanical and electromechanical technologies, not in digital computers. The Aiken project at Harvard was to create a machine that could do calculations in physics (Aiken's department). Aiken was looking for a calculation firm, and turned to IBM only after Monroe (the calculator company) turned him down. The Aiken project used IBM's existing electromechanical technologies, so the direction of technical progress here represented the recombination of IBM technologies with scientists' needs, not the other way. The point here is absolutely not to belittle the inventiveness and foresight of this project. Instead, the point is to say what this project was not: an investment by IBM in technologies to be useful in business data processing. It was only much later, as we shall see following, that IBM turned to the overlap between electronic computing and business data processing.[20]

The core distinction here between scientific calculation and business data processing at the earliest stages concerns the presence of actionable entrepreneurial knowledge. Military demand for scientific calculation had it; Aspray and Campbell-Kelly (2004) correctly begin their chapter entitled "inventing the computer" by saying "World War II was a scientific war." In contrast, their next chapter, entitled "The Computer Becomes a Business Machine," begins with a story about Thomas Watson (sr.) of IBM. After about 1951, IBM became very aware of the potential of the computer as

19. It is, of course, not true of scientific and engineering tools in general. Those are often built in interdisciplinary teams where one knows the purpose and the other the methods. Entrepreneurial knowledge is needed for that.

20. IBM did not take up the burst of technical opportunity that arose in World War II; it was not until the Korean War that "government sponsored competition" prompted IBM to move into computing.

a business machine and played a central role in its reconstruction "to be a data-processing machine rather than a mathematical instrument" (Aspray and Campbell-Kelly 2004, 106). How this reconstruction was undertaken is well understood: how it was enabled is an important part of the inversion that created the data-processing machine.

13.4.3 Openness

The sense in which the scientists and engineers invented a GPT was that they invented and improved *tools* that they could use in scientific and engineering calculations. As is the habit of scientists, they designed the tool to be general calculating engines. A scientist does not make a tool general because she or he foresees all its uses; on the contrary, generality is often motivated by a sense that others may take up the tool for their own uses. The essential role of science here was the openness with which the tool was delivered to the rest of the economy, including other scientific and engineering disciplines, and ultimately to unrelated commercial application.[21]

This tool turned out to be suitable for recombination outside the range of science and engineering. That recombination led to a very large spillover from the scientific sector to the rest of the economy (to which we shall turn in a moment) but the spillover did not flow through application of the science itself. The essential role played by the scientific-ness of the original inventors in the spillover process was not the new scientific knowledge itself. The spillout was the recombination of an input into science. This is not "the commercialization of science" as often understood, but the beneficial effects of scientific openness in widespread dissemination of a tool.[22] The organizational structures and values that supported openness, generality, and disclosure, which exist in scientific communities, to be sure, but also in some other invention communities, can form very important parts of a market work-around when the linear path is blocked by lack of entrepreneurial knowledge. In this case, IBM's λ_2 would be quite large, and the original inventors of many critical computing technologies did not command much of a λ_1 once the computer was recombined into business data processing.

Once the computer had been invented and was being applied to an every widening circle of computations, the knowledge state of the economy changed. What had been scarce k became very widely held K. Many people could now see the possibility of the general purpose computer as a business

21. It was thought for a time that Eckert and Mauchly had a patent as a result of the Electronic Numerical Integrator and Computer (ENIAC), but this turned out to be incorrect. Some say the commercially-oriented Eckert and Mauchly invented the stored program computer, others say it was John von Neuman. There is no doubt, however, that it was von Neuman who sought to have the concept and engineering of the stored program computer available to all.

22. The discovery and associated inventions of the semiconductor effect, the transistor, and the integrated circuit were an extremely important spillout from science to the computer industry, and were very much the commercialization of science.

tool, at least in applications that were obviously computational, such as accounting, finance, and some operations management tasks like inventory control. To be sure, the electronic computer would have to overcome serious disadvantages relative to electromechanical devices, such as low reliability. That, however, could be conceptualized as a technical/engineering problem.

Perhaps more importantly, once the technical knowledge about the computation itself was made open, it could be combined with other knowledge about business data processing. This was a far more difficult problem than scientific calculation. Most managerial applications of business data processing have a very complex relationship between the business logic of the application and the technical capabilities of computer hardware and software. The simplest are accounting and finance and even they have a more complex interface with calculation than do typical scientific or engineering calculations. This very complex problem was, however, partly solved by the invention of the electronic computer as a mathematical engine. A decentralized path of invention could take advantage of the widely distributed knowledge in the economy, and now firms with knowledge of business data processing entered the picture in a very important way.

It is a mistake, a very common mistake, to think that the only entrepreneurial information problem at an early stage is a shortage of "vision" on the part of "visionaries"—that is, individuals or firms who foresee the future. This misses a central important point about entrepreneurial knowledge. Market economies can, with the help of enough openness, achieve breakthroughs that were unforeseeable to any individual because knowledge was widely distributed. Of course, those breakthroughs that arise through an inversion come later than they would have if there had been a single individual with all the knowledge of both technical possibility and demand needs. The distributed state of ex ante knowledge is a social cost, but at what a high rate and in what an excellent direction technical progress can proceed ex post an inversion. That improvement arises from opportunity pent up while the social return to invention is above the private return, opportunity unleashed by the changing knowledge state of the economy.

13.5 A Planned Initiative Succeeds

Once an inversion is completed, the newly created information about technical progress may lead, through decentralization, to recombinant invention by distinct inventors than those who participated in the original inversion. Those new inventions can lead to an acceleration, completing the circuitous route to the founding of a market.

A wide number of firms, with an extremely wide range of knowledge bases and capabilities, entered a race to be the leading computer vendor in business data processing. IBM, though its technical knowledge base lay in mechanical and electromechanical business data processing, won this race.[23] IBM took advantage of newly public knowledge about computers, its own existing knowledge about the needs of business data processing, and undertook significant recombination.

Open knowledge about the electronic computer did not just benefit IBM. The openness created a large number of recombinatory experiments in competition with one another. No one knew exactly what a business data processing computer looked like even after they saw a successful scientific computer. The competitive experimentation race to establish a successful business data processing business around the mainframe computer worked well in such a knowledge-challenged environment.

In the case of business data processing there was still a great deal of invention to be undertaken in computers themselves and in their commercial applications to build a complete GPT cluster. What is quite interesting about those next steps is that they took a radically different form: IBM undertook a planned initiative to construct a GPT cluster centered on the mainframe computer and induced customers, primarily large firms, to create applications. That planned initiative won a competitive race among a number of distinct business data processing firms that ended with an IBM standard.[24]

IBM went to work to create the general purpose components that could be used by its corporate customers to build applications. IBM also built a very good computer design and engineering technical capability, though IBM was rarely the technical leader in computers, narrowly understood. Yet IBM offered a complete set of complementary general-purpose inputs, including hardware, software, storage, and other peripherals that reflected its knowledge of the kind of problems its customers were trying to solve. Further, IBM put in place an organizational support system that let its customers lower the risks of undertaking experiments in the applications of computers—this is a general purpose complement unmatched by any significant competitor worldwide. The creation of the IBM mainframe standard was an example of how a planned initiative can build a GPT cluster. To underscore the key point here, once IBM understood the technical prospects for electronic computing reasonably well, that single firm had the entrepreneurial knowledge to undertake a planned initiative. It combined preexisting knowledge of its customers' needs with new, generally available knowledge about what was technically feasible.

Of course, there was continuing feedback between technical knowledge and knowledge of user needs in computing for decades after this. There was a dramatically high rate of technical progress in computing, even if we think

23. See Bresnahan-Malerba on the nature of this competition, especially on the point that IBM formed an organization designed to link knowledge of customers' business needs to knowledge of what was technically feasible in computing.

24. This articulation of IBM's success draws heavily on Usselman (1993) and on my work with Franco Malerba (1998).

of a narrow definition like the speed of the computer. More important, the structures created by IBM to feedback user needs into technical improvements—to create new entrepreneurial knowledge—led to many new product features and technologies.[25] This planned initiative succeeded admirably until the late 1980s. Even the difficult transition out of the IBM mainframe computer era into the current "server" era was characterized by scarce entrepreneurial knowledge. I do not treat that transition in detail here, though Shane Greenstein and I have argued (1996) that its information needs were daunting and that the relevant information was highly dispersed.[26]

13.5.1 A (Different) Example Where Entrepreneurial Knowledge Was Less Scarce

It is worth pointing out the contrast to another GPT cluster in the computing industry that did not supply business data processing customers, but instead supplied technical, scientific, and engineering customers. The "minicomputer" industry was staffed by scientists and engineers and its customers were also primarily technical people, with technical problems to solve. Thus the minicomputer industry followed reasonably directly out of the original scientific and engineering knowledge basis of the electronic computer. Based on technical people selling to technical people, the minicomputer industry did not need elaborate structures to create new entrepreneurial knowledge. The relative scarcity and importance of entrepreneurial knowledge in WCA explains much of the difference of firm and industry structure between the business data processing sector dominated by IBM and the much more competitive minicomputer segment.[27] Ironically, the same shortages of entrepreneurial knowledge about customer needs that made scientific openness essential to the invention of business data processing (BDP) made entry and competition against IBM's position, once established, very difficult.

If not for the recombination of the electronic computer into a business data processing machine, society would "only" have gotten the kinds of

25. Perhaps the most important solution to the problem of scarce knowledge about applications/technology overlap was IBM's invention of the closed, modular platform. This invention reduced the risk of customer experimentation dramatically. If a customer discovered that a particular business application worked, but that it required a larger or smaller computer, larger or smaller data storage, and so forth, they could move to those components without losing their initial investment in invention. This supported one of the most important forms of experimentation in business data processing, the construction of a complex high value system on top of a simple system. A customer might build an accounts receivable system that just kept track of who owed what, and then build a complex decision-support system on top of it to guide the extension of trade credit. If the trade credit system worked, IBM could offer the larger computers and data storage, and so forth needed to run it in a modular fashion.

26. Bresnahan and Greenstein (1996) concluded from our empirical analysis that the most valuable computer applications were also the most difficult to invent given a new computer technology. We also concluded that technical progress in computing and technical progress in the uses of computing are very different bodies of knowledge.

27. I am grateful to Shane Greenstein and to Franco Malerba in this regard; without our collaborations I would never have come to understand this.

$V(A,G)$ returns we got from scientific and engineering computing mostly supplied with minicomputers, not the much larger value associated with BDP. At this stage it is perhaps useful to reiterate what $V(A, G)$ means in this chapter. As a first point, what is *not* important is a judgment about the ultimate social value of business data processing versus scientific calculation. Instead, it is the area under the demand curve for BDP versus scientific, engineering, and other technical calculations (which takes the budget for science as given). Whatever the ultimate importance of science, science had significantly less willingness to pay for computers than did commerce over the second half of the twentieth century. However, at the crucial moment when the computer was being invented, scientists and engineers had the entrepreneurial knowledge (and the military demand) to fund the invention.

13.5.2 Invention of the PC as a Business Tool

The personal computer has found new bodies of demand a number of times. I focus here on the circuitous route to the first large markets for the PC as an individual productivity tool for white-collar workers.[28] As with other GPTs for WCA, it followed a circuitous route.

I revisit the familiar history of the very early PC industry with analytical goals in mind, taking repeated advantage of the gap between what we now know about the uses of the personal computer and what industry participants knew during the 8-bit era, roughly the late 1970s. That lets us understand the role of the information structure of invention at the time. The critical event still in the future was the invention and widespread distribution of personal productivity applications for white-collar workers. Market events during the 8-bit era were based on contemporary knowledge of demand—and on contemporary uncertainty about the future of demand.

That information structure of invention helps explain a number of market outcomes in the 8-bit era. Those include the importance of entrepreneurship, market selection of the more open platforms, firms' motivations for supplying open systems, and recombination. Accordingly, I will start with investigation of contemporary information, and then turn to examination of the supply of the two most successful platforms of the era.

There is real analytical value in understanding what suppliers did not know in the early days of the industry. That lets us understand firm strategies which were enabling rather than a planned initiative. It was commonplace in the 8-bit era to think of the main market of the PC as being hobbyists. Here is Microsoft founder Paul Allen in 1977: "The personal computer user finds himself at the leading edge of a new computer applications and technology, He is becoming a source of expertise and innovation. He is

28. The history of these advances is carefully treated in a number of secondary sources, on which I rely heavily in this section. My account draws on Freiberger and Swaine (2000), on Ceruzzi (1998), Aspray and Campbell-Kelly (2004), on Langlois and Robertson (1992), and on other secondary and contemporary sources.

not merely a passive, casual user of hardware and software developed by others."[29] Around the same time, the founder of the commercial PC industry, Ed Roberts, forecast most business growth in "inventory, accounting, that sort of thing" (i.e., IBM mainframe-like applications for small business). With the candor and self-confidence characteristic of important inventors in computing, Roberts pointed out that no one present at the founding had a solid forecast of later developments (most pointedly, not his collaborator Bill Gates).

The most important platforms of the 8-bit era, commercially, were the Apple II and CP/M computers (running the CP/M operating system on a wide variety of brands of computers). Apple had a sponsored platform but a very open approach to developers. The design of the Apple II made it a mass market PC. The computer came in a plastic case, not metal, and looked like an office appliance more than a hobbyist's technology. It required no soldering, had a keyboard and a monitor, and could run programs. As a result the Apple II was dramatically easier to use than earlier personal computers (though still quite difficult to use by modern standards). Accordingly, it appealed to a far larger market than the hobbyist kits could. An important differentiator for Apple was that it used color, which appealed to game developers, but it appealed to the home and school user as well. On the other hand, the Apple II had a 40-column screen, fine for games and school but very problematic for word processing and spreadsheets. These design trade-offs reflected current technical levels, of course, but—as would be realized later during a scramble to make different trade-offs—also the key fact that demand forecasts were for hobbyist, home, and game.

Ken Olsen, founder and chairman of Digital Equipment Corporation (DEC), famously said in 1977, "There is no reason anyone would want to have a computer in their home." This remark is universally quoted to show that Olsen missed the opportunity represented by the PC. That dinosaur! This gives us an opportunity to be clear on who foresaw what. Contrast with Olsen's remark a contemporary explanation from Apple computer about the uses of its new PC, in a press release titled "Product Close-Up: Apple II Microcomputer" from the June 1978 issue of *Personal Computing*:

> Applications include using the computer as a teaching aid for students and for entertainment through interactive games . . . paddles and joysticks can be interfaced . . . a built in speaker sounds when the ball is hit or a photon torpedo is fired at a klingon. Manufacturers [Apple] also suggest home business applications such as financial and bookkeeping analysis, charting the Dow Jones average and home budget tracking. . . . [W]hen the Apple II is equipped with soon to be announced added components, it will be able to monitor home systems such as heating, cooling,

29. "Software Column" by Paul Allen, VP of Microsoft: Personal Computing, January/February 1977, 66. At the time, Allen was Microsoft's "big think" person, while Bill Gates was more in charge of implementation.

> burglar alarm, fire and smoke detectors and lighting. When you're away, the computer can randomly light parts of the house on different days to give the appearance that someone is in residence.

Apple's description of the uses of its machine in this quotation include (a) immediately visible uses (games and educational software); (b) uses that still have not had any widespread commercial importance for the PC (burglar alarms, home heating, lighting, and cooling); and (c) uses that would find a mass market a decade or two later (home finance, which would become a mass market after the introduction of Quicken, and mass market use of online financial services, which would come with widespread use of the Internet).

The other main platform sponsor, selling CP/M, did not have Apple's marketing savvy, and simply admitted that it was up to others to figure out what the PC was for. "Statistics" and "Economics Research" were among the top uses of CP/M machines in a survey, suggesting a market somewhat smaller than 100s of millions of PCs. The point is, it was not merely Apple and DEC who lacked what we now know was key entrepreneurial knowledge about the use of PCs in offices. The lack was universal.

The founders of the PC industry did not particularly have white-collar automation in mind. (Except in the sense that they had everything in mind.) The first important platform sponsors in the PC industry, who built substantial (hundreds of thousands of units) commercial markets did not particularly have white-collar automation in mind. This leads me to the second central point, the widespread distribution of knowledge.

It was the invention of the word processor and the spreadsheet by new inventors—not the founders of the industry, nor people they had ever met—that turned the PC toward WCA. Interestingly, even the first inventor of a PC word processor, Michael Shrayer, who wrote Electric Pencil as a tool for printing manuals for his *real* software products, developer tools, did not really have WCA in mind. He had the immediate need to print manuals.

However, the creation of the PC and of a nonkit PC (Roberts; Jobs and Wozniak at Apple) and of key software (Gary Kildall at Digital Research Inc., Gates and Allen at Microsoft) led to the creation of an enormous amount of market *K*. This, together with the open systems approach of early PCs, led to an explosion of applications software, but most particularly to the invention and commercialization of software for WCA. The inventor of the first spreadsheet, VisiCalc, absolutely had the automation of accounting work in mind. So did the effective commercializer of word processing, Seymour Rubenstein, seller of WordStar, who quickly entered and competed away Electric Pencil's business. The invention and commercialization of these very widely used applications turned the PC into a tool for the individual white-collar worker in the corporation. They were not anticipated by the founders of the industry. Indeed, once the inevitable consequences of the conversion of the PC into a white-collar tool occurred—IBM's entry, the professionalization of hardware and software supply—many of the founders reacted very negatively. Far from planned, this was a market outcome. If I have mentioned many of the inventors, it is to drive home the point that knowledge was very distributed and that decentralization was essential.

The entrepreneurs of WordStar and VisiCalc built large volume (by then PC standards) businesses because the main PC types, the Apple II and CP/M machines, were open to it and had rapidly growing installed bases. Existing PC firms—neither the inventors of the Apple or of CP/M, nor Micro Instrumentation and Telemetry Systems nor Microsoft, themselves pioneering and entrepreneurial—did not invent the new markets, nor did they commercialize them. The shortcomings of these firms (and of established firms like IBM and DEC) were not a limitation on what the market system could accomplish, however, as new firms opened up the new markets. Existing personal computer industry firms were a source of trained managers and potential distribution partners and technical collaborators for the new firms. This specialized and loosely linked structure worked well. It did not need planning nor central coordination to gain economies of scale in multiple products.

Through this inversion, a very valuable GPT cluster, the PC industry used (primarily) by white-collar workers was invented. Once again the first inventions served a technically-oriented community, hobbyists and hackers, with narrow goals. This time, that community was not academic science or military demand, but a self-organizing group much like modern open-source movement. They used some of the organizing principles of open science, however, including open systems. Some entrepreneurs would have liked to close systems, but the resource constraints of small firms in a small market left them compelled—recognizing that they did not know everything—to let outsiders innovate. Not only was there a shortage of entrepreneurial knowledge, the shortage was recognized and impacted business practice in a first order way.

With an important overlap between technical possibility and demand needs seen by no one, the early PC industry followed a circuitous route. The original invention for hobbyists and the commercialization for home users were inverted by the invention of the word processor and the spreadsheet. This invention was inherently decentralized, as early movers did not anticipate what followed, and it led to a profound acceleration once the high value business PC markets were identified.

13.6 Major Mass Market E-Commerce, E-Content, E-Communication Initiatives

I turn now to the invention of a successful mass market platform: electronic commerce, content, and communications (hereafter EC^3), the widely-used Internet. To date, the Internet is the most important technology for the extension of WCA into markets. This famous example of recombination—the Internet had been used for other purposes for decades—lets us address two important analytical areas.

First, examining this invention, and the many failed planned initiatives that proceeded it, permits us to sharpen the concept and role of entrepreneurial knowledge considerably. The list of failed planned initiatives is remarkable, both remarkably long and remarkable for containing highly capable, knowledgeable firms with many resources. They all had *almost enough* entrepreneurial knowledge to start an EC^3 GPT cluster. They all knew that there was a broad mass market opportunity to create some kind of EC^3 GPT cluster. As in the case of the founding of the PC industry described earlier, we can take up the question of what inventors did not know when they did not know it. While all the planned initiatives failed, the actual creation of the successful EC^3 platform on the Internet was an inversion, following a highly decentralized, circuitous route. Attributing the success of the ultimately successful set of inventions to superior knowledge and foresight on the part of its early inventors is incorrect. Instead, the inversion was, as we shall see, a market work-around of important shortages of entrepreneurial knowledge.

Second, this important example lets us examine the role of openness in platform creation. This is considerably sharper than the cases examined before, because in this example entrepreneurial knowledge was not terrible, just not sufficient to permit success. Many of the planned initiatives were closed in ways that would have served the interests of platform sponsors or other early participants. Even when they were not extremely closed, and even when entrepreneurial knowledge was not terrible, they failed. The interaction between modest shortcomings of entrepreneurial knowledge and modest departures from open systems worked to block innovation. At the end of this section I discuss the theoretical salience of this finding.

The same history also shows that a circuitous route can invent something that is not obvious. Here I focus on two aspects of the widely used Internet. An innovation that satisfies a long-felt need, unsatisfied by many prior innovation attempts, is likely nonobvious. When the last key invention in the successful innovation is, from a strictly technical perspective, not a hard problem, the inference of nonobviousness is overwhelming. We shall see that the entrepreneurial knowledge needed to design a successful mass market EC^3 platform is what rendered it nonobvious. Open-systems innovation, which economizes on scarce entrepreneurial knowledge, was the key to success.

13.6.1 E-Commerce, Notably in Finance

The potential social value of mass-market electronic commerce was a long-felt need for many years before the widespread use of the Internet. Potential innovators knew that there was value in a platform for mass market electronic commerce. What they did not know, with adequate precision to guide a planned initiative, was the technical features of that platform and its relationship to other uses.

Mass-market e-commerce was a long-felt need in part because of the earlier success of e-commerce outside mass markets. Decades before the widespread use of the Internet, treasurers at large corporations could have access to bank account information electronically. Similarly, an airline reservations system could be accessed both by employee sales agents and by external (to the airline firm) travel agents. There were also some limited e-commerce applications that were used by the consumer, such as bank automatic teller machines. These applications crossed the boundary of the firm, which is why I call them e-commerce. What they did not do is reach a mass market of individuals using a common device. These applications did make it clear that one goal for WCA was crossing the boundary of the firm and automating markets (most white-collar work is in buying and selling bureaucracies). The invention and widespread adoption of the PC suggested to a wide variety of potential innovators that a GPT cluster of mass market e-commerce applications was feasible.

Many firms engaged in retail finance (banking and brokerage) saw this opportunity in the 1980s and first half of the 1990s and attempted to create a GPT cluster to fulfill it. These were not trivial undertakings, and often involved very large investments by very successful retail banking and brokerage firms, such as Chemical Bank, Bank of America, Banc One, Shawmut Bank, and so on. They also included Citibank, which had successfully pioneered the ATM network, one of the most successful mass-market e-commerce applications (but without a general-purpose "client" device) of the prior era. Many of these firms made very substantial investments in systems, and through much of this long era, these initiatives were always about to succeed. A 1983 article in *Time* entitled "Armchair Banking and Investing" (Alva, Ungeheuer, and Koepp 1983, n.p.) pointed out that

> Bankers believe that financial services will eventually be part of futuristic home information packages like Viewtron that supply everything from recipes to movie reviews. Therefore they are scrambling to organize joint ventures with communications firms.

You can see from that very brief 1983 quote that the shock of the Internet was not the "vision" of delivering mass market EC^3 to consumers. These very early initiatives failed, as did their successors over the dozen or so years between this quote and the success of the Internet. One might think that the initiatives were technically too early or the attainable market too small before PCs diffused. However, over the relevant time period PCs got easier to use, diffused very widely, and became connected on better and better modems.

If the "vision" was present, what was the bottleneck? How was the bottleneck removed by the widespread use of the Internet? The *Time* quote, like many discussions by contemporary observers over the next dozen years, has several clues. Contemporary observers thought that a mass market financial e-Commerce system would need to be part of a larger "package" of online services to attract sufficiently many users to be economic. Bankers and brokers believed, rightly, that banking/finance applications alone, including checking brokerage account balances, online trading, online banking, and online bill paying, did not appear to offer enough value to end users.

The bankers and brokers solved this by turning potential collaborators in "home information systems" to offer users a "package." Conceptualizing the offering as a "package" for consumers captures much of the thinking at the time; that is, a planned initiative led by a consortium of applications developers. Turning to information firms for "home information systems" brought more knowledge of demand into the planned initiatives, a topic to which I now turn.[30]

13.6.2 Electronic Content (Mass) Markets

The potential social value of mass-market access to information and entertainment online was also, as a broad general idea, obvious for many years. There had been a number of online information systems in smaller markets, and their diffusion to mass markets was broadly forecast. There were even platforms for the sale of specific information services to their markets, and the expectation that a similar platform would emerge in the mass market arena was widespread.[31] None took off. This, too, permits a deep investigation of what the many failed potential innovators knew, and did not know, beforehand.

The conceptualization of many initiators of home information systems closely followed that of already existing business information systems of offering a subscription "package." High value information that already exists somewhere (stock prices on trades in the last 20 seconds) was already being sold at high prices to specialized audiences (traders, by Bloomberg). Surely lower value information that already exists somewhere could be sold to a mass market. For example, the editorial content of *Readers' Digest*

30. This section has emphasized a mass market platform for home use because of the dramatic growth in home use post-Internet. There were, however, parallel initiatives for at-work use, also of limited success pre-Internet.

31. A number of special-purpose online services had prospered, selling high-value information in narrow markets. One thinks of Lexis/Nexis selling information to attorneys, Bloomberg to the financial industry, DIALOG, and so on. By the late 1980s, there were hundreds of online databases. DIALOG was a database platform; searchers and readers would pay between $35/hour and $500/hour depending on the database. Bloomberg, founded in 1981, was founded by a former financial market participant (at Salomon brothers) who saw the benefits of delivering already existing information to financial market participants. They would lease a "Bloomberg machine" (i.e., a special-purpose terminal), and get rapid 24 hour access to financial and related information. These successful commercial online services had themselves been invented by circuitous paths (e.g., DIALOG started at Lockheed).

already existed in machine readable form: surely it could also be sold somehow at lower prices to a mass market online audience? The *Readers' Digest* example is real, and a large number of publishers of consumer-oriented media content sought to move online over the 1980s and early 1990s.

Many of these existing publishers of consumer-oriented media recognized the limitations of their entrepreneurial knowledge and sought to overcome those limitations by undertaking joint ventures or alliances with technology firms. Knight-Ridder, CBS, and Times-Mirror all had collaborations with AT&T. Many other firms had collaborations with IBM. Harrigan (2003) has a very useful review of the wide list of joint ventures (JVs) and alliances that arose in this area. Like the other media firms that sought to create mass markets on a go-it-alone basis, these collaborations did not succeed in creating a mass market.

The plethora of attempts at mass-market e-content typically set up the online services as closed, with particular attention to the unauthorized copying of content, which often gave control rights to the owners of a particular kind of content. While those contractual protections may have had a good economic purpose looking only at local knowledge, they were problematic for creating a broad general GPT cluster involving different kinds of content and service. The other potential suppliers of e-commerce services, for example, would not necessarily have adopted a subscription model nor would they have emphasized the prevention of copying. Making this problem more difficult—as we now know from watching the struggles of "content" providers from magazines to Hollywood adapt to the Internet, the iPad, and so forth—is that the entrepreneurial knowledge of exactly how existing content will be sold in a new medium is hard to come by. How much harder when the medium has yet to be invented! There were many of these initiatives, spread out over a wide variety of content companies, joint ventures with existing telecommunications companies, and computer firms. I will not attempt a complete list here because the economically important point is that, even taken together, these initiatives did not attract sufficient end-user interest to start a positive feedback loop around mass-market e-content.

13.6.3 Electronic Communication for Mass Markets?

Similarly, a wide number of firms offered electronic communications services to consumers and/or to firms in the period preceding the widespread use of the Internet. Many of these looked like modern e-mail, and indeed shared some technology with the development of e-mail in not-for-profit settings on the Internet. None of the for-profit ones were as large as the user-built e-mail network serving existing Internet users (largely in universities and related places). The end result was also low usage, and the network effects of communications systems create much more value in widely used systems. By the early 1990s, one could see the odd result that scientists and engineers, surely not the most communicative of people, had excellent access to e-mail on the Internet, but that other classes of users, whether as employees or as consumers, had much more limited access. This makes it clear that mass market electronic communications was also a long-felt need. Direct efforts to push it to firms and consumers were, however, proceeding slowly.

I have reviewed just a few of the many planned commercial initiatives in the dozen or so years before mass use of the Internet took off. Many firms were throwing large R&D budgets at one aspect of EC^3. None of them had quite the right knowledge to pull it off; all knew the social return was high, but no one could find quite the right direction of technical progress to unleash it. In this long era, technologies that might make the PC into a communications, real-time entertainment, or information gathering tool existed but were narrowly distributed. The Internet ones were narrowly distributed to academic and related communities. The commercial ones were narrowly distributed because of their proprietary or top-down nature. There were huge network effects benefits that could follow from a data communications network—being able to e-mail pretty much anyone, for example. Yet these remained latent because no network was ubiquitous.

13.6.4 Planned Initiatives as a Coordination Device

The previous subsection pointed to a number of mass market EC^3 initiatives that were most strongly pushed by a particular kind of application. Bankers pushed mass market e-commerce, publishers pushed mass-market e-content, and technology firms pushed mass market e-communications—and many others not reviewed here. None drew a widespread enough audience to ignite a mass market. This problem of fragmentation was not lost on contemporary observers who noted that, to attract sufficiently many consumers to create a positive feedback loop, e-commerce sites would need e-content and e-communications services, and vice versa. We now know that this problem was solved by the Internet inversion, which drew in sufficiently many users to create many opportunities for all three kinds (C^3) of applications both reaching consumers and workers, and whose openness permitted rather than coordinated the supply or applications.

One might think that this problem could be solved by coordination and the creation of a general mass market online platform. The most important lesson of mass market EC^3 is that this intuition, too, is wrong when entrepreneurial information is scarce. To see this, I now examine the two most successful planned initiatives led by a platform sponsor before the widespread use of the Internet, America Online (AOL), and Microsoft Network (MSN).

Each of these was an "online service," meaning a closed, proprietary platform for EC^3 applications. Online services provided infrastructure for EC^3 applications. They were set up to take advantage of central control of the platform. Following ideas like those in the "two-sided markets" literature, online services would have contracts both with applications developers and with users. They would collect revenues from the users and pay the developers. Control permits complex pricing schemes in such a platform. Users typically paid a monthly subscription fee, and could also pay by the minute they were connected to the service or value added charges based on what services they used, content they looked at, or applications that they ran. A large service could license in many applications from a wide variety of third-party inventors. Online services also provided infrastructure so that subscribers could communicate with one another. For example, they may have e-mail services or online discussion areas or forums. Each online service was a closed system, in competition with the other closed systems, and content was typically local to each online service (though there was some multihoming) and the communications services offered were also local to the specific online service.

While online services followed the program suggested by the "two-sided market" literature in economics—that is, a benevolent dictator platform sponsor offering complex prices to both sides (users and applications) and competing with other platform sponsors, they were only moderately successful. That is not to say they failed as businesses, but all of these online services now seem to us to be smaller, less rich, and more expensive than the commercial Internet.

The most successful online service for end consumers before the widespread use of the Internet was AOL. America Online was marketed to consumers as a general online service, and it provided e-mail (to other AOL users) and related communications services. America Online also offered content providers and e-commerce merchants the opportunity to put materials inside AOL's "walled garden." America Online would then distribute those materials online to consumers. Startup AOL was not the only online service, as computer heavyweight IBM and retailing heavyweight Sears collaborated to build one. Many firms saw the broad, general opportunity.

America Online was successful enough to draw competitive imitation from Microsoft. Microsoft created an AOL-imitation online service, called MSN, which followed the walled-garden model. There would be e-communications tools for users, and authoring tools for e-commerce and e-content providers who wanted to sign a contract with Microsoft to share revenue. An important advantage of Microsoft's plan was the widespread distribution of the MSN "client" software, which, starting with the release of Windows 95, would be distributed with new computers, an obvious mechanism to build a mass market. The idea of widespread distribution to consumers was also responsive to the biggest problems faced by existing EC^3 initiatives; that is, getting enough users to attract a wide variety of developers. Another reason to examine MSN is that, technologically, it was newer than the widespread use of the Internet. When Microsoft launched it the Internet inversion was already almost completed. Microsoft Network did not fail because it used earlier-vintage technology nor because it had no good plan for mass usage. It failed because the "Internet tidal wave" rolled over it.

We did not get to see the AOL-MSN competition that would have followed but for the widespread use of the Internet. Both were quickly competed into irrelevance by the Internet. MSN was withdrawn (confusingly, there was a later Internet website with the same name from Microsoft) and AOL became a "gateway" to the Internet. Absent the widely used Internet, would the AOL-MSN competition have led to widespread EC^3 with as much innovativeness, breadth of uses, and usage? While it is always difficult to answer a historical counterfactual, at least two important considerations make it clear that the likely outcome would have been significantly slower to develop, less innovative, less flexible and changing, and smaller than today's Internet.

13.6.5 Why Planned Initiatives Failed

The last pre-Internet initiative also offers us an opportunity to hear the insider perspective from Bill Gates of Microsoft on the disadvantages of MSN versus the Internet (emphasis in original):[32]

> Subject: Internet as a business tool
> I know I am a broken record on this but I think our plans continue to underestimate the importance of an OPEN unified tools approach for the Internet. The demo I saw today when Windows 95 was showing its Internet capability was someone calling up the Fedex page on the Internet and typing in a package number and getting the status. Imagine how much work it would have been for Fedex to call us up and get that running on MSN and negotiate with us. Instead they just set it up. A very simple way to reach out to their customers. The continued enhancement of the browser standards is amazing to me. Now its security and 3d and tables—what will it be within the next several years? Intelligent controls, directory—everything we are trying to define as standards.

Gates makes two arguments here that are salient to our inquiry. First, he sees the advantages of the permissive nature of a new application development in an open environment (in his discussion of Fedex.) The attempt to keep control slows innovation by lowering λ_2. Second, he sees the open Internet as being as effective as a planned initiative in creating a "unified tools approach" and in "continued enhancement of . . . standards." This is analytically important because many advocates of planned GPT initiatives assert that planning will produce superior architectures. There are, of course, cases in which planned initiatives are better in that regard, as we saw

32. This is an e-mail from Gates on April 6, 1995 to a number of senior Microsoft executives including those responsible for MSN. It was published as a result of the Antitrust case and is located in Government Exhibit 498. I cite it as Gates (1995).

in the IBM business data processing example earlier, but open decentralized market innovation can be very good for standards, as it was in the PC. It can offer an important competitive alternative.

Latent in Gates' remark is also a serious problem of centralized contracting. Solving fragmentation through a planned initiative would call for entrepreneurial knowledge of the possible developments in e-content, e-commerce, and e-communications to attract many complementary applications, and also for sufficient knowledge of the relevant consumer marketing issues to create a widespread mass market. That is a lot of entrepreneurial knowledge to get together in one place. Openness economizes on it—no one would need to know the potential invention possibilities at Fedex and at millions of other firms to know how to structure the platform contract.

A related point about the difference between walled gardens and open systems is the potential for transformative recombinant innovation by providers of complements. We saw this in the PC example and also here. The open Internet has given us a wide number of innovations that run on the server; one thinks immediately of Yahoo, Google, Ebay, Amazon, WikiPedia, and Craigslist. The first four of these would have been perceived as duplicative or as competitive threats by a walled garden online service provider, and the last two would have faced difficulty at the time of their founding, paying for space in a walled-garden environment. The distributed innovation essential to the acceleration of an inversion would have been problematic for MSN or AOL.

Another reason to believe the pre-Internet initiatives would have gone less far and much less fast is that their proponents anticipated a long, slow growth path. Microsoft, for example, thought that the diffusion of broadband connections to the home would be an important growth driver for MSN, and was (wisely, given their entrepreneurial knowledge) investing in online systems in advance of that development. Broadband diffusion would have been even slower than it has been historically if not for the explosion in telecommunications demand driven by the Internet.

13.6.6 The Internet Inversion

In the earlier sections, I noted many participants who lacked entrepreneurial knowledge at an early stage. It is worth considering how knowledge changed as a result of the Internet inversion.

To begin, let me very briefly recount the familiar steps leading to an Internet suitable for mass-market use. After beginning as a military technology, the Internet spent much of its youth as a partly National Science Foundation (NSF)-sponsored network in universities, military installations, and some technical companies. In this era, a number of important developments occurred, including valuable add-on facilities for e-mail, for discussion and "social" networking (like Usenet—which is "social" in the sense engineering communities can be, not in the sense of Facebook), and for sharing data sets and the like among scientists. Two important steps moved the Internet closer to mass market use. The first was the creation of the World Wide Web (WWW) in the computer department of CERN, a physics laboratory. The World Wide Web runs on top of the Internet and provides for a system of interlinked hypertext documents. The WWW was clearly envisioned by its inventors as entirely general (like a number of other networks of the era) and had several useful features that permitted generality, including the use of URLs, a broad open capacity for adding materials, and so on. The application that paid for the development of the WWW, however, was to permit physics researchers to share data sets.

The final step toward mass market use was the invention of the web browser at another computer department of another physics laboratory, this one at the University of Illinois. The web browser was almost purely a recombination of existing elements. However, to quote Schumpeter again, while there are "numerous possibilities for new combinations" they are only obvious ex post. Before the recombination, ex ante, "most do not see them." As a technical matter, the browser's inventors recombined the idea of a graphical user interface with some inventions and improvements in that interface (the "back" button) with existing hypertext protocols. This was the last step in the inversion that was entirely within the technical world, and it was adequately simple to invent that the resources available to one physics lab at one university could pay for it.

The web browser and the open WWW were sufficiently suitable to mass market that they began to draw many users, creating the so-called "Internet mania." A number of applications were quickly available, many involving user-generated content. The availability of e-mail as an already developed application—and a free one—was also a driver of rapid adoption.

One of the inventors of the browser first searched for jobs in interactive television, the Silicon Valley rage of the moment, and then became a founder of Netscape, the commercializers of the browser.[33] (Entrepreneurial knowledge is about overlaps, not about envisioning the whole thing.) A venture capitalist who backed Netscape, L. John Doerr noted the dramatic change in the state of knowledge after the creation of the noncommercial "Mosaic" browser (Cusumano and Yoffie 1998, n.p.):

> I'd seen Mosaic, the UNIX version of it. . . . Marc earned $3.65 an hour, or whatever the University of Illinois had paid him . . . and 2 million people were using it. You would have to be dumb as a door post not to realize that there's a business opportunity here.

33. There were many, many false starts for online content. I have skipped the enormous category of them related to "convergence" of traditional mass media with computing. That a key figure in the commercial development of the Internet mass market almost worked in one of them is as telling about entrepreneurial knowledge as the broad ignorance of WCA possibilities at the founding of the PC industry.

That is the hallmark of a change in knowledge, ex post obviousness. Decentralization was essential here again, as the commercializers of the browser quickly drew criticism from Internet and especially WWW technologists (in much the same spirit that many inventors of the early PC or of early computers criticized IBM) for being commercial. The problem with open systems from a first-inventor perspective is not that recombination may create something unanticipated, but that it may create something undesired.

Mass market electronic commerce, content, and communication is one of the great triumphs of recombination. It represents a dramatic increase in the value-in-use of a wide number of preexisting technologies, from the telephone network to the PC, from the server and the database management system to the marketing knowledge of a number of existing retailers. The invention of those preexisting technologies was financed with knowledge of and in anticipation of their own original markets, not primarily in anticipation of mass market EC^3 returns, and their recombination represents a social boon.

Mass market EC^3 was triggered by a series of GPT component inventions: the browser, the WWW, and the Internet. Each of these was invented or innovated in low-resource environments but environments where (a) entrepreneurial knowledge showed how a particular problem could be solved in a general way and (b) openness was a natural way to compensate for resource scarcity.

The Internet mass market platform for EC^3 has several important features that sharpen our understanding of entrepreneurial knowledge in the case of "platform" industries. The failures that preceded the mass market use of the Internet had the feature that many firms

- Knew that some kind of platform for mass market EC^3 would be valuable.
- Knew that any such platform would need to recombine some aspects of business data processing, telecommunications, and the PC.
- Knew many of the applications areas in which value would arise.
- Did not know, however, what mix of applications (i.e., what services, content, and e-markets), would draw mass user participation.
- Did not know what "business models" would be successful in many of the key applications sectors.

The problem of entrepreneurial knowledge is knowing what product will sell in a new market. This problem is ratcheted up in the platform creation or GPT context. A platform entrepreneur needs to know what group of applications (including content) will attract a group of users that will in turn be attractive to creators of the relevant applications. The scope of knowledge required ex ante appears daunting. Small surprise, then, that there have been elements of decentralized exploration, even to the point of inversion, in the creation of many important platforms. The opportunity to recombine, as much as the vision to create, are central to the invention of many of the most valuable modern GPT clusters.

13.6.7 Relationship to Recent Literature

If the planned initiatives followed the directions of the "two-sided markets" literature and failed for that reason, where is the gap? The literature investigates the benefits of a platform sponsor creating a set of incentives for market participants, under the assumption that the appropriate platform sponsor is known, or can be determined by ex ante competition, and has sufficient entrepreneurial information (which need not be perfect) to set incentives for participants, including incentive to invent applications. Thus, for example, Weyl and Tirole (2010) have a careful treatment of the relationship between the social optimum incentive scheme and the one that would be picked by a platform sponsor. They point out that an effectively designed incentive scheme can efficiently reward applications or content creators, and that the platform sponsor is in a position to create and to benefit from an incentive scheme that benefits both users and creators. Like earlier work by, for example, Baumol and Willig (1981), they note that incentives to discriminate across groups can be efficiently used by discriminating monopolists. Their central policy proposal, creation of a local set of incentives by a platform sponsor, is also the best description of how the mass market EC^3 planned initiatives studied in this section failed.

The important point is that innovation sometimes calls for decentralization, not planning. The path to creating a new platform often calls for shifts in leadership, something that cannot be left to a platform sponsor as their incentive is to maintain leadership. The creation of new platforms, under conditions of distributed knowledge, calls for permitting not coordinating. Both of these economic effects take us outside the assumptions of the "two-sided markets" literature.

The history of efforts to start mass-market electronic commerce, content, and communication is revealing about the knowledge needed for a planned effort to create a new GPT cluster. The first successful mass-market e-commerce, e-content, and e-communication GPT cluster, the widely used Internet, emerged by a circuitous route marked by inversion. A long series of planned efforts to create such a GPT cluster failed. The planned efforts reviewed in this section were closed commercial initiatives that drew on the entrepreneurial and technical knowledge of some very impressive market participants. The failures, as we see in this section, arose because their entrepreneurial knowledge was limited, even though it was almost right. Examining them permits us to sharpen the concept of entrepreneurial knowledge considerably. It also shows, once again, the importance of openness in permitting multiple innovators to create what no single planner could.

13.7 Smartphones

Sometimes an entrepreneur has sufficient entrepreneurial knowledge for a planned initiative, particularly when many of the market pieces are already in place. West and Mace (2007), in an interesting history of the invention of the Apple iPod, show that one firm succeeded in creating a digital music player with Internet distribution. Previous efforts had either failed with consumers or with music studios. Apple's understanding of the incentives of music studios was deep, and it takes nothing away from their accomplishment to say that songs, while hard to invent, have as a group more easily forecast demand than do WCA productivity apps. In this instance, the problem of entrepreneurial knowledge formation was solvable, and solved. Apple's formidable ability to design for consumer use, and canny observation that computer power and storage were now low enough for a device, were congruent with the needs of building a mass music platform. All the more impressive is the same firm's building upon that base to create a smartphone applications platform by building on the base in music and on the technical infrastructure put in place by mobile carriers. The mobile carriers had "app stores," but never ones with much volume. Important early applications such as games were, once again, not impossible to foresee, but one firm did see the platform opportunity with enough clarity about complementors' incentives to start a planned initiative. That there are so few examples of successful planned initiatives illustrates the difficulty of coming up with sufficient entrepreneurial knowledge in computing in general.

In computing, the biggest shortages of entrepreneurial knowledge have arisen at the founding of the WCA GPT clusters, as we have seen. Founding science and engineering platforms or consumer entertainment platforms has been easier. The variation arises, not in the technology itself, but in the market problem of foreseeing what technology will bridge to the very hard-to-forecast automation of white-collar work in bureaucracies and markets.

13.8 Conclusion

The GPTs call for invention both in general components and in applications sectors. This raises the possibility that the founding of GPT clusters may, like recombination, be held back by scarcity of entrepreneurial knowledge. Ex ante, there may be no single locus of knowledge of the precise direction of technical progress into the overlaps between technical opportunity and growth needs. This lack of anticipation does not follow from irrationality or similar phenomena, but instead reflects the distribution of knowledge across many agents in a market economy. Some know technical opportunity; others know the growth needs.

I have brought forth both a very simple theory of this and undertaken historical investigations to foreground an important fact about late twentieth century and early twenty-first century economic growth. The ex ante problem of scarce entrepreneurial information has led each of the major white-collar automation technologies in computing to be invented by a circuitous route of inversion, decentralization, and acceleration. Important recombinations of these technologies into new, more complex systems have also been characterized by much better knowledge ex post than ex ante. Since WCA will continue to be one of the central growth poles of the twenty-first century, this is an important lesson. Little can be done to solve the problem of scarce entrepreneurial knowledge in this area.[34] Much can be done, however, to preserve the openness and decentralization that have been so important.

Many observers are tempted to conclude that the Internet inversion, the general purpose computer inversion, or the PC inversion involved pivotal steps. To take the largest of three very large literatures, a number of observers have argued that the "countercultural" (in the 1960s political sense) communities involved in the development of the PC were pivotal. I admire the achievements of many countercultural inventors of the PC revolution, just as I admire the achievements of scientists in creating the computer or the widely used Internet. But we should be careful before we conclude anything was pivotal. The logic of an inversion does not say that the particular circuitous route taken to found any particular GPT cluster is pivotal. It is close to saying the opposite—there are a wide variety of paths to collective discovery of a valuable GPT. The "countercultural" nature of some PC innovators, the technical nature of many others, the military and scientific nature of key inventions of the general purpose computer (or Internet) innovators play two roles in the analysis. The first is that they are examples of diversity, especially diversity in entrepreneurial knowledge. The importance of diversity means that few are pivotal. Second, they used open approaches, often because of the very limitations of their entrepreneurial knowledge or their capabilities. Openness is crucial but likely no inventor was pivotal.

A similar problem applies to the common argument that small historical accidents in the founding of GPTs and in recombination are determinative of events for decades if not centuries afterward. While there was clearly some inertia around the IBM computer standard and there is some inertia around the Windows PC, those came at the exploitation stage, not at the earliest stages of exploration. More broadly, a decentralized and diverse economy will find and exploit large overlaps between technical opportunity and growth needs. The lesson we should take away from the particular paths used historically are first, that openness was important to market solutions,

34. There have been numerous failed efforts over the last fifty years to improve ex ante knowledge about WCA. Most have used an engineering approach to organizational design or customer relations.

and second, that the apparent maturation of some industries (such as the IBM mainframe and, one can only hope, the Windows PC) can itself be an intermediate stage. Abandoning openness at this stage would be a major error.

References

Acemoglu, D. 2002. "Directed Technical Change." *The Review of Economic Studies* 69:781–809.

Alva, Marilyn, Frederick Ungeheuer, and Stephen Koepp. 1983. "Armchair Banking and Investing." *Time,* November 14. www.time.com/time/magazine/article/0,9171,952268,00.html.

Arora, A., A. Fosfuri, and A. Gambardella. 2001. *Markets for Technology: The Economics of Innovation and Corporate Strategy.* Cambridge, MA: MIT Press.

Aspray, William, and Martin Campbell-Kelly. 2004. *Computer: A History of the Information Machine,* 2nd ed. Boulder, CO: Westview Press.

Baumol, William J., and Robert D. Willig. 1981. "Fixed Costs, Sunk Costs, Entry Barriers and Sustainability of Monopoly." *Quarterly Journal of Economics* 96 (3): 405–31.

Bresnahan, T. F. 2010. "General Purpose Technologies." In *Handbook of the Economics of Innovation,* edited by Bronwyn Hall and Nathan Rosenberg, 761–92. Amsterdam: North Holland Elsevier.

Bresnahan, T. F., E. Brynjolfsson, and L. M. Hitt. 2002. "Information Technology, Workplace Organization, and the Demand for Skilled Labor: Firm-Level Evidence." *The Quarterly Journal of Economics* 117 (1): 339–76.

Bresnahan, T. F., and S. Greenstein. 1996. "Technical Progress and Co-Invention in Computing and in the Uses of Computers." *Brookings Papers on Economic Activity: Microeconomics* 1996:1–83.

Bresnahan, T. F., and F. Malerba. 1998. "Industrial Dynamics and the Evolution of Firms' and Nations' Competitive Capabilities in the World Computer Industry." In *The Sources of Industrial Leadership,* edited by D. Mowery and R. Nelson, 79–132. Cambridge: Cambridge University Press.

Bresnahan, T. F., and M. Trajtenberg. 1995. "General Purpose Technologies: Engines of Growth?" *Journal of Econometrics* 65 (1): 83.

Brynjolfsson, E., and L. M. Hitt. 2000. "Beyond Computation: Information Technology, Organizational Transformation and Business Performance." *The Journal of Economic Perspectives* 14 (4): 23–48.

Ceruzzi, Paul E. 1998. *A History of Modern Computing.* Cambridge, MA: MIT Press.

Cohen, W., and D. Levinthal. 1990. "Absorptive Capacity: A New Perspective on Learning and Innovation." *Administrative Science Quarterly* 35:128–52.

Cusumano, Michael A., and David B. Yoffie. 1998. *Competing on Internet Time: Lessons from Netscape and Its Battle with Microsoft.* New York: Free Press.

Dosi, G. 1982. "Technological Paradigms and Technological Trajectories: A Suggested Interpretation of the Determinants and Directions of Technical Change." *Research Policy* 11 (3): 147–62.

Fleming, Lee. 2001. "Recombinant Uncertainty in Technological Search." *Management Science* 47 (1): 117–32.

Freiberger, Paul, and Michael Swaine. 2000. *Fire in the Valley: The Making of the Personal Computer,* 2nd ed. New York: McGraw-Hill.
Harrigan, K. R. 2003. *Joint Ventures, Alliances, and Corporate Strategy.* Lexington: Beard Books.
Hayek, F. A. 1945. "The Use of Knowledge in Society." *American Economic Review* 35 (4): 519–30.
Jones, Benjamin. 2009. "The Burden of Knowledge and the 'Death of the Renaissance Man': Is Innovation Getting Harder?" *Review of Economic Studies* 76 (1): 283–317.
Jovanovic, B., and P. Rousseau. 2005. "General Purpose Technologies." In *Handbook of Economic Growth,* Volume 1B, edited by Philippe Aghion and Steven N. Durlauf, 1181–222. Amsterdam: Elsevier B.V.
Langlois, R. N., and P. L. Robertson. 1992. "Networks and Innovation in a Modular System: Lessons from the Microcomputer and Stereo Component Industries." *Research Policy* 21:297–313.
March, J. 1991. "Exploration and Exploitation in Organizational Learning." *Organization Science* 2 (1): 71–87.
Mokyr, J. 2002. *The Gifts of Athena: Historical Origins of the Knowledge Economy.* Princeton, NJ: Princeton University Press.
Nelson, R., and S. Winter. 1982. *An Evolutionary Theory of Economic Change.* Cambridge: Belknap Press.
Romer, P. M. 1987. "Growth Based on Increasing Returns Due to Specialization." *The American Economic Review* 77 (2): 56–62.
Rosenberg, Nathan. 1963. "Technological Change in the Machine Tool Industry, 1840–1910." *Journal of Economic History* 23 (4): 414–43.
———. 1996. "Uncertainty and Technological Change." In *The Mosaic of Economic Growth,* edited by R. Landau, R. Taylor, and G. Wright, 334–52. Stanford: Stanford University Press.
Schumpeter, J. 1939. *Business Cycles.* New York: McGraw-Hill Book Company, Inc.
Scotchmer, S. 2004. *Innovation and Incentives.* Cambridge, MA: MIT Press.
Usselman, S. 1993. "IBM and Its Imitators: Organizational Capabilities and the Emergence of the International Computer Industry." *Business and Economic History* 22:1–35.
Weitzman, M. L. 1998. "Recombinant Growth." *Quarterly Journal of Economics* 113 (2): 331–60.
West, Joel, and Michael Mace. 2007. "Entering a Mature Industry through Innovation: Apple's iPhone Strategy." DRUID 2007 Summer Conference. http://www2.druid.dk/conferences/viewpaper.php?id=1675&cf=9.
Weyl, E. Glen, and Jean Tirole. 2010. "Materialistic Genius and Market Power: Uncovering the Best Innovations." Working Paper.

Comment Benjamin Jones

This chapter has a "big think" orientation and reveals numerous insights about the innovation process. The starting point is to recognize that knowl-

Benjamin Jones is associate professor of management and strategy at the Kellogg School of Management, Northwestern University, and is on leave from the National Bureau of Economic Research.

edge required for successful innovation is distributed across many agents. These agents do not know each other, so their individual knowledge is not easily aggregated or shared. The chapter then makes a distinction between two types of knowledge that are relevant to innovation. There is technical knowledge—the actual engineering and scientific know-how to actually make something. And there is entrepreneurial knowledge—knowledge about whether there is a market for the new thing and, if there is a market for it, whether there might be other, associated markets and complementary recombinant innovations that further justify going down the initial path.

Note immediately that there are some standard innovation flavors here. There is uncertainty about the innovative possibilities. Ex ante, it is ambiguous what these innovative opportunities are, technically and in the market. There is also an emphasis on complementarity, both the interdependence of knowledge and the consequent interdependence of agents across whom the knowledge is divided up.

But the key addition of the chapter is a flavor of Hayek, asking how distributed knowledge can be brought together and emphasizing the role of the market. If someone actually delivers an innovation to the marketplace, then distributed agents see the innovation and recombine it with their own ideas. Before the innovation is delivered to the market, there is an absence of knowledge. The core idea in this chapter is that in making the thing and bringing it to the market, the information burden on everybody else is relieved. This action turns one agent's entrepreneurial knowledge—perception of a particular opportunity—into widespread knowledge, making it easier to recombine and build into additional innovations. Another theme of the chapter is that this process may be especially critical for general purpose technologies.

The following simple formalization can capture many of the main ideas in the chapter and demonstrate the generality of applications that emerge from Bresnahan's analysis. Imagine you are considering an innovation A with value $V(A)$, which can be obtained for a cost r. Furthermore, imagine there is some possibility of combining innovation A with some other innovation B, giving your initial effort some additional value $V(A, B)$. The analysis of the chapter hinges on whether you can expect, in this world of decentralized knowledge, to capture this $V(A, B)$.

Write the expected return on the innovation A as[1]

$$\{V(A) - r\} + V(A,B) * \lambda * K.$$

Let your bargaining power be measured by $\lambda \in [0,1]$, defining the share of the additional income $V(A, B)$ that you would capture. Define $K \in [0,1]$ to represent the probability that you will perceive the opportunity of $V(A,B)$.

1. This notation and setup is not quite what was used in initial drafts of the chapter, but is simple and sufficient to capture some key ideas.

The issue is thus partly one of bargaining power over future innovations, for example, due to intellectual property rights. The issue is also one of knowledge—you may not know that the recombinant possibility even exists.

The interesting case, of course, is where $V(A)$ is less than r. Then, on your own, you may choose not to produce innovation A given its expense. Yet there may be substantial value in the recombination of A and B. The challenge is either that you do not look forward to a large share of the value (λ is low) or you do not readily perceive the combination itself (K is low).

The bargaining problem suggests that you need high λ to encourage the investment in A. However, while high λ means that you can appropriate most of the market—the $V(A,B)$—it also implies that other would-be innovators become less inclined to create B, because now they cannot get much of the recombination benefit for themselves. This trade-off, and its implications, has been studied extensively by Suzanne Scotchmer.

The emphasis and novelty of this chapter surrounds the question of knowledge itself, represented by K. Even if we solve the bargaining problem, you still will not get innovation if K is low. The innovator has little or no idea what this B is. This lack of knowledge could surround technical aspects of B, market knowledge for B, and/or B's recombinant prospects with A. These possibilities may be very hard to foresee, especially when knowledge is distributed.

Returning to the Hayek theme, one (imperfect) solution to this knowledge problem is for someone to simply create B and bring it to the market. Then people see it, resolving the K problem, and now may create A. The marketplace thus helps unleash recombinant innovation.

The general purpose technology (GPT) version of this analysis is to imagine that there are lots of potential innovations that could recombine with A (the GPT),

$$\{V(A) - r\} + \sum_i V(A,B_i) * \lambda_i * K_i.$$

This setup suggests a natural story for "inversion" as the initial step for the spread of a GPT. The GPT is originally produced with a narrow application in mind. This is the case where $V(A) > r$ and the innovation goes ahead without consideration of the recombinant possibilities. For example, computers were originally developed to perform narrowly defined calculations, and government researchers created the precursor of the Internet for their own narrow purposes. There was little knowledge about the ultimate potential (the K_i were low). But having produced A, these areas started witnessing decentralized innovation. While the A people did not see the B_i—and likely were not even thinking about B_i—suddenly there are all these agents thinking about A, because now they can see it. So the decentralized B_i people dive in and innovation accelerates; if A is a general purpose technology, decentralized innovations can really take off.

The rest of my comments will depart from the general purpose technology focus of the chapter and consider some other applications of this simple framework, which can further demonstrate its use.

Consider basic research. Basic research typically shows little or no market value directly ($V(A) < r$) but may have lots of recombinant possibilities for commercial innovations (the $V(A,B_i)$ may be large). That is often how economists describe basic research and the reason it may be underprovided. The standard policy solution is subsidization: public institutions pay scientists a wage and provide research funds. In addition, we make A freely available: we set $\lambda = 0$ for producers of basic research. Thus the distributed Bs capture the full value of recombination, incentivizing their activity. This perspective provides a standard description of the "public, open science" model, which is a good description of many national innovation systems.

The additional nuance that Bresnahan's approach reveals centers on the dissemination of basic scientific knowledge. With basic science, the output is not presented as a standard good or service, demonstrating revenues, costs, and profits in the marketplace. Rather the output is a paper, a seminar, an informal chat with colleagues. How does the commercial market learn about the new idea or whether it is valuable? That is, how successfully does the "public, open science" model solve the "low K" problem? Papers and conferences are part of the solution but may be incomplete; for example, they do not convey tacit knowledge. One solution for commercial enterprises may be geographic agglomeration around universities. Private firms locate around Stanford and Berkley, MIT, and so forth, explicitly to increase their K.

In this view, the effectiveness of agglomeration will depend on the capacity of private firms to search the university for good ideas. That is, the agglomeration solution—using a local network in place of an arms-length market—is not the Hayek-like solution. Recall the starting point of the chapter—knowledge is distributed across agents. The market may solve this problem when an innovation is sold, but if direct communication is important to acquire basic science ideas (hence explaining agglomeration) then firms' acquisition of researchers' ideas depends on the researcher's willingness to engage. If the researcher's interests or incentives are defined by producing additional basic research, why exactly does the researcher take the firms' phone calls? Does the researcher want to spend hours and hours talking to private firms?

Here the issue of openness becomes more complicated. Namely, the K issues and λ issues start to interact. Can you tell the basic researcher "you have to publish your ideas for free" ($\lambda = 0$) and also say "you still need to take calls from all these commercial people who are going to make all the income from your idea"? That is not easy. So perhaps we need to think about giving some λ back to the basic researchers, which would result in higher K for others.[2] Alternatively, we can imagine that firms will simply pay researchers for their time (i.e., a consulting fee), which would also raise K. This solution might be difficult in practice, however, given the substantial compensation and costly bargaining that might be needed with each researcher, the breadth of search the firm must undertake, and the bias expansive (and thus expensive) search may impose against small firms. These are key questions for understanding possible market failures in the commercialization of university research and the ultimate returns to basic science.

One can also think about standard setting through this lens. Think of a standard as an innovative output, A. By publicly agreeing to A, the market enhances recombinant possibilities by raising K. This knowledge is not standard marketplace knowledge based on profits from a new innovation, but rather acts to reduce market uncertainty about what the standard is going to be, facilitating recombination. By providing standards for free, one also solves the λ problem and creates stronger incentives for further innovation. One may then see a role for nonprofit or government institutions in helping set standards.

A last comment regards possible market failures. Ex ante, if a bargaining problem (λ) stymies innovation, then one could integrate the firm and achieve the first best. With Bresnahan's starting point, however, the nature of knowledge distribution is such that one does not even know who to integrate with. That is the key problem: the fact that you cannot identify the recombinant possibilities ex ante means that you cannot easily solve the bargaining problem in practice—you cannot integrate your way around it. So innovation faces a serious market failure in the sense that socially profitable innovation does not occur. At the same time, it is not clear how a government realistically solves this problem directly, given that a government cannot obviously create a better information set (especially given the advantage of decentralized firms in perceiving innovative opportunities in their markets). Given the positive spillovers from the initial innovation, coupled with these fundamental information constraints, the government's role may then be limited to subsidizing innovation broadly—not just basic science, but also commercial innovation, through such policies as research and development tax credits.

In sum, this chapter points to knowledge distribution as a key feature in understanding innovation, with applications to general purpose technologies and other areas. This framework also points toward the tension between the openness that can allow recombination and the protection of one's own commercial interest that can incentivize the individual innovations themselves. In market settings, the profitability of the initial innova-

2. This consideration would suggest, for example, some value of the Bayh-Dole Act.

tion will be sufficient for some innovative activity, and the market then acts to encourage recombination. In basic research settings, the institutions of public, open science can be understood in the same framework, but the analysis suggests that these science institutions may need a further look in helping to ensure that firms and publicly-supported researchers actually engage in efficient knowledge interchange.

VII

Panel Discussion
The Art and Science of Innovation Policy

The Art and Science of Innovation Policy
Introduction

Bronwyn H. Hall

In this introduction to the panel discussions, I would like to make a few opening remarks on the topic of the panel. I am very grateful to the organizers for including me on the program, since the book we are honoring has been very important in determining the direction of my career. I first discovered *The Rate and Direction of Inventive Activity* when I was a graduate student at Stanford, after I had been working in the innovation economics field already for about five or six years. Although there is also much of interest in the rest of the volume, Arrow's paper in particular did much to shape my thinking on the relationship between innovation/invention and welfare, and therefore innovation policy. His observations on the financing of inventive activity formed the basis of part of my research program (Hall 2009) and when I began teaching, this paper served as the framework for a course I created at Berkeley in the economics of innovation.

In these opening remarks, I raise two aspects of innovation policy that seem to me important and sometimes understudied. Perhaps our panelists will say more about them.

First, I would like to recall the full title of the 1962 Nelson volume: *The Rate and Direction of Inventive Activity: Economic and Social Factors.* The use of the word social draws attention to the fact that any innovation policy may need to consider noneconomic as well as economic drivers of innovative behavior. Such drivers include the following: (a) the range of motivations of scientists, inventors, and innovators motivations (which can vary, about which see Machlup's article in the Nelson volume); (b) resistance to change

Bronwyn H. Hall is professor in the graduate school at the University of California at Berkeley; professor of economics of technology and innovation at the University of Maastricht, Netherlands; and a research associate of the National Bureau of Economic Research.

on the part of individuals and firms that is not simply due to sunk costs considerations, leading to slower than optimal diffusion of new technologies in some cases; and (c) "culture" or norms. The latter often shows up as societal attitudes toward failure, which have frequently been identified as an important factor in explaining the differing levels of entrepreneurial activity in the United States and Europe (e.g., Reynolds et al. 2000). In addition, we now have considerable evidence that the returns to innovative activity can be very skewed, owing to the extreme uncertainty and serendipity of the innovative process. The large element of chance poses a considerable challenge for ex ante project selection as well as ex post research evaluation. Those of us who have spent a lot of time trying to answer policymakers' questions about the returns to R&D are very aware of the desire for a single numeric estimate of this quantity (possibly with a standard error) and the impossibility of delivering such an animal. When the conference organizers entitled this session the "art and science of innovation policy," I am sure they had observations like these well in mind.

Second, I want to remind us that the breadth of policies that influence innovative activity is very wide, and in some cases, nontargeted policies can be more important than those specifically targeted to innovation. For example, the Science, Technology, and Economic Policy Board of the National Academies was in fact founded and funded initially by a couple of entrepreneurial industrialists whose firms had suffered during the period of high interest rates of the early 1980s, Ralph Landau and George Hatsopoulos (National Research Council 2010). Their concern was not primarily innovation policy, but the effects of macroeconomic policy on entrepreneurial and technology-intensive businesses.

I have recently spent a considerable amount of time on a European Commission expert group panel on "Knowledge for Growth" that addressed itself to a range of policies in this area (European Commission 2009). Key among the problems considered was the perceived underperformance in R&D and innovation in Europe, which has brought home the aforementioned observation forcefully. The expert group (and others who have looked at this problem) identified a scarcity of fast-growing young innovative firms as one explainer of European underperformance in this area. But this finding in turn suggests that policies like labor market and entry regulation (Djankov et al. 2002; Klapper, Laeven, and Rajan 2006), financial market conditions (Gorodnichenko and Schnitzer 2010), and even building codes can be important factors in stimulating or discouraging innovative activity. These arguments suggest that there are limits to the effectiveness of innovation policies that are introduced without consideration of the economic environment as a whole.

With that brief introduction to the topic, I turn now to our panelists, Glenn Hubbard, Dominique Foray, and Manuel Trajtenberg.

References

Djankov, S., R. La Porta, F. Lopez-de-Silanes, and A. Shleifer. 2002. "The Regulation of Entry." *Quarterly Journal of Economics* 117 (1): 1–37.

European Commission, DG Research. 2009. "Expert Group 'Knowledge for Growth.'" http://ec.europa.eu/invest-in-research/monitoring/knowledge_en.htm.

Gorodnichenko, Y., and M. Schnitzer. 2010. "Financial Constraints and Innovation: Why Poor Countries Don't Catch Up." NBER Working Paper no. 15792. Cambridge, MA: National Bureau of Economic Research, March.

Hall, B. H. 2009. "The Financing of Innovation." *European Investment Bank Papers* 14 (2): 1–23. (Reprinted 2010 in the *Review of Economics and Institutions* 1(1). http://www.rei.unipg.it/rei.)

Klapper, L., L. Laeven, and R. Rajan. 2006. "Entry Regulation As a Barrier to Entrepreneurship." *Journal of Financial Economics* 82 (3): 591–629.

National Research Council, Board on Science, Technology, and Economic Policy. 2010. "Policy and Global Affairs." http://sites.nationalacademies.org/pga/step/index.htm.

Reynolds, P. D., M. Hay, W. D. Bygrave, S. M. Camp, and E. Autio. 2000. *Global Entrepreneurship Monitor: 2000 Executive Report.* Kansas City: Kauffman Center for Entrepreneurial Leadership at the Ewing Marion Kauffman Foundation.

Putting Economic Ideas Back into Innovation Policy

R. Glenn Hubbard

When Josh Lerner asked me to offer panel remarks, he wanted me to discuss both the art and science of innovation policy. That is an enormous subject, and Bronwyn Hall made it even larger by now encompassing social factors in her introduction. As an economist, I'll stick to my own narrower knitting.

Some of the themes from earlier in the conference about basic science and engineering, importantly about diffusion through both professional talent and entrepreneurs, set up very nicely what I want to talk about. As an economist who has also been in a policy chair and who is a business school dean, when I speak to businesspeople who want to discuss innovation, they are generally people who benefited from the serendipity of a good draw, or they would not be seeing me—I rarely see the bad draws in my job. And policymakers, I think, face the same issue.

When I hear the phrase "innovation policy," based on my time in Washington, where I heard it on more than a few occasions, my antennae go up. That is because sometimes this discussion is as much about entrepreneurship, a related but not entirely coincident subject or, worse in my experience, it is actually about rent seeking. The role of policy, when thinking about innovation, is less about innovation's per se features, which interest us as economists, but more about links to economic growth and productivity growth. And policy discussions, in this regard, I think are often very specific. I will give some examples in a moment of how that might be unfortunate.

Despite the admonition from our profession that we should more narrowly focus on what I think of as conditions supporting innovation and

R. Glenn Hubbard is dean as well as the Russell L. Carson Professor of Finance and Economics at Columbia Business School, professor of economics at Columbia University, and a research associate of the National Bureau of Economic Research.

technical change—or, as I will try to argue, on the diffusion of innovation—I think there is also value in thinking about it first in a very big picture way, like in Joel Mokyr's work over many years. I am also thinking of the more pointed discussion of the organization of innovative cultures that you will find in my colleague Ned Phelps' Nobel lecture.

I think the good news for us as economists is that both the economics of innovation and the economics of innovation policy do have sound empirical bases for discussion. But I think we need to apply the arguments in the right setting, and we need to focus, with growth in mind, on diffusion.

So let me start first by asking what we mean by "innovation," because policymakers often use this word in very different ways. What you might mean are individual acts of innovation. I think of solo inventions, like Willis Carrier with air conditioning, like entrepreneurship. I think that is what many policymakers mean when they start to ask questions. Or we might mean something more like a *process* of innovation or a *climate* for innovation in which continuous change is made. From a policy perspective, we need to be interested in both, but policies that promote individual entrepreneurship or risk taking are not necessarily the same as those that enhance the climate for innovation. And we should be interested as much in the diffusion of innovation as the overarching policy concern should be with growth and not about innovation per se.

But the second thing to ask is what we mean by policy. When I was Chairman of the Council of Economic Advisers, John Doerr, as an eminent venture capitalist, came with many business leaders in tow to meet with me. The business leaders gave a long presentation about the tech bubble and the meltdown, after which John turned to me and asked, "So what are your ideas to do about it?" I looked at them, and I said, "Gee, I thought it was the other way around: I thought that was what I was asking you!" Part of the policy discussion, then, often calls for individual policy responses to particular issues or situations. I think that is unwise.

A second type of concern comes up when policymakers talk to the business community. Generally, there the emphasis is often on very macro concerns. I was joking with Bronwyn that whenever I have the privilege to visit my friends at the Hoover Institution, I invariably hear that if only we could reduce the capital gains tax another percentage point, a torrent of innovation would hit the country. And I am quite sympathetic as an individual to such tax arguments, but I am skeptical from an overall policy perspective.

There are other things that we could do: I think here of the work the World Bank does in looking closely at business indicators, their approach being what I think of as more a kind of "league table" for thinking about zthe overall climate for innovation. This approach is probably less relevant for the United States, where conditions are much better, but definitely relevant in thinking about policies abroad. In that regard, I think we have to be careful about slipping from a discussion of innovation policy, a hard enough term to define, into the word "competitiveness," which makes me very nervous. Such a term is easy for us to think about for a firm: survive for a long time, you are competitive. If you lose money and go out of business, you are not competitive. But it is a much harder thing to think about as a public policy for a country.

So how, then, should we think about the scope of innovation, and then policy? There are three things one needs to think about in innovation policy. The first is obvious to policymakers. The others, I think, may be as important, if not more important.

The factor that grips policymakers is to think about the product market, first the development of new products or technological change. It is in the product market where we often see, too, somewhat unfortunate interventions to which I come to in a moment. What I think are probably as important, if not more important, are what I would call enablers. By this I mean policies about the labor market (which might, for example, be policies that encourage mobility) and, particularly, management practices and productivity growth. I also think of financial markets in this regard, not financial innovation on its own but markets for risk capital and risk taking. From a policy perspective, in this regard, thinking about innovation and productivity growth is not just about technical change. It really takes a village.

Second, in terms of the scope of policy, there are three considerations. One often discussed factor is the encouragement of *R&D*. Tax policy is usually the lever discussed in Washington, and it has a moderate effect. A bigger deal is, of course, the intellectual property regime and things that we learn from individual regulatory environments, like the energy environment or health care. A second policy discussion returns to *innovation,* and therein lies a number of significant policy concerns, ranging from tax policy to patent regimes to antitrust policy. And, third, on disseminating innovation, the policy environment toward management and labor practices is very important. Here, I am thinking about the work of Nick Bloom and John Van Reenen and others who study the substantial cross-country and within-country differences in productivity growth that I think of as at least largely related to the speed of diffusion of innovation led by management practices.

In terms of policy, there have been some successes in promoting innovation in the United States. Some of those successes relate to deregulation—in telecommunications, for example. However, some waves of innovation actually come from regulation. The financial services sector comes to mind, where many waves of innovation were stimulated by regulation. And then I think of the policy we have had toward intellectual property—the Bayh-Dole Act and Defense-University collaborations come to mind. The biggest failures come from the problems of being specific in interventions; here, I would think of industrial policy failures, like the Synthetic Fuels Corporation or today, General Motors.

Now recalling Edison's mix between inspiration and perspiration, policy, like many teachers of entrepreneurship, tends to be so focused on the former and not the latter, and it might be the latter that's more important. And by that I mean not just science, but also about business and management and the policy environment. That is also a more straightforward, if more humble, role for policy. I think of Bob Solow's famous line, "I know there are a lot of industries where there's $4 worth of social output for every dollar worth of private output, I just don't know which ones they are." Rarely do policymakers have that kind of humility.

Third, I wanted to close by discussing an important and underemphasized element, which is the policy process. This is something that as economists we do not often think about but that turns out to be critical in talking about the policy of innovation. Normally, at least in a US setting, there are interagency processes for anything involving economic matters. But voices for innovation in Washington typically are often limited to people who write Greek letters on their blackboard. To narrow down who that might be in Washington, one might be the Council of Economic Advisers—at least one hopes. Another might be the science advisors. Interagency processes approaches have tended to be much more successful in things related to finance than to technology, and one might look to success stories of longer-term interagency working groups. I am thinking about just such an experience in the George W. Bush administration, a long-term working group on antitrust and innovation on environmental policy and how to promote low-cost innovation for Homeland Security.

But I will close where Bronwyn Hall led off. Policy is equally likely to involve art as science.

Why Is It So Difficult to Translate Innovation Economics into Useful and Applicable Policy Prescriptions?

Dominique Foray

Bronwyn Hall already mentioned the "Knowledge for Growth" Expert Group at the European Commission in which I participated for four years as cochairman, together with Bronwyn, Paul, and people like Philippe Aghion, Jacques Mairesse, Ramon Marimon, Reinhilde Veugelers, André Sapir, Stan Metcalfe, and a few others. As part of our activities, every two or three months we held discussions with the Research Commissioner Janesz Potocnik. As he was very committed to our group, we were all quite motivated, not to give any policy prescriptions but to discuss interesting innovation policy issues. And so I will take this experience as a basis for what I want to say: how difficult it is to translate the findings of innovation economics into well-understood and potentially exploitable policy prescriptions. And in doing so I will address three categories of difficulties.

I would like to start with this quotation from George Stigler in his paper, "Economists and Public Policy" in 1982 to discuss a first difficulty: "*Once the practice of testing our predictions by examining the evidence became general practice, economists' advice—that is, the advice that survived the empirical tests—would be heeded by the society*" (13). Of course, Stigler argued, this is a myth based on a misperception of how our results can attract the attention of policymakers and society as a whole, and can only be applied to innovation policy research. Once innovation policy research and innovation economics reach the point of becoming a strong empirically disciplined science, it becomes much more difficult to ensure that its results and findings are understood and properly used by policymakers. In fact, the vast majority of

Dominique Foray holds the chair in Economics and Management of Innovation at École Polytechnique Fédérale de Lausanne (EPFL).

policymakers still proceed on the basis of only casual understanding, uninformed by systematic empirical inquiries into the process of innovation.

I would like to take an example of this problem and then discuss why it might be amplified in our discipline. An illustration of Stigler's argument concerns the progress achieved by innovation policy research in the domain of the evaluation of government support for commercial R&D.

Some economists have made the point that some of these programs are not expanding the amount of R&D but simply transferring the cost of commercial R&D to the government. This is a great, but difficult to understand, empirical result: a funded project that is successful says nothing about whether the project needed a subsidy. But this is something that is very hard to take for a policymaker, who is used to interpreting the success of a funded project as evidence that the public program is great and useful in stimulating innovation. And so it might be very difficult for a policymaker and also for a government to take the opposite view, which in a sense is the view consistent with this empirical finding, that a high rate of failures of projects subsidized by a program is an indication that the public program targeted high-risk projects with little chance of being successful.

And so I think that it is quite clear that the more our prescriptions are based on the fine empirical analysis of what is going on—with quite complex results—the less likely they will be heeded by policymakers and government. And perhaps the difficulty highlighted by Stigler and illustrated by the case just described is even greater in our field because we have competitors in this business of translating findings into policy prescriptions; competitors who are delivering far more simple messages that policymakers care to listen to. Here an interesting episode in the history of the "Knowledge for growth" Expert Group comes to my mind. This concerns a Booz Allen Hamilton report on R&D spenders, to which we wrote a response with Bronwyn Hall and Jacques Mairesse. This report had much greater impact in the European press, by the way. It is an empirical study relating to a large population of top R&D spenders about the relationships between R&D and firms' performance and it concludes that the share of spending devoted to R&D has no relationship to the economic performance of firms. Firms that spend less on R&D than competitors have superior performances, or these companies that spend less than their competitors on R&D, yet outpace their industries across a wide range of performance metrics. And so the idea that R&D is just an input and does not tell us anything about innovation is floating in the air, and policymakers like the simple message: Do not invest so much in R&D and you will perform better.

There are a great many methodological problems in the empirical study, as well as misinterpretations of their own results. Our chairperson could explain that better than I. However, it had a big impact on policymaking discussion, in spite of the bulk of evidence accumulated by empirical research since the conference whose anniversary we are celebrating in this volume.

And I think one reason is that the message on this topic, coming from the economics of innovation, is much more complex. Our message is that (a) the uncertainty inherent in the processes of research and innovation implies an equivalent uncertainty in the profitability of these investments at the level of an individual firm; and (b) there is no doubt that such profitability when measured at the aggregate level or for society as a whole has been shown to be as high as, or higher than, the profitability of investment in the physical capital. In short, do not confuse what is true for the forest as a whole with what is true for each individual tree! This is a more complex message for a policymaker and is made even more complex by all the footnotes he or she can read about the difficulties of measuring R&D output at firm level and interpreting the results—in particular difficulties related to the measurement of prices in the case of new products, or to the question of the lag between investment in R&D and its contribution to performance; all footnotes involving plenty of nuances that do not appear in the Booz Allen Hamilton report.

And I would like to close this story with its final anecdotal "fireball," which illustrates part of the problem of the difficulties of competing for policy attention with companies like Booz Allen Hamilton. We responded to this report with a paper written with Jacques and Bronwyn,[1] and started discussions with *Harvard Business Review* to publish it because, indeed, there are sometimes papers in this journal that are intended to explain methodological issues of empirical research in economics and management to managers. So we started talking with the editorial board, which was nice, but at some point, there was a long silence from the journal. And then we learned that—let's call him Mr. X—who was the editor we had dealt with, had left the journal. And where do you think he went? To Booz Allen Hamilton as a senior consultant!

And so we abandoned our efforts to find a journal to publish our response. So that is the first difficulty involved in translating our findings into policy prescription, largely based on Stigler's myth.

The second point is really simple. It concerns the inherent limitation of what we can generate as policy prescription from some interesting and useful findings. Let's take as an example the case of coordination failure. I think this is an important concept. Listening to Tim Bresnahan, it is obvious that coordination between different classes of agents is needed, although it is not easy, to ensure the full deployment of a GPT involving plenty of coinvention of application processes.

Now understanding the basic principles of coordination problems obviously does not take one very far in the direction of useful, practical conclusions as to how to construct a technology policy.[2] And so the practical

1. See Hall, Foray, and Mairesse (2007).
2. See Klette and Møen (1998).

implementation of a policy to deal with coordination involves answering a set of questions that is not simple. What activities in what firms need to be coordinated, and in what way? An appropriate choice of policy tools requires a detailed understanding of the externalities and innovation complementarities. And so the information requirements, at a practical level, raise serious questions about the possibilities for government policies to correct coordination problems in the real world. And so in many cases, the practicality and costs of policy intervention make some failures that we have identified too expensive or too difficult to correct. We made this point with Philippe Aghion and Paul David in a paper published recently in *Research Policy*.[3]

My last point about our difficulties in translating research findings into policy prescription is in a sense more our fault. This concerns our biased research agenda. For at least thirty years and particularly in Europe, it seems to me that the policy research agenda in academia focused almost exclusively on the design, development, and evaluation of tools, instruments, and programs aimed at increasing the rate of innovation in the system.

But beyond the infinite sophistication regarding the questions of the design, effectiveness, and impacts of these tools and instruments aimed at increasing the rate of innovation (such as fiscal measures, direct subsidies, and the improvement of framework conditions), the other area, which relates to the direction of inventive activities, has been relatively unexplored in policy research discussion.[4] At this conference, it is quite tempting to recall that the seminal book of our profession, which we are celebrating today, was entitled *The Rate and the Direction of Inventive Activities!*

Why such a bias in the agenda? The arguments are as follows: yes, there are market failures, particularly in the area of R&D in the form of positive externalities (knowledge spillovers), which drive a wedge between private and social returns from R&D investment. Because of these positive externalities, some socially useful investments will not appear as being privately profitable, so the market will not sufficiently support the activities and policy needed to correct this failure. But the next argument is that government failures are expected to be greater than market failures (although there is little evidence as to how much greater they are). And so the main message relates to neutrality; the resources allocated through the policy mechanism must respond to market signals rather than bureaucratic directives. An efficient policy does not select projects according to preferred fields but responds to demand that arises spontaneously from the industry. Departing from neutrality in order to influence the direction of innovation—providing subsidies to favored firms or sectors—is prone to misallocate sources since it implies guessing future technological and market developments. This opens the door to all

3. See Aghion, David, and Foray (2009).
4. See Foray (2009).

those little monsters that economists always try to eradicate, which they call wrong choices, picking winners, and market distortions.

In short, the message was: "Do not undertake actions to influence the direction of innovation but let market prices reflect the future scarcity of commodities so that certain kinds of innovation will be induced by changes in relative prices." There is obviously evidence of inducement—for instance, some kind of correlation between energy prices and energy-related innovations can be found—but in many cases the price system does not do the job (does not reflect future scarcity) and therefore has little effect on the direction of innovation. And when there are inducement effects, the timescale seems to be decades. So for policies that deal with prices, taxes, and standards to have maximum impacts, long periods of time are required.

Thus in the area of policy research and discussion the last three decades have been dominated by the argument that market failures need to be corrected in order to reach the desirable level of investments, but where these investments should go should not be a concern for policies. It is much better to leave this issue to the magical chaos of the "blind watchmaker." Any notion of specialization policy or top-down strategic initiatives has become a taboo in policy discussion, particularly in the large international policy forums as well as in the European Commission.

But this economist's discourse is radically out of step with reality. While economists claim to be the most assiduous partisans of neutral R&D and innovation policies, which therefore do not distort the logics of market-driven resource allocation, the share of resources allocated to missions and large programs has always accounted for a large share of central government R&D spending within the Organization for Economic Cooperation and Development (OECD). Thus, as D. Mowery has shown, 90 percent of federal R&D expenditure in the United States is not allocated based on a principle of market failure but has rather been oriented by a "mission" logic.

The result of this discrepancy between "economists' fantasies and political and industrial realities" is that not enough attention and effort have been devoted to this very important aspect of R&D and innovation policies, since economists have excluded it from their ideal world in which the market (or its "failures") must be the sole mechanism of resource allocation. This is not to say that nothing has been done. There were a few grand exceptions in the case of scholars like Dick Nelson or Dave Mowery. But it is fair to say that this topic has been largely neglected by the profession.

But we are now entering the era of crises and Grand Challenges—climate change, food, water, and health. These Grand Challenges make a good case for revising our agenda. Increasing the rate of innovation is not enough; we do not necessarily want to increase the rate *randomly* in the system but in certain domains and sectors such as climate change or health—such areas where the centrality of R&D is emerging as a solution to structural problems. There may be a stronger case today than in the past for targeting innovation policy in particular directions.

And because of our biased research agenda, many issues regarding the design and organization of policies aimed at responding to a Grand Challenge remain largely unexplored. While on the one hand there are now many calls for government to marshal our capabilities in science and technology to deal with problems like AIDS and global warming, on the other hand only scattered research exists on how mission-oriented government R&D programs have in fact worked out. Our research deficit on this topic means that many issues are still poorly understood and that we are now thus perhaps unlikely to be very effective in helping to construct effective and efficient technology policies designed to respond to these Grand Challenges.

So we have the three problems, the first one known as Stigler's myth, the second concerning the inherent limitations of the exercise of translating scientific findings into the construction of a concrete innovation policy, and the third related to our own bias in the research agenda. These are obstacles but also challenges for translating innovation economics and innovation policy research into useful and applicable policy prescriptions.

References

Aghion, P., P. A. David, and D. Foray. 2009. "Science, Technology and Innovation for Economic Growth: Linking Policy Research and Practice in 'STIG systems.' " *Research Policy* 38 (4): 681–93.

Foray, D. 2009. "Structuring a Policy Response to a Grand Challenge." In *Knowledge for Growth, Prospects for Science, Technology and Innovation,* 67–75. ERA, EUR 24047, Bruxelles.

Hall, B., D. Foray, and J. Mairesse. 2007. "Pitfalls in Estimating the Returns to Corporate R&D Using Accounting Data." First European Conference, Knowledge for Growth. October.

Klette, J., and Møen, J. 1998. "From Growth Theory to Technology Policy: Coordination Problems in Theory and Practice." Discussion papers 219, Statistics, Norway.

Stigler, G. J. 1982. "Economists and Public Policy." *Regulation,* May/June, 13–17.

Can the Nelson-Arrow Paradigm Still Be the Beacon of Innovation Policy?

Manuel Trajtenberg

The Nelson-Arrow (N-A) paradigm, as espoused in the volume commemorated in this conference, is widely regarded as one of the most consequential developments in economics, shaping the views on innovation and on science and technology (S&T) policies prevalent ever since, and generating an enormous volume of subsequent research. It has justly earned its place in the dual "hall of fame" of economics and public policy, and constitutes a worthy sequel to the much celebrated *Science, the Endless Frontier* by Vannevar Bush, the outstanding science guru of President Franklin Roosevelt.

The N-A paradigm basically postulates that the production of new knowledge entails significant externalities that are difficult to appropriate, thus opening up a wide gap between social and private rates of return to inventive activities. Such a gap, coupled with acute risk and the specter of moral hazard in financing R&D, results in systemic underinvestment in R&D, lower than socially desirable rates of innovation, and hence slower economic growth. Two types of policy instruments are thus needed to counteract those failures: the first to *increase appropriability,* mostly via intellectual property (IP) protection; the second to address *underinvestment in R&D* directly via various forms of government subsidies, the more so the more basic the nature of research is. This is postulated implicitly in the context of a closed economy; that is, one lacking significant international flows or leakages that could alter this basic line of reasoning. Fifty years later the logic of N-A is still intact, but there are a number of question marks that have arisen in the past few decades that deserve careful consideration:

Manuel Trajtenberg is chairman of the Planning and Budgeting Committee of the Council for Higher Education in Israel, professor at the Eitan Berglas School of Economics at Tel Aviv University, and a research associate of the National Bureau of Economic Research.

1. How much underinvestment in R&D is there, really, and hence what is the "optimal" amount of R&D at the macro level?

2. What sort of R&D should we promote; that is, is there room to deviate from neutrality and do some form of "targeting"?

3. How does diminished appropriability fare vis à vis widespread sharing activities associated with the Internet, to be labeled "wiki-motives"?

4. How do the policy prescriptions of the N-A paradigm, predicated basically for a closed economy, hold up in the face of globalization of S&T?

5. Is the N-A paradigm relevant also for developing economies?

1 How Much Underinvestment in R&D?

As already mentioned, the N-A paradigm generated a very large amount of subsequent research, both theoretical and empirical, but little of it was *directly* concerned with policy, certainly with macro policy. Thus, whereas the broad strokes of policy are quite clear, the devil is in the details, and in that regard available research offers rather poor guidance. Take the presumed underinvestment in R&D—what do we know about the magnitude of the gap? Is the 2000 Lisbon goal of R&D/GDP = 3 percent a reasonable one? Does the fact that Israel displays the highest R&D/GDP ratio in the world (4.8 percent) necessarily mean that it is doing the right thing in this respect? We have to admit that we have a very limited conceptual and empirical base to address these and related questions, which are further complicated by the following considerations:

- It is very hard to tell apart (and we often tend to confound) average and marginal effects in this context (from spillovers to appropriability to subsidies), and what we typically need for policy are the marginal effects.
- What we truly care about is not formal R&D per se, but rather the overall amount of innovation and its implementation. "Tweakers" (to paraphrase Joel Mokyr) may be as important as R&D personnel, but the former barely find their way into economic statistics, and are hard to target via economic policy.
- As argued by Paul Romer, spending more on formal R&D may end up just inflating wages of R&D personnel, and not producing more innovation.
- Clearly, it cannot be that high R&D/GDP rations are necessarily a good policy prescription for every economy: comparative advantage holds in this context as much as in any other, and besides, it is not a bad idea to free ride on international spillovers.

The unpleasant truth is that we may have to admit ignorance in this regard, at least until further research brings in some useful insights, and thus leave aside aggregate, macro targets (such as the Lisbon one). Instead, we should focus on micro aspects that may have economy-wide effects, such as improving the institutions that facilitate innovation, with the R&D/GDP ratio being just one end result of that.

2 What Sort of R&D? Neutrality versus Targeting

R&D is widely heterogeneous, as are innovations themselves, ranging from basic scientific research in esoteric fields to mundane development. We presume that the gap between social and private returns is wider the more basic research is, and conversely for applied research. But that may not be quite so: to begin with, social and private returns may be highly correlated: for example within some lines of research in biotech the returns are surely "high social," "high private", whereas in some obscure research area in economics these might well be "low," "low". It is not clear which of them deserves more support, if at all: after all, if private returns are sufficiently high, they may be enough to generate "enough" R&D. On the other hand, if public returns are low there is no reason to support research to begin with. What we should be looking for are fields where there is a *negative correlation* between the two: high social but low private returns. If we could identify them, we would have a powerful tool for targeting. The message is clear: we should devote more research efforts not only to the overall gap between social and private returns to innovation, but to assessing the nature of the gap for specific research fields.

3 IP and Appropriability versus "Wiki Motives"

Many in this conference as well as others have voiced increasing concerns in recent years that the means for IP protection may be actually stifling innovation rather than encouraging it (e.g., too many patents, too much fragmentation of IP for every bit of knowledge). If so, one of the key policy prescriptions stemming from the N-A paradigm is seriously questioned. On the other hand, *sharing* knowledge and information in cyberspace have become a widespread driving force, as manifested in social networks, open source ventures, the "wiki" movement, and so forth, involving collaborative activities of vast numbers of people. Sharing as a powerful motive is truly novel, and was nearly inexistent in this context as recently as a generation ago. We are only beginning to understand the incentives that may underlie such behaviors, and there is a long way to go in that regard.

To the extent that innovation involves "recombinant ideas" (as suggested by Martin Weitzman), cyber-sharing may become a powerful countervailing factor to the appropriability deficit. Furthermore, the Internet, search engines, and related technologies are turning knowledge more and more into a true public good, thus enormously increasing the social (worldwide) value of both the stock of knowledge and increments to it. An apparent paradox arises in this respect: on the one hand cyber-sharing should increase the gap between social and private returns as traditionally defined. But if private returns include (as they seem to do) nonpecuniary elements that are positively related to the extent of sharing, then in fact the gap may have narrowed as a consequence. If so, perhaps S&T policy should be aimed more at making sure that cyberspace remains wide open, encouraging sharing, and so forth, and not at fostering more IP protection. Be as it may, there clearly are sharp trade-offs between the two, which need to be further investigated in order to inform policy.

4 Globalization of Innovation versus National S&T Policies

There is a basic incongruence between S&T policies being formulated for the most part at the *national* level, and the fact that the objects of these policies (e.g., science, R&D, innovation) take place in a global dimension, and are governed by forces that escape to a large extent national control. Suppose, for example, that a particular country wants to attract multinational corporations, and in particular that it offers incentives to set up R&D labs in its territory. Who will actually benefit from the R&D done there? Will it be mostly the local economy? Who will ultimately own the IP generated in such a lab? The answers to these and similar questions are far from clear, and yet absent hard evidence or reasonable presumptions in that respect we cannot assess such policies. One can easily replicate this dilemma in virtually all other areas of S&T policy: the fact is that both the inputs and the outputs of R&D and innovation do not respect borders, are increasingly mobile and fluid, and devoid of clear institutional or geographic anchors. To insist, this creates a fundamental incongruence between country-level policies and the objects of such policy.

One telling aspect of this incongruence is the fact that virtually all players, big and small, developed or emerging, are deeply concerned about the implications of globalization in science, technology, and R&D. Thus the United States is concerned about the fact that significant portions of innovative activities have moved to other countries, driven by the wide availability of talent elsewhere. On the other hand, emerging economies are disturbed by the fact that innovations generated in their midst by guest multinationals end up benefiting somebody else. "Host" and "guest" (for R&D) countries can easily be discussing the same sort of concerns from diametrically opposed standpoints. Likewise, brain gain for one is obviously brain drain for others, but then in a further twist returning diaspora scientists and engineers may undo the flow and generate opposite anxieties.

The proliferation of government support to R&D in ever more countries is certainly good for world innovation, but for individual players it assumes at times the nature of a race that only a few can win, if at all. We know very little about this brave new global world, we do not possess enough data, our models are not yet tailored to fit the bare contours of these evolving phenomena, and hence can offer little help for framing policies. Again, much more research on these issues is badly needed.

5 Innovation Policy in the Context of Development

The N-A paradigm refers implicitly to a developed economy, and therefore innovation entails the production of new knowledge *for the world.* Not so for developing countries, where issues of transfer, imitation, diffusion, "new for the country" (or for the region, or for the firm) are as, if not more, important. In fact, innovation for development should be construed as a broad notion that includes widely distributed innovations of all stripes, both in products and in processes, generated by rank and file workers as much as by R&D labs. Furthermore, the economic rationale for government support of R&D needs to be adapted to the economic environment of developing countries, the notion of spillovers should be reexamined in view of globalization, and the same goes for the working of General Purpose Technologies (GPTs). The Israeli economy offers a fascinating illustration of extraordinary success in innovation, particularly in information and communications technology (ICT), yet the benefits from the high tech sector eluded the rest of the economy, giving rise to a "dual economy." Understanding this outcome provides valuable insights for the design of growth-promoting innovation policies.

6 A Call for Policy-Oriented Research

The common thread that runs through the issues just discussed is the acute need for much more policy-oriented research in the area of innovation. How are we faring in that respect? How relevant is ongoing economic research in this area for today's and tomorrow's innovation policy? I must confess that I changed my mind in this respect in the course of the conference: having arrived with a low prior, I realized that there is quite a lot going on that may be relevant for economic policy, if still mostly embryonic. That is encouraging but limited, because the prevalent perception among many of our peers is still that policy-oriented research is second rate, and is looked down upon, particularly when it comes to promotion decisions.

We should recall that in the life sciences what motivates most research is the quest to find cures to disease, a fact that is widely appreciated and heralded as a beacon of science policy. In economics, by contrast, we seem to be ashamed by the explicit quest for better policies, for curing of economic or social diseases. Let me argue that being motivated by true policy issues may bring us to push the frontiers of economic knowledge no less than being motivated by the elegance of formal models, or the degree of sophistication of stereotyped economic agents. Thus, I want to encourage all of us to go for it, to assume responsibility, and not leave policy making in the hands of bureaucrats, only to self-congratulate ourselves from the safety of ivory tower for knowing better . . . we do not. During the conference I partially recovered my faith in the economics profession, please help me turn into a true believer.

Contributors

Daron Acemoglu
Department of Economics
Massachusetts Institute of Technology
50 Memorial Drive
Cambridge, MA 02142-1347

Philippe Aghion
Department of Economics
Harvard University
1805 Cambridge Street
Cambridge, MA 02138

Kenneth J. Arrow
Department of Economics
Stanford University
Stanford, CA 94305-6072

Pierre Azoulay
Sloan School of Management
Massachusetts Institute of Technology
100 Main Street
Cambridge, MA 02142

Kevin J. Boudreau
London Business School
Regent's Park
London NW1 4SA United Kingdom

Timothy F. Bresnahan
Department of Economics
Stanford University
579 Serra Mall
Stanford, CA 94305-6072

Luis Cabral
Stern School of Business
New York University
44 West 4th Street
New York, NY 10012

Iain M. Cockburn
School of Management
Boston University
595 Commonwealth Avenue
Boston, MA 02215

Paul A. David
Department of Economics
Stanford University
579 Serra Mall
Stanford, CA 94305-6072

Giovanni Dosi
Istituto di Economia
LEM, Laboratory of Economics and Management
Sant'Anna School of Advanced Studies
Piazza Martiri della Libertà 33
56127 Pisa, Italy

Alexander J. Field
Department of Economics
Santa Clara University
Santa Clara, CA 95053

Dominique Foray
Management of Technology and Entrepreneurship Institute
Ecole Polytechnique Fédérale de Lausanne (EPFL)
Odyssea 1.16–Station 5
CH–1015 Lausanne, Switzerland

Jeffrey L. Furman
School of Management
Boston University
595 Commonwealth Avenue
Boston, MA 02215

Joshua S. Gans
Rotman School of Management
University of Toronto
105 St. George Street
Toronto ON M5S 3E6 Canada

Joshua S. Graff Zivin
University of California, San Diego
9500 Gilman Drive, MC 0519
La Jolla, CA 92093-0519

Shane Greenstein
Kellogg School of Management
Northwestern University
2001 Sheridan Road
Evanston, IL 60208-2013

Bronwyn H. Hall
Department of Economics
549 Evans Hall
University of California, Berkeley
Berkeley, CA 94720-3880

Rebecca M. Henderson
Harvard Business School
Morgan 445
Soldiers Field
Boston, MA 02163

R. Glenn Hubbard
Graduate School of Business
Columbia University, 101 Uris Hall
3022 Broadway
New York, NY 10027

Adam B. Jaffe
Department of Economics, MS 120
Brandeis University
415 South Street
Waltham, MA 02454

Benjamin Jones
Kellogg School of Management
Northwestern University
2001 Sheridan Road
Evanston, IL 60208

Shulamit Kahn
School of Management
Boston University
595 Commonwealth Avenue
Boston, MA 02215

William Kerr
Harvard Business School, Rock Center 212
Soldiers Field
Boston, MA 02163

Samuel Kortum
Department of Economics
University of Chicago
1126 East 59th Street
Chicago, IL 60637

Karim R. Lakhani
Harvard Business School
Morgan Hall 433
Soldiers Field
Boston, MA 02163

Josh Lerner
Harvard Business School
Rock Center 214
Boston, MA 02163

Megan MacGarvie
School of Management
Boston University
595 Commonwealth Avenue
Boston, MA 02215

Ralf R. Meisenzahl
Division of Research and Statistics
Board of Governors of the Federal Reserve System
20th Street and Constitution Avenue, NW
Washington, DC 20551

Joel Mokyr
Departments of Economics and History
Northwestern University
2003 Sheridan Road
Evanston, IL 60208

Petra Moser
Department of Economics
Stanford University
579 Serra Mall
Stanford, CA 94305-6072

David C. Mowery
Haas School of Business, Mail Code 1900
University of California, Berkeley
Berkeley, CA 94720-1900

Fiona Murray
Sloan School of Management
Massachusetts Institute of Technology
100 Main Street
Cambridge, MA 02142

Richard R. Nelson
Columbia Earth Institute
2910 Broadway
New York, NY 10025

Paul W. Rhode
Economics Department
University of Michigan
611 Tappan Street
Ann Arbor, MI 48109-1220

Nathan Rosenberg
Landau Economics Building
Stanford University
579 Serra Mall
Stanford, CA 94305

Bhaven N. Sampat
Department of Health Policy and Management
Columbia University
600 W. 168th Street
New York, NY 10032

Antoinette Schoar
Sloan School of Management
Massachusetts Institute of Technology
100 Main Street
Cambridge, MA 02142

Suzanne Scotchmer
Department of Economics, Evans Hall
University of California, Berkeley
Berkeley, CA 94720-3880

Carl Shapiro
Haas School of Business
University of California, Berkeley
Berkeley, CA 94720-1900

Daniel F. Spulber
Kellogg School of Management
Northwestern University
2001 Sheridan Road
Evanston, IL 60208

Paula E. Stephan
Department of Economics
Andrew Young School of Policy Studies
Georgia State University
Box 3992
Atlanta, GA 30302-3992

Scott Stern
Sloan School of Management
Massachusetts Institute of Technology
100 Main Street
Cambridge, MA 02142

Manuel Trajtenberg
Eitan Berglas School of Economics
Tel Aviv University
Tel Aviv 69978 Israel

Peter Tufano
University of Oxford
Saïd Business School
Park End Street
Oxford, OX1 HP
United Kingdom

Michael D. Whinston
Department of Economics
Northwestern University
2001 Sheridan Road
Evanston, IL 60202

Author Index

Subject Index

Page numbers followed by the letter *f* or *t* refer to figures or tables, respectively.